BRITISH POETRY
AND
THE AMERICAN REVOLUTION

BRITISH POETRY
AND
THE AMERICAN REVOLUTION

A Bibliographical Survey of
Books and Pamphlets,
Journals and Magazines,
Newspapers, and Prints

1755-1800

by

Martin Kallich

Volume I

The Whitston Publishing Company
Troy, New York
1988

Copyright 1988
Martin Kallich

Library of Congress Catalog Card Number 86-50943

ISBN for set of two volumes 0-87875-318-4
ISBN for Volume I 0-87875-363-X

Printed in the United States of America

Contents

Preface vi
Introduction xii
References xxxii
Keys to the Entries xxxiv
Key to Abbreviations of Newspapers, Journals and Magazines xxxvi
Key to Abbreviations of Verse Forms xxxvi
Key to Locations of Libraries xxxvii

Prologue: 1755-1762 1

British Poetry and the American Revolution: 1763-1783
    1763 59
    1764 99
    1765 122
    1766 153
    1767 186
    1768 199
    1769 230
    1770 290
    1771 341
    1772 373
    1773 398
    1774 428
    1775 483
    1776 562
    1777 665
    1778 747
    1779 884
    1780 1014
    1781 1120
    1782 1182
    1783 1282

Epilogue: 1784-1800 1355
Supplement: Additions 1433

Index 1504
    I.   Authors and Their Poems, Titles of Anonymous Pamphlet Poems . . 1504
    II. Topics: Persons, Places and Events; Themes and Subjects 1541
    III. Verse Forms and Other Forms 1705

PREFACE

This project on British poetry and the American Revolution began about sixty-five years ago in Brooklyn, New York, where I was born and raised. There as a child and young man I would often walk portions of the King's Highway to and from school. This avenue was one of the longest of the very old thoroughfares of the town of Brooklyn before it was incorporated as a borough into New York City. The road arched many miles from the northeast to the southwest, extending across almost all of western Long Island, or the old King's County now coterminous with the present-day borough. Somewhere off this road and still standing, if only in the romantic mists of memory, was an ancient rural-type ranch building, a wooden-frame farmhouse, which deeply impressed my imagination because local legend dated its construction in the Revolutionary era.

I also recall walking in another direction to an old borough subdivision with the quaint name of New Utrecht, not far from my home. I was thrilled to note that a village of this name, the only remaining vestige of Dutch colonial settlements of the seventeenth century (like the name Breucklyn or Brookland, and other Dutch place names) was identified along with the King's Highway on an old sketch that passed for a British map used by General Sir William Howe during his Long Island campaign. This campaign was the one in which George Washington's forces were almost annihilated on August 27, 1776. If my memory is not playing me false, the plat of the section just off the western end of the highway, where my father (a modest entrepreneurial developer of the 1920's) had constructed a few houses, still clearly showed the extension of the road further west in the direction of the area between New Utrecht and Bath Beach. That part of the old highway, now disappeared and buried in old and forgotten maps, apparently affected the shape of the property on which several homes were constructed, so that my father's home, squeezed into a smaller than usual odd-shaped lot, appeared eccentric as a two-story almost square box amidst longer and conventionally shaped rectangular structures.

Such apparently trivial memories as these, redolent of the past, have continued to haunt me, to pique my curiosity, and nostalgically carry me back to the source of an irrepressible archetypal quest in which my personal history and the early history of our country have become inextricably merged. Triggered by these details, the archetype would be evoked and transport me unwittingly to the Revolutionary period time and again. Naturally, I felt obliged to visit the historic sites in Brooklyn where Continental soldiers died and were buried -- like the monument on the slope of Lookout Hill in Prospect Park, a shaft which commemorates the Maryland soldiers who formed the valiant rear-guard of the American army in the Battle of Long Island; and the Martyr's Monument designed by Stanford White and dedicated to the Continentals who died on the Wallabout Bay prison ships during the Revolution; and several sites elsewhere in New York, New Jersey, and New England and the eastern seaboard associated with the leaders and significant events of the American War of Independence.

Not to be ignored is the fact that, for twenty-five years up to the present time, I have lived in a small Illinois town, which for some strange reason has been named DeKalb, after the foreign volunteer Major General Baron Johann DeKalb. The commander of the Virginia militia when killed at Camden, South Carolina, August 16, 1780, Baron DeKalb was one of the many casualties of

British General Cornwallis's crushing victory over the American southern army led by General Horatio Gates.

In the town of DeKalb, I edited a source book entitled The American Revolution Through British Eyes (Evanston and New York: Row, Peterson, 1962) with the assistance of Andrew MacLeish. Then I proceeded with a few essays on Horace Walpole and later eighteenth-century British history -- "Horace Walpole Against Edmund Burke: A Study in Antagonism," Studies in Burke And His Time IX:2-3 (Spring & Winter 1968), 834-63, 927-45; and "The Whig Politician," in Horace Walpole (New York: Twayne Publishers, 1971), pp. 34-63, both of which prepared me for deeper and more extensive academic studies in the field. At this point I may have become aware of what I really wanted to do -- something different from Frank Moore's Songs and Ballads of the American Revolution (1856) or his Diary of the Revolution From Newspapers and Original Documents 1775-1784 (1860), or James Gaston's London Poets and the American Revolution (1979), or Thomas Adams' American Controversy (1980). Thus I was encouraged to continue with the development of the idea of the Anglo-American connection, but in a much more substantial manner than before, the result being this comprehensive work based on a collection of British poetry on the American Revolution, of which this bibliography (the first of its kind) is the initial phase, the next phase being an edition of the poetry.

Many people and institutions have assisted me in the preparation of this bibliography. Certainly, without their help, I could never have completed the task as I have outlined it in the introduction that follows. I am obliged to the National Endowment for the Humanities for its confidence in my ability to complete this enormous task and awarding me a substantial grant. I was thereby enabled to travel to several libraries here and abroad where research had to be conducted, particularly the surveys of the ephemeral publications, journals and newspapers. I wish also to express my thanks to the Graduate School of Northern Illinois University for several small research grants over the years to make countless short trips to Chicago and the Newberry Library, and to help defray expenses for photocopying, and for typing the manuscript.

I owe several individuals a debt of gratitude for assisting me in a variety of ways: Thomas Adams of the John Carter Brown Library for his guidance with his Preliminary List of Pamphlets on the American Controversy (1966), which was followed by his refined and finished American Controversy: A Bibliographical Study of the British Pamphlets About the American Disputes, 1764-1783 (1980); and to Helen Louise McGuffie of Bethany College, Bethany, West Virginia, who generously shared her expertise gained over many years working with eighteenth-century British periodicals and pamphlets for her bibliography on Samuel Johnson in the British Press, 1749-84: A Chronological Checklist (1976). Dr. McGuffie's detailed professional advice on British newspapers to be found in America and in England steered me in the proper directions and spared me much grief and frustration. I owe a debt of gratitude also to Donald Baker of Sutton Poyntz, Weymouth, England, and Frank Baker of Duke University, Durham, North Carolina, who have introduced me to the numerous anti-American poems of Charles Wesley (most still in manuscript); to James Gaston of the Air Force Academy for his innovative dissertation, An anthology of Poems on the American Revolution Taken from Prominent London Journals and Newspapers 1763-1783 (1975), which he had published five years later -- a work which I accepted as a challenge to improve upon; and to Peter Stanlis of Rockford College (and the Council of the

National Endowment for the Humanities), John Riely of Boston University, and Alfred Young of Northern Illinois University, all experienced scholars in the field of eighteenth-century studies, for their useful advice on certain problems arising during the course of this research and their constant and unflagging interest and encouragement.

I am heavily in debt to many staff members of the British Library, especially those of the Photographic Department for the efficient processing of my many orders of microfilm, and to the Department of Prints of the British Museum, where I spent two months poring over the Stevens-George Collection of Political and Personal Satires; to the staff members of the Beinecke Rare Books Library of Yale University and the Yale-Walpole Library at Farmington, Connecticut, where I have met with patience and unfailing courtesy and, as well, the New York Public Library, and the Bodleian of Oxford University. Other libraries whose staff have been especially cooperative must also be thanked for their assistance in answering questions about their holdings or providing photographic copies: the Huntingdon Library at San Marino, California; the University of Illinois Library at Urbana; Indiana University Library at Bloomington; the John Carter Brown Library at Providence, Rhode Island, the Library Company of Philadelphia; and Harvard University Library of Cambridge, Massachusetts.

My special thanks to the Newberry Library for granting me storage space, thereby facilitating my work, and to the Interlibrary Loan Office of Founders Library, Northern Illinois University, particularly Mrs. Eileen Dubin and her chief assistant, Mrs. Myrtie Podschmidt, for providing an efficient liaison with the Center for Research Libraries in Chicago; and to Dr. William Dubois, Curator of Rare Books, Founders Library, for performing various tasks such as screening some of the materials, among others, that helped lighten the load.

Finally, I wish to acknowledge with thanks the work of Mr. Juris Lidaka, who volunteered his time and placed his editorial expertise at my disposal as he assisted in the onerous task of preparing the manuscript, patiently working over the innumerable details on thousands of cards and presenting them in a seemly manner, and to my wife Harriett Sclar Kallich for giving the manuscript a last careful proofing and for bearing with me during many difficult years of a long travail.

Northern Illinois University
DeKalb, Illinois

INTRODUCTION

The purpose of this bibliography is to make readily accessible to scholars and lay readers interested in Anglo-American cultural history a substantial part of the poetry published in Great Britain between 1763 and 1783 about its American colonies and about domestic political and social affairs that affected the colonies (including selections from 1755 to 1762 and 1784 to 1800). The poetry covers a critical period of time when these colonies reacted vigorously to Britain's new imperial policies upon the termination of the Seven Years' War, revolted, and achieved independence.

Specifically, what follows is a comprehensive bibliography of the poetry published in Great Britain related to the American Revolution in the period 1755-1800 in book or pamphlet form, in broadside prints, and in more than 35 journals and 25 newspapers -- a total of approximately 5,600 poems. In the register of entries, I have tried to locate and describe every relevant verse pamphlet, every book of poems, every broadside with accompanying verse that is relevant, and every relevant poem in these journals and newspapers that published poetry in the period; and to enter all appropriate bibliographical data useful for handy reference, including brief annotation to specify relevance.

Such a bibliography should contribute to a solid basis for a systematic understanding, appreciation, and assessment of this neglected area of scholarship, thus stimulating fresh professional concern. To date, British students of their own literature and American students of British literature have, with very few exceptions, avoided this method of illuminating this subject. American cultural historians of the eighteenth-century colonies focus on the native colonial literature; and only occasionally and casually do they refer to the British poetry for evidence. This work should bring British and American literary interests together, and, as it imposes a degree of bibliographical control on the subject and indicates in one sharply delineated area an unexplored intercultural relationship, should encourage the efficient and continued pursuit of the theme.

Method of Research

Pamphlets and Books. In this survey of the British poetry published in the period of the American Revolution, I have expanded the rigorous norms used by Joseph Sabin and his followers in the basic bibliographical tool, *Bibliotheca Americana. A Dictionary of Books Relating to America, From its Discovery to the Present Time* (Amsterdam: N. Israel, 1961-62 [first published 1868-1936]), and by Thomas Adams in his more specialized enumerative and analytical bibliography on the subject, *The American Controversy, A Bibliographical Study of the British Pamphlets About the American Disputes, 1764-1783* (Providence, R. I.: Brown University Press, 1980), so that the suspiciously low yield in both (about 100-115 poetry titles) has been considerably enlarged. The result is, in my opinion, not only a more comprehensive coverage than that offered by either Sabin or Adams, but also a more accurate reflection of the political and social poetry related to America that was published for the edification and amusement of the British public at the time.

I have concluded that the best source of information is to be found in the original contemporary journal reviews, particularly the *Monthly Review* and the

Critical Review. Published without interruption throughout the years covered by this bibliography, these two reviews provided the most useful clues for the identification of relevant poems on the subject because of their systematic and consistently comprehensive coverage of London publications. However, because of cultural or political bias, their commentary could be misleading. Thus the reading of pamphlet poems brushed aside with a demeaning and distorting sentence or two was mandatory and often rewarding. Furthermore, these reviews often reprinted excerpts from poems regarded as significant.

Occasionally, also, newspapers printed announcements of poems to be published and excerpts from published poems that were highly regarded and that the editor wished to bring to the attention of his readers, thereby providing additional clues to identification. So too, according to the practice of some journals -- for example, the brief reviews in the Scots Magazine and the Gentleman's Magazine, which were sometimes useful. Moreover, I have screened the numerous volumes of the Bodleian Godwyn Pamphlet Collection for pertinent titles. Finally, whenever authors were identified -- for example, Robert Colvill or Bryan Edwards -- an attempt to read their works was made, in order to discover likely candidates for inclusion.

Altogether, this varied search yielded about 500 poems published as pamphlets and books that included information of some use to an understanding of the Anglo-American relationship in the period of the American Revolution.

Serials: Journals and Magazines. In general, research into the journals and magazines of the period is rendered easy because of the lists in the New Cambridge Bibliography of English Literature (Cambridge: University Press, 1974-77), Volume 2, and because many libraries in America and in England have complete files of many of them -- for example, the Bodleian and the British Library in England and the Newberry in Chicago, the New York Public Library, and the Yale University Library, all these locations where I have conducted my surveys. Also available for reading are the major microfilm collections like English Literary Periodicals and Early British Periodicals, processed by Xerox University Microfilms International and circulated by the Center for Research Libraries in Chicago. Many journals set aside a special section for the poetry contributions, thereby facilitating survey -- for example, Gentleman's Magazine and Scots Magazine, "Poetical Essays"; the Town and Country Magazine, "Poetical Pieces"; the Edinburgh Weekly Magazine, "Poetry." Some, on the other hand, scattered the poems in each issue. I have concluded that the following journals are useful sources of information. The list includes the years of active publication within the terminal periods of this study, all being complete and unbroken files.[1]

Annual Register 1758-85.
Arminian Magazine 1778-85.
British Magazine, Or Monthly Repository, 1760-67.
British Magazine and Review 1782-83.
Court Magazine (Court & City Magazine; Court, City & Country Magazine) 1761-65.
Court Miscellany 1765.
The Crisis 1775-76.
The Critical Review 1760-85.
Edinburgh Magazine 1757-62.
Edinburgh Magazine and Review 1773-76.
English Review of Literature 1783-85.
European Magazine & London Review 1782-85.
Every Man's Magazine 1771-72.
Freeholder's Magazine 1769-70.
Gentleman's Magazine 1758-85.
Hibernian Magazine 1771-85
Lady's Magazine 1770-84.

[1] But some numbers of the rare Freeholder's Magazine in the British Library are imperfect, Chatterton's poems unfortunately being missing!

London Magazine 1758-85.
London Museum 1770-71.
London Review 1775-80.
Matrimonial Magazine 1775.
Monthly Review 1760-85.
New Annual Register 1780-85.
North Briton 1762-63.
Oxford Magazine 1768-76.
Political Magazine 1780-85.
Rambler's Magazine 1783-85.
Royal Magazine 1759-69.
Ruddiman's Weekly Mercury 1777-83.
St. James's Magazine 1762-64, 1774. (Two journals.)
Scots Magazine 1758-85.
The Scourge 1780.
Sentimental Magazine 1773-77.
Town & Country Magazine 1769-84.
Universal Magazine 1758-85.
Weekly Amusement 1763-67.
Weekly Entertainer (Sherborne) 1783-84.
Weekly Magazine (Edinburgh) 1768-84.
Weekly Miscellany (Sherborne) 1773-82.
Westminster Magazine 1773-85.

Of these journals, by far the greatest number originate in England. Included are one journal from Ireland and five from Scotland.

Serials: Newspapers. Regarding research into newspapers for evidences of poetry relating to the American Revolution, my task involved working with the Charles Burney Collection of Newspapers in the British Library at London, simply because it is the greatest concentration of eighteenth-century English newspapers, particularly those published in London. (This huge collection has recently been made available in microfilm.) The survey of the newspapers, therefore, was largely conducted at the British Library, supplemented by reading, whenever the need arose, in the Bodleian, the Beinecke Library of Yale University, and, to a lesser extent, the Newberry Library in Chicago. The Center for Research Libraries also supplied film from its archives (e.g.,

Gazetteer, Public Advertiser, Caledonian Mercury) as well as one original (Lloyd's Evening Post), all secured through the Interlibrary Loan Office of the Founders Library of Northern Illinois University.

The following list includes those papers that had published poems somewhat regularly at the least. The extent of the survey is indicated by those dates after the first, which records the year the newspaper was established. (I have tried to simplify these details on the list. Any additional data on the birth, life, death, or mergers and incorporations of the papers, as well as the breaks in the continuity of the files, will only obscure the clarity of the list.)

London Dailies:
  Gazetteer 1735. 1763-84, 1785 (scattered nos.).
  (Parker's) General Advertiser 1776. 1776-77 (occasional nos.), 1777-79 (to Jul), 1780 (occasional nos.), 1782-83 (to May).
  London Courant Nov 1779. 1779 (Nov) -82 (to May, thereafter occasional), 1783 (occasional nos.)
  Morning Chronicle Dec 29, 1770. 1771 (only two issues in Burney!), 1772-85.
  Morning Herald Nov 1, 1780. 1780 (Nov) -84.
  Morning Post Nov 2, 1772. 1773 (scattered nos.), 1774 (Jan-Jun, Jul-Dec scattered nos.), 1775-80, 1781-84 (scattered nos., but 1782-83 is fairly good).
  Public Advertiser Nov 4, 1734. 1760-85.
  Public Ledger Jan 12, 1760. 1760-61, 1765 (Jul-Dec), 1774, 1775 (scattered nos.).

London Tri-Weeklies:
  English Chronicle Jan 2, 1779. 1782-83 (occasional nos.).
  General Evening Post 1733. 1770-84, 1785 (Jul-Dec).
  Lloyd's Evening Post Jul 22, 1757. 1759-85.
  London Chronicle Jan 1, 1757. 1760-85.
  London Evening Post 1727. 1760-67, 1770-80, 1782 (occasional nos.).
  London Packet Oct 1769. 1772-78, 1779 (Jan, Oct-Dec), 1780 (Jan-Mar, Jul-Dec; missing nos. in these months), 1781-84 (occasional nos.)
  Middlesex Journal Apr 4, 1769. 1769 (Apr) -76.
  St. James's Chronicle Mar 12, 1761. 1761 (Apr) -85 (Jun-Dec).
  Whitehall Evening Post 1746. 1760-61, 1769 (Jun-Dec), -85.

London Weeklies:
  Baldwin's London Weekly Journal Jan 1762. 1768 (scattered nos.), 1769-74.
  Bingley's Weekly Journal Jun 9, 1770. 1770-72.
  Craftsman: or Say's Weekly Journal Jul 1758. 1771-76 (to Jun), occasional nos. thereafter to 1783.
  Westminster Journal 1763-64. 1771 (Sep-Dec), 1774-84.

Other Newspapers, Scots, Irish, and Provincial:
  Adams Weekly Courant (Chester) 1732-33. 1774 (Sep-Dec), 1775 (Jan, Nov-Dec), 1776 (occasional nos.), 1780 (Jun-Dec).
  Caledonian Mercury 1720. 1759, 1776-85.
  Chester Chronicle May 2, 1775. 1776 (Jan-Jul).
  Cumberland Pacquet Oct 20, 1774. 1774 (Nov-Dec), 1775-83.
  Faulkner's Dublin Journal 1725. 1760-85.
  Kentish Gazette May 4, 1768. 1772-76.
  Freeman's Journal (Dublin) Sep 10, 1763. 1763-85.

In this period, the second part of the eighteenth century, especially with the beginning of the reign of George III in 1760, the feature of the newspaper that held the greatest interest was political. In satisfying this expectation, the printing of a variety of political sentiment, including reports of the debates in Parliament, poetry played a significant role. That newspaper publishers and editors regarded poetry as of some significance is demonstrated by the fact that they did not use it as mere "fillers" meant to pad out space within the format. Poems, especially political poems, appeared too consistently to be considered as frivolous evidences of taste. They contributed to the political debate. Furthermore, many poems have received multiple publication, suggesting pressure to reprint to satisfy reader demands. Lastly, many papers regularly devoted a column to poetry, although equally many would print the poems on any page of the usual four or eight page format. The special columns were often identified with a title: for example, Freeman's Journal, "The Parnassiad"; General Advertiser, "Poet's Column"; London Packet, "Post from Parnassus"; Middlesex Journal, St. James's Chronicle, and Gazetteer (1780 and after), "Poet's Corner; <u>Morning Post</u> and <u>Public Advertiser</u>, "Poetry"; <u>Whitehall Evening Post</u>, "The Helicon Bag"; <u>Westminster Journal</u>, "The Helicon Mail."

Altogether, these journals and newspapers yielded approximately 5075 individual poems with relevance to America during this period. Many of the poems received multiple printings; but these are not counted in the total. Nor does this count include the excerpts from the pamphlet poems that appeared in the monthly reviews and newspapers.

<u>Prints</u>. Practically all of the poems in prints are filed with the Department of Prints at the British Museum, London. These prints have been assigned numbers, which now correspond with the numbers in the comprehensive <u>Catalogue of Political and Personal Satires</u> (1870-1954), prepared in over eighty years' time by Frederick George Stephens and Mary Dorothy George, eleven large volumes listing thousands of prints with detailed analyses and commentary. A few additional poems in prints -- originals or copies -- are located elsewhere: e.g., in America: the Lewis-Walpole Library in Farmington, Connecticut; the Colonial Williamsburg Foundation, as listed in the catalogue by Joan D. Dolmetsch, <u>Rebellion and Reconciliation</u> (1976); the Pierpont Morgan Collection in New York City; and, in England, the British Library (as distinguished from the British Museum). However, omissions and oversights have been rarely detected, thereby attesting to the thoroughness of the work performed by these two distinguished English scholars.

About one hundred poems in prints are listed in my register. Included in the entries are references to a few relatively recent books with useful illustrations. (It should be noted that the prints assembled and catalogued by Stephens and George are now available for study on microfilm.)

Miscellanies. In addition to all the sources of information listed above, the numerous collections of the miscellanies published throughout the period sometimes proved to be useful. Poems published in the presumably more durable form of miscellanies reprinted versions of the originals appearing in the ephemeral journals and newspapers. These collections of miscellaneous "fugitive" texts are additional evidences of popular taste -- that is, of material deliberately selected by an editor for contemporary readers in the belief that it was valuable enough to preserve effectively for posterity, thus a reflection of the impact on popular taste by what some regarded as memorable poetry of some significance and merit. Further, the miscellaneous collections assured that few, if any, quality poems of value would slip through the wide net used for this bibliography.

The following list, arranged chronologically, includes the most useful miscellanies consulted in this bibliographical survey. This list, not exhaustive, is meant to be suggestive. Textual differences between one edition and another and between the original and the reprinted poem, and variations in the contents are to be expected, because of the often casual nature of the publication. Like the newspapers, miscellanies generate bibliographical problems that are too numerous and too complicated for discussion here.

A Genuine Collection of the Several Pieces of Political Intelligence Extraordinary, Epigrams, Poetry, &c. that have Appeared before the Public in Detached Pieces; Now carefully selected together in one View, by An Impartial Hand. London & Westminster: Butcher, Russell, 1766.

The Battle of the Quills: Or Wilkes Attacked and Defended. An Impartial Selection of all the most Interesting Pieces, Argumentative, Declamatory, and Humourous, in Prose and Verse, Relative to John Wilkes Esq; . . . London: J. Williams, 1768.

The New Foundling Hospital for Wit. Being a Collection of Fugitive Pieces, in Prose and Verse, Not in any other Collection. London: Debrett, 1768[-86]. Part I (1768), II (1769), III (1769), IV (1771), V (1772), VI (1773). Published also in 1784 and in 1786 in six volumes, "With several pieces never before published. A new edition, corrected and considerably enlarged."

A Collection of Poems In Two Volumes. By Several Hands. London: G. Pearch, 1768. Second edition: In Four Volumes, 1770. Also other editions, In Four Volumes, 1775, 1783.

The Patriotic Miscellany. Being a Collection of Interesting Papers, Jests, Anecdotes, Epigrams, &c. In the Case of John Wilkes, Esq; . . . London: Booth, 1769.

A Companion For a Leisure Hour: Being A Collection Of Fugitive Pieces, in Prose and Verse. By Several Gentlemen. London: Almon, 1769.

The Humours of the Times, Being a Collection of Several Curious Pieces, in Verse and Prose. By the Most Celebrated Geniusses, for Mirth, Wit, and Humour . . . London, 1771.

Stevens, George Alexander. Songs, Comic, and Satyrical. Oxford, 1772. Another ed., 1782. Two American editions, 1777 & 1778.

Baratariana. A Select Collection of Fugitive Political Pieces, published during the Administration of his Excellency Lord Viscount Townshend in Ireland. Dublin, 1772. Second edition, "Corrected and enlarged," Dublin, 1773. Third edition, "Corrected and enlarged," Dublin, 1777.

The Fugitive Miscellany. Being a Collection of such Fugitive Pieces, in Prose and Verse, as are not in any other Collection. With many pieces never before published. London: Almon, 1774. Also published in 1775.

The Caledoniad. A Collection of Poems. Written Chiefly by Scottish Authors. London: W. Hay, 1775. Three volumes.

An Asylum for Fugitives. Published Occasionally. London: Almon, 1776.

The Repository: A Select Collection of Fugitive Pieces, of Wit and Humour, in Prose and Verse. By the most eminent Writers. London: Dilly, 1775. Two volumes. Second edition, Volumes 3 & 4 added in 1783.

The Muse's Mirror: Being A Collection of Poems By [39 names in 3 columns]. London: R. Baldwin, 1778. Two volumes. Second edition, 1783.

<u>The Vocal Magazine; Or, British Songster's Miscellany, Containing all the English, Scotch, and Irish Songs, Cantatas, Glees, Catches, Airs, Ballads, &c., deemed any way worthy of being transmitted to Posterity. Volume the First.</u> London: Harrison, Bew, 1778. [c. 1300 texts.]

<u>The Lady's Poetical Magazine, or Beauties of British Poetry.</u> London: Harrison, 1781-82. Four volumes.

<u>The Convivial Songster, Being a Select Collection of the Best Songs in the English Language: Humourous, Satirical, Bacchanalian, &c. &c. &c. With the Music Prefixed to each song.</u> London: Highley, [c. 1782].

<u>An Asylum for Fugitive Pieces, in Prose and Verse, Not in Any Other Collection. With Several Pieces never before Published. A new ed.</u> . . . London: J. Debrett, 1785-86.

Dunstan, Jeffery (pseud.). <u>Fugitive Pieces, Written by Sir Jeffery Dunstan, Member of Parliament, And Mayor for Garrat; Now Collected together for the First Time; Among Which Are Inserted A Few Pieces Written By The First Wits of The Nation</u> . . . London: Printed For Sir Jeffery, and Sold By the Booksellers, 1789.

<u>Poems, Chiefly by Gentlemen of Devonshire and Cornwall.</u> Bath: Cruttwell, 1792. Two volumes.

An unstated assumption underlying this bibliography is that the claim of superiority for one type of publication over another cannot be substantiated. It is, of course, impossible to assess precisely the relative effect on public opinion of the several different kinds of press formats -- including the broadsides of graphic satiric prints and popular songs. But it could be readily assumed that a good many of the pamphlets, being more expensive than serials and having a smaller market, required subsidy but not necessarily more subtlety and intellectual sophistication, and were generally polished and finished literary works, perhaps, therefore traditionally elitist rather than merely popular. However, with regard to volume sales, newspapers effectively cut across class distinctions and clearly outperformed all other types of publication, demonstrating their great importance in the literary market place. Indeed, there was so much give and take between serials and pamphlets, so much borrowed and reprinted, that it really makes little difference in the determination of value whether a literary work first reached the public in this or that format. Presenting the quantitative facts about the varied press production given British poetry about the American Revolution can only suggest the intensity with which the subject was pursued to satisfy the emotional and intellectual demands of a complex and multifaceted public. Thus we can only conclude, perhaps lamely but undeniably, that each form taken by the press certainly permitted the venting of personal emotion and contributed its mite to the moulding of public opinion and feeling. Clearly, if anything, it has been the bad fortune of eighteenth-century British newspapers to be generally unavailable for present-day study that accounts for whatever prejudice there is against them. Moreover, measured against norms derived from experience with modern newspapers, they are not considered the repositories of the kind of "high" literature usually deserving of respect. As a result, mistakenly underestimated to begin with, this poetry has been ignored.

Regarding Irish, Scottish, and English provincial newspapers of this period, my original plan included a survey of some sources outside of London; and as can be seen from the list of consulted titles, a few of these have been substantially examined -- two Irish, one Scottish, and a few English. I thought that the Burney Collection would have enough evidence from the provinces to satisfy my original plan. But this was not to be. Burney focuses on London newspapers and appears to have, for the most part, only occasional and scattered issues from the provincial English press, and these published little or no poetry. The newspaper division of the British Library at Colindale stores these provincial resources. A reading of the provincial press may rightfully be considered a desideratum of contemporary scholarship, along with the completion of the files of certain valuable London papers and the addition of a few more appropriate Irish and Scottish newspapers.

At the present time, because newspaper resources for this period are scattered in several libraries here and abroad, it would take a good deal of money and time to bring order out of the chaos that characterizes this area of eighteenth-century British studies. Unless he has the Burney volume in front of him, a reader never can be sure when a hiatus in a file of papers will appear, occasional numbers appearing only too often, as well as pathetically large gaps. Thus it is not possible to function efficiently and systematically without great effort. Also the bibliographical sources of information are woefully inadequate, because the details on the holdings are not always recorded completely in the reference tools that must be used. Nor are they up-to-date. The numerous questions indicated on the list of newspapers in the New Cambridge Bibliography of English Literature (Vol. 2, pp. 1331-36) may be cited as an example. In this respect, perhaps the most useful reference source at present for these newspapers in American libraries is the National Union Catalogue, which records locations as well.

Only relatively few newspapers have been filmed so that almost perfect, if not entirely perfect, runs are made conveniently available. The London Gazetteer and Public Advertiser, and the Dublin Freeman's Journal can be cited in this respect; but unfortunately, the film of the Gazetteer was processed quite some time ago and leaves much to be desired for quality. The British Library has recently filmed the entire Burney Collection; but gaps in the Burney files have not been filled by splicing film from other libraries like the Bodleian in order to produce a comprehensive synthesis. Nevertheless, despite these complaints, much has been done in this register of newspaper poetry. Should this plea for the improvement of certain types of eighteenth-century study be effective, perhaps in the years to come significant additions may be made to my work.

The Scope and Nature of this Bibliography.

A bibliography that records almost every poem on America and almost every poem about domestic affairs that possessed an obvious potential for affecting America can never satisfy every expectation. First, there will be disagreement about the definition of the chronological period of the American Revolution. Should it begin at 1763? This is the year of the Peace of Fountainebleau that brought an end to the Seven Years' War (known also as the Great War for Empire, or as the French and Indian War); and among historians, this is the conventional year of the beginning of a new era in the relations between the American colonies and the mother country that eventually led to war between them and permanent separation. If this is true, then the question could rightfully be asked, why not 1755 as the important year when the Seven Years' War began -- particularly when the English and their American colonial allies began to react to the so-called French "encroachments" on the settlements in the Ohio River valley claimed by the British crown?

Regarding this new problem in western Pennsylvania, we should think of General Edward Braddock assisted by a young Virginian, twenty-three old Colonel George Washington, on the way in July 1755 to attack the invading French in their new Fort Duquesne (renamed Pittsburgh after William Pitt). We should also think of General Augustus Howe (brother of the later General Sir William and Admiral Sir Richard Howe), assisted by Major Israel Putnam of Connecticut in an attempt in July 1758 to force the French from their new Fort Carillon (renamed Ticonderoga by the British), which controlled the inland water route between Canada and the American provinces. Both British commanding officers died with the Americans at their side. The year 1759, when General James Wolfe died before Quebec at the moment of victory, may also be considered crucial, because it signaled the real end of French hegemony in Canada and the end of the threat to colonial American expansion westward. But it also set the stage for an appreciation of the great irony of 1778 -- the Franco-American alliance -- of which so much was made in the poetry.

With this idea in mind, I have offered a <u>selection</u> of poems on the preliminary events in the years 1755-1762 that laid the groundwork for an understanding of the American troubles to come -- of British attitudes and emotional commitments that certainly contributed to the intensity with which opinions were held and to the behavior of the people who expressed them. Thus in this collection, readers will note poems on Edward Braddock and George Augustus Howe. They will also note poems about William Pitt, Earl of Chatham, the chief minister who is credited with the tremendous gains of the British in the Seven Years' War; about the new King George III; about King George's attempt to strengthen the monarchy by controlling Parliament through a new system of politics engineered by his mentor, John Stuart, Earl of Bute; about Lord Bute, the peace he made with France, and the corruption of Parliament; about the Scots "invasion" of England; about Tories, tyranny, and Jacobites, and Whigs, liberty, and republicans; about the opposition to Bute initiated by John Wilkes and the ensuing excitement lasting many years when Wilkes, prosecuted (or persecuted) by the government in power because he objected to Bute's peace, appeared to achieve the status of a martyr to idolizing London mobs.

Readers of this bibliography will be able to follow the careers in poetry of not only those political figures already cited but also Edmund Burke and Charles James Fox, Lord Frederick North and Lord George Germain. They will be able to see the connection made with the Puritan Revolution and the execution of Charles I, the Glorious Revolution of the Williamites and the deposition of James II, the last Stuart tyrant, and the American Rebellion, the resort to arms, because the connection with these revolutionary precedents was made in numerous poems on the subjects. In addition, such allied themes as emigration; the freedom of Ireland; the freedom of the press, and the threats to civil rights; the integrity of elections (or corruption and bribery) and the inadequate system of representation; the budget, fiscal policy, and taxation will be seen in the poetry.

All these central themes and all these important political leaders were of interest to the colonial Americans of the time because America was affected by them; and, being British, many Americans read British papers and journals and pamphlets and many of their publications reprinted items from the British press, and vice versa. Where, then, should a line be drawn on poems about individuals like the premier Lord North, the American Secretary Lord Germain, or the rabble rouser John Wilkes, or poems about themes such as corruption and bribery when America is <u>not</u> specifically cited? Surely, as Thomas Adams has written about pamphlets in "The British Pamphlet Press and the American Controversy, 1764-1783," because "the British pamphlets debated a whole range of related topics, . . . an understanding of the impact of this substantial output of published matter on these topics is relevant to an understanding of what happened to both Anglo-American relations and to Britain itself during these twenty years." (American Independence: The Growth of an Idea [1980], pp. 214-5.)

The same can be said about the poetry. If a strong sense of oppression is the predominant American emotion energizing the movement first towards resistance to tyranny and then towards war against the parent country and separation from her, the answer must be clear: readers of this bibliography should have made available to them all the relevant sources showing how certain Englishmen also reacted to oppression and communicated their fears of tyranny in various forms, including poetry. I choose at random one poem that illustrates the difficulty of defining too narrowly the nature of the American troubles: The Favourite; A Character from the Life (1778), entered as 78-16, a poem that reflects on numerous themes and personalities of great importance to an understanding of the American problem. A scurrilous lampoon on the Earl of Bute, and a panegyric on Lord Chatham, this work reviews past history from a Whig and anti-Scottish posture; blames the Earl of Mansfield for the war against America; sees Lexington as a massacre of American innocents; remarks on General Burgoyne and his disastrous defeat, on the failures of Lord Germain (the Secretary of State responsible for overall policies regarding the campaigns of the war), on the Carlisle Peace Commission (which conveyed Lord North's propositions for a peace to the Congress), on Admiral Augustus Keppel and the state of the fleet, all significant and inter-related topics bearing on the American War. This typical tangle of topics suggests that any attempt at isolating the American factor from the complex of associated ideas will inevitably produce distortion.

Or considering this matter solely according to the British Establishment, a quotation from the prose introduction to a long poem attacking Benjamin Franklin, *The Traitor. A Poetical Rhapsody* (1781), entered as 81-15, demonstrates that it is essential to provide a broad context for the proper illumination of the colonial issue. In this work, the author not only vents his spleen at Franklin in France but also the rebel's English supporters at home -- John Almon, the radical publisher, and Richard Price, the celebrated libertarian and dissenter who opposed coercion; and he concludes with an observation on the necessary relationship between British domestic and foreign affairs and America, which is the object of exploration in this research project:

> That the Americans depend less on the <u>Spartan</u> Wisdom of the Congress, the <u>Roman</u> bravery of their Troops, the <u>solid</u> Alliance with France, the <u>golden</u> Friendship of Spain, and, which is now their favourite topic, the armed Neutrality, than on the Disunion of the British People. This is the Rock of their Confidence. The Provincial Associations, the Discontents of Ireland, the London Tumults, inflammatory Speeches, and antiministerial Publications, have been, and are, the principal sources of Life to their sanguine expectations.

Indeed, because the issue of the North American colonies was often at the center of British affairs in this historical epoch, this work has in effect become a survey of almost all the political poetry of the time, that on America as well as that affecting America. Readers interested in the Anglo-American relationship, faced with this complex of ideas must then decide for themselves how they wish to use them. This bibliography is meant to be as comprehensive and complete as it can possibly be, limited only by and relative to the sources from which it is drawn.

Regarding the chronological boundaries of this survey, as understood by students of the American Revolution, a question similar to that about 1763 can be raised about the conventional terminal year of 1783. This year brought the Peace of Paris that gave formal international recognition to the independence of the United States of America. Thus it marked the end of the revolutionary period and the beginning of a new era with new faces, new ideologies, new contests. I have no quarrel with this view, should only America be considered. But we must remember that, basically, this is a bibliography of the later eighteenth-century <u>British</u> relation to America. Thus it is easy to show that the formal end of the American War did not abruptly bring a loss of memory to British politicians and poets. They were still affected by the attitudes and events of the disastrous war years. This effect can be seen with the entrance of the younger William Pitt into the political arena and the way in which poets interpreted or reported his behavior against the norm of those who favored or opposed coercion of America. Their reaction to the surprising coalition of Charles James Fox, the great Opposition leader and critic of the ministry during the period of the American War, and Lord North, the former premier at the time and Fox's major target, is equally relevant. Also, such problems as Negro slavery and the ill-treatment of Loyalists irritated some British writers and poets. Others hoped for reconciliation and reunion. Still others saw Great Britain at the height of its power and prosperity in 1763 and pessimistically mourned the loss of an empire and wept over its decline after 1783. Feeling continued to run high. So the Poet Laureat James Pye in 1800 bitterly blames the seditious Opposition for treacherously undermining the Government and encouraging the Americans who,

> Rear'd, like the pelican, with parent blood,
> Turn their wild vengeance 'gainst Britannia's heart,
> And aim with fatal rage, the parricidal dart.
> <u>Carmen Seculare for the Year 1800</u>.

To illustrate the continuing influence of the American Revolution, and to provide a proper termination of this bibliography, I have included an epilogue with appropriate verse from a variety of sources to the year 1785, and from the pamphlet literature in some instances beyond that year. It is my hope that those who are attracted to the possibility of the effectiveness of British poetry in demonstrating the validity of their hypotheses concerning Britain and the American Revolution will find this to be a well-rounded and comprehensive catalogue of riches.

Finally, let us not forget that there are the purely literary possibilities of this enormous amount of material -- the experimentation with forms, the various kinds of classical and medieval imitations, the parodies; the sonnet, blank verse, and heroic couplet, the Hudibrastic octosyllabic couplet, and satire, the use of the rhetoric of poetry -- all attest to the real presence of a creative literary imagination and of a variety of literary skills with which the writers from almost all the classes practiced the art of poetry. The question of value, which is daily debated about all literature of any time, can now be raised about British poetry on the American Revolution as we will begin to read and understand it.[2]

[2] A supplement includes added entries of poems that have been overlooked or located too late to be placed among the main entries. These poems are listed alphabetically within the year of publication in an <u>Addenda</u> section at the end of the bibliography.

References

Adams, Thomas R. The American Controversy. A Bibliographical Study of the British Pamphlets about the American Disputes, 1764-1783. Providence: Brown University Press; New York: The Bibliographical Society of America, 1980. Two volumes.

The American War of Independence 1775-83. A Commemorative Exhibition Organized by the Map Library and the Department of Manuscripts of the British Library Reference Division 4 July to 11 November 1775. London: British Museum Publications, 1975.

Bailey, D. W. British Public Opinion on the American War in Prints. [London:] British Museum, [c. 1976].

Bristol, Roger P. Supplement to Charles Evans American Bibliography. Charlottesville: University of Virginia Press, 1970.

The British Look at America During the Age of Johnson. Providence: Brown University, 1971. [Catalogue.]

The Dictionary of National Biography . . . From the Earliest Times to 1900. Ed. Sir Leslie Stephen. Oxford: Oxford University Press, 1885-1901. Twenty-two volumes.

Dolmetsch, Joan D. Rebellion and Reconciliation: Satirical Prints on the Revolution at Williamsburg. Charlottesville: University of Virginia Press, 1976. [Illustrated catalogue.]

Evans, Charles. American Bibliography. A Chronological Dictionary of all Books, Pamphlets, and Periodical Publications Printed in the United States of America. From the Genesis of Printing in 1639 to and Including the Year 1820. With Bibliographical and Biographical Notes. New York: Peter Smith, 1941. Fourteen volumes. [First published 1903.]

Halkett, Samuel, and John Laing. Dictionary of Anonymous and Pseudonymous English Literature. New and enlarged edition. Edinburgh: Oliver and Boyd, 1926-62. Nine volumes.

Halsey, Richard T. H. The Boston Port Bill as Pictured by a Contemporary London Cartoonist. New York: Grolier Club, 1904.

Namier, Lewis, and John Brooke. The History of Parliament: The House of Commons 1754-1790. New York: Oxford University Press, 1964. Three volumes.

The New Cambridge Bibliography of English Literature. Ed. George Watson. Cambridge: University Press, 1974-77. Five volumes.

Pearson, Kenneth, and Patricia O'Connor. 1776: The British Story of the American Revolution. London: Times Newspapers, 1976. [Catalogue.]

Sabin, Joseph. Bibliotheca Americana. A Dictionary of Books Relating to America, From its Discovery to the Present Time. Begun by Joseph Sabin, Continued by Wilberforce Eames, and Completed by R. W. G. Vail for the Bibliographical Society of America. Amsterdam: N. Israel, 1961-62. Twenty-nine volumes. [First published 1868-1936.]

Stephens, Frederic George, and Mary Dorothy George. Catalogue of Political and Personal Satires Preserved in the Department of Prints and Drawings in the British Museum. London: British Museum, 1870-1954. Eleven volumes. [Vol. 3, Pt. ii (1751-60); Vol. 4 (1761-70); Vol. 5 (1771-83); Vol. 6 (1784-92). Stephens prepared the volumes to 1770; George prepared the volumes to 1792 and thereafter.]

Valentine, Alan. The British Establishment 1760-1784. An Eighteenth-Century Biographical Dictionary. Norman, Oklahoma: University of Oklahoma Press, 1970. Two volumes.

Wynn Jones, Michael. The Cartoon History of Britain. London: Stacy, 1971; New York: Macmillan, 1973.

Wynn Jones, Michael. The Cartoon History of the American Revolution. New York: Putnam, 1975.

Key to the Entries

Books and pamphlets.
63-1. Catalogue number. Name of author (if identified).
   Title.
   Place of publication; Publisher, date. Number of pages.
   First line and number of lines.
   Notices: Reviews in CR, MR, ERL, excerpts printed in journals and newspapers. As a rule, I do not include announcements advertising future publication.
   Sabin and Evans catalogue numbers, if available.
   Copies: British Library Shelf Number, Bodleian Shelf Number, National Union Catalogue locations in American libraries.
   Annotation: An outstanding feature of the form -- the meter or the stanzaic pattern and a brief summary of the contents. Information presented in the title and first line probably needs no repetition here: for example, acrostic, satire, imitation, epigram, epitaph, ode, song, ballad, as well as ideas, themes, names of people and places.

Serial poems.
63-75. Catalogue number. Author (if identified).
   Title.
   First line and number of lines.
   Sources: Publication in journals and newspapers, with date.
   Annotation: Same as above.

Poems in prints.
63-150. Catalogue number. Title of print or accompanying poem.
   First line and number of lines.
   Nature of the broadside -- usually engraving or etching. Name of artist (if identified. Date of composition.
   Catalogue number in Department of Prints, British Museum: Stephens or George. A reference to Dolmetsch and some other modern reprinting may be added.
   Annotation: Brief comment on the contents of the poem and print.

Special Problems: Inconsistencies.
   The title. Because of the multiplicity of sources for some poems, the titles may vary. Occasionally, the same poems are both titled and untitled, should there be numerous sources. Readers are urged to consider the first-line to help clarify confusion regarding identification of a poem. First lines are, of course, crucial for those poems having no title in any of the sources. Here bracketed first lines have been adopted as the title and indexed accordingly.

   The date. The date of publication, as a rule, has determined the year in which a poem has been recorded. Occasionally, however, a few exceptions have been made. (1) When the date of composition is part of the title or when the year of the content is clearly at odds with the year of publication of a poem, so that there appears to be an obvious disparity between the date of composition or time of the content and the year of publication, the significant determining factor for the chronological record is the year of composition and content. For example, see 58-9. (2) Another problem involves dating of some of the newspaper sources, especially the triweeklies. It should be understood that triweekly, weekly, and monthly publications appeared at the end of an interval. The London triweekly afternoon or evening papers were published at the end of a two or three day interval (Jan 10-12, 1776). But here, in this bibliography, for the sake of convenience and rapid identification, it is the first day or beginning of the interval that has been recorded in order to shorten the entries. An exception to this practice is the recording of the New Year poems (Dec 30, 1776-Jan 1, 1777), where it would be obviously misleading to use the first date. Thus I have often given both dates for poems published at the turn of the year, when I thought it might appear more logical to do so.

Spelling. Because of the great variety of texts, the spelling of names and places will often be inconsistent in the entries. No adjustments for consistency have been made in the transcriptions of titles and first lines; here the original spelling (as well as the original punctuation) has been copied. Other adjustments, however, do appear: raised letters have been lowered, abbreviations of names expanded, apostrophes modernized. It may be safe to say that the copied titles are correct with respect to the words that appear in the original. Variation in spelling reflects the failure to achieve orthographic standardization in the eighteenth century. The accepted modern spelling of names and places (Germain, Germaine; Prescot, Prescott; Savile, Saville; Thurloe, Thurlow; Barre, Barré; Ticonderago, Ticonderoga; Guadeloupe, Guadaloupe) will be found in the index.

Key to Abbreviations of Newspapers, Journals and Magazines

AM	Arminian Magazine	LR	London Review
AR	Annual Register	Mat M.	Matrimonial Magazine
AWCour	Adams Weekly Courant	M Chron.	Morning Chronicle
B&BM	Bristol & Bath Magazine	MH	Morning Herald
BLJ.	Baldwin's London Journal	MJ	Middlesex Journal
BM (BMag)	British Magazine, or Monthly Repository	MP	Morning Post
		MR	Monthly Review
BM&R	British Magazine and Review	NAR	New Annual Register
		North Br	North Briton
BWJ.	Bingley's Weekly Journal	Ox M	Oxford Magazine
		PA	Public Advertiser
Cal Merc	Caledonian Mercury	PL	Public Ledger
C Chron.	Chester Chronicle	PM	Political Magazine
Court M.	Court Magazine	Ram M.	Rambler's Magazine
Court&CM	Court & City Magazine	RM (R Mag)	Royal Magazine
Court C&CM	Court, City, and Country Magazine	RWM.	Ruddiman's Weekly Mercury
		St J's C	St. James's Chronicle
Court Misc	Court Miscellany	St J's M	St. James's Magazine
CR	Critical Review	Say's	Craftsman, or Say's Weekly Journal
Crisis	Crisis		
Cumb Pacq	Cumberland Pacquet	Sent M	Sentimental Magazine
DJ	Dublin Journal	SM	Scots Magazine
E Chron.	English Chronicle	T&C	Town & Country Magazine
Edin M	Edinburgh Magazine	UM	Universal Magazine
Edin M&R	Edinburgh Magazine & Review	WA	Weekly Amusement
		W Ent.	Weekly Entertainer
EM (Eur Mag)	European Magazine	WM	Weekly Magazine [Edinburgh]
E Man's M.	Every Man's Magazine	W Misc	Weekly Miscellany
ERL	English Review of Literature	West G	Westminster Gazette
		West J	Westminster Journal
Free M	Freeholder's Magazine	West M (West Mag)	Westminster Magazine
Freeman's J.	Freeman's Journal	W Eve Post	Whitehall Evening Post
G.	Gazetteer		
GA	General Advertiser		
G Eve Post	General Evening Post		
GM	Gentleman's Magazine		
HM	Hibernian Magazine		
KG	Kentish Gazette		

Abbreviations of Verse Forms

HC	Heroic Couplets
OC	Octosyllabic Couplets

Lady's M	Lady's Magazine
Lloyd's	Lloyd's Evening Post
L Chron.	London Chronicle
L Cour	London Courant
L Eve Post	London Evening Post
LM (L Mag)	London Magazine
L Mus.	London Museum
LP	London Packet

Key to Locations of Libraries

The abbreviation BL refers to the British Library Catalogue, the source of all the BL shelf numbers indicated in this bibliography. The Godwyn Pamphlet Collection is the basic source for relevant titles located in the Bodleian, with a few exceptions. NUC refers to the National Union Catalogue, the source of the locations and the abbreviations used to identify libraries in the United States and Canada. The Lewis-Walpole Library is now an adjunct of Yale University, but because its holdings (especially the prints) are not located at Yale in New Haven, but in Farmington, CT, it is given a separate listing. The libraries marked with an asterisk are most useful for studies on British Poetry and the American Revolution.

*BL	The British Library, Reference Division, London, England. [Formerly identified as BM, the British Museum.]
*Bod	Bodleian Library, Oxford, England.
CLU	University of California, Los Angeles.
CLU-C	University of California, Los Angeles, Clark Memorial Library.
*CSmH	Henry E. Huntington Library, San Marino, CA.
CU	University of California, Berkeley.
CU-A	University of California, Davis.
CU-S	University of California, San Diego.
CaBVaU	University of British Columbia, Vancouver, Canada.
CaOt	Toronto Public Library, Canada.
*CtY	Yale University Library, New Haven, CT.
DFo	Folger Shakespeare Library, Washington, D.C.
*DLC	Library of Congress, Washington, D.C.
FU	University of Florida, Gainesville.
*ICN	Newberry Library, Chicago, IL.
ICU	University of Chicago, IL.
IEN	Northwestern University, Evanston, IL.
*IU	University of Illinois, Urbana.
InU	Indiana University, Bloomington.
IaU	University of Iowa, Iowa City.
KU	University of Kansas, Lawrence.
MB	Boston Public Library, Boston, MA.
MBAt	Boston Athenaeum, Boston, MA.
*MH	Harvard University, Cambridge, MA.
MHi	Massachusetts Historical Society, Boston.
MU	University of Massachusetts, Amherst.
MWA	American Antiquarian Society, Worcester, MA.
MWelC	Wellesley College, Wellesley, MA.

MWiW-C	Williams College, Chapin Library, Williamstown, MA.
MdBP	Peabody Institute, Baltimore, MD.
MiD	Detroit Public Library, MI.
MiD-B	Detroit Public Library, Burton Historical Collection, MI.
MiU	University of Michigan, Ann Arbor.
*MiU-C	University of Michigan, Clements Library, Ann Arbor.
MiEM	Michigan State University, East Lansing.
MsU	University of Mississippi, University.
N	New York State Library, Albany.
NB	Brooklyn Public Library, Brooklyn, NY.
NIC	Cornell University, Ithaca, NY.
*NN	New York Public Library, NY.
NNC	Columbia University Library, New York, NY.
NNU-W	New York University Libraries, Washington Square, New York, NY.
NcD	Duke University, Durham, NC.
NcU	University of North Carolina, Chapel Hill.
NjP	Princeton University, Princeton, NJ.
OCU	University of Cincinnati, Cincinnati, OH.
OClW	Case Western Reserve University, Cleveland, OH.
OU	Ohio State University, Columbus, OH.
OrU	University of Oregon, Eugene.
PHi	Historical Society of Pennsylvania, Philadelphia.
PPL	The Library Company of Philadelphia, PA.
PPRF	Rosenbach Foundation, Philadelphia, PA.
PPULC	Union Library Catalogue of Pennsylvania, Philadelphia.
PU	University of Pennsylvania, Philadelphia.
RPB	Brown University, Providence, RI.
*RPJCB	John Carter Brown Library, Brown University, Providence, RI.
*TxU	University of Texas, Austin.
ViU	University of Virginia, Charlottesville.
ViW	College of William and Mary, Williamsburg, VA.
WU	University of Wisconsin, Madison.
Lewis-Walpole Library	Wilmarth S. Lewis-Horace Walpole Library, Yale University, Farmington, CT.

Prologue   1755-1762

1755   Books & Pamphlets

55-1. [Duncombe, John]
Horace, Book the First, Ode the Twenty-ninth. Imitated and Addressed to the Honourable William Hervey, Esq; on his Setting Out for North America, 1755.

"And has my Friend, uncheck'd by fear." (30)

In 67-2: Works of Horace, vol. I, pp. 116-17.

Notices: Lloyd's Eve Post, April 15, 1763; L Eve Post, April 15, 1763.

Regular Horatian ode. Hervey volunteered to be chaplain under Braddock, who was ordered to stop the encroaching Gaul on the Ohio. Has he had any contact with the Indians? Has his desertion of the church for the army bound France to its treaty with England?

55-2. [Prime, Benjamin Young]
On General Braddock's Defeat, A.D. 1755.

"Erewhile from Eastern shores well-pleas'd we heard." (86)

In 64-7: The Patriot Muse, pp. 9-11.

Blank verse. Protests criminal French and Indian incursions in the western regions of colonial America (near the Monongehela River, Fort DuQuesne), where Gen. Braddock and others died, "A sacrifice to Gallic perfidy!" Prays for a successful resistance.

1756 Books & Pamphlets

56-1. Averay, Robert.
   Britannia and the Gods in Council; A Dramatic Poem: Wherein Felicity is Predicted to Britain, the Causes of the present Disputes in Europe and America are Debated, and their Issue prophetically determined.
   London: Kinnersly, 1756. 32p.

   "O Thou Supreme! unlimited in Pow'r." (c. 600)

   Notices: MR 15 (Jul 1756), 84-5; GM 26 (Jun 1756), 308.

   Copies: BL 11630.e.5 (7); NUC CSmH, DFo, MiU-C.

   Blank verse. A patriotic poem meant to animate the British to an impending war with the French, who are blamed for their aggression "on the confines of Virginia's land"—their construction of forts on the "Ohio's Banks"—thereby encroaching Britain's rights. Cited are Boscawen, Acadia.

1757 Books & Pamphlets

57-1. Britain, a Poem; in three books.
Edinburgh: Ruddiman, Jun., 1757. vii+84+2p.

"'Twas on the day, when, every care at rest." (1606)

Notices: CR 4 (Sep 1758), 279-80; MR 16 (May 1757), 462.

Copies: BL 994.d.40.

Blank verse. On the French successes that began the Seven Years' War, "the ruin and depredation of our Indian colonies" and "the sacking of an out-settlement." Blames France for starting the war, noting that Britain's "western empire [was] spoil'd and deeply gor'd." Refers to the defeat of Braddock on the Ohio and Mercer at Oswego, and Indian attacks (encouraged by French gold) upon the colonial planters, leading to the provincial call for aid and counsel from the parent country.

57-2. [Prime, Benjamin Young]
On the Surrender of Fort William-Henry, A.D. 1757.

"What awful sound is this comes issuing forth." (176)

In 64-7: The Patriot Muse, pp. 12-17.

HC. Mourns the loss of Ft. William-Henry (on Lake Champlain) to the French under Montcalm, and the defeat of Braddock near the Monongahela River and of Schuyler at Oswego, the loss of Minorca. Describes savage Indian warfare.

1758 Books & Pamphlets

58-1. [Prime, Benjamin Young]
  An Ode on the Surrender of Louisbourg, July 27, 1758.

  "'Tis done, 'tis done." (204)

  In 64-7: The Patriot Muse, pp. 32-9.

  Regular Horatian ode. Exults in the British victory over the French at Louisbourg, Cape Breton. Praise of Pitt's navy, which made it possible, and Amherst, Wolfe, Boscawen, and others.

58-2. [-----]
  To General Amherst Passing through Long Island.

  "Amherst, while crouds attend you on your way." (41)

  In 64-7: The Patriot Muse, pp. 39-41.

  HC. A tribute to Amherst's generalship for his successful campaign against Cape Breton.

58-3. [-----]
  The Unfortunate Hero. An Ode Sacred to the Memory of Viscount Augustus Howe . . . Who was Slain in a Skirmish near Carillon, July the 6th, 1758.

  "Come, weeping muse, descend and bring." (184)

  In 64-7: The Patriot Muse, pp. 26-32.

  Irregular Pindaric ode. Mourns the death of noble Howe near Carillon (the French fort later renamed Ticonderoga), a defeat for America. Originally published New York: Parker & Weyman, 1758. 15p. Evans B1993 (Supp.); Sabin 97745.

Serials

58-4. A Ballad for the Year 1758.

"Last year all the cry." (60)

The Vocal Magazine; or British Songster's Miscellany (1778), Song #745, p. 195; SM 21 (Jan 1759), 34; UM 24 (Feb 1759), 100.

1757 was terrible--the British were defeated; but then Pitt came, Howe challenged France, and British spirit was restored. Boscawen, Louisbourg and Cape Breton, Frontenac, Senegal are signs that 1759 will see France humbled.

58-5. The Glorious Twenty-sixth of July, 1758.

"Britannia's sons rejoice." (21)

SM 20 (Aug 1758), 421-2; UM 23 (Aug 1758), 84.

Song honoring Amherst and Boscawen for taking Cape Breton (Canada).

58-6. An Ode Written on the 27th of December 1757.

"The Laureat dead! ah well a day." (48)

GM 28 (Jan 1758), 35.

Quatrains. When laureate Colly Cibber died, Whitehead was chosen to take his place. Advises the new poet laureate's "ballads" be "some for music, some for sense."

58-7. On reading Lady Howe's address.

"Now, Nottingham, assert your country's cause." (7)

SM 20 (Sep 1758), 483.

HC. Support of Lady Howe's request that Nottingham electors vote for her son William as their representative in Parliament because George Augustus Howe had been killed.

58-8. On the death of Lord Howe.

"Britannia mourns her youthful hero slain." (42)

SM 20 (Oct 1758), 530.

HC. Britain and America mourn the death of young Howe, killed in action near Ticonderoga, July 6, 1758. His brothers, Richard and William, will avenge his death upon "Gallia's sons." George Augustus Howe was an Irish peer, member for Nottingham, Colonel of the 55th regiment of foot, and a Brigadier on the American establishment.

58-9. On the Taking of Louisbourg.

"Stand round, my brave boys! let us sing and rejoice." (28)

The Vocal Magazine (1778), Song #466, p. 124.

Ballad narrates the conquests of Cape Breton and Louisbourg (Nova Scotia) over the French.

58-10. On the Taking of Louisburgh. By the Rev. Mr. Pullein.

"Hail, western world! begin thy better fate." (46)

GM 28 (Aug 1758), 372; SM 20 (Aug 1758), 421.

HC. Celebrates the coming of British liberty to Louisburgh. Praise of Pitt.

58-11. A Prophecy.

"Fifty-seven to this poor nation." (8)

LM 27 (Jan 1758), 44.

The year 1757 brought several reverses to Britain, but the next year should improve.

58-12. The Toast.

"Let Sweden, Vienna, and France join in league." (6)

SM 20 (Jan 1758), 20.

Anapest tetrameter couplets. Britain, with its allies -- Prussia, Denmark, and Holland -- should defy the triple alliance of Sweden, Austria, and France.

58-13. True Blue. A New Song.

"I hope there's no soul met over this bowl." (30)

UM 22 (Mar 1758), 143.

Song against selfishness, corruption (bribe, pension, place), and slavery; but praise of trade.

1759. Books & Pamphlets

59-1. Colvill, Robert.
  Verses for General Wolfe's Monument. November, 1759.

  "Here rests the CHIEF, with civic honours crown'd." (16)

  In 79-7: The Caledonians, p. 41; also in his Poetical Works (London: Dodsley, 1789), pp. 119-20.

  Panegyric on Gen. Wolfe whose successful campaign extended Britain's empire over Canada. At end dated "Sept. 7, 1760." See 72-A, Colvill on Wolfe again.

59-2. [Duncombe, John]
  Horace, Odes I: 37 Imitated. On the Defeat of the French Army in Canada, by General Wolfe. (1759)

  "Now let each pious Briton praise." (40)

  In 67-2: Works of Horace, vol. I, pp. 146-7.

  Horatian ode in quatrains. Britons rejoice that Montcalm was defeated by Wolfe, for now America is safe from Canada to Boston and to Georgia.

59-3. [-----]
  Horace, Odes V: 10. On Sir Edward Hawke's Victory over the French Fleet off Belleisle.

  "Say, Veteran Friend, belov'd Remain." (56)

  In 67-2: Works of Horace, vol. II, pp. 303-4.

  Horatian epistle, tetrameter couplets. Praise is due Hawke, Keppel, and Howe for their defeat of the French fleet off Belleisle, thereby preventing an invasion.

59-4. Lockman, John.
  To the Honourable General Townshend, on his arrival from Quebec.
  London: n.p., 1759. Broadside.

  Copies: MH.

  See 60-23.

59-5. [Prime, Benjamin Young]
An Acrostic. [William Pitt]

"W ho's this to whom the helm of state is giv'n." (11)

In 64-7: The Patriot Muse, p. 56.

HC. Praise of Pitt for his leadership in the war against France. "Though Amherst wields, 'tis he directs the lance."

59-6. [-----]
Britain's Glory, or Gallic Pride Humbled. A Pindaric Ode. Composed on the taking of Quebec. 1759.

"While injur'd Britain's indignation glows." (311)

In 64-7: The Patriot Muse, pp. 41-50.

Irregular Pindaric ode. Celebrates Wolfe's great victory over Montcalm in Quebec. Reviews the losses of the early years of the war and the reversal with the victory at Louisbourg, followed by other victories -- Guadeloupe, Niagara, Ticonderoga, and now Quebec.

Serials

59-7. An Acrostic. [General Wolfe]

"Greatest in fame! and to thy country dear." (12)

Edin M 3 (Nov 1759), 591; GM 29 (Nov 1759), 539; SM 21 (Dec 1759), 643.

Eulogy on Wolfe, who died before Quebec, September 13, 1759.

59-8. The best Defence, that has yet been made, or even can be made, for a late Noble Commander. Address'd to -----.

"Of pamphlets what shoals! what debates pro and con." (6)

UM 25 (Oct 1759), 212.

Debates on Sackville's conduct at Minden are useless; it was his "nature" that was at fault, meaning that he is cowardly. For an Abstract of the Trial of Lord George Sackville, see UM 26 (Apr 1760), 204-16.

59-9. Britain's Glory, or the Year 1759.

"The Genius of Britain's triumphant once more." (37)

RM 1 (Dec 1759), 320; UM 27 (Jul 1760), 40-1 (with music).

Song. Quatrains celebrating the victories of Britain over France in the War for Empire everywhere--in Europe, in America, in India. Cited are Pitt, Niagara, Cape Breton, Crown Point, Quebec, Saunders, Wolfe.

59-10. The Contrast. [Anagram]

"B-y base retreat how were those honours stain'd." (12)

Edin M 3 (Jun 1759), 308; UM 24 (Jun 1759), 320.

HC. Anagram contrasts the inglorious behavior of Byng with the heroic actions of Boscawen, and other British officers: Keppel, Howe, Wolfe, Clive, etc.

59-11. Description of a Ninety-Gun Ship.

"Amidst a wood of oaks with canvas leaves." (50)

Edin M 3 (May 1759), 247; GM 29 (May 1759), 229; SM 21 (Jul 1759), 363.

HC. A description of a large and powerful British battleship.

59-12. Designed for the Monument of General Wolfe.

"Here intomb'd a Soldier lies." (4)

RM 1 (Dec 1759), 321.

A simple epitaph on Wolfe.

59-13. Elegy on the death of Gen. Wolfe.

"On yonder plain what awful form appears." (36)

SM 21 (Oct 1759), 526.

Elegiac quatrains. Britain mourns the death of Wolfe.

59-14. An Essay to an Epitaph on the Truly Great and Justly Lamented Major General Wolfe, who fell victoriously before Quebec, Sept. 13, 1759.

"Here rests from toil, in narrow bounds confin'd." (22)

AR 1759, p. 452; Edin M 3 (Nov 1759), 591; GM (Nov 1759), 539.

HC. Honors Wolfe who defeated Montcalm at Quebec.

59-15. Extempore. Upon the news of the Generals Wolfe and Montcalm being both killed in the same action.

"The great Epaminondas conqu'ring, dy'd." (4)

SM 21 (Oct 1759), 527.

Epigram. Wolfe matches Epaminondas, as "The vanquish'd Montcalm swells the victor's [funeral] train."

59-16. The French Invaders, A New Song.

"'Tis rumour'd the French will soon visit our coast." (44)

UM 25 (Sep 1759), 141-2.

Song, in praise of Amherst, Boscawen, Keppel, Wolfe, Townshend, Barrington, Saunders, who with others will fight off the French in Europe, Africa, and America.

59-17. [Goldsmith, Oliver ?]
On the Taking of Quebec.

"Amidst the clamour of exulting joys." (12)

The Busy Body, No. 7, Oct. 22, 1759.

Quatrains. Wolfe's victory and death produce an ambiguous feeling -- exultation mixed with grief. (Wolfe's mother was a Goldsmith; Wolfe was allied to the Goldsmith family.) Also in The Poetical and Dramatic Works of Oliver Goldsmith (London: Evans, 1780). Roger Lonsdale, ed., The Poems of Thomas Gray, William Collins, and Oliver Goldsmith (London: Longmans, 1969), p. 768, considers it a poem of doubtful authenticity.

59-18. Hints to the Sculptor, for erecting a monument to the memory of the much-lamented Gen. Wolfe.

"Raise to his mem'ry and deathless name." (53)

RM 1 (Dec 1759), 320.

HC. Directions for the construction of a worthy monument to Gen. Wolfe.

59-19. [Inscription for Wolfe's Monument in Westminster Abbey.]

"This Monument / Sacred to the Memory." (c. 18)

Edin M 3 (Nov 1759), 609.

The monument for Wolfe was voted for by the House of Commons. Another inscription: 59-23.

59-20. Inscriptions on six windows during the illuminations, in London, Oct. 17, 1759.

"Praise the only Giver of Victory." (c. 15)

SM 21 (Oct 1759), 528.

Inscriptions honoring British victories in Europe, Asia, Africa, and America, including Wolfe's victory at Quebec.

59-21. Lines occasioned by the death of Gen. Wolfe.

"Amidst these triumphs, this excess of joy." (44)

SM 21 (Oct 1759), 526-7.

Blank verse. Britain mourns the death of Wolfe, the "pattern of heroism."

59-22. Lines occasioned by the Dispute between York and Kent about the Birth Place of Gen. Wolfe.

"Around the world when Homer's genius shone." (12)

Edin M 4 (Jan 1760), 35; GM 29 (Dec 1759), 593.

HC. Quebec is a second Illium. Now there is a dispute as to where Wolfe was born.

59-23. A Monumental Inscription, to perpetuate the Memory of General Wolfe.

"Stop, passenger." (c. 60)

UM 25 (Dec 1759), 305-6.

Traces the military contributions of Wolfe -- Minden, Louisbourg, Cape Breton, Quebec -- "The Conqueror of Canada."

59-24. A New Song, Occasioned by the late Victory obtained over the French Army, by the brave and intrepid Prince Ferdinand of Brunswic.

"Come fill ev'ry glass." (42)

UM 25 (Sep 1759), 143-4.

Song in sixains. Celebrates the victory at Minden, August 1, 1759.

59-25. An Ode on our Glorious Successes; as it was performed at Cuper's-gardens, on the 30th of August last.

"Hark, Truth her trump sounds." (56)

Edin M 3 (Sep 1759), 484.

Regular (Horatian) ode in octaves. Celebrates the victories over the French from the banks of the Weser to those of the Thames. Hawke has also blocked the French fleet under Conflans; Prussia fights valiantly; and peace will come only when America is won.

59-26. An Ode to Miss L-----. On the Death of General Wolfe.

"Britons, the work of war is done." (30)

AR 1759, pp. 451-2; LM 28 (Nov 1759), 613; SM 21 (Nov 1759), 585.

Regular (Horatian) ode in sixains. Wolfe died bravely.

59-27. Old England's Glory revived.

"Fame blow up thy trumpet, at Britain's command." (28)

LM 28 (Dec 1759), 674.

Song. Celebrates the great triumphs of Britain in the East and West -- North America and Asia, as well as Africa. But Wolfe lost his life at Quebec and many died at Minden. Closes with a hope for "a lasting good peace."

59-28. On the Defeat at Ticonderoga, or Carilon. By a Lady in America.

"Neglected long had lain my useless lyre." (51)

Edin M 3 (Feb 1759), 77; LM 28 (Feb 1759), 102.

HC. Mourns the defeat of the British at Ticonderoga (July 1758) by the French general Montcalm. Young George Augustus Howe, whose aide was Putnam, died in this action, like that in which Braddock lost his life. (Howe lost his life July 5, 1758.)

59-29. On the Monmouth's Cutting Out Four Swedish Vessels . . . in Sight of the French Fleet in Brestwater.

"Britannia heard the piercing voices of fame." (42)

Edin M 3 (Jul 1759), 361.

HC. Description of a naval action led by Hawke and Augustus John Hervey against the French in Brest harbor in which the enemy lost some auxiliary vessels.

59-30. Quebec. An Hero-Elegiac Poem on the Conquest of that Place, and the Death of General Wolfe.

"With soul of anguish, and with weeping eyes." (130)

L Chron 7 (Jan 3, 1760), 21; RM 1 (Supplement 1759), 370-1.

HC. Panegyric on Wolfe, apotheosized for his great victory at Quebec.

59-31. A Simile.

"Corinna, in the country bred." (74)

Edin M 3 (Feb 1759), 78; SM 21 (Feb 1759), 89-90; UM 24 (Feb 1759), 95.

Hudibrastics. This poem illustrates Pitt's bon mot that America was won in Germany.

59-32. The Tears of Britannia. An Ode Sacred to the Memory of General Wolfe.

"Where Albion's sea-girt cliffs, with tow'ring pride." (36)

Edin M 3 (Nov 1759), 589.

Regular (Horatian) ode in quatrains. Mourns Wolfe's death.

59-33. To Fame. An Ode. In Memory of the Late Victory obtained by Ferdinand over the French, Aug. 1, 1759. By Mr. Weller.

"Hear now the distant shouts of war." (56)

Edin M 3 (Oct 1759), 537; GM 29 (Sep 1759), 483.

Regular (Horatian) ode in octaves. Celebrates Anglo-Allied victory over the French at Minden, a German town on the Weser River. The Anglo-Allied army was commanded by Duke Ferdinand of Brunswick and the French under Marshal Contades. (This is the famous battle in which the British cavalry commander, Lord George Sackville, refused to obey Ferdinand's order to advance, thereby robbing the victory of decisive results.)

59-34. To Mr. Urban, on compleating the Twenty-Ninth Volume of the Gentleman's Magazine.

"'Tis done! unclouded sets the radiant year." (60)

GM 29 (1759), [ii]; SM 22 (Mar 1760), 125.

HC. Sylvanus Urban, the pseudonymous proprietor of the Gentleman's Magazine, receives a poem summarizing the glorious achievements of 1759 all over the world: Goree (Keppel), Minden, Madras, Guadeloupe, Cape Lagos, Quebec (Wolfe), Belleisle. See 60-39, the same verses.

59-35. To Mrs. Wolfe.

"Forbear with unrelenting sighs." (16)

SM 21 (Oct 1759), 528.

Quatrains. Mrs. Wolfe should cease mourning because her son has achieved a deathless fame.

59-36. To the Lady of Lord George Sackville.

"Grieve no more if ills depress." (30)

SM 21 (Sep 1759), 474-5; PA, Mar 17, 1779.

Trochaic three-stress couplets. Sympathy for the wife of Lord Sackville because of the scandal caused by his behavior at Minden, and a defence of Sackville who "Stands condemn'd without a cause." Dated Sept. 24, 1759.

59-37. To the Memory of an Officer Killed before Quebec.

"Ah me! what sorrows we are born to bear." (74)

Edin M 3 (Oct 1759), 537-8; SM 21 (Oct 1759), 527.

HC. The beloved mourns the death of an officer killed before Quebec, a casualty in the Seven Years' War.

59-38. To the Memory of Gen. Wolfe.

"If nobly fighting in a nation's cause." (16)

Edin M 3 (Oct 1759), 540.

HC. Honors Wolfe for his achievement: he died as he conquered Quebec.

59-39. To the Memory of General Wolfe.

"From envy, and from chance remov'd." (18)

GM 29 (Nov 1759), 539.

Sixains. Honors Wolfe for "The western world to've won."

59-40. To the Rt. Hon. Wm Pitt, Esq; on Col. Clavering's arrival with an Account of the surrender of the Island of Guadaloupe.

"Lo! Neptune smooths the raging of the deep." (28)

GM 29 (Jul 1759), 334; SM 21 (Jul 1759), 363.

HC. Praise of Pitt's leadership.

59-41. The Triumvirate. Addressed to Mrs. Wolfe.

"Rome has beheld her much-lov'd Cato bleed." (8)

SM 21 (Oct 1759), 528.

HC. Wolfe's compeers in the list of fame are King Frederick of Prussia and Prince Ferdinand.

59-42. The Year Fifty-Nine. A New Song.

"Come all ye brave Britons, let no one complain." (36)

Edin M 3 (Dec 1759), 645; UM 25 (Dec 1759), 321.

Song. A summary of the several defeats suffered by the French when engaging the English army and navy: Senegal, India, Minden; De la Clue defeated by Boscawen, Montcalm defeated at Quebec; Niagara, Crown Point, Ticonderoga, Belleisle; Conflans defeated by Hawke.

Prints

59-43. The Mistake a Satyrical Print on a late Battle near M--D-N in G-RM--Y.
1 Aug. 1759.

   "Whilst Marshal C[on]t[ade]s and ye Gallant gay B[rog]lio." (8)

   Engr. with couplets. August 1, 1759.

   Stephens 3684 (III: 2, 1199-1200).

   Sackville's unacceptable behavior at the Battle of Minden from this time received
the attention of the satirists. (The battle was fought between the Anglo-Allied
army commanded by Duke Ferdinand of Brunswick and the French under Marshal Contades,
the latter being defeated. Lord George Sackville, the British cavalry commander,
refused to obey the order to advance, sent several times by Ferdinand, thereby
robbing the victory of decisive results.)

1760   Books & Pamphlets

60-1. Cockings, George.
   War: An Heroic Poem, from the taking of Minorca, by the French; to the Reduction of the Havannah, by the Earl of Albemarle, Sir George Pocock.
   London: Say, Cook, 1760. xiv + 174p.

   Copies: NUC NN.

   See 60-3.

60-2. -----.
   -----. Second Edition, to the Raising of the Siege of Quebec: With large Amendments and Additions.
   Boston: Adams, 1762. xvi + 190 + 46p.

   Copies: NUC DLC, MH, MiU-C, NN, RPJCB.

   See 60-3.

60-3. -----.
   War: An Heroic Poem. From the Taking of Minorca by the French, to the Reduction of Manilla; In Ten Books. [4th ed.]
   London: Hooper, 1765. 240p.

   "Of Providence, and Britain's happy state." (c. 4500)

   Sabin 14110-11, 101257.

   Copies: BL 11643.h.21.

   HC. The campaign against Louisbourg and Cape Breton, Quebec--the death of Howe before Ticonderoga and Wolfe before Quebec; the taking of Martinico and of Havannah (Cuba)--among other campaigns are narrated. The emphasis is on the fighting--English bravery, French treachery, and Indian cruelty. Occasionally the provincial contributions to British successes are mentioned, but rarely.

60-4. -----.
   Britannia's Call to Her Brave Troops & Hardy Tars.
   Boston: Adams, 1762. 46p.

   Copies: NUC IU, NN.

   An excerpt from his War, 2nd ed, 60-2 above.

60-5. [Duncombe, John]
Horace IV: 4 Imitated. On the Conquest of Louisbourg, Quebec, and all Canada, by the Generals Amherst and Wolfe.

"As Western Orellana, King of Floods." (76)

In 67-2: Works of Horace, vol. II, pp. 208-11.

Notices: L Mag 35 (Sep 1767), 475-6.

Horatian ode, HC. The French mourn their defeat everywhere by the British--especially in Canada where Wolfe and Amherst were the conquerors.

60-6. [Patrick, J.]
Quebec: A Poetical Essay, in Imitation of the Miltonic Style: being a regular Narrative of the Proceedings and Capital Transactions performed by the British Forces under the Command of Vice-Admiral Saunders & Major-General Wolfe, in the glorious Expedition against Canada, in the year 1759.
London: Whitridge, 1760. 30p.

"Once more celestial Maid, whose sacred Ray." (439)

Sabin 59075.

Copies: NUC CaOt.

Miltonic blank verse. "A volunteer on Board his Majesty's Ship Somerset," Patrick describes the combined sea and land operations under Saunders and Wolfe in the summer of 1759. Participants cited are Monckton, Montcalm, Holmes, Townshend, et al.

60-7. [Prime, Benjamin Young]
The Lamentation of Louis XV. On Occasion of the Conquests of the English, A.D. 1760.

"Pensive, trembling and embarrass'd." (132)

In 64-7: The Patriot Muse, pp. 59-71.

Quatrains, in French and English. Persona of King Louis XV of France reflects on the war--the gains at the beginning, and then the losses and the threat of an invasion of the homeland.

60-8. [-----]
Loyal Tears shed over Royal Dust, or An Elegy on the Death of his late Majesty King George II, of Glorious Memory, Who departed this Life, Oct. 25, 1760, Aetat 76.

"Why heaves my bosom with continual sighs." (175)

In 64-7 : The Patriot Muse, pp. 72-77.

HC. The king dies while "fame resounded Amherst's glorious arms"--amidst all the victories against France. The next George will "complete the vengeance his grand-sire began." May Pitt continue to stand near the throne!

Serials

60-9. Acrostic. [Granby]

"Granby, the Gen'rous, Gentle, Great, and Good." (6)

DJ, Sep 9, 1760.

Praise of the Marquess of Granby, a genuinely noble patriot.

60-10. Browne, Moses.
Verses (written the evening of the royal funeral) on occasion of the late King's death, and proclaiming his present Majesty.

"Where the beach-brows Hantonia's soil o'erlook." (62)

PL, Nov 18, 1760; RM 3 (Nov 1760), 265.

HC. Britannia mourns the death of George the Second, but his grandson George the Third assumes the throne and resumes the war against France.

60-11. A Call to the Poets. On the taking of Quebec.

"While to brave Wolfe such clouds of incense rise." (28)

L Chron 7 (Jan 17, 1760), 71; SM 22 (Jan 1760), 33.

HC. Others besides Wolfe deserve praise for the victory at Quebec -- Monckton and Townshend.

60-12. Cunningham, John.
An Elegiac Ode on the Death of his late Majesty.

"England! thy Genius vested like despair." (144)

Edin M 4 (Nov 1760), 589-90; Works of the English Poets, ed. S. Johnson (London: Wright, 1790), 69: 162-8.

Elegiac quatrains. The nation mourns the death of "the venerable King" George II; but another George will "hold the reins of regal power" and be "As good, as glorious, as the parent King."

60-13. Epitaph on General Wolfe . . . in the Parish Church of Westerham, in the County of Kent.

"Whilst George in sorrow bows his laurell'd head." (4 + 8)

GM 54 (Oct 1784), 731; UM 26 (Apr 1760), 203.

Inscription and HC on the birth and death of the "Conqueror of Quebec."

60-14. Extempore on Two Naval Victories Last Year.

"What wonders brave Hawke and Boscawen have done." (2)

Edin M 4 (Jun 1760), 316.

Hawke and Boscawen destroyed the ships of two French admirals, De la Clue and Conflans.

60-15. A Farewell to General Murray, Governor of Quebec, 25 of Sept. 1759.

"'Twas Wolfe's, the pow'r of British troops to try." (20)

PL, Jul 5, 1760.

HC. Praise of Gen. James Murray, who had with Wolfe shared the dangers of the Canada campaign: Quebec.

60-16. [Garrick, David]
   Song. [Heart of Oak. Sung in Harlequin's Invasion.]

"Come cheer up, my lads, 'tis to glory we steer." (24)

RM 2 (Mar 1760), 153; UM 26 (Mar 1760), 152-3 (with music); The Vocal Magazine (1778), Song 540, p. 141.

A patriotic naval song of the Great War for Empire, one of the famous and enduring songs against the French; the music was by William Boyce, Master of the Royal Band.

60-17. Horace. Ode XV. Imitated.

"As Lewis slumber'd o'er the plans." (40)

GM 30 (Aug 1760), 384; L Chron 8 (Aug 12, 1760), 155; SM 22 (Aug 1760), 424.

Joan of Arc prophesies the doom of King Louis of France. He will be destroyed by Pitt and Newcastle, Prince Ferdinand (Minden), Wolfe, Barrington, Boscawen, Hawke. But, "Hot Braddock [only] may thy fate delay," in the west.

60-18. Inscriptions on an Obelisk at Lord Amherst's Seat, Riverhead, Kent.

"Louisburg surrendered." (c. 20)

W Misc 17 (Dec 31, 1781), 326-7.

Amherst advertises all the British victories over the French in which he had a part: Louisbourg, Fort du Quesne, Niagara, Ticonderoga, Crown-Point, Quebec, Montreal, etc.

60-19. The Junto.

"A council was lately assembled at Marli." (28)

BM 1 (No. 5, 1760), 265; Edin M 4 (Apr 1760), 213.

Hexameter couplets. The French ministry agree that they are beaten and can only continue to fight in despair.

60-20. Lockman, John.
An Ode: On the Birth-Day of His Royal Highness George Prince of Wales 4th June 1760.

"O'rjoy'd, my artless Lyre I strung." (72)

PA, Jun 30, 1760.

Regular (Horatian) ode in octaves. On the future George III, soon to be king of England at a time of great glory in 1759. Some stanzas allude ironically to rebellion.

60-21. Lockman, John.
A Sixth Loyal Song: Viz. Admiral Hawke's Welcome to Old England.

"Behold where Britannia points, joyful, her Lance." (48)

PA, May 7, 1760.

Song. In praise of Hawke's triumph over the French navy, the 20th of November, 1759, a great year for the British.

60-22. Lockman, John.
A Song on the taking of Mont-Real by Gen. Amherst.

"I fill not the glass, to some favourite lass." (48)

BM 1 (Oct 1760), 603; The Vocal Magazine (1778), Song 857, p. 233.

Song. Amherst has taken Montreal, and now Britain has won Canada.

60-23. Lockman, John.
To the Honourable General Townshend, on his Arrival from Quebec.

"Thrice welcome! Hero! Patriot! every name." (44)

RM 2 (Jan 1760), 43-4; L Chron 22 (Sep 17, 1767), 280; DJ, Oct 3, 1767.

HC. Panegyric on General Townshend, second in command to Wolfe, in the Quebec campaign. Reprinted 1767 when Townshend was appointed Viceroy of Ireland.

60-24. The Man of Kent. In Imitation of Pope's Man of Ross.

"P. Why are our thoughts on lords alone intent." (44)

Edin M 4 (Jan 1760), 34-5; GM 30 (Jan 1760), 38; SM 22 (Jan 1760), 33.

HC. Praise of Wolfe, the man of Kent.

60-25. Mathison, T.
A Sacred Ode. By T. Mathison, minister at Brechin. Occasioned by the late successes attending the British arms.

"In thee, great Sov'reign of the skies." (124)

SM 22 (Jan 1760), 31-2.

Quatrains. Celebrates British successes in the war against France. Roused by Pitt, Britain triumphed at Minden (Prince Ferdinand), Lagos (Boscawen), India (Pococke), Goree and Senegal, Guadeloupe (Barrington), at Quebec (Wolfe), and on the seas (Hawke).

60-26. Maubert's Reverie.

"As fam'd Maubert profoundly grave." (24)

PL, Oct 16, 1760.

Quatrains. The French author Maubert is advised by the devil to lie about English victories everywhere, including Montreal and Quebec.

60-27. Merrick, James.
On His Majesty's Accesion [sic] to the Throne.

"Late in yon sequester'd grave." (106)

Edin M 5 (Feb 1761), 93.

Trochaic tetrameter couplets. A lyric panegyric on the new king who has just begun his reign. (Also in John Nichols, ed. A Select Collection of Poems [London: Nichols, 1780], VIII, 205-9; from Pietas Universitatis Oxoniensis [Oxonii, 1761].)

60-28. A New Song, on the Successes of his Majesty's Arms in Canada.

"The projects of France." (66)

UM 27 (Oct 1760), 211.

Song, celebrates all the important victories in Canada: Montreal, Cape Breton, Quebec, but stresses Montreal.

60-29. Occasioned by reading M. Vaudreuil's Letter, which was industriously circulated at Montreal.

"The Gallic commander, with true French parade." (21)

BM 1 (Nov 1760), 664.

Trochaic hexameter couplets. The French commander at Montreal submits to Amherst.

60-30. Occasioned by the Death of General Wolfe.

Blest Liberty! how absolute thy power." (30)

BM 1 (Apr 1760), 213-14.

HC. Wolfe's example has inspired Britain to conquer.

60-31. Ode addressed to the late Gen. Wolfe. Written after the reduction of Louisbourg.

"Sprung from an ancient, honour'd race." (30)

BM 1 (Feb 1760), 98; Edin M 4 (Jan 1760), 35; SM 22 (Jan 1760), 32.

Regular ode, couplets in sixains. Wolfe has inspired the British to continue their victories over France. Also entitled "Ode to General Wolfe."

60-32. Ode on the Death of George II. King of Great Britain, &c.

"Why lours yon cloud upon Britannia's brow." (114)

BM 1 (Nov 1760), 662-3.

Irregular ode. George II is mourned, but another George will continue the dynasty.

60-33. Ode on the New-Year.

"At length the wanton hours appear." (48)

BM 1 (Jan 1760), 42.

Regular ode, couplets in sixains. The King is honored for his great victories over France, especially in Canada, where the Indians, impressed by the British, enlist in the cause of liberty.

60-34. An Ode to the Ever Memorable Year 1759.

"Blow the trumpet, strike the lyre." (56)

BM 1 (Feb 1760), 99-100; Edin M 3 (Jan 1760), 33; GM 30 (Jan 1760), 38; Lloyd's 6 (Jan 21, 1760), 78.

Irregular Pindaric ode, a song. In 1759 the French lost the sea to the British navy. Britain was guided by Pitt. This year will be remembered for the many victories over France.

60-35. On the Death of General Wolfe.

"Amidst these loud acclaims which rend the sky." (40)

GM 30 (Apr 1760), 195.

HC. Mourns brave Wolfe, who will achieve immortality for his victory.

60-36. On the Death of General Wolfe.

"Behold the man! with rev'rence, speak his name." (24)

In Joshua Edkins, ed., A Collection of Poems (Dublin, 1789), I, 26-7.

HC. Praise of Wolfe for his great victory, and mourning for his untimely death.

60-37. On the Death of the King. By the Rev. Mr. Fawkes.

"Ah fatal hour!--we must at last resign." (14)

L Chron 8 (Oct 30, 1760), 428; PL, Nov 1, 1760; UM 27 (Nov 1760), 265.

HC. The end of the reign of George II. It was George II's blessed lot to close a happy reign, triumphant over France. Signed Fra. Fawkes in L. Chron.

60-38. On the Frequent Defeats of the French Army. An Epigram.

"The toast of each Briton in war's dread alarms." (4)

Edin M 4 (Sep 1760), 484; GM 30 (Sep 1760), 431.

The French run for their lives in every battle.

60-39. On the Last Campaign.

"'Tis done! unclouded sets the radiant year." (60)

Edin M 4 (Jan 1760), 34.

HC. Britain has been victorious over France over the wide world; it was a great year for triumphs, greater than any other time. See 59-34, the same verses.

60-40. On the Late Rumour of a Peace, and the Present Seeming Disappearance of an Accommodation.

"Britain, again thou call'st to arms." (42)

GM 30 (Jul 1760), 337; PL, Jul 7, 1760.

Regular ode in sixains. There will be no peace apparently, and so Britain must again prepare for the fight against France, especially for the protection of the colonies.

60-41. On the Taking of Montreal by Gen. Amherst.

"An humble Muse, unus'd to rude alarms." (80)

GM 30 (Oct 1760), 480-1; PA, Oct 13, 1760; SM 22 (Nov 1760), 580.

HC. Praise of Amherst who, conquering Montreal, completed what Wolfe began, thereby defeating France's hope of an American empire. Generals Johnson, Braddock, and Wolfe preceded Amherst in the American campaigns against France, and extended the bounds of the empire.

60-42. Song in the Fair.

"In story we're told." (60)

RM 2 (Jan 1760), 41; UM 25 (Supp 1759), 376, & 26 (Feb 1760), 95-6 (with music); The Vocal Magazine (1778), Song 863, p. 235; L Chron 7 (Jan 1, 1760), 15.

Patriotic song in praise of English victories over the French: in America (Amherst and Boscawen), where Cape Breton, Crown Point, Niagara, Guadeloupe, and Quebec have been taken, and in Africa (Senegal), in Europe (Minden); and Hawke defeats Conflans in the Channel. (By "Paul Whitehead" in L Chron.)

60-43. Spence, Joseph.
On the Death of King George II. And Inauguration of George III.

"In blooming majesty, and graceful State." (90)

In John Nichols, ed., A Select Collection of Poems (London: Nichols, 1780), VIII, 14-17.

Regular (Horatian) ode in dixains. Places the event in a historical context. Spence appears to emphasize the Whig view of history and monarchy. (From Pietas Universitatis Oxoniensis [Oxonii, 1761].)

60-44. To Britannia. An Ode.

"Britannia, queen of ocean, rise." (24)

PL, Mar 20, 1760.

Regular (Horatian) ode in quatrains. Hope that after France is defeated peace will be restored. France will be defeated as Minden and Quebec testify.

60-45. The Trident Restored. To the Right Hon. William Pitt, Esq;

"Halcyons were brooding o'er the silent Deep." (72)

L Eve Post, May 22, 1760.

HC. When Pitt took the helm, Britain (especially because of her navy) assumed her hegemony in Europe.

60-46. Trophy of the Genius of Quebec.

"Where near Quebec St. Lawrence flows." (27)

RM 3 (Jul 1760), 43.

Song. The English will bring liberty to Quebec when their form of government displaces the tyranny of the French.

60-47. Verses occasioned by the Death of Gen. Wolfe.

"Blest Liberty! how absolute thy power." (30)

Edin M 4 (Mar 1760), 145-6.

HC. Praise of Wolfe's inspiring leadership.

60-48. Verses on Sea and Land Officers.

"Sir Edward Hawke. Beneath a ribbon and unsully'd star." (44)

RM 2 (Mar 1760), 154.

Quatrains characterizing heroic naval and military officers participating in the Great War for Empire: Hawke, Boscawen, Saunders, Keppel, Howe, Dennis, Granby, Waldegrave, Amherst, Monckton, and Townshend.

60-49. Verses: Suggested by the two grand National Subscriptions set on Foot in 1759.

"O Year Renown'd! Triumphant Fifty-Nine!" (56)

PA, May 14, 1760.

HC. The subscriptions are for British troops abroad, for widows and orphans of those who died in service, and for French prisoners. The war is just, but now is the time for charity.

60-50. Whitehead, William.
  Ode for the New-Year 1760.

  "Again the sun's revolving sphere." (56)

  BM 1 (Feb 1760), 98; Edin M 4 (Jan 1760), 33; GM 30 (Jan 1760), 38;
L Eve Post, Dec 30, 1759-Jan 1, 1760; LM 29 (Jan 1760), 45; SM 21 (Dec
1759), 644; UM 25 (Supp 1759), 373; W Eve Post, Dec 30, 1759-Jan 1, 1760.

  Pindaric ode celebrating British victories over the French, thereby restoring
the blessing of freedom to various lands.

60-51. The World turned upside-down. A Song.

  "Time was when merit had applause." (24)

  GM 30 (Jul 1760), 337.

  A cynical song about hypocrites who prefer the bad to the good: "Pride,
and self-int'rest rule the roast."

60-52. Woty, William.
  Stanzas, Occasioned by the Death of his Late Most Sacred Majesty.

  "As late I mus'd, from Observation free." (52)

  Edin M 4 (Oct 1760), 542-3; GM 30 (Nov 1760), 534; L Chron 8 (Oct 30, 1760),
428; LM 29 (Dec 1760), 607-8; PA, Nov 1, 1760; SM 21 (Oct 1760), 523; W Eve
Post, Oct 30, 1760.

  Quatrains. I mourn the death of the good old king, but I also welcome the new,
his grandson, who will bring peace.

Prints

60-53. [America! of Wealth thou modern Mine.]

  "America! of Wealth thou modern Mine." (4)

  Engr. with quatrains. C. 1760.

  Lewis-Walpole Library.

  America's savages should not complain were they conquered, for Britons (Europeans?) have become slaves of America's corrupting gold. (See T. Warton's ode on the "Revenge of America," 63-167.)

1761 Books & Pamphlets

61-1. [Duncombe, John]
Horace, Odes, III: 26. Imitated. To the Rev. Mr. Hirst, F.R.S. Chaplain of his Majesty's Ship the Lenox.

"Whither on the Muse's pinion." (32)

In 67-2 : Works of Horace, vol. II, pp. 140-1.

Notices: BM 8 (Jul 1767), 383; L Eve Post, Apr 9, 1767; RM 17 (Jul 1767), 43.

Regular Horatian Ode, tetrameter quatrains with alternating rhymes. References to the British victories over the French in Pondicherry (India) and Canada.

61-2. Evans, Nathaniel.
Ode on the Prospect of Peace. 1761.

"When elemental conflicts rage." (208)

In 72-4 : Poems on Several Occasions, pp. 21-29.

Regular Pindaric ode. Welcomes news of English victories and of the peace. Cited are Canada; Clive and India; Keppel and Goree and Senegal; Elliott, Granby, France (Louisburgh, St. Lawrence, Quebec), Wolfe, Pennsylvania, and the Delaware.

61-3. [Mallet, David]
Truth in Rhyme, addressed to a certain Noble Lord.
London: Millar, 1761. 20p.

"Astrea, eldest born of Jove." (134)

Notices: CR 11 (Jun 1761), 492; MR 25 (Jul 1761), 79; L Chron 9 (Apr 28, 1761), 415.

Copies: BL 11661.d.1; NUC MH, MiU, NjP, OCU, PU.

Octosyllabic couplets. Praise of John Stuart, 3rd Earl of Bute. Counselled by Bute, the young King George III appoints Mansfield to an important official position related to his right to the throne--a sign that Mansfield has attached himself to Bute. (Bute became Prime Minister officially on May 26, 1762.) This poem is mentioned in Churchill's The Ghost (1762-63), III, 497-502.

Serials

61-4. An Acrostic. [Bussy]

"Britannia for Arms, Arts, and Virtue renown'd." (5)

St J's C, Oct 13, 1761.

Bussy, the French chief minister, boasts that England will submit to France.

61-5. Augustus Britannicus. To his Son.

"Far from your sight you'll drive the abject slave." (34)

Edin M 5 (Aug 1761), 426-7.

HC. A character of an ideal king, who is above faction.

61-6. A Card to Louis XV.

"By Bussy, your Servant, it now does appear." (10)

St J's C, Aug 18, 1761.

Hexameter couplets. Ironic satire on King Louis of France. George III sends a card, a message, to Louis XV, warning him not to invade because his wedding and coronation are being planned. Bussy is cited, Louis's chief minister.

61-7. A Coronation Ode.

"Stop, Time." (72)

Edin M 5 (May 1761), 257-8; LM 30 (Apr 1761), 214-15; PA, Mar 30, 1761; SM 23 (Apr 1761), 202.

Irregular Pindaric ode. A native monarch rules Britain who will, it is hoped, bring peace, an end to war with France. By William Havard, an actor (1710-78).

61-8. The Earl of Essex, 1598, commanded and applied to a late Event, 1761.

"Unmov'd at Spanish Arts, at Spanish Arms." (12)

L Eve Post, Oct 27-29, 1761; PA, Oct 29, 1761.

Essex, in Elizabeth's reign, warned of Spanish duplicity; so Pitt, in George's reign, warns of the treacherous French and those British who appear to side with them.

61-9. Epigram.

"My lov'd Boscawen dead! 'tis all a lie." (4)

SM 23 (Feb 1761), 97.

Boscawen lives triumphant at Lagos and immortal at Louisburg.

61-10. Epistle to a Friend, on the Report of the King's Intended Marriage, and the Prospects of a Peace.

"Yes--ev'ry hopeful son of rhyme." (108)

Edin M 5 (Aug 1761), 425; L Eve Post, Aug 27, 1761; St J's C, Aug 25, 1761.

Octosyllabic couplets. Pleased to learn that the King will marry, and likewise pleased that Britain is doing well in the war, not fretting over increased taxes.

61-11. A Fragment found in the Corner of a Palace.

"Thus in my haste I reason'd with despair." (c. 220)

PL, Jan 27, 1761.

HC. Part of this fragment, which is concerned with a character of the new, young King, describes the victory in Canada; but the future, the poet predicts, will be even greater and more dazzling. Corruption, too, will disappear.

61-12. The hunting of Chevy Chace, an old ballad, accommodated to the present times.

"God prosper long our noble King." (152)

SM 23 (Nov 1761), 566.

Ballad on Pitt's resignation and its repercussion, a cause for alarm. Reviews Pitt's successful leadership in the war; but Pitt, "the glory of our land," has "fall'n into disgrace!"

61-13. Inscription, to the Memory of a Great Patriot and Statesman.

"With honesty, and active genius born." (14)

PL, Nov 2, 1761.

HC. Eulogy of Pitt for his character and achievements. (His resignation is not mentioned, but implied in the title.)

61-14. The Letter of a Right Honourable Person versified, and another in Answer to it; with Notes, historical, critical, political, &c. . . .

"Having found, with surprise, that my late resignation." (70)

UM 29 (Dec 1761), 329-30.

Fourteeners. Pitt defends his resignation because of differences over Spain. His advice (to declare war on Spain) was not taken.

61-15. A Loyal Song.

"Huzza my brave lads, with one heart and one voice." (25)

PL, Jun 25, 1761.

Patriotic, anti-Gallican song.

61-16. A Loyal Song.

"Our Henrys and Edwards old history shews." (26)

RM 5 (Aug 1761), 94.

Song. Patriotic lyric directed against the French. Present victories (Goree, Guadeloupe, Senegal, Cape Breton) are in the great tradition of victories over the French.

61-17. A New Song, on seeing Colonel Burgoyne's Regiment of Light Horse reviewed in Hyde-Park.

"Come, ye brave British lads who have courage to fight." (25)

UM 28 (Jan 1761), 41-2.

An anti-Gallican war song.

61-18. [No letters more full or expressive can be.]

"No letters more full or expressive can be." (4)

UM 29 (Nov 1761), 268.

W. P. (Pitt) stands for "wisdom, war, wonder, and wit" and "peerage, and pension, and Pitt."

61-19. [No Letters there are more expressive can be.]

"No Letters there are more expressive can be." (8)

St J's C, Dec 19, 1761.

Hexameter couplets. Pitt has the will, but not the power.

61-20. [Now Pitt with honest warmth's resigned.]

"Now Pitt with honest warmth's resign'd th'important seal." (9)

PL, Oct 8, 1761.

Fourteeners. Britain is dismayed that Pitt has resigned, believing it incredible.

61-21. Old England's Epitaph.

"Hic jacent England's glory, wisdom, wit." (2)

BM 2 (Oct 1761), 553.

Epitaph. England will decline, now that Pitt is out.

61-22. On a late fatal Resignation.

"Temple and Pitt resign, and every brow." (22)

UM 29 (Nov 1761), 268.

HC. Pitt and Temple are pleased to resign from the ministry and do not raise a fuss or stir up faction -- true disinterested patriots!

61-23. On a late Removal.

"When the duke de Choiseul receiv'd the report." (10)

BM 2 (Oct 1761), 552; Edin M 5 (Oct 1761), 548; PL, Oct 8, 1761.

France is pleased at Pitt's removal; England can only be conquered in Pitt.

61-24. On a Late Resignation.

"As Pitt has resign'd--e'en let the thing rest." (6)

PL, Dec 3, 1761.

We should accept Pitt's resignation.

61-25. On a late Resignation.

"Pitt has resign'd, by whose sagacious aid." (30)

BM 2 (Oct 1761), 552; Edin M 5 (Oct 1761), 547-8; PL, Oct 20, 1761; SM 23 (Oct 1761), 536.

HC. Pitt brought victory to Britain; he should be restored.

61-26. On a late Resignation.

"When first, portentous, it was known." (12)

Edin M 5 (Nov 1761), 600; GM 31 (Nov 1761), 528; L Chron 10 (Oct 29, 1761), 423; RM 5 (Nov 1761), 263; SM 23 (Nov 1761), 566.

Epigram in sixains. Perhaps the King's dropping the great diamond of the crown foretells the loss of Hanover, or Pitt. Who would have guessed that Pitt would resign! (The diamond episode assumed great symbolic significance in due time.) Another title is "On the King's Dropping the Great Diamond of the Crown."

61-27. On a slur thrown on Mr. Pitt's name, in some late verses of Lord L-----.

"Say, high fam'd L-t---n, whose courtly lays." (10)

SM 23 (Mar 1761), 55.

HC. Objects to the "ill-nature" of "such fond, such wanton jests" in a satire on Pitt.

61-28. On Mr. Pitt's Resignation.

"Aegyptian Darkness cover'd all the Land." (26)

L Eve Post, Oct 17, 1761; LM 30 (Oct 1761), 555.

HC. Pitt led the country and it prospered, triumphant over France. We pray that he be restored, for the King is righteous and virtuous.

61-29. On Mr. Pitt's resignation.

"Britain, by conqu'ring Gallia scorn'd." (20)

SM 23 (Oct 1761), 536.

Quatrains. Churchill (Duke of Marlborough) "in midst of conquest fell"; so Pitt. "The rest our enemies will tell."

61-30. On Mr. Pitt's Resignation.

"Britain, with ev'ry Blessing crown'd of late." (18)

L Eve Post, Oct 13, 1761; PL, Oct 16, 1761.

HC. A "factious few" are responsible for Pitt's resignation, after so many successes as leader.

61-31. On Mr. Pitt's Resignation.

"Britons, 'tis done! the fatal Stroke is giv'n." (6)

St J's C, Oct 13, 1761.

Only France can gain from Pitt's resignation. Bussy is cited.

61-32. On Mr. Pitt's Resignation.

"Whence does the Gaul exult? Can Broglio boast." (4)

BM 2 (Oct 1761), 552; PL, Oct 9, 1761.

Pitt has resigned; France exults.

61-33. On Mr. Pitt's resigning the Seals.

"Ne'er yet in vain did heav'n its omens send." (4)

LM 30 (Oct 1761), 555; SM 23 (Oct 1761), 536.

Epigram. When Pitt resigned, the nation lost "the noblest jewel in the crown." An allusion to the ill omen of a jewel falling from George III's crown at his coronation, a great diamond on top of the crown.

61-34. On Seeing the Heralds declare War against Spain.

"Since the parties for peace from Augsburg are gone." (4)

UM 29 (Supp 1761), 384.

Epigram. Now Britain declares war on Spain, which was Pitt's wish months ago (the cause of his resignation). Spain declared war on Great Britain January 16, 1762.

61-35. On the Death of Admiral Boscawen.

"Long France did conquer'd India coast." (12)

Edin M 5 (Jan 1761), 34; Lloyd's 8 (Jan 19, 1761), 70; PL, Jan 24, 1761.

Quatrains. Praise of Admiral Boscawen for driving the French from India and America.

61-36. On the False Appellation given to a late Mark of Royal Magnificence.

"Prithee, my friends, no more dissention." (4)

PL, Nov 20, 1761.

Reward is the proper word, not "that hated word" pension. (Pitt is the reference, of course.)

61-37. On the late Successes of the British Arms.

"Again the wide-mouth'd trump of fame." (48)

Edin M 5 (Aug 1761), 425; RM 5 (Aug 1761), 94.

Regular Horatian ode in praise of British victories in Europe, America (Canada, West Indies), India, Africa: Britain will bring peace and prosperity and civilization as a result of its triumphs.

61-38. On the Present Military Preparations.

"Still must the martial banner be display'd." (64)

Lloyd's 8 (Apr 10, 1761), 348.

HC. An objection to destructive war.

61-39. A Pindaric Ode on the Gallant Behavior of the Highlanders in N. America.

"Descend, ye nine! 'tis yours to raise." (114)

Edin M 5 (Apr 1761), 201-2.

Irregular Pindaric ode patriotically celebrating the victories of the Highlanders in the Ohio -- which please Oscian (Ossian).

61-40. [The Romans thank'd their Chief, with glorious Pride.]

"The Romans thank'd their Chief, with glorious Pride." (12)

DJ, Oct 24, 1761.

Heroic quatrains. Deplores Pitt's resignation -- "his Country's Glory is his Crime."

61-41. A Royal Soliloquy after Coronation.

"To reign is fix'd--but how to reign's the question." (48)

SM 23 (Sep 1761), 489.

Blank verse. Parody in part of Hamlet's soliloquy. The poet hopes the new King's rule will be tempered by love and justice. At the end, the King is made to say, "I will know my subjects, and be known to them."

61-42. To his Countrymen. On a late Resignation.

"Well, well, my good countrymen! -- Prithee don't fret." (32)

GM 31 (Nov 1761), 528; L Chron 10 (Oct 29, 1761), 423-4.

Doggerel, hexameter couplets. Pitt leaves the war in good hands, the King's! (Are these verses ironic?)

61-43. To Mr. P[itt].

"Great man, with glory crown'd, in dangers try'd." (10)

L Chron 10 (Nov 3, 1761), 436; RM 5 (Nov 1761), 263.

Pitt's resignation recalls the fall of Churchill in Anne's reign, and bodes ill for the country in George's reign.

61-44. To the Rt. Hon. Wm Pitt, Esq;

"Let Rome and Carthage boast no more." (14)

Edin M 5 (Mar 1761), 147.

Simply a brief boast of British military and naval successes over the French -- Minden and "the Western ocean," under the leadership of Pitt.

61-45. To the Tune of the Merry toned Horn.

"While the French are all cursing the Wars." (32)

PA, Oct 13, 1761.

A patriotic war song makes the point that George the Third must negotiate a good peace with France before the war can be concluded.

61-46. Verses address'd to the Authors of Apology, Examiner Triumvirate, &c. &c. &c.

"You that are blest with Learning, Taste and Sense." (16)

St J's C, Nov 17, 1761.

HC. Satire now has some subjects to ridicule: corruption, faction, party. The poets should assert the cause of Pitt and the patriots.

61-47. Verses addressed to the Author of the Pindaric Ode on the Royal Nuptials.

"Whilst you, great Bard, advent'rous, sing." (24)

Lloyd's 9 (Nov 30, 1761), 531.

Octaves. Praise of Pitt, retired at Hayes, for subduing France and Spain.

61-48. Verses occasioned by a late Resignation.

"Where are the fleets of France? All cover'd o'er." (13)

GM 31 (Nov 1761), 528; L Chron 10 (Oct 29, 1761), 423; RM 5 (Nov 1761), 263; SM 23 (Oct 1761), 536.

HC. Pitt's resignation is deplorable just when France has been terribly defeated, and the new administration will sell out.

61-49. Warton, Thomas.
To Mr. Secretary Pitt.

"So stream the Sorrows that embalm the brave." (104)

LM 30 (Feb 1761), 97-8; PA, Feb 5, 1761; RM 4 (Feb 1761), 93-4; SM 23 (Jan 1761), 40. Also L Chron 9 (Jan 31, 1761), 117.

Praise of Pitt in the reign of the new king. (From the <u>Oxford</u> <u>Verses,</u> <u>on</u> <u>the</u> <u>Death</u> <u>of</u> <u>his</u> <u>late,</u> <u>and</u> <u>Accession</u> <u>of</u> <u>his</u> <u>present</u> <u>Majesty</u>.)

61-50. Whitehead, William.
Ode for the New-Year 1761.

"Still must the Muse, indignant, hear." (76)

BM 2 (Jan 1761), 47; Edin M 4 (Dec 1760), 653; GM 31 (Jan 1761), 38; L Eve Post, Dec 30, 1760-Jan 1, 1761; LM 30 (Jan 1761), 46; PA, Jan 1, 1761; PL, Jan 2, 1761; RM 4 (Jan 1761), 41; SM 22 (Dec 1760), 653; UM 27 (Supp 1760), 375-6; W Eve Post, Dec 30, 1760-Jan 1, 1761. Also L Chron 9 (Dec 30, 1760-Jan 1, 1761), 6.

Pindaric ode. Britain has conquered France, and another George is on the throne.

61-51. Woty, William.
On the Death of Admiral Boscawen.

"Oh! say Melpomene! thou queen of tears." (45)

L Chron 9 (Jan 22, 1761), 87; LM 30 (Jan 1761), 48.

Blank verse. Admiral Edward Boscawen died January 10, 1761. He was naval commander of the expedition which captured Louisburg.

1762 Books & Pamphlets

62-1. [Bayly, Mary]
   Old Woman's Loyalty: Or, a Few Lines Made on the Birth of the Illustrious Prince of Wales; Born August 1st, O.S. 1762. . . . To which is added A Poem on the Taking of the Havannah and the Re-Taking of Newfoundland.
   London: Lewis, 1762. 16p.

   "Rouse up, my muse, rejoice and sing." (114)

   "With Deborah let Britons join and sing." (144)

   Sabin 57148.

   Copies: NUC RPJCB (2nd ed, 1762)

   HC, OC. In the first, Bayly rejoices in the birth of an heir to the throne, expresses fierce anti-Papist sentiments, and prays for a "glorious" peace.
   In the second, she declares the year 1762 brought victories like those of 1759 against the Papist Bourbon allies, the victory over the Spanish in Havannah (Cuba), and over the French in New Foundland, thereby saving the "fishing trade."

62-2. [Duncombe, John]
   Horace, Odes, I: 2 Imitated. In the Character of a Portuguese.

   "Too long has this devoted State." (68)

   In 67-2: Works of Horace, vol. I, pp. 15-18.

   Horatian ode, alternating deca- and octosyllabic lines in couplets. A Portuguese asks the English to come to the aid of his country against Spain in the Seven Years War--especially Granby, Townshend, Howe, and Burgoyne.

62-3. [Evans, Nathaniel]
   Ode, on the late Glorious Successes of his Majesty's Arms, and Present Greatness of the English Nation.
   Philadelphia: Dunlap, 1762. 14p.

   "Hail sacred Muse! thou harbinger of Fame." (180)

   Notices: GM 33 (May 1763), 251-2 (extract of 108 ll.).

   Evans 9113; Sabin 23178.

   Copies: NUC MHi, PPL, PPRF.

   Heroic stanzas. Panegyric on Britain for the defeat of France and Spain--

44

in the West Indies--Cuba and Martinico, led by Monckton and Albemarle. (Also appears in 72-4 : <u>Poems</u> <u>on</u> <u>Several</u> <u>Occasions</u>, pp. 64-71.)

62-4. Evans, Nathaniel.
Verses for the New-Year 1762.

"Still as emerges from the womb of time." (80)

In 72-4 : <u>Poems</u> <u>on</u> <u>Several</u> <u>Occasions</u>, pp. 55-59.

HC. Verses written for the newspaper delivery boys, celebrating the victories over France. The English came to the aid of the Americans and restored the peace. The English were victorious in Europe and India, too.

62-5. The Minister of State. A Satire.
London: Howard, 1762. 15p.

"While Freedom echoes from each venal Throat." (c. 525)

Notices: CR 14 (Oct 1762), 316; MR 27 (Nov 1762), 390-1.

Copies: BL 11630.f.38; NUC CtY, DFo, ICN, IU, MH, NN, TxU.

HC. Cynically surveys the corrupting influence of the ministerial form of government, of "Faction's Pow'r," and believes that "under a wise, virtuous, and magnanimous Prince" an "arbitrary Plan of Government is by far the most eligible." Cited are Sir Charles Wyndham, 2nd Earl of Egremont; John Russell, 4th Duke of Bedford; Philip Yorke, 1st Earl of Hardwicke; George Montagu Dunk, 2nd Earl of Halifax; William Pitt, and Bute.

62-6. An Ode to Lord B***, On the Peace. By the Author of the Minister of State, a Satire.
London: Howard, 1762. 15p.

"Hail England, darling isle of heaven!" (180)

Notices: CR 14 (Nov 1762), 394; MR 27 (Dec 1762), 460.

Copies: Bod BS 10 (2); NUC CtY.

Regular Horatian ode. Satire on Lord Bute and the Scots. Urges that France be crushed, never to rise against England again. But "Scottish slaves" wish to have peace and to restore English conquests. Notes the opposition between Pitt and Bute.

62-7. Ogden, James.
The British Lion Rous'd; or Acts of the British Worthies, A Poem in Nine Books.
Manchester: Whitworth, 1762. 223p.

"Great-Britain's worthies, an illustrious train." (c. 4000)

Notices: MR 26 (Apr 1762), 316-7.

Sabin 56808.

Copies: BL 11623.k.10; NUC MB, MiU-C, NN, RPJCB.

HC. A patriotic epic celebrating the national successes on land and sea during the Seven Years War. Includes remarks on the French causing the war by her attacks on English settlements in America and English allies in Europe, and by aid to Jacobite rebels. Parts show how provincial and regular troops (including the Scottish) unite to defeat the French in North America. Cited are Pitt, Townshend, Wolfe, Amherst, Saunders, Monkton, Braddock, and Sackville (at Minden); the fighting at Ticonderoga, Niagara, Crown Point, and especially Quebec, which gave Canada to Britain. The year 1759 is significant. (Incidentally, refers to America as Columbia, p. 68.)

62-8. [Prime, Benjamin Young]
On the Peace of Fountainebleau.

"Oft has the muse her country's conquests sung." (275)

In 64-7: The Patriot Muse, pp. 86-94.

HC. In this last poem of his collection of poems on the French and Indian War, Prime strenuously objects to the shameful peace, betrayed by false friends and deluded by foes. Predicts that the French in Canada will prove to be "perfidious rebels," and France will become strong again as Guadeloupe and Martinique in the West Indies are restored. Even Spain was restored Havannah in exchange for Florida--a poor bargain! Cited are Pitt, King George, Canada.

62-9. [-----]
On the Surrender of the Havannah. A.D. 1762. An Ode.

"While the triumphant silver trump of fame." (24)

In 64-7: The Patriot Muse, pp. 85-6.

Regular Horatian ode. Spain is defeated in Cuba, and should "tempt [Britain's] wrath no more."

62-10. The Royal Favourite; a Poem; or a Blot in the Great Favourite's Scutcheon.
London: Pridden, 1762. 11p.

"Encircled by the Silver Sea." (138)

Notices: CR 14 (Dec 1762), 476-7; MR 27 (Dec 1762), 460; L Eve Post, Nov 30, 1762, and Jan 27, 1763.

Copies: NUC IU.

Hudibrastics. Defence against the reviling satirists of George III and Bute, whose only fault is that he is a Scotsman.

62-11. The Wandsworth Epistle. In Metre. By Oswald Fitz-James, Esq;
London: Finmore, 1762. 12p.

"The City, I'm told, Sir, exclaims at the Peace." (168)

Notices: CR 14 (Sep 1762), 239; MR 27 (Sep 1762), 228; Court&CM 1 (Sep 1762), 614-15; Edin M 6 (Sep 1762), 455-6; GM 32 (Sep 1762), 441-2; SM 24 (Sep 1762), 458-60.

Copies: NUC ICN, MdBP.

Hexameter couplets, doggerel burlesque. Elaborate ironic satire on the Scots and Bute for wishing to conclude an ignominious peace with France, and a defence, in effect, of Pitt. Notes how the war began with "the encroachments of France . . . on America's plains," spread to Europe (Germany), and ended favorably "all around the world," except Westphalia. In the negotiations for peace, however, "North America's empire . . . the firmest support of our greatness and trade,/ Is . . . undervalu'd, despis'd."
    The original prose is in GM 32 (Sep 1762), 405-6 (dated Sept. 5 [1762]) and SM 24 (Sep 1762), 455-8. Oswald Fitz-James is a pseudonym.

Serials

62-12. An Acrostic, Addressed to the Four Gallant Brothers, on the Important Acquisition of the Havannah.

"Heroic Chiefs of honor'd Keppel's name." (8)

L Eve Post, Oct 5, 1762.

The Keppel brothers (Augustus, George, William, and (?) are paid tribute for their capture of the Havana from Spain, a rich prize.

62-13. Advice to Modern Country Politicians.

"Go weed your corn, and plough your land." (12)

Edin M 6 (Nov 1762), 572; LM 31 (Nov 1762), 619.

Sixains. Country farmers should take care of their business and leave politics to the king.

62-14. A Ballad. To the old Tune of Chevy-chase.

"God prosper long this Free-born Isle." (46)

UM 31 (Sep 1762), 148.

Ballad. Questions the value of the peace treaty: it does not appear to be "worth the while."

62-15. [Be chearful my lads, let our glory increase.]

"Be chearful my lads, let our glory increase." (16)

L Eve Post, Nov 4, 1762.

Quatrains. We must not have a peace, when our work is only half done.

62-16. [Be thine then Bute, to follow virtue's lead.]

"Be thine then Bute, to follow virtue's lead." (56)

L Eve Post, Nov 4, 1762.

HC. An optimistic view of the role of Bute. Advice to Bute to help improve the country: mend the Marriage Act, lessen taxes, reduce time for suits in litigation, banish corruption in England and persecution in Scotland.

62-17. The Call. To Mr. P[itt].

"O Pitt (thy country's guard, and genius) rise." (43)

L Eve Post, Oct 12, 1762.

HC. Questions the peace, which benefits France. Who shall inform the heroic dead of this inglorious peace? Boscawen, Wolfe. Pitt should complain directly to the King. See 63-17.

62-18. The City Grumbler's Reply to the Epigram in the St. James's Chronicle.

"You told us Affairs would soon wear a new Face." (14)

L Eve Post, Nov 18, 1762.

Hexameter couplets. A complaint at the peace, which benefits France. Pitt must come back in place of Bute. Rigby is cited.

62-19. An Epigram.

"Base Growlers may of Newfoundland complain." (4)

L Eve Post, Aug 21, 1762.

There are complaints at giving Newfoundland to France; but we shall have it at peace by granting France the fishery (of the Grand Bank).

62-20. An Epigram.

"Hang, hang, those English Geese." (8)

L Eve Post, Nov 27, 1762.

Henry Fox wishes to suppress those in Parliament who are warning the people about the role of Bute. These old Whigs will save the nation. Cf. 62-28.

62-21. Epigram.

"Let Numsculls dispute." (6)

L Eve Post, Jul 24, 1762.

A cynical view of the dispute over Pitt and Bute. The writer will support anyone who gives him a place.

62-22. Epigram.

"My Voice is still for War, 'Sempronius cries.'" (4)

L Eve Post, May 29, 1762.

The English wish for a continuation of the war; the Scotch wish for peace.

62-23. An Epigram.

"Spain jealous and proud, sorely vex'd to be told." (10)

BM 3 (Oct 1762), 552; DJ, Oct 26, 1762; Edin M 6 (Nov 1762), 572; L Eve Post, Oct 23, 1762.

The Spanish commander at Havannah gives as an excuse for his surrender the fact that Keppel and Pocock were there.

62-24. An Epigram.

"We must ascribe the loss of Newfoundland." (4)

L Eve Post, Aug 12, 1762.

Pitt is responsible for the loss of Newfoundland because of his resignation.

62-25. An Epigram on the Times.

"Says France's monarch to the King of Spain." (8)

Edin M 6 (Dec 1762), 628; GM 32 (Dec 1762), 594; UM 31 (Dec 1762), 326.

On the peace. The English conquer in the war, but they lose the peace.

62-26. The following Verses, written a little before the Reduction of Martinico, containing a good deal of Humour, we have here re-published them, at the Request of a Correspondent, from the Antigua Gazette.

"Welcome all my good Friends! Welcome Gentlemen all." (42)

St J's C, Apr 10, 1762.

Hexameter Couplets. A list of the French losses to the English: St. John (Newfoundland), Quebec, Goree, Belleisle, Martinique.

62-27. [From the prospect of peace what discords arise.]

"From the prospect of peace what discords arise." (20)

L Eve Post, Dec 14, 1762.

Quatrains. An ambiguous position is here taken on the controversial peace, but in effect the writer supports it.

62-28. Honest P[elha]m's Advice to the Geese of Old England.

"Cackle, on, my brave Geese, of Reynard ne'er be afraid." (4)

L Eve Post, Nov 23, 1762.

Henry Fox was parliamentary manager for Bute. Cf. 62-20.

62-29. I am for Peace; but, when I speak, They are for War.

"What can the Sons of Albion mean." (114)

St J's C, Dec 28, 1762.

Octosyllabic couplets. On the controversy over the peace. Argues for the need for generous attitudes towards a peace with France so that it will be enduring.

62-30. [If Pitt will take the helm once more.]

"If Pitt will take the helm once more." (13)

L Eve Post, Aug 14, 1762.

Octosyllabic couplets. If Pitt will assume the leadership once more, the French and Spaniards will be defeated everywhere and will sue for peace.

62-31. [Inscription on a Monument to Don Lewis de Velasco, Governor of the Moro Castle, The Havannah.]

"Sacred to the memory of / Don Lewis de Velasco."

L Eve Post, Oct 26, 1762.

Commemorates the fall of the Moro Castle Fort, July 30, 1762, under de Velasco, and the surrender of Havana August 13 to George (Keppel), Earl of Albemarle, and Sir George Pocock. Ironic it will be if the peace compels Britain to return Havana to Spain!

62-32. The Lion, the Cock, and the Mule. A Fable. Most humbly addressed to his Catholic Majesty.

"Since you, seduc'd by France's specious lore." (42)

Court M 1 (Jan 1762), 227-8.

HC, animal fable. The British lion will teach the Spanish mule a lesson after the defeat of the Gallic cock.

62-33. The Menace. To the Earl of B---.

"What tho' you taught the Royal youth." (20)

GM 32 (Jun 1762), 288; L Chron 11 (Jun 24, 1762), 607; L Eve Post, Jun 26, 1762; SM 24 (Jun 1762), 324.

Quatrains. Bute is being maliciously maligned. (A defence of his integrity.) He taught "the Royal Youth . . . the love of liberty and truth."

62-34. A New Ballad. Wrote on the Spot at the Attack of Martinico.

"Strange stories we're told." (36)

L Chron 11 (Mar 27, 1762), 303; L Eve Post, Mar 30, 1762.

Song. Admiral Rodney and General Monckton attack Martinique and will succeed.

62-35. A New Song.

"In vain N[iver]noise." (18)

L Eve Post, Sep 28, 1762.

Song. Britons refuse to be finessed into a peace by the French diplomat Nivernoise; they will continue the war.

62-36. A New Song: On the Reduction of Martinico.

"What nation shall dare with Old England compare." (30)

UM 30 (Supp 1762), 371-2. With music.

General Monckton, February 13, 1762.

62-37. A New Song. Sung by Mr. Lowe at Vauxhall.

"On the white cliffs of Albion, see Fame where she stands." (28)

UM 30 (Jan 1762), 39-40. With music.

Song. The King ends the war.

62-38. An Ode to the British Nation.

"Hail! gen'rous nation, resolutely true." (48)

LM 31 (Sep 1762), 502; RM 7 (Sep 1762), 149-50; St J's C, Sep 14, 1762.

Regular Horatian ode in quatrains. As long as Britain behaves honorably and without tyranny, it will prosper: its people free, enjoying peace, and practicing the true religion. (Really, this is directed at France.)

62-39. On a Late Glorious Minister.

"His measures check'd, with keen resentment fir'd." (20)

L Eve Post, Dec 21, 1762.

HC. A defense of Pitt against scurrilous criticism for accepting a pension for his great service to the nation.

62-40. On General Monckton's Success at Martinico. Addressed to Great Britain.

"Hail happy isle! surrounded by the sea." (10)

Edin M 6 (Feb 1762), 100.

In 1762 the Hon. Robert Monckton commanded the expedition against Martinique and other West Indian islands. These lines simply record the fact of the success over the French in Martinique.

62-41. On reading the Extraordinary Gazette, of the taking the Havannah.

"Now to my arms submits the pride of Spain." (30)

SM 24 (Oct 1762), 542.

HC. Let us celebrate this victory and the peace that comes with it.

62-42. On the Present Peace.

"We still presume a dismal peace is sign'd." (17)

L Eve Post, Nov 27, 1762.

HC. A protest at the poor peace which benefits France.

62-43. On the Reduction of the Havannah by the British Arms; by Peter Blackburn, an English merchant's Son, of Lisbon, under fourteen years of age.

"When fair Britannia's martial band." (60)

Edin M 6 (Nov 1762), 572; GM 32 (Nov 1762), 546; SM 24 (Nov 1762), 605.

Regular Horatian ode. Celebrates the conquest of Havana.

62-44. The Opinion of Hope. A Political Cantata.

"Fix'd on the summit of a rocky steep." (48)

Court M, Nov 1762, p. 720; Edin M 6 (Nov 1762), 569-70.

Song. Cantata, two recitatives and two airs. Britain complains of the politicians torn apart by contentious factionalism, and Hope urges them to unite to face the enemy, France, and conclude a glorious peace.

62-45. The Patriot King, or George the Third.

"Three Georges now for Britain's Welfare born." (10)

LM 31 (Jan 1762), 44; St J's C, Jan 30, 1762.

HC. The third George, a youth, has virtue; he could be a Patriot King.

62-46. [Pitt, Pelham, Ca'ndish, scorn the vile abuse.]

"Pitt, Pelham, Ca'ndish, scorn the vile abuse." (6)

L Eve Post, Nov 6, 1762.

A defense of the resignation of Pitt, Cavendish, and Pelham (Duke of Newcastle).

62-47. The Poet turn'd Politician.

"What, Churchill, wilt thou leave the Flow'r-strewn Tracks." (8)

St J's C, Aug 24, 1762.

Quatrains. Advice to Churchill not to engage in political poetry.

62-48. The Scotch Bonnet. A New Ballad. Tune, -- He that has the best Wife.

"'Tis in vain to dispute, of a shoe or a boot." (35)

L Eve Post, Jul 8, 1762; LM 31 (Jul 1762), 398.

Song. Light satire. The Scotch have come to court and are favored by the King.

62-49. A Short Method for a Long Peace.

"Tho' Britons their foes are famous for beating." (8)

Edin M 6 (Feb 1762), 100; GM 32 (Apr 1762), 187; SM 24 (Nov 1762), 605.

Epigram. Advises that nothing that the British have conquered and seized from France should be returned.

62-50. A Song, entitled, Barbadoes Voluntiers. By an Officer of the Corps that went upon the Expedition against Martinico. To the Tune of, -- Push about the brisk Bowl.

"My lads of Barbadoes, remember your Blood." (30)

St J's C, Mar 27, 1762.

Led by Monckton, volunteers from Barbadoes help in the conquest of Martinique.

62-51. Song. On Our Success in the Present War. Tune, -- Britannia rule the Waves.

"With shouts of gladness rend the Sky." (22)

LM 31 (Nov 1762), 619-20; St J's C, Oct 19, 1762.

A patriotic celebration of the heroic valor of the British victors in the war. Britain is mistress of the seas.

62-52. A Song. On the Conquest of the Havannah.

"Now England's victorious." (42)

BM 3 (Oct 1762), 551-2; L Eve Post, Oct 12, 1762.

Praise of Britons who conquered the Spaniards at the Havannah.

62-53. A Song, on the Taking of the Havanna, in the Character of a Sailor. By Mr. Wignell. To the tune of, -- As I derrick'd along.

"Come on, brother Tar, and I'll tip you a stave." (24)

L Eve Post, Oct 19, 1762.

A patriotic song against the French and Spaniards. Commander-in-Chief Lord Albemarle (George Keppel, older brother of Augustus Keppel) is praised, along with Admiral George Pocock, who had the naval command.

62-54. Song. To the Tune of, Ye commons and peers.

"Unbounded ambition, thou turbulent maid." (20)

Court M 1 (Jan 1762), 226-7; Edin M 6 (Jan 1762), 44.

Britain shall defeat Spain.

62-55. Stanzas to Peace.

"Downy Peace, extend thy pinions." (32)

RM 7 (Dec 1762), 310.

Quatrains in praise of the peace and victory over France, which should bring trade and prosperity and the reduction of taxes.

62-56. [This George the Third I hate -- detest.]

"This George the Third I hate -- detest." (13)

St J's C, Jan 9, 1762.

Quatrains. Supported by the Devil, France and Spain threaten the young King George, whose country needs to be unified.

62-57. To Lord Bute.

"Tho' versed in science, and in morals great." (8)

L Eve Post, Nov 23, 1762.

HC. In statesmanship and politics, Bute is inferior to Pitt. Bute should therefore resign his position to Pitt.

62-58. To the Genius of Britain.

"Genius of Britain, spread thy guardian wing." (18)

RM 7 (Sep 1762), 150; SM 24 (Oct 1762), 542.

HC. Britain will have an honorable peace with Bourbon France and Spain.

62-59. To the King.

"Who can attempt a more exalted Theme." (12)

St J's C, Mar 4, 1762.

Quatrains. Panegyric on King George III. May he be protected from his enemies, "exulting foes" (France and Spain).

62-60. To the Memory of Capt. Sh-d-ly Mackenzie, Who died of the Wounds he received at the Taking of Newfoundland.

"St. John, thy sandy banks, and spawning train." (30)

Edin M 6 (Dec 1762), 628.

HC. It is no consolation to have Newfoundland at the cost of Mackenzie's life.

62-61. To the Readers of the Edinburgh Magazine.

"When listed in the literary field." (104)

Edin M 6 (1762), iii-iv.

HC. A summary of the conquests by the British in the war: Canada, Ticonderoga and Duquesne (Ohio), Quebec, West Indies, India, Africa, Havana; and Europe, with Prussia as ally (praise of Frederick the Great's military genius).

62-62. To the Right Hon. J. E. of B[ute].

"From scenes of blood, and all the ills of war." (24)

L Eve Post, Sep 14, 1762.

HC. Support of Bute's peace. Let us have peace and reduce taxes.

62-63. To the Right Hon. William Pitt, Esq; at Hays.

"Envious of honours they can never claim." (20)

L Chron 12 (Dec 9, 1762), 564; RM 7 (Dec 1762), 310-11.

HC. Panegyric on Pitt, retired at his country estate, Hayes: virtuous, pure, and incorruptible.

62-64. Triplets addressed to the Right Hon. Lord Bute, With a singular Present, By one Retiring from Political Controversy.

"Ye baneful Censors of a Patriot Age." (6)

St J's C, Nov 20, 1762.

Triplets. Bute, loyalty, and peace should prevail, it is hoped, guarded by Magna Charta, the Act of Settlement (Hanover), and the Act of Union (Scotland).

62-65. Verses addressed to Mr. Pitt on his Resignation.

"Great Pitt, whose patriot Cares, divinely blest." (35)

St J's C, Mar 4, 1762.

HC. Questions the wisdom of Pitt's resignation; another leader like him is needed at the helm of the ship of state, or he must be restored.

62-66. Whitehead, William.
   Ode for the New Year. 1762.

"God of slaughter, quit the scene." (60)

Edin M 6 (Dec 1761), 649; GM 32 (Jan 1762), 39; Lloyd's 10 (Jan 1, 1762), 5; L Eve Post, Dec 31, 1761-Jan 2, 1762; LM 31 (Jan 1762), 47; PA, Jan 1, 1762; St J's C, Dec 31, 1761-Jan 2, 1762; SM 23 (Dec 1761), 656; UM 29 (Supp 1761), 382. Also L Chron 11 (Dec 31, 1761-Jan 2, 1762), 1.

Pindaric ode. The laureate welcomes peace: "Enough of glory Albion knows."

62-67. Wrote in America, on a Great Man.

"An humble bard, unpractic'd and obscure." (90)

RM 6 (Jun 1762), 306.

HC. Panegyric on Pitt for his virtuous character and statesmanship.

British Poetry and the American Revolution
1763-1783

1763 Books & Pamphlets

63-1. [Bentley, Richard]
Patriotism: A Mock Heroic. In Five Cantos.
London: Hinxman, 1763. 66p.

Notices: CR 16 (Nov 1763), 390; MR 29 (Dec 1763), 409-11.

Copies: BL 840.k.5 (17); Bod Godwyn Pamph. 1706; NUC CtY, DFo, ICN, IU, MH.

See 63-2.

63-2. [-----]
----- in Six Cantos. The Second Edition.
London: Wilkie, 1765. xviii + 83p. + Index.

"'Twas night; the voice of jollity was hush'd." (1290)

Copies: BL 991.1.27; Bod Godwyn Pamph. 1749b (1); NUC CtY, NN, OU, PU.

HC. Mock-heroic satire directed against the opposition. Patriotism and self-interest are the same; faction is motivated by pride and raises the mob against George III and the peace provisions. Cited are Pitt, Grenville, Bute, Halifax, Egremont, Pelham, Walpole, Mansfield, Wilkes, Sandwich, et al. (Also in The Repository [London: Dilly, 1783], IV, 68-128; and School for Satire [London: Jacques, 1802], pp. 269-358.)

63-3. The Crisis: An Ode, To John Wilkes, Esq;
London: Williams, 1763. 12p.

"Let the keen lightning's ruddy fire." (216)

Notices: CR 16 (Nov 1763), 389; MR 29 (Nov 1763), 398.

Copies: BL 11631.g.26; NUC DLC, MH, MiU-C, NN.

Quatrains. Panegyric on John Wilkes from the popular side of the question. On Wilkes' press battle with Bute and the Scots, against whom the poet rails. Compares Wilkes to Cicero, and asserts that the threat to punish him creates the crisis.

63-4. [Dalrymple, Hugh]
Rodondo; Or, The State Jugglers.
London: Nicoll, 1763-70. 44 + 47 + 35p.

"When Learning grew to such a head." (c. 2200)

Notices: CR 15 (Feb 1763), 126-7; MR 28 (Jan, Feb 1763), 73, 161; Lloyd's Eve Post, Jan 24, 1763; L Eve Post, Mar 1 & 5, 1763; L Mag 39 (Feb 1770), 104; SM 25 (Feb, Jun, & Sep 1763), 106-7, 340-5, & 499-504, & 32 (May 1770), 261-6.

Copies: BL 1077.k.40; NUC CtY, DLC, IU, NN, RPJCB.

Hudibrastic doggerel. Humorous, vulgar, allusive satire on Pitt (Rodondo), with remarks on Churchill and Wilkes, Bute and the Scots. Cantos I and II are meant to counterbalance Churchill's Prophecy of Famine; Canto III is obscure. In general, this is a highly allusive satire on individuals; America is not the concern. Also in Walter Ruddiman's Collection of Scarce . . . Pieces (Edinburgh, 1773).

63-5. Evans, Nathaniel, and Paul Jackson.
An Exercise; containing, A Dialogue [by Evans] and Ode on Peace [by Jackson]. Performed at the Public Commencement in the College of Philadelphia, May 17th, 1763.
Philadelphia: Steuart, 1763. 8p.

"When flourish'd Athens with the Grecian reign." (108)

"Smiling Pleasure's festive band." (48)

Evans 9484.

Copies: PU, PPL.

HC. A classical dialogue in praise of academia in America, where, now that peace has come (for "George gave the word"), the arts can be cultivated. King George is praised for subscribing with a "regal bounty" to the establishment of the Colleges of Philadelphia and New York. (Also in 72-4, his Poems, pp. 72-81.)
Jackson's Ode celebrates the end of the war as it comes to America, bringing peace to the Indians in the regions of the Erie, Ontario, and the Mississippi.

63-6. [Greene, Edward Burnaby]
The Tower: A Poetical Epistle, inscribed to John Wilkes, Esq;
London: Ridley, 1763. 13p.

"Ye solemn Mansions, where the Northern Mind." (134)

Notices: CR 15 (May 1763), 407; MR 28 (Jun 1763), 487; PA, May 26, 1763.

Copies: BL 1500/282 and 1481.e.14; NUC CtY, MH.

HC. Praise of Wilkes, now a prisoner in the Tower, for insisting upon the principle (of a free press); criticism of the venal and corrupt court--dominated by the Scots--for undermining freedom. Cited is the term, "Warrants."

63-7. Satires on the Times in Two Parts.
London: Dodsley, 1763. 48p.

I: "Titles of Yore thro' Great Possessors fam'd." (c. 570)

II: "O Jewel of inestimable worth." (c. 460)

Notices: CR 16 (Nov 1763), 392-3; MR 29 (Dec 1763), 466-8.

Copies: BL 163.m.76; NUC IU, TxU.

HC. A general moral satire on the vicious times, with only occasional relevant political remarks. Inveighs against corruption and luxury of empty-headed but wealthy aristocrats, idle, mean, and despicable, who buy and sell votes. Merit, intrinsic worth, has fled the land as these people are guided by infamous "Int'rest."

63-8. Verses addressed to No Minister.
London: Nicoll, 1763. 7p.

"Great Mr. Pitt, no more thy name." (78)

Notices: CR 16 (Sep 1763), 232; MR 29 (Sep 1763), 227.

Copies: BL T.1554.(8); NUC DFo, IU, MH.

Sixain stanzas. A satire on Pitt, out of office and deserted except by Wilkes. "On what New Scheme of Politicks / With Whigs and Tories, would'st thou fix, / To gull this Simple Nation?"

Serials

63-9. An Address to the Right Hon. Mr. Pitt.

"A Muse unknowing in the paltry ways." (c. 150)

Lloyd's 13 (Aug 29, 1763), 210-11; L Chron 14 (Aug 9, 1763), 142-3; PA, Aug 30, 1763.

HC. A tribute to Pitt, a complaint at the poor peace treaty. Churchill (Duke of Marlborough) suffered the same fate in Queen Anne's reign as Pitt in King George's reign. Bribery, corruption, and Bute are blamed. Urges Pitt to return to Parliament and inquire into the Peace and present policy.

63-10. An Answer to an Epigram in the Gazetteer on the Burning of a Boot at Temple-Bar.

"'Tis said that the State and the Mob did dispute." (6)

L Eve Post, Dec 15, 1763.

Epigram. Satire on Bute. The State burnt the North Briton, the mob a boot (Bute); but the mob really did little. Liberty will be asserted only when Bute's head is cut off.

63-11. An Answer to the Quiet Man's Opinion of the Times.

"Mr. Timothy Cautious,/ You Say, you think in Time of Peace." (36)

PA, Jul 18, 1763.

Triplets, plus fragmented fourth line rhyme. Timothy Cautious writes meaninglessly and ignorantly about Wilkes, the King, and Bute. See 63-133.

63-12. [Britannia pensive lean'd upon her Spear.]

"Britannia pensive lean'd upon her Spear." (16)

Freeman's J, Oct 18, 1763.

Quatrains. A complaint at chaos, taxes, and a sense of hopelessness because the country lacks leadership. S---- is recommended as a leader.

63-13. Britannia to her Sons.

"My sons you nobly did engage." (48)

GM 33 (Jul 1763), 356.

Stanzas in sixains. Now that peace has come, there is dissension in the country: protests against the excise tax and against Bute, and oppression of the patriot Wilkes.

63-14. Britannia to his Grace the Duke of Bedford.

"To fair Britannia's fertile Shore." (30)

St J's C, Apr 26, 1763.

OC. The Duke of Bedford is praised for bringing the peace with France to a happy conclusion.

63-15. The British Ambassadress's Speech to the French King.

"Hail! tricking Monarch, more successful far." (61)

L Chron 13 (Jun 18, 1763), 590; St J's C, Mar 3, 1763, & Jun 16, 1763.

HC. The June printing appeared with revisions and additions, and a prose introduction. Ironic satire on the Tories and Jacobites (of Queen Anne's reign) for being pro-French. The persona of the Duchess of Shrewsbury expresses her bias for the French at the end of Queen Anne's reign.

63-16. [B(ute) has resign'd (God save the King.)]

"B[ute] has resign'd (God save the King)." (64)

St J's C, Apr 26, 1763.

OC. Satire on Bute and the Scotch. An expression of pleasure in the resignation of that Scotch Jacobite, and a summary of the causes of the English prejudice against the Scotch: their culture, food, clothing, religion, intolerance, and Jacobitism.

63-17. The Call: To Mr. Pitt.

"O Pitt! (thy country's guard and genius) rise." (45)

Freeman's J, Oct 1, 1763; St J's C, Jul 12, 1763.

HC. A complaint at corruption and faction that are destroying Britain, and an invitation to Pitt for assistance to present a grievance to the King. Also a complaint that the treaty of peace benefited France. See 62-17.

63-18. Cancelled.

63-19. A Collection of Modern Epigrams.

UM 33 (Dec 1763), 325.

Twelve on Wilkes and the North Briton affair, most of which have been recorded: e.g., "A Scots Epigram," "On Seeing the North Briton Burnt," "On a Late Publication," "On a late Duel," etc.

63-20. The Comparison between John Churchill, Duke of Marlborough, and Charles Churchill, Anticaledonian.

"In Anna's Wars immortal Churchill rose." (8)

LM 32 (Aug 1763), 443; St J's C, Jul 28, 1763.

HC. Another comparison between Churchill the warrior and Churchill the poet -- one superior in arms, one in wit.

63-21. A Conversation. [Between a Noble Lord and Wilkes.]

"O Wilkes! my Lord **** is so wounded and hurt." (14)

PA, May 17, 1763.

Hexameter couplets. The noble lord, Bute, offers Wilkes a bribe, Canada, to stop writing; but Wilkes, offended, insists upon being true to the Whigs. See [A Minister of State grown sore], 63-77.

63-22. The Dedication.

"My Lord, as my Elvira's Story." (86)

St J's C, Feb 22, 1763.

OC. Ironic anti-Scotch satire on Bute and the peace, and on literary figures (Hume, Smollett, Mallet).

63-23. A Double Acrostick.

"With Scottish Insolence and Pride." (12)

L Eve Post, May 26, 1763; PA, May 28, 1763; St J's C, May 24, 1763.

Quatrains. Wilkes and Temple are praised for saving the country from the ruin brought on by Bute and the Scots.

63-24. An Elegy. On the death of General Wolfe.

"Begin, begin the sorrow-soothing theme." (108)

AR, 1763, 239-41.

Elegiac quatrains. Eulogy on Wolfe.

63-25. Epigram.

"As at the Exchange, beside the Pile of Wood." (6)

Freeman's J, Dec 20, 1763; LM 32 (Dec 1763), 670; St J's C, Dec 10, 1763; UM 33 (Dec 1763), 325.

HC. The hangman agrees with the protesting mob that he would rather burn twenty Scotsmen than Wilkes's *North Briton*, No. 45.

63-26. An Epigram.

"Behold our apples and our pears." (7)

L Eve Post, Apr 12, 1763.

OC. Objects to the excise tax on apples and pears, for which Scottish Bute is responsible. (Cider is made from apples, perry from pears.)

63-27. An Epigram.

"Guadaloupe, Martinique, and of conquests a score." (6)

GM 33 (Feb 1763), 91; L Eve Post, Feb 8, 1763; UM 32 (Feb 1763), 99.

Mixed verse. The French got back Guadaloupe and Martinique, etc., and returned nothing except one culprit (who is pro-French Bute).

63-28. Epigram.

"Hail! happy modern ministers of state." (4)

L Eve Post, May 19, 1763.

Quatrain. Satire on the ministry. Wilkes has been elevated from an infamous scribbler into a hero by the blunders of the state.

63-29. An Epigram.

"Lo now, three various years have pass'd away." (10)

L Eve Post, Nov 3, 1763.

HC. Satire on Bute and the Scots, responsible for demeaning Britain.

63-30. Epigram.

"O Grief of Griefs! -- the Parson cries." (4)

BM 4 (Dec 1763), 662; Freeman's J, Dec 20, 1763; LM 32 (Dec 1763), 671; St J's C, Dec 13, 1763; UM 33 (Dec 1763), 325.

Quatrain. Satire on Parson Kidgell, who hypocritically exposed the alleged blasphemy of Wilkes's Essay on Woman.

63-31. Epigram.

"Pow'r always us'd to go with places." (4)

L Eve Post, Sep 13, 1763.

OC. Satire on Bute. Bute rules from behind a screen.

63-32. Epigram.

"Says Forbes to Wilkes, ye are a scoundrel." (10)

L Eve Post, Sep 27, 1763; PA, Sep 30, 1763; St J's C, Sep 29, 1763.

OC. Captain Forbes challenges Wilkes to a duel for denigrating the Scots; but Wilkes declines. Satire on the Scot.

63 33. Epigram.

"Sc[otc]h Pavement is good, 'tis granted; what then." (8)

St J's C, Sep 13, 1763.

HC. A protest at the Scotch pavement, although it is cheap.

63-34. Epigram.

"Since by the Peace we're scalp'd again." (4)

Freeman's J, Sep 27, 1763; L Eve Post, Sep 17, 1763; LM 32 (Oct 1763), 555; PA, Sep 22, 1763; St J's C, Sep 20, 1763.

OC. Objection to the poor peace will stop upon the punishment of the person responsible (Lord Bute).

63-35. Epigram[s].

"That Wilkes will fight, the Scots deny." (2)

"In spite of Art, in erring Scotchmen's Spite." (2)

St J's C, Nov 17 & 24, 1763.

OC. Wilkes will accept the challenge to a duel with Martin (a Scots bully and assassin).

63-36. Epigram.

"To what dirty Tricks have some great Ones descended." (4)

BM 4 (Dec 1763), 662; Freeman's J, Dec 20, 1763; LM 32 (Dec 1763), 670; St J's C, Dec 13, 1763; UM 33 (Dec 1763), 325.

Hexameter couplets. The Government has stooped very low to ruin Wilkes for defending the subjects' rights. (Essay on Woman frame-up.) But Pratt will defend him and liberty.

63-37. Epigram.

"W. Roars for Liberty -- d'ye ask the reason." (5)

PA, Jun 2, 1763.

Irregular stanza. Judge Pratt, in ordering Wilkes's release from confinement, has granted Wilkes permission to commit all crimes but treason.

63-38. Epigram.

"What Halcyon days, they cried, would follow Peace." (4)

Lloyd's, Apr 6, 1763; LM 32 (Apr 1763), 211; PA, Apr 8, 1763; UM 32 (Apr 1763), 214.

HC. Satire on the Scots. Instead of prosperity after the peace, we see an excise tax on apples. Signed "An old Westminster."

63-39. Epigram.

"What Walpole could not do, the S[overeig]n tries." (6)

L Eve Post, Apr 7, 1763.

HC. The English will not permit an excise tax, regardless of the Scottish Administration and the King.

63-40. Epigram on a Late Affair.

"If Wilkes had ne'er a Champion stood." (14)

LM 32 (Dec 1763), 670; St J's C, Dec 8, 1763.

OC. Wilkes is being persecuted because of his attacks on the government. His Essay on Woman is an excuse to prosecute him for blasphemy.

63-41. Epigram. On a Late Publication.

"Let pious Kidgell preach, or write, or fawn." (4)

See 63-42.

63-42. Epigram. On the Same.

"What to the Jakes had better been confin'd." (2)

BM 4 (Dec 1763), 662; St J's C, Nov 26, 1763; UM 33 (Dec 1763), 325.

Hexameter couplet. In defense of Wilkes and against Kidgell. (Kidgell gave a copy of Wilkes's Essay on Woman to Lord March, who passed it on to Lord Sandwich.)

63-43. Epigram on Bribery in P[arliament].

"That votes for money now are sold." (4)

L Eve Post, Oct 22, 1763.

Quatrain. Satire on corruption. Members of Parliament buy and sell votes. Parliament is corrupt.

63-44. Epigram. On Mr. Wilkes being in Danger of Assassination from Alexander Dun. [On the Late Attempt to Assassinate Mr. Wilkes.]

"Alas, poor Wilkes! how singular thy Lot." (2)

"That Johnny Wilkes, as Fame has spread around." (4)

"When Dun's attempt abortive prov'd, each Scot." (4)

St J's C, Dec 15 & 27, 1763.

HC & quatrain. Three epigrams on Dun's attempted assassinatin of Wilkes. A joke is made at another attempt to kill Wilkes, this time by a Scotsman named Dun. That is, Wilkes is not afraid of his duns, or creditors, except this Dun, a Scot. The Scots wish he had succeeded.

63-45. Epigram. On Seeing the North Briton Burnt.

"Earth, Rocks and Mountains, all with Fire shall burn." (12)

St J's C, Dec 3, 1763.

HC. Even if Wilkes's North Briton is burnt (by the common hangman), because of its attack on Bute's policies, its message is still true and will live on.

63-46. Epigram. On Seeing the North Briton, No. 45, Burnt by the Common Hangman.

"Because the North-Briton inflam'd the whole nation." (4)

Freeman's J, Dec 13, 1763; LM 32 (Dec 1763), 670; St J's C, Dec 1, 1763; UM 33 (Dec 1763), 325.

Anapest tetrameter couplets. Anti-Scotch satire. England would have been more pleased if the real North Briton were burnt.

63-47. Epigram on the Return of the Flat-Bottom'd Boats with the French Prisoners.

"On these dread Boats, once Terror of our Isle." (4)

Lloyd's, Apr 27, 1763.

HC. The French prisoners are returned on the flat-bottomed boats that were built for the invasion of England.

63-48. Epigram on the Two Contending Parties.

"Both make the public good their plea." (4)

L Eve Post, Oct 6, 1763.

Quatrain. Satire on politics. The two contending political parties want the rewards of office; neither is disinterested.

63-49. Epistle to a Friend in the Country.

"Whilst you, dear S. calmly wise retreat." (54)

L Eve Post, Jun 18, 1763.

HC. Today we need the guidance of men of integrity like Sidney and Hampden in the past, because the country's politics is corrupted by self-interest and gold.

63-50. Epitaph.

"Near this Place is deposited." (26)

PA, May 20, 1763.

Inscription. Satire on Wilkes. An imaginary epitaph for Wilkes, who died for liberty "by abusing his Sovereign." But the spirit of faction has also died with him.

63-51. Epitaph for General Wolfe.

"Rest, happy Shade! while round thy early tomb." (6)

Lloyd's 13 (Dec 5, 1763), 545.

HC. Wolfe will never be forgotten.

Epitaph on Gen. Wolfe, In the Church of Westerham, in Kent. Conqueror of Quebec. "While George, in sorrow, bows his laurel'd head." (4 + 8) Lloyd's 13 (Nov 14, 1763), 473. Inscription and HC on Wolfe. Reprint of 60-13.

63-52. Extempore.

"When virtuous S[andwich] pleads the cause of Truth." (6)

Freeman's J, Dec 13, 1763; LM 32 (Dec 1763), 671.

Irregular verse. Because of their exposure of Wilkes as author of the Essay on Woman, the author is sceptical of the alleged reformation of immoral Sandwich and hypocritical Kidgell.

63-53. An Extempore Definition of a Libel.

"A Libel is a brat begot of hate." (8)

Lloyd's 13 (Jul 18, 1763), 71; L Eve Post, Jul 19, 1763.

HC. A libel is noxious, and our cider feels it; even liberty and virtue are affected. Hogarth is cited as attacking liberty.

63-54. An Extempore Epigram. On the Sale of Rice's Black Boy.

"To distant ages should it e'er be told." (4)

L Eve Post, Feb 3, 1763.

HC. Indignation at the sale of a black boy in England, the land of liberty, in the ministry of Scottish Bute.

63-55. Extempore on an Officer.

"War is over, peace is come." (10)

L Eve Post, Mar 1, 1763.

OC. A soldier has only scars to show for the Seven Years' War; but peace compensates for all.

63-56. Extempore, on the Late Verdict at Westminster-Hall.

"Blest be the Man, whose gen'rous Soul disdains." (10)

Freeman's J, Dec 20, 1763; St J's C, Dec 15, 1763.

HC. Reaffirms the British subject's natural freeborn rights. Rejects the verdict against Wilkes, the "slavish yoke" of the Court. (Reference to the burning of Wilkes's North Briton.)

63-57. The Fable of the Trees.

"Once on a Time, when great Sir Oak." (64)

LM 32 (May 1763), 271; St J's C, Apr 30, 1763; UM 32 (May 1763), 265.

OC. A sylvan fable meant to illustrate the factional divisions caused by elevating the Scots over the English. The King is urged to restore the balance.

63-58. The First Ode of Horace Imitated. Addressed to the Redoubtable E[arl] T[emple], by the Invincible J[ohn] W[ilkes], Esq.

"T[emple] in Form, in Mind, alike elate." (56)

St J's C, Jun 14, 1763.

HC. Satire on Wilkes. Wilkes's persona confesses to his patron Earl Temple his motivation and explains the strategy of his political campaign to become a popular leader.

63-59. [Freeth, John.]
A New Song. Tune of, -- Roast Beef of Old England.

"When factious cabals roar aloud in the State." (22)

L Eve Post, May 7, 1763.

Satirical song on the difficult Scotch politics of the times: Churchill, H---d (?), and Wilkes were made to suffer.

63-60. From the Cambridge Verses on the Peace; lately presented to his Majesty.

"High on a cliff, whose solitary brow." (78)

GM 33 (Jun 1763), 306.

HC. Praise of Britain and King George for victory in the late war, which brings freedom to India and "Truth" to Canada (referring to the "true" religion).

63-61. The Glorious Verdict. A Song. Inscribed to Liberty.

"The Court were all met." (30)

BM 4 (Dec 1763), 661; L Chron 14 (Dec 13, 1763), 570; PA, Dec 14, 1763; UM 33 (Dec 1763), 333.

Tune is not given. On the jury's and Judge Pratt's decision favoring Wilkes, who had charged administration with a breach of the peace when seizing his papers.

63-62. The Goddess Liberty to the Author of the North Briton, No. 41. whoever he may be.

"Scribbler! in whom unite mad Lilburn's rage." (28)

PA, May 27, 1763.

Blank verse. The goddess Liberty disavows Wilkes, the seditious subversive.

63-63. A Hint to the Annalists of the Year 1763. A Poem. Inscribed to John Wilkes, Esq;

"Whether ambition, pride, or vanity." (c. 140)

L Eve Post, May 24, 1763.

HC. Praise of Wilkes and satire on the Scotch and Bute, and the times corrupted by the poor peace. The unsatisfactory peace is the cause, together with the abuse of power, of the threats to liberty and of the new taxes. But Wilkes is the patriot who fights the good cause.

63-64. The Hist -- Story, call'd Peacemaking. A Fragment.

"God prosper long our noble King." (52)

Freeman's J, Sep 10, 1763.

Quatrains. Pitt should be restored to leadership, and the Scotsmen should return home. (N. B. This is the very first issue of this Irish newspaper -- volume I, issue number 1.)

"The same dislike the lambkin bears." (24)

L Chron, 14 (Sep 27, 1763), 311; PA, Oct 1, 1763.

OC. Captain Forbes, a Scotsman, has fought against England in the French service, and has nothing to offer England but infamy. He should "fly" into exile.

63-66. Intelligence Political. Whig and Tory.

"A Minister of State, grown sore." (18)

St J's C, May 10, 1763.

OC. Two views -- the Tory Government's and the Whiggish Wilkes's -- on the use of General Warrants, ending with a poem expressing the same opposition in terms of broad principles -- Power vs. Liberty.

63-67. The Jewel in the Tower. A Song [By Countess Temple].

"If what the Tower of London holds." (24)

Letters from the Year 1774 to the Year 1796 of John Wilkes, Esq. . . . With a Collection of Miscellaneous Poems (London: Longman et al., 1804), I, 190-2.

Quatrains. Tune not given. In praise of Wilkes, imprisoned in the Tower of London.

63-68. Johnson, Walter.
On the Peace.

"Hail joyful Peace! now all complaints are vain." (10)

Court&CM 1 (May 1763), 255.

HC. Objects to the satires directed at the peace. Britain fights for honor more than gain; complaints at the peace must end, for even the gods are honorable after storms.

63-69. Justice and Privilege. A Fable.

"Justice and Privilege t'other day." (35)

PA, May 24, 1763.

OC. In a conflict between justice and privilege, the latter appears to win. An oblique commentary on the Wilkes episode.

63-70. [Kidgell so fear'd the Poem should come out.]

"Kidgell so fear'd the Poem should come out." (4)

Freeman's J, Dec 20, 1763; St J's C, Dec 8, 1763.

Quatrain. Epigram. Satire on Parson Kidgell, who had secured Wilkes's <u>Essay on Woman</u>, gave it to Lord March, who gave it to Sandwich; this brought the action against Wilkes. Kidgell, wishing to ruin Wilkes, is a hypocrite.

63-71. The Late Administration Epitomized: An Epistle in Verse To the Rt. Hon. William Pitt, Esq;

"Then dastard B--- said it was in vain." (22)

L Eve Post, Jan 20, 1763.

HC. A selection made by the newspaper editor from a poem on Pitt's resignation that defends and explains his behavior as a result of Bute's corrupt administration.

63-72. The Letter P.

"An honoured Letter would we mention." (20)

Freeman's J, Nov 1, 1763.

OC. Clever account of the importance of the letter P, which stands for a variety of good and bad things, concluding with the need for "probity." Behind it is the strong scent of corruption.

63-73. Liberty; a Song. To the Tune of, Hearts of Oak.

"Come, chear up, my lads, to our country be firm." (24)

BM 4 (May 1763), 267; GM 33 (Jun 1763), 308.

A liberty song, versus bribes and excise tax.

63-74. Liberty, Property, and No Excise.

"A Courtier profess'd, much esteem'd by the Great." (20)

UM 32 (Apr 1763), 214.

Hexameter couplets. Satire on the ministry. A courtier is made (ironically) to express his support of the cider tax, along with Sir Francis Dashwood.

63-75. Lines to Mr. Hogarth.

"On Faction's pinions rais'd above the croud." (8)

PA, May 24, 1763.

HC. Satire on Wilkes. Hogarth portrays Wilkes as a hypocrite who cries "George and Liberty." But Wilkes's real intent is to betray his king and country.

63-76. Lord Warkworth: or, the Westminster Election. A New Toast. The Tune, Hearts of Oak are our Ships, Hearts of Oak are our Men.

"Ye Westminster Men." (42)

PA, Mar 14, 1763.

An election song for Lord Warkworth, a Percy, heir of Northumberland, who had fought in Germany.

63-77. [A Minister of State, grown sore.]

"A Minister of State, grown sore." (18)

PA, May 11, 1763.

OC. Dialogue between Wilkes and Bute. Bute, angry at Wilkes for his North Briton, wishes to imprison him; but Wilkes asks for a judgment between Bute and himself. He dares to bleed for Liberty. This is perhaps the first poem on the Wilkes troubles. See "A Conversation," 63-21.

63-78. [The mob with state power will always dispute.]

"The mob with state power will always dispute." (2)

G, Dec 14, 1763; PA, Dec 15, 1763.

HC. Epigram. The "mob" will have its way: it burnt a boot (Bute), while the state burnt the North Briton.

63-79. A New Loyal Song. By R. Lewis. To the Tune of, -- Rule Britannia.

"Fair albion's genius, deign to smile." (32)

L Eve Post, Sep 13, 1763.

A criticism of the late dishonorable peace.

63-80. A New Song. Sung at a certain Theatre Royal, in the character of a Frenchman. Tune, -- Doodle, doodle, doo.

"See me just arrive from France-e." (45)

LM 32 (Feb 1763), 99; St J's C, Feb 3, 1763.

Satire on Bute and the peace for favoring France. The persona of France expresses pleasure at having Bute, Tories, Scots, and Jacobites as allies.

63-81. Ode, to John Wilkes, Esq; On his Dismission from the Command of the Buckinghamshire Militia.

"Must thy rich Plume and bold Cockade." (68)

St J's C, Sep 13, 1763.

Regular (Horatian) ode in quatrains. Wilkes lost his command of the Buckinghamshire militia, but he can still fight battles with his pen, especially against Bute and the Scots.

63-82. On a Certain Wish.

"No greater honour do I crave." (6)

L Eve Post, Sep 6, 1763.

Epigram. Sixain. Satire on Bute for his poor peace. All parties would be pleased, should he get his wish to die as one who made the peace.

63-83. On a Late Cavalcade.

"In Scarlet Gowns the servile Turncoats came." (20)

L Eve Post, May 14, 1763.

HC. The cavalcade is a funeral procession flowing from the late peace that must be rejected because it favored France. Cited are Liberty, Faction, Corruption, and all the conquered lands restored to the enemy.

63-84. On a Late Duel.

"Quoth Sam M[artin], it's right, I'm determin'd to fight." (4)

L Eve Post, Dec 1, 1763.

Quatrain. Satire on Bute. Samuel Martin, MP & sec of the Treasury, denounced by Wilkes in the North Briton for corruption in the peace proceedings, challenged Wilkes to a duel and almost killed him, Nov 16, 1763. (Wilkes retired to France, Dec 6-10.)

63-85. On a Late Glorious M[iniste]r.

"His measures check'd, with keen resentment fir'd." (20)

LM 32 (Feb 1763), 100; SM 25 (Feb 1763), 111.

HC. Panegyric on Pitt, who allows his merit to speak for itself.

63-86. On a late Jury.

"Ye brave supporters of your country's cause." (10)

BM 4 (Jun 1763), 382; DJ, Jul 19, 1763; L Eve Post, Jul 9, 1763.

HC. The jury and Chief Justice Pratt deserve praise for the verdict against the tyranny of arbitrary writs. (The issue was illegal searches and seizures.)

63-87. On a Late Resignation.

"The opposition, cries the Scot." (8)

L Eve Post, Apr 26, 1763.

OC. Bute is forced to resign, but behind the curtain he intends to pull strings and control King George.

63-88. On a Late Transaction.

"Brave Hampden, with the Love of Virtue fir'd." (6)

St J's C, Nov 17, 1763.

HC. Wilkes was wounded in his duel (with Samuel Martin), but he will recover, unlike great patriot Hampden, with whom he shares the same ideals.

63-89. On a Modern Patriot.

"Behold him out of place! see how he glows." (11)

L Eve Post, Jul 23, 1763.

HC. Satire on corruption. A portrait of a corrupt politician -- out of place, he is a patriot; in place, he is for taxes and against liberty.

63-90. On a Noble Peer's going to the Beef-Steak Club, and the Company all leaving the Room.

"See [Sandwich] good and K[i]d[ge]ll nice." (8)

St J's C, Dec 20, 1763.

Quatrains. Sandwich and Kidgell are avoided at the Beef Steak Club (for their behavior regarding Wilkes and the Essay on Woman).

63-91. On a Scotch Bonnet.

"Maidens should sing in tuneful sonnet." (15)

L Eve Post, Aug 6, 1763.

Only the Scots benefit in the present dispensation. To be a Scot is to be awarded favors.

63-92. On a Septennial Election.

"This is the harvest of the venal tribe." (8)

L Eve Post, Jun 23, 1763.

HC. Satire on a Parliamentary election for corruption.

63-93. On a Warrant from a Certain Office.

"Thou brat of pow'r! thou child of lawless force." (13)

L Eve Post, Jul 2, 1763.

HC. Satire on arbitrary and despotic General Warrants issued by the ministry.

63-94. On Burning the North Briton, No. 45. A Scots Epigram.

"Ah! mickle is the Power and Force that lies." (8)

Freeman's J, Dec 20, 1763; LM 32 (Dec 1763), 670; St J's C, Dec 10, 1763; UM 33 (Dec 1763), 325.

Epigram. HC. The Scots rebelled in 1715 and 1745; and now Wilkes's North Briton, No. 45, is burned by the common hangman. A North Briton burns again!

63-95. On Juries.

"While Juries are the Judges of the land." (7)

L Eve Post, May 24, 1763.

HC. Opposition to Mansfield's decision. Juries must be allowed to judge the law, not the judges.

63-96. On Liberty.

"Water may fishes, air may birds content." (4)

L Eve Post, Nov 24, 1763; St J's C, Nov 22, 1763.

Epigram. Quatrain. Liberty is a Briton's natural element.

63-97. On Mr. Wilkes's Safe Return to England.

"Welcome Britannia's friend, in thee we see." (14)

L Eve Post, Oct 1, 1763.

HC. Praise of Wilkes, who -- loyal to England, the throne (King), and the law -- returns from France.

63-98. On Occasion of the Peace. A Poem.

"Peace o'er the world her olive wand extends." (108)

UM 32 (Feb 1763), 97-8.

HC. General praise of peace. The end of the war brings peace and prosperity.

63-99. On Reading a Poem called Truth in Rhime; By S---- J-----, Esq;

"Well, now I think we shall be wiser." (26)

St J's C, Apr 30, 1763.

OC. Truth in Rhime is flat stuff because the times are not propitious for satire. The King is virtuous and likewise his court, where service and merit are rewarded. The author may be Soame Jenyns. See 61-3.

63-100. On Seeing the Picture of Lovat and Wilkes, drawn by Hogarth.

"From Forty-five to Sixty-three." (8)

AR 1763, p. 236; St J's C, Jun 11, 1763; UM 32 (Jun 1763), 323.

Epigram. An observation on the changing times. Before, Hogarth satirized a Scotsman who loved the Stuarts, Lovat, the rebel Jacobite; now, he satirizes Wilkes, the hater of Stuarts and Scots.

63-101. On Septennial Parliaments.

"Thou child accurst! thou brat replete with ill." (15)

L Eve Post, Jun 2, 1763; WA, Mar 28, 1767, p. 208.

HC. Septennial Parliaments are blamed for the ills of the nation: corruption, threats to liberty, taxes, and tyranny.

63-102. On the Apple.

"The Apple, says the Earl of Bute." (5)

L Eve Post, Jun 14, 1763.

Epigram. OC & triplet. Ironic lines about the apple (cider tax) that turned the Earl of Bute out of place.

63-103. On the Burning the North Briton.

"To burn that vile inflammatory paper." (4)

L Eve Post, Dec 15, 1763.

Epigram. Quatrain. To have the hangman burn the North Briton will really kindle the flame (of liberty).

63-104. On the Grand Question: Who is to be IN, and Who OUT.

"The Peace coming on." (24)

BM 4 (May 1763), 267; L Eve Post, May 19, 1763.

Sixains. There is no difference between the Outs and the Ins.

63-105. On the Liberty of the Press.

"Thou friend of truth! thou friend of liberty." (12)

L Eve Post, May 26, 1763.

HC. Defence of the liberty of the press, which is the source of the Brunswick line and the liberty of the subject against arbitrary power.

63-106. On the Lord Chief Justice P[ratt].

"Bless'd with the clearest head, and soundest heart." (7)

L Eve Post, May 17, 1763.

HC. Justice Pratt is praised as a guardian of English liberty (because he declared General Warrants illegal).

63-107. On the New Dancing Exercise.

"As Soldiers now to our surprise." (14)

DJ, Oct 1, 1763;   Freeman's J, Oct 1, 1763;   Lloyd's 13 (Sep 21, 1763), 293;   L Eve Post, Sep 17, 1763;   LM 32 (Oct 1763), 555;   UM 33 (Sep 1763), 154.

OC. Corruption must have been involved in the loss of the conquered lands to France and Spain.

63-108. On the New Excise on Cyder and Perry.

"Sad sons of Devon -- your hard fate deplore." (18)

L Eve Post, Apr 26, 1763;   St J's C, Apr 14, 1763.

HC. Satire on the Scots. Objection to the new tax on apples (cider) and pears (perry). The Scots benefit. Bute is cited.

63-109. On the only Provision for our Discharged Soldiers and Sailors.

"Should those, who bravely for their country bled." (6)

L Eve Post, May 31, 1763.

HC. A protest against inhumanity. Some provision should be made for the veterans of the war.

63-110. On the Out's and In's.

"The Out's, much like an empty stomach are." (8)

L Eve Post, Jun 25, 1763.

Mixed, quatrains and couplets. The In's are content and quiet; the Out's fret and are noisy.

63-111. On the Parliament(s) of France.

"We ne'er can call or think that people [are] free." (10)

Freeman's J, Oct 18, 1763;   L Eve Post, Oct 8, 1763.

HC. Tyrants cannot enslave the people when Parliaments are honest. Greater evil springs from evil Parliaments than from evil kings.

63-112. On the Patriot Statesman.

"If Pitt accepts, 'tis plain he wants a place." (4)

L Eve Post, Sep 27, 1763.

Epigram. HC. Pitt (the patriot) will be in the wrong if he accepts or rejects the King's offer to join the government.

63-113. On the Peace.

"Ye Malecontents! your murm'rings cease." (8)

L Eve Post, May 28, 1763.

OC. Satire on those corrupt hacks who accept bribes to praise the peace.

63-114. On the Power of Bribery.

"All animals alike pursue their gains." (7)

L Eve Post, Nov 12, 1763.

Epigram. HC. Satire on bribery and corruption. Money will corrupt men and even transform a vile treaty into a glorious peace.

63-115. On the Present Discord of the Nation.

"Whilst each side, heated with malicious zeal." (6)

L Eve Post, May 19, 1763.

Epigram. HC. The abuse of power will bring continuing discord.

63-116. On the Present Opposition.

"Tho' Grumblers and Growlers still rail at the Peace." (12)

St J's C, Sep 10, 1763.

Anapest tetrameter couplets. Satire on the peace. The present Opposition should stop criticizing the peace. We got cold Canada from France.

63-117. On the Present Peace.

"Hail, Peace! of heav'n thou darling firstborn child." (52)

RM 8 (May 1763), 158.

HC. A generalized non-political panegyric on peace, concluding with a pledge of loyalty to the King.

63-118. On the Present Times.

"The Law should guard the weak, restrain the strong." (12)

G, Nov 28, 1763; WA, Jan 28, 1764, p. 96.

Triplets. Mansfield and Pratt are serving well, and the people are protected according to law.

63-119. On the Report of a Coalition of Parties.

"When place and pension bear no longer sway." (11)

L Eve Post, Jul 19, 1763.

HC. Whig and Tory will never unite. There cannot be a coalition of parties, because of corruption.

63-120. On the Report of Lord B---'s Resignation.

"Lord B---, they say, has now resign'd." (32)

St J's C, Apr 12, 1763; UM 32 (Apr 1763), 214.

Quatrains. Bute will still rule behind the curtain.

63-121. On the Word Faction.

"Faction! What art? to whom dost thou belong." (12)

L Eve Post, Jun 4, 1763.

HC. "Faction" is always maligned, but it is really honest, sincere, incorruptible, etc.

63-122. On the Word Libel.

"Libel! child of the tongue and pen." (12)

L Eve Post, May 21, 1763.

Quatrains. On the libel issue taken up by the Courts. Truth cannot be a libel, the poet alleges, in defense of press freedom.

63-123. On the Word Oeconomy.

"Tell me, child of prudence! and tell me true." (8)

L Eve Post, Jun 9, 1763.

HC. The word "oeconomy" applied to private life means prudence, order, and frugality; but applied to public life it means the opposite -- extravagance.

63-124. On the Word Representative.

"To represent, is but to personate." (6)

BM 4 (Jun 1763), 326; L Eve Post, May 31, 1763.

HC. Ironic statement of belief that MP's who accept bribes represent their constituents as well as those who are honest.

63-125. The Pack; or, the Sensible Ass: A Fable.

"Those who have read the books of yore." (26)

L Eve Post, Nov 8, 1763.

OC. Animal fable. Urges Pitt to be the country's guide in the nation's interest.

63-126. [Parody on Cato.]

"It must be so. -- Patriots you reason well." (24)

St J's C, Aug 2, 1763.

Parody on Addison's Cato, Act V, Cato's soliloquy. Satire on the Scots. Britannia chooses liberty over gold, but Scotsmen choose the money.

63-127. A Parody on Romeo and the Apothecary.

"I'll publish Treason straight." (40)

GM 33 (Jun 1763), 307-8; St J's C, Jun 16, 1763.

Parody on Shakespeare's Romeo and Juliet, in which Wilkes urges a poor publisher to print "Treason" for him against the Ministry.

63-128. Party Chit-Chat.

"Says one, who will pretend to say." (8)

BM 4 (Dec 1763), 662.

Epigram. OC. A Scotsman accuses Churchill of joining Wilkes in France and becoming archbishop to the devil.

63-129. Peace.

"Rejoice, O Isles! and be your praises heard." (46)

Lloyd's 12 (Mar 18, 1763).

Blank verse. Praise of peace and the arts which will make it enduring.

63-130. A Political Parley.

"K. That all clamour may cease; and to make your friends easy." (22)

Court&CM, Sep 1763, p. 448; L Eve Post, Sep 15, 1763; LM 32 (Sep 1763), 498; St J's C, Sep 10, 1763.

Hexameter couplets. The King refuses to accept Pitt's conditions for returning to the Court. Townshend, Temple, Newcastle, and the inadequate peace are cited.

63-131. Pratt and Liberty. A New Song. To the Tune of Ge-ho Dobbin.

"When late at Guildhall Britain's freedom was try'd." (26)

BM 4 (Jun 1763), 382; L Eve Post, Jul 14, 1763.

Song. The jury declared General Warrants illegal, and Judge Pratt (later Lord Camden) awarded the plaintiff Wilkes £2900.

63-132. Price of Stocks At the Political Exchange.

"Bute's Fears -- above Par." (9)

L Eve Post, Sep 13, 1763.

A prose-poem summary of the times: Bute, Peace, Corruption (Placemen, Pensions and Places).

63-133. A Quiet Man's Opinion of the Times.

"I think, indeed, 'tis very odd." (16)

GM 33 (Jul 1763), 356; PA, Jul 13, 1763; UM 32 (Supp 1763), 374.

Quatrains. Signed Timothy Cautious. That taxes increase is odd. Neither Bute nor Wilkes is disturbing. Both the King and Wilkes have merit. For an answer, see 63-11.

63-134. A Rebus.

"When Heav'n blest the land with peace." (8)

L Eve Post, Dec 8, 1763; St J's C, Dec 6, 1763.

OC. Bute has succeeded with taxes where Robert Walpole failed.

63-135. Rules for Preferment.

"Would'st thou be rais'd, these rules regard." (10)

L Eve Post, Jun 11, 1763.

OC. In order to be elevated to a place, praise the peace, engage in corruption, and support the Ministry.

63-136. The Sc[otc]h Pavement. An Epigram.

"Fragments of Rocks from Northern Albion torn." (6)

St J's C, Jul 19, 1763.

HC. Satire on the Scots, who exchange their stone for English bread.

63-137. The Scot's Resolve.

"I have a salve shall answer all intents." (6)

L Eve Post, May 21, 1763.

HC. Epigram. Satire on the Scots. They will place the blame for all their evil measures on the King, and take the credit for good measures.

63-138. The Scot's Revenge.

"The mob are all against me, says the Scot." (7)

L Eve Post, May 12, 1763.

HC. Satire (ironic) on the Scots. They take revenge against English abuse by imposing taxes and passing laws that abridge their liberties.

63-139. [Sometime, I think some Time last year.]

"Sometime, I think some Time last year." (53)

St J's C, Dec 17, 1763.

OC. Satire on the Scots and Kidgell, scurrilous and vulgar, because of Kidgell's nasty behavior regarding Wilkes. He provided Sandwich with the _Essay on Woman_, upon which Wilkes was to be tried for blasphemy.

63-140. A Song. By a Devonshire Cyder-Maker. Tune -- Hearts of Oak.

"Cheer up, English hearts, and your liberty prize." (34)

St J's C, Aug 23, 1763; UM 33 (Aug 1763), 102.

A song for liberty against Bute and Scotch tyranny and the tax on cider.

63-141. Song. For those who approve it, On November 15, 1763. To the Tune -- Smile, Smile, Britannia, &c.

"Come, come, the Song of Joy." (36)

St J's C, Nov 17, 1763.

Song. The King is toasted and the hope expressed for his integrity and his support of freedom. But there is the Scottish threat that must be fought off with the help of Pitt and Prince William.

63-142. A Song on Liberty. Tune, -- The Lillies of France.

"Come each honest Briton, assist me to sing." (28)

L Eve Post, Jun 2, 1763.

Song. In defense of liberty, Wilkes, and Lord Temple against "Court Minions" and corrupt placemen.

63-143. A Song on the Present Times. Tune, Hearts of Oak.

"Come all English Hearts, independent and free." (31)

L Eve Post, Apr 5, 1763; PA, May 6, 1763.

Signed W. M. in the first copy. A song protesting the Cyder Bill, a proposed new tax burden after the war.

63-144. Sonnet V. To Mr. F.

"While party rage, my F. distracts the state." (14)

PA, Jun 9, 1763.

An Italian sonnet praising good fellowship and deploring political conflicts between Whigs and Tories, Pitt and Bute.

63-145. [Sore from the fight see wounded W(ilkes) retreat.]

"Sore from the fight see wounded W[ilkes] retreat." (14)

PA, Jun 7, 1763.

HC. Wilkes is compared to Pitt in trying to get support from the mob; only satirists really have the freedom or privilege to censure.

63-146. [Stevenson, John Hall.]
Queries to the Critical Reviewers.

"Ye judging Caledonian Pedlars." (64)

St J's C, Feb 12, 1763.

Quatrains. Satire on Scotch Jacobites and Tories. A corrected version of the same poem published February 8, 1763. Anti-Scotch satire, with a satiric postscript addressed to Smollett, editor of the Critical Review. (Also printed in his Works [London: Debrett, 1795], I, 134-7.)

63-147. The Surry Address to their Members Imitated.

"Most worthy Sirs! accept the tribute due." (20)

Court&CM 1 (Sep 1763), 449.

HC. A petition by Surrey freeholders to their MP's remarks on North American details of the treaty of peace accepted by Bute and now begs that Wilkes, as a result of his North Briton No. 45, be protected through parliamentary immunity.

63-148. [A Tax on Loyalty should Senates pay.]

"A Tax on Loyalty should Senates pay." (4)

St J's C, Dec 27, 1763.

HC. Satire on Bute. Should Parliament tax loyalty, Bute would not have to pay much.

63-149. [That Jemmy Twitcher should his Comrade peach.]

"That Jemmy Twitcher should his Comrade peach." (10)

St J's C, Dec 17, 1763.

HC. A protest at the really immoral behavior of Kidgell and Sandwich in their frame-up of Wilkes (Essay on Woman). See 63-139.

63-150. [This Wilkes has rais'd such a Dust.]

"This Wilkes has rais'd such a Dust." (10)

PA, Jun 7, 1763.

OC. Hopes that Wilkes will hang or his writings be burned by the common hangman.

63-151. The Thistle.

"Thistles, curst weed! on barren ground." (6)

L Eve Post, Jul 2, 1763.

OC. Satire on the Scotch penetration into English politics through the royal family.

63-152. The Times. A New Song.

"A Truce with your nonsense of Pitt and of Bute." (32)

Court&CM 1 (Oct 1763), 496.

A drinking song for a club of London Irishmen. Let the times be what they will regarding Pitt and Bute, Wilkes and Talbot, the English and the Scots, Forbes, Churchill, and Hogarth, the press and the clergy -- the Irish will flourish under the Earl of Northumberland (recently appointed Lord Lieutenant of Ireland).

63-153. To a Friend, on the Day Peace was Proclaimed.

"How can you better spend the day." (30)

Lloyd's 12 (Jun 1, 1763); LM 32 (Jun 1763), 327; St J's C, Jun 2, 1763.

Regular (Horatian) ode in sixains. Rejoice (ironically advised) at the peace; but let us drink to Pitt, and to the Scotch who should return to their country.

63-154. To Mr. Churchill.

"Great Churchill's Sword to vanquish'd France gave Law." (10)

St J's C, Feb 10, 1763.

HC. Epigram. John Churchill, Duke of Marlborough, conquered France; John Churchill, poet, conquered Rome and its satirists.

63-155. To Mr. Pitt.

"Who'll credit Lies, aim'd but to wound thy Fame." (6)

Lloyd's 13 (Sep 19, 1763), 281; L Chron 14 (Sep 20, 1763), 287.

HC. Defense of Pitt, who cannot be easily defamed.

63-156. To Mr. Wilkes on his Commitment to the Tower.

"Wilkes! hast thou not deserv'd this place." (5)

L Eve Post, Apr 30, 1763.

Ironic lines on Wilkes, committed to the Tower for his North Briton No. 45. Bute, it is predicted, will be imprisoned within a year.

63-157. To Mr. William Hogarth, On some late Political Productions. A Fable.

"A Monkey once, by Heav'n design'd." (60)

PA, Jun 13, 1763; St J's C, Jun 11, 1763.

OC. Animal fable to illustrate the mistake Hogarth made on entering politics with his satire on Wilkes.

63-158. [To praise, Great Peer! where Merit claims the strain.]

"To praise, Great Peer! where Merit claims the strain." (24)

Lloyd's 12 (May 11, 1763).

HC. A defense of Bute by a Scotsman. (Possibly ironic.)

63-159. To the Gentlemen, Clergy, and Freeholders, of the County of Gloucester.

"A Courtier profess'd, much esteem'd by the Great." (20)

GM 33 (Apr 1763), 196; St J's C, Apr 19, 1763.

Hexameter couplets. An expression of opposition to the new cider tax, another source of irritation with Bute.

63-160. To the People of England.

"The insignificant Dispute." (18)

Lloyd's 13 (Oct 12, 1763), 366.

Sixains. A cynical view of the dispute over Pitt and Bute -- a plague on both their houses! What is needed is union.

63-161. To the Right Honourable William Pitt, Esq; at Hayes.

"Envious of honours they can never claim." (20)

L Eve Post, Jan 20, 1763.

HC. Upon his resignation, Pitt is retired to his estate at Hayes. These lines defend the patriot who left with virtue intact. Administration is called "a vicious band."

63-162. A True Character of Lord C. J. P--tt.

"A Friend to all whom Justice can defend." (12)

BM 4 (Dec 1763), 662; St J's C, Dec 17, 1763; UM 33 (Dec 1763), 326; WA Jan 14, 1764.

HC. Panegyric on Lord Chief Justice Pratt for his good judgment and for impartially maintaining the rights of the subject.

63-163. Verses occasioned by the Cyder-Bill.

"When Cornwall did his fav'rite red-streak fell." (16)

St J's C, Apr 12, 1763; UM 32 (Apr 1763), 214.

HC. Opposition to the proposed tax on cider.

63-164. Verses written by a Lady in America, after the defeat of the brave, tho' unhappy General Braddock.

"No more I'll paint in soft descriptive strains." (55)

RM 8 (Jun 1763), 317.

HC. Describes the defeat of Braddock's forces and the slaughter of his officers by French and Indians, who used base tactics unfamiliar to the British.

63-165. Versification of Mr. W----s's Letter.

"I little could think, when I told you my Hardships." (26)

St J's C, May 12, 1763.

Anapest tetrameter couplets. Wilkes complains of his treatment by Government and asserts his principles.

63-166. The Warrant.

"With Wisdom fraught a Warrant went." (8)

L Eve Post, May 3, 1763.

Quatrains. Ironic verses on the General Warrant (among the earliest comments in verse). It was issued for "Nobody," but "Somebody," Wilkes, was served with it.

63-167. Warton, Thomas.
The Revenge of America.

"When Cortez' furious legions flew." (22)

Court&CM 1 (Oct 1763), 496; Court Misc 1 (Dec 1765), 338-9.

OC. The Genius of Old India predicts that ruin will overtake the Europeans who, to satisfy a lust for gold, have plundered America.

63-168. [When Andrew shall unite with James.]

"When Andrew shall unite with James." (16)

North Briton, No. 41 (Mar 12, 1763).

OC. A satire on the Scots administration: that is, Bute, who is responsible for the poor peace, a sell-out. Cited are Canada, France, fishing rights, Florida, Jamaica, and Stuart.

63-169. [When P. no Longer was allow'd to Guide.]

"When P. no Longer was allow'd to Guide." (12)

St J's C, Jun 14, 1763.

Quatrains. Ironic comment on Pitt, no longer Premier, condescending to guide Wilkes.

63-170. Whitehead, William.
Ode for the New Year, 1763.

"At length th'imperious Lord of War." (62)

BM 4 (Jan 1763), 43; Edin M 6 (Dec 1762), 625; GM 33 (Jan 1763), 37; Lloyd's 12 (Dec 31, 1762-Jan 3, 1763); LM 32 (Jan 1763), 44; RM 8 (Jan 1763), 43-4; RWJ, Jan 8, 1763; SM 24 (Dec 1762), 663; UM 31 (Supp 1762), 375-6; & L Chron 13 (Jan 1, 1763), 5.

Irregular Pindaric ode. The war is over. Peace comes. And now there is an heir to the throne. King George is praised as one providing a good example of a ruler, "whose paternal sway / Despises regal art."

63-171. Wilks, Periwinkles, and Buckies, i.e. a small round Fish. A Poem. Or,

Claudero to Mr. Wilkes.

"Discord fly on sooty Pinions." (64)

PA, Jun 4, 1763.

OC. A satire on Wilkes, beloved by Discord and Satan, the Lord Mayor of London and London merchants.

63-172. Written Extempore, on being asked What is the Liberty of Great Britain?

"What is Old English Liberty? Friend, you now ask." (18)

LM 32 (Dec 1763), 671; St J's C, Dec 10, 1763.

Hexameter couplets. Satire on Bute and the Scots, who are subverting English liberty. Cited are the French, the peace, tyranny, taxes, and Wilkes.

Prints

63-173. Canada or the Tower. Kaw Jack, have Canada or to the Tower.

"B**t humbly entreats you will now condescend." (12)

Etching with quatrains. April 1763.

Stephens 4041 (IV, 266-7).

Bute offers Wilkes a bribe for his silence: the governorship of Canada. But Wilkes refuses it to remain true to the Whigs and the King.

63-174. The Devil to Pay; or, The State Indifference. By Thomas Appletree, of Herefordshire. Liberty, Property, and No Excise. An Old English Motto.

"Recitative. Britons give ear; I sing in doleful lay." (86)

Engr. with 4 columns of verse. March 1763.

Stephens 4013 (IV, 238-40).

The cantata laments the taxing of Englishmen by Scots, denounces the excise and the Peace, and expresses a wish for the return of Pitt to power.

63-175. Englands Scotch Friend. A New Song. Tune When mighty Roast Beef &c.

"Now Peace it is finish'd it surely doth tend." (25)

Etching with engraved ballad. 1763.

Stephens 3961 (IV, 178-9).

Bute's sell-out to France in the Peace of Paris is deplored in this ironic satire.

63-176. Excise A-la-Mode; or, Sawney's Oeconomy. A New Song. To the Tune of The Old Woman of Grimstone.

"All the Friends of the Land, who Corruption withstand." (40)

Broadside with engr. design. March 28, 1763.

Stephens 4009 (IV, 235-6).

An example of the numerous prints on the Peace of Paris, the conditions of which included restoration to the French and Spaniards of many places conquered during the Seven Years' War. These conditions in the Peace evoked dissatisfaction in England, hostility towards the Scotch responsible for it being fanned by Wilkes' North Briton. This song takes exception to the new taxes, especially the excise on cider.

63-177. An Exciseman made out of the Necessaries of Life now Tax'd in Great Britain.

"When Fame first the Olive Branch held o'er the Land." (10)

Engr. with couplets. March 1763.

Stephens 4015 (IV, 240-1). Repr. Wynn Jones, Cartoon Hist. of Brit. (1971), p. 50.

The Treaty of Paris (signed Feb. 10, 1763) was expected to decrease taxes. But increased taxation was proposed, thereby insuring the overthrow of Bute. He resigned April 8, 1763. Taxes on cider, candles, beer, wine, perry, mum, leather, soap, coffee, tea, chocolate, and land were proposed, according to this print. The Excise Bill was enacted March 31, 1763.

63-178. The Execution.

"What has Britannia left to hope." (8)

Etching with engr. couplets in quatrains. November 15, 1763.

Stephens 4066 (IV, 298-9).

Satire on the Earl of Sandwich, here denominated Jemmy Twitcher, for accepting the bribe of Henry Fox, Paymaster-General of the Army. Sandwich is accused of betraying his friend Wilkes (thus having "peached" on Wilkes, he is hereafter called Twitcher, the celebrated character from Gay's Beggar's Opera).

63-179. The Extraordinary Address of the Wise and Learned Aldermen, Merchants, Traders, &c. of the City of Gotham.

"Forgive us, dread Sir, that at last we're agreed on it." (48)

Broadside verses with engr. May 12, 1763.

Stephens 4058 (IV, 290).

Fourteeners. A mock account of a deputation of London citizens to the Court, to whom they praised the Peace of Paris. (William Beckford, Lord Mayor, refused to take part in these proceedings.) The ceremony was performed May 12, 1763. The new taxes are praised ironically, too.

63-180. France and England, or a prospect of Peace.

"Tho' Crestfallen at present the Spaniards and France." (8)

Engr. with verses. 1763.

Stephens 4002 (IV, 227).

Hexameter couplets. A protest at "our Bunggling [sic] Peace-makers, Bedford & Bute," who appear to be giving the advantage to France and Spain. Meanwhile, English soldiers, neglected, "Beg, Murder, or theave."

63-181. The Grand Triumvirate or Champions of Liberty.

"What reward to him is due." (17)

Engr. with acrostic verses. April 1763.

Stephens 4035 (IV, 259-60).

Acrostic spelling the names of Wilkes, Bute, and Hogarth. Wilkes is eulogized, but Bute and Hogarth are censured: Bute for his poor Peace, and Hogarth for his satiric engraving of Wilkes and for holding the place of Serjeant-Painter to the King.

63-182. In and Out, and Turn About; or the Game of Bob-Cherry. As it is now performing by the greatest Actors in the Nation.

"Of all the Games which now go down." (48)

Engr. with verses. April 1763.

Stephens 4032 (IV, 256-7).

A satirical ballad occasioned by the retirement of Lord Bute, who had sold out to France and Spain. Also BL 1876.f.1 (169).

63-183. Mass-Aniello or the Neapolitan Insurrection. Liberty, Property and no Excise.

"It happen'd at Naples when Taxes [were] high." (16)

Engr. with couplets. March 1763.

Stephens 4014 (IV, 240).

One Massaniello began an insurrection over excessive taxes in Naples, committing terrible atrocities. Bute is asked to draw a lesson from this event because of his oppressive excise on cider, passed March 31, 1763.

63-184. The Politicians.

"Britannia's Sons of all Conditions." (17)

Engr. with couplets in quatrains, except first stanza. March 1763.

Stephens 4018 (IV, 243-4).

These lines provide evidence of the interest taken by all classes of the English people in the Peace just concluded and the new taxes it brought, and in the central figures of Bute and Pitt.

63-185. The Proclamation of Proclamations, or the most glorious and memorable Peace that ever was proclaimed in this or any other Metropolis throughout the World.

"See here Fellow-Subjects, (so fine and and so pretty!)." (12)

Engr. with quatrains in couplets. April 1763.

Stephens 4007 (IV, 233-4).

A protest at Scotch domination of the English and the poor peace "patch'd up" by Bute, so "That our Foes may take Breath and our Taxes increase." Peace was proclaimed March 22, 1763; Lord Bute resigned April 8, 1763.

63-186. The Tyburn Interview: A New Song. By a Cyder Merchant, of South-Ham, Devonshire. Dedicated to Jack Ketch. To the Tune <u>A Cobler there was</u>, &c.

"As Sawney from Tweed was a trudging to Town." (60)

Broadside engr. with quatrains and "Derry down" chorus. March 1763.

Stephens 4017 (IV, 242-3).

A satire on the Scotch who are invading England seeking their fortune at the expense of tax-payers like the Devon apple-farmers.

63-187. View of the Present Crisis Representing the Heroes of the Times supposed to be concern'd in the Grand Political Uproar.

"Britons behold the hated Monster rise." (24)

Engr. with sixains in couplets. April 1763.

Stephens 4037 (IV, 261-2).

Wilkes and others (Churchill, Newcastle, Cumberland, Pitt) attack the monster "General Excise" and "his venal Tribe." Bute retires because of the discord he provoked. Henry Fox plays a crafty game.

63-188. Wilkes, and Liberty. A New Song. To the Tune of, Chevy-Chace.

"In George Street, Westminster, there liv'd." (36)

Broadside, engr. and two columns of ballad verse. May 1763.

Stephens 4029 (IV, 253-4).

On Bute's persecution of Wilkes and a counterthreat by Wilkes' supporters. Wilkes was imprisoned in the Tower on April 29, 1763, for publishing the North Briton, No. 45, April 23, which was alleged to be a libel on the King. But he was soon released (on May 6) by Lord Chief Justice Pratt, afterwards Earl Camden.

63-189. Wilkes, and Liberty. A New Song. To the Tune of, Gee ho Dobbin.

"When Scottish Oppression rear'd up its d--n'd Head." (60)

Broadside with engr. above two columns of ballad verse. May 1763.

Stephens 4028 (IV, 252-3).

Narrates the history of Wilkes' prosecution for his publishing the North Briton, No. 45, emphasizing his patriotism, his imprisonment in the Tower, the conduct of his patron Earl Temple, his arraignment at Westminster, and his acquittal.

1764   Books & Pamphlets

64-1. The Crisis: Being three State Poems on the Following Subjects; I. The Northern Dictator. A Dialogue between a Highland Peer, and his Vassals. II. On the Reduction and Surrender of the Havannah, and Conclusion of the late Peace. III. Caledonia. A Description of that fertile and beautiful Kingdom. Written on the Dismission of the present glorious Minority. And humbly addressed to the Honourable Assembly in Albemarle-Street.
London: Williams, 1764. 32p.

I: "Near Hyde-park-corner soars a lofty pile." (c. 340)

II: "From Britain's annals blot the fatal day." (c. 225)

III: "Thy rugged hills now, Scotia, meet my eye." (c. 240)

Notices: CR 17 (Jun 1764), 471.

Copies: BL 1077.k.14 (2); NUC CSmH, CtY, MH, MiU-C.

HC. Three satires on Bute, the Scots, and the peace. I. On Bute for providing needy Scots funds from the English treasury, which is being filled by the "Cyder Tax"; on the enemies of Temple, Wilkes, Pitt. II. Protest at the peace which benefits the Scots and England's enemies. Wolfe has died in vain, for even Canada is not secure, since Indians attack the inhabitants. Bute is responsible for it, and even the City did not celebrate this peace, which will simply bring on more war. III. The impoverished Scots are being enriched by the English treasury. Pitt must return to save the nation.

64-2. [Duncombe, John]
Horace, Odes, III: 4 Imitated. To Liberty (1764).

"O Liberty, to Britain's favour'd Land." (90)

In 67-2: Works of Horace, vol. II, pp. 32-6.

Notices: Lloyd's Eve Post 20 (Mar 6, 1767), 228.

Horatian ode. Written in 1764. English liberty is associated with three rivers: Runnymeade, where Magna Carta was signed, the Boyne, where William III defeated the French Papists, and the Spey, where Prince William (Duke of Cumberland) defeated the Papists and Scotch at Culloden.

64-3. [Gentleman, Francis]
The General. A Poem.
London: Nicoll, Bristow, Etherington, 1764. 36p.

Notices: CR 18 (Aug 1764), 159; MR 31 (Sep 1764), 231; GM 34 (Aug 1764), 392; R Mag 11 (Aug 1764), 102-3; St J's Chron, Aug 18, 1764; L Chron 16 (Aug 14, 1764), 154-5; SM 26 (Sep 1764), 508.

Copies: Bod Godwyn Pamph. 1725; NUC DLC, MH, NcD.

HC. On and to John Manners, the Marquis of Granby. Discusses the beginning of the Seven Years War, the chief events, and the heroes who fought in it-- Minden in which Granby fought with gallantry; Wolfe and Howe, both killed in America. Concludes with a panegyric on Granby, King George, Pitt, Pratt (Lord Camden), et al. C. Churchill is cited.

64-4. Goldsmith, Oliver.
The Traveller, or A Prospect of Society. A Poem. Inscribed to the Rev. Mr. Henry Goldsmith.
London: Newbery, 1765. iv + 22p.

"Remote, unfriended, melancholy, slow." (c. 450)

Notices: CR 18 (Dec 1764), 458-62; MR 32 (Jan 1765), 47-55; BM 5 (Dec 1764). 659-6; Freeman's J, Jan 22, 1765; L Chron 16 (Dec 18, 1764). 589; LM 34 (Feb 1765), 106-7; RM 11 (Dec 1764), 323-4.

Copies: BL T.12*. (1); NUC CLU-C, CtY, FU, IaU, ICN, ICU, InU, MH, MWiW-C, MiEM, NjP, TxU, ViU.

Published 19 Dec 1764; 11 editions to 1775, et al. HC. Goldsmith's travels in Italy, Switzerland, France, and Holland bring him back to Britain, and his conclusion is that all is not ideal--that even in Britain the great Whig chieftains are factious and greedy for power, the law severe and unjust, the wealthy corrupt, the poor slavish, and the rural peasantry forced to emigrate to America (Oswego and Niagara are cited) where they are endangered by the savage Indians. He turns to the King for redress.

64-5. [Latter, Mary]
Liberty and Interest. A Burlesque Poem on the Present Times.
London: Fletcher, 1764. 20p.

"Ye nameless Grubstreet Muses! hear." (c. 380)

Notices: CR 17 (Jan 1764), 76; MR 30 (Jan 1764), 69; GM 34 (Feb 1764), 91-2; L Chron 15 (Mar 1, 1764), 214.
Copies: BL 1486.l.3; NUC MH.

Hudibrastic doggerel. The Muse sings the joys of liberty and begs that the excise on cider and perry, for which Bute is exorcised, be removed. But self-interest is a far more powerful motive of behavior than the love of liberty.

64-6. The Patriot Poet, A Satire. Inscribed to the Reverend Mr. Ch-----ll. by a Country Curate.
London: Wilkie, 1764. 35p.

"No more, my friend--yes, tho' no muse inspire." (c. 600)

Notices: CR 17 (Apr 1764), 314-16; MR 30 (Mar 1764), 240.

Copies: NUC CU, CtY, ICN, TxU.

HC. Satire on the Whig opposition; defense of the monarch against factious republicans; attack on Churchill for his vicious treatment of Hogarth. Cited are Hampden, Pitt, Churchill, Wilkes, Hogarth, Pratt, Mason, et al.

64-7. [Prime, Benjamin Young]
The Patriot Muse, or Poems on Some of the Principal Events of the Late War; Together with A Poem on the Peace. By an American Gentleman.
London: Bird, 1764. vi, [9]-94p.

Notices: CR 19 (Jan 1765), 71; MR 32 (Feb 1765), 153-4.

Sabin 65528.

Copies: NUC DLC, PPL, RPJCB.

Many poems in a variety of forms (HC, blank verse, Pindaric and Horatian odes, acrostics, quatrains). On General Braddock's Defeat (1755), the Surrender of Fort William Henry (1757), the Death of Viscount Howe (July 6, 1758), the Surrender of Louisbourg (July 27, 1758), the Taking of Quebec (1759), the Surrender of the Havannah (1762), and the Peace of Fountainebleau (1762-3), which trace English fortunes from defeat to victory, and to defeat at the peace. Key figures are Wolfe, Amherst, and Pitt. Poems listed individually above.

64-8. The True-Born Scot: Inscribed to John Earl of Bute.
London: Sumpter, 1764. 22p.

"To you, my Lord, I dedicate this Verse." (c. 400)

Notices: CR 18 (Aug 1764), 159; MR 31 (Sep 1764), 232.

Copies: NUC CtY, ICU, InU, NjP.

HC. Ironic satire on the Scots and Bute, the favorite and still a power in the government. Cited are Mansfield, (Philip Carteret) Webb, Temple, Wilkes (who has fled to France), Pitt, et al.

64-9. Wilkes and Liberty: Or, The Universal Prayer.
London: Williams, 1764. 28p.

"In black reflection lost, with eye unclos'd." (c. 375)

Notices: CR 17 (May 1764), 397; MR 30 (May 1764), 415; St J's M 4 (Jun 1764), 388.

Copies: CtY (not in NUC).

HC. Dedicated to the Minority Club, held at Wildman's in Albemarle Street. Satiric advice to a would-be poet on the proper way to advance in a corrupt world--including bespattering Wilkes and undermining liberty. Prays that the King receive good counsel and beware Scots and the Earl of Bute, and that the nation be protected by William, Duke of Cumberland, and that Wilkes and Liberty return safely to England.

Serials

64-10. [A is for attainder, axe, and asunder.]

"A is for attainder, axe, and asunder." (22)

Freeman's J, Sep 25, 1764; L Chron 16 (Sep 20, 1764), 279; L Eve Post, Sep 15, 1764.

Alphabet poem. Satire on Bute and a corrupt parliament for arresting Wilkes, among other targets like the Scots. By "Philo-Pitt."

64-11. An Acrostick. [Freeman's Journal.]

"F reedom's Assertor." (15)

Freeman's J, Oct 30, 1764.

Dimeter couplets. The Freeman's Journal presents its liberty platform: opposition to "Scotch Rogues," defense of Ireland, integrity, and freedom.

64-12. Answer to the Epigram in our Paper of Tuesday, December 18.

"Should Heav'n to Whigs a Place not give." (4)

St J's C, Dec 27, 1764.

Epigram. Quatrain. The conflict of policy between Whigs and Tories; but Tories (it is ironic), being for prerogative, might keep them out of hell. (The Dec. 18 issue is wanting.)

64-13. [Beneath a nameless Shrine are laid.]

"Beneath a nameless Shrine are laid." (52)

Freeman's J, Nov 24, 1764.

Epitaph. Quatrains. A tribute to Churchill who, like James Thomson, wrote for freedom.

64-14. The Cause.

"Why all this prate of Whig and Tory." (8)

L Eve Post, Jan 5, 1764.

Satire on corruption and party divisions. The party strife between Whig and Tory is all about places.

64-15. Characters in St. Giles's Jack Wildfire and Jemmy Twitcher.

"Of lofty Themes let lofty Poets dream." (23)

GM 34 (Mar 1764), 140; St J's C, Mar 13, 1764.

HC. A contrast between the characters of licentious Wilkes and hypocritical Sandwich, and a satire on Sandwich.

64-16. Cancelled.

64-17. [Come, strike me a March, and I'll tell of the Times." (27)

"Come, strike me a March, and I'll tell of the Times." (27)

Freeman's J, May 5, 1764.

Hexameter couplets. Pitt, a sturdy Whig of the spirit of '88, has restored glory to Britain; but it is being threatened by Bute.

64-18. Crabtree, Christopher.
The Feast of Fancy, A Pastoral Elegy, To the Memory of Mr. Charles Churchill.

"Ye echoes my sentiments hear." (64)

Court C&CM 1 (Nov 1764), 461; Freeman's J, Dec 4, 1764; LM 33 (Nov 1764), 588-9; RM 11 (Nov 1764), 270-1; BM 5 (Nov 1764), 603-4; L Chron 16 (Nov 15, 1764), 476.

Elegiac quatrains, in praise of Churchill despite his rough satire which painted Bute black and scourged the Scots. But he painted Wilkes white as the purest snow.

64-19. Dialogue between Churchill and His Friend [Wilkes].

"F. When, Churchill, when wilt thou lay down thy Pen." (8)

St J's C, Feb 23, 1764.

HC. Churchill will continue stubbornly to defend Wilkes and English laws (freedom and the rights of the subject).

64-20. An Epigram.

"As our Conquests which cost us such Treasure and Blood." (4)

L Eve Post, Jul 14, 1764.

Hexameter couplets. Sandwich is aping Bute in benefitting the enemy -- this time Spain.

64-21. Epigram.

"If vice should ever meet with foul disgrace." (4)

L Eve Post, Dec 15, 1764.

HC. Pun that demeans Sandwich, who for his vice is recommended as the "Vice-roy . . . of all America."

64-22. Epigram.

"On the Essay on Woman pray why all this Spite." (2)

St J's C, May 31, 1764.

Irregular couplet. On Wilkes and Kidgell.

64-23. Epigram.

"Pitt conquer'd nobly, you agree." (4)

L Chron 16 (Sep 6, 1764), 238; RM 11 (Sep 1764), 160.

Quatrain. Although Pitt's motives were poor, he had conquered nobly; should Bute succeed as well, his motive can be what it will.

64-24. Epigram.

"Say, when will England be from faction freed." (4)

GM 34 (Jul 1764), 344; St J's C, Jul 5, 1764.

Quatrain. England will be free of faction when Bute dies.

64-25. Epigram.

"They quite Mistake brave Conway's case." (4)

L Eve Post, May 3, 1764; St J's C, May 1, 1764.

Quatrain. Support of Henry Seymour Conway, who voted against General Warrants (Feb. 6 and 18, 1764), and was therefore dismissed from the King's service, his regiment and his place in the bedchamber.

64-26. Epigram.

"When Scotland's Cross 'midst England's Peers was seen." (6)

Freeman's J, Dec 18, 1764; L Chron 16 (Dec 15, 1764), 578.

HC. Anti-Scots and anti-Bute satire: a wish for Bute to be crucified.

64-27. Epigram.

"Wit, Satire, Humour, Poetry, are fled." (2)

St J's C, Nov 29, 1764.

HC. Praise of Churchill, who has just died, for wit, satire, humor, and poetry.

64-28. Epigram. On a Late Proclamation.

"Since, spite of Pistols, Duns, and Laws." (6)

Freeman's J, Sep 1, 1764; St J's C, Aug 23, 1764.

Sixain. Wilkes ran from the Tories for safety, and now they attack him for irreligion; but he will endure. (It is the alleged blasphemy of the *Essay on Woman* that is the reference.)

64-29. An Epigram on General Conway's Dismission.

"Why grumble, ye Whigs, at brave Conway's hard lot." (4)

L Chron 15 (May 5, 1764), 439; PA, May 7, 1764.

Hexameter couplets. Bute was responsible for Conway's dismissal from his place.

64-30. Epigram on the Death of Mr. Churchill.

"Great Churchill gone! Ye Ministers rejoice." (6)

Freeman's J, Dec 18, 1764; St J's C, Dec 13, 1764.

HC. Churchill's targets, the ministers of state, should repent, being warned. Churchill had inspiration from Heaven.

64-31. Epigram. On the Florist's naming a Thistle "Lord Bute."

"Plain Dealer, Briton, Auditor, Scrutator." (4)

L Eve Post, Aug 11, 1764; St J's C, Aug 9, 1764.

Anapest tetrameter couplets. Anti-Scottish and anti-Bute satire.

64-32. Epigram on the New Pavement.

"The new Scottish pavement is worthy of praise." (4)

LM 33 (Nov 1764), 590.

Anapest tetrameter couplets. Satire on the Scots, who have taken all the "posts" in the Government.

64-33. Epigram on the Scotch Pavement.

"By Scotland's Thane we've long been led." (8)

Court C&CM 1 (Aug 1764), 313; Lloyd's 15 (Aug 13, 1764), 158; L Chron 16 (Aug 14, 1764), 157; L Eve Post, Aug 14, 1764; PA, Aug 15, 1764.

Quatrains. A whiggish complaint at the domination of English Government by the Scotch. Bute and Wilkes are cited.

64-34. Epigram. On the Sudden Migration of those Celebrated Champions of Religion and Liberty, the Rev. Mr. Kidgell, and John Wilkes, Esq.

"When Faction was loud, and when Parties ran high." (4)

LM 33 (May 1764), 262; St J's C, May 1, 1764; UM 34 (May 1764), 268.

Quatrain. Both Kidgell and Wilkes escaped (to France) to avoid prosecution.

64-35. [Epigrams on Pitt and Bute.]

"Pitt's War our Charges did increase." (4)

"Pitt conquer'd nobly you agree." (4)

L Eve Post, Sep 6, 1764; PA, Sep 8, 1764.

Epigrams printed together. Quatrains. Objects to Bute's poor peace treaty at the termination of Pitt's triumphs in the war with France. For the second epigram, see also 64-23.

64-36. Epitaph[s] to the Memory of the late Mr. Charles Churchill.

"Prose-driving Dunces, waddling fools in rhime." (4)

"Churchill no more! O cruel death, 'twas hard." (4)

Court C&CM 1 (Nov 1764), 460; Freeman's J, Nov 20, 1764; Lloyd's 15 (Nov 16, 1764), 486; RM 11 (Nov 1764), 272; St J's C, Nov 15, 1764; BM 5 (Nov 1764), 604; L Chron 16 (Nov 17, 1764), 483.

Quatrain and quatrain in couplets. Churchill, the scourge of dunces, fools, and scoundrels, is dead. His equal has yet to be found.

64-37. A few Lines inscribed to the Right Hon. John Montagu, Earl of Sandwich, one of his Majesty's Principal Secretaries of State, &c. &c. by an admirer of his Lordship's infinite Virtues.

"Nor Brunswick's praise, nor Prussia's warlike King." (10)

L Eve Post, Aug 11, 1764.

HC. Satire on Sandwich. Ironic praise of the Earl of Sandwich for "never betraying his friend" Wilkes (which he did, of course), and for other accomplishments.

64-38. The Force of Fate [and Answer].

"Of Freedom fond, England, in Days of old." (14)

Freeman's J, Feb 2, 1765; PA, Jan 3, 1765; St J's C, Dec 29, 1764, & Jan 12, 1765.

HC. Liberty continues to be in conflict with tyranny, the divine right of kings to rule, the royal prerogative. Fate is against it, yet the Stuarts and Bute still support the prerogative. See 65-58: "A Freeman's Wish."

64-39. A Fragment.

"Says George to Charles the other day." (32)

PA, Mar 16, 1764.

Quatrains. King Charles Stuart (Charles I) advises King George to be content and patient with the state of affairs.

64-40. [Freeth, John]
The Statesmen. A Satirical Ballad.

"Amongst the Rulers of the State." (128)

L Chron 16 (Sep 29, 1764), 315; PA, Oct 4, 1764; UM 35 (Oct 1764), 206-7; Freeth, Warwickshire Medley (1776), pp. 58-62.

Double quatrains, ballad satire on the trends in politics from the time of Sir Robert Walpole and William Pulteney, Earl of Bath, to the administration of the Duke of Newcastle (Pelham-Holles), Henry Fox, Pitt, Bute, until the domination by the Scots and Tories, to the dismay of the Whigs.

64-41. Griffith, Richard.
[Crown'd with Laurels see the Brave.]

"Crown'd with Laurels see the Brave." (20)

PA, Sep 25, 1764.

Quatrains. Britain has been victorious in the East and the West; her fighting men now return home. Should Britain be united, no other country could match her naval power ("wooden Wall") and destroy her.

64-42. [His wish'd Return the Sons of Freedom claim.]

"His wish'd Return the Sons of Freedom claim." (24)

L Eve Post, Jan 10, 1764; PA, Jan 13, 1764.

HC. Praise of Wilkes, who had fled to France for safety. He should return and trust the supporters of freedom, English laws, and juries against tyranny, "proud Prerogative." (Nine and a half lines are censored.)

64-43. An History of the Last Session of Parliament.

"Who says the Parliament the Nation bilks." (4)

L Eve Post, May 19, 1764.

Epigram. Quatrain. Ironic satire on Parliament. The last Parliament merits praise for persecuting Wilkes and reforming franked letters.

64-44. Horace, Book i. Ode 14, freely paraphras'd, and inscribed to OLD ENGLAND. Written after an Inglorious Peace.

"Ah! luckless ship, that from the boist'rous main." (34)

Lloyd's 15 (Sep 7, 1764), 242; L Eve Post, Sep 8, 1764.

HC. The ship of state is in danger (not being assisted by Pitt, Temple, and Churchill) as a result of "A Peace inglorious, or the Nation's Debt." We must have Pitt as our pilot.

64-45. Hymn to Liberty.

"Sister of Jove! Aetherial Flame." (24)

Freeman's J, Aug 7, 1764.

Song. A protest against corruption that threatens to destroy liberty.

64-46. Lines to C. Churchill.

"Few are the Bards, whatever Age we trace." (12)

PA, Jan 27, 1764.

HC. Churchill, honest and consistent patriot unlike Dryden, will never prostitute his verse to "wicked power," to tyrants.

64-47. Majority to the Minority. [And] Answer to the Address to the Minority. [And] Appeal, In Answer to the Verses to the Minority.

"Great Men are like the stately Oak." (6 + 4 + 6)

St J's C, Sep 8, 20, & 25, 1764.

Sixains & quatrain. "Great Men" are unmoved by factional strife; but they are protected (by the King). However, stemming corruption is all that matters.

64-48. The Means to Rise.

"If you, my Friend, in B---- C---- would thrive." (35)

Freeman's J, May 5, 1764; St J's C, Apr 19, 1764.

HC. Satire on the Tory ideology. The only way to secure a place at court is to adopt Tory policies. This poem is a good summary of the issues and basic themes of the time: Bute, taxes, the King's prerogative, Pitt, the peace, faction, and the City of London.

64-49. The Minority. An Epigram.

"O my poor Country -- Churchill cries." (4)

St J's C, Oct 2, 1764.

OC. Satire on Churchill, who simply supports another corrupt group wanting pensions, the Minority.

64-50. A Mistake Rectified.

"Whilst Pitt sat Ruler at the Helm of State." (7)

St J's C, Nov 29, 1764.

HC. There were no parties under Pitt; but under the Scots, there is a good deal of factional strife. However, all agree that Bute is responsible.

64-51. The Moderator; or Advice to Mechanical Patriots.

"Of Pitt or Bute why all this rage." (16)

PA, Jun 13, 1764; UM 34 (Jun 1764), 320.

Quatrains. The King has broken no law; you so-called patriots are deceived. It makes little difference who is in power, Pitt or Bute, for we must still pay taxes.

64-52. Modern Progress of Patriotism.

"In days of yore, and not long since." (36)

L Chron 16 (Jul 24, 1764), 83; St J's C, Jul 19, 1764; UM 35 (Aug 1764), 100.

Sixains. The so-called Patriots try (undeservedly) to dominate the court from their clubs at several coffee and chocolate houses: George's, White's, Arthur's, Almack's.

64-53. O Tempora! O Mores!

"Since madness reigns, and Britain's sons complain." (24)

Lloyd's 14 (Feb 15, 1764), 161; UM 34 (Feb 1764), 94.

HC. Satire on the times, corrupt and undermined by faction. A solution for the times is a tax on fools and knaves, for "of debt 'twill set us free."

64-54. An Ode, 1764.

"Whence can arise these dread alarms." (91)

Lloyd's 15 (Dec 3, 1764), 538; L Chron 16 (Dec 6, 1764), 546; PA, Dec 7, 1764; New Foundling Hospital for Wit (1786), IV, 52-5.

Regular (Horatian) ode in seven-line stanzas. Satire on the Opposition, who are out of office and place. The author prefers the "strongest side, / Be't either Whig or Tory."

64-55. Ode to Lord Clive.

"When Pindar pour'd his rapid strain." (36)

Lloyd's 14 (Apr 16, 1764), 374.

Regular (Horatian) ode in sixains. Panegyric on Clive, who subdued "the Nabob fierce" and made available India's wealth to Britain.

64-56. An Old Story new revived.

"When Tory Oxford rul'd the Roast." (42)

GM 34 (May 1764), 244; L Chron 15 (May 1, 1764), 421; St J's C, Apr 26, 1764.

OC. Satire on Tories and Scots, and Bute. A way to get rid of them is suggested.

64-57. On a Certain Jury.

"Let others chant of this or that." (19)

L Eve Post, Jun 2, 1764.

OC. Praise of the Middlesex jury for defending liberty.

64-58. On a Late Distinguished Financier.

"No Ways and Means against the Tyrant Death." (12)

GM 34 (Sep 1764), 443; St J's C, Sep 8, 1764.

HC. Epitaph on the death of Henry Legge, August 23, 1764. (He was Chancellor of the Exchequer, 1754-5, 1756-7, and 1757-61.)

64-59. On a Late Rencounter. [And] Epigram.

"You'll own the great Churchill possesses, I hope." (4 + 4)

St J's C, Oct 27 & Nov 3, 1764.

Hexameter couplets and quatrain. Epigrams. Churchill is superior even to Dryden -- perhaps.

64-60. On Choosing a New Member of Parliament for Aylesbury.

"A Second Member chosen! -- well." (12)

St J's C, Feb 14, 1764.

OC. The character of a model MP: a man of integrity, honest and incorruptible, and a lover of freedom.

64-61. On Churchill's Times.

"Sodom by Angels was destroy'd." (12)

RM 10 (Sep 1764), 159; St J's C, Sep 20, 1764.

Quatrains. Churchill should not satirize the innocent, nor be guilty of crimes he attacks.

64-62. On General Conway's Dismission.

"Should future Annals the strange Story tell." (8)

GM 34 (May 1764), 244; St J's C, May 19, 1764.

HC. It is incredible that a man of Conway's high character and integrity should be dismissed from service to the King. (Implied is that it casts a shadow on the court.) "Tho' neither Coward, Traitor, Rebel, Scot."

64-63. On General Conway's Dismission.

"When virtue can't exist in place." (4)

L Eve Post, May 29, 1764.

OC. Epigram. Defense of Conway for his vote against General Warrants.

64-64. On Hearing of a Conference between Mr. Pitt and the Earl of [Bute].

"Deluded Britain, see thy Patriot Friend." (6)

"The great Patriot, thinking he's low in Repute." (2)

L Chron 16 (Jul 5, 1764), 18; PA, Jul 6, 1764.

Hexameter couplets. Epigrams. Bitter taunts at Pitt for apparently courting Bute, contrary to his avowed policies.

64-65. On Judge Jefferies.

"Was Jefferies e'er to visit us again." (7)

L Eve Post, Aug 14, 1764.

HC. Satire on Judge Mansfield for his Tory views on the freedom of the press and English juries: "English Juries are not Judges of the Law."

64-66. On Mr. Churchill's Death.

"Farewell, great Bard -- ye sons of Science mourn." (34)

PA, Nov 24, 1764; WA, Dec 15, 1764, p. 832.

Epitaph. HC. Churchill, the independent and incorruptible freedom fighter, is dead.

64-67. On Perjury.

"The Wretch who robs me of my Store." (8)

St J's C, Feb 9, 1764.

Quatrains. Perjury is worse than theft or libel. Thus, one (Sandwich?) who testified with lies against Wilkes deserves to be punished. But Wilkes deserves mercy.

64-68. On the Death of Mr. C. Churchill.

"Churchill is dead, Apollo heaves a groan." (32)

L Eve Post, Dec 18, 1764.

HC. Mourns the death of Churchill. Praise of his independence.

64-69. On the Death of the late famous Churchill.

"If Genius, Worth, be held to Britons dear." (14)

PA, Nov 22, 1764.

Epitaph. HC. Churchill died prematurely; those who love freedom mourn, but others, the ministers, are pleased.

64-70. On the Late Additional Window-Tax.

"God gave us Light, and bade that Light to roll." (4)

L Chron 16 (Sep 22, 1764), 295; St J's C, Sep 20, 1764

HC. Epigram. Satire on the ministry for their new window tax.

64-71. On the Proclamation made at St. Margaret's Church, Westminster.

"Be quick, ye Ministerial band." (8)

Court C&CM 1 (Aug 1764), 316; L Chron 16 (Aug 11, 1764), 150; L Eve Post, Aug 14, 1764.

Quatrains. Epigram. Satire on Kidgell and the Tories. It is not new for Tories to go into exile; so Wilkes will have Kidgell to prepare the way for him.

64-72. On the Scotch Pavement.

"Had paving London Streets in Taste." (4)

L Chron 16 (Nov 13, 1764), 468; PA, Nov 14, 1764; St J's C, Nov 10, 1764.

Quatrain. Epigram. Satire on Bute and the Scots, who should provide the pavement for English pedestrians!

64-73. A Parody on Verses of Sir Walter Raleigh. Written in 1764.

"Go, truth, unwelcome guest." (29)

Freeman's J, Aug 26, 1769; The Humours of the Times (London, 1771), pp. 386-7.

Sixains. Parody of Raleigh's "Go, soul, the body's guest." Satire on the Tories and Bute, but praise of Pitt. The Tory faction, which supports arbitrary power, has had its day; Bute, too, will fall and die; but Pitt will live forever.

64-74. The Patriot. A Poem. Inscribed to the Right Hon. William Pitt.

"One Briton yet asserts that awful name." (50)

L Eve Post, Apr 12, 1764.

HC. Against corruption and for Pitt. Pitt can restore purity and integrity to the nation, and can compel the Scots to return home.

64-75. Perjury A-La-Mode. A Cantata.

"Happy the Rogue (whate'er betide)." (19)

St J's C, May 22, 1764.

Song. Satire on the corruption of the court, and on Sandwich, especially, for alleged perjury against Wilkes.

64-76. The Prescription. Occasioned by a Late Death.

"The Nation is disorder'd all agree." (12)

St J's C, Jul 7, 1764.

Hexameter couplets and HC. The minority and majority should go to the devil. Their platforms are absurd: more war and complacent peace. The death of Henry Bilson Legge, former Chancellor of Exchequer, is probably the reference.

64-77. A Prophecy.

"When England's bold Sons, once Lords of the Waves." (16)

L Chron 15 (May 10, 1764), 452; PA, May 11, 1764; St J's C, May 8, 1764.

HC. England will mourn the loss of its freedom because the King and the court, the Lords, control Government and Parliament.

64-78. A Prophecy from Merlin's Cave.

"When proud St. Andrew rules the Roast." (46)

St J's C, May 10, 1764.

OC. Satire on the character of the court, corrupt and Tory. It appears that King George is a Stuart (or Jacobite).

64-79. A Pun.

"'You're surpriz'd,' do ye say, 'Jemmy Twitcher should 'Peach.'" (6)

St J's C, Feb 28, 1764.

Anapest tetrameter couplets. Satire on the Earl of Sandwich for testifying against Wilkes in regard to the Essay on Woman.

64-80. The Question.

"When Nassau, favouring the Land." (7)

St J's C, Jan 31, 1764.

OC. Who can, like William assisted by Lord Dorset, dissipate discord and end faction? (King George and Lord Bute cannot.)

64-81. The Rats and the Cheese.

"If Bees a Government maintain." (40)

DJ, Nov 24, 1764; GM 34 (Nov 1764), 539; L Chron 16 (Nov 13, 1764), 468; PA, Nov 14, 1764; St J's C, Nov 13, 1764; WM 2 (Nov 17, 1764), 211.

Hudibrastics. Animal fable that cynically satirizes politicians of both parties who are not guided by genuinely patriotic motives but merely by self-interest.

64-82. A Recipe, Occasioned by Mr. Churchill's being taken ill at Bologne, and attended by four Physicians.

"Great Churchill sick! O cruel Fate." (8)

St J's C, Nov 6, 1764.

Quatrains. Churchill is ill in France; he needs to be leeched.

64-83. A Salve for the Minority, on the Loss of their Legge. [And] Answer to the Salve for the Minority.

"The Minority's Bruises, Diseases and Sores." (6 + 4)

St J's C, Sep 6 & 25, 1764.

Sixain and quatrain. Epigram. Satire on the minority upon the death of Henry Legge; only pensions will be a salve for their losses.

64-84. Semper Idem.

"Such little, dirty, trumper'y tricks." (24)

L Eve Post, May 29, 1764.

Quatrains. Satire on Bute (always the same), the King's favorite, for hypocrisy.

64-85. Serious Thoughts on True Nobility and False.

"Not all, who are accounted great." (28)

G Eve Post, Jun 28, 1770; KG, Nov 5, 1774; L Cour, Feb 16, 1782; L Eve Post, Aug 14, 1766, & Jul 10, 1773; Say's, Jul 31, 1773; UM 35 (Oct 1764), 209, & 46 (Supp. 1770), 374; W Eve Post, Feb 14, 1782; LM 39 (Jul 1770), 380.

Quatrains. Satire on slavish and hypocritical courtiers. See 70-167.

64-86. A Short Essay on Charles Churchill. Written in 1764. With Notes and Alterations in 1774. To a Friend.

"A Thousand sheep, if bards say true." (c. 180 + c. 150)

GM 50 (Sep 1780), 433-4, & (Oct 1780), 485-6.

OC. Two installments. A tribute to Churchill's character as a satirist.

64-87. Some Reflections which occurred to one of the Electors of the Borough of Ashburton on . . . the Peace.

"Must the ----- be address'd." (72)

L Eve Post, Feb 2, 1764.

Sixains. Objection to the new taxes (on cider and perry), the first results of a poor peace treaty.

64-88. Sung Extempore at a certain Tavern, by four of Macheath's gang. Tune, --

Begging we will go.

   "Crook Finger'd Jack. Come, here's a sparkling bumper." (22)

   L Eve Post, May 19, 1764.

   Song. Satire on the corrupt and immoral ministers, Sandwich and others.

64-89. [There's S------- the pious, the chaste, and the wise.]

   "There's S------- the pious, the chaste, and the wise." (4)

   St J's C, Feb 4, 1764.

   Anapest tetrameter couplets. Epigram. Satire on Sandwich, Jeremiah Dyson, and Gower (?), as "humble Servants of Bute."

64-90. To a General Officer on his Dismission.

   "When ----- and ----- hold the reins of state." (50)

   GM 34 (Jun 1764), 294; L Chron 15 (May 3, 1764), 427.

   HC. A defense of Conway.

64-91. To his Country's Friend.

   "Welcome, dear Stuart, to our open Arms." (4)

   St J's C, Nov 29, 1764.

   Quatrain. Satire. Ironic advice to the Scots now guiding British policy to restore the pretender Prince Charles to the throne.

64-92. To John Wilkes, Esq.

   "If e'er Oppression, with her desperate Tools." (8)

   St J's C, Feb 23, 1764.

   HC. Wilkes will endure, despite oppression.

64-93. To the E[arl] of S[andwich].

   "If thee religious Peer, thy Passion calls." (11)

   St J's C, Feb 14, 1764.

HC. Counsels Sandwich to join the Medmenham sect. These verses must be ironic. Wilkes for a time was Sandwich's crony in this libertine club.

64-94. Tunbridge Verses. Epigram on a Late Death: Addressed to the Minority. [And] Answer to the Tunbridge Verses. [And] Epitaph on the Same.

"The rotten Cause that you maintain." (8 + 4 + 4)

St J's C, Aug 25 & 28, 1764.

Quatrains. Satire on the minority upon their loss of Philip Yorke, Earl of Hardwicke, and of Henry Legge.

64-95. The Twin Scots. A Tale.

"When Charles had on the Block resign'd his Breath." (12)

Freeman's J, Jul 28, 1764; L Chron 16 (Jul 24, 1764), 84; L Eve Post, Jul 24, 1764; St J's C, Jul 21, 1764.

HC. One Scot doomed Charles I; another (Bute) dooms George III (by an inglorious peace treaty).

64-96. Upon Wilkes.

"Great in his Fall, his End he still obtains." (2)

St J's C, Feb 23, 1764.

HC. Epigram. Wilkes has lost his liberty, but England gains thereby.

64-97. Verses addressed to Freedom.

"Whether reclining on the mould'ring tomb." (c. 215)

G, Apr 21, 1764.

Blank verse. A general complaint against oppression. Those who betray the freedom of the people in the country for gold are "venal souls." The poet asks that the Goddess of Freedom "Dash these domestic spoilers from their pride!"

64-98. Verses inscribed to L[or]d B[u]te.

"Hail, Happy B[u]te! blest in the Pedigree." (8)

St J's C, Oct 23, 1764.

HC. Ironic satire on Bute, Tory Stuart, supporter of despotic rule.

64-99. Verses on the Twin Stars Disappearing. Humbly Address'd to the Common Council.

"Cockney's, your Patriot W[ilke]s is fled to France." (75)

PA, Jan 17, 1764.

HC. Satire on Wilkes and Churchill, who have gone to France. The satirist excoriates them and asks these incendiaries to create trouble in Paris as they have in London.

64-100. The Viziarate.

"W--E had Talents to corrupt a State." (16)

St J's C, Jul 5, 1764.

HC. A defense of King George. All the King's ministers have served him well. A patriot, why should any fear the King? Cited are the two Grenvilles, Sandwich, Pitt, Bute, and others.

64-101. The Voice of Freedom. Verses wrote in the Year 1764.

"The midnight bell had toll'd from far." (44)

Lloyd's 14 (Mar 5, 1764), 225.

Quatrains. Hampden and Sidney are recalled to inspire the struggle against oppression.

64-102. The Walls of Troy. Written in July, 1764. Found among the Papers of a Deceased Clergyman.

"In English 'tis unsafe to speak." (48)

Freeman's J, Nov 10, 1764.

Quatrains in OC (with same rhymes for second couplet). The walls of Troy are being breached by corruption, but Pitt and Pratt, two columns, are intact. The threat of Roman Catholicism is cited.

64-103. [Whilst W(ilke)s supports a nation's injur'd laws.]

"Whilst W[ilke]s supports a nation's injur'd laws." (10)

Lloyd's 14 (Feb 13, 1764), 160.

HC. Epigram. Objects to Wilkes's impiety, but supports his fight for freedom: "in the Libertine the Patriot's lost."

64-104. Wildman's: A Fragment of a Political Dialogue.

"A. Whence, my good Lord." (32)

St J's C, Feb 11, 1764.

HC, dialogue. The Opposition is centered at the gambling club Wildman's, a Whig establishment.

64-105. [Worn quite to Shreds the hackney'd Theme of Scot.]

"Worn quite to Shreds the hackney'd Theme of Scot." (10)

St J's C, Apr 10, 1764.

HC. The supporters of Pitt against Bute have exhausted their theme. Now license appears to blaspheme God, and the King avenges God (by convicting Wilkes).

64-106. Written in the Budget. (A New Pamphlet) and Sent to a Great Man.

"How great's the praise of Grenville, born to pay." (2)

L Eve Post, May 19, 1764.

HC. Epigram. George Grenville (First Lord of Treasury, April 1763-July 1765) is praised, if ironically, for his way of paying the nation's debts.

64-107. Wrote at the Proclamation of the Late Peace in London.

"The Peace proclaim'd! no English shouts arise." (16)

Freeman's J, Dec 18, 1764; LM 33 (Dec 1764), 653; St J's C, Dec 8, 1764.

HC. Criticism of the late peace treaty because it benefitted France and Spain.

1765 Books & Pamphlets

65-1. [Bridges, Thomas]
The Battle of the Genii. A Fragment. In three canto's. Taken from an ancient Erse manuscript, supposed to be written by Caithbat, the Grandfather of Cuchullin. . . . Done into English by the author of Homer Travestie.
London: Hooper, 1765. 63p.

"E'er Time began his infant race." (c. 1380)

Notices: CR 19 (Feb 1765), 151; MR 32 (Apr 1765), 276-9; L Chron 17 (May 28, 1765), 516.

Copies: BL 11630.e.9 (6); NUC IU, PLL, RPB, TxU.

Hudibrastics. Burlesque modeled on Milton's Battle of the Angels (Paradise Lost, Book 6). The action covers the years 1763-65. A vulgar satire on the Scots for their proclivity to rebel against the Hanoverian family, crudely distorting the political warfare in these years and explaining how Bute, in the reign of George II, became the tutor of the future king, George III. Characters who appear are Bute, Pitt and Chatham (in two capacities), Wilkes, Burke, Rockingham, Temple, Pratt, et al. There are no allusions to the American troubles.

65-2. [-----]
The Battle of the Bonnets, A Political Poem, From the Erse.
London: Bingley, [1768?]. 64p.

Copies: BL 11630.d.3 (3); NUC CLY, ICN, OU.

See 65-1. Another edition, but caption title is "The Battle of the Genii."

65-3. [Duncombe, John]
Horace, Odes, IV: 15 Imitated. To his Majesty.

"When stretch'd beneath the Beechen shade." (48)

In 67-2: Works of Horace, vol. II, pp. 268-70; L Chron 21 (Mar 12, 1767), 253.

Horatian ode in octosyllabic couplets. Dated 1765. Duncombe celebrates the acquisitions gained by the late peace (Canada and "Mississippi to the Pole"), and the virtues of George II.

65-4. [Greene, Edward Burnaby]
The Laureat. A Poem. Inscribed to the Memory of Charles Churchill.
London: Ridley, 1765. 28p.

"With ancient Bards, establish'd names, who sit." (c. 550)

Notices: CR 19 (Feb 1765), 87; MR 32 (Feb 1765), 153.

Copies: BL 840.k.16. (8.); NUC DLC.

HC. Satire on William Whitehead and Samuel Johnson; Scottish authors David Mallet, David Hume, and Tobias Smollett; Mason, the Whartons. They all do not measure up to Churchill, who really deserves the laurel for his satires.

65-5. [-----]
The Scourge, A Satire. Part I.
London: Almon, 1765. 22p.

"Churchill's no more!--Corruption rears her head." (c. 375)

Notices: CR 20 (Dec 1765), 470; MR 33 (Dec 1765), 488-9; Freeman's J, Jan 4, 1766 (entire poem).

Copies: BL 11633.ee.5; Bod Godwyn Pamph 1745 (8); NUC CtY, DFo, DLC, ICN, IU, MH, PU.

HC. Mourns the death of Churchill, "Satire's dread Scourge," who was "a staunch Whig, and bred on Freedom's plan." Celebrates satire, which is needed to lash the Tory politics of the time. A whole army of names is cited--Johnson, Hume, Smollett, Twitcher (Sandwich), James Scott, Kidgell, Bute; the Stuarts, Tories, Jacobites; King George; Pitt and Temple; Mansfield and Pratt. The Second Part was never published.

65-6. Lovibond, Edward.
To Laura. On Politics.

"From moments so precious to life." (44)

In 85-8: Poems on Several Occasions, pp. 167-70.

Quatrains. Written about 1765. Lovibond rejects politics--Churchill, Wilkes, Bute, Pitt--for the love of Laura.

65-7. An Ode to the People of England.
London: Langford, 1765. 7p.

"Faction avaunt!--A hopeful race." (114)

Notices: CR 20 (Aug 1765), 154; MR 33 (Aug 1765), 165; G, Aug 17, 1765; L Chron 18 (Aug 13, 1765), 158; SM 27 (Aug 1765), 432.

Copies: BL 1600/985; NUC IU, NN.

Regular Horatian ode. Ironic expression of hope, now that the Opposition is in power, that amends will be made for the disgrace suffered from the peace. But

this administration cannot last. A very allusive poem, full of personalities.
A brief reference is made to the colonies, who have "misus'd" Britain.

65-8. Oppression. A Poem. By an American. With Notes, by a North Briton.
London: Moran, 1765. 34p.

"'When private faith and public trusts are sold." (c. 670)

Notices: CR 19 (Apr 1765), 315-6; MR 32 (May 1765), 392; GM 35 (Apr 1765),
193; PA, Apr 1, 1761.

Evans 10112, 10113; Sabin 57416.

Copies: Bod Godwyn Pamph 1745 (9); NUC CtY, DLC, MB, MH, MiU-C, NN, RPB.

HC. Satire on the ministry regarding treatment and taxation of the American
colonies. Has possibly the first known use of the term Yankee ("the Portsmouth
Yankey"--this text quoted in the OED, s.v., A. 1. a). Cited are Grenville, Bute,
Mansfield, Pitt, Conway, Fox, Egremont, Wilkes, Sackville, Temple, Grafton,
Albemarle, Sandwich, Norton. (Reprinted in Boston and New York, 1765.)

65-9. [Shaw, Cuthbert]
The Race. By Mercurius Spur, Esq. With Notes. By Faustinus Scriblerus.
London: Flexney, 1765. 36p.

"Aid me, some honest sister of the nine." (c. 600)

Notices: CR 19 (Jan 1765), 73; GM 35 (Jan 1765), 40; St J's Chron, Jan 29,
1765.

Copies: BL 011653.o.68.

See 65-10.

65-10. [-----]
-----. The Second Edition. With Large Additions and Alterations.
London: Flexney, 1766. 40p.

"Ye puny things, who self-important sit." (c. 700)

Notices: CR 21 (Apr 1766), 315; MR 34 (Apr 1766), 321-3; St J's Chron,
May 6, 1766.

Copies: NUC CSmH, CtY, DFo, MH.

HC. A satire, partly imitative of Pope's Dunciad: the race is simply an
imagined competition for fame among the writers of the time. Some of the
authors characterized have a degree of political relevance: William Whitehead,
John Wilkes, Samuel Johnson, David Mallet, Churchill. The 2nd ed is prefixed

by an attack on the critical reviewers; in this edition, Churchill wins the prize.

Spur, Mercurius. The Race. See 65-9 and 65-10.

65-11. [Stockdale, Percival]
Churchill Defended, a Poem: Addressed to the Minority.
London: Flexney, 1765. 23p.

"Only weak Men, or Men of wicked Views." (c. 440)

Notices: CR 19 (Jan 1765), 71; MR 32 (Jan 1765), 76.

Copies: BL 644.k.19 (6); NUC CtY, WU.

Advertisement dated Nov 22, 1764; largely written before Churchill's death (Nov 4, 1764). HC. Defense of Churchill's character for candor, against the criticism of the clergy; praise of his manly and unaffected poetry for supporting freedom, outperforming Pope but modeled on Dryden, and superior to Scottish Macpherson and John Home and English Mason. Closes with a wish to write for the "Minority."

65-12. Wodhull, Michael.
The Equality of Mankind: A Poem.
Oxford: Jackson, 1765. 33p.

"There was a time when those hapless schools." (530)

Notices: CR 20 (Dec 1765), 468-9; MR 34 (Jan 1766), 22-4; GM 35 (Dec 1765), 584; UM 37 (Supplement 1765), 373-4, & 38 (Feb 1766), 100-1.

Copies: BL 11630.d.2 (7); Bod Godwyn Pamph 1487 (22); NUC CtY, MH, NcU, OCU.

HC. Monarchy and the "baleful reign of Stuart Kings" are questioned. Illustrates Whig-Tory divisions or attitudes; but this is a strong Whig poem. (Rev ed in 1798, and with appendix in 1799 [1800 in colophon]; also in his Poems [London: Bowyer & Nichols, 1772], rev ed 1804; and in A Collection of Poems . . . By Several Hands [London: Pearch, 1770], IV, 231-51, and [1775], IV, 265-85.)

Serials

65-13. Acrostick on the Death of the late Mr. Charles Churchill.

"Come all ye Opposers of the public Good." (16)

PA, Feb 18, 1765; RM 12 (Feb 1765), 104.

Acrostic. Now that Churchill, the champion of liberty, has died, the vicious friends of Bute rejoice.

65-14. Advice from the Country; a Song sung at Boston, in New-England.

"Amid this loud clamour." (78)

GM 35 (Dec 1765), 575; L Chron 18 (Dec 17, 1765), 575-6; PL, Dec 17, 1765.

Song. Opposition by Americans to the Stamp Act. (From the Mass. Gazette Extraordinary, Oct. 31.)

65-15. Advice to the Marquis of Rockingham, upon a late occasion. By an old courtier.

"Well may they, Wentworth, call thee young." (36)

AR 1765, pp. 279-80; Lloyd's 17 (Nov 1, 1765), 434; PA, Nov 2, 1765; St. J's C, Oct 24, 1765.

Sixains. Ironically advises the naive Rockingham not to be kind or humane.

65-16. Advice to the Presbyterians.

"Now is the time! begin your works." (48)

L Eve Post, Mar 2, 1765. (Supplement to the Advice in L. Eve. Post, April 20, 1765.)

Quatrains. An attack on Presbyterians for policies like those of republican whigs, using whatever issue they can to gain their ends, such as General Warrants and the liberty of the press. (By R. Cole.)

65-17. Advice to the Thane.

"Call in all their cringing graces." (4)

L Eve Post, Jun 11, 1765.

Epigram. Satire on Bute, who is asked to bribe some nobility in order to have some "tasks," favors, performed.

65-18. Advice to the Writers in favour of the Late and Present Ministry.

"Cease, cease this Wrangling, Strife, and Rout." (4)

PA, Aug 27, 1765.

Epigram. No matter who is *in* or *out* of power, Bute remains behind the throne.

65-19. An American Squib.

"Jove fixt it certain, that whatever Day." (2)

PL, Dec 18, 1765.

A couplet ends a prose paragraph on the hanging of an effigy of a Virginia Stamp Tax collector. "Virginia is determined to be free."

65-20. An Antient Prophecy of Merlin's.

"When from the North a cruel bird call'd [Stewart]." (12)

L Eve Post, Feb 23, 1765; Freeman's J, Mar 23, 1765.

HC. Summary of what could happen, should the Scots Stuarts rule: there will be oppression in Britain, corruption and bias, influence on the King, increase of taxes, slackening of trade, packed juries and harsh justice, loss of freedom of the press.

65-21. The Ass Overladen. A Fable.

"A Loaden basket long an ass had bore." (18)

Freeman's J, Jul 9, 1765; L Chron 18 (Jul 4, 1765), 14; L Eve Post, May 23, 1765; UM 36 (Supplement 1765), 376; WA, Jun 6, 1767, p. 368.

HC. Animal fable. Objection to the oppressive stamp tax.

65-22. The British Toast.

"Replenish your glasses, and crown them to Pitt." (16)

Court Misc 1 (Aug 1765), 103-4.

Song, in praise of Pitt's leadership.

65-23. [Churchill is dead, but still survives his fame.]

"Churchill is dead, but still survives his fame." (20)

Court C&CM 1 (Jan 1765), 558.

HC in praise of Churchill who has just died: a poet of great integrity and a friend of freedom, never prostituting his pen to serve vicious men.

65-24. Conclusion of a Letter from a Gentleman in America, to his Friend in London.

"In vain, ye writers, you your proofs produce." (18)

L Eve Post, Dec 3, 1765.

HC. On the Stamp Act which has caused a conflagration in America. What it bodes no one is sure of.

65-25. The Contest of the Trees. A Political Fable. Inscribed to the Right Hon. Mr. P---.

"'Tis said--the Muse forgets the Page." (82)

PA, Sep 14, 1765; PL, Sep 16, 1765.

Octosyllabic couplets. Nature fable. The trees, wishing for a monarch to rule and impose order, finally choose the orange for its modest merit. So Britons should choose Pitt to settle party squabbles and end corruption.

65-26. The Contrast. A Tale.

"Within our time, and in this realm." (72)

PL, Dec 18, 1765.

Hudibrastics. Praise of Rockingham. A story of one who sought a place in Robert Walpole's government in vain illustrates the nearly impossible contrast--one who acts unselfishly, Rockingham.

65-27. The Courtier's true Vade Mecum.

"Those fine-spun Notions which so high you rate." (62)

L Chron 18 (Aug 1, 1765), 118; PA, Aug 2, 1765.

HC. Satire on the game of politics. Only cunning is required for preferment at court. See 65A, An Old Experienced Courtier's Advice.

65-28. Dialogue.

"A. O Boote! the Post of Pow'r since thou possest." (5)

Freeman's J, Apr 6, 1765.

Satire on Bute's bribery with public funds.

65-29. Dialogue, Air, and Chorus. At the Commencement in the college of Philadelphia, May 30, 1765.

"'Tis done--your patient ear we greet no more." (c. 75)

SM 27 (Aug 1765), 434; PA, Aug 1, 1765.

Thanks to the King, the Archbishop of Canterbury Secker, and William and Thomas Penn for their large financial contributions to the seminary in Philadelphia.

65-30. Dialogue between the Guardian of Albion and a Stranger.

"A. Guardian of Albion, say, what new Distress." (19)

St J's C, Apr 13, 1765.

HC. Britain is threatened by France and Spain (because of the late peace treaty), and by corruption within--bribery, selling votes.

65-31. The Dog and Cat, a Fable.

"A Dog, who long time had been used to steal." (20)

Freeman's J, May 4, 1765.

HC. Animal fable. Both Ins and Outs are only interested in pensions and places, not in the public welfare.

65-32. [England already long enough hath kept.]

"England already long enough hath kept." (14)

L Eve Post, Feb 23, 1765.

HC. On the freedom of the press. England has a new martyr to take the place of Charles I, J. Williams, pilloried owner of a London newspaper.

65-33. An Epigram.

"Accurst be They, the Scripture says." (6)

PA, Aug 2, 1765.

Satire on Bute. Those are accurst if they receive the world's praise; thus Bute must be blest because he's cursed and hated.

65-34. Epigram.

"'Bout quart'ring troops why all this clamour made." (8)

L Eve Post, Apr 27, 1765.

The colonists have no real complaints against new taxes and quartering troops. (One of the first poems on the American contest.)

65-35. Epigram.

"Four Circumstances England greatly bless." (4)

St J's C, Apr 11, 1765; Freeman's J, Apr 20, 1765.

England is greatly blessed with free juries, Parliaments, and press, and the Test Act (toleration).

65-36. Epigram.

"The Helm let Pitt or Sandwich guide." (4)

L Chron 17 (Jun 11, 1765), 563; PA, Jun 12, 1765; St. J's C, Jun 8, 1765; Freeman's J, Jun 29, 1765.

Bute still pulls the strings behind the curtain, regardless of the premier, Pitt, or Sandwich.

65-37. Epigram.

"In sacred prophecies of yore we find." (4)

PL, Sep 13, 1765.

Pitt is being exalted (by his supporters, presumably in preparation for being recalled to office).

65-38. Epigram.

"No Favourite! but if it be our Lot." (4)
"In vain to Harrogate the Fav'rite flies." (4)

Freeman's J, Feb 9, 1765; St J's C, Feb 2, 1765.

Objection to Bute as the King's favorite--a Scot and a Stuart! Bute has retired to Luton-Hoo, near Harrogate--Bute, a Stuart with an itch for tyranny.

65-39. Epigram.

"Quoth the Outs to the Ins ye cannot stay." (4)

L Eve Post, Jul 25, 1765; Freeman's J, Aug 17, 1765.

On the change of ministry--the Outs are Grenville, Sandwich, and others, the Ins are the Rockinghamites.

65-40. Epigram.

"That Nation blest in Politicks has been." (2)

Freeman's J, Oct 8, 1765; St J's C, Sep 10, 1765.

Satire on the instability of English politics in the last four years--four ministries in this period!

65-41. Epigram.

"While the Ins and the Outs are disclaiming the Thane." (4)

St J's C, Sep 17, 1765.

Bute may be criticized by all the politicians in and out, but he is behind or beneath everything.

65-42. Epigram.

"Why from the North alone do all promotions role." (2)

L Eve Post, Mar 2, 1765; Freeman's J, Mar 23, 1765.

Satire on the Scots who have secured many places in administration.

65-43. Epigram.

"With horrid buz the Ins and Outs." (12)

L Chron 18 (Aug 1, 1765), 120; PL, Aug 6, 1765.

Quatrains. Satire on party factionalism, especially the patriots.

65-44. Epigram.

"Ye Rebel Picts, whom William lately bang'd." (2)

St J's C, Feb 9, 1765; Freeman's J, Apr 6, 1765.

Anti-Scots satire for greed and rebellion. Reference to William, Duke of Cumberland, who had helped suppress the '45.

65-45. Epigram.

"You say the Ministry are young: 'Tis Truth." (6)

St J's C, Jul 23, 1765; Freeman's J, Aug 6, 1765.

Satire on slavish ministries, dominated by Bute. But the youthful Rockingham ministry does not deserve this kind of criticism.

65-46. Epigram. Advice to Friends Abroad.

"Wand'rers, forlorn, with Stockings out at Heels." (8)

St J's C, May 21, 1765; Freeman's J, Jun 8, 1765.

Advice to Wilkes to return from abroad and be careful not to libel the Great Ones.

65-47. An Epigram. By Moderator.

"Betwixt the Patriot Parties why this pet." (4)

L Eve Post, Sep 12, 1765; Freeman's J, Oct 8, 1765.

Questions the need for the patriot factions to argue about how the national debt is to be paid: Chathamites, Rockinghamites, Wilkesites.

65-48. Epigram. Occasioned by those of Tom T'Otherside . . . .

"Tom T'otherside of the right true Tory Leaven." (4 & 4)

St J's C, Jan 17, 1765.

Two epigrams satirizing Tories. On Whig and Tory differences regarding the monarchy.

65-49. Epigram. On the Publication of Mr. Legge's Papers.

"Papers from Legge--and for the public Eye." (8)

St J's C, Jan 10, 1765.

HC. Henry Legge died Aug 23, 1764. He was Chancellor of the Exchequer 1754-55, 1756-57, 1757-61. Here he is eulogized as a patriot, and Bute cursed as a treacherous Scot.

65-50. An Epitaph upon the Duke of Cumberland.

"Here by the side of Kings entomb'd lies." (16)

PL, Nov 27, 1765.

HC. Eulogy of Cumberland for suppressing the (Jacobite) rebellion and upholding the flag of liberty against (Stuart) tyrants. (Many poems on the Death of William Duke of C. I give a selection only.)

65-51. The Exile.

"See! wounded Wilkes! an out-law'd Exile roam." (4)

L Eve Post, May 16, 1765; Freeman's J, May 28, 1765.

Quatrain. Wilkes is in exile where he has more freedom than at home.

65-52. Extempore on Reading the Last Birth-Day Ode.

"How near ally'd are Indolence and Theft." (2)

St J's C, Jun 27, 1765.

Epigram. Satire on Whitehead for his poorly written and plagiarized laureate ode.

65-53. A Fable, Modernized.

"Where force has fail'd, th' alluring smile." (58)

PL, Aug 8, 1765.

Hudibrastics. A fable illuminates the effect of bribery upon politics.

65-54. The Four Ages inverted, in Ad[ministratio]n.

"In old N[ewcastle]'s Dotage we might see." (9)

St J's C, Sep 10, 1765.

HC. The several changes since Holles, Duke of Newcastle's time are traced through

Pitt, then Halifax and Sandwich, and now Wentworth (Rockingham) and Grafton. The point is made that the last are very young.

65-55. A Fragment.

"Hark to the Maxim of the Stuart Line." (5)

Freeman's J, Apr 20, 1765.

HC. King William opposed the Stuart maxim of rule by divine right and set the English free through the House of Hanover.

65-56. Fragment of an Epistle to a Friend.

"What, then, no longer single must I tarry." (24)

L Eve Post, Feb 21, 1765.

HC. Light satire. The poet refuses to marry a fair Presbyterian because she is a republican and hypocrite.

65-57. France to England. A Card.

"Whilst other Nations seem to act by Chance." (10)

L Chron 17 (May 30, 1765), 523; LM 34 (Jun 1765), 315; St J's C, May 28, 1765.

HC. France confesses that she will <u>cheat</u> England, if she can't <u>beat</u> her. Cited is the peace treaty of 1763.

65-58. A Freeman's Wish. In Answer to the Force of Fate.

"The Wretch, who England's Freedom would revoke."

St J's C, Jan 12, 1765; Freeman's J, Feb 2, 1765.

HC. Objection to anyone who will re-introduce despotism in England. (See Force of Fate, St. James's Chronicle Dec. 29, 1764, which this poem should follow.)

65-59. Free(th), John.
The Ins and Outs. A Song. Tune, Caesar and Pompey.

"What a noise has there been! What a great consternation." (42)

Cumb Pacq, Sep 3, 1782; G, Dec 26, 1767; GM 36 (Jan 1766), 34; L Chron 19 (Jan 4, 1766), 23; PA, Dec 25, 1765; Dec 25, 1767; UM 37 (Supp. 1765), 370-71; 39 (Dec 1766), 318; The Warwickshire Medley (1776), pp. 3-4. Also L Chron 22 (Dec 26, 1767), 623. See 76-13.

Song. The competition for political power and position is like a horse race in which all (Whigs, Tories, Scots, bishops, Wilkes) are motivated by self interest.

65-60. Free(th), John.
The State Jockeys. Tune, Shawnbree.

"Ye lads who delight in a whip and a spur." (48)

The Warwickshire Medley (1776), pp. 33-35. See 76-13.

Song. A review of the state jockeys, or premiers: Newcastle, Pitt, Bute; and now the Scots dominate the field, and the Whigs are out. See Freeth's The Statesmen: 64-40. (This song could have been composed between 1761-63.)

65-61. From a Gentleman in the Country to his friend in London.

"What our good Parliament is doing." (56)

G, Jun 8, 1765.

Epistle. Octosyllabic couplets. An introduction to significant themes in the year 1765. The gentleman from the country asks if politics is still disturbed and factious; if Pitt and Grenville have compromised their differences. Corruption is cited.

65-62. The Genius of England.--To a Freeman.--To be Sung or Said.

"My son, to whom freedom is sweeter than pelf." (84)

L Chron 18 (Aug 29, 1765), 212; PA, Aug 30, 1765; UM 37 (Sep 1765), 154.

Sixains in couplets. Objects to the new ministry ("boys and old women"): Rockingham, Dowdeswell, Conway, Newcastle, et al. Bute is mentioned.

65-63. The Independent and Happy Cobler.

"Places and Pensions I despise." (14)

Freeman's J, Apr 16, 1765; L Eve Post, Apr 9, 1765.

Octosyllabic couplets. The happy cobbler loves his freedom and independence, hates politics and lies and the Scotch.

65-64. An Indian's Speech to his Countrymen. Imitated from the second Vol. of the Idler.

"While in a soft Savannah's cool retreat." (c. 100)

GM 35 (Nov 1765), 526; PL, Dec 3, 1765.

Blank verse. An American Indian complains of the white man's evil incursions that destroy the Indian way of life and expresses pleasure over disputes to the title of lands usurped by the fierce and fraudulent invaders.

65-65. The Inn's.

"There's Spectacle Pres." (17)

L Eve Post, Jul 27, 1765.

Trimeter couplets. A list of the new Rockingham Administration--but the suspicion is that Bute is still behind the curtain.

65-66. Kenrick, William.
Verses to a Gentleman, who desired the Author to write Politics.

"You ask me, why I spend my time." (54)

PL, Dec 28, 1765 (Signed W.K.); BM 6 (Dec 1765), 660.

Sixains. Kenrick declines to engage in party writing, to serve ministers and party, preferring philosophy and literature.

65-67. A Late Wonderful and Extraordinary Dialogue Between the English and Scotch Stones in the Strand.

"Quoth a petrified Pitt--G-d rot your Scots faces." (12)

G, Dec 13, 1765.

Hexameter couplets. Satire on the Scotch at court who, it is asserted, will next aim at the crown.

65-68. Liberty and Independence. A Song. Addressed to the Inhabitants of the Borough of Southwark.

"While trifles prevail with a whimsical town." (28)

PL, Oct 28, 1765.

Song. The Borough of Southwark never sells a vote, being unbiased, unbribed, independent, and free; and will support a candidate who is equally honest.

65-69. Lines Written Extempore on the present disturbances Relative to the Stamp-Act in North-America.

"Pitt said, as ev'ry Patriot shou'd." (16)

L Eve Post, Dec 21, 1765.

Quatrains. Indignation at the American rejection of a moderate tax (the Stamp Act).

65-70. Lloyd, E.
On Mr. Churchill's Death.

"Unfeeling Witlings, who are all Out-side." (99)

St J's C, Jan 8, 1765.

HC. Eulogy of Churchill for his talent for political satire. These lines were written shortly before Lloyd's death.

65-71. Ludus Mirabilis.

"O Rock[ingha]m! whom all must love that know." (24)

PA, Aug 2, 1765.

Quatrains. Britain loses as a result of the messy juggle for power in which Rockingham, Henry Fox, Pitt, and Bute are engaged.

65-72. Modern Politics: An Epigram.

"The constant Will of rend'ring each his own." (9)

Freeman's J, Apr 20, 1765.

HC. Satire on Bute and the peace treaty which benefited France.

65-73. A Monody.

"Begin, my Muse, a solitary Strain." (160)

PA, Jun 14, 1765; Freeman's J, Jun 22, 1765; St J's C, Jun 11, 1765.

Irregular ode, on the death of Churchill. The poet Churchill represents the ideals of Whiggish republicanism and freedom against lawless tyranny.

65-74. A New Ballad.

"Make haste, O my muse, and begin." (24)

PA, Nov 6, 1765; UM 37 (Nov 1765), 266.

A cynical song about political lies and hypocrisy--in defense of the old administration against the lies of its critics. Cited are Conway, Dowdeswell, Newcastle, Temple, Pitt.

65-75. A New Ballad; Entitled, A Letter from a Newmarket Jockey to his Brother at York. Tune,--Larry Grogan.

"Brother Harry, I send you most terrible News." (56)

L Eve Post, Aug 24, 1765.

Song. A rollicking ballad satire on the Rev. James Scott (Anti-Sejanus) and "Estimate" Brown for their diatribe on horseracing (Grafton and Rockingham) as a corrupting influence--instead of preaching against real corruption.

65-76. A New Ballad, on the Change of the Ministry in July 1765.

"Attend, fellow subjects, glad tidings I bring." (64)

G, Jul 19, 1765; Lloyd's 17 (Jul 19, 1765), 74; L Chron 18 (Jul 18, 1765), 70; PA, Jul 20, 1765; PL, Jul 20, 1765; UM 37 (Jul 1765), 43-4.

Song. Ballad celebrates the change to the Rockingham ministry. The preceding ministry is berated as "bunglers in politics, botchers of peace"--Grenville, Bute; the new are approved, "Cumberland's friends," and supported by Pitt, Grafton, Conway, Charles Townshend, Pratt, Dowdeswell, Keppel.

65-77. [No prudence the late Ministry possess'd.]

"No prudence the late Ministry possess'd." (4)

L Eve Post, Nov 12, 1765.

Brief extemporaneous comment on the last ministry which imprudently antagonized the colonies and ruined trade; the present ministry may do better with prudence.

65-78. Non nos à Regibus, sed Reges à nobis.

"Jack English I think both a Fool and a Sot." (4)

St J's C, Apr 23, 1765.

Satire on Bute, who deserves his grand motto--"We go not to Kings, but Kings go to us."

65-79. The Northern Conjurer.

"Ye Romish Jugglers, who from Days of yore." (23)

L Chron 17 (May 28, 1765), 514; St J's C, May 25, 1765; Freeman's J, Jun 8, 1765.

HC. Anti-Bute satire. Bute is corrupting Parliament with gold, and will soon have France, Spain, and Rome against England.

65-80. An Occasional Song. On the Birth Day of Little Master Hinchinbrook, Son and Heir to Jemmy Twitcher, Ap 8, 1765.

"Come on jolly Days, let's get drunk and be mad." (17)

St J's C, May 9, 1765.

Satire on Sandwich on the coming of age of his son. Sandwich is satirized for his immorality and his treacherous treatment of Wilkes. (This song is a parody of Hearts of Oak.)

65-81. [Ode against Oppression.]
A Translation of the Ode against Oppression. By N.M.

"What hideous sight, O Deity on high." (42)

PL, Oct 10, 1765.

Regular (Horatian) ode. A complaint at oppression in France, and praise of liberty in England.

65-82. An Ode, which was performed at the Castle of Dublin, on Tuesday, the Fourth of June, being the Birth-Day of . . . George III . . . By Benjamin Victor, Esq; . . .

"Ye Pow'rs, that on the Virtuous wait." (37)

Freeman's J, Jun 8, 1765.

Irregular Pindaric ode. It is ironic to see this official Establishment Ode beside the other poems critical of the state of affairs at the same time.

65-83. On a Prophecy of Merlin's.

"When victors shall unto the vanquish'd sue." (11)

L Eve Post, Mar 21, 1765; Freeman's J, Apr 6, 1765.

HC. Satire on the peace and the Scots. As a result of the poor peace treaty which benefited France, terrible things will happen--France will dominate and the Scots will overrun Britain.

65-84. On General Warrants.

"Let the good of the State." (6)

L Eve Post, Feb 7, 1765.

Sixain. General Warrants are illegal, although they may be rationalized as good for the state.

65-85. On Hearing that Mr. Pitt was to be employed in Affairs of State very soon again.

"Fly, Tyranny, no more be known." (20)

St J's C, Nov 2, 1765.

Ode in Sixains. The rumor that Pitt will come back to politics gives pleasure--he will restore justice and remove tyranny.

65-86. On King Charles the First.

"Would you this blessed Martyr truly paint." (4)

Freeman's J, Mar 23, 1765; L Eve Post, Mar 7, 1765.

Epigram. Charles I, the so-called martyr, was a good man; but as a king he was a tyrant.

65-87. On Mr. C. Churchill.

"Since the mighty Churchill to Dust is blown." (4)

PA, Jan 19, 1765.

Epitaph. Only England suffers from Churchill's death; Scotland rejoices.

65-88. On Reviewers and Reviews.

"O Bard! revise not ev'ry faulty line." (8)

L Eve Post, May 2, 1765.

Quatrains. Reviewers look for faults to ridicule. (Applicable to the pamphlet poems.)

65-89. On Seeing Several Letters in the Public Papers, Soliciting to Abolish the Observance of the Thirtieth of January. [By R. Cole.]

"That day, when smote by Sectaries' pow'r." (24)

L Eve Post, Jan 31, 1765.

Quatrains. A defense of the day meant to commemorate the martyrdom of Charles I, and an attack on the Presbyterians and sectaries.

65-90. On Seeing the List of Ins and Outs in the Several Daily Papers.

"A Pretty List, upon my word." (18)

L Eve Post, Aug 24, 1765; PL, Aug 31, 1765.

Sixains. General satire on party politics.

65-91. On the Alterations at Court. [Altered from Sir Charles Hanbury Williams.]

"More Changes, better Times we wait." (6)

L Eve Post, Jul 11, 1765; Freeman's J, Jul 23, 1765.

Sixain. Epigram. "Bleeding Britain" awaits the better times to come upon a new ministry--of Temple, James Grenville, Pitt.

65-92. On the Change of the Ministry.

"All for the best! The Candid say." (4)

PA, Jul 19, 1765.

Epigram. If Temple and Pitt had power, instead of Bute, the government would be improved.

65-93. On the City of Bristol presenting Lord Chief Justice Pratt with his Freedom in a Gold Box.

"When London, Mistress of our Isle." (25)

Freeman's J, May 19, 1765; St J's C, May 12, 1765.

Octosyllabic couplets. Lord Chief Justice Pratt deserves the Freedom of London and Bristol because he preserves freedom for others.

65-94. On the Death of his Royal Highness the Duke of Cumberland.

"Now faction rejoice--he is dead." (32)

L Eve Post, Nov 5, 1765.

Quatrains. Eulogy of Cumberland (son of George II) who had defeated the French and the Scots in the '45 rebellion, opposed the Tory faction as a patriot, supported Devonshire, Temple, and Pitt.

65-95. On the Death of his Royal Highness the Duke of Cumberland. Inscribed to the Favorite.

"At William's Fall while Britain's Sons stand mute." (4)

PL, Nov 28, 1765.

Bute will never meet William, Duke of Cumberland, in Heaven.

65-96. On the Death of Mr. Churchill.

"Churchill! -- If aught can reach Thee in thy Tomb." (16)

PA, Jan 19, 1765.

HC. One Scotsman mourns Churchill's death and regrets the debasing of his satire by politics.

65-97. On the Death of the late Mr. Churchill.

"That Churchill's dead, Apocrypha don't lie." (6)

St J's C, Mar 19, 1765.

HC. Panegyric on Churchill: the British Juvenal will sting eternally.

65-98. On the Monthly Reviewers.

"To write without Style, to read without taste." (5)

St J's C, Mar 7, 1765; Freeman's J, Mar 19, 1765.

Satire on the Monthly and Critical Reviewers for pretended learning and hasty censures, without taste or style.

65-99. On the Much--Lamented Death of his Royal Highness William, Duke of Cumberland.

"Bold Faction rear'd her guilty head." (12)

L Chron 18 (Nov 2, 1765), 438; L Eve Post, Nov 2, 1765; PL, Nov 5, 1765.

Quatrains. Freedom asserts that the death of Cumberland will not permit the Tory traitors to Britain to rise, so long as George III prudently leads the country.

65-100. On the New Excise on Cyder.

"Why meddle with the apple, mighty B[ute]." (4)

L Eve Post, Feb 28, 1765.

Objection to the new tax on apple cider--which will cause Bute's downfall.

65-101. On the New Ministry.

"To serve the State and save this Land." (4)

Freeman's J, Aug 3, 1765; L Eve Post, Jul 20, 1765; PA, Jul 24, 1765.

Epigram. The new Rockingham ministry should have the support of Pitt and Temple.

65-102. On the Report of a General Change in the Ministry.

"O Bless'd Report! what joy, should'st thou prove true." (8)

Freeman's J, May 28, 1765; L Eve Post, May 21, 1765.

Quatrains. The Irish are pleased with the rumor of a change in administration, for it will mean a revival of trade and prosperity. (The Americans were directly concerned, too.)

65-103. On the Times.

"What is't to us who guides the State." (6)

Freeman's J, Mar 19, 1765; L Eve Post, Mar 5, 1765; PA, Mar 8, 1765.

Epigram. No matter who may be in power, knaves rule and fools compete to be their slaves.

65-104. [O Thou, who lately, for thy private Gain].

"O Thou, who lately, for thy private Gain." (8)

Freeman's J, May 4, 1765.

HC. Anti-Bute verses. Bute is responsible for the poor peace-treaty which will only be broken again and bring on another war.

65-105. The Outs.

"There's Gren, the Budget-maker." (13)

L Eve Post, Jul 30, 1765.

Trimeter couplets. The former George Grenville administration, now going out, was controlled by Bute.

65-106. [Parliaments, whilst free, are, of all good things the first.]

"Parliaments, whilst free, are, of all good things, the first." (2)

Freeman's J, Apr 6, 1765; L Eve Post, Mar 16, 1765.

Epigram. Objection to corruption which destroys free Parliaments.

65-107. [Peace begets Poverty.]

"Peace begets Poverty." (6)

PL, Nov 21, 1765.

A revision of an old adage about peace, poverty, war, riches.

65-108. A Poem on the Death of his Royal Highness, William Duke of Cumberland; Composed and Spoken by one of the Gentlemen of Mr. Rule's Academy in Islington, at their public Examination at Christmas, 1765.

"Now mourn, Britannia, just is thy cause of grief." (24)

PL, Dec 21, 1765.

HC. Praise of William, Duke of Cumberland, for beating the Scots rebels after the defeats at Falkirk, Carlisle, Preston-Pans.

65-109. A Prophecy of Merlin's.

"When Holland shall a Journey take to France." (5)

Freeman's J, Aug 17, 1765; L Eve Post, Aug 3, 1765.

Before Scotland dominates England, Bute will be executed. The Peace is condemned, too.

65-110. The Scotch Bagpipe.

"By Music's magic pow'r, old Poets tell." (12)

L Eve Post, May 9, 1765.

HC. Satire on the Scots, who have the power to end the war, sue for a treaty with France, impose the cider tax, persecute Wilkes, corrupt Parliament and the King.

65-111. The Senator Enlightened, or Julius Caesar's Salve.

"At Rome, in antient times, as Poets say." (24)

L Eve Post, May 4, 1765.

HC. Satire on corruption. A moral fable illustrating the power of a bribe, meant to show how corruption fortifies tyranny.

65-112. [Shall only my poor friends of Sodom now.]

"Shall only my poor friends of Sodom now." (10)

L Eve Post, Feb 21, 1765.

HC. A defence of Williams in the pillory--triumphant, unlike prostitutes who are punished.

65-113. A Short Account of a Late Administration.

"G-----e mere Pelf, B----d lov'd Pelf and Power." (2)

St J's C, Sep 5, 1765.

Epigram. The late administration (Bedford, Dunk [Halifax], Sandwich, and Grenville) were greedy whoremongers.

65-114. A Short Story to the Politicians.

"A many, many years ago." (40)

L Eve Post, Nov 26, 1765; PA, Nov 29, 1765; PL, Dec 2, 1765.

Quatrains. Urges silence in the dispute over the ministry--the King chose this Administration; he is just and the ministry do not deserve consure.

65-115. Spoken Extempore.

"Since tuneful Churchill is no more." (6)

LM 34 (Jan 1765), 47.

With Churchill dead, Wilkes banished, no one can prevent us from emulating the greedy Scotch.

65-116. Stanzas on our present Unhappy Divisions.

"See! where Britannia weeping sits, the while." (32)

PA, Nov 28, 1765.

Heroic quatrains. The near anarchy brought on by factional disputes and by the problems with America may destroy the nation, and only France will triumph. The nation must unite. Duke of Cumberland's death is cited.

65-117. Supplement to the Advice to the Presbyterians.

"Suppose on Pop'ry you descant." (28)

L Eve Post, Apr 20, 1765.

Quatrains. R. Cole accuses the Whig Republicans and Presbyterians of treachery --i.e., for blaming Popery rather than the sectaries as threats to the state.

65-118. XXXth [Thirtieth] of January.

"By Maxims new, and fatal counsels led." (6)

St J's C, Feb 7, 1765.

HC. A warning to the Tories, based on the experience of Charles I, that tyranny is not permitted in England.

65-119. [A Thousand shapes, like Proteus, Jemmy wears.]

"A thousand shapes, like Proteus, Jemmy wears." (20)

L Eve Post, Feb 12, 1765.

HC. Satire on Sandwich, who assumes many shapes, but he is (chiefly) a treacherous hypocrite who has betrayed Wilkes.

65-120. The Times.

"Veterans suffer, good men grieve." (4)

Freeman's J, Jun 8, 1765; PA, May 27, 1765.

Epigram. Satire on the Scots. The patriot Pitt is needed to save the country from fools and Scots.

65-121. The Times: A Satire.

"When Pope and Swift lay number'd with the Dead." (44)

Freeman's J, Aug 17, 1765; St J's C, Aug 3, 1765.

HC. Satire on the peace, Scots, Bute; & praise of Pitt, and a hope he will become the leader again.

65-122. To any Minister or great Man.

"Whether you lead the patriot band." (56)

L Chron 17 (May 4, 1765), 434; LM 34 (May 1765), 258; PA, May 6, 1765 (42); St J's C, May 2, 1765 (42); also AR 1765, p. 278.

Sixains. The minister or great man must expect faction and detraction.

65-123. To -----, Argumentum ad Hominem.

"With Patriotic Fumes replete." (22)

L Chron 17 (Mar 9, 1765), 242; PA, Mar 13, 1765.

Octosyllabic couplets. Nicholas Neitherside believes that there is no difference between the ins and the outs. Both are corrupt, false patriots guided by self-interest.

65-124. To General Conway on his being made Secretary of State.

"Undaunted chief, to Britain dear." (8)

St J's C, Jul 13, 1765; The Muses's Mirror (London: Baldwin, 1778), II, 106.

Epigram. Quatrains. Not long ago the King removed Conway from his places, but now he has returned to favor!

65-125. To Mr. [R.] Cole, in Answer to his Lines on the Observance of the 30th of January.

"Yes, Cole, there are a miscreant race." (32)

L Eve Post, Feb 2, 1765.

Quatrains. We should ever have before us the lesson of Charles I--he was a tyrant and tyranny is abhorrent to English freedom. Cited are Strafford and Charles I.

65-126. To Mr. [R.] Cole, in Reply to his Two Excellent Pieces on King Charles's Martyrdom.

"Is there a power whose presence charms." (76)

L Eve Post, Feb 14, 1765. (Signed Nishes Spoon.)

Octosyllabic couplets. Praise and defence of freedom. Charles I should have died in battle with Cromwell and Hampden; then he would not now be pitied for his execution. But he was a tyrant and deserved his fate. (See comment on this poem in L Eve Post, Feb 21, 1765.)

65-127. To Mr. Spoon, on his Verses in the London Evening Post, on the 5th Instant.

"That you, Sir, by the muse have chanc'd." (24)

L Eve Post, Feb 7, 1765.

Quatrains. Response to Spoon's stanzas "To Mr. Cole, In Answer . . ." and a defense of the day commemorating Charles I's martyrdom, and attack on the Presbyterians, and (Whig) libertarians.

65-128. To My Lord [Sandwich].

"Hail Twitcher! may the brazen Trump of Fame." (8)

St J's C, Jan 12, 1765.

HC. Satire on Sandwich for his dishonesty. (Indirect allusion to his exposure of Wilkes's "Essay on Woman.")

65-129. To Sir J. Williams, Knight of the Most Elevated Order of the Pillory, &c.&c. &c.

"See the -- coach in silence move along." (8)

L Eve Post, Feb 16, 1765.

HC. Applause for Williams, in the pillory, Feb 14, 1765--a martyr for freedom of the press.

65-130. To the Right Hon. the Earl of Bute.

"Of Wealth and Peace he saw th'united Charms." (8)

St J's C, Mar 21, 1765.

HC. Ironic satire on Bute. The Peace made Bute wealthy so that he could purchase and adorn his estate at Luton-Hoo (in 1763).

65-131. To the Right Honourable Jack Ketch, &c. &c. of Old Palace-Yard.

"The time will come, tho' time creep ne'er so slow." (12)

Freeman's J, Feb 26, 1765; L Eve Post, Feb 14, 1765.

HC. A threat to punish the Scots for their tyranny.

65-132. To the Wise Men of Gotham.

"The Gothamites mistook the Case." (26)

L Chron 17 (Feb 19, 1765), 178; Freeman's J, Apr 6, 1765.

Octosyllabic couplets. It is no disgrace to be pilloried by an oppressive government for exercising the freedom of the press. (By Thomas Cunningham.)

65-133. Toasts at a Certain Club.

"That P--- may soon possess the [premie]r's place." (8)

L Eve Post, Aug 1, 1765.

HC. Toasts express the hope that Pitt will be premier joined with Earl Temple.

65-134. A Translation.

"The Lord of Sandwich guideth me." (24)

L Chron 18 (Nov 12, 1765), 459.

Quatrains. Parody of the 23rd Psalm, on the stamp tax. Sandwich's writer, James Scott, whose pen-name was Anti-Sejanus, is the target of this satire.

65-135. [Verses on the Reception of the Stamp Act in Boston.]

"Your servant, Sirs, do you like my Figure." (26)

L Chron 18 (Dec 12, 1765), 567; PA, Dec 13, 1765.

Reprint of octosyllabic couplets affixed to effigies of two ministers hung on the Liberty Tree in Boston on the day the Stamp Act was to take effect. The figures are not named in these verses damning those responsible for the tax.

65-136. The Vision. A Ballad.

"No more of the Taxes, I've done with the Times." (32)

L Eve Post, May 11, 1765; PA, May 14, 1765.

Song. The vision is of an attractive land of freedom, plenty, and peace; but when Bute, the Scot, comes on the scene, it disappears.

65-137. What is an Ex Officio Innuendo?

"An Innuendo in such Mint." (13)

L Chron 17 (Feb 7, 1765), 138; L Eve Post, Feb 5, 1765.

Octosyllabic couplets. A protest at the way in which the government attempts to limit the freedom of the press--by penalizing innuendoes.

65-138. [Whate'er may be the humble Tories fate.]

"Whate'er may be the humble Tories fate." (4 + 4)

St J's C, Jan 8, 1765.

Epigrams. Satire on the Whigs. Republican Whigs must realize Heaven is Tory, a monarchy.

65-139. [While Heavy Dulness spreads her leaden Wings.]

"While heavy Dulness spreads her leaden Wings." (32)

Freeman's J, Aug 13, 1765.

HC. Satire on the times, from the Whig perspective. This bard hopes to take Churchill's place. Pro-Wilkes, anti-Bute and corruption. (Probably an extract from a pamphlet satire on the times.)

65-140. Whitehead, William.
Ode for the New-Year, performed before their Majesties Jan 1, 1765. By William Whitehead, Esq; Poet Laureat.

"Sacred to thee." (45)

GM 35 (Jan 1765), 39-40; LM 34 (Jan 1765), 45; PA, Jan 1, 1765; Freeman's J, Jan 5, 1765; L Chron 17 (Dec 29, 1764-Jan 1, 1765), 6.

Irregular Pindaric ode. Celebrates English commerce, which is greater than that of Spain and brings treasure to London from America and India.

65-141. The Wish and the Reply.

"Says Bute to Pitt, I wish you'd join with me." (8)

Freeman's J, Jun 18, 1765; L Eve Post, May 28, 1765; PA, May 31, 1765.

Quatrains. Bute asks to be allowed to ally with Pitt to head a government, but Pitt declines the invitation.

65-142. [With joy, illustrious Pratt, we see.]

"With joy, illustrious Pratt, we see." (8)

PL, Jul 24, 1765.

Octosyllabic couplets. Honor to Lord Chief Justice Pratt, now Baron Camden. (Camden denied the legality of General Warrants, a judgment that pleased the patriots.)

65-143. Written Extempore, on hearing the melancholy news of the Death of the Duke of Cumberland, in the 45th year of his age.

"In Forty-Five great William's sword." (8)

L Eve Post, Oct 31, 1765.

The Duke of Cumberland defeated the Scots in 45; Wilkes was forced into exile as a result of No. 45; would that Bute had died at the age of 45.

65-144. Written Extempore on the Death of his Royal Highness the Duke of Cumberland.

"When our Sweet William dy'd, that Royal Flower." (4)

St J's C, Oct 31, 1765.

Quatrain. The death of the Duke of Cumberland gives the Scotch great pleasure.

65-145. Wrote Extempore with a Pencil whilst Mr. Williams stood in the Pillory.

"Martyrs of old for Truth thus bravely stood." (6)

Freeman's J, Feb 26, 1765; RM 12 (Feb 1765), 104.

Praise of John Williams who was made to suffer the pillory for reprinting Wilkes' No. 45, after it had been burnt by order of Parliament.

65-146. Wrote Immediately after Mr. Williams's Standing in the Pillory.

"By pride impuls'd, when knaves and fools." (12)

L Eve Post, Feb 16, 1765.

Quatrains. Honest John Williams is honored for being pilloried for freedom. (He had reprinted Wilkes' No. 45 after it had been burnt by order of Parliament.)

Prints

65-147. The Great Financier, or British Oeconomy for the Years 1763, 1764, 1765.

"Our Budget is empty, and upward it flies." (24)

Etching with six quatrains. 1765.

Stephens 4128 (IV, 359-61).

Because of great debts, the government through George Grenville, Chancellor of the Exchequer, imposes a new economy over American objections. America, portrayed as a half-naked Indian with feathered head-dress and a collar marked "Taxed without Representation," says,"Commerce will outweigh it." The Stamp Act is being enforced. General Warrants are also cited.

65-148. The Pillory Triumphant: Or, No. 45 For Ever. Tune, There was a jovial Beggar, &c.

"Ye Sons of Wilkes and Liberty." (50)

Engr. with ballad and chorus. February 14, 1765.

Stephens 4115 (IV, 349-50).

On the pillorying of John Williams, bookseller, in Palace Yard, Westminster, for printing Wilkes' No. 45. The poem emphasizes the function of the press as the guardian of liberty, and attacks the government for unjustifiably punishing Wilkes.

65-149. The State Nursery.

"First you see Old sly Volpone--y." (40)

Engr. with triplets and doodle chorus.

Stephens 4133 (IV, 364-5).

Satire on the Rockingham administration. Dowdeswell, Chancellor of the Exchequer, had promoted the repeal of the Cyder Act. Lord Holland, the sly fox, rides on the shoulders of Bute. Rockingham is portrayed as an infant in a cradle rocked by the Duke of Newcastle.

1766 Books & Pamphlets

66-1. Cockings, George.
  The Conquest of Canada; or the Siege of Quebec. An Historical Tragedy of Five Acts.
  London: Cooke & Haysell, 1766. vi + 76p.

  "Then you resolve to leave me?" (c. 2000)

  Notices: CR 21 (Jun 1766), 471-3; MR 35 (Jul 1766), 76-8; GM 36 (Jun 1766), 288.

  Evans 12355, 12729 (American eds 1772-3)

  Copies: BL 841.d.19 (1), 161.h.10; NUC CtY, DLC, MH, RPJCB, et al.

  Includes one patriotic naval song about Hawke and Saunders leading the attack on the Quebec fortress--"Come on my brave Tars! let's away to the Wars" (44 lines at the conclusion of Act I, pp. 16-17).

66-2. The E[ar]l of C[hatha]m's Apology: A Poem.
  London: Almon, 1766. 3-18p.

  "The western sun had sought his ev'ning grave." (c. 280)

  Notices: CR 22 (Nov 1766), 382-3; MR 35 (Nov 1766), 407.

  Copies: BL 1488.i.26; NUC CSmH, CtY, MH, PU.

  HC. Satire on Pitt. The ghost of Pynsent appears to Pitt and castigates him for accepting the peerage, for corruption, and for breaking the faith by surrendering the cause of liberty. Chatham is terrified and thereupon apologizes. (Also in New Foundling Hospital for Wit, Part I [1768], pp. 108-17, and in The Humours of the Times [1771], pp. 139-51.)

66-3. An Elegy on the Late Rt. Hon. W[illiam] P[itt], Esq.
  London: Kearsly, 1766. 16p.

  "If when the stern relentless hand of fate." (236)

  Notices: CR 22 (Aug 1766), 154-5; MR 35 (Aug 1766), 163-4; B Mag 7 (Aug 1766),

437-8; G, Aug 18, 1766; L Chron 20 (Aug 14, 1766), 168; PA, Aug 18, 1766; R Mag 15 (Aug 1766), 101-3; St J's Chron, Aug 16, 1766.

Copies: BL C.108.e.9; NUC IEN, KU, MH, NN, OCU.

Elegiac quatrains. Criticism of Pitt for his elevation to the peerage. Pynsent, one of the titles conferred on Pitt, is cited; also the Ohio. There is a dedication to Richard, Earl Temple.

66-4. An Epistle to the Rt. Hon. the Earl of Chatham, Lord Keeper of the Privy-Seal, and One of His Majesty's Most Honourable Privy-Council.
   London: Bladon & Blyth, [1766]. 5-18p.

"While cringing courtiers at your levee wait." (c. 230)

Notices: CR 22 (Oct 1766), 319-20; MR 35 (Oct 1766), 325; L Chron 20 (Oct 18, 1766), 392.

Copies: NUC ICN.

HC. An independent poet, unpensioned and unplaced, pays tribute to Pitt, and notes that America is indebted to him. Pratt, Earl of Camden, is also praised.

66-5. An Essay on Patriotism, in the Style and Manner of Mr. Pope's Essay on Man. In Four Epistles. Inscribed to the Rt. Hon. the E--- of C------. By a Member of a Respectable Society.
   London: Wilkie, 1766. 28p.

"Awake, my CH-TH-M! leave all meaner things." (338)

Notices: CR 22 (Sep 1766), 226-7; MR 35 (Oct 1766), 325; G, Sep 26, 1766; GM 36 (Sep 1766), 430; Lloyd's Eve Post 19 (Sep 24, 1766), 299; L Chron 20 (Sep 20, 1766), 295; WA Oct 18, 1766, pp. 691-2.

Copies: NUC MH.

HC. In defense of Chatham as a patriot--his policy guiding English conduct in the last war--that America might be preserved in Germany, and his politics after the war. This is a Whig poem in support of Whig principles against Bute and the Tories.

66-6. An Extraordinary Ode to an Extraordinary Man on an Extraordinary Occasion.
   London: Cooke & Jones, 1766. 7p.

"The Country Girl that's well inclin'd." (102)

Notices: CR 22 (Aug 1766), 153; MR 35 (Aug 1766), 163; B Mag 7 (Aug 1766), 438-9; L Chron 20 (Aug 2, 1766), 128; PA, Aug 6, 1766; St J's Chron, Aug 5, 1766.

Copies: BL 11633.h.15 (2); NUC CtY.

Regular Horatian ode. Criticism of Pitt for being seduced by a bribe--the offer of a peerage--thereby losing his virtue, popularity, and power, his "best Friend the Mobb," and the confidence of the Whigs and the fear of the Tories.

66-7. [Falconer, William]
  The Demagogue. By Theophilus Thorn, Esq.
  London: Robinson & Roberts, 1766. 27p.

"Bold is th'attempt, in these licentious times." (c. 420)

Notices: CR 21 (Feb 1766), 137-9; MR 34 (Mar 1766), 243; B Mag 7 (Feb 1766), 103-4; L Chron 19 (Mar 1, 1766), 213; St J's C, Mar 8, 1766.

Copies: BL 1346.i.13; NUC CtY, ICN, PU.

HC. Censures Pitt for espousing the American cause in the colonial disputes, and accuses him of fomenting sedition and rebellion. Spares neither Churchill nor Wilkes, too. The Seven Years' War, the Stamp Act, and Bute also appear. (A 2nd ed London, 1766, and another ed in The Caledoniad [London: Hay, 1775], vol. II, pp. 205-25.)

66-8. A Genuine Collection of the Several Pieces of Political Intelligence Extraordinary, Epigrams, Poetry, &c. that have Appeared before the Public in Detached Pieces; Now carefully selected together in one View, by An Impartial Hand.
  London & Westminster: Butcher & Russell, 1766. 102 + 1p.

Copies: BL 8138.de.5 (1); NUC CSmH, CtY, DLC, NN.

About 65 poems, most fairly short: epigrams, epitaphs, HC, extempores, odes, satires, panegyrics, extracts from long poems. (I have located at least 44 in the serials, journals and newspapers.) On the elevation of Pitt to the Earldom of Chatham. See esp. An Inscription which is to be put on the Statues preparing to be sent to America: "In Memory of / W. P." (pp. 59-61), a satire.

66-9. [Greene, Edward Burnaby]
  The Politician: A Poem. Addressed to Mr. James Scott, Fellow of Trinity College, Cambridge.

London: Ridley, 1766. 24p.

"The Patriot falls--each gay Delusion dies." (c. 400)

Notices: CR 21 (May 1766), 394; MR 34 (Jun 1766), 482.

Copies: BL 1490.ee.8; NUC CtY, DLC, MH, NjP, NN.

HC. Satire on the corrupt times. Praise of the youthful Rockingham ministry, which had repealed the Stamp Act, for which America was grateful. James Scott is Anti-Sejanus, the name assumed by the hack hired by the Earl of Sandwich to write for the government and the Stamp Act. (Also in Greene's Poetical Essays [London: Ridley, 1771], pp. 239-59.)

Hedge, Simon. See 66-12.

66-10. Ode to the Legislator Elect of Russia, On his being prevented from entering on his high Office of Civilization, by a Fit of the Gout.
London: Nicoll, 1766. 11p.

"O thou! who, thron'd in priestly state." (108)

Notices: CR 22 (Aug 1766), 155; MR 35 (Oct 1766), 322; Lloyd's Eve Post 19 (Aug 29, 1766), 211; PA, Aug 29 & Sep 2, 1766; UM 39 (Sep 1766), 149; also L Chron 20 (Aug 30, 1766), 223.

Copies: NUC CtY, MH.

Regular Horatian ode. Refers to Pitt who, despite his gout, spoke against the Stamp Act, "Preserv'd the colonies," and restored "expiring trade." Now that he is in the ministry again, he will try to save the ship of state in spite of being ill.

66-11. Political Epistles on Various Subjects of the Present Times.
London: Nicoll, 1766. 20p.

"Man first in virtue, 'tis believ'd." (c. 350)

Notices: CR 21 (Feb 1766), 156; MR 34 (Feb 1766), 164-5, & (Mar 1766), 242; PA, Apr 2 & Sep 3, 1766.

Sabin 63772.

Copies: NUC IU.

Octosyllabic couplets. Only one epistle, the first, and that praises the King. However, later others appeared--the third in April 1766. (See PA, Apr 2, for an announcement and Sep 3 for an extract in defense of Pitt.) But these epistles are not located. A defense of the British system of government in King, Lords, and Commons. But as the emphasis appears to be on justifying the King's prerogative, the poem becomes somewhat Tory in its bias. King George is cited.

66-12. The Poor Man's Prayer. Addressed to the Earl of Chatham. An Elegy. By Simon Hedge, A Kentish Labourer.
London: Payne, 1766. 9p.

"Amidst the more important toils of state." (100)

Notices: CR 22 (Sep 1766), 232; MR 35 (Oct 1766), 323-6; B Mag 7 (Sep 1766), 495-6; Freeman's J, Sep 20, 1766; G, Sep 16, 1766; GM 36 (Sep 1766), 430; Lloyd's Eve Post 19 (Sep 15, 1766), 270, & (Sep 22, 1766), 288; L Chron 20 (Sep 11, 1766), 264; L Eve Post, Sep 11, 1766; L Mag 35 (Sep 1766), 482; PA, Sep 16, 1766; R Mag 15 (Sep 1766), 159-60; St J's Chron, Sep 16, 1766; UM 39 (Sep 1766), 150-1; W Misc 2 (May 16, 1774), 163-4.

Copies: BL 1489.tt.46; NUC ICN, NN, OCU, PU.

Quatrains. Hedge (a pseudonym) implores Pitt to help the poor tenant farmer, like himself, starving amidst plenty. The cause of his poverty is the exportation of "our harvest to a foreign shore."

66-13. Pynsent. A Poem.
London: Williams, 1766. 16p.

"In youth's full bloom himself glad PYNSENT saw." (c. 180)

Notices: CR 21 (Feb 1766), 156; MR 34 (Mar 1766), 243; GM 36 (Feb 1766), 90; L Chron 19 (Feb 20, 1766), 183.

Copies: BL 11630.e.5 (21); NUC CtY.

HC. Review of the peace, for which Bute was responsible, ending the glorious victories of Pitt, who has now assumed Pynsent's mantle against the Tories. Lines at the end "were added in the heat of Colony disputes." (Sir William Pynsent, Bart., whose title and fortune were passed on to Pitt, is also discussed.)

66-14. Pynsent's Ghost: (A Parody on the Celebrated Ballad of William and Margaret:).

London: Almon, 1766. 14p.

"'Twas at the silent midnight hour." (80)

Notices: CR 22 (Sep 1766), 233; MR 35 (Oct 1766), 325; GM 36 (Sep 1766), 430; Lloyd's Eve Post 19 (Sep 1, 1766), 223; L Chron 20 (Aug 30, 1766), 224; St J's Chron, Sep 4, 1766.

Copies: BL 644.k.19 (5); NUC CU, ICN, MH, NN, PU.

Quatrains. Satire on Pitt. Parody of David Mallet's ballad; the two ballads face each other on opposite pages. Upon his death, Pynsent passed his title and estate to the Earl of Chatham. He returns to haunt Chatham, castigating him for greed, selfishness, hypocrisy, and for serving Bute.

66-15. [Rogers, Major Robert]
Ponteach: Or The Savages of America. A Tragedy.
London: Millan, 1766. 110p.

"So Murphey, you are come to try your Fortune." (c. 3000)

Notices: CR 21 (Feb 1766), 150; MR 33 (Mar 1766), 242; GM 36 (Feb 1766), 90; Lloyd's 19 (Feb 28, Mar 10, 1766), 211, 243; L Chron 19 (Feb 8, 1766), 143.

Sabin 72729.

Copies: BL 1342.o.5; NUC CtY, DLC, MB, MiU-C, NN.

On Pontiac's Conspiracy (1763-5). Includes "The War Song. To the Tune of Over the Hills and far away," sung by Tenesco, the Head Warrior, at the end of Act III (pp. 65-7): "Where-e'er the Sun displays his Light" (44).

66-16. Scott, John.
Sonnet. To Britannia. [Sonnet V. To Britain. 1766]

"Renown'd Britannia! lov'd parental land." (14)

On Reading Mrs. Macaulay's History of England. 1766. [Stanzas . . .]

"To Albion's Bards the Muse of History spoke." (16)

In George Pearch, ed., A Collection of Poems in Four Volumes (London: Pearch, 1770), IV, 130-1; (London: Pearch, 1775), IV, 114-15.

Also in 82-23: John Scott, Poetical Works, pp. 317-19 (with revisions of both poems, and titles as bracketed above). The sonnet is reprinted in The Lady's Poetical Magazine (London: Harrison, 1781-2), II, 469.

"Sonnet": written in social and political protest. Britain is suffering as freedom is subverted by the class division between the helpless working poor and the powerful rich. Britain's fall is threatened by corrupt senators who are bribed to encourage oppression and corrupt ministers, "slaves in office," who deny "freemen's rights." Should Britain lose its freedom, it will destroy itself. (Scott probably has in mind the Wilkes episode and the rise in the cost of food.)

"Stanzas": Scott agrees with Mrs. Macaulay's Whig reading of history. He praises her history for its emphasis on the struggle for freedom against tyrannical oppression.

Thorn, Theophilus. See 66-7.

Serials

66-17. Advice to the Scriblers.

"Ye graphists of Grub-street, who scrawl about what." (8)

UM 39 (Sep 1766), 150.

Epigram. Satire. Advises the Grub Street satirists to focus on a real abuse--the exporting of "corn" by farmers and landlords, which increases the price of bread oppressively--rather than criticizing Chatham.

66-18. Alteration.

"Oh, hear the Muse, illustrious Pitt." (24)

L Eve Post, Aug 7, 1766.

Quatrains. A protest at Pitt's elevation to the peerage--the destruction of Pitt's Cato image of integrity.

66-19. America Triumphant; or, Old England's downfall. -- Tune, There was a jovial beggar.

"This world is like a whirligigg." (72)

GM 28 (Feb 1766), 98; L Chron 19 (Feb 18, 1766), 175; PA, Feb 20, 1766. (60)

Song. Britain must now bow down to America, and so we should go there to avoid taxes.

66-20. Anniversary Song on the Repeal of the Cyder-Act. The Tune -- Bumper, 'Squire Jones.

"Ye Cyder-land men." (50)

L Chron 20 (Jul 1, 1766), 16; PA, Jul 3, 1766.

Dowdeswell and Cornwall are toasted for providing tax relief and protecting property.

66-21. An Apology for Mr. P[itt].

"The Tories 'od rat' em." (12)

L Chron 20 (Aug 16, 1766), 175; L Eve Post, Aug 14, 1766; New Foundling Hospital for Wit (1768-1773) Pt. 1 (1768), p. 97; The Humours of the Times (1771), p. 123; Genuine Collection (1766), p. 45. See 66-8.

Sixains, epigram. Defense of Pitt against tory criticism of his richly deserved elevation to the peerage. But it has an ironic twist. See [The Tories adrat'em], 66-125.

66-22. [Around thee, Pitt, is such a Glory spread.]

"Around thee, Pitt, is such a Glory spread." (8)

St J's C, Nov 20, 1766.

HC. Defense of Pitt--who is great and incorruptible, despite pension, bribes, titles.

66-23. Britain's Fate.

"To warn poor Britain of her fate." (4)

L Eve Post, Jul 15, 1766.

Quatrain. General warning of a dangerous political situation: schemes being devised to enslave Britain.

66-24. Britannia's Ghost. To a Late Great Man.

"While C---m, seeking soft repose." (36)

PA, Aug 11, 1766; Genuine Collection (1766), pp. 29-31; WA, Sep 13, 1766, p. 611.

Quatrains. Sir Charles Hanbury William's remarks on Chesterfields' acceptance of a bribe adapted to Pitt's acceptance of a peerage: Pitt has lost his reputation as a patriot for wealth, titles, power and has betrayed his country. See 66-8.

66-25. Cato's Soliloquy imitated. Scene the senate-house in B[osto]n. America sola, sitting in a thoughtful posture: In her hand the Resolves of the House. The Stamp-Act on the table by her.

"It must be so--my sons ye reason well." (31)

L Chron 19 (Mar 16, 1766), 225; SM 28 (Mar 1766), 149.

Blank verse, imitation of Addison's Cato. America complains that her liberty is menaced by the Stamp Act and defiantly declares that liberty will "flourish in these western climes." For a non-political humorous parody of Cato's soliloquy, see Freeman's Journal, Nov 1, 1766.

66-26. [Chatham's a title, stedfast Pitt remains.]

"Chatham's a title, stedfast Pitt remains." (18)

G, Aug 22, 1766; Genuine Collection (1766), p. 53. See 66-8.

HC. Pitt does not deserve his loss of reputation because of his elevation to the peerage.

66-27. [Chatham once survey'd, with seeming dread.]

"Ch--m once survey'd, with seeming dread." (12)

G, Aug 21, 1766.

HC. A criticism of Pitt for corruption, for accepting a peerage and a pension.

66-28. The Coalition. A New Song, in Praise of the New M--y.

"In the year sixty-three." (42)

L Chron 20 (Sep 20, 1766), 292.

Song, in praise of the coalition ministry, because Chatham joined it! Bute and the Scots are cited.

66-29. The Cock and the Owl. A Political Fable.

"A Cock who long had rul'd the Roast." (36)

PA, Aug 21, 1766; G, Aug 22, 1766; Genuine Collection (1766), pp. 52-53. See 66-8.

Sixains. On Pitt's apparent retirement from noisy politics. His retirement brought only abuse!

66-30. [The Colossus.] To the Tune of The Old Woman of Grimstone. [Timothy Trimwell, pseud.]

"The Magog of the City." (42)

PA, Feb 14, 1766.

Song. Refers to engraving against Pitt who courts America in his attempt to return to political power. See print: 66-137.

66-31. [Come Pitt and Pratt, illustrious Pair!]

"Come Pitt and Pratt, illustrious Pair." (8)

St J's C, Mar 20, 1766.

Quatrains. Pitt and Pratt are asked to lead the country, defend freedom and foster trade. (See The Congratulation, 66-32.)

66-32. The Congratulation: Addressed to the Sons of Freedom, on the Change of the Ministry in 1766.

"Thank heav'n! at length the paltry farce is o'er." (42)

Asylum for Fugitive Pieces (London: Debrett, 1785), I, 62-3.

HC. The weak and negative Rockingham ministry collapses, and the writer (John Almon) is glad because he wants Pitt and Camden to lead the new ministry. (The Rockingham ministry falls at end of July 1766.)

66-33. The Coronet: Or, the Patriot Metamorphos'd. A New Song.

"How happy a State does Lord C--m possess." (56)

St J's C, Aug 23, 1766; Genuine Collection (1766), pp. 71-74. See 66-8. The Humours of the Times (1771), pp. 126-29. New Foundling Hospital for Wit (1768), pp. 99-101.

Song. Satire on the history of Pitt, from Sir Robert Walpole's time to the present when he became Earl of Chatham. Cited are Grenville, patriot, bribery.

66-34. A Counter-Epitaph on the late W. P.

"Chatham, best friend to truth, of soul sincere." (6)

G, Aug 9, 1766; L Eve Post, Aug 7, 1766; Genuine Collection (1766), p. 25. See 66-8.

Epitaph. Chatham (Pitt) gained a title, but deserved the honor. The Gazetteer published another counter-epitaph beneath this one: "'Tis False! He is not fallen from what HE was." (6)

66-35. The Court Dance; or, Perpetual Change.

"You first lead up, then turn about." (6)

L Eve Post, Nov 29, 1766; UM 39 (Dec 1766), 318.

Epigram. Sixain. Ministers come and go; but Bute is always "behind the curtain." Slightly changed in 82-66, 83-64.

66-36. Death and the Shepherd: A New Song. To the Tune of, Death and the Lady.

"Come, Shepherd, lay your Folly now aside." (96)

St J's C, Mar 29, Apr 1, 1766.

Song. Satire on Earl of Sandwich. Dialogue in quatrains. The situation is the repeal of the Stamp Act, which Sandwich opposed. This poem dramatizes the efforts of Sandwich to prevent the repeal and death of his child, the Stamp Act.

66-37. A Dialogue between a Lord of a Manor and his Labourer.

"Well, John, I'm glad thou'rt not so misled." (24)

L Eve Post, Nov 1, 1766; PA, Nov 5, 1766.

HC. The Labourer complains that he gets scarcely enough wages for food and drink; the Lord objects to paying a living wage.

66-38. A Dialogue between Ralph and Hodge.

"Adzooks! Master Hodge, you're welcome to town ----." (16)

G, Aug 14, 1766; L Chron 20 (Aug 14, 1766), 159; PA, Aug 13, 1766; UM 39 (Aug 1766), 95; LM 35 (Aug 1766), 432; Genuine Collection (1766), p. 38. See 66-8.

Quatrains. Satire. -- How Pitt's elevation is seen by the lower class who have lost their leaders: Pitt is buried in Chatham, and Wilkes is still away.

66-39. The Earl: An Ode. Imitated from Horace.

"My Lord! Great Commoner no more." (30)

PA, Aug 18, 1766; Genuine Collection (1766), pp. 46-7. See 66-8; The Humours of the Times (1771), pp. 124-5; New Foundling Hospital for Wit, Part I (1768), pp. 97-8.

Imitation of Horace, Lib. 1, Od. 29. Satire on Pitt who, having betrayed his good name for money and titles, is subjected to scorn, contempt, raillery.

66-40. An Elegy on the Much Lamented Death of Anti-Sejanus. By Mr. Kingsley.

"Come, mournful Muse! an Onion bring." (24)

L Eve Post, Mar 13, 1766; Freeman's J, Mar 22, 1766.

Hudibrastics. Mock-elegy, personal satire on the Rev. James Scott (Anti-Sejanus), Sandwich's hired hack.

66-41. An Elegy on the Stagnation of News, in Virginia. To Benjamin Bailey, Esq;

"The death of politics to mourn, O! Ben." (118)

L Eve Post, Feb 27, 1766.

HC. The effect of the Stamp Act here is allusively and humorously described -- the non-importation agreement.

66-42. An Elegy to the Unlamented Memory of that Poor Poet, Priest, Pander, and Politician, Anti-Sejanus.

"Ye cinder Sisters, dear to Gray's-Inn Lane." (44)

St J's C, Mar 13, 1766; Freeman's J, Mar 22, 1766.

HC. Mock elegy, satire on Anti-Sejanus, the Rev. James Scott, supposedly dead. Scott wrote for Sandwich (Twitcher), cited in the poem, against the repeal of the Stamp Act.

66-43. Epigram.

"In Germany the Patriot said." (4)

L Eve Post, Jan 25, 1766.

Pitt should be heeded -- America may conquer England.

66-44. Epigram.

"That John Wilkes loves Liberty, sure we must say." (2)

St J's C, Jan 11, 1766.

Wilkes remains in exile in order to be free (to stay out of jail).

66-45. Epigram.

"When Peace was made and Britain sav'd." (6)

St J's C, Apr 12, 1766.

Ironic satire on Bute's pride in the peace (of 1763).

66-46. Epigram on a late Promotion [Pitt]; on the Great Commoner being made Lord Privy Seal and Earl of Chatham.

"Some folks still aver." (12)

Lloyd's 19 (Aug 1, 1766), 119; L Chron 20 (Jul 31, 1766), 119; L Eve Post, Jul 31, 1766; PA, Aug 1, 1766; Genuine Collection (1766), p. 10. See 66-8.

Sixains. Satire on Pitt, who has what he wants--a position in the administration, pension, place, and peerage.

66-47. Epigrams.

"The Commoner took in, and Wilkes away." (2)
"To turn the Heart of Pitt! Ah! Who could do't." (2)
"Trust not in Man, the holy Scripture says." (4)

L Eve Post, Aug 5, 1766; PA, Aug 6, 1766; Genuine Collection, p. 19. See 66-8.

Some in the nation are pleased that Wilkes is away and Pitt taken out of politics. Who could do it but Bute!

66-48. [Epigrams on Pitt].

"No more as a fool, let Lord B--- be pitied." (2)
"By stern Contempt of Titles, said the Sage." (4)
"Some say, that B--- made P--tt a Peer." (8)
"Tis too apparent in this Age of Vice." (4)

PA, Aug 6, 1766; PA, Aug 11, 1766; Genuine Collection (1766), p. 31; L Eve Post, Aug 9, 1766; PA, Aug 11, 1766; St J's C, Aug 7, 1766; Genuine Collection (1766), p. 28; PA, Aug 13, 1766; L Chron 20 (Aug 7 & 9, 1766), 144, 151.

66-49. [Epigrams on Pitt.]

"Condemn not Pitt before his actions prove." (4)
"Mourn England, Old and New--from shore to shore." (10)
 On a Quondam Commoner--"Uncommon wisdom, honesty." (6)
"When Pitt for Liberty held forth." (6)

G, Aug 21, 1766; Genuine Collection (1766), p. 56; G, Aug 6, 1766; L Chron 20 (Aug 5, 1766), 135; Genuine Collection, (1766), pp. 19-20; G, Sep 12, 1766; Genuine Collection (1766), p. 102; G, Aug 16, 1766.

66-50. Epigram on the Death of the Duke of Cumberland.

"When Legge and Devon fell, great was our Grief." (4)

Freeman's J, Jan 11, 1766.

Anti-Bute. Death has cut off Henry Legge, Duke of Devonshire (William Cavendish), and the Duke of Cumberland -- would that it cut off Bute!

66-51. Epigram on the Report of L[ord] C[hatham]'s Being to be Advanced To the Honour of the Garter.

"Rais'd as he is by Fortune, Country, King." (2)

St J's C, Oct 21, 1766.

Satire on Pitt, elevated to the peerage, now craving to be led.

66-52. Epigram. Upon the Reconciliation of a Merchant and his Wife at the Time of the Repeal of the Stamp Act.

"The Stamp-Act repeal'd? says a Merchant, odd life, Sir." (6)

L Chron 19 (Mar 22, 1766), 279.

If a mother country cannot tax her colonies, then a husband cannot exact obedience from his wife.

66-53. An Epistle to a Friend in the Country, containing Sundry Matters of Weight and Moment.

"Having heard that your Doggerel's in mighty Renown." (c. 118)

G, Aug 26, 1766; PA, Aug 27, 1766; St J's C, Jul 14, 1767; Geniune Collection (1766), pp. 67-70. See 66-8; New Foundling Hospital for Wit, Part I (1768), pp. 101-05.

HC. Light satire on politics--Pitt, orations in Parliament, America's respect for Pitt, Pitt's elevation and the effect on his reputation.

66-54. [Epitaphs on Pitt.]

"Here lies interr'd, never to rise again." (6)
"To the memory of the late W--m Pitt, Esq." (45)
"C[hatha]m, no friend to truth, in fraud sincere." (6)

G, Aug 16, 1766; L Chron 20 (Aug 14, 1766), 167; Geniune Collection, p. 40; G, Aug 22, 1766; Geniune Collection, pp. 54-55; G, Aug 7, 1766; Geniune Collection (1766), p. 25.

Satires on Pitt.

66-55. An Epitaph on the Death of Anti-Sejanus.

"Here lies a Scot who curs'd a Bute." (4)

L Eve Post, Feb 18, 1766.

A mock epitaph on James Scot, Anti-Sejanus, who wrote without good sense. (Scot defended the Stamp Act.)

66-56. Extempore, on the Report of the Death of Mr. Wilkes, in Exile at Paris.

"When Wilkes! a Name to Patriots ever dear!" (6)

St J's C, Aug 12, 1766; PA, Aug 13, 1766; Genuine Collection (1766), p. 35.

Wilkes, shocked at Pitt's apostasy, dies fearing for the country.

66-57. The Feasting Faction, A Parody on Cato. Act 1, Scene 1.

"The dawn is overcast, the morning lowrs." (50)

L Chron 20 (Jul 3, 1766), 20.

Blank verse. Satire on Pitt and Wilkes.

66-58. A Fragment.

"But now (Oh! what a falling off was there)." (23)

L Eve Post, Aug 29, 1766; Genuine Collection (1766), pp. 89-90.

HC. Satire on Pitt for accepting the peerage--and now he is silenced by Bute. "All lov'd the Patriot, but detest the Lord."

66-59. [Freeth, John.]
A Dialogue between a Briton and a North American. To the Tune of Push about the brisk bowl.

"To judge at this crisis which England's the best." (40)

L Chron 19 (Apr 8, 1766), 340; The Warwickshire Medley (1776), pp. 56-7. See 76-13.

Song. An American defends the colonies' stand on taxes and the blessings of liberty, despite the opposing view that England has done more than her share in protecting America from France.

66-60. The Gentle Shepherd. A Parody.

"A Gentle Shepherd (that's his proper name.) (80)

L Chron 19 (Apr 26, 1766), 396; PA, Apr 24, 1766.

HC. Parody of Pope's Second Pastoral applied to present times. Satire on the effect that the repeal of the Stamp Act had on the political situation. George Grenville, the father of the Stamp Act, is the Gentle Shepherd. Cited are Dowdeswell, Bedford, Sandwich, Rigby, Pitt.

66-61. The Hat and Crown. A Political Parallel. By the Author of the Review of Dr. Johnson's Shakespeare.

"The Hat, is Manners to the Crown." (36)

St J's C, Feb 22, 1766.

Sixains. The King should be spared Pitt, a threat to him, for he resembles Oliver Cromwell. America, "ingrate," is cited. With a versified answer.

66-62. [Have ye forgot, ye venal tribe.]

"Have ye forgot, ye venal tribe." (36)

G, Mar 28, 1766; Lloyd's 18 (Mar 28, 1766), 306; L Eve Post, Mar 27, 1766.

Sixains. Defense of Pitt. Have the British people forgotten what Pitt accomplished in the last war against France?

66-63. [Here continueth to rot.]

"Here continueth to rot." (24) and Procession (c. 50)

Freeman's J, Mar 15, 1766; Lloyd's 18 (Mar 10, 1766), 243 (see also p. 347); L Eve Post, Mar 11, 1766; St J's C, Mar 8, 1766.

Epitaph on Anti-Sejanus. Satire on James Scott at the time of the debate on the repeal of the Stamp Act.

66-64. Hopkinson, Thomas.
An Exercise, containing a Dialogue, and two odes, performed at the publick Commencement in the College of Philadelphia, May 20, 1766.

"This is done, bright Science, now with roseate Hand." (c. 150)

L Chron 20 (Jul 19, 1766), 73; PA, Jul 25, 1766.

Blank verse, two odes. In praise of freedom in America, an immediate reaction to the news just received in Philadelphia of the repeal of the American Stamp-Act. Pitt is extolled, and Rockingham, Grafton, Shelburne, Camden, Conway, Barre, Thomas Howard (Earl of Effingham).

66-65. An Inscription for the New-York Play-House.

"In this refin'd, excelling manly age." (11)

L Eve Post, Dec 16, 1766.

HC. An invitation to the variety of drama at the New York Playhouse. (Of general cultural interest.)

66-66. Kenrick, William.
The Political Magnet. A Simile.

"Lodg'd in the Northern Pole, the wise." (24)

G, Sep 3, 1766; Lloyd's 19 (Sep 1, 1766), 223; L Chron 20 (Aug 30, 1766), 217; PA, Sep 3, 1766; St J's C, Aug 30, 1766; Genuine Collection (1766), p. 88. (See 66-8.) William Kenrick, Poems; Ludicrous, Satirical and Moral (London: J. Fletcher, 1768), pp. 39-40. Also 1770 ed., pp. 39-40. (See 68-15.)

Sixains. A satire on Pitt, now Earl of Chatham, who is attracted to Bute, the magnet.

66-67. Martin, Alexander.
America: A Poem. By Alexander Martin, Esq. Published by the Earnest desire and generous subscription of some of the principal gentlemen of the province of Wilmington in North Carolina.

"As on the broad Atlantic's beaten shore." (403)

G, Sep 29, 1766. Entire poem; Evans 11323 (Philadelphia: Andrew Steuart, 1769). Second ed.

HC. Reviews British history, protests American loyalty during the several struggles for liberty in Britain, and concludes with praise of Pitt for restoring liberty to America and supporting the American resistance to the Stamp Act. Cited are General Braddock, Lord George Augustus Howe, General Wolfe. (Martin was Deputy King's Attorney in 1766, a judge in 1774, and Governor of North Carolina in 1782. See DAB.)

66-68. A Never-Failing Receipt to Make a Ministry Popular.

"Let them make cheap our beer, our bread and meat." (3)

L Eve Post, Sep 20, 1766.

Triplet. A common person's view of politics. Lower prices on food and drink will make a ministry popular.

66-69. A New Song, entitled and called, The Best Exchange: The Old Fumblers for Young Lovers. To the Tune of Doodle, Doodle, Doo.

"Old Lady England late so drooping." (40)

G, Jan 6, 1766; St J's C, Jan 2, 1766.

Song. On the welcome change to the young Rockingham ministry; Grafton, Conway, Cavendish, Onslow, Dowdeswell, Charles Towns[h]end.

66-70. A New Song. To whatever Tune you will.

"Come, pluck up my Muse, 'tis of Chloe I sing." (20)

St J's C, Jan 14, 1766.

Song. The American colonists are no longer children requiring the protection of their mother; but of late they are rebelling against her. The Stamp Act is cited.

66-71. The Newsman's New-Year's Gift.

"Masters, I must in my dull rhymes." (62)

L Eve Post, Dec 31, 1765-Jan 2, 1766.

Hudibrastics. Light comment on the times, including hostile remarks against the Stamp Act.

66-72. An Ode from an American to the Right Honourable W. P---.

"Now, Clio, now resume the lyre." (72-78)

PA, Feb 27, and Mar 3, 1766.

Regular (Horatian) ode in sixains. Praises Pitt, guardian of Boston and the Colonies from unjust and unnatural taxation, successful in bringing about the repeal of the Stamp tax. A stanza was added and the complete poem printed March 3, 1766.

66-73. Ode to a late Great Man.

"If Virtue be an empty Name." (78)

St J's C, Sep 2, 1766; Genuine Collection (1766), pp. 90-2. See 66-8.

Regular (Horatian) ode in sixains. Satire on Pitt for accepting a peerage.

66-74. Ode to the Respectable Populace of America. By one of colonial principles.

"Yes, pow'rful vulgar, I subscribe." (60)

PA, Feb 21, 1766; SM 28 (May 1766), 263.

Regular (Horatian) ode in sixains. Advises the English who petitioned against the Cider Tax to follow the example of the rebellious and successful resistance by Americans to the Stamp Tax. Pitt and Conway are cited.

66-75. Ode, Wrote at Boston in New-England, On the Repeal of the Stamp-Act.

"Black as when Northern Tempests frown." (88)

PA, Jul 1, 1766.

Regular (Horatian) ode in octaves. Praises the Patriot Opposition, now at the helm, for repealing the Stamp Act, citing Wolfe, Pitt, Grafton, Conway, Barre, Rockingham, Camden, Chesterfield, Dartmouth.

66-76. [Oh! might a Spark of that bright Flame.]

"Oh! might a Spark of that bright Flame." (24)

PA, Aug 27, 1766; Genuine Collection (1766), p. 76. See 66-8.

Sixains. Ironic remarks on Pitt's elevation to the peerage; Pitt, bribed by money and tempted by power to change his principles.

66-77. On a Late Event.

"Shall Pitt, to sacred Freedom late so dear." (4)

L Eve Post, Aug 2, 1766; Genuine Collection (1766), p. 10. See 66-8.

HC. Worried questions about the effect of Pitt's elevation to the peerage upon his integrity.

66-78. On a Late Promotion.

"The Court, to please old talking Will." (4)

L Chron 20 (Aug 2, 1766), 127; L Eve Post, Aug 2, 1766; Genuine Collection (1766), p. 23. See 66-8.

Epigram. Satire on Pitt. The Court, to silence Pitt, elevated him to the peerage.

66-79. On a Quondam Great Commoner.

"A Patriot, that so firmly stood." (4)

L Eve Post, Aug 19, 1766; Genuine Collection (1766), p. 48. See 66-8.

Epigram. Satire on Pitt for accepting the peerage, as well as places and pension.

66-80. On Reading Mr. P[it]t's Speech.

"Methinks the Roman, (O take care of my Pen." (18)

Freeman's J, May 3, 1766.

HC. Praise of Pitt's oratory. ("Liberty is understood.")

66-81. On Reading that Artists intend to set up a Striking Likeness of the late Mr. Charles Churchill, in Westminster Abbey.

"Though ye finish the Work with masterly Skill." (2)

St J's C, Apr 5, 1766.

Epigram. A place for Churchill's monument in Westminister Abbey is not proper.

66-82. On Seeing Lord R-k-g-m and the Duke of G--n, at Newmarket.

"Upon the Turf, the other Day." (8)

St J's C, Apr 29, 1766.

Epigram. Satire on Rockingham and Grafton whose real business, it appears, is at the Newmarket racetrack.

66-83. On Seeing Mr. Pitt upon a Pocket Handkerchief.

"When lost was Britain's Fame in Arms." (8)

St J's C, Jun 12, 1766.

Epigram. Quatrains. Ironic lines on Pitt, now being demeaned.

66-84. On Seeing Two Prints Basely Designed to Defame Mr. Pitt.

"S-db-y, who lash'd in Prints, in Rhymes." (24)

St J's C, Feb 27, 1766.

Regular (Horatian) ode in sixains, in defense of Pitt, and an attack on the artist who has switched sides from Pitt to Bute and the Scots, Sandwich and Grenville, and the Tories. Hogarth, Churchill are cited.

66-85. On the Change of the Administration.

"Oh Pitt! whose great parts ev'ry Briton adores." (16)

L Eve Post, Jul 17, 1766.

Hexameter couplets. Satire on Pitt regarding the difficulty of forming a new government upon the collapse of the Rockingham Administration.

66-86. On the Earl of Chatham.

"Regardless of a factious Roar." (4)

L Chron 20 (Sep 20, 1766), 253; L Eve Post, Sep 6, 1766; PA, Sep 10, 1766; Genuine Collection (1766), p. 101. See 66-8.

Epigram. Chatham stands firm, despite the blasts of critics.

66-87. On the Great Commoner, lately created an Earl, and made Lord Privy Seal.

"What! -- then is Virtue but an empty Name." (22)

Freeman's J, Oct 11, 1766.

HC. A defense of Pitt's elevation to the peerage: it was merited.

66-88. On the new-discovered Island in the South-Sea.

"Since peace throughout Europe now seems to remain." (20)

Lloyd's 19 (Jul 9, 1766), 33.

Quatrains. Admiral Byron is celebrated for discovering an island of gold in the South Seas, which will save England from taxes and hunger.

66-89. On the Present Ministry.

"O'er envy, malice, impudence and lies." (4)

L Eve Post, Mar 8, 1766.

HC. General praise of the Rockingham ministry.

66-90. On the re-admission of a Great Commoner to the administration.

"Let Faction inculcate, to gratify spite." (88)

SM 28 (Aug 1766), 437.

Quatrains in couplets. Satire on Pitt and his policies. America is cited.

66-91 A Pastoral-Elegiac Dialogue, between the Gentle Shepherd, and Jemmy Twitcher, on the unfortunate Death of Fair Miss Amie Stamp.

"Tell me, dear Jemmy, tell me what to say." (40)

G, May 19, 1766; L Chron 19 (May 17, 1766), 475; PA, May 19, 1766; St J's C, May 15, 1766.

The search for new taxes continues, now that the Cyder and Stamp Taxes cannot be collected. Sandwich (Twitcher) and Anti-Sejanus will continue to try to raise revenue--and incite riots. George Grenville is the Gentle Shepherd.

66-92. The Perils of Poetry [By James Scott]: An Epigram.

"While Scot, like a Strumpet, bawls Whore first aloud." (4)

St J's C, Mar 4, 1766.

Satire on Anti-Sejanus, James Scott. Scott's poem, The Perils of Poetry, is easy to criticize.

66-93. A Political Litany. Spare us, good Lord!

"From all Monopolizers, Forestallers and Regrators, and from all Want of the Necessaries of Life." (18 Paragraphs.)

L Eve Post, Jul 26, 1766; Freeman's J, Aug 9, 1766; Genuine Collection (1766), pp. 6-7. See 66-8.

Spare us from corruption, taxes, long parliaments, tyranny, popery, high food prices for the poor.

66-94. Political Squibs.

"'Tis too apparent in this age of vice." (c. 60)

BM 7 (Aug 1766), 440; RM 15 (Aug 1766), 104; UM 39 (Aug 1766), 95 (6 selected).

Nine epigrams or mock epitaphs, informal extemporaneous stanzas on the politics of the time, especially on Pitt, the Great Commoner, who had recently been elevated to the peerage.

66-95. Postscript.

"From the black caves of night and Hell." (42)

L Chron 20 (Sep 27, 1766), 320.

Quatrains. Defense of Pitt, who is really the same despite his elevation. Only he can save the nation.

66-96. Postscript.

"Shall P--t, to sacred Freedom late so dear." (6)

L Chron 20 (Jul 31, 1766), 120.

HC. Should Pitt temporize with freedom, he will simply be like Grenville, Bute, Bedford.

66-97. The Prophecy, or New Coalition.

"Says the Thane, one day in his closet confin'd." (10)

L Eve Post, Aug 9, 1766; Genuine Collection (1766), pp. 34-35. See 66-8.

Hexameter couplets. Bute got Satan, friend of the tories, to trap Pitt. (Ref: Pitt's elevation to an earldom.)

66-98. Proposals for Printing by Subscription (taken from Mr. Hogarth's famous Picture of Mr. Garrick, in the Character of Richard III) the Print of a Late Great Commoner.

"Enter the Ghost of Sarah Duchess of Marlborough." (44)

PA, Aug 28, 1766; St J's C, Aug 28, 1766; Genuine Collection (1766), pp. 85-87; New Foundling Hospital for Wit, Part I (1768), pp. 106-08; WA, Sep 27, 1766, pp. 643-4.

Parody of Shakespeare's ghosts in Richard III. The ghosts of several people who had something to do with Pitt's career denounce him for wrongs committed and complain of his apostasy, his elevation to the peerage: Sarah, Duchess Marlborough; Robert Walpole, Earl of Orford; Ralph Allen; Sir William Pynsent; William Pulteney, Earl of Bath.

66-99. Remark on the Reviewers.

"To convince us that Chatham to Dagon now bends." (2)

St J's C, Oct 11, 1766.

Epigram. The reptilian reviewers, once Pitt's enemies, are now his friends.

66-100. The Rose and Thistle. A Song. To the Tune of, ---- the Lillies of France.

"The Rose of Old England so dearly caress'd." (24)

L Eve Post, Jun 17, 1766; Freeman's J, Jun 24, 1766.

Song. The decline of England is attributed to Scotland's domination of British politics. Wilkes's appearance in England gives pleasure.

66-101. The St. James's Dance. A Song; As Performed at Court.

"Pray observe our new-made dance, Sir." (35)

L Eve Post, Sep 4, 1766; Genuine Collection (1766), pp. 97-98. See 66-8.

Song. A cynical view of politics, including Pitt's work for America to advance his own interest. Cited are Charles Townshend, Fletcher Norton, Fox, Wilkes, Rockingham, and others.

66-102. [Says Great William Pitt, with his usual Emotion.]

"Says Great William Pitt, with his usual emotion." (6)

L Eve Post, Aug 21, 1766; Genuine Collection (1766), p. 57. See 66-8.

Hexameter couplets. Satire on Pitt for accepting the peerage.

66-103. Scene Blackheath.

"August advanc'd! Pynsent, beware." (16)

Freeman's J, Aug 30, 1766.

Quatrains. A simile. The enemies of Chatham and England, France and Spain, are like mad dogs kenneled by Bute.

66-104. Shaw, Cuthbert.
Answer to the Verses entitled, Enquiry after the Author of an Epigram, who calls himself Author of the Race.

"An honest Man -- not Fear's or Envy's Slave." (10)

St J's C, Jan 4, 1766.

HC. Shaw, author of The Race, writes a favorable character of himself.

66-105. [Should this (which Heaven avert!) prove true.]

"Should this (which heaven avert!) prove true." (12)

L Eve Post, Feb 18, 1766.

Placed in the context of Samuel Foote's loss of a leg is a semi-humorous allusion to the serious consequences of the Stamp Act -- civil war!

66-106. A Sketch. Written Immediately after Reading the History of the Late Minority.

"How vain are Hopes! How changeable is Man!" (30)

PA, Jul 4, 1766; Humours of the Times (1771), pp. 95-97; New Foundling Hospital for Wit, Part I (1768), pp. 77-78.

HC. The minority now in power is completely to be distrusted -- Rockingham, an inexperienced youth interested in cock-fighting and horse-racing; Chesterfield, a corrupt "hoary dotard." They are unable to dismiss Bute's friends. (Richard Grenville, Lord Temple, wrote the History of the Late Minority.) Another subtitle for this poem is "Written on the Change of the Ministry in 1765."

66-107. [Some say, that Bute made Pitt a Peer.]

"Some say, that Bute made Pitt a Peer." (8)

L Eve Post, Aug 9, 1766; PA, Aug 11, 1766; St J's C, Aug 7, 1766; Genuine Collection (1766), p. 28. See 66-8.

Epigram, quatrains. Bute raised Pitt to ruin Pitt's reputation; but Pitt's elevation will never improve Bute's reputation.

66-108. A Song from the Virginia Gazette, May 2. Tune -- Hearts of Oak.

"Sure never was picture drawn more to the life." (41)

Lloyd's 19 (Jul 14, 1766), 50; PA, Jul 9, 1766; The Vocal Magazine (1778), Song 374, p. 101. ("An American Song.")

Song. An expression of hostility for the Stamp Act and of loyalty to the King.

66-109. Sonnet.

"Mansfield! thou Senator fit to have stood." (14)

PA, Mar 11, 1766.

Modified Italian sonnet. Judge Mansfield (Wm. Murray, Lord M.) is praised for sustaining the constitution in the face of factional disputes.

66-110. Stamp All.

"As the Grand Financier he sat thinking one day." (60)

G, Jan 23, 1766.

Song. Grenville's new stamp tax on America has been successfully resisted in the colonies. The Scotch are cited.

66-111. The State Quacks.

"Britannia was sick, for a doctor they sent." (20)

The Muse's Mirror (London: Baldwin, 1778), II, 218-219.

A ballad narrating the several changes of the ministry from the time of Bute and Pitt, and their inability to make Britain prosper.

66-112. [The States of Old England, by Authors that Write on't.]

"The States of Old England, by Authors that write on't." (16)

St J's C, Sep 4, 1766.

Hexameters, quatrains, in ironic praise of the mob, the fourth estate. Cited are King, Lords, Commons.

66-113. The Tinker.

"A Tinker is thought a black man, and what not." (20)

L Eve Post, Apr 29, 1766.

Song. Humorous allusion to America's claims and quarrels with Britain and recourse to Pitt. (The feeling is that Britain has botched up the situation regarding America.)

66-114. To Anti-Sejanus.

"By thy tropes and thy figures, thy scandal and lies." (6)
"You tell us you're sickly, and soon like to depart." (5)

L Eve Post, Feb 20, 27, 1766.

HC. Satire on James Scott, Anti-Sejanus, ambitious for a bishopric from his political essays. He is patronized (paid) by Lord Sandwich.

66-115. To be Sold, "A Negro Woman . . ."

"When Rice to France was forc'd to fly." (28)

L Eve Post, Apr 8, 1766.

Quatrains. Indignation at evidence of real slavery in Britain -- a Negro woman is advertised for sale in a newspaper.

66-116. To L[ord] B[ute].

"Retire, good B[ute], no longer --- the Throne." (8)

St J's C, Nov 25, 1766.

HC. Advises Bute to retire from the Court and the King's presence in order to please the King and pacify the nation.

66-117. To Lord Ch---m.

"Hail best of men! resume thyself." (44)

L Chron 20 (Aug 23, 1766), 196; PA, Aug 27, 1766; Genuine Collection (1766), pp. 77-78. See 66-8.

Blank verse. In defence of Pitt transformed into Chatham, who will continue to demonstrate his leadership.

66-118. To Mr. Scott -- on the Criticisms that have been published against the Perils of Poetry.

"When the Vine's luxuriant Boughs." (12)

St J's C, Mar 11, 1766.

Sixains. A defence of James Scott's poem, The Perils of Poetry. (James Scott was being vilified as Anti-Sejanus at this time. One substantial critique of Scott's poem appeared in St J's C, Mar 15, 1766, p. 2.)

66-119. To the Author of the Demagogue.

"What frenzy could thy wrathful muse provoke." (30)

G, Mar 22, 1766, PA, Mar 22, 1766.

HC. Protests Falconer's satire on Pitt; there are fitter targets, such as Sandwich, Grenville, James Scott, and Bute.

66-120. To the Cavillers at The History of the Late Minority.

"Rail, ye unlearned Asses! still rail on." (30)

L Eve Post, Jul 8, 1766; PA, Jul 10, 1766; Freeman's J, Jul 26, 1766.

HC. Satire on the government that repealed the Stamp Act -- Rockingham, Conway, Richmond, Pitt, and others.

66-121. To the Earl of Chatham.

"Great Pitt, thou Guardian of the public weal." (29)

Lloyd's 19 (Oct 17, 1766), 378.

HC. Notes Pitt's great accomplishments, among them successfully pleading the cause of the American colonies. He is needed now to save the nation.

66-122. To the Late Minority, alias the Present Ministry, On reading the History of their Conduct. By a Quondam Friend.

"And does it gall you then, ye venal Crew." (36)

L Eve Post, Jul 3, 1766; PA, Jul 2, 1766; The Humours of the Times (1771), pp. 97-99; New Foundling Hospital for Wit (1768), pp. 78-79.

HC. Satire on the Rockingham ministry for its hypocrisy, its failure to support freedom's cause and Wilkes, as well as Pitt against Bute. No one in the Rockingham ministry is so well qualified to lead as Pitt.

66-123. To the People. On their Suspicion of the Late Great Commoner.

"Judge not in haste, but wait, and see." (4)

L Chron 20 (Aug 16, 1766), 175; L Eve Post, Aug 14, 1766; Freeman's J, Aug 19, 1766; Genuine Collection (1766), p. 45. See 66-8.

Epigram. Quatrain. Defense of Pitt -- who should not be judged until his conduct, after his elevation, is seen.

66-124. To the Present Ministry.

"Boast not, my Lords, that Courage you inherit." (2)

St J's C, Mar 20, 1766.

Epigram. Satire on the Rockingham ministry. The present ministry lacks spirit, even to do wrong!

66-125. [The Tories, adrat'em.]

"The Tories, adrat'em." (6)

St J's C, Aug 30, 1766.

Sixain. The Tories lack common sense in accusing Chatham without cause. This is a straightforward defense of Pitt against his critics. See the negative, An Apology for Mr. Pitt, 66-21.

66-126. The Trout. A political Allegory.

"A Trout, a dainty well-fed fish." (24)

Lloyd's 19 (Aug 1, 1766), 119.

Sixains. Like the shy trout, Pitt was finally hooked.

66-127. True Nobility. Addressed to the Earl of Chatham.

"Tho' from his birth no mean applause." (12)

L Chron 20 (Aug 16, 1766), 175; L Eve Post, Aug 14, 1766; Genuine Collection (1766), p. 44. See 66-8.

Quatrains. A criticism of Chatham (Pitt) for accepting the peerage. True nobility comes from one's own achievement, not from birth.

66-128. [Ungrateful Athens, void of Faith or Trust.]

"Ungrateful Athens, void of Faith or Trust." (10)

St J's C, Sep 18, 1766.

HC. Defense of Pitt. The great Athenians, Socrates and Aristides, could not reform a venal state; nor can Pitt.

66-129. Verses, by an American Bellman, on the Recent Reconcilement of the modern Brutus with the modern Cassius, who, like their Namesakes of old were once unfortunately at Variance.

"O Blest Event, that none could hope." (4)

PA, Feb 26, 1766.

Epigram. It is a miracle to see Pitt and Barré reconciled.

66-130. [What a pother of late, has been in the State.]

"What a pother of late, has been in the State." (8)

Lloyd's 19 (Sep 1, 1766), 219.

Epigram, quatrains. Satire on Pitt, and defense of Bute.

66-131. What Should Be: Addressed to Him Who Can.

"Yes, there are Men, untainted, firm, and free." (38)

St J's C, Jul 5, 1766.

HC. Panegyric on Pitt, Temple, Camden, Lyttelton -- the first three praised for their virtue and integrity in Burke's History of the Late Minority. (This poem is really an attack on the new Grafton ministry.)

66-132. [Why all this Censure? why this Flux of Wit.]

"Why all this Censure? why this Flux of Wit." (20)

L Chron 20 (Aug 21, 1766), 192; PA, Aug 25, 1766; Genuine Collection (1766), pp. 63-4. See 66-8.

HC. Pitt really merits the honor of a peerage.

66-133. Wilkes's Return. A Song. Tune, -- The Sun was in the Firmament.

"It happen'd near that festival." (32)

L Eve Post, May 20, 1766.

Song. Acclaim for Wilkes. Wilkes, after two years' exile in France, decides to return home. He has recovered from the wound received in the duel with Samuel Martin (Secretary of the Treasury, and a Bute supporter) in November 1763.

66-134. The World turned upside down; or, the Old Woman taught Wisdom. A Ballad.

"Goody Bull and her Daughter together fell out." (52)

GM 36 (Mar 1766), 140-41; L Chron 19 (Mar 8, 1766), 236; PA, Mar 10, 1766; SM 28 (Mar 1766), 150.

Song. Ballad narrates the quarrel between "Goody Bull," Great Britain, and her daughter, America, who seeks a degree of freedom. Britain reluctantly is forced into a reconciliation (repeal of the Stamp Act) with her rebellious colonies. See print, 66-139.

66-135. [Ye venal Slaves, far hence away.]

"Ye venal Slaves, far hence away." (24)

L Chron 20 (Sep 2, 1766), 227; PA, Sep 6, 1766.

Sixains. Pitt, tired of the House of Commons, quits it for the higher House of Lords, a promotion he merits.

Prints

66-137. Commonwealth: The Colossus.

"Tell to me if you are witty." (20)

Etching with triplets and doodle chorus. 1766.

Stephens 4162 (IV, 399-400). Repr. Jones, Cartoon History of Britain (1971), p. 52.

An anti-Pitt cartoon. Pitt encourages American resistance to the Stamp Act, encourages the commercial interests rather than the landed class, encourages sedition through demagoguery. He is satirized as a statesman on stilts, an American colossus. He is mounted on the stilts of "Sedition" and "Popularity," the former extending to New York in America.

66-138. The New Country Dance, as Danced at Court. July the 30th, 1766.

"Here you see de Country Dance, Sir." (32)

Engr. with quatrains and doodle chorus. July 30, 1766.

Stephens 4147 (IV, 380-1).

Amidst other figures including Wilkes, Pitt tells America, a half-naked young woman with a feathered head-dress and holding a bottle of rum, "I stood staunch in your Cause." America replies, "Yes, We finely hum'd old England." The Earl of Winchelsea gives up his post as Lord President of the Council under the Rockingham administration to the Earl of Northington.

66-139. The Wheel of Fortune or England in Tears.

"Adieu fair England, Queen of every Isle." (5)

Engr. with HC and triplet. August 1766.

Stephens 4154 (IV, 391-2).

A protest at the economic distress in England that is causing emigration of the poor to America. This recession or depression is blamed on "Monopoly and Oppression," the selfishness and corruption of Lord Bute (that is, the pensioners bribed by Bute), and the Scotch. Pitt promises relief and a new Parliament, and even Wilkes (writing in exile abroad) declares he will not allow England to be ruined.

66-140. The World turned upside down, or The Old Woman taught Wisdom. [In Goody Bull or the Second Part of the Repeal.]

1767 Books & Pamphlets

67-1. Bruce, Michael.
  Ode: To Paoli.

"What man, what hero shall the Muses sing." (100)

In his Poems on Several Occasions (Edinburgh: Robertson, 1770), pp. 101-7; 1782 ed, pp. 111-7.

Copies: BL 11634.de.2; NUC CU-A, DLC, MWelC, MsU (1782 ed, CtY, ICN, InU, NjP, PPL).

Written c. 1767 by this young Scottish poet, at a time when there was hope that the Corsicans would "lay the proud oppressor low," the poem eulogizes the heroic Paoli, leader of the freedom-loving Corsicans, "A rising nation of the brave."

67-2. [Duncombe, John]
  The Works of Horace, in English Verse, by Mr. [Wm] Duncombe, Sen. J. Duncombe, M.A. The Second Edition. To which are added, Many Imitations, now first published.
  London: White, et al., 1767. 4 vols.

Notices: CR 24 (Oct 1767), 266-75; MR 37 (Jul 1767), 1-8.

Copies: BL 237.e.23-26; NUC CtY.

The 1st ed (2 vols, 1757-9) did not include the 8 poems on Canada and the Seven Years War, which are discussed separately above: 55-1, 59-2, 59-3, 60-5, 61-1, 62-2, 64-2, & 65-3.

67-3. [Gough, James]
  Britannia: A Poem. With Historical Notes. Inscribed to the King, Queen, and Royal Family. The Lords and Commons of Great Britain and Ireland. The Governors and Members of British Colonies.
  London: Millar & Baldwin, 1767. 32p.

"Since mighty Realms have left, a lonely Waste." (c. 580)

Notices: CR 25 (Jan 1768), 72-3; MR 38 (Jan 1768), 70; GM 38 (Jan 1768), 28-9; Lloyd's Eve Post 20 (Dec 21, 1767), 604; L Chron 22 (Dec 17, 1767), 585.

Sabin 28076.

Copies: BL 11626.h.14 (1); Bod Godwyn Pamph 1716 (5); NUC CSmH, KU, MH, NjP.

HC. Reviews British history from Alfred to the present, praises national advantages (highways, canals, industry, farms) and Britain's glory--liberty--imploring legislators to be "good guardians" and invoking blessings on the nation, including the colonies and Ireland.

67-4. An Ode to the Earl of Ch----m. By the Author of the E--l of Ch----m's Apology.
London: Almon, 1767. 7p.

"Forgive, my Lord, an homely Muse." (84)

Notices: CR 23 (Apr 1767), 297-8; MR 36 (Apr 1767), 331-2; L Chron 21 (Apr 4, 1767), 333.

Copies: BL 1489.m.22; NUC CtY, OCU.

Regular Horatian ode. Ascribed to Henry Seymour by Horace Walpole. The Muse addresses Chatham as an equal--bold, candid, independent--and is harshly critical. Chatham's powers have declined since the great days of the last war, misdirected to fostering America's hostility to Britain: "She wounds that mother to despair, / Who gave her ease and wealth." But Britain now has found a genuine friend in Grenville, concerned for the public good, liberty and law. (Also in New Foundling Hospital for Wit, Part 1 [1768], pp. 118-20, & Vol. I [1786], pp. 81-4; and in The Humours of the Times [London, 1771], pp. 152-5.)

67-5. Patriotism: A Political Satire. By Cato Redivivus.
London: Williams, 1767. xix + 25p.

"Learning's great Ornament, and Virtue's Friend." (c. 480)

Notices: CR 24 (Nov 1767), 381-2; MR 38 (Jan 1768), 71; GM 37 (Dec 1767), 600-1; PA, Nov 30, 1766.

Copies: Bod Godwyn Pamph 1725 (6) & 1745 (11); NUC CSmH, DLC.

Public Advertiser, Nov 30, 1766: "N.B. Whatever Copies are not signed in the Author's Handwriting with the name Cato-Redivivus, are spurious and pirated."
HC. An "old Whig" mourns party spirit, corruption, threats to free elections,

taxation, increase in public debt, continental wars; he defends the free-born Briton living in a monarchy under law. Cited are Rockingham, Thynne (Viscount Weymouth), Pratt (Earl of Camden), and Onslow. Once, he objects to tyrannical treatment of the Americans (p. 19).

67-6. The Prospect of Liberty. Addressed to The Gentlemen of the County of H[u]n[tin]gd[o]n.
London: Bladon, 1767. 64p.

"Peace to the man, from ev'ry anguish free." (c. 1250)

Notices: CR 24 (Jul 1767), 72-3; MR 37 (Oct 1767), 315; L Chron 22 (Aug 11, 1767), 149.

Copies: BL 11602.gg.21 (2); Bod Vet A.5d.345 (11); NUC CtY.

HC. Rambling essay, satire and panegyric alternating. Praises liberty and its champions, especially Sir Robert Bernard. Useful for establishing local, regional, party politics at the time of the Parliamentary elections. Bernard helped found the Bill of Rights Society (1769). His politics are favored by the poet, an admirer of Churchill. America is not mentioned.

Redivivus, Cato. See 67-5.

Seymour, Henry. See 67-4.

67-7. State Necessity Not considered as a Question at Law. A Political Sketch.
London: Kearsly, 1767. 16p.

"A Grecian Sage, while Authors wrote." (c. 200)

Notices: CR 23 (May 1767), 225-6; MR 35 (Dec 1766), 473-4, 36 (Mar 1767), 241-2; L Chron 21 (Mar 14, 1767), 264.

Copies: NUC MH, PPL.

Octosyllabic couplets. Fate only appears to have made Pitt, who has accepted a peerage, a slave to Bute. But he really will not turn from freedom to allow the Stuarts to rule the nation. Besides, it matters not who is in power, for the people always lose. Reference to Grenville's (?) stabbing "the infant colonies." See prose pamphlet State Necessity Considered as a Question at Law (London: Bladon, 1766).

67-8. Underwood, Thomas.
The Impartialist. A Poem. By T. Underwood, Author of the Snarlers. London: Webley, 1767. 22p.

"Thanks to the kind Indulgence of the Town." (c. 370)

Notices: CR 23 (Feb 1767), 143; MR 36 (Mar 1767), 239.

Copies: BL 1490.e.44; Bod Godwyn Pamph 1492 (8) & 1745 (10); NUC CtY, MH.

HC. General satire. Wishes for Churchill's genius for satire; asserts his independence and integrity; defends the function of satire to expose evil and corruption, regardless of the importance of the targeted person; and, again, takes after the monthly reviewers, as in The Snarlers (1767), which is not relevant to this bibliography. (Also in his Poems [Bath: Archer, 1768], pp. 24-41. For additional comment on this, see "An Epistle, To a Friend, who was pleased to approve of the Author's Snarlers and Impartialist," in his Poems, pp. 143-5.)

67-9. Underwood, Thomas.
Extempore upon the Much-lamented Death of the Right Honourable Charles Townshend, obit Friday, Sept. 4, 1767.

"With gushing Eyes, and Heart-felt Grief." (4)

In Poems, &c. By T. Underwood, (Bath: Archer, 1768), p. 64.

Britain mourns the death of worthy Townshend.

Serials

67-10. Alas! Poor England.

"Who can allay Britannia's Fears." (6)

St J's C, Mar 14, 1767.

Sixain. Fears that Britain will suffer, now that both Chatham and Bute rule.

67-11. The Analogy between Legislation and Horse-Racing.

"The swift pac'd Hours convoke again." (52)

BM 8 (Apr 1767), 215-6; PA, Apr 22, 1767; RM 16 (Apr 1767), 215-6; St J's C, Apr 18, 1767; WA, May 23, 1767, p. 335; L Chron 21 (Apr 21, 1767), 387.

Octosyllabic couplets. The making of laws by Parliament resembles horse-racing: betting and legislation require a good mind, the saddle and taxes have something in common, etc.

67-12. [A--y the Revolution Likes].

"A--y the Revolution likes." (12)

St J's C, Nov 17, 1767,

Quatrains. An objection to a whig who supports the principles of freedom yet uses Press Warrants for a private end, to keep poachers off his land.

67-13. A Catch.

"Heaven and Hell might strive to catch him." (10)

GM 37 (Sep 1767), 472.

Song. On the death of Charles Townshend, author of the celebrated tea tax, etc.

67-14. Change upon Change.

"See Bob-cherry play'd at court." (6)

L Eve Post, Feb 17, 1767.

Satire on political changes, ins and outs, --meaningless "sport."

67-15. The Christ-Cross-Row, 1767.

"Since everyday great examples affords." (35)

L Eve Post, Aug 4, 1767.

HC. An alphabet poem on politics--general, mild, and moralistic. However, corruption, court, and Chatham are placed together.

67-16. Dialogue between two neighbouring Offices.

"Dear Sister, you're older and wiser than me." (13)

PA, Oct 13, 1767.

Hexameter couplets. The Pay Office complains that the Treasury has taken all its best men, Townshend and North.

67-17. [Enraptur'd Senates oft had heard.]

"Enraptur'd Senates oft had heard." (12)

St J's C, Sep 5, 1767.

Sixains. Eulogy on Charles Townshend, who recently died. Townshend's oratory is especially praised.

67-18. An Epigram.

"Provisions are dear, and our Taxes are high." (4)

L Eve Post, Jul 4, 1767.

Another protest at high food prices--but one person objects to the tax on beer.

67-19. An Epigram.

"Quoth Ben to Hodge, I have forgot." (7)

L Eve Post, Aug 18, 1767.

Satire on the Men in Power. Another objection to the high cost of food--meat this time.

67-20. An Epigram.

"While the Poor for want of Provisions are crying." (4)

L Eve Post, May 16, 1767.

The poor cry for lower food prices, the rich try for power. (This was a difficult period for the working class.)

67-21. An Epigram.

"Writers have often said, the frame political." (4)

L Eve Post, Feb 10, 1767.

Satire on the government--which is ill.

67-22. A Farewell.

"Farewell, Old England! soon should some kind Fate." (16)

St J's C, Dec 12, 1767.

HC. A complaint at the corruption of politics--poor ministers, increased taxes, selling votes--because of the desire for power and riches.

67-23. Hilary Term, 1766, P versus C, in the Common Pleas.

"Two Ministers in the republick of letters." (c. 140)

Lloyd's 20 (Jan 23, 1767), 82; L Eve Post, Jan 22, 1767; L Chron 21 (Jan 20, 1767), 79.

Hexameter couplets. Humorous verses on Pitt vs. Chatham, P vs. C, concluding that Pitt and Chatham are still the same man.

67-24. The Humble Petition of a Poor Rioter, now under Sentence, addressed to his most gracious Sovereign.

"Father of Britain, bend thine Ear." (32)

L Eve Post, Jan 24, 1767; PA, Jan 23, 1767.

Quatrains. An imprisoned rioter petitions for mercy because he protested only out of hunger and poverty. He pleads for transportation, against execution, so that he can work and be productive.

67-25. Inscriptions At Sir Jeffery Amherst's New Montreal, near Riverhead, in Kent.

"To that most able Statesman." (32)

SM 29 (Dec 1767), 643; GM 37 (Dec 1767), 602.

The obelisk is dedicated to Pitt, and the victories over the French in Canada are commemorated.

67-26. [Kenrick, William.]
P[itt] and Proteus.

"Chousing, cheating, chopping, changing." (72)

St J's C, Jan 6, 1767; Kenrick, Poems; Ludicrous, Satirical and Moral (London: T. Fletcher, 1768), pp. 44-46. (Also 1770 ed., pp. 44-46). See 68-15.

Hudibrastics. Satire on Pitt for his peerage--Pitt notorious for transformations political. A humorous summary of Pitt's political career. Cited are Bute, Charles Townshend, tory and whig.

67-27. King Bladude to William Pitt, sendeth greetynge.

"Much wond'rous goode to the founte dispense." (9)

New Foundling Hospital for Wit (1768-1773), Sec. ed., Pt. 1 (1768), p. 121.

Medieval imitation, dated July 18, 1767. A hope that Pitt will remain uncorrupted to restore liberty to England.

67-28. [Lockman, John]
Albion to Cynthia. An Ode. On the Passage of his Excellency the Lord Viscount Townshend, to his Government in Ireland.

"Thou Silver Moon! fair Queen of Night." (36)

DJ, Oct 17, 1767; L Chron 22 (Oct 17, 1767), 384; PA, Oct 22, 1767.

Quatrains. Panegyric on Lord George Townshend who helped defeat the French and acquire Canada for Britain and protect Ireland from French invasion.

67-29. The Loyal Pair. An Epigram.

"I'll list for a Soldier, says Robin to Sue." (4)

G, May 28, 1767; L Chron 21 (May 26, 1767), 512.

Robin will enlist to escape from his wife. (This vacuous epigram reappeared often through the years.)

67-30. Mother Goose's Budget Open'd. Part I. Or, A New Set of Tales and Fables for Grown Gentlemen.

"Behold, good Folks! my Budget I display." (36)

L Eve Post, Mar 7, 1767.

Ironic song about the budget which has good things for everyone.

67-31. The Nation's Wish. By a Lady.

"Curs'd be the Wretch that's bought and sold." (24)

L Eve Post, Nov 28, 1767; PA, Nov 6, 1767; Freeman's J, Jan 2, 1768.

Octosyllabic couplets in six-line stanzas. The technique of bribing electors undermines liberty and creates factions and party divisions. We wish for unity.

67-32. A New Year's Address to the News-Paper Letter-Writers, for 1767.

"Enough of Chatham and Bute." (24)

L Eve Post, Jan 1, 1767.

Quatrains. An expression of distaste for politics, for the wrangling over Chatham and Bute, over Ins and Outs.

67-33. On a Late Promised Resignation.

"Will Prudens resign, or continue in Place." (4)

St J's C, Aug 22, 1767.

Quatrain. Indicates the continuing suspicion of Lord Bute's influence.

67-34. On the Earl of Chatham.

"Save, save your Country and your King." (6)

PA, Mar 13, 1767; St J's C, Mar 10, 1767.

Sixain. Chatham should not be intimidated by criticism, because his principles are right and his heart is incorruptible.

67-35. On the Much Lamented Death of the Right Hon. Charles Townshend.

"Weep all ye Witty, all ye Wise deplore." (62)

G, Sep 8, 1767.

HC. Epitaph. Praise of Townshend, who as chancellor of the exchequer in the Grafton-Chatham ministry did much to increase American resentment, died suddenly September 4, 1767. North succeeded him.

67-36. On the Partiality of Scots, To Scots Authors.

"It makes me mad to hear such partial Fools." (18)

St J's C, Jan 20, 1767.

HC. Anti-Scots satire. A negative given to partial Scots critics. (This is literary criticism with a political slant.)

67-37. Plantation News.

"A Tribute due to / The illustrious Pitt." (6)

Freeman's J, Mar 31, 1767.

Inscription on an obelisk. A tribute to Pitt for reconciling the colonies with the mother country--parent and children.

67-38. The Present Age.

"No more, my Friend! of vain applause." (72)

Lloyd's 21 (Aug 19, 1767), 170; L Chron 22 (Aug 18, 1767), 176; PA, Aug 20, 1767; SM 29 (Aug 1767), 433-4; UM 41 (Aug 1767), 99-100.

Quatrains. A satiric picture of the times, including all classes of society and many professions. Ironic comment on the famine, on hard times. Reprinted 75-219.

67-39. The Price of Stocks at the Political Exchange.

"The Necessaries of Life--200 per cent. Pre." (12)

L Eve Post, Jun 20, 1767.

Prose-poem. A period of depression is summed up in this list about difficult times for all.

67-40. A Song. To be sung by the poor of Great Britain.

"Come, let us songs of triumph sing." (36)

G, Sep 30, 1767.

The poor, objecting to monopoly which keeps prices high and exports food needed at home, look to the King for redress.

67-41. The Thane's Dance.

"Lead up, join Hands." (16)

L Eve Post, Oct 27, 1767.

Dimeter quatrains. Bute is responsible for the numerous changes in government.

67-42. To a Modern Politician.

"I grant Corruption sways Mankind." (72)

Freeman's J, Dec 26, 1767.

Octosyllabic couplets argue that he who intends the public good does not have to accept bribes.

67-43. To Charles Townsend.

"They wrong'd you, Friend Charles, who with Sneer." (4)

St J's C, Mar 19, 1767. (Spelling *sic*.)

Epigram. Defense of Charles Townsend's consistent conduct.

67-44. To the Earl of Chatham.

"O thou! whatever Title please thine Ear." (4)

St J's C, Apr 28, 1767.

Epigram. Criticism of Pitt for accepting the peerage title and losing his reputation.

67-45. To the Earl of Chatham.

"Take care, my good Lord, for your Lordship's own Sake." (4)

St J's C, Jan 3, 1767.

Epigram. A warning to Pitt, now Chatham, to share the cake, the awards, with other whigs.

67-46. To the Earl of Chatham.

"That Faction ceas'd, that love combin'd." (18)

LM 36 (Aug 1767), 424; SM 29 (Aug 1767), 435.

Octosyllabic couplets. Pitt deserves praise for his past service to the nation, but now that he has lost his reputation as a patriot he receives only insults and pity.

67-47. To the Right Hon. the Earl of Chatham, on Reading the Swarm of Absurd and Virulent Pamphlets published against him and the present patriotic Ministry. An Epigram.

"Flint struck on steel but wakes its innate fire." (6)

L Eve Post, Mar 28, 1767.

HC. A defense of Chatham and his government. Chatham and the present ministry will become stronger as a result of criticism.

67-48. To the Tories.

"Come, my dear Friends, whilst Sol darts forth his Rays." (8)

St J's C, Nov 26, 1767.

HC. A hope that Bute will return from his travels abroad and provide leadership (to the Tories).

67-49. [Whilst great men for themselves are carving].

"Whilst great men for themselves are carving." (13)

L Eve Post, Jul 16, 1767.

Tetrameter couplets. The rich in power want sense--it makes no difference who among them are in power because their measures are the same. Meanwhile the poor suffer.

67-50. Whitehead, William. Ode for the New Year, 1767. By William Whitehead, Esq; Poet Laureat.

"When first the rude, o'er-peopl'd, North." (56)

G, Jan 2, 1767; Lloyd's 20 (Dec 1766-Jan 3, 1767), 1; L Chron 21 (Dec 30, 1766-Jan 1, 1767), 8; L Eve Post, Dec 30, 1766-Jan 1, 1767; LM 36 (Jan 1767), 34; PA, Jan 1, 1767; St J's C, Dec 30, 1766-Jan 1, 1767.

Regular (Horatian) ode. Britain colonizes the western world and is an asylum of freedom for exiles from other countries.

1768 Books & Pamphlets

68-1. The A[lderma]n's Letter To The L[ord] M[ayo]r, Relative to His Polite Treatment of Mr. Wilkes. Versified by Another A[lderma]n.
[London:] Hooper, 1768. 20p.

"My very Worshipful Lord Mayor." (c. 390)

Notices: CR 25 (May 1768), 390-1; MR 38 (May 1768), 406.

Copies: BL 840.k.11 (6); NUC NN.

Octosyllabic couplets. Defense of Wilkes' character and politics; satire on Lord Mayor Thomas Harley (1767-68) for being a Tory and Jacobite and favoring "the Popish Party" of the Stuart Pretender, and for his hostility towards Wilkes because of pure "interest"--i.e., his fear of losing a contract and a place at court for his brother. The poem illustrates how corruption affects London politics.

68-2. The Battle of the Quills: or, Wilkes Attacked and Defended. An Impartial Selection of all the most Interesting Pieces, Argumentative, Declamatory, and Humorous, in Prose and Verse, Relative to John Wilkes, Esq; Written by his Adversaries, his Partisans, and Himself, From the Time of His declaring himself a Candidate to represent the City of London in Parliament to his being elected Knight of the Shire for the County of Middlesex. To which is prefixed, An Account of the Nature of Outlawry.
London: Williams, 1768. 74p.

Notices: CR 25 (Apr 1768), 308; MR 38 (Apr 1768), 323; L Chron 23 (Apr 7, 1768), 343; LM 37 (Jun 1768), 334.

Copies: BL 113.d.58; NUC CSmH, DLC, NN, NcD.

Five songs and three other pieces of verse from the newspapers:

Wilkes and Liberty. "With longing look and falt'ring speech." (30) p. 6
For Wilkes and our Country. "Hear Liberty, waving her cap to us all." (20) p. 7
Wilkes and Freedom: A New Ballad. "Come all ye good friends to your country's cause." (21) p. 7
The Joiners Joined; or, Jack Gimlet, the Joiner Triumphant. "Ye Joiners of England, and Joiners of France." (84) p. 32
A New Ballad by 'Squire Buckhorse, in honour of 'Squire Wilkes. "Come all ye brave boys who obey Wilkes's nod." (30) pp. 33-34
[O Sacred walls! while in your midnight gloom.] (24) pp. 34-35

Britannia to John Wilkes, Esq. "Droop not, my son, thy laurels cannot fade." (10) pp. 59-60
Inscription for a Pillar to be erected in Dorsetshire. "Sacred to the eternal infamy of the City of [London]." p. 60.

68-3. Britannia's Intercession for the Deliverance of John Wilkes, Esq. from Persecution and Banishment. To which is added A Political and Constitutional Sermon: And A Dedication to L*** B***. The Fifth Edition.
London: Woodgate, [1768]. 17p.

Psalm 151: "All people who on the earth do dwell." (20) p. 10

Copies: BL P.P. 5640.ba (2); 12315.m.8 (4th ed); 8133.d.25 (1) (9th ed); NUC ICN, MHi, MWA, & MiD (6th ed); NjP (7th ed).

Satire on Bute, the Scots, and the oppressive ministry. A ceremonial prayer for Wilkes and liberty, including an imitation of Psalm 151. Allusion in the sermon to the violence of the St. George's Fields riot, in which a crowd waiting for Wilkes to be released from the King's Bench prison was fired upon by a detachment of foot-guards. (The original, without the sermon, was entitled A New Form of Prayer, and Thanksgiving for the Happy Deliverance of John Wilkes, Esq. [London: Woodgate, 1768].)

68-4. Churchill, Charles.
[Lines from several poems--Prophecy of Famine, Epistle to Hogarth, The Conference, The Duellist, The Candidate, Gotham--on Wilkes.]

In The North Briton, XLVI Numbers Complete. By John Wilkes, C. Churchill, et al. (London, 1772), vol. IV, pp. 138-43.

These extracts totalling 68 lines, with a prose introduction, were originally published in St. James's Chronicle, June 2, 1768.

68-5. The Complaint of Liberty.
London: Cadell, 1768. 5-23p.

"Hark! how the growling blast with hollow roar." (c. 290)

Notices: CR 26 (Dec 1768, 472-3; MR 40 (Jan 1769), 88; L Chron 25 (Jan 12, 1769), 47; LM 37 (Dec 1768), 666.

Copies: NUC DLC, IU.

HC. The goddess Liberty mourns French oppression of Paoli's Corsicans. In the past, Belgium fought off the tyranny of Spain, Switzerland that of some petty rulers, Sweden under Gustavus that of Denmark. Free Britain must help the Corsicans resist oppression: "Where Freedom, Glory call, they point their course."

68-6. [Delamayne, Thomas Hallie]
  The Banished Patriot, Or, The Exile Returned. An Heroic Fragment.
  London: Williams, [1768]. 27p.

  "The Patriot now to Gallia's utmost verge." (c. 450)

  Notices: CR 25 (May 1768), 390-1; MR 38 (May 1768), 406.

  Copies: NUC CtY.

  Blank verse and HC. Before Wilkes leaves France, Churchill's spirit reveals the future, providing estimates of the politicians with whom Wilkes must compete upon his return from exile. Then, after reaching England, Wilkes is warned by Britannia that the King will not pardon him, admonishes him to continue in the cause of freedom and justice, begs him to have the Colonists recalled to "their duteous love," and expresses hostility for Bute.

68-7. Eleutheria: A Poem. Inscribed to Mrs. Macaulay.
  London: Kearsly et al., 1768. 8p.

  "I snatch the Pen, impatient to record." (c. 170)

  Notices: CR 25 (Apr 1768), 309; MR 38 (May 1768), 409-10.

  Copies: BL 11630.e.7 (8); NUC CtY, MH, MiU, OCU.

  Blank verse. Dated Feb. 20, 1768. In a dream vision, Jove orders Eleutheria (Liberty) to England to save the country from the evils of corruption and oppression. The goddess is attended by English patriots, all in the Whig tradition-- Milton, Pym, Hampden, Ludlow, Harrington, Sidney, Locke, Russell, et al.--rides in triumph through the city, and then speaks in Parliament, where she warns of many dangers: injustice, corruption, the loss of the colonies. Finally, she assumes the form of Macaulay, who has become her oracle.

68-8. The Exile Triumphant: or Liberty Appeased. A Poem Humbly Inscribed to the Worthy Liverymen of the City of London.
  London: Steare, 1768. 23p.

  Notices: CR 25 (May 1768), 227; MR 38 (Mar 1768), 245.

  Copies: NUC CtY, NNU-W (these copies cannot be located).

68-9. The Expostulation; A Poem.
   London: Bingley, 1768. 30p.

   "When Guilt abroad, in native Hue, hath flown." (c. 500)

   Notices: CR 25 (May 1768), 390-1; MR 38 (Jun 1768), 498; L Chron 23 (May 12, 1768), 464.

   Copies: NUC CtY, DLC, IU.

   HC. A rambling, generalized satire that starts with a diatribe against corrupting luxury in evil times. Government is grounded on self-interest, money, and power. Even peace does not bring blessings, proving to be "our Spoiler"-- e. g., the policy governing the colonies estranges them (p. 14n), arts and commerce fade, public trust is abused by those in high office and the nobility, and the King relies too heavily on his favorite Bute and on the Scots.

68-10. ---------- For Ever! A Poem. "In the approaching Election of Representatives, I doubt not but My People will give me fresh Proofs of their Attachment to the true Interest of their Country." The King's Speech.
   London: Newbery, [1768]. 13p.

   "Hark! how the silver-toned bells proclaim." (190)

   Notices: CR 25 (Mar 1768), 227; L Chron 23 (Apr 7, 1768), 343; LM 37 (Jun 1768), 334.

   Copies: NUC NN.

   HC. On the approaching parliamentary election. Urges the young peers to lead the country with integrity. Curses those who corrupt and damn the cause of liberty, including Bute; asserts that only Grafton can save the country. Cited are Rockingham, Bedford, Grenville, North, Chatham.

68-11. [Greene, Edward Burnaby]
   Corsica. An Ode.
   London: Ridley, 1768. 7p.

   "Rebels!--avaunt th'inglorious name." (144)

   Notices: CR 26 (Nov 1768), 378-9; MR 39 (Nov 1768), 401; GM 38 (Nov 1768), 533; L Chron 24 (Nov 5, 1768), 445, & 26 (Oct 28, 1769), 420; WM 2 (Dec 8, 1768), 305.

   Copies: NUC MH.

   See 68-12.

68-12. [-----]
   -----.

   In 71-2 : his Poetical Essays, pp. 36-42.

   Regular Horatian ode. Acclaims the heroic struggle of the Corsicans against the oppression of Genoa, and urges Britain to come to their assistance in their struggle for liberty before France intervenes. Refers to Boswell and America, and to Paoli as an incorruptible model for those who believe in freedom.

68-13. Hollway, James.
   Merit. A Poem Inscribed to his Grace the Duke of Grafton.
   London: Lewis, 1768. iii-iv, 5-16p.

   "When honest truth and justice hold the scale." (c. 260)

   Notices: CR 24 (Dec 1767), 471; MR 38 (Jan 1768), 70.

   Copies: BL 644.k.19.

   HC. A flattering panegyric on Grafton, who has "assum'd the ministerial pow'r," and his politics--honorable, incorruptible, just, "steady in freedom's cause," and unselfish.

68-14. Howard, Middleton.
   The Conquest of Quebec: A Poem.
   Oxford: Fletcher, 1768. i + 12p.

   "Farewell ye Naiads who your Tresses lave." (216)

   Notices: CR 26 (Dec 1768), 472; MR 40 (Feb 1769), 139-40; L Chron 24 (Dec 20, 1768), 593; LM 38 (Feb 1769), 104.

   Sabin 31097.

   Copies: BL 11649.f.17 (2); NUC CtY, DLC, MH, MiU-C, RPJCB, TxU.

   HC. Awarded the prize by the Earl of Litchfield, Chancellor of the University of Oxford, for the best poem on the subject. Narration of Wolfe's victory at Quebec and his death. Cited are General Townshend (who assumed command upon Wolfe's death), fierce Scottish troops, and Montcalm.

68-15. Kenrick, William.
   Poems, Ludicrous, Satirical, and Moral.
   London: Fletcher, 1768.

Notices: MR 38 (Apr 1768), 334; LM 37 (Feb 1768), 113.

Copies: BL 994.c.15.

Includes three relevant poems, the first two published earlier in the serials, the third apparently for the first time in this collection:

The Political Magnet. A Simile. Written in the Year 1766. "Lodg'd in the northern pole, the wise." (24) pp. 39-40. See 66-66.
P[itt] and Proteus. *Mutatas dicere formas*. Written in the year 1767. "Chousing, cheating, chopping, changing." (72) pp. 44-46. See 67-26.
The Loaded Ass; or Public Credit. A Political Fable. "A mottled ass, in days of yore." (98) pp. 262-66. UM 43 (Oct 1768), 208-9.

68-16. -----.
-----. [Another ed]
London: Williams, 1770. viii, 324p.

Copies: BL 11632.d.23; NUC CtY, IU, MB, MH.

The three poems in 68-15 are reprinted (pp. 39-40, 44-46, 262-6 again), and three additional relevant poems are included from the serials:

The Lion in the Toils. A Political Fable. *Ex ungue leonem*. "Committed by the hand of power." (40) pp. 308-9. See 68-63.
The Political Scapegoat. An Epistle to Sir William Draper. "How's this?-- the learn'd Sir William Draper." (c. 120) pp. 310-15. See 69-106.
An Epistle to Mr. Wilkes, on the Confirmation of his Sentence in the House of L---s. Written during a Fit of the Gout. "In spite of error, quirk, and flaw." (106) pp. 320-4 (mispaginated). See 69-105.

68-17. The Lamentation of Britannia for the Two-and-Twenty Months Imprisonment of John Wilkes, Esq. in the King's Bench Prison.
London: Woodgate, [1768]. 8p.

Notices: LM 37 (Jun 1768), 335.

Copies: BL 1481.f.5, 8133.d.25; NUC NN (first portion missing).

A ceremonial complaint (in Biblical style) at Wilkes's imprisonment, concluding with two poems, "Songs of Britannia. Long and common measure": [1] "Right sad I was, when that my eye" (20) and [2] "Now hath mine ears" (24). Britannia predicts revenge for the violence and slaughter at St. George's Fields, protests the government's use of force, or the people will go elsewhere, taking trade with them.

68-18. Liberty Deposed, or The Western Election: A Satirical Poem. In Three Books.
London: Almon et al., [1768]. 59p.

"Of liberty the direful fate." (276 + 467 + 509)

Notices: CR 25 (Mar 1768), 227; MR 38 (Apr 1768), 334.

Copies: BL 11642.cc.43 (4).

Hudibrastics. Generalized satire on bribery and on the corruption of liberty in rotten boroughs during an election in western shires, including Cornwall. However, Chatham is often cited favorably, and Cornish politicians are once alluded to (II, 400 ff.--p. 36).

68-19. An Ode to Liberty, Inscribed to The Right Hon. Thomas Harley, The Lord Mayor of the City of London.
London: Wilkie, 1768. 11p.

"O Thou whose Spirit-stirring Name." (78)

Notices: CR 25 (Apr 1768), 309; MR 38 (Apr 1768), 334; L Chron 23 (Apr 16, 1768), 376.

Copies: BL 163.m.37; NUC DLC, MH.

Regular Horatian ode. Inscribed to Harley April 12, 1768. A protest at oppression and the threat to the liberty and rights of English subjects as laid down in Magna Charta. But no one in the Grafton ministry cares, and Camden and Shelburne have disgracefully retreated; G-----t (?) particularly has not supported Harley.

68-20. Plain Truth, in Plain English. A Satire. By a Plain Man, in a Plain Dress.
London: Bingley, [1768]. 22p.

"While Europe's trembling with tumult'ous Throes." (c. 580)

Notices: CR 26 (Dec 1768), 473; MR 39 (Dec 1768), 489.

Copies: NUC CSmH.

HC. Satirizes Bute and the Scots for self-interest, and notes that in America is to be seen impending ruin, or a civil war. Wilkes is cited.

68-21. A Poetical Epistle to The Right Hon. Lord M[ansfield]. By a Gentleman of the King's Bench Prison.
   London: Bingley, 1768. v-xii + 13-36p.

   "My Lord, how abject is the present time." (c. 350)

   Notices: CR 26 (Nov 1768), 383; MR 39 (Nov 1768), 401.

   Copies: BL 11630.d.12 (13); NUC IU.

   HC. Dedication to John Earl of Bute, dated Sept. 15, 1768, from the King's Bench Prison. Ironic satire on Bute and Judge Mansfield, "congenial in their suspension of politics, principles, and dispositions," the enemies of Wilkes and his supporters. Mansfield is made to appear responsible for the massacre in St. George's Fields--which is described. Cited are the young Allen who was murdered, his father, and Wilkes. Praise of the integrity of Camden. At the end, hope is expressed for the execution of Bute and Mansfield. Pretends to be written from the prison in St. George's Fields.

68-22. [Shaw, Cuthbert]
   Corruption. A Satire. Inscribed to the Right Honourable Richard Grenville, Earl Temple. By the Author of The Monody to the Memory of a Young Lady.
   London: Nicoll, Davis, et al., 1768. 37p.

   "Accept, O Grenville, no dishonest strain." (c. 430)

   Notices: CR 26 (Dec 1768), 473; MR 39 (Dec 1768), 487-8; L Chron 24 (Nov 29, 1768), 525.

   Copies: NUC MH.

   HC. Satire on the corrupting influence of avarice. Wilkes' patron, Earl Temple, is invoked for assistance in S's campaign against corruption, bribery, and injustice, after the last war. Major attacks are made on Bute, "his SECOND"-- Mansfield (?), and Chatham. Concludes with a panegyric on Wilkes, the incorruptible martyr in the cause of freedom. Others favored are John Glynn and Sir Jeffrey Amherst.

68-23. Stevenson, John Hall.
   Makarony Fables; Fables for Grown Gentlemen. With the New Fable of the Bees. In Two Cantos.
   London: Almon, 1768. vii + 9-58p.

   "I never yet beheld that man." (c. 500)

Notices: CR 25 (Jan 1768), 69-70; MR 38 (Mar 1768), 247; L Chron 23 (Jan 16, 1768), 64.

Copies: NUC CtY, IEN, MH, MiU, TxU.

(The New Fable of the Bees, pp. 47-58.) Octosyllabic, alternate rhymes. Humorously discusses, in I, monarchy, specifically reflecting on the relationship between Bute and the Queen Dowager; Bute's conflict with Pitt; the colonies, the Scots, George Grenville, and court politics for 1761-66, when the favorite Bute exerted his influence. In II, the years covered are 1766-67, when Chatham's illness disrupted his ministry. But Bute's secret influence still operates, and the piece closes with the supposed coalition of Bute and Chatham in 1767. (2nd & 3rd eds 1768, another ed 1772. See also his Works [London: Debrett, 1795], vol. I, pp. 218-48.)

68-24. Underwood, Thomas.
Liberty, A Poem.
London: Bladon, Blyth, et al., 1768. 5-34p.

"Th' expected Storm blown over--the Reviews." (c. 510)

Notices: CR 25 (Feb 1768), 152; MR 38 (May 1768), 248, & 39 (Jul 1768), 80; L Mag 37 (Feb 1768), 111.

Copies: NUC CtY, MH.

HC. Rambling satire on various themes--severity of the reviewers, liberty, the King's humanity, Wilkes and his followers' hostility to the good King due to a supposed threat to their liberty. Also, the uncertainty of present ministries, Pitt too ill to provide leadership, and Pitt's accepting peerage--bad and good. Hopes for unity and the end of faction, a model being the Corsican struggle for liberty. He admonishes the selfish and mercenary not to undermine the state. Closes with objections to the reviewers' despotic power, their venality, and lack of candor, and with an assertion of his freedom. (Also in his Poems [Bath: Archer, 1768], pp. 199-221.)

68-25. The Victim. A Poem. Inscribed to John Wilkes, Esq.
London: Staples Steare, 1768. 31p.

"In vain the muse, with all her charms invite." (c. 340)

Notices: CR 25 (Apr 1768), 309; L Mag 37 (Jun 1768), 334.

Copies: BL 1600/310.

HC. Dedicated to Wilkes in exile, "the most intrepid assertor of his country's liberty." The poet complains of despotic oppression, monopoly reducing food production and causing famine, and the breakdown of commerce. He satirizes luxury and adoption of effeminate French fashions. Bute, too, is criticized for his "despotic principles" responsible for discord since he is "so near the throne." There are those who, besides Wilkes, maintain British liberty--Camden.

68-26. Wheatley, Phillis.
To the King's Most Excellent Majesty. 1768.

"Your subjects hope, dread Sire." (15)

In 73-11: Poems, p. 17.

HC. Thanks and blesses King George for the repeal of the Stamp Act.

Serials

68-27. An Address from the London Mob to the Mob of Edinburgh, on the late Rejoicings.

"While ev'ry English hearts with pleasure glows." (39)

RM 18 (May 1768), 231.

HC. The English rejoice that Wilkes has been freed; but the Scots do not, false and perfidious Jacobites. Cited are North-Britons, Wilkes, Forbes, Dunn, King Charles, King George.

68-28. Answer to the Pun on the Vicar of Brentford.

"When Wilkes drew his Goose-quill, intrepid and free." (6)

St J's C, Dec 24, 1768.

Epigram. Wilkes's reputation is exalted by Parson Horne of Brentford. See "The Vicar of Brentford," St. James's Chronicle, December 15, 1768: 68-111.

68-29. The Aspiration.

"When shall the happy Times arrive." (22)

RM 18 (Nov 1768), 519-20.

Octosyllabic couplets. When Wilkes and Liberty arrive, utopia shall prevail. (Possibly ironic.)

68-30. Ballad on the General Election.

"Hail, glorious time." (24)

GM 38 (Mar 1768), 135; Lloyd's 22 (Mar 16, 1768), 265; SM 30 (Mar 1768), 153; New Foundling Hospital for Wit (1768), IV, 100-1; A Companion for a Leisure Hour (1769),, pp. 150-1.

Song in sixains. An ironic satire describing the effect of electioneering on those who seek votes. Hypocrisy and bribery prevail.

68-31. Britannia to John Wilkes, Esp.

"Droop not, my Son, thy Laurels cannot fade." (10)

GM 38 (Mar 1768), 136; Lloyd's 22 (Mar 21, 1768), 287; Battle of the Quills (1768), pp. 59-60; A Companion for a Leisure Hour (1769), p. 149.

HC. Britannia declares that only when she falls and freedom dies will Wilkes fail.

68-32. A Card to John Wilkes, Esq. on Hearing the Rampant Exultation of a Club of Scotchmen, on his Receiving Sentence last June.

"Such are the Honours thy lov'd Country pays." (20)

LM 37 (Sep 1768), 492-3; BLJ, Sep 17, 1768.

HC. Praise of Wilkes, despite his imprisonment by his enemies, the Scots.

68-33. [Comes yonder Time, or Politician queer.]

"Comes yonder Time, or Politician queer." (45)

RM 18 (Nov 1768), 520.

HC, celebrating Wilkes' birthday and 45. Cited are William Whitehead, Newton, Charles Churchill.

68-34. A Conversation.

"Quoth H-y to G-n, your counsel I ask." (15)

St J's C, Apr 7, 1768; SM 30 (Apr 1768), 211.

Hexameter couplets. Augustus John Hervey asks Grafton the way to treat the mob. Grafton recommends that the mob be given freedom, as in New York and Boston.

68-35. Directions to the Heralds for new painting the City Arms.

"Out with that Cross from London's shield." (12)

L Chron 23 (Jun 16, 1768), 583.

Quatrains. Criticism of Bute and his supposed mistress, the Queen Dowager, for dominating the City of London.

68-36. DuBois, Dorothea.
The New Year's Gift. By Lady Dorothea DuBois.

"To fair Britannia's best of Kings." (32)

Lloyd's 22 (Jan 1, 1768), 10.

Octosyllabic couplets. Hopes for a good year and redress of grievances suffered by the poor.

68-37. The Election: A Ballad. To the Tune of "Chevy Chace."

"God prosper long our Noble King." (76)

G, Dec 21, 1768; Lloyd's 23 (Dec 19, 1768), 595; L Chron 24 (Dec 17, 1768), 592; PA, Dec 20, 1768; The Humours of the Times (London, 1771), pp. 338-41.

Ballad narrates an election riot with the candidates on the hustings--Sir William Proctor and Serjeant John Glynn. Parson Horne opposes Proctor. Another title is "The Middlesex Election."

68-38. Epigram.

"Should Truth, Wit, Wisdom, all unite." (6)

St J's C, Jun 23, 1768.

Sixain. Mansfield supports the Establishment, regardless of wisdom, and makes liberty a slave.

68-39. Epigram on Mr. Wilkes's Confinement.

"No more let England vainly boast." (4)

St J's C, Jul 5, 1768.

England cannot boast of her liberty when Wilkes is confined in prison.

68-40. Epigram on the Death of the Late Duke of Newcastle.

"Newcastle dead! Confusion seize." (4)

St J's C, Nov 24, 1768.

Because Thomas, the Duke of Newcastle has died, while John Stuart, Third Earl of Bute is still alive, England must worry. (Thomas Pelham Holles, Duke of Newcastle [1693-1768] was premier at the time Pitt earned his reputation as an efficient, inspiring, and brilliant national leader in the Seven Year's War. In May 1762 he was removed from office so that Bute could take his place and proceed to the negotiation of the Peace Treaty of 1763.)

68-41. Epigram on the Fate of the Celebrated Patriot.

"Of old the Man who serv'd fair Freedom's Cause." (4)

St J's C, Nov 29, 1768.

Wilkes, the great patriot, is ill-served by his country, which pays him with exile and prison.

68-42. An Epigrammatical Prophecy, occasioned by a Report of the Duke of G---'s new House being tumbled down.

"'Beware, sly Proverb saith, to bring!" (16)

RM 18 (Nov 1768), 530.

Quatrains. Rumor of the Duke of Grafton's house having fallen occasions fears that the empire will crumble, that the colonies will be lost.

68-43. Epistle to John Wilkes, Esq.

"Bless'd by the anxious Croud that murm'ring wait." (c. 130)

L Chron 24 (Jul 21, 1768), 79; PA, Jul 22, 1768; St J's C, Jul 19, 1768.

HC. Satire on Bute who is responsible for Wilkes' imprisonment. However, Wilkes has support in Middlesex and eventually will be freed.

68-44. Epistle to John Wilkes, Esq; in Confinement.

"While ev'ry truly English breast." (30)

LM 37 (Jul 1768), 377; PA, Jul 8, 1768; St J's C, Jul 5, 1768; The Humours of the Times (London, 1769), pp. 324-5; New Foundling Hospital for Wit, Part 3 (1769), pp. 37-8.

Sixains. Wilkes bravely suffers the malice of oppressors in Parliament; he will, it is hoped, be freed despite the ministry and the court.

68-45. Extempore. On the Frequent Reports of Changes in the Ministry.

"Tho' Changes of Ministers still will go on." (4)

PA, Dec 6, 1768.

Epigram. The changes in the ministry are apparent, not real; the ministers are still the same: semper eadem.

68-46. An Extempore. Written on Friday night at a Select Society of '45.

"Behold the Man, whose great intrepid Soul." (8)

PA, Oct 31, 1768.

HC. Let us, the Select Society of '45, praise Wilkes on his birthday, October 28.

68-47. [Freeth, John]
The Birmingham Cut; Or, Navigation Extended.

"When fam'd Columbus first the sails unfurl'd." (36)

Lloyd's 22 (Mar 25, 1768), 298; L Chron 23 (Mar 22, 1768), 287.

HC. A celebration of industrious Birmingham, now opened to sea-trade by a canal. Britain builds its greatness on trade, the sale of its manufactured goods to America and other lands.

68-48. A Friendly Caution to the Free Electors of the City of Litchfield, by W. J.

"O! leave, my Muse, thy dear Arcadian plains." (76)

L Chron 23 (Jan 7, 1768), 28.

HC. A warning to Litchfield electors to have a free and uncorrupted election, for corruption had ruined Greece and Rome.

68-49. [Hail, Corsica! than whose recorded name.]

"Hail, Corsica! than whose recorded name." (32)

Lloyd's 22 (May 25, 1768), 508.

HC. Boswell, in quoted lines from Pride, A Poem, celebrates Paoli's fight for Corsican freedom against the Genoese. (From Boswell's Account of Corsica [1768], p. 225.) See 66-A.

68-50. [Hail, freeborn Spirit! lovely Freedom, Hail!]

"Hail, freeborn Spirit! lovely Freedom, hail." (33)

St J's C, Apr 2, 1768.

HC. Invocation to Freedom and praise of John Wilkes and John Glynn vs. the Stuarts.

68-51. [If it be true, that Wilkes and Pitt agreed.]

"If it be true, that Wilkes and Pitt agreed." (4)

St J's C, Apr 5, 1768.

Epigram. Satire on Pitt and the court. Wilkes would be sent to prison, Pitt awarded a coronet, if they were to be factious. Such is justice in England.

68-52. Imitation. Anacr. Od. 46 To J[ohn] W[ilkes.] Esq.

"Would you wish to serve the State." (28)

New Foundling Hospital for Wit, Part 3 (1769), pp. 36-7; A Companion (1769), pp. 145-6.

Quatrains. Dated Sept. 12, 1768. A curse upon corruption. Gold turned Pitt into a villain and confined Wilkes in jail.

68-53. Impromptu on Mr. Wilkes being Elected for Middlesex.

"Thy Fortune, O Wilkes! has been wonderous strange." (6)

St J's C, Mar 26, 1768.

Epigram. Praise of Wilkes who, returned from exile, is repulsed by London, but accepted by Middlesex.

68-54. Impromptu. On Mr. Wilkes's Birth-Day.

"The Foes of Wilkes affirm with Scorn." (4)

PA, Oct 31, 1768.

Epigram. His foes scorn Wilkes for being a rake; but his friends say he has reformed.

68-55. Impromptu. To Liberty.

"Say, sacred Goddess! on what happy Isle." (6)

St J's C, May 10, 1768.

HC. Sympathy for Wilkes. Paoli has come from Corsica to gain freedom in England; but Wilkes has been put in prison.

68-56. An Impromptu. To Sir Joseph Mawbey . . . .

"Mawbey, the Muse's Glory and her Pride." (4)

PA, Dec 12, 1768.

Mawbey, MP for Southwark, London, is praised for presenting Wilkes's petition to the King for redress of grievances.

68-57. [In days of yore, when for the commonweal.]

"In days of yore, when for the common weal." (44)

L Chron 23 (Jan 12, 1768), 47.

HC. A warning against corruption in the coming election. The nature of the corruption is explained--the way votes are purchased.

68-58. [In proud -------'s Despight.]

"In proud -----'s Despight." (12)

PA, Jul 20, 1768.

Sixains. Wilkes is supported by the people despite his vice.

68-59. An Inscription For a Monument dedicated to the Memory of Modern Patriotism.

"Here Lieth / Wisdom!--Virtue! Popularity." (c. 60)

G, Oct 4, 1768; GM 38 (Oct 1768), 468; L Chron 24 (Oct 4, 1768), 335; PA, Oct 3, 1768; SM 30 (Oct 1768), 537; UM 43 (Oct 1768), 207.

Attack on Pitt for allowing "Domestic Faction" to ruin his country.

68-60. Inscription for a Pillar to be erected at -----, Dorsetshire.

"Sacred / To the eternal Infamy of the city of ******." (c. 20)

RM 18 (Mar 1768), 136; Battle of the Quills (1768), p. 60. See 68-2.

An inscription honoring Wilkes, freedom fighter, and damning a city in Dorsetshire for not defending the rights of freeborn Englishmen.

68-61. An Inscription For the Statues Sent To America.

"In Memory of / W.P." (c. 50)

G, Oct 4, 1768; The Humours of the Times (London, 1771), pp. 120-2; New Foundling Hospital for Wit, Part 1 (1768), pp. 95-6.

Satire on Pitt for betraying the people for "pension, place, and coronet," July 30, 1766.

68-62. The Joiners Joined.

"Ye Joiners of England, and Joiners of France." (32)

PA, Mar 21, 1768; Battle of the Quills (1768), p. 32. See 68-2.

A Wilkes election song.

68-63. Kenrick, William.
The Lion in the Toils. A Political Fable.

"Committed by the hand of power." (40)

G, Dec 5, 1768; PA, Dec 6, 1768; St J's C, Dec 1, 1768; New Foundling Hospital for Wit, Part 3 (1769), pp. 39-41; Kenrick, Poems; Ludicrous, Satirical and Moral (London: J. Fletcher, 1770), pp. 308-9; also LM 37 (Dec 1768), 659. See 68-16.

Octosyllabic couplets. Animal fable, Wilkes being the lion confined in prison and seeking the law's protection. But ministerial power has difficulty in coping with Wilkes.

68-64. [Let Amherst go, his Sov'rain said.]

"Let Amherst go, his Sov'rain said." (64)

G, Oct 1, 1768; A Companion for a Leisure Hour (1769), pp. 157-9.

Ballad on Amherst's loss of place. He deserved better treatment.

68-65. [Let Britons ever hail the glorious Hour.]

"Let Britons ever hail the glorious Hour." (13)

PA, Jun 27, 1768.

HC. The conclusion of an essay on Wilkes' release from confinement. Let us praise those Middlesex freeholders who supported Wilkes and espoused his cause, the curbing of "imperious Pow'r."

68-66. Lines addressed to that great Patriot of England, Mr. Wilkes.

"To Thee, great Wilkes! a Tribute due I bring." (33)

PA, Sep 24, 1768.

HC. Despite the oppression of his enemies, Wilkes bravely continues the struggle for the cause of Freedom, even in prison.

68-67. Lockman, John.
Ode on the Administration of Ireland, under his Excellency the Lord Viscount Townshend.

"My Locks, tho' silver'd o'er by Time." (66)

DJ, May 17, 1768.

Regular (Horatian) ode. Praise of Townshend's administration for cleansing Ireland of corruption and encouraging trade, agriculture, and industry.

68-68. London to Wit. Extract from the Dialogue between the Two Giants.

"To all and ev'ry." (56)

RM 18 (May 1768), 231.

Tetrameter couplets. The persona of Wilkes ironically speaks and betrays himself as he asks for the support of the London livery while running for election to parliament.

68-69. Cancelled.

The Nation's Wish. By a Lady. "Curs'd be the Wretch that's bought and sold." (24)
Freeman's J, Jan 2, 1768. Also L Eve Post, Nov 28, 1767; PA, Nov 6, 1767.
The same poem as 67-31.

68-70. A New Ballad composed by 'Squire Buckhorse, in honour of 'Squire Wilkes.

"Come all ye brave boys who obey Wilkes's nod." (24)

G, Mar 18, 1768.

Song. Satire on Wilkes and his followers, destructive blasphemers all.

68-71. New Year's Ode.

"Whilst Whitehead slumbers o'er his sack." (118)

Ox M 1 (Supplement 1768), 274-5.

Irregular ode. The violence in the term of Thomas Harley as Lord Mayor of London is summed up. The poet objects to the oppression of Harley, complains that Wilkes is in prison, that young Allen died in the St. George's Fields riot. Praises Glynn for his opposition to the ministry.

68-72. Oakman, J. [pseud.]
To the Nobility, Gentry, &c. The Humble Petition of Want and Misery.

"While thro' the drear of frost and snow." (36)

Lloyd's 22 (Jan 13, 1768), 51.

Sixains. A poem of social protest by the poor who look to the humane and charitable rich for help.

68-73. Occasioned by Mr. Wilkes being Elected for Middlesex.

"In the bleak Shade by adverse Fate." (40)

L Eve Post, Apr 2, 1768.

Quatrains. Praise of Wilkes and expression of joy over his March 1768 victory in the Middlesex election for Parliament.

68-74. Ode on the Dissolution of the British Parliament.

"As the rich Web, the curious Matron's Pride." (102)

St J's C, Dec 3, 1768.

Regular (Horatian) ode in sixains. Invocation to Liberty upon the suspension of the power of Parliament for a while, for she brings peace to the multitude--with allusion to Wilkes in jail.

68-75. On a Late Promised Resignation.

"Will Ch--- resign, or continue in place." (4)

G, Oct 27, 1768; L Chron 24 (Oct 25, 1768), 400.

Epigram. Chatham resigned as Lord Privy Seal on October 14, 1768, and was replaced by a supporter of Bute (Augustus John Hervey, Lord Bristol).

68-76. On hearing that Mr. W---s, after having been disappointed at Westminister and London, intended standing for the county of Middlesex.

"Quoth angry W---s, How damn'd hard fated." (6)

SM 30 (Apr 1768), 211.

Epigram. Sixain. Wilkes, hated by women and outlawed by men, is accepted by Middlesex.

68-77. On John Wilkes, Esq; offering himself a Candidate For the County of Middlesex.

"Fir'd with a truly patriotic Zeal." (16)

PA, Mar 28, 1768.

HC. Wilkes deserves support as the patriotic defender of liberty against lawless tyranny.

68-78. On Lord B--t's being appointed Governor of V--a, in the room of G--l Sir J--y Am---t, dismissed.

"New trouble, colonists! your time is come." (6)

WM 1 (Sep 1, 1768), 274.

Epigram. HC. Botetourt displaces Amherst as Gov. of Virginia. The colonists should beware--they no longer have Conway to speak for them.

68-79. On Mr. Wilkes's Birth-Day, Oct. 28, 1768.

"In fair October, George the Great was born." (16)

St J's C, Oct 25, 1768.

HC. George II was born in October, like Wilkes; the Scots ruined the peace and the country; but Wilkes saved the country from them, although in jail now.

68-80. On Reading the Papers, that a number of English Church Bells are to be sent to Corsica.

"While o'er the globe old England tells." (12)

L Chron 23 (Apr 19, 1768), 383.

Sixains. The English should be ashamed because they are not helping the Corsicans in their struggle for liberty.

68-81. On the Birth-Day of John Wilkes, Esq; By a Young Lady.

"Nature, with all her Toil, (expert and sage)." (10)

PA, Nov 2, 1768; St J's C, Oct 29, 1768.

Wilkes, a genuine patriot, will endure, despite opposition, persecution, violence, to keep England free. Allusion to death of Allen in St. George's Fields' riot.

68-82. On the Death of England's Prince of Whigs.

"Ye Tories laugh! Whigs sigh, and drop a Tear." (4)

St J's C, Nov 26, 1768.

Epigram. The Tories are pleased at the news of Newcastle's death--the Prince of Whigs. Signed Andrew Marvel (pseud.).

68-83. On the Removal of the Guards from before the King's Bench Prison.

"Let Tyrants keep their Guards for Pomp and State." (4)

BLJ, Sep 17, 1768.

Epigram. Wilkes, unlike hated tyrants, needs no guards for he has his country's love.

68-84. On Wilkes, Candidate for Middlesex.

"Wilkes, rejected at London, to Middlesex flies." (8)

St J's M, Apr 12, 1768.

Hexameter couplets. Comment on Wilkes's candidacy for MP from Middlesex, after being rejected by London. [Following the verse is this comment--"It is very remarkable that Mr. Wilkes polled   For Middlesex 1292
                                      For London   1247
                                                45."]

68-85. The Parody Parodized; or, The Massachusetts Song of Liberty.

"Come, swallow your bumpers, ye Tories! and roar." (53)

G, Nov 8, 1768; Freeman's J, Nov 12, 1768; L Chron 24 (Nov 3, 1768), 438; St J's C, Nov 5, 1768; SM 30 (Nov 1768), 599-600; WM 2 (Nov 17, 1768), 211.

A parody of the Tory "Song, which made its appearance from a garret at Castle William." From the Boston Gazette, Oct 6, 1768. ---- A Boston song that encourages continuing resistance to the oppression of tyrants and their minions. See 68-95.

68-86. The Particulars of a Happy Government.

"Blest is that Government where greedy Knaves." (20)

BLJ, Oct 22, 1768; Freeman's J, Oct 22, 1768; UM 43 (Oct 1768), 208.

HC. Ironic praise of a debased and corrupt government.

68-87. Pascal Paoli to his [Sacred] Majesty. An Epistle.

"Bold with just firmness in the glorious cause. (c. 110)

RM 18 (Nov 1768), 517.

HC. Verse epistle praise of Paoli and Corsica and their fight for Freedom from France. Britain should assist them in their struggle against French tyranny.

68-88. Percy and Sandys. A Ballad. For the Westminster Election, 1768. Tune, Bumper 'Squire Jones.

"My Westminster Friends." (36)

L Chron 23 (Mar 5, 1768), 232.

Election song for Hugh Percy and Edwin Sandys, boasting that in Westminster there's no corruption, no faction.

68-89. Query.

"The Scottish Kirk treat Wilkes--just like a Pope." (6)

St J's C, May 21, 1768.

HC. The Scottish Kirk feels Wilkes deserves punishment; but the Presbyterians in the city adore Wilkes. Why the difference, it is asked.

68-90. Ranger's Visit. A New Song. Tune, The Old Woman at Grinstead.

"A Visit I made." (36)

Lloyd's 22 (Apr 18, 1768), 382.

A drinking song for Wilkes and freedom.

68-91. The Rape of the Boot and Petticoat. (with a Copper-plate annexed)

"Sing thou, my muse, the dire contested fray." (38)

Ox M 1 (Jul 1768), 35.

HC. Satire on Lord Mayor Thomas Harley for his disapproval of Wilkes and liberty and his support of Bute. See Catalogue of Political and Personal Satires, ed. F.G. Stephens (London: British Museum, 1883), IV, 425-7 (#4190), for commentary.

68-92. Ryley, J.C.
An Acrostic. [Wilkes.]

"I sing the Patriot, who with all the Pride." (10)

L Eve Post, Jul 16, 1768.

HC. Praise of Wilkes, patriot, freedom-fighter.

68-93. [Says a Scotchman to Wilkes, as he brush'd by his Side.]

"Says a Scotchman to Wilkes, as he brush'd by his Side." (4)

St J's C, Apr 16, 1768.

Epigram. Anti-Scots satire--from Bute down to the peasant clod.

68-94. Song, For Mr. Wilkes's Birth-Day. To the Tune of--The Belleisle March.

"Huzza, for St. George!--let us drink and be gay." (20)

St J's C, Oct 25, 1768; BLJ, Oct 29, 1768.

Drinking song, praising Wilkes, in prison, and Serjeant John Glynn (counsel for the printers of the North Briton in 1764 and for Wilkes in 1768).

68-95. A Song, Now much in vogue in North America.
Tune, Hearts of Oak.

"Come, join in hand, brave Americans all." (43)

G, Sep 1, 1768; L Chron 24 (Sep 3, 1768), 219; L Chron 38 (Jul 8, 1775), 40; LM 37 (Sep 1768), 492; SM 30 (Sep 1768), 488; WM 1 (Sep 29, 1768), 405; W Misc 3 (Dec 12, 1774), 255-6.

By John Dickinson, the first American patriotic song; first published in the Boston Gazette, July 18, 1768. It was known as "The Liberty Song; Or, In Freedom We're Born," and was written in reaction to the Townshend Acts. -- A loyalist parody appeared in the Boston Gazette, Sep 26, 1768, which was itself parodied in the St J's C, Nov 5, 1768, etc. -- The song complains of "tyrannous acts," unjust taxation, coming pensioners and placemen, and insists that Americans will unite in defense of their liberty. -- See The Parody Parodized, 68-85.

68-96. A Song, which made its appearance from a garret at Castle William [Boston], Sept. 22.

"Come shake your dull noddles, ye pumkins, and bawl." (53)

PA, Nov 8, 1768; SM 30 (Nov 1768), 599.

"From the Supplement Extraordinary to the Boston Gazette of Monday, Sept. 26." -- A loyalist parody of John Dickinson's "Liberty Song," or "A Song, Now much in vogue in North America." -- This song satirizes the rioting Boston mob, bent on plunder and destruction.

68-97. Spoken Extempore by a poor debtor in the King's Bench, on seeing the presents brought to Mr. Wilkes.

"Here, as in fortune's wheel, observe." (8)

G, Nov 8, 1768.

Quatrains. Satire on Wilkes who eats well because he "libell'd God and King."

68-98. [That man who would a tyrant be].

"That man who would a tyrant be." (16)

L Chron 24 (Oct 18, 1768), 384.

Epigram, moral fable. In union there is strength. Britain should be cautious and not mistreat the colonies. (From the New-York Gazette.)

68-99. Thou Art the Man!

"Say, Bute-born Anarchy, confusion say." (26)

St J's C, Apr 12, 1768.

HC. Satire on Bute for causing dissension and anarchy.

68-100. To Jack Cade, jun. in the King's Bench.

"Half of our Aim obtained is some Success." (8)

PA, Jul 1, 1768.

HC. Wilkes, compared with Jack Cade, the seditious rebel, deserves imprisonment and hopefully will die. His "Forty-Five" recalls the year 1745, when another unsuccessful attempt was made on the throne.

68-101. To John Wilkes, Esq.

"If e'er Oppression, with the desp'rate Claws." (22)

St J's C, Jul 12, 1768.

HC. Eulogy on Wilkes, imprisoned; and an attack on the enemies of freedom, "court parasites" and "tools of power," corrupt characters.

68-102. To John Wilkes, Esquire.

"If writing and fighting in Liberty's Cause." (4)

L Eve Post, Apr 30, 1768.

Epigram. Wilkes should be proud to be called a rebel, for he defends liberty and the laws.

68-103. To John Wilkes, Esq. Member of Parliament for the County of Middlesex, and Prisoner in the King's Bench.

"In every age true sense is always blest." (158)

RM 18 (Jun 1768), 276-7.

Heroic couplets. Wilkes' friend Churchill is praised for writing effectively about liberty; and Camden, for his judgment against illegal general warrants and his assertion of freedom for all Englishmen whether of high or low degree. Algernon Sydney and John Hampden are invoked against the Scots and Bute, and Wilkes joins them. (A Whig poem!)

68-104. To John Wilkes, Esq. On the 20th of April, 1768.

"And all the World in Chains, but Cato, see." (2)

St J's C, Apr 12, 1768.

Wilkes, like Cato, wishes to be free.

68-105. To John Wilkes, Esq. Upon his Birth-Day, October 28, 1768.

"Livy, no more thy Heroes Deeds proclaim." (42)

St J's C, Oct 25, 1768.

HC. Eulogy on Wilkes, "The Scourge of Fav'rites, and the Rod of Tools," for his integrity as a freedom-fighter. Signed by Andrew Marvel (pseud.).

68-106. To the Administration on Mr. Wilkes's Confinement.

"All Scotland may stare, and all England may rail." (4)

St J's C, Dec 31, 1768.

Epigram. It is certainly poor politics to keep a smart man like Wilkes in jail, when he belongs in the administration.

68-107. To the Author of "The Present State of the Nation."

"To plan the Safety of the tott'ring State." (32)

PA, Dec 21, 1768.

HC. Let us praise George Grenville for preparing the country for future wars. The obvious way to lessen our debts is to increase our strength. (William Knox wrote the pamphlet; Burke answered it in 1769.)

68-108. To the Conqueror of Louisbourg, Newfoundland, and Canada, on the late noble Reward for all Victories.

"Let Amherst fall! Corruption said." (60)

G, Sep 27, 1768; PA, Sep 26, 1768; A Companion for a Leisure Hour (1769), pp. 154-8.

Ballad. A complaint because of the fall from grace of Lord Amherst who, through the machinations of Hillsborough, was removed from court. But he will be remembered in America. See 68-64, [Let Amherst go, his Sov'rain said].

68-109. To the Gentlemen, Clergy, and Freeholders of the County of Middlesex.

"Ye Voters of Middlesex, who Liberty love." (18)

PA, Jul 25, 1768.

Hexameter couplets. Waxes ironic at "Liberty Jack" Wilkes and his subversive bullies.

68-110. Verses on the Times, A.D. 1768.

"Breathing Sedition, a rash fiery Band." (24)

PA, Dec 6, 1768.

HC. Pessimistically describe the chaotic political scene, when liberty becomes license as a result of riots and demagoguery. (Wilkes, "the Mob-led Patriot," may be guilty.) From A Sketch of the Times: 69-18. Like "A Sketch for A.D. 1769": 69-199.

68-111. The Vicar of Brentford.

"Heretofore Wilkes, to work in his Country's Destruction." (4)

St J's C, Dec 15, 1768.

Epigram. Anti-Wilkes satire. Now Wilkes has an ally in Horne for his sedition.

68-112. Wilkes and Freedom: A New Ballad. Addressed to the Constitutional and Unbiassed Liverymen of London. Tune, -- <u>Geho</u>, <u>Dobbin</u>.

"Come all ye good Friends to your Country's Cause." (19)

PA, Mar 16, 1768; Battle of the Quills (1768), pp. 7-8. See 68-2.

An election song urging the London livery to choose Wilkes as their alderman because of his past record as an intrepid freedom fighter. (The "troubles" will begin anew.)

68-113. Wilkes and Liberty. To the tune of, -- When all the Attic Fire was fled, / And all the Roman Virtue dead, / Fair Freedom lost her Seat, &c.

"With longing look and fault'ring speech." (30)

L Chron 23 (Mar 10, 1768), 248; St J's C, Mar 10, 1768; SM 30 (Mar 1768), 153; Battle of the Quills (1768), p. 6. See 68-2.

Song in sixains. Wilkes returns to England from exile in France and hopes to be elected by the liverymen of London as alderman.

68-114. Wilkes in Masquerade. An Epigram.

"Wilkes, warm'd with patriot fire, had he been there." (4)

Ox M 1 (Oct 1768), 154.

Wilkes' merits are obscured by his jail sentence.

68-115. The whole present Dispute in Law and Politics.

"To contradict Wilkes, now M---- replies." (13)

St J's C, Jul 7, 1768; The Humours of the Times (London, 1771), p. 326; New Foundling Hospital For Wit, Pt. 3 (1769), p. 39.

HC. Satire on Judge Mansfield and the court. Mansfield is contradicted by Wilkes who insists Bute wishes to dominate the court.

68-116. [Ye Men of Middlesex prepare].

"Ye Men of Middlesex prepare." (6)

St J's C, Apr 12, 1768.

Epigram, sixain. Middlesex will suffer for supporting Wilkes.

Prints

68-117. [Avaunt ye troublers of a World's repose.]

"Avaunt ye troublers of a World's repose." (4)

London Magazine 37 (1768), frontispiece. Dolmetsch, pp. 44-5.

Britannia weeps because of the struggle for freedom in Corsica and the American colonies. The explanation of the print is given in the "Preface" to the 1768 volume of the London Magazine. After the complaint at "burdensome and oppressive taxes" and corruption, the explanation continues as follows: "The enemies of liberty have been but too successful in the late year. Our colonies have, hitherto, in vain, held out their supplicating hands for redress; and the brave Corsicans, who have so many years struggled for freedom, seem abandoned to Gallic tyranny."

68-118. Cancelled.

68-119. Liberty Revived. Tenax propositi.

"When Bute and his Faction had ravag'd the Land." (32)

Engr. broadside with quatrains in hexameters and derry down chorus. March 1768.

Stephens 4192 (IV, 430-1).

Song in praise of Wilkes, who stood up for freedom against the malicious Scotch, including Judge Mansfield, and returned from exile to stand for election as MP in March 1768. Others cited are those involved in Wilkes' history: Kidgell, Samuel Martin, Alexander Dunn, and Bishop Warburton (who was critical of the blasphemy in Wilkes' Essay on Woman).

68-120. The Many Headed Monster of Sumatra, or Liberty's Efforts against Ministerial Oppression; A Vision.

"The Shades of Night had long prevail'd." (28)

Engr. with OC. June 10, 1768.

Stephens 4231 (IV, 473-4).

OC. Dream vision. On the contest between Wilkes and the Duke of Grafton's ministry during Wilkes' imprisonment and his election for Middlesex. The monstrous dragon "Arbitrary Power" has many heads, among them Lord Bute, Sir Fletcher Norton, Judge Mansfield, and John Dunning (a lawyer).

68-121. The Scotch Victory. An Elegy wrote on reading the Inscription on the Tomb-Stone erected in Newington Church-yard to the Memory of William Allen junior.

"Arms, and the youth I sing, who guiltless fell." (76)

Engr. with quatrains. 1768.

Stephens 4196 (IV, 435-6).

On May 10, 1768, a numerous crowd of persons assembled before the King's Bench Prison, Southwark, and proposed to deliver John Wilkes, who, having surrendered himself prisoner, was there confined. The guards were sent for, the Riot Act was read. A disturbance followed, the soldiers were ordered to fire, and a youth named Allen was killed. In the poem, Grafton, Weymouth, and Barrington of the ministry are held responsible.

68-122. The Scots Triumph, or A Peep behind the Curtain.

"The Ancients had triumphs in Story we're told." (18)

Engr. with hexameter couplets. May 20, 1768.

Stephens 4195 (IV, 433-5).

Pro-Wilkes verse. The "true Sons of Liberty" pull Wilkes' triumphal carriage, but the oppressive foes of Liberty (Bute, Mansfield, Halifax, Fox, Sandwich, and the Devil) still continue to threaten Wilkes and Liberty. Wilkes was imprisoned in May 1768.

68-123. The Times, or 1768. [Plate 1]

"Behold corruption openly profest." (24)

Etching with HC. June 8, 1768.

Stephens 4242 (IV, 486-7).

The times are in a parlous state, and Bute is to blame. Wilkes, the King, General Warrants, Lord Mansfield, Scotland, and William Allen are cited.

68-124. -----. [Plate 2]

"The prickear'd [Ass] an honest Brute." (c. 90)

Etching with rebus in OC. 1768.

Stephens 4243 (IV, 487-8).

Satire on the viciousness of the present age, caused by Bute and his bribery. The satire includes Pitt who "sold his Country for a Name," and many others who bartered honesty for gold. But as Temple, Wilkes, Glyn, Rockingham, and Granby defend the cause of freedom, there is still hope that the monumental column of liberty with the names of the Whig heroes, Hampden, Sidney, Russell, Marvell (with Cromwell looking down from above) will continue to stand.

1769   Books & Pamphlets

69-1. Alves, Robert.
The Miseries of War: An Elegy. Written anno 1769.

"Whither advance yon hosts in gleaming arms." (124)

In 82-1: Poems, pp. 78-86.

Elegiac stanzas. A protest by a Scottish poet at destructive war, including civil war, brought on by "Ambition" and causing "Rage and Tumult," etc. Bids "sweet Charity" to inspire "on earth the sparks of heavenly love." But "Still Europe sends her madding sons to war"--in Germany, in "both Indies"--and now Britain is infected as the American colonies, "her rebel-sons their parent scorn," and the French bloody Corsica, "Paoli's isle." (Printed in the collected poems, this elegy takes on added significance.)

69-2. [Barbauld, Anna Laetitia (Aikin)]
Corsica. (Written in the year 1769.)

"Hail generous Corsica! unconquer'd isle." (c. 190)

In her Poems (London: Johnson, 1773), pp. 1-12.

Notices: CR 35 (May 1773), 192-5; MR 48 (Jan 1773), 54-6.

Copies: BL 643.k.9 (9), 11656.e.77 (reissue, 1773), 11633.bb.3 (3rd ed, corrected); NUC CSmH, CtY, ICN, ICU, IU, MB, NN, PPL.

(Five editions by 1777; I have used the 3rd.) Blank verse. Celebrates the Corsican struggle for liberty. Britons should catch the contagion of the heroic ardor from the Corsicans, and Boswell is commended for taking this view. The primitive nature of Corsica is where Liberty loves to range; so if the Corsicans are determined to be free, they will never succumb to oppression, French or Genoese. However, although led by such a gallant chief as Paoli, Corsica was overwhelmed, "by numbers crush'd,/ Admired, unaided fell."

69-3. The Blessings of Liberty Displayed; With the Fall of Corsica: A Poem.
London: Bladon & Gardner, 1769. 41p.

"Deign, heav'n-born LIBERTY, to aid my song." (c. 800)

Notices: CR 28 (Nov 1769), 379, & 30 (Jul 1770). 71 (3rd ed); MR 41 (Nov 1769), 394; G, Nov 10-11, 1769; L Chron 26 (Nov 16, 1769), 488.

Copies: NUC IU.

HC. Addressed to the Liverymen of London. Begins with attack on Grafton, prime minister, and "his patron Bute," and then proceeds to themes significant to liberty: the blessings of constitutional liberty, natural rights protected by law; objections to the tyrannizing and plundering of India, which enables nabobs to threaten the constitution with their enormous wealth and power; further objections to a standing army, the worst foe to liberty (but a navy is fine); objections to the slave trade and the cruelty of slavery, urging that slavery be made illegal in Britain. Regarding America (a strong section in this poem), notes the colonists are oppressed by placemen, warships, hostile troops, and bishops, "priestly Lords," who would undermine their religion. Urges the Americans to resist this tyranny and the merchants to assist them. Liberty, pleased to have the support of London, asks that the Scots not suffer unjust criticism, for they too love freedom; concludes with a mournful narrative of the defeat of Paoli and the Corsicans by the French, blaming the failure to secure British help upon the oppressors at home. The exiled Paoli is welcomed to Britain.

69-4. Cockings, George.
  The Paoliad, or Corsican Memoirs: A Poem.
  London: Cooke, 1769. 5-44p.

"Whene'er the Muse with martial transport fir'd." (c. 1100)

Copies: Bod Godwyn Pamph 1280; NUC IU, MH.

HC. Narrative history of the Corsican resistance to tyranny, with a detailing of the struggle against Genoa and France, until final defeat by the French forces, to the dismay of the British who, he hopes, will some day assist the Corsicans and Paoli in their fight for freedom. Refers to Boswell's account of Corsica.

69-5. Cooke, William.
  The Conquest of Quebec: A Poem. Occasioned by the Premium offered by the Right Honourable the Earl of Litchfield, Chancellor of the University of Oxford.
  London: Davis & Reymers, 1769. 34p.

"Thrice happy! who no future ills descry." (514)

Notices: CR 27 (Jun 1769), 467-9; MR 40 (Jun 1769), 515-17.

Copies: BL 11630.d.16 (10), 11632.g.13; NUC DLC, MH, RPJCB.

HC. The poet honors the British commanders (Howe, Townshend, Murray, Monckton) who succeeded in defeating the French at Quebec. Describes the St. Lawrence River, and relates in detail the ascent up the heights to the Plains of Abraham and the battle that ensued, in which Wolfe, Monckton, and Montcalm died. Wolfe is made to say that "The sword of the Sons of Freedom . . . defends . . . the injur'd Colonies" (ll. 265-6). The description of the Indian allies of the French forms an interesting section.

69-6. Greene, Edward Burnaby.
Liberty.

"Here on my much lov'd native shore." (234)

In 71-2: *Poetical Essays*, pp. 3-13.

Irregular Pindaric ode. Probably written 1769. A generalized hymn to Liberty, celebrating the spirit from ancient Greek and Roman times to the present in an apparently non-political manner except when it becomes egalitarian (or levelling) and asserts themes that defend the function of satire to express thoughts that are anti-Gallic, anti-Stuart, anti-Papal, and hostile to faction and corruption. In the contemporary context of "Wilkes and Liberty" and the Whig objections to the secret influence of Tory Bute, this sublime poem may have significant political relevance.

69-7. Hazard, Joseph.
The Conquest of Quebec. A Poem. By Joseph Hazard, of Lincoln College, Oxford. Oxford: James Fletcher; London: J. Fletcher, 1769. 5-20p.

"Wrapt in Oblivion's Shroud the youthful Muse." (c. 260)

Notices: CR 27 (Jun 1769), 469; MR 40 (Jun 1769), 517-19; Lloyd's Eve Post 24 (May 10, 1769), 454.

Sabin 31097.

Copies: BL 11633.h.6; NUC CtY, DLC, RPJCB.

Blank verse. Another poem that competed for the Earl of Litchfield's award at Oxford. Details Wolfe's ascent to the Plains of Abraham, the battle between the French and English forces before Quebec, the defeat of the French, and the death of Wolfe. A map of Quebec accompanies the text.

69-8. The Middlesex Freeholder; or, the Triumph of Liberty. Addressed to the Leading Members of the Society at the London Tavern, Supporters of the Bill of Rights. By a Gentleman of Middlesex.
London: Bladon, 1769. 5-18p.

"Ye men of Middlesex--a noble train." (c. 210)

Notices: CR 27 (Mar 1769), 234; MR 40 (Mar 1769), 251.

Copies: NUC MH, PU.

HC. Praise of the Middlesex voter who has courageously supported Glynn and restored Wilkes despite bribes and threats to his life (the fearful St. George's Fields massacre ordered by Bute is mentioned in this context). A Briton will not stand unconcerned when his rights are invaded and his country sold. If need be, he will give his life for freedom: "Kings may make LORDS--but cannot make a MAN." (The occasion is the election victory of Wilkes, and the continued fear of violent suppression after the St. George's Fields massacre.)

69-9. The Middlesex Petition Inversed.
London: Bladon, 1769. 23p.

"The Middlesex Freeholders' humble Petition." (186)

Notices: CR 28 (Jul 1769), 71; MR 41 (Aug 1769), 160; G, June 29, 1769; Lloyd's Eve Post 24 (May 29, 1769), 521; L Chron 25 (Jun 25, 1769), 615; R Mag 19 (Jun 1769), 276-8.

Copies: NUC InU, MH.

Dactylic tetrameter. The Middlesex Petition (May 24, 1769) against arbitrary government, signed by 1565 freeholders led by Wilkes, John Glynn, and John Horne, accompanies the verse rendition. The petition to the King complains of all those grievances suffered in the county, the nation, "the whole British empire," including America--arrests under a general warrant, homes invaded, bodies imprisoned illegally, habeas corpus eluded, printers punished without a jury trial, attacks on the liberty of the press, trial by jury discountenanced, execution by the military, etc. See #34 for the specific reference to America. This petition sums up all the grievances against the arbitrary government of the time, similar to those expressed by the Americans. It is essentially a Whig assertion of liberty.
For other publications of the prose, see, e. g., L Chron 25 (May 30, 1769), 517, and GM 39 (Jun 1769), 289-92, where a comparison with American grievances is made.

69-10. An Ode to the People of England.
London: Kearsly et al., 1769. 12p.

"Ye guardian Powers! who us'd to smile." (168)

Notices: CR 28 (Dec 1769), 460; MR 42 (Jan 1770), 75; L Chron 26 (Dec 14, 1769), 580; LM 38 (Dec 1769), 642.

Copies: NUC   CtY, IU, PPL.

Regular Horatian ode. Complains of the way law and freedom are trampled down in "these debas'd, inglorious days" by "the foes of Liberty . . . with Discord at their head." Steers a middle course between Mansfield and Camden, Chatham and Grafton. A severe criticism of Bute is made in stanzas 23-24.

69-11. An Ode upon the Present Period of Time; With A Letter to The Right Honourable George Grenville.
   London: Almon, 1769. iii-iv, 5-12p.

"In Times like these, when party rage." (126)

Notices: CR 27 (Jan 1769), 72; MR 40 (Jan 1769), 87; GM 39 (Mar 1769), 157; L Chron 25 (Jan 1769), 16; LM 38 (Feb 1769), 104; W Eve Post, Jan 28, 1769.

Copies: BL 1488.i.28 (2); NUC   CtY, IU, MH.

Regular Horatian ode. Panegyric on George Grenville, for his "Public Virtue." Britain's true friend, unlike the Bedfords, Grafton, he must return to active political life in order to "avert a Nation's fall." Ascribed to "the Hon. Henry Seymour, half-brother of the Earl of Sandwich," by Horace Walpole. (Also in New Foundling Hospital for Wit, Pt. 3 [1769], pp. 161-6, & [1786], vol. I, pp. 85-9.)

69-12. A Poem Humbly inscribed to John Wilkes, Esq.

"Bless'd by the anxious crowd that murm'ring wait." (102)

In English Liberty: Being a Collection of Interesting Tracts, From the Year 1762 to 1769. Containing the Private Correspondence, Public Letters, Speeches, and Addresses of John Wilkes, Esq. (London: Baldwin & Woodgate, [1769]), pp. vii-xi.

Copies: NUC CSmH, CtY, ICN, ICU, MB.

HC. Dedicated to Wilkes, this--the only poem in the collection--urges him to pursue his plan, because his cause and liberty's are identical. Reviews the struggle for Wilkes, now serving his sentence in the King's Bench Prison, and for liberty, emphasizing the influence of Bute, and the role of Barrington, Mansfield, and Norton in suppressing the patriot mob and free speech. (The murder of Clarke at Brentford and of young Allen, by Scotch soldiers, at St. George's Fields on

May 10, 1768, are understood.) Wilkes had won the Middlesex election; but, being in prison serving a sentence, he was denied his seat, which was given to Luttrell. Yet Wilkes will be free, his sentence now half-expired, and it is hoped the King will pardon him.

69-13. Political Society: A Poetical Essay. Addressed to John Wilkes, Esq;
  London: Flexney, 1769. 40p.

"While the whole Nation's fill'd with dire alarms." (c. 700)

Notices: CR 27 (Feb 1769), 154-5; MR 40 (Apr 1769), 336-7; L Eve Post, May 7, 1771; W Eve Post, Feb 4, 1769.

Copies: Bod Godwyn Pamph 1703; NUC CtY.

HC. A Whig statement on government arguing against Tory ideas--divine hereditary right to rule, passive obedience to a tyrant, servility. Objects to the "shameful peace" and corruption; insists on virtue and merit as measures of honor and worth, the models being Hampden, Sidney, Paoli. Praises Whig leaders--Savile, Burke, Rockingham, Camden, and Wilkes who stands for "Firmness" against "licentious pow'r" and "the Idol Thane," Bute. America is cited as "Columbia." Perhaps by Archibald Maxwell.

69-14. Pottinger, Israel.
  Stanzas Sacred To Liberty. To Which Are Added, The Farringdon Election, a Ballad. The Poet's Curse, a Fragment. By I. Pottinger.
  London: Bingley, 1769. 20p.

Stanzas. "Is Churchill dead--and shall no other pen." (128) pp. 5-13.

Farringdon Election. "God prosper long our good Lord May'r." (64) pp. 14-18.

The Poet's Curse. "Lives there a wretch so dead to England's weal." (20) pp. 19-20.

Notices: CR 27 (Feb 1769), 155; MR 40 (Feb 1769), 176; LM 38 (May 1769), 268; Ox M 2 (Feb 1769), 51, 71.

Copies: NUC CtY.

Dedication to George Bellas, alderman, asserts Pottinger's loyalty to Wilkes and liberty. Heroic stanzas declare for patriot integrity against power and corruption; for Wilkes as the exemplar of freedom against Bute. The poet curses Bute and treacherous Scotsmen who endanger the throne.

69-15. [Richardson, William]
  Corsica: A Poetical Address.
  London: Almon, 1769. 5-18p.

Notices: CR 27 (May 1769), 234; MR 40 (May 1769), 250.

Copies: NUC CtY, InU, TxU.

69-16. [-----]
-----. The Second Edition.
   Glasgow: Foulis, 1769. 5-15p.

   "Briton's awake! shake off th'unseemly bands." (c. 280)

   Copies: BL 992.b.21.

   Blank verse. This edition is enlarged and corrected. The poet grieves for the Corsicans, defeated by the French, their freedom and independence gone; but he urges Britain to assist them in achieving liberty. (Also in 74-14: Poems, Chiefly Rural [Glasgow: Foulis, 1774] and [1781], entitled "Corsica. Written at St. Petersburgh, 1768.")

69-17. The Siege of Quebec.
   London: Allen, Fletcher, & Walter, 1769. 30p.

   "Descend, Apollo, and ye tuneful Nine." (c. 530)

   Notices: CR 28 (Dec 1769), 464; MR 42 (Jan 1770), 76.

   Copies: NUC CtY, DLC, RPJCB.

   HC. Celebrates the great English success at Quebec by Wolfe, Monckton, Townshend, and Murray of the army, and Saunders, Holmes, and Durell of the navy. A narrative of the campaign in epic style, from beginning to end--the defeat of the French, the capitulation of the town, the funerals of Wolfe and Montcalm. Closes with a panegyric on Pitt.

69-18. A Sketch of the Times, For A.D. 1769, Corrected and Enlarged: And now reprinted for A.D. 1771.
   London: Dodsley, 1771. 11p.

   "Breathing sedition, a rash fiery band." (100)

   Copies: CtY, MH.

   HC. A severe indictment of the hypocritical, rebellious, and seditious rioters crying for liberty but only succeeding in exercising license and falling into lawlessness and anarchy--to the dismay of a kind, humane, just King who himself cherishes freedom. These so-called patriots, tools of faction, believe in equality (or levelling) and wish to abolish the nobility, yet at home they rule like brutal, petty tyrants. Horace Walpole identifies his brother Sir Edward as the author of this poem. See 69-199 for a possible first version.

69-19. Stevenson, John Hall.
A Tory Ode.

"I tried to sing, and touch'd my strings." (48)

Ode.

"Full long to laughter-loving fancy wed." (40)

In <u>Lyric Consolations, with the speech of Alderman W[ilkes] delivered in a dream at the King's Bench Prison the evening of his inauguration</u> (London: Almon, 1769), pp. 30-5, 65-6. Also in Stevenson's <u>Works</u> (London: Debrett, 1795), II, 23-5, 48-50.

Notices: CR 27 (May 1769), 396-7; MR 40 (Apr 1769), 351-2.

Copies: NUC CtY, ICN, IEN, MH, NIC, NcD.

Both poems are imitations of Horace. "A Tory Ode" alludes to the accession of the Tories to power and places soon after the accession of George III. The Scottish Tories have driven out the Whigs; Bute and Mansfield rule, imposing (their kind of) civic order as far west as the lands across the Atlantic. (Indians at Niagara are cited.)
"Ode," an elegy, mourns officers who died in the last war: Braddock, Wolfe, Howe, and others.

69-20. The Times. A Poem.
London: Almon, 1769. 23p.

"While fame, O Britain, hovers o'er." (318)

Notices: CR 27 (Jun 1769), 471; MR 40 (Apr 1769), 335-6; Lloyd's Evc Post 24 (Apr 7, 1769), 341; L Chron 25 (Apr 6, 1769), 336.

Copies: CtY, MiU, NcD.

Sixains, made of octosyllabic couplets. Address to Britons to rouse and save their country from the corruption of the despots. Oppression is preparing coercion; the laws are perverted by ruffians; assassins hired for public murder, the rights of the people invaded; and Wilkes, the pattern of virtue and only friend of his country, unjustly imprisoned, falsely charged with sedition, impiety, and obscenity. The Scotch and Allen are cited.

69-21. Tournay, Thomas.
Ambition. An Epistle to Paoli. By the Rev. T. Tournay.
London: Dilly, 1769. 30p.

"Illustrious Chief! whose firm undaunted soul." (c. 360)

Notices: CR 27 (Apr 1769), 311-13; MR 40 (Apr 1769), 339-40; L Chron 25 (Mar 21, 1769), 273.

Copies: NUC CtY, ICN, MiU, NjP, NIC, PU.

HC. Inscribed to John Sawbridge. Although Corsica's struggle against the French has been betrayed by the Scotch influence over British government, there are Britons still who sympathize with the cause of Paoli. Ambition--the desire for conquest, the "rage for pow'r," ruthless oppression, arbitrary power that subverts "the native rights of human kind" and "the unalienable rights of all"--destroys freedom. (Asserts Algernon Sidney's Whig ideology over Robert Filmer's Toryism.) T. objects to slavery, black and white, and declares that Britain, motivated by freedom, should not "seek t'enslave the western hemisphere." Finally, he urges Paoli to continue the good fight for freedom and justice.

Serials

69-22. [A was Ambition, that Foe to Mankind.]

"A was Ambition, that Foe to Mankind." (24)

St J's C, Sep 28, 1769.

HC. Alphabet (Abcedarian) poem, reviews the politics in a generally moral way --faction, knavery, lying, grumbling, etc., -- and particularly belittles Junius, Horne, and Wilkes.

69-23. An accurate Account of the several Monies expended by a certain Society from the time of its Foundation, to the 1st Day of April, 1769.

"To three months allowance of mutton and beef." (62)

W Eve Post, Apr 1, 1769.

Hexameter couplets. Satire on the followers of Wilkes and Horne. A bill by the Society for the Support of Magna Charta and the Bill of Rights listing charges. Cited are Allen and Clarke.

69-24. An Acrostic. [Grafton.]

"Gen'rous and frank when int'rest is thy aim." (7)

MJ, May 20, 1769.

HC. Satire on Grafton.

69-25. An Acrostic. [Wilkes.]

"Wicked, and much too wicked for a Rake." (6)

PA, Jun 2, 1769.

HC. Wilkes, wicked rabble rouser, should stay in prison.

69-26. An Address to a Provincial Bashaw.

"When elevated worth commands esteem." (104)

LM 38 (Aug 1769), 441-2.

Quatrains, "addressed to the Governor of a North American Colony," Francis Bernard. A personal satire that originated in America.

69-27. An Address to Liberty.

"Dear Liberty, thou sacred name." (12)

MJ, Apr 8, 1769.

Quatrains. The people are willing to risk their lives for liberty.

69-28. Address to Lord Bute.

"See, mighty Bute, how Stripling Grafton sweats." (4)

St J's C, Jul 25, 1769.

Epigram. Satire on Grafton, disciple of Bute, both of Stuart origin. (Augustus Henry Fitzroy, 3rd Duke of Grafton, 1st Lord of the Treasury, July 1766-Jan. 1770.)

69-29. An Alphabet for Little Masters.

"A stands for Asses and Administration." (26)

Freeman's J, Aug 19, 1769.

Alphabet poem, naming politicians and newsworthy persons--e.g., Allen (killed in St. George's Fields), Grafton, Chatham, North, Mansfield, Fletcher Norton, Wilkes. Corruption also is cited.

69-30. Another Ode. To the Same Tune as that in the Public Advertiser of Wednesday Last.

"Fit Tool for such a wicked Cause." (42)

PA, Aug 28, 1769; St J's C, Aug 26, 1769.

Ode in sixains. A reaction to Col. Luttrell who was chosen to take Wilkes's seat in the Commons. He should be forgotten, despite his support of several politicians and courtiers -- Mansfield, Grafton, and others. (The ode is written against the "Ode to Colonel Luttrell," in PA, Aug 23, 1769.)

69-31. Answer to the Verses on Paoli's Arrival, inserted in this Paper of the 6th. By the Author of the First.

"I am the Man, if impious, 'tis my Pride." (20)

PA, Oct 10, 1769.

HC warning Paoli not to trust the English King and his court.

69-32. [Astraea, fairest of the heav'nly race.]

"Astraea, fairest of the heav'nly race." (46)

MJ, Oct 5, 1769.

HC. Astraea, the Goddess of Justice, has no place in England, and the court is to blame.

69-33. [At the Great London Tavern in Bishopsgate Street.]

"At the Great London Tavern in Bishopsgate Street." (18)

PA, Apr 29, 1769; W Eve Post, Apr 27, 1769.

Hexameter couplets. Ironic satire on the Society for the Support of the Bill of Rights who resolve (lamely) to ignore those who wish to suppress the organization.

69-34. [Augment the Army. Pay for Swords and Guns.]

"Augment the Army. Pay for Swords and Guns." (4)

Freeman's J, Oct 3, 1769.

Epigram. Objects to the attempt to enlarge the army at the expense of freedom. St. George's Fields cited.

69-35. A Ballad.

"Ye Pot Politicians, who Forty-five roar." (16)

W Eve Post, Jan 3, 1769.

Song. Anti-Wilkes satire. Wilkes' supporters are "the spawn of Old Nol" (Cromwell), and hypocrites (Presbyterians.)

69-36. [The Battle of Brentford let others record.]

"The Battle of Brentford let others record." (38)

St J's C, Apr 11, 1769.

Song. A ballad narrating the problems of the electoral process in Brentford involving Serjeant John Glynn.

69-37. [Beneath a neighbouring Oak.]

"Beneath a neighbouring Oak." (33)

Ox M 2 (May 1769), 188.

Epitaph inscription on the political death of Wilkes.

69-38. Boswell, James.
Verses in the Character of a Corsican, at Shakespeare's Jubilee, at Stratford upon Avon, Sept. 6, 1769.

"From the rude banks of Golo's rapid flood." (46)

Lloyd's 25 (Sep 8, 1769), 244; L Chron 26 (Sep 12, 1769), 344; PA, Sep 11, 1769; RM 19 (Sep 1769), 392-3; SM 31 (Sep 1769), 488; WM 6 (Oct 12, 1769), 51; W Eve Post, Sep 9, 1769.

HC. Boswell carries his plea for Paoli and Corsican freedom to Stratford.

69-39. Boyce, Samuel.
An Ode. Addressed to Sir Joseph Mawbey, Bart.

"Curst be the man that bends with awe." (24)

MJ, Apr 4, 1769.

Regular (Horatian) ode in sixains. Praise of Mawbey, Alderman of London, for his patriotic support of freedom and the people's rights. (Mawbey was also MP for London.)

69-40. [Britain, thou'st seldom seen thyself thus fated.]

"Britain, thou'st seldom seen thyself thus fated." (2)

St J's C, Apr 29, 1769.

A paradox--the King is "more lov'd," but his ministers are "more hated."

69-41. Britannia Deploring the Fate of Mr. Wilkes.

"And O my Wilkes, dear injur'd, honour'd name." (34)

Free M 1 (Sep 1769), 49-50; MJ, Aug 29, 1769.

HC. Praise of Wilkes, the martyr for freedom, imprisoned by Mansfield.

69-42. Britannia's Sigh.

"While Law and Liberty's made Sport on." (4)

St J's C, Feb 14, 1769.

Epigram. It is not fair that corrupt Norton is favored, but Wilkes still persecuted.

69-43. [But if there rise some public Discontent.]

"But if there rise some public Discontent." (20)

St J's C, Apr 13, 1769.

Quatrains. "Imperfect" poem. Advice from a Tory politician in the ministry on how to deal with the Opposition: Anyone who opposes us is called factious. Cited are Mc-Quirk (who attempted assassination of Wilkes), Allen and Clark (the martyrs of freedom).

69-44. The Caps of Liberty. A new Birth-day Ballad on a famous Patriot. To the Tune of Moll Spriggins.

"When the Vicar of Horne had lost." (81)

RM 19 (Nov 1769), 317; W Eve Post, Nov 11, 1769.

Song, protesting Wilkes' demagoguery that has cheapened and prostituted liberty. He is to be distrusted like Cromwell. Parson Horne also cited. The destruction of the Roman republic is the parallel case.

69-45. A Card to John Wilkes, Esq.

"Thou know'st, O Wilkes, th' Event of thy Dispute." (8)

St J's C, Apr 13, 1769; The Patriotic Miscellany (London: Booth, 1769), p. 25.

A declaration of sympathy for Wilkes, who has borne much mistreatment for his opposition to Bute and tyranny. "Right will prevail at last."

69-46. The Character of Cato.

"No stings of private hate his peace infest." (29)

W Eve Post, Dec 16, 1769.

HC. The character of Cato -- a genuine disinterested patriot, the ideal political hero. The image of Cato is the classical icon of the patriot. The portrait, by implication, is a criticism of the corrupt politician.

69-47. Character of John Wilkes, Esq;

"Sure Wilkes's character is hard to know." (6)

L Chron 25 (Feb 2, 1769), 120; WM 3 (Mar 2, 1769), 276.

HC. It is difficult to assess Wilkes' character -- some praise him as patriot, others damn him as devil.

69-48. A Circular Letter. To ----- -----, &c.

"We having infring'd on your freedom and laws." (66)

Ox M 2 (Apr 1769), 150.

Hexameter couplets. Ironic satire. The persona of a member of the ministry betrays corruption as he asks for support in the persecution of Wilkes. The letter is apparently addressed to the aldermen of London.

69-49. The Consolation.

"Britannia, bid thy Sons take Heart." (4)

St J's C, Feb 14, 1769.

Epigram. As Britons continue to fight for Magna Charta, King George will soon espouse the cause of liberty. (Vain hope!)

69-50. Corsica. An Ode.

"Rise, Muse, and in immortal Lays." (36)

PA, Jun 22, 1769.

Regular ode in sixains in praise of the unconquerable Paoli and his Corsicans who, despite France, still maintain the spirit of liberty. Paoli seeks safety in a foreign country.

69-51. Cunningham, John.
Occasional Stanzas for the Play, performed at Sunderland, for the Benefit of those glorious Sons of Liberty, the Corsicans.

"Who can behold with an unpitying eye." (24)

Lloyd's 24 (Feb 15, 1769), 170.

Sixains. Expression of sympathy for the Corsicans fighting for freedom against the French. Britain should help!

69-52. Curtius and Felton.

"When Earth yawn'd wide, to swallow antient Rome." (10)

St J's C, Sep 12, 1769.

HC. Curtius and Felton, two patriot martyrs, are contrasted, but British Felton was greater because he smote a tyrant.

69-53. Dialogue between the two Heads on Temple Bar.

"The dull dismal watchmen were going their rounds." (46)

MJ, May 2, 1769.

Hexameter couplets. Two Scotch rebel traitors, Fletcher and Townley, executed twenty-three years ago, think it strange that now the Scotch are prospering at court, that the Tories have displaced the Whigs. See 69-A, A Conversation between the Two Heads. . . .

69-54. The Dover Freemen. A New Song.

"Come let's join hand in hand, my brave Freemen all." (31)

Lloyd's 25 (Sep 25, 1769), 300.

An election song, adapted by the Americans: "Not as Slaves, but as Freemen, our Votes we will give."

69-55. The Dream. (In imitation of Chevy Chace.)

"Three nights ago, full tir'd and spent." (88)

MJ, May 16, 1769.

Ballad. On Wilkes' election, but rejection by the Commons. Cited are Luttrell and Glynn.

69-56. An Elegy written in St. Bride's Churchyard; in imitation of Gray's Elegy on a Country Church Yard.

"The bell tolls six, the knell of parting day." (44)

WM 3 (Feb 16, 1769), 214.

Elegiac quatrains. Satire on the city rulers, the mayor Harley and the aldermen, for failing to help Wilkes and side with Glynn.

69-57. An Englishman's Soliloquy. Inscribed to Doctor Musgrave.

"What am I, say? -- or on what spot of land." (46)

Free M 1 (Nov 1769), 162-3; Ox M 3 (Nov 1769), 191.

HC. A patriot describes his conditioning in English liberty -- as opposed to French tyranny, and his willingness to die for the continuation of liberty. (Musgrave was a physician and political polemicist.

69-58. An Epigram.

"The children of England, with Danger beset." (4)

L Chron 25 (Mar 23, 1769), 287; PA, Mar 24, 1769.

The people are attracted to Wilkes, Allen, and Horne, neglecting religion and the King.

69-59. Epigram.

"From east to west, from north to south." (8)

MJ, Jun 8, 1769.

Quatrains. Everyone knows Allen was murdered upon the orders of Weymouth, and his murderers were paid by Barrington.

69-60. Epigram.

"Says vaunting Bute, 'In times to come.'" (8)

Free M 1 (Sep 1769), 51.

Satire on Bute's boast that he made a glorious peace.

69-61. Epigram.

"Tortur'd with ease, most nobles daily live." (4)

MJ, Jul 8, 1769.

Satire on Grafton who has no time to enjoy his wealth.

69-62. Epigram on the Conquest of Corsica.

"Some Points by Gold you've gain'd; some few by Fight." (2)

PA, Sep 14, 1769.

France conquered Corsica by force and fraud, not by right.

69-63. Epigram on the Scarcity of Poetical Writers against the Present Administration.

"Th' indignant Muse has left to simple Prose." (6)

St J's C, Dec 14, 1769.

HC. Satire on Grafton about whom the poetic muse finds it difficult to write. (The reference is to Junius' essays.)

69-64. Epigram III of the First Book of Martial imitated. To John Wilkes, Esq; Alderman of Farringdon Ward Without.

"O Thou! acknowledg'd Great as well as good." (9)

PA, Apr 7, 1769.

Triplets. Praise of Wilkes for his patriot virtues -- incorruptible, unselfish, honest, poor. Thus he has been elected three times by the people, although rejected by the House of Commons.

69-65. Epigrams. For the Tomb of James the First.

"Here lies that wretched Fav'rite-ridden Thing." (8)

PA, Jan 6, 1769.

Three satires against the King and the court.

69-66. Epitaph.

"Here rests his Head upon the Lap of Earth." (12)

L Chron 26 (Jul 27, 1769), 103; St J's C, Jul 25, 1769.

Elegiac stanzas. Parody of the epitaph in Gray's Elegy in which Gray is satirized for the flattery of his Installation Ode (69-135 & Gray, 69-A), evidence of corruption because it allegedly secured him a large pension.

69-67. Epitaph for the Late Mr. Charles Churchill, buried at Dover in Kent.

"Here when his conqu'ring Bands proud Julius led." (12)

BLJ, Sep 2, 1769; W Eve Post, Aug 26, 1769; PA, Aug 25, 1769; St J's C, Aug 24, 1769.

HC. Grieve for Churchill, the last and best of patriot poets. See 69-A, Underwood.

69-68. Epitaph, occasioned by a Demise mentioned in a Late Publication of Letters.

"Here, underneath, great Ch---m lies." (4)

St J's C, Dec 14, 1769.

Wilkes has dug Chatham's political grave.

69-69. An Epitaph on L[ibert]y.

"Here lie the remains of Constitutional L-----y." (23)

L Chron 25 (Apr 18, 1769), 376; Ox M 2 (Apr 1769), 149; WM 4 (Apr 27, 1769), 116; W Eve Post, Apr 18, 1769.

Inscription on the death of liberty occasioned "by a Wound . . . received in France" by Bute six years ago. (Reference is to the peace.)

69-70. An Epitaph to be inscribed on the Sepulchre of J. W. in 45 lines.

"Who lyes here." (45)

WM 4 (Apr 13, 1769), 53.

Inscription. A satire on Wilkes whose political death is "unregretted."

69-71. Extempore.

"Great is the man, and great is his reward." (6)

The Patriotic Miscellany (London: Booth, 1769), p. 70.

HC. Panegyric on Wilkes, like Cato a fighter for freedom against despots.

69-72. Extempore.

"Shall a curst ministry infringe our laws." (8)

MJ, May 30, 1769.

HC. The people will continue to support Wilkes against the ministry.

69-73. Extempore. [And] On Reading Some Verses in which Mr. Wilkes is compared to Cato.

Great is the man, and great is his reward." (10)

MJ, Apr 13 & 15, 1769.

Wilkes is our Cato, a freedom-fighter against ministerial tyranny. But he must not suffer Cato's fate.

69-74. Extempore. On Mr. Wilkes Being Made an Alderman.

"An Alderman in Chains! -- I've heard of such a Sight." (4)

PA, Jan 7, 1769.

Epigram. Praise of Wilkes, an alderman with brains.

69-75. Extempore. On Mr. Wilkes's Birth-Day.

"The Patriot band in festal chorus join." (4)

MJ, Oct 26, 1769.

Epigram. Wilkes is toasted -- the patriot in prison is still "great" and free.

69-76. Extempore. On Seeing a Pardon for MacQuirk in the Papers.

"A Pardon fortune gives MacQuirk." (12)

MJ, Apr 25, 1769; The Patriotic Miscellany (London & Norwich: Booth, 1769), pp. 72-3.

Epigram, sixains. The injustice of pardoning MacQuirk, who attempted to assassinate Wilkes, and of imprisoning Wilkes for his political writings is patent.

69-77. Extempore on Seeing Junius's Last Spirited Letter.

"Great Churchill's Pen for Satire was renown'd." (6)

BLJ, Dec 30, 1769; St J's C, Dec 26, 1769.

HC. Junius is equal to Churchill as a satirist -- the one in prose, the other in verse.

69-78. Extempore, on the Report that a Certain Unpopular Baronet would be advanced to the Peerage.

"In former times, (but heaven be praised)." (8)

MJ, Apr 4, 1769; The Patriotic Miscellany (London & Norwich: Booth, 1769), p. 68.

Quatrains. Satire on the contemptible nobility.

69-79. Extempore on the Times.

"Tories, who Brunswick's house oft damn'd." (8)

MJ, May 20, 1769.

Quatrains. Tories are now favored because of Bute, while Whigs are in disrepute.

69-80. Extempore. On Three Brewers Voting for a Late Expulsion.

"When men their votes thus prostitute." (8)

MJ, Apr 28, 1769.

Quatrains. The three brewers in Parliament joined with Stephen Fox, Baron Holland, a tool of Bute, and voted to expel Wilkes. They should be boycotted. They are John Calvert, Samuel Whitbread, and Henry Thrale, friend of Samuel Johnson.

69-81 Extempore, spoken among Mr. Wilkes's and Mr. Glynn's Hearty Well Wishers at Cowbridge in Glamorganshire.

"If Wilkes and Liberty should e'er be bought." (8)

St J's C, Jan 3, 1769.

HC. "Wilkes and liberty" can never be bribed. Cited are Mansfield, Fletcher Norton, Grenville, Beauchamp Proctor (who was defeated by Glynn).

69-82. A Fashionable Wish.

"With forty thousand Acres not content." (6)

St J's C, Jan 12, 1769.

HC. Satire on the voting system, on rich landowners who engage in bribery. A mock wish for a huge estate to control votes.

69-83. The Female Politician.

"Or in, or out." (18)

RM 19 (Mar 1769), 135-6.

Sixains by a female politician who couldn't care less for Wilkes and Horne, Coates and Glynn, Broughton or Allen and the politics that fire up mobs.

69-84. The Following Lines Appeared in all the American Papers, immediately upon a Government Officer's taking leave of a certain House of Assembly, in one of the Provinces there.

"Go hated ---, by all countries curs'd." (6)

Lloyd's 25 (Sep 13, 1769), 260.

HC. An unpopular government officer leaves for Britain and is cursed by the American poet. (The officer is Francis Bernard, Governor of Massachusetts.)

69-85. Forty-five Dozen of Candle. To Mr. Alderman White of Winchester, on his Present to Mr. Wilkes, of forty-five Dozen of Candle.

"What Hero, what King." (30)

L Chron 26 (Oct 21, 1769), 393; RM 19 (Oct 1769), 270; St J's C, Oct 19, 1769.

Song. For his birthday, Wilkes has been given a gift of 45 dozen candles; but the giver should beware of Wilkes.

69-86. The Fox Chace. To the Tune of, ---- "The Hounds are all out."

"Ye Hunters so bold who delight in a Chace." (37)

Free M 1 (Dec 1769; Feb 1770), inserts post 220 & 322.

Song. Lyric with music. The freeholders and livery of Coventry follow those of London and York and Devon in chasing Bute to France.

69-87. [Freeholders of Middlesex.]

"Freeholders of Middlesex." (c. 50)

MJ, Apr 15, 1769; Free M, Apr 29, 1769.

Inscription. The printer of the Middlesex Journal urges the people to assert their natural rights, for they are "the Fountain of Power."

69-88. [The Friend of Liberty! What Nobler Name: Verses Addressed to John Wilkes, Esq.]

"The Friend of Liberty! what nobler Name." (10)

BLJ, Aug 12, 1769; Lloyd's 25 (Aug 9, 1769), 142; St J's C, Jun 13, 1769, repeated Aug 8, 1769.

HC. Panegyric on Wilkes who will prevail over "The Rage of Time and Courts/And make bold Pow'r and future Ministers pale."

69-89. The General Gaol-Delivery; or W--kes chosen Alderman. To the Tune of Green grows the Rushes-O.

"We've chose brave Wilkes our Alderman." (30)

SM 31 (Jan 1769), 38; L Chron 25 (Jan 3, 1769), 11.

Song. A semi-literate follower of Wilkes glories in the choice of Wilkes as alderman of Farringdon Without.

69-90. General Paoli's Hat.

"Britons, behold a Patriot true." (40)

PA, Oct 28, 1769.

Octosyllabic couplets. Paoli needs a new hat and Britons can supply it with the help of several leading politicians, Thomas Townshend and Chatham, and others; and so Paoli may be restored.

69-91. The Genius of America to her Sons.

"Who'd know the sweets of Liberty." (12)

L Chron 25 (Jun 3, 1769), 536; SM 31 (Jul 1769), 377.

Sixains. The spirit of America is described in non-political positive terms emphasizing "the sweets of Liberty."

69-92. The Genius of England, To Law and Liberty.

"A. What thus abus'd, and in your Guardian's Eye." (4)

St J's C, Apr 29, 1769.

Extempore. Law and liberty, so it is believed, can no longer be found in England --because of oppression, the Scots, and politicians. (Where can they be found? Presumably in America.)

69-93. [Happy! had all our boasted Patriots been.]

"Happy! had all our boasted Patriots been." (8)

LM 38 (Mar 1769), 164-5; St J's C, Mar 4, 1769.

HC. Wilkes and Glynn, of Middlesex, provide models of genuine patriotism.

69-94. Hint to the People of the Country of Baetica, 1769.

"When in the midst of thee thy children seek." (10)

RM 19 (Oct 1769), 472; St J's C, Oct 24, 1769.

HC. The evidence of current events suggests that England is moving towards tyranny and slavery. References to Wilkes, St. George's Fields and Allen, tyranny, liberty.

69-95. Horace, B. III. Ode 24 Imitated. [On the Times.]

"Though richer than Arabia's Store." (108)

Freeman's J, Mar 25, 1769.

Imitation of Horace in octosyllabic couplets. The times are corrupted by luxury, -- and politics, and the colonies are affected.

69-96. The Humble Address of the Fishermen of Brentford to John Wilkes, Esq;

"Dear Sir, to you is our ardent Wishes." (21)

PA, May 12, 1769.

HC. Ten fishermen present the "Son of Liberty," Wilkes, with forty-five smelts.

69-97. Impromptu.

"John Wilkes -- a patriot is, all must allow." (16)

MJ, Jul 15, 1769.

HC. We should unite behind "the four Johns" -- Wilkes, Glynn, Free, and Horne, in the struggle against tyranny.

69-98. Impromptu.

"Let slav'ry's sons on slavish measures dwell." (4)

MJ, Apr 27, 1769.

Epigram. Although Wilkes may be expelled from Parliament, he remains in every Briton's heart.

69-99. Impromptu. Occasioned by the Defeat of the French by the Corsicans.

"Two famous Chiefs for Liberty contend." (6)

MJ, Jun 6, 1769.

HC. Wilkes is linked with Gen. Paoli's fight for freedom.

69-100. [In fam'd St. George's Fields young Allen fell.]

"In fam'd St. George's Fields young Allen fell." (4)

Freeman's J, Mar 21, 1769.

Epigram. Allen and Clark were murdered [by soldiers], and the government is responsible. George Clark died December 14, 1768, after receiving a head blow on December 8, 1768.

69-101. The Injured Ghost of Liberty in 1769 at the Bar of the H---- of C------.

"When all was closed in dreadful Night." (144)

G, Jul 10, 1769; PA, Jul 12, 1769; W Eve Post, Jun 10, 1769.

Ballad protests Wilkes' expulsion from his seat in the House of Commons, blaming Bute among others.

69-102. Injur'd Innocence.

"To Clark's pale reeking shade thus Allen." (10)

St J's C, Feb 21, 1769; The Patriotic Miscellany (London: Booth, 1769), p. 25.

HC. Clark and Allen, martyrs of tyrannical oppression in 1768, are glad to be in heaven -- not suffering oppression, injustice, and arbitrary power, or not fearing bloody Irish and Scots.

69-103. In-tempore, on the truly renowned Minister of Brentford, in humble imitation of some Elegant Extempore Lines in Tuesday's Whitehall Evening-Post on the Same Happy Subject.

"How inauspicious was the morn." (14)

W Eve Post, Jan 19, 1769.

Octosyllabics rhyming on "Horne." Satire on Parson Horne, "Sedition's trusty friend," and Wilkes's friend.

69-104. [John Wilkes and Horne set out, Whip and Spur.]

"John Wilkes and Horne set out, Whip and Spur." (6)

PA, Sep 7, 1769.

Epigram. Satire. Wilkes and Horne wish to set up a triumvirate with Jack Ketch (the public hangman of the days of Charles II).

69-105. [Kenrick, William.]
An Epistle to John Wilkes, Esq; On the Confirmation of his Sentence in the House of L[ord]s. Written during a Fit of the Gout.

"In spite of error, quirk and flaw." (106)

Lloyd's 24 (Feb 10, 1769), 152; WM 3 (Feb 23, 1769), 241; William Kenrick, Poems; Ludicrous, Satirical and Moral (London: J. Fletcher, 1770), pp. 320-4.

Octosyllabic couplets. Ironic satire. Kenrick is glad he has the gout and cannot act in behalf of Wilkes. Unengaged in politics, he is safe.

69-106. [Kenrick, William.]
The Political Scape-Goat. An Epistle to Sir William Draper.

"How's this? -- the learn'd Sir William Draper." (c. 120)

Ox M 2 (Apr 1769), 150-1; William Kenrick, Poems; Ludicrous, Satirical and Moral (London: J. Fletcher, 1768), pp. 310-15.

Octosyllabic couplets. Kenrick waxes sarcastic over Draper's plan for bringing concord to the nation by reconciling Wilkes and Bute, by "making Wilkes a tool of state." Whigs and Tories are fundamentally irreconcilable. Then Kenrick offers his own plan.

69-107. The Lamplighter of Gra[. . . .]. To L[or]d H[ollan]d.

"In vain O Holland are thy Wiles." (44)

PA, Sep 20, 1769.

Quatrains. Fox, Lord Holland, steals the public's money, and although he escapes censure now, he will be eventually cashiered for corruption, like others (Grafton) who failed to support Wilkes in the last Middlesex election. Bute is cited. (The printing of the title is imperfect.)

69-108. The Lion and Subject Beasts. A Fable.

"A Lion, tamest of his kind." (74)

G, Jul 26, 1769; Ox M 3 (Jul 1769), 31-2.

Octaves. Animal fable. A review of politics from the peace to the present time. The lion, who represents King George, swears he will rule "with gentle hand" and "guard the laws," if he has the "loyalty and love" of his subjects. Bute, Grafton, Sandwich, Bedford are cited. See "The Assembly of Beasts," Catalogue of Political & Personal Satires, ed. F. G. Stephens (London: British Museum, 1883), IV, 542-4 (#4303).

69-109. The Lion, the Fox, and the Fat-Hog. Fable III.

"Young Leo -- a most gracious Sovereign." (68)

Freeman's J, Mar 25, 1769.

Hudibrastics. Animal fable, about King George under Bute's influence making the peace with France. Bedford negotiates the peace; the hound Liberty thereupon hunts the fox Bute, traitor to the state.

69-110. Middlesex. A Ballad. Sung this Day at a Meeting of Gentlemen, called the Patriot Jubilee, in Honour of Mr. Wilkes's Birth-Day.

"Ye Middlesex lads and ye lasses." (35)

L Chron 26 (Oct 26, 1769), 416; PA, Oct 28, 1769; W Eve Post, Oct 26, 1769.

Song. Wilkes is in the tradition of Algernon Sidney and John Hampden as a defender of freedom and the rights and laws of the people.

69-111. The Middlesex Freeholder's Farewell and Address to his Family, on the Second Morning of the Brentford Election, after the Murders of the First.

"See from his seat th' indignant Briton start." (54)

Free M 1 (Oct 1769), 105-6.

HC. The brave freeholder, indignant at the murder of Allen and Clark, must continue to press for freedom despite the danger to his life (in the election of Wilkes).

69-112. The Modern Champion of Liberty.

"While False alarms to madness drive each dunce." (146)

G, Jan 31, 1769.

HC. Satire on Wilkes as a lying demagogue and his followers as rioters, and a defense of the King. Cited are General and Press Warrants, Proctor, North Briton 45.

69-113. Modern Patriotism.

"The man who would aspire to fame." (48)

Lloyd's 24 (Feb 1, 1769), 119; PA, Feb 2, 1769.

Octosyllabic couplets. Cynical anti-Wilkes satire. Wilkes is portrayed as a lying and seditious demagogue who "Abus'd his King, revil'd his God."

69-114. A Modest Hint of Advice to the High and Mighty.

"Must one unknown teach men in pow'r." (16)

L Chron 25 (Jan 28, 1769), 103; WM 3 (Mar 16, 1769), 338.

Quatrains. The ministers should cease persecuting Wilkes.

69-115. A Monody; or, The Tears of Sedition on the death of Junius.

"And are those periods fill'd with tuneful care." (28)

GM 39 (Apr 1769), 207-8; SM 31 (Apr 1769), 207; PA, Apr 10, 1769.

Elegiac quatrains. His Wilkite followers mourn the death of Junius, for Junius has been silenced, bribed by ministerial gold. (In a letter to PA, Apr 12, 1769 Junius denies that he is a partisan of Wilkes and that he has been bought off by the ministry.) Signed "Poetikastos," a writer in opposition to Wilkes, who replies to Junius in GM for Apr 1769. (See Letters 14 and 15 in The Letters of Junius Complete, ed. John Almon [London: Richard Phillips, 1806], 1: 128-30.)

69-116. [Mr. Wilkes's Address to the County of Middlesex, versified.]

"Gentlemen, The remarkable Series of very strange things." (c. 112)

Lloyd's 24 (Mar 31, 1769), 320-1.

HC. Wilkes, from jail, insists that he should sit in Parliament for Middlesex, contrary to the wishes of a tyrannical ministry. He complains of the St. George's Fields Massacre. (See another version in "Mr. Wilkes's Celebrated Address . . . " in PA, Jan 24, 1769.)

69-117. Mr. Wilkes's Celebrated Address to the Freeholders of Middlesex, versified.

"Freeholders and gentry of Middlesex county." (70)

PA, Jan 24, 1769; SM 31 (Jan 1769), 38-9.

Hexameter couplets. Satire on Wilkes. His persona betrays his political chicanery. He describes his reaction to the death of Allen in the St. George's Fields riot. (This poem is about the same episode as "Mr. Wilkes' Address to the County of Middlesex, versified," Lloyd's, Mar 31, 1769.)

69-118. A New Liberty Song. To the Tune of -- Rule Britannia.

"When our Forefathers fled the Land." (32)

Lloyd's, Jun 30, 1769; PA, Jun 29, 1769, (From the Boston Weekly News-Letter.)

Song. In the tradition of those forefathers who fled to America for freedom, Boston will never submit to tyranny. Francis Bernard is cited.

69-119. A New Song. Sung at Several Loyal Societies in this City, on the 28th of October last, the Birth Day of that Inflexible Patriot John Wilkes Esqr. The Words by a Patriot, set to music by H. B. Esqr.

"Here's a Health to our King, let's rejoice, drink, and sing." (20)

Free M 1 (Dec 1769), insert post 172.

Damns Bute, the King's Scottish adviser, and petticoat rule; but praises the patriot Wilkes.

69-120. Occasional Lines, Spoken at Chichester on the Birthday of Mr. Wilkes.

"Wrapt in poetic fire, fain would I sing." (26)

MJ, Apr 22, 1769.

Blank verse. Panegyric on Wilkes in prison in the tradition of Raleigh, Drake, Hampden, Russel, and Sidney.

69-121. Occasioned by the News of Mr. Wilkes's being chosen Alderman.

"Had pious Kidgell liv'd this Day to see." (12)

St J's C, Feb 7, 1769.

HC. Now that Wilkes has joined the Establishment, Bute can return. His demeanor will be bland.

69-122. Cancelled.

69-123. Ode.

"Bold was the man, as Horace somewhere sings." (54)

Ox M 2 (May 1769), 190-91.

Regular (Horatian) ode in Spenserian stanzas. Britain, unlike Spain and Holland, does not exploit the inhabitants of the New World. Believing in freedom, she hopes the savage will assert his natural rights and "nobly dare be free." This poem is applicable "to the unhappy differences subsisting between England and her Colonies."

69-124. An Ode, by Sedition.

"Alas! my faithful squinting friend." (24)

G, May 3, 1769.

Regular (Horatian) ode in sixains. Satire on Wilkes and Horne and their factious followers.

69-125. An Ode on Mr. Wilkes's Birthday, Oct. 28, 1769.

"Doff your hats and shew your manners." (50)

T&C 1 (Nov 1769), 608; WM 6 (Dec 21, 1769), 371-72.

Irregular ode, lyric in style, in celebration of Wilkes's birthday. Advice to his followers among the working class to show their contempt of the ministry.

69-126. Ode on the Birth-Day of John Wilkes Esq;

"Pierian maids, to whom belong." (60)

Free M 1 (Oct 1969), 103; MJ, Oct 26, 1769.

Regular ode in sixains. Praise of Wilkes, imprisoned by Mansfield, and praise of his supporters -- Wilson, Glynn, Beckford, Townshend, Sawbridge, Bellas.

69-127. Ode on Wilkes's Birth Day. Inscribed to the Supporters of the Bill of Rights.

"Bells shake your steeples; and with brazen mouths." (48)

Ox M 3 (Nov 1769), 191.

Regular (Horatian) ode in twelves. Let us celebrate Wilkes' birthday. Wilkes is in the tradition of Sydney, Hampden, Marvell.

69-128. An Ode. Sacred to Modern Patriotism on the auspicious 9th of November, 1769.

"With brazen Tongue let Hydra Faction shout." (64)

PA, Nov 9, 1769.

Elegiac quatrains. Satire on Wilkes and his "Rabble Scum," those factious patriots who arraign Grafton and Harley.

69-129. Ode to Colonel Luttrell.

"Fit for a just and generous cause." (90)

BLJ, Aug 26, 1769; Lloyd's 25 (Aug 21, 1769), 182-3; L Chron 26 (Aug 22, 1769), 191-2; LM 38 (Aug 1769), 440-1; PA, Aug 23, 1769, (Commentary Aug 26, 1769); St J's C, Aug 22, 1769; WM 5 (Sep 7, 1769), 306-7.

Regular ode in sixains. A vindication of Col. Henry Lawes Luttrell who was seated in the House of Commons despite the fact that Wilkes received the majority of votes in the by-election for Middlesex in 1769. Cited are James Townsend, Beckford, Burke, Barre, Mawbey, Sawbridge, et al. See "Another Ode, To the same Tune," 69-30.

69-130. Ode, to Colonel Luttrell. (By a Friend to Liberty.)

"O Luttrell! still in freedom's spite." (36)

MJ, Aug 26, 1769.

Regular ode in sixains. Colonel Luttrell, who was chosen MP for Middlesex, despite losing the election to Wilkes, is wrong to accept the seat, evidence of the abuse of power by Grafton, Bute. (This thoroughly Whig poem asserts the rights of man.)

69-131. Ode to Colonel -------- [Luttrell].

"O Thou, whom adverse Fates ordain." (108)

PA, Sep 4, 1769.

Regular ode in sixains, abusing Luttrell, the tool of the government, of Grafton, Norton. But L. will regret taking his seat, for Glynn and Burke will speak against him in the Commons and none of his assumed allies will come to his defense. Still, he is a threat to freedom, for he symbolizes the return of the spirit of Stuart tyranny.

69-132. Ode to John Wilkes, Esq; Member of Parliament for Middlesex.

"Ye Nymphs, who haunt Parnassus Hill." (84)

MJ, Aug 24, 1769.

Regular ode in sixains. Praise of Wilkes for defending the cause of liberty against the Scotch and the venal court. (But he was not to be MP until 1774!)

69-133. Ode to Liberty.

"O Goddess on whose steps attend." (58)

WM 3 (Mar 16, 1769), 337.

Regular ode in dixains. A general assault on tyranny. May liberty stand on "deep foundations" in Britain.

69-134. Ode to Liberty, Written by a Freeholder of Middlesex, and Most Humbly Inscribed to John Wilkes, Esq; our Truely Worthy Representative.

"Brightest Offspring of the Skies." (41)

St J's C, Nov 23, 1769.

Irregular ode to the spirit of liberty (embodied in Wilkes).

69-135. Cancelled.

Ode, to Music. Performed in the Senate House at Cambridge, July 1, 1769. At the Installation of Augustus Henry [Fitzroy], Duke of Grafton, Chancellor of the University. Written by Mr. Gray, Author of the Elegy in a Country Church-yard: Set by Dr. Randall, Music Professor. "Hence! avaunt! 'tis holy ground." (94) GM 39 (Jul 1769), 359; LM 38 (Jul 1769), 378-80; St. J's C, Jul 1, 1769. For pamphlet, see Gray's Ode, 69-A.

69-136. Ode to Music. To be performed in St. George's Fields, May 10, 1770, before A--g--s F--r--y, D--e of G--n, P--e M-n-st-r.

"Hence! avaunt! 'tis sacred Ground." (94)

PA, Jul 17, 1769; St J's C, Jul 13, 1769.

An elaborate parody of Gray's Ode to Music in honor of the Duke of Grafton, at Cambridge, July 1, 1769. Certain MP's are satirized besides Grafton; the Scottish interest is cited, corruption is deplored. Two additional satiric parodies appeared: they are noted in the commentary on Gray's Ode, 69-A.

69-137. An Ode to the D[uke] of G[rafto]n.

"Arm'd with that courage which of yore." (20)

PA, May 11, 1769; W Eve Post, May 9, 1769.

Regular ode in quatrains, in praise of the Duke of Grafton for restoring dignity to the nation.

69-138. Ode to the Minister of Brentford.

"When Heaven's inevitable rage." (84)

Lloyd's 24 (Mar 8, 1769), 240; LM 38 (Jun 1769), 328-9; RM 19 (Mar 1769), 135-6.

Regular ode in sixains, in praise of Parson Horne. The martyred young Allen, killed in a St. George's Fields riot, prophesies vengeance upon his guilty murderers and success to Horne's defense of freedom and the rights of man.

69-139. Ode to the Minister of Brentford, occasioned by Certain Stanzas at the End of the North Briton, Number 92.

"Proceed, sage Prelate, we beseech." (36)

Lloyd's 24 (Feb 24, 1769), 200; PA, Feb 25, 1769.

Regular ode in sixains. Allen's ghost warns Wilkes and Horne and their seditious supporters of the lessons to be learned by those who followed Cromwell, Wat Tyler, Jack Cade: they may be hanged.

69-140. The Offer of a Young Minister to the Public, In This Time of Necessity.

"Since the state is in want of some bold forward youth." (36)

New Foundling Hospital for Wit, Part 2 (1769), pp. 1-3.

Hexameter couplets in six-line stanzas. The young minister is formed by advice from many leading politicians -- Rockingham, Grafton, Shelburne, Burke. And "From Chatham he learnt to harangue and dispute/For American rights."

69-141. On a Late Election.

"Our old Mother Country (good Heaven relieve her)." (16)

St J's C, May 2, 1769.

Hexameter couplets. An allegory describing the sick condition of England -- the use of oppressive force in St. George's Fields and the Brentford election (of John Glynn).

69-142. On a late Occasion.

"Great King and noble lords 'tis time to look about ye." (23)

MJ, Jun 6, 1769.

HC. The House of Commons appears to be all-powerful and needs not the King or Lords. (Alludes, perhaps, to Wilkes' failure to be seated.)

69-143. On a Late Occasion. Wrote between Sleeping and Waking.

"Hour came it, Tom Dingle." (24)

BLJ, Apr 1, 1769; St J's C, Mar 25, 1769.

Regular ode in sixains. Advice to someone not to be a tool of the ministry, because it cannot be trusted. The point is that the ministry is oppressive and willing to invade the rights of the freeholders.

69-144. On Hearing that a Gentlemen of Humour had Lately Furnished a Certain Out-House in His Garden with a Great Number of the Late Present Addresses.

"Ye base-born sycophants, ye witless things." (8)

MJ, Apr 18, 1769.

HC. Epigram. Satire on politicians who support the ministry in its measures against Wilkes.

69-145. On John Wilkes, Esq. being elected Alderman in the Room of the Late Sir Francis Gosling, Knight.

"The Gosling gone, his Place is well supply'd." (4)

St J's C, Jan 5, 1769.

Epigram. Pleasure that Wilkes was elected alderman, upon the death of Sir Francis Gosling.

69-146. On John Wilkes, Esq; in Confinement.

"Courtiers, uncourtly and civil." (6)

BLJ, Oct 14, 1769; RM 19 (Oct 1769), 472; St J's C, Oct 7, 1769.

Epigram. Satire on the court. Because squint-eyed Wilkes could see too many ways, he was imprisoned by the court.

69-147. On Mr. Wilkes.

"His steadfast Purpose Terrors cannot shake." (10)

PA, Feb 25, 1769.

HC. Epigram. Praise of Wilkes, the devoted fighter against tyranny.

69-148. On our Great Patriot in the King's Bench.

"For the Good of Old England Wilkes toils." (4)

PA, Feb 6, 1769.

Epigram. Wilkes in prison appears to fight for freedom; but he is a squinting hypocrite.

69-149. On our Present Unhappy Divisions.

"Shall restless Faction, rous'd on every side." (35)

W Eve Post, Dec 12, 1769.

HC. Defence of the court and Grafton. The people should not rail at Grafton, for he tries to preserve the peace; they are being seditious.

69-150. On Paoli's Arrival [September 18, 1769].

"On Albion's shore King Theodore." (16)

L Chron 26 (Sep 26, 1769), 312; PA, Sep 28, 1769; RM 19 (Sep 1769), 424; WM 6 (Oct 12, 1769), 52; W Eve Post, Sep 26, 1769.

Quatrains. Paoli should be warned of the fickle British; they had mistreated King Theodore before, and they are not to be trusted to treat Paoli well.

69-151. On Reading in the Papers that a Scotch Regiment was Speedily to Embark for Corsica, to assist Paoli against the French.

"Have Scotia's Sons then caught th' Alarm." (12)

St J's C, Jan 31, 1769.

Quatrains. The Scots may atone for their murder of Allen and others in the St. George's Fields' massacre by helping Paoli against the French.

69-152. On Reading that the Portrait of Thersites was to be drawn in Imitation of J. Wilkes, Esq;

"How witty the invention! just the thought." (12)

W Eve Post, Jan 31, 1769.

HC. Anti-Wilkes satire. Wilkes is compared to ugly and dissident Thersites.

69-153. On Seeing a Print of Mr. Wilkes in Alderman's Robes.

"Here though we view the peaceful robe." (8)

L Chron 25 (Feb 2, 1769), 120; WM 3 (Feb 16, 1769), 212.

Epigram. Satire on Wilkes. Despite his election to the position of alderman, Wilkes is still a vicious creature.

69-154. On Seeing in the Papers that Sir Francis Blake Delaval, Knight of the Bath, was Chairman of the Society of Supporters of the Bill of Rights, at the London Tavern, on the 25th Day of April.

"Brave Delaval on hostile Shore." (20)

PA, May 20, 1769.

Quatrains praising Sir Francis Blake Delaval for chairing a meeting of the Society of Supporters of the Bill of Rights.

69-155. On Seeing some Lines in the St. James's Chronicle on Mr. Wilkes being made an Alderman.

"From his own Ashes see a Phoenix rise." (6)

St J's C, Jan 27, 1769.

HC. Light comment on Wilkes taking Mr. Gosling's aldermanic seat.

69-156. On the Abuse of Satire. A Fragment.

"Satire, for general good by heaven design'd." (38)

Ox M 3 (Oct 1769), 151.

HC. Satire has a noble constructive purpose, "To show fair Virtue in the clearest light." But it is often abused.

69-157. On the Conquest of Corsica by the French.

"France! by thy brib'ry spreading o'er." (4)

G, Sep 14, 1769; PA, Sep 12, 1769. (In Latin and English.)

Epigram. France conquered the Corsicans by force and fraud; and "right" was not on her side.

69-158. On the Cry of Wilkes and Liberty at the Great Masquerade.

"The night approach'd, -- and now the motley crew." (10)

The Patriotic Miscellany (London: Booth, 1769), p. 76.

HC. Wilkes' candor stands against ministerial hypocrisy.

69-159. On the Enemies of Mr. Wilkes perpetually Harping on the Essay on Woman, and Repeating the crime of Blasphemy.

"What can we little, of the great folks say." (8)

W Eve Post, Feb 11, 1769.

HC. To continue to accuse Wilkes of blasphemy and overlook the blasphemy of the aristocracy is dishonest.

69-160. On the Late Promotion of Sir Fletcher Norton.

"Norton preferr'd! Fame, catch the pleasing sound." (11)

W Eve Post, Feb 4, 1769.

HC. Norton, a Bute man, was counsel for the crown against Wilkes and spoke against Wilkes. He is praised for meriting a promotion to P.C. (Privy Councillor)

69-161. On the Piety of the Times.

"'Tis said, if right I understand." (12)

W Eve Post, Feb 9, 1769.

Sixains. Satire on the times, on greed and on sedition ("state blasphemy"). (There may be an allusion to Wilkes in these lines -- the blasphemy of his Essay on Woman, for which he had been prosecuted.)

69-162. On the Present Commotions.

"While factious men, the meteors of an hour." (48)

UM 44 (Apr 1769), 210; WM 4 (Apr 20, 1769), 83; Lloyd's 24 (Mar 22, 1769), 288.

HC. A complaint directed at party and faction, destabilizing irrational forces in the political arena.

69-163. On the 10th of May, 1769, being the Anniversary of the Murder of Mr. William Allen, and the Massacre in St. George's Fields, both on the 10th of May 1768.

"This the sad returning day." (24)

MJ, May 20, 1769; W Eve Post, May 18, 1769.

Trochaic tetrameter couplets. This is a sad day when, a year ago, young Allen was murdered by the Scotch in the St. George's Fields riot.

69-164. On the Times.

"Britannia sought the other day." (16)

PA, Nov 1, 1769; W Eve Post, Oct 31, 1769.

Quatrains. Because Wilkes and his faction profane liberty, she has deserted Britain. But seditious faction will be suppressed and the monarchy protected.

69-165. On the Times.

"Britons could once to justice bring." (18)

MJ, Apr 22, 1769; The Patriotic Miscellany (London: Booth, 1769), p. 72.

Sixains. Give Wilkes his liberty, hang Bute, and the times will improve.

69-166. On the Times, 1769.

"'O Times! O Manners!' honest Cicero cry'd." (10)

BLJ, Sep 30, 1769; RM 19 (Sep 1769), 424; St J's C, Sep 26, 1769.

HC. There is no cause for complaining at terrible times in the present reign of King George, for the country is at peace and prosperous.

69-167. On the Times, 1769.

"We all must remember the late happy Day." (4)

PA, Mar 8, 1769.

Epigram. The disturbing times are not caused by religion and liberty. (The allusion is to Wilkes and Parson Horne.)

69-168. On the Two Patriotic Writers, Junius, and Junius Americanus.

"See, with a like refulgent light." (12)

Free M 1 (Oct 1769), 106; MJ, Oct 10, 1769.

Epigram. Quatrains. Praise of the two Juniuses. (The American was Arthur Lee.)

69-169. On the Unanimous Re-election of John Wilkes, Esq; to the High Office of Alderman of the Ward of Farringdon Without.

"Without! -- Without what! -- fill up th'un finish'd Sentence." (2)

St J's C, Feb 7, 1769.

Couplet. Wilkes became alderman without engaging in venal bribes and without repentance of past behavior.

69-170. On the University of Cambridge.

"Fixt to one Point is Alma Mater still." (10)

L Chron 25 (Jun 8, 1769), 551; St J's C, Jun 6, 1769.

HC. Satire on the University of Cambridge for its vile self-interest, "her end [being] partial Good." (The event that triggered this criticism is the election of the Duke of Grafton as Chancellor of the University.)

69-171. On the Verses on Mr. Wilkes's Chain . . . .

"Why chain poor Johnny? 'tis unkind." (16)

W Eve Post, Jan 19, 1769.

Quatrains. Wilkes deserves to be hanged. (A reaction to satire on Wilkes as possible alderman -- in W Eve Post, Jan 3, 1769; see 69-208.)

69-172. On Two Murders.

"Say, Clarke and Allen, say illustrious Dead." (8)

PA, Apr 7, 1769.

Epigram. HC. Justice for the murders of Clarke and Allen, the result of tyranny, is inevitable, though slow in coming.

69-173. On Wilkes and his Patrons and Partizans.

"How rashly they run into dang'rous Extremes." (32)

PA, Oct 3, 1769.

Quatrains. Wilkes and his faction are really motivated by self-interest and an aversion to monarchy that will result in tyranny like Cromwell's government. They are not to be trusted.

69-174. Once and Now.

"Once for Alderman stood." (6)

PA, Feb 3, 1769; St J's C, Jun 17, 1769.

Epigram. Sixain. In the past, the London City aldermen were good people; but today to be an alderman one must revile King and God. (Indirect allusion to the Wilkes faction.)

69-175. O Yes! O Yes! O Yes!

"This is to give Notice." (23)

L Chron 25 (Mar 14, 1769), 256; PA, Mar 16, 1769; Freeman's J, Mar 21, 1769.

Unusual quatrains. The merchants of London petition to be rid of Wilkes and the Supporters of Rights.

69-176. Parody [Contrasted] on the Hunting Song in Thomas and Sally.

"The voice of corruption calls scribblers abroad." (16)

MJ, Aug 31, 1769.

Song. Ironic parody of the anti-Wilkes parody (PA, Aug 29, 1769). This parody attacks Grafton, oppression and corruption. See 69-177.

69-177. Parody on a Favourite Hunting Song in the Farce of Thomas and Sally.

"The clamorous Horn calls the Rebels abroad." (18)

L Chron 26 (Aug 26, 1769), 207; PA, Aug 29, 1769.

Ironic anti-Wilkes song urging mob action for Wilkes now that Parliament is in session; a satire on the republicanism of the City petitioners of the King.

69-178. Parody on a Favourite Hunting Song in the Farce of Thomas and Sally.

"Hark! Justice's Horn calls the Patriot abroad." (16)

L Chron 26 (Aug 31, 1769), 224; PA, Sep 2, 1769; RM 19 (Sep 1769), 423; St J's C, Sep 2, 1769.

Parody, pro-Wilkes song, in response to the anti-Wilkes parody of August 26, 1769. Urges action by the patriot supporters of liberty.

69-179. Parody on a Favourite Hunting Song in Thomas and Sally.

"The Patriots Horn calls the Freemen abroad." (17)

Lloyd's 25 (Sep 8, 1769), 244.

Urges action in the struggle to maintain "rights," linked with "America's groans."

69-180. Parody on Cato.

"Act 1. Scene Brentford." (46)

G, Apr 13, 1769; WM 4 (Apr 20, 1769), 84.

Blank verse. Two freeholders of Brentford deplore the threat of ministerial tyranny directed at Wilkes and liberty.

69-181. Parody on Some Stanzas of Pollio, an Elegy. Applyed to the Brentford Election.

"Near Thames' smooth Stream where late Freedom's Sons." (28)

St J's C, Apr 8, 1769.

Elegiac stanzas. A complaint by Liberty that the Court Interest, through bribery, is destroying freedom. But Glynn won in Brentford and there freedom flourishes, although it fails in Scotland.

69-182. The Pedigree of a Ministerial Address.

"The Thane begot a Ministry." (5)

L Chron 25 (Apr 4, 1769), 327; The Patriotic Miscellany (London: Booth, 1769), p. 30.

Prose poem. The great political turmoil over "arbitrary measures" is traceable to Bute and ministerial corruption.

69-183. A Petition of Grievances and Apprehensions, Humbly submitted to your R---l consideration.

"Most gracious Sire, we condescend." (60)

Lloyd's 24 (May 3, 1769), 430; PA, May 3, 1769; RM 19 (May 1769), 232; SM 31 (May 1769), 231; W Eve Post, May 2, 1769; also L Chron 25 (May 2, 1769), 420.

Octosyllabic couplets. The Middlesex Petition to the King, signed by 1565 Freeholders, in verse form. Whimsical, ironic petition to the King for the protection of liberty. James Townsend, Parson Horne, Serjeant Glynn are cited. See 69-9, The Middlesex Petition Inversed, another version, serious and complete.

69-184. The Petition of the Mile-End Male-Contents, versified.

"We of Mile-End and Bishopsgate." (122)

L Chron 25 (May 4, 1769), 431; PA, May 6, 1769.

Octosyllabic couplets. Satire on the London mob, supporters of Wilkes who fear the end of Trial by Jury and oppose the use of the standing army to suppress their riots. (The poem is apparently incomplete.)

The Petition of the Supporters of the Bill of Rights to his Majesty.

See 69-185: A Petition said to be Delivered to King Charles II.

69-185. A Petition said to be Delivered to King Charles II.

"In all humility we crave." (8)

DJ, Apr 20, 1769; L Chron 25 (Apr 13, 1769), 359; RM 19 (Nov 1769), 520; SM 31 (Apr 1769), 207.

An ironic anti-royalist petition from the people demanding that the King give up his power. With the King's Answer: "Charles at this Time having no Need / Thanks you as much as if he did." (2) Dublin Journal, April 22, 1769.

69-186. A Political Ballad. To the Tune of -- Chevy Chace.

"God save the King, and bless the Land." (72)

LM 38 (Apr 1769), 206; BLJ, Apr 8, 1769; St J's C, Apr 1, 1769.

Ballad, narrative of an eventful riot caused by Wilkes's followers, leading to the calling of the guards. (A picture of the times.)

69-187. A Political Prayer, by J. P.

"Thy aid, high Heav'n! I now implore." (32)

W Eve Post, Mar 14, 1769.

Quatrains. A prayer against corruption and arbitrary power (murders), and for the protection of virtuous patriots like Allen, who was murdered in the St. George's Fields riot.

69-188. The Power of Woman, Exemplified in Lord B---.

"Undone by woman, faithful records tell." (6)

Free M 1 (Sep 1769), 51.

HC. Bute surpasses Charles I and Anthony, for through his relationship with the Queen Mother, he dominates King and country.

69-189. A Prophecy of Merlin Versified.

"When Gotham's sons their K[ing] shall live to see." (23)

MJ, Oct 12, 1769.

HC. An awful prophecy of doom brought on by the imprisonment of Wilkes, an injustice, and the corruption of Grafton, criminal and profligate, and the indifference of the ministry to City remonstrances.

69-190. The Question.

"If Freeholders return what the House will make void." (2)

BLJ, Apr 15, 1769; St J's C, Apr 6, 1769.

Epigram. Questions [the validity of] denying Wilkes his seat in the Commons after being elected.

69-191. A Riddle.

"Name me the Prince, who never from his Youth." (2)

St J's C, Apr 29, 1769.

Epigram. Satire on the King -- incapable of hearing or speaking the truth.

69-192. Rowling, R. R.
An Address. To the Gentry, Clergy, and Freeholders of the County of Kent, and to the Freemen of the City of Canterbury.

"Rouse up ye men of Kent." (36)

MJ, May 20, 1769.

Octaves. Praise of Wilkes in which the poet says he will leave Kent for Middlesex where freedom is defended zealously.

69-193. Rowling, R. [R.]
Nell of Kent.

"To visit a relation." (48)

MJ, Jul 18, 1769.

Ballad. In London Wilkes' No. 45 is very popular. Wilkes, Glynn, Liberty, and 45 is the common cry.

69-194. [Sacred to the memory of William Allen.]

"Sacred to the memory of William Allen, with Observations on the Death of Mr. William Allen, junior."

L Chron 26 (Jul 20, 1769), 75; Ox M 3 (Jul, Aug 1769), 39, 53; W Eve Post, Jul 18, 1769.

Inscription for the tomb of the martyr (to tyranny), William Allen, killed in St. George's Fields, May 10, 1768. With copperplate of the monument. See F. G. Stephens, Catalogue of Political and Personal Satires (London: British Museum, 1883), IV, 438 (# 4199).

69-195. A Sale.

"Dame Liberty's breaking up House." (44)

Lloyd's 24 (Mar 24, 1769), 298; St J's C, Mar 21, 1769.

Quatrains, attacking the Scotch for undermining liberty in England.

69-196. [Says a jolly Jack Tar, to a half-starved Scot.]

"Says a jolly Jack Tar, to a half-starved Scot." (6)

MJ, Jun 24, 1769.

Epigram. A British sailor drinks to Wilkes but refuses a health to Bute.

69-197. The Sense of Millions, Most Humbly Addressed to a Great Personage.

"M[onarch] belov'd, whose Sires with gentle Hand." (35)

Free M 1 (Sep 1769), 49; St J's C, Jun 1, 1769.

HC. An address to the King, begging him to be gentle and gracious, to end the tumults over Wilkes by allowing a free election of the man chosen.

69-198. Sherratt, Thomas.
On Seeing the Picture of Pascal Paoli, General of the Gallant Corsicans. Addressed to Barlow Trecothick, Samuel Vaughan, and James Boswell, Esquires.

"Break thro' each mental Cloud, bright heav'nly Beam." (32)

PA, Jun 8, 1769.

Quatrains, praising James Boswell and others for supporting the Corsicans in their struggle for freedom.

69-199. A Sketch for A. D. 1769.

"Breathing sedition, a rash fiery band." (38)

GM 39 (Apr 1769), 208; PA, Apr 15, 1769; SM 31 (Apr 1769), 208; WM 4 (May 25, 1769), 244; W Eve Post, Apr 13, 1769.

HC. A severe criticism of the rebellious mob which endangers true liberty. The King is defended. -- There is no indication that this poem may be part of a longer work. A longer version was published in 1771; for this version, see 69-18.

69-200. [Sly Junius sculks behind the Scenes.]

"Sly Junius sculks behind the Scenes." (12)

BLJ, Sep 30, 1769; St J's C, Sep 26, 1769.

Quatrains. Sir William Draper should, it is hoped, expose Junius as a coward.

69-201. Song for Mr. Wilkes's Birthday. To the tune of the Bellisle march.

"Huzza! for St. George, let us drink and be gay." (21)

Free M 1 (Sep 1769), 49-50; MJ, Oct 24, 1769.

Praise of Wilkes and Glynn who support the cause of freedom.

69-202. A Song for the brave and honest Liverymen of the City of London, on the Election of a Mayor, Sept. 29, 1769.

"Come, come, one and all." (35)

MJ, Sep 26, 1769.

Trecothick and Beckford, two patriots, stand for the mayoralty. The city of London asserts its rights in opposition to the court.

69-203. A Song. For the Freeholders of the County of Devon. Tune -- Hearts of Oak.

"Ye friends to bless'd freedom, who nobly despise." (38)

W Eve Post, Oct 24, 1769.

Song against the Scots and corruption, and for Wilkes and liberty, in support of Samuel(?)Musgrave of Devon.

69-204. The Song of the Wilkites, at their Club. To the Tune -- Come, jolly Bacchus.

"Where are the Muses? they must not be dumb." (24)

BLJ, Dec 9, 1769; St J's C, Nov 30, 1769.

A song for Wilkes who stands for liberty against oppressive and tyrannical government.

69-205. Song. To John Wilkes, Esq. Tune, The Miller.

"How hopeful a state does the patriot possess." (24)

G, Sep 18, 1769; PA, Sep 15, 1769; SM 31 (Oct 1769), 546; W Eve Post, Sep 14, 1769.

Satire on Wilkes who depends on the mob and the devil for support, "laughs at all order," and "baffles all laws."

69-206. Song. To the Tune of Doodle, doodle, doo, etc.

"You Politicians, grave and wise." (36)

Lloyd's 24 (Mar 15, 1769), 264.

Quatrains on the deceitfulness of Wilkes, a demagogue who writes against church and state and prompts rebellion.

69-207. A Specific for National Grievances.

"Since Doctor Musgrave has prescrib'd in vain." (12)

RM 19 (Oct 1769), 472.

HC. Satire on supporters of Wilkes. Should Britons attend to Jack Ketch as they protest their grievances, they will suffer hanging -- an effective cure "For av'rice, fraud, corruption, and ambition."

69-208. Spoken Extempore on Hearing that Mr. Wilkes was a Candidate for the office of Alderman.

"Good Lord, what a whim this of his'n." (4)

L Chron 25 (Jan 3, 1769), 15; SM 31 (Jan 1769), 39; W Eve Post, Jan 3, 1769.

Epigram. Satire on Wilkes for wishing to be alderman of London. (See reaction, "On the Verses on Mr. Wilkes's Chain," Whitehall Evening Post, January 19, 1769: 69-171.)

69-209. Stanzas.

"If melting monodies could soothe his soul." (16)

GM 39 (Apr 1769), 208; PA, Apr 18, 1769; SM 31 (Apr 1769), 207.

Heroic quatrains. Junius is not dead. No poetry can succeed in doing honor to his powerful and patriotic theme.

69-210. Stanzas.

"When black oppression rear'd it's head." (18)

L Chron 25 (Jan 5, 1769), 23; PA, Jan 7, 1769.

Sixains. Wilkes educated the people in their rights against the oppression of arbitrary government.

69-211. Stanzas, Addressed to the Minister of Br[entfor]d.

"Though void of Virtue, Wit, and Parts." (24)

PA, May 5, 1769.

Quatrains. A satire on Parson John Horne, the anti-Court City politician.

69-212. Stanzas, in Answer to Stanzas addressed to the Minister of Br[entfor]d.

"By native worth call'd forth the cause." (28)

PA, May 9, 1769; W Eve Post, May 6, 1769.

Quatrains. Praises Parson Horne, incorruptible freedom-fighter and ally of Wilkes and Glynn.

69-213. The Te Deum of Sedition, on the Resuscitation of Junius.

"Arise, ye Spirits of the Song." (24)

L Chron 25 (Apr 13, 1769), 356; PA, Apr 14, 1769; SM 31 (Apr 1769), 208.

Quatrains. Satire on Junius who is not dead, as he asserts; but he wishes a greater bribe for his silence -- to be a minister of state.

69-214. [A Theatrical Announcement.]

"Acted but once." (c. 30)

MJ, May 9, 1769.

Parody. A satire on the oppressive government and its Scotch minions -- regarding Wilkes. Cited are St. George's Fields Massacre, Barrington, Weymouth, Allen, Pitt, and others.

69-215. [Tho' in my Life I never car'd about.]

"Tho' in my Life I never car'd about." (32)

PA, Sep 6, 1769.

Mixed forms. Abuse of Wilkes, immoral and dishonest, and motivated solely by self-interest. Wilkes is a mock patriot.

69-216. The Times. A Picture.

"Freedom in fetters -- black determined white." (4)

MJ, May 30, 1769.

Epigram. Honest Britons are sickened at the way in which the Commons, influenced by Bute, refused to accept Wilkes' victory in the Middlesex election and sat Luttrell instead.

69-217. [The times seem drawing on again.]

"The times seem drawing on again." (15)

L Chron 25 (May 4, 1769), 432; WM 4 (May 18, 1769), 212.

Octosyllabic couplets. A warning that these times may be like those of King Charles' reign in which civil war and anarchy ruined the nation.

69-218. To a Certain Lieutenant Colonel of -----.

"O Thou, whatever Name thy Pride may suit." (16)

Free M 1 (Sep 1769), 51; Freeman's J, Nov 4, 1769.

HC. Damning satire on McQuirk, the bravo and tool of Bute, who challenged Wilkes to a duel -- a blatant attempt at assassination. (McQuirk was convicted of murder but pardoned.) The title in the Free Mag is "To a Certain Captain of Dragoons."

69-219. [To address, or not to address.]

"To address, or not to address? That is the question." (22)

W Eve Post, Mar 23, 1769.

Parody on Hamlet's soliloquy. Satire on corruption and self-interest in government. (The idea is, should we risk losing contracts and loans if we address grievences to ministers?)

69-220. To all Honest Freeholders.

"While hackney'd Pens fair Freedom's Cause assail." (26)

St J's C, Dec 23, 1769.

HC. A plea to honest freeholders to persist in the defence of liberty (Wilkes) against corrupt and tyrannical administration and placemen.

69-221. To Candidus.

"My Friend, if I am not too free." (30)

W Eve Post, Jun 15, 1769.

Regular (Horatian) ode, addressed to a newspaper correspondent, praising him for his support of Junius.

69-222. To Henry Lawes Luttrell, Esq;

"Your accepting a place is a cursed disgrace." (4)

MJ, Apr 11, 1769.

Satire on Luttrell. The Middlesex voters will not support anyone (Luttrell) brought in by Bute.

69-223. To John Wilkes, Esq.

"By shuffling and slipping and playing the Knave." (4)

L Chron 25 (Mar 16, 1769), 259; BLJ, Mar 18, 1769; St J's C, Mar 14, 1769.

Epigram. Wilkes should persist, despite attacks from the Establishment.

69-224. To John Wilkes, Esq.

"If prayers to Heav'n from heart sincere avail." (16)

MJ, Jul 29, 1769.

Quatrains. Praise of Wilkes, defender of freedom.

69-225. To John Wilkes, Esq.

"No Hopes thou'lt ever dine with Speaker Cust." (10)

St J's C, May 20, 1769.

HC. The poet is indignant that Wilkes was "ejected" by the House of Commons (influenced by Bute) four times, and Luttrell chosen instead.

69-226. To John Wilkes, Esq.

"While, nobly suff'ring for thy country's good." (32)

MJ, Aug 3, 1769.

HC. Wilkes is praised, and entertained in prison by these verses.

69-227. To John Wilkes, Esq. A Sonnet.

"In these vile Times, when to deceive the Throne." (14)

St J's C, Jun 15, 1769.

An Italian sonnet, in praise of Wilkes and liberty, to which the "guilty Great" are indifferent. Probably by William Sharp of the Isle of Wight.

69-228. To John Wilkes, Esq; in the King's Bench Prison.

"Hail! thou great martyr in thy country's cause." (12)

Lloyd's 24 (May 10, 1769), 455; PA, May 11, 1769; W Eve Post, May 9, 1769; The Patriotic Miscellany (London: Booth, 1769), p. 73.

HC. Lines dedicated to brave Wilkes, "the Guardian of Liberty" against an arbitrary government.

69-229. To John Wilkes, Esq; On his Birth-Day.

"Let the dread Thunder fly." (48)

PA, Oct 31, 1769.

Irregular Pindaric ode honoring Wilkes on his birthday. Wilkes was born to protect freedom in a sinking country.

69-230. To John Wilkes, Esq. on his Receiving a Present of Four Turkies and Two Geese from a Gentleman in Schropshire.

"Since Fortune, dear Sir." (6)

L Chron 25 (Jan 26, 1769), 91; St J's C, Jan 24, 1769.

Epigram. Light satire on Wilkes. Now that he is an alderman, he must eat well.

69-231. To John Wilkes, Esq; Prisoner in the King's Bench.

"Let venal sons conspire to shade." (24)

Ox M 2 (Jan 1769), 32.

Quatrains in eight-line stanzas. Wilkes will persevere because of his courage and virtue. He will not be a slave to tyrants. The poet concludes, "I will not give/My Liberty till Death."

69-232. To Junius.

"Cease, Junius, cease, envenom'd Darts to throw." (12)

PA, Aug 4, 1769.

HC. Hidden, Junius cowardly attacks Granby, who does not deserve such vicious treatment.

69-233. To Junius.

"The generous Junius will not, sure, refuse." (114)

MJ, Oct 7, 1769; PA, Oct 5, 1769.

HC, inspired by Junius' avowed mission of exposing corruption in high places and defending man's inherent rights; expresses pleasure, too, in his lively satiric style.

69-234. To Junius.

"Go on, worthy sir, in defence of our cause." (38)

Ox M 2 (May 1769), 190.

Hexameter couplets. Praise of Junius for exposing "the vile hirelings," the hack writers, "mask'd hypocrites" and villains, and urges him to be the champion of those who defend the laws.

69-235. To Junius.

"Have Mercy, Junius, withdraw thy honest Pen." (8)

PA, Aug 4, 1769.

Quatrains. Junius need not attack the political hack writers; their writings once caused laughter, now pity.

69-236. To Junius.

"How dar'st thou, Junius, in this dangerous Time." (38)

PA, Aug 17, 1769; W Eve Post, Aug 15, 1769.

HC. Praise of Junius and his satiric mission, which is to expose the villains and rogues in high station and to defend liberty.

69-237. To Lord Chatham.

"Pitt, thou wert once the nation's darling! how." (42)

W Eve Post, Apr 8, 1769.

Blank verse. Pitt must restore security in the realm by protecting the rights of subjects against courtiers usurping those rights and denigrating the people to the King.

69-238. To Marcellus.

"Accept the tribute of a female hand." (4)

MJ, Oct 31, 1769.

Praise of Marcellus for his "Ode on the Birth-Day of John Wilkes, Esq;" in MJ, Oct 26, 1769: "soul-enchanting bard." See 69-126.

69-239. To Marcellus. On his Ode to John Wilkes, Esq;

"While thou, Marcellus, charms't a wond'ring rage." (12)

MJ, Oct 28, 1769.

Quatrains. One poet praises another for his "Ode on the Birth-Day of John Wilkes, Esq;" in MJ, Oct 26, 1769. Marcellus drew his "pen in freedom's cause." See 69-126.

69-240. To Mr. Fell.

"Shall wicked minions of the court." (24)

MJ, Jun 20, 1769.

Sixains. Bute has returned from his visit to the Pope in Rome. Now is the time to resist arbitrary power. Allusion to Allen's murder. Isaac Fell is the publisher of the Middlesex Journal.

69-241. To Mr. Wilkes.

"Be cautious, Wilkes, and bear with steady Head." (18)

L Chron 25 (Jan 5, 1769), 20; PA, Jan 6, 1769.

HC, warning Wilkes to distrust the mob but to trust the King whose judgment is reliable. -- This poem is prophetic of Wilkes' last phase in London politics. It was reprinted in LP, Nov 4, 1774 -- when Wilkes was elected Mayor of London -- in protest against a plagiary in LP, Nov 2, 1774.

69-242. To Paoli.

"Alas! poor Paoli, thou'lt curst this shore." (4)

Ox M 3 (Supplement 1769), 283.

Epigram. Paoli will rue the day he came to Britain, for Grafton will not prevent his downfall.

69-243. To Pascal Paoli.

"Let poets sing of Philip's warlike son." (c. 60)

WM 5 (Jul 27, 1769), 113.

HC. Paoli joins "the patriot, hero, and the man," as he fights for freedom against France.

69-244. To Poetikastos.

"Poetikastos, fie for shame." (30)

W Eve Post, Jun 1, 1769.

Regular (Horatian) ode in sixains. Objects to one poet's biased political verse, but then proceeds to praise Junius, who is "Inspir'd in Freedom's cause."

69-245. To the Freeholders of Middlesex.

"Obstinate Middlesexians, to dispute." (2)

St J's C, Apr 29, 1769.

Epigram. Satire on Bute's power. The Middlesex freeholders cannot dispute the law of England, that is, Bute.

69-246. To the Good People of Britain.

"Of parties the tools, of passions the slaves." (8)

L Chron 25 (Jan 7, 1769), 31; WM 4 (May 25, 1769), 245.

Quatrains. A wish that the people "were not so easily cullied" (deceived and led by the nose).

69-247. To the Lord Mayor and Common Council of the City of London.

"While many a venal Pen prepares Applause." (22)

St J's C, Apr 18, 1769; BLJ, Apr 22, 1769.

HC. Praise of the patriotic London Mayor and Common Council for integrity in the face of the corrupt court's pressures. Cited are Stuart maxims, prerogative, corruption, Scots, the inglorious peace.

69-248. To the People of London: To Divert them from Mobbing.

"Say, whither wou'd you run, ye fools." (26)

L Chron 25 (May 18, 1769), 479; PA, May 20, 1769; WM 4 (Jun 22, 1769), 370.

Octosyllabic couplets. A loyal poem. A complaint directed at mob violence, discord, rebellion -- and a reminder of the fate of Charles I.

69-249. To the Tune of Chevy Chace.

"God save our Sov'reign -- bless the Realm." (104)

PA, Apr 12, 1769.

Song. Ballad, narrating the evil history of Wilkes, the demagogue. It would be good for the nation to be rid of him and his supporters. Then England may help Corsica.

69-250. To the Wou'd-be Peer, Parolles.

"Hence! and forever hide that brazen brow." (30)

RM 19 (Oct 1769), 471.

HC. A satire on a cowardly peer who is supporting Wilkes and his followers, Sawbridge and Townshend, and encouraging the mob and sedition. (Is he Lord Temple?)

69-251. [To thee, dear Wilkes, in rustic dress.]

"To thee, dear Wilkes, in rustic dress." (18)

MJ, Jun 17, 1769.

Triplets. On Wilkes' persecution -- but he will endure in his fight for freedom.

69-252. To W. W[hitehea]d, Esq; Poet Laureat.

"<u>Whitehead</u>, you every year improve." (12)

MJ, Jun 13, 1769.

Sixains. Satire on Whitehead for his dull odes.

69-253. The Triumvirate: Occasioned by Seeing the Print of W--s, G--n, and H--e, in Conversation together.

"W--s, G--n, and H--e, all met one Morn." (80)

PA, Mar 3, 1769.

Ballad stanzas. Satire on Wilkes, Glynn, and Horne who, joined by the Devil, plan to disturb the peace by raising a mob and slandering the ministry. -- This poem is not the same as that accompanying the print, "The Triumverate" (1769): see 69-270. The print may be in F. G. Stephens, Catalogue of Political and Personal Satires (London: British Museum, 1883), IV, 468 (# 4226).

69-254. Verses by a Lady, upon reading the Rev. Dr. Free's Anniversary Sermon, just published, for the year 1769, against political murder.

"So Tully thunder'd at a Cataline." (35)

MJ, Jun 15, 1769.

HC. The Rev. Free, who preached at Allen's funeral, is praised for his defense of freedom, his association with Wilkes and Churchill.

69-255. Verses, Occasioned by Reading the Names of the Speakers For and against a Late Public Measure.

"Ye venal tribe, false guardians of the laws." (16)

MJ, Apr 18, 1769.

HC. An attack on corrupt politicians, including Grafton; and praise of Wilkes. The reference is Wilkes' denial of a seat in the Commons.

69-256. Verses on Seeing the Print of James Boswell, Esq; in the Corsican Dress.

"Boswell, thy figure, thus display'd." (18)

L Chron 26 (Oct 19 & 24, 1769), 344, 403; WM 6 (Oct 19, 1769), 86.

Sixains. Apparently, the writer takes exception to some aspect of Boswell's Corsican dress and criticizes Boswell's "black" character. For the print, see F. G. Stephens, Catalogue of Political and Personal Satires (London: British Museum, 1883), IV, 551 (# 4310).

69-257. Verses on the Gracious Reception of the Middlesex Petition.

"To our lov'd Monarch, to whose praise belong." (28)

L Chron 25 (Jun 17, 1769), 584.

HC. This poet is confident that the King will redress the grievances of his Middlesex subjects.

69-258. Verses on the State of the Nation.

"Quoth Ll[oy]d, one day, to trusty K[no]x." (32)

Lloyd's 24 (Feb 24, 1769), 202; PA, Feb 27, 1769.

Quatrains against the fragmented opposition which must remain <u>out</u> until they can decide on their leader. Burke may be able to respond effectively to William Knox's <u>Present State of the Nation</u> (1769), but he cannot elevate Rockingham to a position of leadership. (Charles Lloyd was George Grenville's secretary; William Knox wrote the pamphlet with the assistance of Grenville; and Burke answered it with his <u>Observations on the Late State of the Nation</u> [1769].)

69-259. Verses written on the Day of Colonel Luttrell's Admission for Middlesex.

"Why am I dull, why in this pensive mood." (16)

BLJ, Aug 12, 1769; Lloyd's 25 (Aug 9, 1769), 142; PA, Aug 11, 1769; St J's C, Aug 8, 1769.

HC. The poet is distressed to "see fair Freedom hence depart," as Luttrell assumes the seat in Parliament that belongs rightfully to Wilkes.

69-260. A Very Old Prophecy.

"When spawn of Picts from o'er the Tweed." (18)

Freeman's J, Apr 18, 1769.

Octosyllabic couplets. A prophecy of ruin for England should Scotch Jacobites and Tories suborn the government and oppress the Whigs.

69-261. A Well-Known Character.

"In pow'r and mischief lo! his second stands." (26)

Free M 1 (Sep 1769), 50.

HC. Strong satire on the character of a courtier, "second to Earl Bute" in greed and corruption, Henry Fox, Baron Holland.

69-262. [When a Minister treads on the Toes of a State.]

"When a Minister treads on the Toes of a State." (12)

St J's C, Jan 12, 1769.

Quatrains. A justification for Wilkes' dissidence, supported against ministers taking illegal action. Cited are Bute, Lord Halifax, Wilkes.

69-263. [When B(ute), the nation's curse, shall rule the roast.]

"When B[ute], the nation's curse, shall rule the roast." (12)

MJ, Jun 17, 1769.

HC. The nation is doomed because of the numerous government abuses and evidences of repression, among them Luttrell's assumption of Wilkes' seat in Parliament, Wilkes' imprisonment. Cited are Scotch, Bute, Murray (Chief Justice, Lord Mansfield), Grafton.

69-264. Why a Patriot Should Squint.

"A One-ey'd Watchman will suffice." (4)

St J's C, Nov 30, 1769.

Epigram. Wilkes is cross-eyed so that he can more effectively be watchman of the state.

69-265. The Wished-For Change.

"When Nature working without art or grace." (20)

Free M 1 (Sep 1769), 51; MJ, Aug 31, 1769.

HC. Invective against Grafton's character.

69-266. [With Honour clad with Innocence array'd.]

"With Honour clad, with Innocence array'd." (6)

PA, Oct 10, 1769.

Epigram. Honorable and innocent, Grafton has nothing to fear from Wilkes, Horne, or Junius.

69-267. [Without Offence to the Majority.]

"Without Offence to the Majority." (62)

PA, Feb 17, 1769.

Octosyllabic couplets. Satire on the Scotch who are being favored at the English court.

69-268. [The year of wonder is advanc'd.]

"The year of wonder is advanc'd." (64)

MJ, May 13, 1769, repr. Jan 16, 1770.

Ballad quatrains. Originally published in the New York Gazette. Satire on Tories -- Scotch Jacobites (such as Bute and Kidgell), High Church clergy and papists, who create difficulties even for the Americans abroad, much less Wilkes and his friends at home.

Prints

69-269. The British Bull Baited by Mungrels.

"Behold the Bull, Britannia's delight." (24)

Etching with HC. 1769.

Stephens 4328 (IV, 569-71).

Allegory. Wilkes as a bull with a collar of "Liberty" is baited by dogs: Sir Fletcher Norton, Mansfield, Bute, and others. William Allen's murder is also noted. At this time, Wilkes was confined in the King's Bench Prison, pending a decision on his outlawry since 1763.

69-270. Epigram 3, of the 1. Book of Martial, Imitated. To John Wilkes, Esq. Alderman of Farringdon Ward Without.

"O thou! acknowledg'd Great as well as Good." (9)

Engr. with verses in triplets.

Stephens 4286 (IV, 525).

Wilkes' election for Middlesex was declared void four times, the last being on April 14, 1769, despite his integrity as a poor but honest patriot. The House of Commons considered Henry Lawes Luttrell elected, April 15, 1769, although he received far fewer votes than Wilkes.

69-271. The Triumverate or Britan[n]ia in Distress.

"O Muse inspire me while I write." (69)

Engr. with verses. July 5, 1769.

Stephens 4298 (IV, 537-8).

The supporters of the Bill of Rights, meeting at the London Tavern, are celebrated. America also appears, "trampling on the Stamp Act."

1770   Books & Pamphlets

70-1. Bruce, Michael.
  Poems on Several Occasions.
  Edinburgh: Robertson, 1770. 117p.

  See 67-1.

70-2. The Dialogue addressed to John Wilkes, Esq.
  London: Wilkie, 1770. 35p.

  "Poet. Farewell to Patience! must I ever stay." (c. 500)

  Notices: CR 29 (Feb 1770), 147; MR 42 (Feb 1770), 145; L Chron 27 (Feb 3, 1770), 125; WM 7 (Feb 15 & 22, 1770), 209-11, 241-5.

  Copies: BL 1481.e.15.

  HC. Imitation of Horace, a dialogue between the poet and his friend on the political state of affairs at this time, when Grafton was about to resign and to be superseded by North. The poet insists upon writing satire in "these dang'rous times" against "Faction," believing that Wilkes, the so-called "Patriot," is vicious and his liberty rebellious license directed at a good King. He also detests Junius and Horne. Saville, he believes, countenances "new Treasons, meaning well." He insists upon being impartial in his expression of the truth, thereby being superior to Churchill. Nor does he have kind words for Chatham and Wentworth (Rockingham).

70-3. An Epistle to Lord Holland. MDCCLXIX.
  London: Brown, 1770. 16p.

  "Why clos'd like Janus' is Apollo's fane." (c. 220)

  Notices: CR 29 (Feb 1770), 146; MR 42 (Feb 1770), 144.

  Copies: NUC CtY, MH.

  HC. Believes that "most love daring Satire's blasting pow'r," and he would love Churchill, had this satirist engaged on the side of truth and virtue. However, he confesses he has no capacity for satire; instead, he writes a friendly essay in praise of Stephen Fox, Lord Holland, who unlike others still sides with "order, decency, and respect for kings," regardless of faction and Wilkes.

70-4. [Goldsmith, Oliver]
   The Deserted Village, A Poem. By Dr. Goldsmith.
   London: Griffin, 1770. vii + 23p.

   "Sweet Auburn, loveliest village of the plain." (c. 440)

   Notices: CR 29 (Jun 1770), 435-43; MR 42 (Jun 1770), 440-5; L Chron 27 (May 26, 1770), 505-6.

   Evans 12060.

   Copies: BL T.666 (14), 11630.d.3 (12), 643.k.9 (2); NUC CtY, ICN, InU, MB, MH.

   Six authorized editions were published during 1770. Eleven authorized editions appeared by 1784. Four American editions appeared: 1771 (Philadelphia & New York), 1782 (Philadelphia), and 1784 (Providence).
   HC. Social satire and commentary. G. attributes British social problems to the engrossers, wealthy merchants or "spoilers" with "tyrant's power," who have forced enclosures on the common lands in order to enlarge their estates. Thus as they take land out of cultivation in order to indulge their luxurious taste for conspicuous aggrandizement--that is, for landscaping parks on a grand scale--at the same time they force the impoverished villagers, the "bold peasantry," to emigrate to the city, where the women are prostituted, and to America, "To distant climes," a wild, untamed, and terrifying land "beyond the western main." (G. cites the "Altama" river, Georgia.)

70-5. The Poetical Retrospect, or the Year MDCCLXIX. A Poem.
   London: Noble, 1770.

   Notices: CR 29 (Apr 1770), 313-4; MR 42 (Apr 1770), 327.

   Copies: none located.

70-6. The Remonstrance. A Poem.
   London: Wheble et al., 1770. 5-39p.

   "Deluded Britons! can you then suppose." (c. 540)

   Notices: CR 29 (Apr 1770), 312-13; MR 42 (Apr 1770), 326; L Chron 27 (Apr 12, 1770), 360.

   Copies: BL 840.k.11 (15), 164.n.28; NUC CtY, 1U, RPJCB.

   HC. Attributed by Boswell to Percival Stockdale. Britons are deluded if they think that "impious" Wilkes and slavish Beckford are real patriots who believe in freedom. Disparages Mrs. Macaulay and eulogizes Samuel Johnson for his honesty, which truly merited a pension (cites Johnson's False Alarm). Defends the King's reputation and asks that he be respected, despite human errors. Closes with severe remarks on the ambiguity and capriciousness of Chatham, "detested, dreaded, and despised." The poet takes the unpopular side of the question.

70-7. [Rushton, Edward?]
Party Dissected; Or Plain Truth. A Poem. By a Plain Dealer.
London: Bell et al., 1770. 5-35p.

"Descend, my muse, assist my artless tale." (c. 400)

Notices: CR 30 (Jul 1770), 68-71; MR 42 (Jun 1770), 486.

Copies: NUC MH.

HC. With an "Apology to the Reviewers" (34). The intention of this generalized satire is, as explained in the "Apology," to reconcile "jarring diff'rence," to suppress division, discord, and faction, and to bring peace. His is no "venal pen," swayed by party. He asks Junius to restrain his "ranc'rous pen," moved as it is by base self-interest. A reasonable moderate, he believes designing men, "pretending freedom," stir up their tools among the people who, led astray, neglect their work--like "Jobson," an artisan or cobbler, who is misled by Wilkes.

70-8. Sedition; A Poem.
London: Nicoll, 1770. 5-16p.

"To soften manners, harmonize the soul." (c. 220)

Notices: CR 29 (Mar 1770), 233; MR 42 (Apr 1770), 327.

Copies: NUC CSmH, CtY, IU.

HC. Employs the weapon of satire against "mad Sedition and her bawling crowd," against Mrs. Macaulay, Wilkes, Beckford, Junius. Closes with praise of honest statesmen: Grenville, Murray (Mansfield), North, Camden, Grafton.

70-9. Sharp, William, Jun.
The Livery's Remonstrance. Verses Written immediately after Reading their noble Address to the King. March 14th, 1770.
London: Flexney, [1770]. 16p.

"Was there an hour which dear remembrance owns." (122)

Copies: NUC CtY.

Includes "Preliminary Lines written on the day of Harry Luttrell's first sitting as Member [of Parliament] for Middlesex" (16 ll.), dated 1769. Sharp complains that freedom, a birthright of the English, is compelled to depart because everyone is "to a Stuart sold." But in the dedication, dated from the Isle of Wight, March 16, 1770, he takes pleasure in the remonstrance, the assertion of grievances, and "zeal for the preservation of our insulted rights."

In the poem, HC, Sharp declares that "Bute's proud clan" controls the King's council, protests corruption, and hopes the King will grant redress. (The reference is to the 1769 by-election for Middlesex, in which Luttrell polled 296 votes against 1143 for Wilkes; but the House of Commons ruled Wilkes ineligible and declared Luttrell elected.)

Serials

70-10. Acrostic. [Junius.]

"In language pure, in sentiment refin'd." (6 + 6)

L Eve Post, Mar 27, 1770.

Acrostics. Two acrostics, the one praising, the other criticizing Junius.

70-11. An Acrostic. [Wilkes.]

"In days of yore how greatly Cato fell." (10)

MJ, Mar 10, 1770.

Acrostic on Wilkes, in prison, and compared with Cato. Bute is cited.

70-12. The Address and Remonstrance of the Grumbletonians to the King.

"Dread Sir,/You know." (30)

G Eve Post, Mar 20, 1770; Lloyd's 26 (Mar 16, 1770), 168.

Sixains. A protest at corruption again by the Grumbletonians. See Lloyd's, Feb 21, 1770: 70-166.

70-13. An Address to the good People of England on the Present Crisis of Affairs.

"Rouse, Britons, rouse! and, with becoming zeal." (18)

Lloyd's 26 (Jan 1, 1770), 11.

HC. Advice (from the Government) to turn from "base Junius" and his lies and to end discord, faction, sedition.

70-14. Cancelled.

70-15. Advice from the Liberty, or the Weaver's Garland.

"My dear Fellow-subjects, who love to be free." (104)

Freeman's J, Jun 14, 1770; Fugitive Pieces of Irish Politics, During the Administration of Lord Townshend (London: Almon, 1772), pp. 157-65; Baratariana. A Select Collection of Fugitive Political Pieces, Published during the Administration of Lord Townshend in Ireland. Second ed., Corr. & enl. (Dublin, 1773), pp. 291-9. Also third ed. (Dublin, 1777), pp. 268-75.

Song. Ballad by Dick White, weaver, critical of the political scene -- of Lord Bute's domination, treatment of America, England, Ireland (attempting "to enslave our American friends"), including praise of several Irish politicians on the side of liberty. An illustration of the problems facing the Irish, similar to those the Americans were having with the English government: the use of "Star-chamber warrants," the corruption of the right of election.

70-16. Advice to Mr. Wilkes.

"Wilkes, like a meteor." (4)
"Would Wilkes approve himself his country's friend." (4)

Lloyd's 26 (Apr 2, 4, 1770), 327, 334.

Wilkes, when freed from prison, should be like a mere common star; he should disappear and be heard of no more.

70-17. An Alphabet for Little Masters and Misses.

"A Stands for an axe, to chop off bad men." (22)

L Eve Post, Dec 6, 1770.

An alphabet poem that satirizes Bute, Mansfield, North -- and asks that the King get good counsel.

70-18. Another Ode to St. Stephen.

"First Martyr of unlawful Power." (78)

BLJ, Dec 15, 1770; BWJ, Dec 22, 1770; L Eve Post, Dec 8, 1770; PA, Dec 12, 1770; St J's C, Dec 11, 1770; New Foundling Hospital for Wit, Part 5 (1772), pp. 55-9; New Foundling Hospital for Wit (1786), IV, 192-5.

Sixains. A Whig poem on the opening of Parliament, praying that the Whig tradition be maintained against Grafton and his "jockey" North. Others cited are Onslow, Barrington, Conway; and war with Spain is supported. Signed "Anti-Bribe Dentatus." See Ode to St. Stephen, 70-113.

70-19. An Answer to a Late Remonstrance.

"Be it known to one and all." (30)

L Eve Post, May 29, 1770.

Trimeter couplets. Satire on the King, whose persona speaks, for rejecting a remonstrance.

70-20. An Answer to a Late Remonstrance.

"My subjects' requests shall be always received." (20)

L Eve Post, Mar 27, 1770.

Quatrains. The persona of the King expresses displeasure at a late petition, but asserts that he follows the law of the land.

70-21. An Apology for a certain great Personage wanting good manners.

"Petitioners of Westminster, be not at all concern'd." (12)

L Eve Post, Mar 31, 1770.

Dactylics and quatrains. A criticism of the tyrannical King for refusing to receive petitions.

70-22. A Ballad.

"As North, Bute, and Grafton, in Council were met." (35)

L Eve Post, Sep 22, 1770; Freeman's J, Sep 29, 1770.

Song about how a deal was made to get Luttrell to oppose Wilkes, gain his seat in the Commons, and receive an Irish place as a reward.

70-23. A Bellman's Verses on New Year's Day [1770].

"I drink no sack, and therefore cannot sing." (26)

L Eve Post, Dec 30, 1769-Jan 2, 1770.

HC. Prophecies which, according to this paper, are the significant issues of the year: Luttrell turned out; Wilkes returning, pardoned by the King; a triennial Parliament; corruption and placemen controlled; grievances redressed; Bute to leave the Queen Dowager; concord at home.

70-24. The Boot. To the Right Honourable the Lord Rockingham.

"Boot, and the men I sing, the first who bore." (165)

L Mus, Mar 1770, pp. 173-7.

HC. Satire on the Scots and their Tory domination of the court. The Whigs should be restored to leadership -- Pitt, Temple, Rockingham. In large part, "the Boot" refers to Bute.

70-25. Britannia to the Freeholders of Middlesex.

"Go forth my sons! no light, no low-born care." (10)

MJ, Apr 19, 1770; Ox M 4 (Apr 1770), 153.

Epigram. Britannia urges Middlesex freeholders to vindicate their rights -- in the tradition of Hampden and Sidney.

70-26. Britannia's Comfort.

"What! Beckford gone? -- My Granby also fled." (c. 100)

L Eve Post, Nov 6, 1770.

HC. Britain mourns the death of Granby and Beckford, among her best allies in the struggle against the corruption of the present ministry -- Bute, North, Grafton, and the Carlton House cabal.

70-27. Britannia's Complaint.

"If those who behold my distress." (48)

L Eve Post, Jul 7, 1770.

Imitation of Shenstone's Pastoral. Britain mourns the loss of the Duke of Cumberland who had stopped the Scots invasion from the north in 1745, and the pathetic state of affairs in the present reign -- tyranny, disregard of petitions for redress, the failure of trade.

70-28. Britannia's Lamentation. An Epigram.

"How hard, alas! is poor Britannia's fate." (10)

L Eve Post, Aug 9, 1770.

Satire on Mansfield, Hillsborough, Barrington. Here the issues of press freedom and colonial freedom are associated to illustrate the difficulties faced by the spirit of British Freedom.

70-29. [Britons fear not the force of Spain.]

"Britons fear not the force of Spain." (4)

Lloyd's 28 (Dec 31, 1770-Jan 2, 1771), 4.

Epigram. Britain need not fear Spain because it has sailors like Hawke and Saunders.

70-30. Butler's Ghost.

"When titled Scoundrels first grew great." (223)

Freeman's J, Sep 22, 1770.

Hudibrastic satire, fragments commenting on contemporary politics, abuses of arbitrary government in Ireland and England.

70-31. The Call of Liberty. A Cantata.

"Briton's attend! your fav'rite Goddess hear." (60)

Free M 2 (Jul 1770), 258-9.

Song. Liberty complains of British slaves to corruption and being forced to leave Britain -- where it is not made clear.

70-32. The Caterpillars, A Ballad.

"Boot. God, but this is wond'rous pretty." (104)

L Eve Post, Jun 23, 1770.

Song. A satire on all the leading statesmen -- Bute, Grafton, North, Mansfield, Norton, Fox, Hillsborough, Barrington, Rigby -- of the present ministry for various vices. Hillsborough refers to the American colonies.

70-33. A Character. [Grafton.]

"O Thou, whose name in future times will stand." (10)

Free M 1 (Jan 1770), 275; MJ, Jan 25, 1770.

HC. Satire on the premier, the Duke of Grafton, profligate, libertine, Jacobite.

70-34. Characteristics. An Allegorical Poem.

"Once on a time the Gods were met." (96)

MJ, Feb 27, 1770.

Ballad, allegorical narrative of the corrupt court of the gods. Wilkes' unjust imprisonment by Judge Mansfield and Wilkes' struggle for liberty are at the heart of the narrative.

70-35. [Chatterton, Thomas.]
The Consuliad. An Heroic Poem.

". . . Twitcher, superior to the venal pack." (10)

Free M 1 (Jan 1770), 273, 274.

HC. A rambling satire on local Bristol politics. Two extracts on major figures in national politics -- Sandwich and Grafton, both presented critically. C. also comments on the St. George's Fields' Massacre, May 10, 1768.

70-36. [Chatterton, Thomas.]
Resignation.

"But Courtiers have a littleness of mind." (822)

Free M 2 (Apr, May 1770), 105-7, 162-3.

HC. Extract, ll. 627-822 (end).
Another rambling satire by Chatterton -- on Bute and the Scots responsible for the grievous ills suffered by the English nation under Grafton and, later, under North. Includes remarks on taxation in America and America's disregarded petitions. The context of these remarks is corruption at court.

70-37. The Complaint. Sung by the Princess Dowager of Wales, six months after the first departure of Lord Bute, to the favourite Scotch tune of -- Dearest Jenny.

"Say, my noble Lord of Bute, to whom I so duly." (25)

BWJ, Sep 8, 1770.

Song. Satire on Bute through the ironic persona of the Princess Dowager of Wales, George III's mother. She asks for his return and his great influence -- evil influence. St George's Fields and corruption are cited.

70-38. Court Patriotism A-la-Mode.

"At Court the great ones jar and quarrel." (14)

G Eve Post, Apr 21, 1770.

Octosyllabic couplets. Satire on the selfish venal nobility at court.

70-39. A Court Soliloquy. Lord N--th solus.

"To war, or not to war? -- that is the question." (29)

L Chron 28 (Dec 1, 1770), 533; WM 10 (Dec 13, 1770), 338.

Blank verse. Parody on Hamlet's soliloquy. North expresses his doubts on a war with Spain over the Falkland Islands.

70-40. [Dark was the night by fate decreed.]

"Dark was the night by fate decreed." (108)

MJ, Jan 23, 1770.

OC. Wilkes's life is being threatened; but Wilkes will be immortal, like the great Whigs Hampden and Sidney, as a freedom fighter. Cited are Bute and the tool of Bute, Samuel Martin, who almost killed Wilkes in a duel, 1763.

70-41. A Dialogue between Old Mother Carlton and her Son.

"Old M. Hold up your head, child! hold it higher." (12)

L Eve Post, May 15, 1770.

Quatrains. Satire on the King for accepting the "secret" influence of his mother and, although not specifically mentioned, her "friend" Bute.

70-42. The Different Reception of Truth and Flattery. A Political Fable. Addressed to John Wilkes, Esq.

"Two men (perhaps in Aesop's days, It matters not)." (64)

Ox M 5 (Nov 1770), 192.

Sixains. The court "Parasite" flatters the ape with lies and is beloved; but the "True Man" (representing Wilkes and "honest Beckford") speaks the truth and is rejected.

70-43. A Display of the learned Doctor Johnson, and his masterly pamphlet, intitled The False Alarm; recommended to the Doctor's own perusal.

"See! against Freedom's struggles, against public hate." (78)

L Eve Post, Jun 14, 1770.

Dactylic couplets. Satire on Samuel Johnson for his attack on Wilkes in The False Alarm, for his pension and corruption.

70-44. Duet Intended to be sung in . . . Newcastle, on the 15th of April. The music taken from the last song of the Maid of the Mill.

"Such a knavish generation." (16)

L Eve Post, Mar 15, 1770.

Song written for Wilkes's release from prison, April 15, 1770.

70-45. The Echo of Freedom. A New Song. To the Tune of the Middlesex Farmer.

"The echo of Freedom calls Britons to rise." (32)

Free M 2 (Aug 1770), 305.

Song, in defense of liberty in general.

70-46. Edmund and Catherine. An Epigram.

"'Thoughts on the present Discontents." (8)

G Eve Post, May 10, 1770; L Eve Post, May 10, 1770; St J's C, May 10, 1770; LM 39 (Jun 1770), 320.

Catherine Macaulay objects to Burke's polemic, Thoughts on the Present Discontents.

70-47. An Elegy on the Death of the Right Honourable William Beckford, Esq; Late Lord Mayor of London, and Member of Parliament for the same. By Miss Maria De Fleury.

"Ye Muses! who in Fonthill's groves reside." (30)

BLJ, Jun 23, 1770.

Elegy on Beckford, guardian of those rights guaranteeing freedom to British subjects. Wilkes and James Townsend will carry the banner of liberty.

70-48. Elegy To the Memory of the Right Honourable William Beckford, Esq; Lord Mayor, and Member of Parliament for the City of London, and Alderman of Billingsgate Ward, who departed this Life June 21, at 39 Minutes past Four o'Clock in the Morning.

"Why hid the sun behind yon gloomy cloud." (40)

Ox M 4 (Jun 1770), 230.

Elegiac stanzas. "Beckford is dead, then mourn all Freedom's sons." He spoke for freedom, "Unplac'd, unpension'd, and untitled."

70-49. [An Elegy Written in St. Patrick's Cathedral.]

"In close cabal now hungry Harpies sit." (42)

Freeman's J, May 26, 1770. [See 70-168.]

Elegiac quatrains, parody on Gray's Elegy. Satire on political corruption, the tendency towards tyranny (the Augmentation Bill), and the King for his petty mind.

70-50. An Elogium on a Late Change in the L----.

"What has sagacious C---n done." (20)

G Eve Post, Jan 23, 1770.

Quatrains. Ironic remarks on Lord Camden's resignation. He is still deserving; he is not disgraced, retiring near Pitt at Hayes.

70-51. Epigram.

"Britons, grown wise, will throw aside their frights." (4)

L Eve Post, Jul 31, 1770.

Satire on the King and Mansfield. Ironic epigram that says the King supports the subject's rights and freedom and Mansfield loves justice. In view of the editorial policy of the L Eve Post and government persecution of its editor, J. Miller, this poem must be ironic.

70-52. Epigram.

"Of Outs and Ins, the common sins." (12)

G Eve Post, Apr 12, 1770; L Chron 27 (Apr 12, 1770), 353; L Eve Post, Apr 10, 1770; WM 8 (May 3, 1770), 146.

Quatrains. Satire on politics. Outs and Ins are both responsible for maladministration.

70-53. Epigram.

"Or war, or peace, the present question is." (4)

L Eve Post, Nov 22, 1770.

The King wants war with Spain over the Falkland Islands; but Carlton House (Bute) does not -- and so we shall have peace!

70-54. Epigram.

"Says Jeff'ries to Bullface, one day at a route." (8)

L Eve Post, Jun 16, 1770.

Satire on Mansfield and Fletcher Norton who, supported by Carlton House, Bute and the King's Mother, have nothing to fear from Chatham.

70-55. Epigram.

"Says outs to ins, 'You're knaves and fools.'" (4)

L Eve Post, Mar 27, 1770.

Satire on outs and ins -- knaves, fools, faction's tools.

70-56. Epigram.

"See! blust'ring North a pow'rful fleet prepare." (7)

L Eve Post, Oct 20, 1770.

HC. Satire on North for being influenced by Bute to call off the war against Spain over the Falkland Islands.

70-57. An Epigram.

"This shew of war will end in smoke." (4)

G Eve Post, Nov 8, 1770; GM 40 (Nov 1770), 534; PA, Nov 10, 1770; Lloyd's 27 (Nov 9, 1770), 458.

The dispute over the Falkland Islands is real, but it will "end in smoke."

70-58. Epigram.

"Thou, Junius, wound'st our Great in seeming Rant." (4)

St J's C, Jan 16, 1770.

HC. Junius cannot be answered by the "Great" enemies he attacks; but he should dread their violence.

70-59. Epigram. Extempore.

"Most think our present heads are fully bent." (6)

Lloyd's 26 (Jan 19, 1770), 78.

HC. The present administration is trying to improve, not to change, the English government.

70-60. Epigram. On Swearing in Mr. Alderman Wilkes Master of the Joiners Company.

"Jack, out of gaol, and out of debt." (4)

Lloyd's 27 (Nov 2, 1770), 438.

Wilkes is sworn in to the Joiners Company as Master, because he has set together three kingdoms -- "by the ears."

70-61. Epitaph.

"Here lieth/A mean and abject wretch." (c. 15)

L Eve Post, Jan 16, 1770.

Inscription. Satire on Junius for faction, sedition, libel, all other sins, including popularity and siding with Wilkes.

70-62. Epitaph for Mr. G. Grenville.

"He who first gave a stamp." (6)

Ox M 5 (Nov 1770), 192.

Sixain. George Grenville, died Nov 13, 1770, had introduced the Stamp Act in 1765, and opposed its repeal in 1766. Signed "Nick Nankeedoodle."

70-63. Epitaph for the late Lord-Mayor.

"This Tomb, what few succeeding ones shall boast." (4)

G Eve Post, Jun 23, 1770; L Chron 27 (Jun 23, 1770), 608; PA, Jun 26, 1770; GM 40 (Jun 1770), 277.

On Lord Mayor Beckford -- a man beloved in Britain. Died June 21, 1770.

70-64. An Extempore.

"'Hard times indeed,' as Falstaff says." (4)

G Eve Post, Nov 17, 1770; L Chron 28 (Nov 15, 1770), 480.

Quatrain. That Wilkes and Horne have fallen out hurts the struggle for liberty.

70-65. Extempore on a Late Majority.

"Ask you why N--- pours his Throat." (20)

PA, Mar 1, 1770.

Quatrains. All are corrupt, all sell themselves to eat at the cost of honor and morality.

70-66. Extempore on reading the K---'s Speech.

"I am sorry to tell you our beasts have the murrain." (12)

Free M 1 (Jan 1770), 275; MJ, Jan 16, 1770; WM 7 (Mar 1, 1770), 276.

Ironic presentation of the King speaking to Parliament and exposing his venal attitude towards his subjects and his view of the "obstinate, troublesome" colonies.

70-67. Extempore on the late seeming Change in the Ministry.

"No sooner does his Grace recede." (4)

Free M 1 (Feb 1770), 321; PA, Feb 20, 1770.

Quatrain. First signs of the new chief minister, young Lord North.

70-68. Extempore, on the Non-celebration of Mr. Wilkes's Birth-Day.

"When Wilkes was safe within the Bench." (8)

PA, Nov 3, 1770.

Epigram. Quatrains. Now that Wilkes is out of prison, he receives little attention.

70-69. Extempore upon a Late Resignation and Appointment.

"At length compell'd to a retreat." (6)

Lloyd's 26 (Jan 31, 1770), 118.

Sixain. Grafton is compelled to resign -- and now North becomes Premier.

70-70. Extempore. Upon Reading No. Forty-five was Inscribed on the Foundation Stone of the New Jail.

"Forty-five, as a number convicted of treason." (4)

G Eve Post, Jun 7, 1770; L Chron 27 (Jun 7, 1770), 552.

Epigram on the celebrated Wilkesian number 45 -- committed to jail forever.

70-71. Ex-Trumpery. On Hearing that the American culprit was undetermined in his Opinion as to Peace or War.

"Undetermin'd is HILL? -- yes. Because, as he'd say." (8)

L Eve Post, Dec 1, 1770.

Hexameter couplets. Lord Hillsborough, Secretary of State for the American Department, is a corrupt courtier guided by self-interest regarding the Falkland Islands dispute. Indecisive, he waits to see how the court inclines.

70-72. Forty-Five. A Ballad.

"To the Worthies of Britain my Song I address." (44)

Lloyd's 26 (Apr 25, 1770), 404.

Song. A humorous ballad sung in the persona of a woman, 45 years old, who wishes to get married. Wilkes and Bute in the background give it an ironic flavor.

70-73. The Glorious Verdict. A Song, inscribed to Liberty.

"The Court were all met." (24)

L Chron 28 (Jul 24, 1770), 88; WM 9 (Aug 9, 1770), 180.

Song in sixains, honoring John Miller, editor and printer of the London Evening Post, because the jury refused to convict him for libel. Reflects the attempt to suppress the freedom of the press to print parliamentary proceedings.

70-74. The Great Fifty-Nine.

"Ye stout British Tars, ever firm in the Wars." (40)

BLJ, Dec 29, 1770; St J's C, Dec 25, 1770.

A song celebrating the defeat in 1759 of a French naval force under Conflans by the British under Admiral Edward Hawke. British officers mentioned are Keppel, Howe, and others.

70-75. A Great Man's Soliloquy on the Event of a Late Address.

"Yes -- it shall live, while mem'ry can retain." (39)

MJ, Mar 24, 1770.

HC, in defense of the City of London against an oppressive court. The "great man" may be the Lord Mayor Beckford.

70-76. The great Messenger of Mortality, or Dialogue between Death and a Lord-Mayor.

"Death. Stern Beckford, lay your Robes and Mace aside." (84)

PA, Jul 10, 1770.

HC. Death exposes all the sins of Beckford, the Lord Mayor of London.

70-77. The Group; or, A slight Sketch of the principal Ministerial Characters from the Year 1755 to 67. Connected by a few Historical Anecdotes of the Times. An Ode. Inscrib'd to several Great Men.

"Come, honest Muse, bring forth to View." (354)

PA, Dec 21, 1770.

Regular (Horatian) ode. Probably by a peer familiar with the internal politics of Parliament, paints a picture from the inside of the governing forces of the period; defines issues and attitudes; and places the American problem in the larger perspective of British politics. -- Abuses "the motley Ministerial Crew" -- Chatham, Newcastle, Bute, Grenville (and American taxation); discusses General Warrants and Wilkes, Sandwich, Rockingham's repeal of Grenville's Stamp Tax, Pitt's support of America, Judge Pratt (Lord Camden).

70-78. [Had tutor Charles into the Prince.]

"Had tutor Charles into the Prince." (12)

L Eve Post, Jul 17, 1770.

Quatrains. If the King had been tutored well, perhaps he could have learned how to spell and write -- but perhaps he's innately dull.

70-79. The Happy Choice.

"Long had the monarch of this isle been bent." (11)

WM 9 (Jul 19, 1770), 84.

HC. Lord North, a man of "sense and honour," becomes premier.

70-80. [Happy the man, who bears a tranquil mind.]

"Happy the man, who bears a tranquil mind. (21)

Lloyd's 26 (Feb 14, 1770), 164.

HC. A portrait of a rational citizen engaged in politics -- one who opposes factional disputes and believes in internal peace.

70-81. A Hint to the Late Premier.

"Grafton, vain Braggart! will it not be read." (24)

L Eve Post, Feb 13, 1770.

Heroic quatrains. Satire on Grafton for deserting politics like a coward.

70-82. The Horned Beasts. An Excellent Old Ballad -- To the Tune of Cheviot-Chace. Humbly Dedicated to the Duke of Grafton.

"God prosper long our noble King." (52)

MJ, Apr 5, 1770.

Ballad, satire on Parson Horne and Duke of Grafton. The issue is not clear. "America's lov'd Hillsborough" is cited.

70-83. [I'll seek out this Junius, this Infant of Hell.]

"I'll seek out this Junius, this Infant of Hell." (6)

Lloyd's 26 (Jan 19, 1770), 78; St J's C, Jan 18, 1770.

Epigram. Junius cannot be caught; or if caught, will prove a great trial.

70-84. An Impromptu.

"G[rafto]n, the meanest of the Courtly throng." (26)

G Eve Post, Jun 21, 1770.

HC. Bitter satire on Lord Grafton. Urges that he not be allowed to assume leadership.

70-85. [In grateful memory . . . William Pitt.]

"In grateful memory." (c. 10)

G, Mar 13, 1770; G Eve Post, Mar 13, 1770; Lloyd's 26 (Mar 12, 1770), 250; W Eve Post, Nov 1, 1770.

An inscription for a statue of Pitt to be sent to South Carolina honoring him for his services to his country and to America, particularly for "defending the Freedom of Americans . . . By promoting a Repeal of the Stamp Act" in 1766.

70-86. [In Whitehead's fate th' effect of Time behold.]

"In W-h--d's fate th' effect of Time behold." (54)

Lloyd's 26 (Jun 28, 1770), 556.

HC. Satire on the laureate Whitehead for being corrupted and for writing fulsome and dull court odes, and for repeating himself with hackneyed lines.

70-87. Inscribed to the M[ar]q[ui]s of G[ra]n[b]y.

"Not many suns since G[ra]n[b]y's warlike hand." (58)

MJ, Aug 9, 1770.

HC. Granby triumphed at Minden, but his conduct since has been infamous, deserving of censure -- e.g., his opposition to Wilkes and his support of despotism, and his deception of Rockingham. A dupe to power!

70-88. Inscription On a Guide-Post to Court.

"Into what wretched Times our Lot is cast." (18)

PA, Dec 15, 1770.

HC. Abuse of the new ministry.

70-89. Inscriptions intended for a great Lawyer's future Monument in Westminister Abbey.

"Too long was wretched mankind led astray." (10)

Free M 2 (Aug 1770), 306.

HC. Satire on William Murray (Earl Mansfield) for his black and ambitious career and for his attacks on the freedom of the press as Chief Justice.

70-90. Intended to be spoke on the ensuing enlargement of Mr. Wilkes.

"In spite of trembling statesmen's horrid hopes." (36)

L Eve Post, Mar 15, 1770.

Irregular Pindaric ode, in praise of Wilkes and all he stood for -- opposition to the Scottish tyranny and unfair taxes, and the struggle for freedom. (Wilkes was to be freed April 15, 1770.)

70-91. Jemmy Twitcher. A Ballad.

"The cream of all virtues is sweet Jemmy O." (21)

L Eve Post, Aug 2, 1770.

Song. Ironic satire on Lord Sandwich, for corruption and for betraying his former friend Wilkes, among other sins.

70-92. Jones, John. [Whilst some on Pleasure's flow'ry lap reclin'd.]

"Whilst some on Pleasure's flow'ry lap reclin'd." (52)

Ox M 4 (May 1770), 195.

Elegiac quatrains lament the corruption of the times -- luxury, exploitation of the poor, "party contests," justice subverted by bribes.

70-93. Junius. A Character.

"When the mask'd Patriots of a former reign." (36)

Lloyd's 26 (Jan 5, 1770), 25.

HC. Satire on Junius, "the foulest [warrior] on the paper plain."

70-94. [Junius again will play th' assassin's part.]

"Junius again will play th' assassin's part." (10)

Lloyd's 26 (Mar 5, 1770), 228.

HC. Junius is vicious and his cause worthless, but his style is attractive.

70-95. The Lamentation of Liberty and Britannia, on the Death of the Right Honourable William Beckford, Esq;

"As sate Britannia on the sea-beat shore." (144)

BWJ, Jul 28, 1770.

HC. Britain and Liberty mourn the death of Beckford, while Mansfield and Bute, enemies of freedom, are still alive. Beckford is placed among the Republican pantheon of Cato, Hampden, Russel, Sidney. Oliver will carry on.

70-96. Letter from Robin Cade, Common-Councilman of London, to his Brother Turpin Cade, Collier at Newcastle upon Tyne.

"Dear Brother, As this was our Day to remonstrate again." (72)

PA, May 26, 1770.

Hexameter couplets. The persona Cade, ironically representing a supporter of Wilkes, reveals how the seditious Wilkite rioters function in pressuring the King so that they can benefit.

70-97. Liberty's Address to the Livery.

"Haste away, my brave Sons, and at Guildhall appear." (16)

G, Jul 11, 1770.

Quatrains in couplets. The London livery, led by Oliver, will carry the torch of liberty despite "vile Courtiers."

70-98. The Lion and the Apes.

"The Apes, a chatt'ring factious sett." (54)

Lloyd's 26 (Dec 29/69-January 1, 1770), 4, (January 31, 1770), 116.

Hudibrastics, animal fable. The British lion advises the factious and idle multitude to behave reasonably and ignore "Junius's treasons."

70-99. The Lion and the Fox. A Fable.

"'Twas in some former days (my cautious rhymes)." (24)

Lloyd's 26 (Feb 16, 1770), 172.

HC. Animal fable teaches a lesson against corruption.

70-100. [Mansfield to Scarb'rough did repair.]

"Mansfield to Scarb'rough did repair." (24)

L Eve Post, Oct 20, 1770.

Quatrains. Satire on Mansfield and the Scottish leadership at court.

70-101. The Marriage of Junius to Miss Laetitia Liberty.

"Ten Dorian flutes." (c. 80)

MJ, Feb 22, 1770.

Inscription, an apparently irregular Pindaric ode, celebrating the nuptials of Liberty to Junius in which the participants are George Savile, Burke, Barre, Mrs. Macaulay, Wilkes, Sawbridge, James Townsend, Bellas, and many others (Chatham, Rockingham, Shelburne, and Americans) -- all in the libertarian cause.

70-102. [Monumentum, Aeternae memoriae sacrum.]

"Monumentum, /Aeternae memoriae sacrum." (46)

L Eve Post, Jun 14, 1770; Freeman's J, Jun 19, 1770.

Inscription. Epitaph on the freedom of the press, outlined in heavy black margins. A protest at the attack on the press.

70-103. A New Patriotic Song on the Times.

"Ye Sons of Britannia now lift up your Voice." (37)

Free M 1 (Jan 1770), insert post p. 276.

A song for Wilkes, Beckford, Savile, Camden, Glynn, Burke, the members of the opposition, and against the court and its "dirty work."

70-104. A New Patriotic Song. To the Tune of Rule Britannia.

"When Freedom's Sons indignant rose." (37)

Free M 2 (Jul 1770), 257.

A song in defense of freedom and in praise of Camden, Chatham, Wilkes, Beckford, Richard Oliver -- all who opposed Parliamentary oppression.

70-105. A New Song.

"When the jugglers of state, and rich court-pension'd knaves." (20)

MJ, Feb 22, 1770.

Song. Satire on the forthcoming change of the ministry -- from Grafton to North. Wilkes and Burke will foil the majority.

70-106. Nortonius Heroum Princeps.

"To raise a deathless name, heroes of old." (8)

L Eve Post, Jun 2, 1770.

HC. Satire on Sir Fletcher Norton, Speaker of the House -- Norton, Chief of Heroes, who deserves a monument of brass.

70-107. Ode. By a Middlesex Politician.

"With anxious speed I left Mile-End." (54)

L Chron 27 (Apr 7, 1770), 340; LM 39 (Apr 1770), 217; PA, Apr 9, 1770; WM 8 (May 3, 1770), 146.

Regular ode in sixains. An expression of disgust at the debates in the House of Commons between the Ins and Outs. Grenville, Dowdeswell, Barre are cited.

70-108. Ode for the Day of Mr. Wilkes's Enlargement.

"Hail to the rosy morn, whose ray." (60)

L Eve Post, Feb 24, 1770.

Song. An oratorio celebrating the release of Wilkes from prison: Wilkes, the patriot follower of John Hampden and Algernon Sydney.

70-109. An Ode For the Year 1770.

"Lo! I, on easy chair reclined." (52)

GM 40 (Jul 1770), 326; Lloyd's 27 (Jul 18, 1770), 67.

Irregular ode in couplets. A cynical view of politics -- which cannot disturb the comfort of an easy life. Grenville and Johnson are cited. Alternative title is Not I, Indeed. An Ode for the Year 1770.

70-110. Ode to Junius.

"O Junius! whilst a venal Tribe." (54)

PA, Dec 29, 1770.

Regular ode in sixains. Asks Junius to return and save the nation from ruin. Cited are Sandwich, Weymouth.

70-111. Ode to Lord Chatham.

"At length th' unequal Strife give o'er." (96)

BWJ, Dec 29, 1770; Freeman J, Feb 9, 1771; L Eve Post, Dec 20, 1770; L Mus 2 (Mar 1771), 239-41.

Regular ode in sixains. Chatham is urged to flee corrupt and ruined Britain for North America and freedom. Cited are Sandwich, Grafton, Bedford, Mansfield, Camden, among others. The myth of America as the land of the free is evoked.

70-112. Ode to Lord North, On His Being Appointed Commander in Chief of The House of Commons, 1770.

"O Thou, whom placemen all adore." (66)

L Eve Post, Feb 27, 1777; PA, Mar 1, 1770; New Foundling Hospital for Wit (1768-73), Part 4 (1771), pp. 37-9; (1786), IV, 170-2.

Regular ode in sixains. North, unlike Grafton, will successfully withstand opposition with the help of bribes -- and Weymouth, Sandwich, Scottish peers, the Bishops, Mansfield, Barrington, Charles James Fox. This is perhaps the first mention of Fox in verse.

70-113. Ode to St. Stephen.

"First Martyr of inhuman Mobs." (77)

BLJ, Dec 8, 1770; L Eve Post, Dec 6, 1770; PA, Dec 5, 1770; St J's C, Dec 4, 1770.

Regular ode in seven-line stanzas. Takes to a degree the Tory side and satirizes the rabble misled by seditious politicians in the Commons. Concludes with a prayer that the House stand firm against the threat from Spain. Cited are Dunning, Barre, Wedderburn, Dowdeswell, Glynn, Burke, James Townsend, among others. See Another Ode to St. Stephen, 70-18.

70-114. Ode to Sir George Saville.

"Lost to each virtue of the mind." (36)

L Eve Post, Mar 15, 1770.

Irregular Pindaric ode. Panegyric on Sir George Saville, a patriot who is uncorrupted.

70-115. Ode to the Sleeping Genius of Britain.

"Lo! where Britain's Genius sleeping." (42)

Lloyd's 27 (Oct 3, 1770), 331.

Regular (Horatian) ode urging Britain not to sleep in the face of French and Spanish menaces, and to unite to prepare for war.

70-116. [Oh grant, kind Heaven! before I close my eyes.]

"Oh grant, kind Heaven! before I close my eyes." (20)

L Eve Post, Apr 24, 1770.

HC. Begs for Bute to be punished for his poor peace and for being a traitor.

70-117. On a Late Occurrence.

"For Britain's good its Delegates." (4)

Lloyd's 26 (Feb 28, 1770), 215.

Epigram. Satire on a weak and ineffectual Parliament (in the face of Spanish incursions).

70-118. On a Report that Lord Mansfield will be appointed Chancellor.

"What honest heart but for his country feels." (12)

L Eve Post, Feb 3, 1770; Ox M, 4 (Feb 1770), 72.

Quatrains. Objects to Mansfield's appointment to the office of chancellor of the exchequer because he is not disinterested.

70-119. On Hearing that Mr. Wilkes's Father was a Distiller.

"Inflam'd alike by Wilkes (the son and sire)." (4)

Lloyd's 26 (Jan 1, 1770), 15.

Epigram. The mob is inflamed by the gin distilled by Wilkes' father and by the son's false British spirit.

70-120. On Hearing the Report of a Great Man's Nails Growing.

"When Barrington the sword conceal'd." (8)

L Eve Post, Oct 16, 1770.

Quatrains. Satire on Barrington and Mansfield for wishing to injure Britain.

70-121. On Junius.

"Like a fell serpent, Junius lost his sting." (4)

Lloyd's 26 (Feb 16, 1770), 172.

Epigram. Satire on Junius, "That monster of Sedition" who has lost his sting.

70-122. On Lord Camden's Dismission.

"When Camden was ordered to give up his charge." (18)

L Chron 28 (Sep 20, 1770), 287; L Eve Post, Sep 15, 1770

Hexameter couplets. Grafton has dismissed Justice Pratt, Lord Camden, but the dismissal casts a shadow on Grafton.

70-123. On L[OR]D C[HATHA]M.

"Strange! C[hatha]m is lame of the gout as fame says." (6)

G Eve Post, Mar 6, 1770.

Satire on Chatham. Pitt, Earl of Chatham, has lost his reputation ever since he accepted a title and pension.

70-124. On Lord Clive.

"Of old proud Asia's mighty Monarch saw." (18)

PA, May 16, 1770.

HC. Panegyric on Lord Clive for conquering India and ruling the country with justice and humanity.

70-125. On Lord North's Naval Armament.

"Spain shall repent her proud and hostile action." (6)

L Eve Post, Oct 16, 1770; Ox M 5 (Oct 1770), 155.

Epigram. Satire on North's boast that he will humble Spain. But the navy is ill-prepared for war.

70-126. On Ministerial Eloquence in Certain Assemblies.

"Though press'd by truth, by argument and sense." (4)

L Eve Post, Dec 13, 1770.

Epigram. North is not swayed by debates in Parliament. He has the majority on his side (through bribery).

70-127. On Mr. Wilkes's Release.

"Splendid as day the sons of freedom shone." (4)

G Eve Post, Apr 24, 1770; L Chron 27 (Apr 24, 1770), 400.

Epigram. Illuminations celebrate the ascent of Liberty to her throne, as Wilkes is released from prison.

70-128. On Patriotism.

"In ancient times, if history tells true." (19)

Lloyd's 26 (Mar 28, 1770), 308.

HC. The present so-called patriots are motivated by sordid self-interest. Discord is caused by corruption.

70-129. On Reading Major Miller's Plans for Regulating the City Militia.

"Britannia's Sons, in Days of Yore." (28)

Lloyd's 27 (Aug 17, 1770), 172; PA, Aug 16, 1770.

Quatrains. Praise of a new plan for restoring order to London undermined by mobs and riots. (In effect an anti-Wilkes poem.)

70-130. On Reading the Letters of Junius.

"Bright as the Sun which through the Zodiac goes." (34)

L Eve Post, Feb 24, 1770.

HC. Praise of Junius, one of the many patriots protecting liberty with Rockingham, Temple, Chatham, Camden.

70-131. On Sir Bullface Doublefee being S[peake]r of the H[ouse] of C[ommon]s.

"Who could have dreamt that Bully N[orto]n." (38)

L Eve Post, Mar 17, 1770.

Satire on Sir Fletcher Norton, for corruption and other sins.

70-132. On the American Contentions.

"Throughout Britannia's wide domain, ingratitude's the fruit." (6)

Lloyd's 26 (Feb 16, 1770), 172.

Fourteener couplets. The colonies are ungrateful to the mother country; but, on the other hand, the mother country cannot rule because of domestic anarchy.

70-133. On the Death of a Late Lord Chancellor.

"Lloyd's 26 (Jan 31, 1770), 118.

HC. Charles Yorke (Attorney-General at the time of the Wilkes case) died Jan. 20, 1770, three days after becoming lord chancellor.

70-134. On the Death of the Much Lamented Lord Mayor.

"Nature unkind, has cast the fatal dart." (12)

Free M 2 (Jun 1770), 210; L Chron 27 (Jun 23, 1770), 605; L Eve Post, Jun 21, 1770.

Quatrains in couplets. Panegyric on Mayor Beckford, independent and incorruptible guardian of liberty.

70-135. On the Death of the Patriotic Lord-Mayor.

"Oh! what a stab is this to Freedom's cause." (12)

G Eve Post, Jun 21, 1770.

HC. Praise of Beckford, a patriot of integrity, who has just died.

70-136. On the Death of the Right Honourable the Lord Mayor.

"And is he dead! O fatal piercing news." (18)

MJ, May 26, 1770.

HC. Epitaph. Weep for Beckford, zealous guardian of the City's rights.

70-137. On the Death of William Beckford, Esq;

"What! Beckford dead! -- who then but must repine." (2)

St J's C, Jun 30, 1770.

Beckford's death is a great loss to Britain.

70-138. On the Debate on the State of the Nation being Put Off for a Ball at the Mansion House.

"Says Tom to Will, how goes the State." (4)

PA, Feb 12, 1770.

Epigram. North's fate is suspended while the patriots attend the Lord Mayor's ball. (North became premier Jan 28, 1770.)

70-139. On the Discovery of Junius, in the St. James's Chronicle of Oct. 26, 1769.

"Ho! now we have you, Junius -- very clear --." (6)

St J's C, Jan 18, 1770.

HC. Who Junius is remains a mystery.

70-140. On the Enlargement of John Wilkes.

"When Greece and Rome triumphant reign'd." (30)

Free M 2 (Apr 1770), 108.

Song. Not the same as poem with same title, MJ, Apr. 19, 1770. Wilkes was freed April 18, 1770.

70-141. On the Enlargement of John Wilkes, Esq; April 18, 1770.

"'Tis past! at length his bonds are o'er." (36)

MJ, Apr 19, 1770.

Sixains. Panegyric of Wilkes, freedom's martyr, released from his imprisonment for blasphemy and libel.

70-142. On the Hanoverian Family.

"To break our Chains and purge our deep Disgrace." (10)

BLJ, Apr 21, 1770; St J's C, Apr 17, 1770.

HC. Some Britons wish for the return of the Stuarts; but King George will continue in the tradition of the first two Georges and not allow the (Jacobite) rebels to operate.

70-143. On the late Arrival of an unpopular Lord.

"Shall wicked minions of the Court." (24)

Ox M 4 (Supplement 1770), 283.

Sixains. A satire on Stephen Fox -- or possibly Charles James Fox.

70-144. On the Late Lord Mayor. [Two poems.]

"All Arts to save his Country Beckford tried." (2)
"Thy future Doom, unhappy Britain, dread." (2)

BLJ, Jul 14, 1770.

Epigrams on death of Beckford. He died when he could not save his country; and Bute, still alive, will cause Britain grief.

70-145. On the Late Lord Mayor. [Three poems.]

"All arts to save his country Beckford tried." (2 + 2 + 5)

G Eve Post, Jul 12, 1770; L Chron 28 (Jul 12, 1770), 41.

Beckford, a great Whig, stood up to the King of England -- but submitted to the King of Terrors, Death.

70-146. On the Late Lord Mayor's Funeral.

"Whilst all the City mourns their Beckford dead." (6)

BWJ, Aug 18, 1770.

HC. All the City mourns Beckford; but no one will mourn the Junto (cabinet or court) should they die.

70-147. On the Oeconomy of the present Administration.

"So saving the minister's grown." (12)

WM 8 (Jun 7, 1770), 308.

Quatrains. Satire on the corruption of the North ministry.

70-148. On the Releasement of Mr. Wilkes.

"Hail! hail! thou steady patriot, Albion's friend." (14)

G Eve Post, Apr 17, 1770.

HC. Praise of Wilkes, hated by courtiers, in the (republican) tradition of Hampden.

70-149. On the Remonstrators.

"On Noise and Riot are the Grumblers bent." (4)

Lloyd's 26 (Apr 13, 1770), 364.

HC. The protestors against Administration should burn their own petitions and grievances. This should end the "mischief."

70-150. On the Report Lately Current of the Death of the Earl of Bute.

"Has then this comet spent its rage at last." (4)

Lloyd's 26 (Jan 19, 1770), 78; St J's C, Jan 18, 1770.

HC. At last the "mighty Stuart" has died -- and so has "Ambition, Avarice, and Pride."

70-151. On the Scum of the Earth.

"The nature of things how the great have mistook." (4)
"The scum of the earth let courtiers despise." (2)

G Eve Post, Mar 31, 1770; LM 39 (Apr 1770), 217; WM 9 (Jul 5, 1770), 20.

Epigrams. Two versions of a republican defiance. The scum always rises to the top.

70-152. On the Times.

"When G[eorg]e with Scotchmen shall converse." (18)

MJ, Mar 10, 1770.

OC. Britons should protest the new ministry, the change to North, for the Scotch are still influential and Tories turning out Whigs. Cited are Bute, Halifax, Sandwich, Norton.

70-153. One Thousand Seven Hundred and Seventy. An Original Satire, Addressed to John Wilkes, Esq;

"When worth like thine survives the rod of pow'r." (66)

Free M 2 (Jul 1770), 259-60.

HC. The satirist is compelled to write (like Juvenal) to expose corruption, but is censored, at which infringement of liberty he complains.

70-154. The Ostrich, the Viper, the Owl and the Fox. A Political Fable. Humbly inscribed to Mr. T. S.

"Accept, dear Sir, a limping lay." (162)

Lloyd's 26 (Feb 5, 1770), 132.

Hudibrastics. Animal fable. Apparently sides with Junius and freedom against faction. (But is too general for the sense to peek through the allegory.)

70-155. The Ox Over Driven. An Original Fable Addressed to a Friend.

"While you, my friend, in country town." (92)

Free M 2 (Jun 1770), 209.

OC. Animal fable, satire on the King for his oppressive government, which will result in the rebellion of the people.

70-156. A Paraphrase on the 22d Ode of the First Book of Horace. Addressed to Sir George Savile, Bart.

"The man whose virtuous soul disdains." (28)

L Eve Post, Mar 3, 1770; Ox M 4 (Apr 1770), 153.

OC. A portrait of a geniune patriot, "Unbrib'd, unpension'd, and unplac'd," fearless George Savile. Reference to "venal Norton" and the (bribed) majority that carries each debate "To ruin . . . the State."

70-157. A Parody from the Fair Penitent, (Act I and II) for to-morrow, the auspicious 18th of April, 1770.

"Joy to thee, Wilkes, Joy to myself!" (42)

L Eve Post, Apr 11, 1770.

Britannia receives Wilkes coming out of prison and embraces him.

70-158. A Parody on Shakespeare.

"Expell'd, or not expell'd, that is the Question." (55)

PA, May 25, 1770.

Blank verse parody of Hamlet's soliloquy satirizes Wilkes and his followers.

70-159. Parody on the Verses written by Dryden on Milton.

"Three Judges in three diff'rent ages born." (6)

L Eve Post, Jul 17, 1770.

Satire on Mansfield, who is slavish to the King, also cruel and villainous.

70-160. Part of a Satyr.

"What is a King? He is chief magistrate." (36)

MJ, Apr 5, 1770.

HC, present a Whig view of a constitutional monarch and his limited prerogative: "Kings from their people all their pow'r derive," etc.

70-161. Cancelled.

70-162. A Patriotic Song. Humbly Addressed to our Two Worthy Sheriffs.

"In our Forefathers Days when the Visage was rough." (35)

Free M 2 (Mar 1770), insert post p. 44.

Song in praise of Mayor Beckford and Sheriffs Townsend and Sawbridge for their boldness and courage in the struggle of the City with the administration.

70-163. Patriotism.

"Oh! could the Muse accustom'd bid to sing." (50)

Lloyd's 26 (Feb 12, 1770), 156.

HC. A portrait of true patriotism -- in generalities; the principle is measures, not men. (Vs. oppression, venality or corruption.)

70-164. The Pedigree of the Ions, or the Proginitors [sic] of the Revolution.

"Evil Ministers begot Oppressions." (10)

L Eve Post, Mar 10, 1770; Free J, Mar 20, 1770.

A prose poem. How the Revolution occurred -- a lesson for the times, for the ministry. Ions=Aeons. For another version, see 73-86 (and 69-A).

70-165. The Pests of Gotham. A Ballad.

"As Jeffries with Bullface and Greybeard once sat." (35)

L Eve Post, Sep 4, 1770.

Song. Ironic remarks on "the Pests" -- Mansfield, Norton, and William DeGrey -- and their persecution of the press. The reference is Mansfield's judgment that the jury can decide only on the fact, not the law involving abuse and libel.

70-166. The Petition of Grumbletonians. To the King.

"Dread Sir,/With submission." (24)

Lloyd's 26 (Feb 21, 1770), 188.

Sixains. Satire on the envious and the selfish who simply wish to be in, and so to stir up trouble. See 70-12.

70-167. The Picture of a Courtier.

"A string of phrases, conn'd with grace." (22)

G Eve Post, Jun 26, 1770); L Chron 27 (Jun 26, 1770), 612; L Eve Post, Jun 23, 1770; WM 9 (Jul 5, 1770), 20.

OC. General satire on a corrupt political peer. This poem matches the poem On True Nobility and False: 64-85.

70-168. Picture of a Dead Monarch.

"Some feeble, head-strong Prince may here repose." (20)

BWJ, Jun 23, 1770; L Eve Post, May 23, 1771; Freeman's J, May 26, 1770.

Elegiac stanzas. An imitation of Gray's Elegy. Satire on the King for all his defects as a ruler, among them being his Jacobitism. An extract from 70-49.

70-169. Piety True Patriotism. An Ode on the Prospect of War.

"No muse I ask to aid my lays." (48)

WM 10 (Dec 13, 1770), 338.

Regular ode in sixains. The pious patriot will reform to save his country and then humble Spain. The reference is the Falkland Islands dispute.

70-170. Poem Addressed to John Wilkes, Esq.

"Genius of England, whither hast thou fled." (102)

Free M 2 (Mar 1770), 49-51.

HC. Praise of Wilkes for standing bravely for freedom unlike mean and weak sycophants who fear Bute. All the good men have left government -- William Beckford, Temple, Pitt (Chatham), as Bute triumphs and Wilkes bleeds.

70-171. A Poem for the First of March, 1770.

"Tho' Poets now commence their flow'ry dance." (34)

L Eve Post, Feb 27, 1770.

HC. A simile. March storms are compared to the storms that rock government. Corruption and the sacrifice of public good will bring on "rude blasts."

70-172. A Political Ballad.

"Ye politic blockheads and asses." (50)

LM 44 (Jun 1770), 320.

Song. Ballad. A cynical view of politicians; they are simply selfish -- Pitt, who is interested in advantage, but not money; Wilkes, who is interested in being a "liberty wit." (A confused poem.)

70-173. The Political Doctor.

"Bolus, a man who lack'd not sense." (38)

Lloyd's 26 (Apr 11, 1770), 356.

OC. Satire on a Wilkes follower who neglects his profession and himself in order to mind Wilkes' business.

70-174. The Present Times.

"While Turks and Russians, fierce in arms." (12)

G Eve Post, Aug 9, 1770; L Chron 28 (Aug 9, 1770), 143; PA, Aug 11, 1780.

OC. Everyone all around the western world is engaged in some type of hostile action but Britain, even Philadelphia and Boston. Britain debates whether to war with Spain for questionable legal rights.

70-175. The Progress of Faction.

"The demon Faction us'd in former times." (46)

Lloyd's 26 (Feb 28, 1770), 212.

HC. An Establishment poem directed against the freedom-loving patriots. Faction has now been refined into Opposition, but it is still the same, motivated by ambition, envy, avarice, and self-interest and causing disorder and anarchy.

70-176. The Prophecy.

"This truth of old was sorrow's friend." (108)

MJ, May 29, 1770.

Sixains in couplets. A satire on the corrupt and oppressive Tory politics of the times. But because the times are at their worst, they must surely mend. Cited are King George and King William, Grafton and Bute.

70-177. A Proposal to the Politicians.

"The great contest through Britain's Isle, is who shall places win." (6)

Lloyd's 26 (Mar 2, 1770), 223.

Fourteeners. The politicians are simply selfish, wanting money and place and thereby corrupting the country. Take the profit out of honors.

70-178. Receipt to make a complete Patriot.

"With Dishonesty begin." (38)

PA, Jan 26, 1770.

OC. Satire on the patriot character which sums up all that is evil in several political figures -- including Sackville, Burke, Barre, Wilkes, Shelburne, Delaval, and James Townsend.

70-179. Reflection.

"The sages all allow for truth." (12)

MJ, Mar 1, 1770.

Sixains. Bute is to be blamed for Grafton's despotism.

70-180. Rehoboam.

"When th'Israelites told Rehoboam." (23)

Lloyd's 26 (Mar 28, 1770), 308.

HC. The King, should he ever prove arbitrary and tyrannical, will bring ruin to himself and the nation. (A general warning growing out of the Wilkes disputes.)

70-181. The Resolutions of the Button-Makers, on a Certain Interloper.

"In club assembled t'other night." (38)

L Eve Post, Feb 17, 1770.

OC. Satire on the King as button-maker and as one who also forms ministries -- as seen by professional button-makers.

70-182. Risum Teneatis Amici! the Answer.

"To hear your complaints I shall ever by ready." (26)

L Eve Post, Mar 24, 1770.

Hexameter couplets. Satire on the King, whose persona speaks, revealing unpleasant traits -- tyranny (refuses to accept petitions), subservience to mother and Bute, corruption and bribery, Toryism.

70-183. The Royal Progress.

"Much like a weight, suspended by a string." (16)

BWJ, Aug 4, 1770.

HC. Ironic satire on the King who can, like Parliament, do no wrong.

70-184. [Says Bullface to North, "My Lord how do you fare?"]

"Says Bullface to North, "My Lord how do you fare." (9)

L Eve Post, Jul 26, 1770.

Hexameter couplets. North confesses to Fletcher Norton that he lacks the support of the public (regarding the Falkland Islands dispute).

70-185. A Second Poem Addressed to John Wilkes Esq;

"Hail, Wilkes! -- than whose recorded name." (c. 90)

Free M 2 (May 1770), 161-2.

HC. Panegyric on manly patriot Wilkes in contrast to the criminal anti-libertarian puppets of Bute at court. The present King does not, unlike Kings of the past, ennoble man.

70-186. 1770: Or, a View of Ireland.

"Yes; I will speak -- nor will I e'er refrain." (c. 70)

Freeman's J, Aug 30, 1770.

HC. Satire in the manner of Pope's *Epistle to Arbuthnot*, on the corrupt maladministration of Ireland, dominated by Bute and his instrument George Townshend. (The author is Lewis, a writer and editor of the *Freeman's Journal*. See To the Author of 1770, 70-210.

70-187. A Short Character of the Late Lord Mayor.

"Sacred to the Memory of the Right Hon. William Beckford, Esq;"

G Eve Post, Jun 23, 1770; L Eve Post, Jun 21, 1770; Owen's Weekly Chronicle, and Westminister Journal, Jun 23-30, 1770.

Epitaph. Praise of Beckford for his independent spirit.

70-188. A Short Dialogue betwixt Atticus and Faction.

"A Minister and virtuous -- 'twas never seen." (26)

L Chron 27 (Feb 10, 1770), 148; PA, Feb 13, 1770.

HC. Atticus (a newspaper correspondent) and Faction agree that the present minister, North, is honest and true -- "so impudently good," as Faction confesses. But despite his merit, North will be damned by Junius, Shelburne, and Wilkes.

70-189. [Sir Fletcher in the chair! -- how I'm amaz'd.]

"Sir F[letche]r in the chair! -- how I'm amaz'd." (12)

MJ, Feb 22, 1770.

HC. Grafton chooses Sir Fletcher Norton as Speaker of the House.

70-190. Smith, William.
A Dialogue, &c. spoken at the Commencement in the College of Philadelphia, June 5, 1770; supposed to be written by Dr. Smith.

"No more in Academic forms we greet." (c. 100)

GM 40 (Aug 1770), 384; Freeman's J, Sep 13, 1770; Lloyd's 27 (Aug 20, 1770), 182; L Chron 28 (Aug 16, 1770), 164; MJ, Sep 6, 1770; WM 9 (Aug 30, 1770), 276-7.

Blank verse dialogue with two airs. First mourns the discord between Britain and America; then celebrates the coming of freedom to "Britain's sons" and the beginning of a prosperous trade -- with an allusion to the colonial non-importation agreement meant to defend the "country's rights."

70-191. [Some say the war is all a hum.]

"Some say the war is all a hum." (9)

G Eve Post, Sep 25, 1770; Lloyd's 27 (Sep 26, 1770), 308; L Chron 28 (Sep 25, 1770), 304.

Triplets, expressing doubt about the war with Spain. Is it a real or manufactured crisis?

70-192. A Song for the 18th of April, the Day of Mr. Wilkes's Release. Intended to be sung at York. To the Tune of Hearts of Oak.

"In Liberty's cause let us raise the glad note." (64)

MJ, Apr 14, 1770.

Song in praise of Wilkes for his bold stand on liberty and arbitrary government. Also in praise of other guardians of liberty: Rockingham, Temple, Burke, Townsend, Sawbridge.

70-193. Song on John Wilkes, Esq.

"Good people of England, your reason awaken." (24)

L Chron 27 (Apr 14, 1770), 368.

Song with "Derry down" chorus. Wilkes should be helped in discharging his debts.

70-194. A Speech to the Worshipful Livery of the City of London, at Guildhall.

"The Lord Mayor being dead, it is always the fashion." (28)

Lloyd's 27 (Jul 2, 1770), 11.

Hexameter couplets. The persona of the London livery comments on the death of Beckford, with some unpleasant remarks on him.

70-195. State of the Nation, 1770.

"Ye Politicians list awhile." (110)

PA, Feb 3, 1770.

Cinquains. A cynical satire on several parasitic individuals who make for a sorry state of the nation: Townsend, Savile, Wedderburn, Barre, Burke, Sackville. Stanza 21 foretells civil war.

70-196. Stevens, George Alexander.
A Christmas Carroll, Called Liberty-Hall.

"Old Homer! but what have we with him to do." (40)

L Chron 27 (Jan 2, 1770), 13; G, Jan 3, 1770; G Eve Post, Dec 30/69-Jan 2, 1770; Stevens, Songs, Comic, Satyrical (Oxford, 1772), pp. 129-31.

A Whig song in honor of Liberty, supported by the cornerstone Magna Charta and the pillars of Independency and Integrity.

70-197. A Sunday Night's Conference at Carlton-House.

"At eve on Sundays, just at eight." (40)

L Eve Post, Mar 10, 1770.

OC. Satire on the King for being (secretly) influenced by his mother and Bute.

70-198. Tait, John.
Ode to Liberty, On the Anniversary of his Majesty's Accession to the Throne, October 25, 1760.

"Welcome, thrice auspicious day." (c. 100)

WM 10 (Oct 24, 1770), 116-7.

An irregular Pindaric ode honoring King George on the tenth anniversary of his accession to the throne. Asks for the end of "discord and factious strife," for concord and unanimity and the maintenance of the British "empire of the main."

70-199. The Titans: A Simile.

"Rawhead and Bloody-bone Petitions." (64)

PA, Mar 24, 1770; Lloyd's 26 (Mar 23, 1770), 290.

OC. A satire on the London council and its inclination to "bellow Remonstrance thro' the City." Beckford is singled out for attack for his use of slaves in Jamaica.

70-200. To Charles Lucas, Esq; M.D. One of the Representatives of the City of Dublin in Parliament.

"From Noise and Business for a while retir'd." (c. 225)

Freeman's J, Sep 15, 1770.

HC. Panegyric on Charles Lucas, patriot member of the Irish Parliament.

70-201. To Junius.

"Junius reflects, ere the tremendous day." (8)

Lloyd's 26 (Feb 21, 1770), 188.

HC. Junius's fine rhetoric against others' failings will not carry him to heaven.

70-202. To Junius.

"Let ev'ry mind, who loves blest freedom's cause." (40)

L Eve Post, Dec 13, 1770.

HC. Praise of Junius for his defense of political liberty and attack on corrupt peers, Junius the guardian of the laws.

70-203. To Junius.

"While Junius lash'd the subject with his quill." (32)

L Chron 27 (Feb 10, 1770), 148.

HC. Junius should direct his satire at the King.

70-204. To Lord Camden.

"Oh, Camden! thou by all mankind rever'd." (99)

L Eve Post, Apr 5, 1770.

HC. Praise of Lord Camden (Pratt) for giving up his place in order to remain honest. He had opposed the use of General Warrants.

70-205. To Lord North. A New Ballad.

"My Lord, fie upon you, you shou'd have more grace." (40)

L Eve Post, Nov 10, 1770.

Song, with "Derry, down" chorus. Satire on Luttrell, the Irish bravo. North should send him back to the army and keep him out of Ireland.

70-206. To Mr. Miller, on his Late Trial. Epigram.

"Boast not you was acquitted by the laws." (4)

BWJ, Oct 27, 1770.

Epigram. John Miller (printer of the London Evening Post) was acquitted; but he should beware of Mansfield. (Liberty of the Press issue.)

70-207. To Mrs. Macaulay.

"Since every critic and severe review." (32)

MJ, May 26, 1770.

HC. Praise of the historical writings of Catherine Macaulay, of which even Pitt approves.

70-208. To Robert Morris, Esq.

"Great Men call'd forth, by great Occasions rise." (36)

BLJ, Sep 22, 1770; St J's C, Sep 18, 1770.

HC. Panegyric on Robert Morris for standing up as a heroic patriot for freedom, unlike slavish courtiers, but like Cato, Hampden, Wilkes.

70-209. To Sir Bull-Face Double-Fee.

"Oh Thou, whose face betrays thy harden'd soul." (18)

MJ, Jan 27, 1770.

HC. Satire on Sir Fletcher Norton, recently elected Speaker of the House. (Churchill had satirized him in The Duellist, III, 269-344.)

70-210. To the Author of 1770: A Political Dialogue. By a Young Lady.

"Lewis, proceed to lash the Age." (38)

Freeman's J, Sep 11, 1770.

OC. Praise of Lewis, the author of "1770," for his fearless satire and defense of Ireland. See 70-186.

70-211. To the Author of "Thoughts on the Cause of our present Discontents."

"Whoe'er thou art, we own thy Power." (14)

BLJ, May 5, 1770; PA, May 12, 1770.

OC. Praise of Burke for his powerful Thoughts on the Cause of our present Discontents, an attack on "Corruption's Sons."

70-212. To the Bedchamber Lord, who, during the time the Lord Mayor replied to his Majesty's Answer to the City Remonstrance, cried out, "Well, this is impudence indeed . . . ."

"What! shall a <u>pensioned</u> Lord presume to scorn." (44)

G, Jun 14, 1770; G Eve Post, Jun 14, 1770.

HC. A defense of Beckford for his integrity against the criticism of "a <u>pensioned</u> Lord."

70-213. To the D[uke] of G[rafton] on his Sudden Retirement.

"All own, my Lord, 'twas right to quit your station." (6)

Lloyd's 26 (Jan 31, 1770), 118.

Epigram. Sixain. Agrees, ironically, that Grafton should resign, and "Decline to give th'encreasing Patriots battle."

70-214. To the Gentlemen of the Long Robe.

"To be quickly dispos'd of, on terms very easy." (20)

L Eve Post, Mar 13, 1770.

Anapest tetrameter quatrains. Satire on the way corruption and bribery destroy the integrity of lawyers and clergymen.

70-215. To the Gentlemen of the Minority in both Houses of Parliament.

"Wou'd those, who, by opinion plac'd on high." (4)

L Eve Post, Apr 24, 1770.

Quatrain. Advises the minority to "persevere" in their opposition.

70-216. To the King of France.

"Since George, engross'd by quacks of State." (50)

L Eve Post, Sep 11, 1770.

OC. Because King George ignores the petitions of his people and the complaints of Ireland and America, the poet invites France and Spain to assist by attacking Jamaica, Minorca, and Gibraltar. Thus, as a result of an outcry on the "gasping trade, and death of loans," the King will give up his false counsellors and concord will reign again in Britain.

70-217. To the Memory of the Right Hon. William Beckford, Esq; deceased, late Lord Mayor of London.

"Hark! hark! what mournful sounds invade my ear." (126)

L Eve Post, Jul 12, 1770.

HC. Mourns the death of patriot Beckford, who is like the Roman Cato. Beckford fearlessly opposed tyranny and protected the rights of British subjects, as well as their laws and liberty, from encroachment by the King.

70-218. To the Memory of William Beckford, Esq; the Late Right Honourable Lord Mayor of London.

"If firm resolves, if unremitted zeal." (10)

BWJ, Jun 30, 1770.

Epitaph, panegyric on Beckford, "great Republican."

70-219. To the Memory of William Beckford, Esq; who Died June the 21st, 1770, Aged LXV.

"What baleful news! alas! our father's dead." (32)

Free M 2 (Jul 1770), 259.

HC. Panegyric on Beckford, upon his death, June 21, 1770.

70-220. To the Rev. Mr. Anti-Sejanus, alias the Rev. Mr. Slyboots, alias the Rev. Mr. ****, chaplain to the pious Jemmy Twitcher.

"Leave off your dull Letters." (30)

G Eve Post, Apr 5, 1770; PA, Apr 6, 1770.

Sixains. Satire on James Scott, "Anti-Sejanus," the parson hackwriter hired by Lord Sandwich. See, e.g., "To Anti-Sejanus," 66-114.

70-221. To the Shabby Doctor.

"My dear Shabby Doctor, of what can you glory." (78)

PA, Feb 12, 1770.

Hexameter couplets. Satire on Doctor John Shebbeare, the Scot hackwriter for the administration, supported by Mungo (Jeremiah Dyson, Tory placeman) who urges the writer to abuse Wilkes' mob.

70-222. To the Third Regiment of the Guards.

"Ye mighty men of the parade." (50)

MJ, Jan 11, 1770.

OC. Satire on the Scotch regiment which was responsible for the violence on St. George's Fields and which supports Bute's repressive policies.

70-223. To the Worthy Aldermen and Common Council of the City of London, the strenuous Supporters of our civil Rights.

"Whilst you, fast Friends to Freedom's sacred Cause." (12)

L Chron 28 (Oct 30, 1770), 423; PA, Oct 31, 1770.

HC. Praise of the elected governors of London City who support its rights against "the courtly Gang."

70-224. To the Worthy Electors of the City and Liberty of Westminister.

"Gentlemen, The very great Honour you've this Day confer'd." (36)

PA, Apr 27, 1770.

Hexameter couplets. Satire on the followers of Wilkes, who are exhibited in a persona representing them engaging in vile machinations simply to create mischief.

70-225. True Blue, or the Press Gang; a Musical Interlude, as Revived at the Theatre Royal in Covent Garden . . .

"Come on, jolly lads, 'tis your country that calls." (20)

BWJ, Nov 24, 1770; G Eve Post, Nov 13, 1770; L Eve Post, Nov 15, 1770; WM 10 (Oct 24, 1770), 117.

Song. Recitative and airs that celebrate naval action. The song patriotically calls for men to join up "to punish the Spaniard." "Let it never be said, . . . that bold British sailors want pressing."

70-226. Truth at Court.

"Now fye upon't, quoth Flattery." (22)

L Chron 28 (Oct 13, 1770), 368; Ox M 5 (Oct 1770), 155, also 9 (Nov 1772), 191.

OC. Flattery is rejected at court; but Truth still embarrasses the King. Also appeared in SM 23 (Apr 1761), 202.

70-227. Upon a certain noble Lord, Late a Most Unpopular Commoner.

"This motley Wretch! with murder'd Fame." (6)

Lloyd's 26 (Feb 19, 1770), 182.

Sixain. Satire on Chatham, who has lost his reputation, because he "Brawls, for the People's right."

70-228. Upon Reading a Late Address of Thanks.

"Sir Robert's Thanks and Declaration." (44)

PA, May 15, 1770.

OC. Praise of an incorruptible recently-elected MP whose identity is not made clear. But the poem is a good comment on the electoral process.

70-229. Upon the Death of the Right Hon. William Beckford, Esq; late Lord Mayor of London.

"Thou last of all the Britons, fare thee well." (17)

L Chron 27 (Jun 23, 1770), 608; PA, Jun 26, 1770.

Epitaph. HC. Praise of incorruptible Beckford, virtuous patriot, a martyr to the cause of Liberty.

70-230. Verses occasioned by the Release of John Wilkes, Esq;

"Still does the Noise of Faction smite mine Ear." (36)

PA, Aug 11, 1770.

Quatrains. Bitter satire on Wilkes who is supported by a disturbing faction that must be suppressed.

70-231. A Vision.

"Tir'd of an indolent, corrupted age." (64)

MJ, Mar 6, 1770.

Quatrains. Allegorical vision of the loss of Freedom and Justice in England, which King George cannot prevent.

70-232. [War, war with Spain, is now the Cry.]

"War, war with Spain, is now the Cry." (4)

PA, Nov 26, 1770.

Epigram, on war with Spain. The King of Spain is the tool of France.

70-233. [What Grief did Beckford's honest Soul oppress.]

"What Grief did Beckford's honest Soul oppress." (6)

BWJ, Jun 30, 1770; Lloyd's 27 (Jul 2, 1770), 11; L Eve Post, Jun 30, 1770; PA, Jul 2, 1770.

Epitaph on Beckford. Grief expressed for the late mayor of London, Beckford, spokesman for the people, who sought redress from the King for Britain's sufferings.

70-234. [When conqu'ring heroes in their country's right.]

"When conqu'ring heroes in their country's right." (32)

G Eve Post, Jul 5, 1770.

HC. Panegyric on Beckford who has just died.

70-235. [When future ages view th' honest page.]

"When future ages view th' honest page." (12)

MJ, Jan 11, 1770.

HC. Grafton is cursed for his oppressive ministry.

70-236. [When haughty Tarquin rul'd the Roman State.]

"When haughty Tarquin rul'd the Roman State." (8)

PA, Jul 6, 1770.

HC. Praise of Mrs. Macaulay for her powerful writings in support of the people's liberty against tyranny.

70-237. Whitehead, William.
Ode for his Majesty's Birth-day, June 4, 1770. Written by William Whitehead, Esq; Poet Laureat, and set to Music by Dr. Boyce, Master of the King's Band of Musicians.

"Discord hence! the torch resign." (45)

BLJ, Jun 9, 1770; BWJ, Jun 9, 1770; Free M 2 (Jun 1770), 209-10; G, Jun 4, 1770; G Eve Post, Jun 2-5, 1770; GM 40 (Jun 1770), 277; Lloyd's 26 (Jun 1, 1770), 533; L Chron 27 (Jun 2-5, 1770), 530; LM 39 (Jun 1770), 322; PA, Jun 4, 1770.

Irregular Pindaric ode. The laureat urges the end of discord, "civil storms," the "madness of the croud."

70-238. Wilkes in Scotland.

"Confound mine Eyes, 'quoth grinning Wilkes, 'I see.'" (6)

PA, Nov 10, 1770; G Eve Post, Nov 8, 1770.

Epigram. Wilkes thinks the Scots are traitors; but it is he who is the traitor.

70-239. William Beckford, Three times Representative in Parliament, and twice Lord Mayor of the City of London . . .

"Behold the man, the glorious man behold." (28)

G, Jul 11, 1770.

Epitaph. HC. Praise of Beckford, who dared tell King George, "He acted wrong."

70-240. Written in the Year 1762.

"In James's Reign a Jefferies rose." (4)

BLJ, May 5, 1770.

Epigram. The hanging Judge Jeffreys of the reign of James II is likened to William Murray, Lord Mansfield, the tool of "King Bute."

70-241. [Ye Whigs and ye Tories, ye placemen and tools.]

"Ye Whigs and ye Tories, ye placemen and tools." (24)

MJ, May 31, 1770.

Song with "Derry down" chorus. Politicians must remember the past when the people fought for their freedom against tyranny. "Give redress to the people before it's too late."

Prints

70-242. Epitaph for William Beckford.

"When Cato died Rome shed the grateful Tear." (8)

Engr. with OC in quatrains. June 21, 1770.

Stephens 4398 (IV, 630).

America is distressed, introduced here because of Beckford's connection with the West Indies and his advocacy of the colonial cause as MP.

70-243. The Fruits of Arbitrary Power; or the Bloody Massacre, Perpetrated in King-Street, Boston, By a Party of the XXIXth Regt. . . .

"Unhappy Boston, see thy Sons deplore." (18)

Engr. with HC in two columns. [May] 1770.

George 4839 (V, 1-2).

British version of Paul Revere's print of the Boston Massacre on March 5, 1770.

70-244. Hall, J. S.
A Game of Skittles.

"Treason and He to Rome are fled." (4)

London Museum 2 (1770), 131.

George 4841 (V, 2-3).

Quatrain. A satire on Bute as a Jacobite who has gone to Rome to visit the Stuart Pretender.

1771 Books & Pamphlets

71-1. [Colvill, Robert]
  The Cyrnean Hero: A Poem. Most Humbly Inscribed to His Grace Charles Duke of Queensberry, &c. By Mr. Colvill. Second Edition.
  Edinburgh: Ruddiman, 1772. ii + 14p.

  "Hail to the CHIEF! whom civic wreaths adorn." (c. 200)

  Notices: L Chron 31 (Mar 24, 1772), 289-90.

  Copies: BL 11633.dd.1, 11633.g.43 (6); NUC CtY, PPULC, PU.

  First published in his Occasional Poems (London: Wilkie et al., 1771), pp. 1-14. HC. Composed when Paoli was on his tour through the west of Scotland, Sep 1771. Expresses the hope that Corsica will be free, despite oppressive French rule, and that Paoli, in exile, will return to win back his countrymen, to the applause of the Scottish and the English people. Praises Boswell for his work in behalf of the Corsican cause. (Also in his Poetical Works [London: Dodsley et al., 1789], pp. 65-74.) See R. C. Cole, Stud. in Scot. Lit. 16 (1981), 112-3.

71-2. Greene, Edward Burnaby.
  Poetical Essays.
  London: Ridley, 1771. xii + 290p.

  Notices: CR 33 (Feb 1772), 173-4; L Chron 31 (Mar 19, 1772), 277.

  Copies: BL 11632.a.16 (2nd ed, 1772); NUC CU, ICN, IU, & MH (1st ed); IEN & MiU (2nd ed, 1772).

  See the individual poems discussed above: 66-9, 68-11, 68-12, & 69-6.

71-3. Murray, Oliver James.
  The Candid Inquisitor, Or, Mock Patriotism Displayed: A Poem.
  London: Shatwell, 1771. iv + 14p.

  "When infant Muses first attempt to sing." (255)

  Notices: CR 32 (Nov 1771), 392; MR 45 (Nov 1771), 412; L Chron 30 (Nov 9, 1771), 457.

  Copies: Bod Godwyn Pamph 1740 (22).

  HC. Dedication (in prose) to the King, whom the poet supports against insidious faction, the "pretended assertors of their rights and liberties." Inspired by freedom, M. bemoans the curse of ambitious pride, which drives "aspiring men" to disturb the peace. Reviews the early years of George III's reign--the victories, marriage, absence of rebellious faction, improved trade, and then the rise of faction and Wilkes on the issue of peace with the Bourbon powers after the war. But Wilkes is a pretended patriot, really guided by self-interest; on the other hand, Savile is a genuine patriot.

71-4. The Patriots Guide. A Poem. Inscribed to the Earl of C[hatha]m, Junius, and John Wilkes, Edq.
   London: Wheble, [1771]. vi + 32p.

   "Shall Kings bear rule, shall Scotchmen places keep." (c. 550)

   Notices: CR 23 (Jan 1772), 85; MR 45 (Dec 1771), 510; L Chron 30 (Nov 21, 1771), 497.

   Copies: BL 11662.d.7.

   HC. Satire on the opposition patriots, demagogues, and republican subversives. The intention of this writer is to expose a "delusive species of patriotism" that inflames the people and destroys order "under the masque of a struggle for liberty." The magistrates of London are guilty of causing this popular madness. As he provides a guide for demagogues, he expresses his distaste for Junius, that great libeller; for Pitt (noting his role in the Stamp Act repeal); for anti-Scotch sentiment because of Bute; for Wilkes, "the squinting patriot," and his rioting mobs demanding redress for grievances.

71-5. Verses Addressed To John Wilkes, Esq; On His Arrival At Lynn.
   Lynn: Whittingham, 1771. 12p.

   "As when the lark, on airy pinions born." (c. 140)

   Notices: CR 31 (Apr 1771), 315; MR 44 (Mar 1771), 259-60.

   Copies: NUC RPB.

   HC. Panegyric on Wilkes. The poet pays tribute to the patriot Wilkes and liberty, and belittles the "great vulgar," "empty lordlings," "Degen'rate slaves." He insists he is "honest, brave, and just," unlike Whitehead and Johnson, in these lines honoring Wilkes for his fight against "despotic rage" and "tyrant pow'r."

Serials

71-6. The Abhorrer's Feast. (Set to music by Alderman Judas.)

"Descend! descend, ye heav'nly nine." (90)

L Eve Post, Apr 23, 1771.

Song. Parody of Dryden's Alexander's Feast. Satire defends Wilkes against the court, dominated by Bute and his mistress (the King's mother at Carlton House), and Grafton, North, Mansfield, Fletcher Norton, Alexander Wedderburn -- all of Carlton House. Cited is corruption: North is "Foul corruption's eldest son."

71-7. An Address to Some Acquaintance on their Return to North-America.

"From ill-concerted plans, untimely laid." (84)

T&C 3 (Apr 1771), 217.

HC. Now that the Townshend Acts have been repealed (Apr 12, 1770), except for the tea-duty, trade between Britain and America revives, and America, from Canada to the Carolinas and Florida, can be developed without French interference.

71-8. Advice to the Premier's Brother, who wants to be a Bishop.

"Wou'd you rise in the church? Be stupid and dull." (8)

L Eve Post, Jun 13, 1771.

Hexameter couplets. Satire on the clerical hierarchy for the manner in which it chooses its leaders. Hypocrisy and meanness are urged as qualifying characteristics.

71-9. Advice to the two Disputing Patriots, from an Old Proverb.

"The Kettle calls the Pot Black A--." (8)

PA, Jun 12, 1771.

Epigram. Wilkes and Horne should cease their farcical dispute.

71-10. Another Inscription for Col. Luttrell's coffin.

"Behold the wretch that here enshrouded lies." (20)

MJ, Feb 14, 1771.

HC. Satire on knavish and slavish Col. Luttrell, who presumably has died. (Henry Lawes Luttrell died in 1821.) See "On Seeing the Coffin, at a late Masquerade": 71-74.

71-11. Ballad. Tune: The Cutpurse.

"Ye Pickpockets, Panders, Whores, Bullies and Pimps." (45)

PA, Jul 13, 1771.

Song. An ironic review of Wilkes's career. Now that Wilkes is sheriff, the lawless will have the freedom to engage in their criminal activities.

71-12. Bob Bowling's Birth-Day Ode.

"Come bring the full pitcher." (36)

MJ, Dec 12, 1771.

Sixains. Praise of Lord Sandwich, recently appointed Lord Admiral.

71-13. [The Boston Massacre.]

"To see the sufferings of my fellow Townsmen." (32)

MJ, Feb 21, 1771.

In a report from Boston, dated Dec 21, 1770. Two parodies of Otway's Venice Preserv'd. Negative reflections on the trial of the British soldiers responsible for the shooting resulting in the Boston Massacre, which these lines believe to be a whitewash.

71-14. Boyce, Samuel.
An Ode: Addressed to Sir Joseph Mawbey, Bart.

"By instinct free, th' exalted Soul." (36)

L Chron 29 (May 30, 1771, 528; PA, Jun 1, 1771; WM 12 (Jun 27, 1771), 403.

Regular ode in sixains. Panegyric on the patriot alderman Joseph Mawbey, and assertion of the virtue and rights of Englishmen against tyranny, corruption, and oppression.

Brackenridge, Hugh Henry. The Rising Glory of America. See 72-14, 78-73, 89-2.

71-15. [Britons, consider well your present State.]

"Britons, consider well your present State." (7)

St J's C, Apr 20, 1771.

Epigram. On the need for reformation. A warning to Britons against civil discord.

71-16. The Butcher and Hog.

"Thus spake the Butcher, in his Hand the Blade." (9)

BLJ, Nov 16, 1771; L Chron 30 (Nov 9, 1771), 457; St J's C, Nov 7, 1771.

HC. An allegorical fable. The butcher blames the hog's resistance to slaughter upon faction and sedition, because hogs have no rights. (The butcher represents power and authority; the hog the English people.)

71-17. The Comparison.

"In taking water, what a mighty stir." (14)

L Eve Post, Dec 17, 1771.

HC. Being a minister of state is like being a passenger taking a boat for transportation, -- welcomed going, but neglected returning, or at his exit.

71-18. The Eagle and other Birds.

"The king that would his subjects bless." (106)

WM 13 (Sep 5, 1771), 305-6.

OC. Animal fable. The moral is that kings must have virtue and wisdom, in order to rule effectively. Cited are Wilkes and Chatham.

71-19. Effusion to Freedom.

"Hail sacred Freedom! -- Friend to Britain's Isle." (10)

G Eve Post, Aug 27, 1771.

HC. Satire on politicians. "A minister of state" cannot (by his very nature) enjoy the blessings of freedom. Nor can he support the cause of freedom.

71-20. Elegy on Patronage.

"In vain for me the linnet tunes his throat." (36)

WM 12 (May 23, 1771), 244-5.

Elegiac quatrains. A complaint by an MP that he must serve in Parliament in order to protect liberty from the despotic forces employing patronage against it.

71-21. English Form of Government.

"King, Lords, and Commons, say ye? no such thing." (6)

BWJ, Sep 7, 1771.

HC. Satire on oppressive government. The King has assimilated Parliament and dominates the government of England. Thus he is a "tyrant of slaves."

71-22. An Epigram.

"The Courtier rails at Wilkes's Crew." (4)

PA, Oct 10, 1771.

Satire on Wilkes and the courtiers. Both are motivated by self-interest.

71-23. Epigram.

"Junius, renown'd for being smart." (4)

St J's C, Sep 3, 1771.

Quatrain. Junius is clever but heartless.

71-24. Epigram.

"Sir Bull-Face, the time that his windows were breaking." (8)

BWJ, May 18, 1771.

Hexameter couplets. Satire on Fletcher Norton, Speaker of the House, who here complains of the mob that breaks the windows of his home. But he deserves this treatment, being a slave of the court.

71-25. Epigram.

"Three Patriot Johns the print shops did adorn." (6)

L Eve Post, May 28, 1771.

Praise of Wilkes and Glynn for their defense of freedom; but satire on Horne for adorning himself with an elegant scarlet coat. (The occasion is a "mezzotinto print" of a Conversation Piece of Glynn, Wilkes, and Horne.)

71-26. Epigram. Dialogue.

"A. Sire, where's our Magna Chart? Your Oath? B. My Mother." (3 + 4)

St J's C, Aug 22, 1771.

Two epigrams. The King is faced with the dilemma of abiding by his oath to defend the realm or giving up Magna Charta, freedom. The King uses his power to place Mayor Brass Crosby in the Tower, but this means tyranny. (The reference is to the City aldermen and mayor imprisoned in the Tower for supporting John Miller, publisher of the London Evening Post, summoned before the bar of the House of Commons for having printed a full report of debates in the House, against its standing order.)

71-27. Epigram. On a Report of the Political Death of Junius, alias Edmund the Jesuit.

"Junius is dead, says common Fame." (2)

PA, Nov 9, 1771.

Satire on Junius, a shameless liar. (The title indicates that Burke is Junius.)

71-28. Epigram on Junius. On Reading his last Letter, which is an Honour to Feeling and Humanity.

"This Patriot-writer of immortal Fame." (4)

St J's C, Sep 28, 1771.

HC. Modest and upright, Junius should also be called Brutus.

71-29. Epigram on Mr. Wilkes's Unwearied Attention to the Public Cause.

"If ancient Poets Argus prize." (4)

Lloyd's 29 (Aug 19, 1771), 183; L Eve Post, Aug 17, 1771; LM 40 (Aug 1771), 419.

Wilkes (Mr. Squintum) is praised for his cross-eyes which permit him to have broader vision.

71-30. Epitaph on a Printer of Boston, in New-England, Written by Himself.

"The Body of /Ben Franklin, Printer." (11)

Lloyd's 29 (Oct 30, 1771), 430; LM 40 (Sep 1771), 465; GA, Oct 14, 1782.

Benjamin Franklin's epitaph in the form of a metaphor, the body as book, is printed in London.

71-31. Epitaph on the Right Hon. George Grenville.

"Whoe'er thou art, Prince, Senator, or Peer." (20)

L Chron 29 (Feb 7, 1771), 143; PA, Feb 9, 1771.

HC. Panegyric on Grenville, who has just died. (Grenville initiated the first proceedings against Wilkes in 1763, introduced the Stamp Act in 1765, and opposed its repeal in 1766.)

71-32. Epitaph, Recommended as a New Style of Monumental Writing Intended for the Vicar of Brentford.

"Passenger, /Stop, read, smile, admire." (24)

Freeman's J, Aug 20, 1771; Lloyd's 29 (Aug 12, 1771), 157; L Chron 30 (Aug 13, 1771), 156; L Eve Post, Aug 10, 1771.

Inscription. Satire on Parson Horne for his ambiguous motives and direction.

71-33. Extempore.

"The Freemen of London, determin'd and bold." (8)

PA, Oct 4, 1771.

Quatrains. The freemen of London will not sell their votes to the vicious court.

71-34. Extempore.

"In Summer's heat our patriots cool." (4)

BWJ, Aug 17, 1771; PA, Aug 23, 1771.

Quatrain. The effect of the four seasons on the politicians.

71-35. Extempore.

"Tho' for a while old Freedom droops her Head." (4)

PA, Oct 10, 1771.

Quatrain. Freedom shall assert itself despite attempts by the venal court to subvert it by bribery.

71-36. Extempore.

"The venal tribe of paltry things at Court." (4)

BWJ, Aug 31, 1771.

HC. Satire on court corruption, which undermines freemen's rights.

71-37. Extempore.

"Warm'd by the Fire of Freedom's sacred Flame." (12)

L Chron 29 (Apr 30, 1771), 420; PA, Apr 29, 1771.

HC. Urges Britons to assert their civil rights against tyranny.

71-38. Extempore.

"When citizens their charter'd Rights support." (2)

PA, Jul 13, 1771.

HC. Epigram. As soon as the people support their chartered rights, the oppressive court measures will disappear.

71-39. Extempore.

"When city Virtue combats courtly Vice." (4)

PA, Jul 9, 1771.

Quatrain. Epigram. The virtuous patriots of London, the honest freemen, are more reliable supporters of the King than his corrupt courtiers.

71-40. Extempore. On Finding Every Poet of the Age silent on the Death of the Earl of Halifax.

"No Monody, no Lamentation." (7)

Ox M 7 (Oct 1771), 152; MJ, Oct 8, 1771.

Epigram. Satire on George Montagu Dunk, 3rd Earl of Halifax, because he neglected liberty. (He was involved from the start in the anti-Wilkes campaign.)

71-41. Extempore, on Reading that the King of Denmark had set apart some Time every Week, to redress his Peoples' Grievances, and receive Petitions.

"For acts like these were crowns and empires given." (42)

E Man's M, Jul 1771, pp. 37-8; Lloyd's 29 (Jul 3, 1771), 20.

HC. King George is urged to follow the good example of the King of Denmark, who heeds the people's petitions and redresses their grievances.

71-42. A Familiar Epistle to the Premier.

"Let me, N--, thy Fortune greet." (112)

PA, Jan 19, 1771.

Tetrameter couplets. Personal abuse of North, creature of Bute and other politicians, greedy for money, and inept.

71-43. A Fragment, Wrote a Hundred Years Ago.

"His Majesty, the King of Spain." (37)

MJ, Feb 2, 1771.

OC. On the confusion of the Falkland Islands affair.

71-44. The Freeman's Resolve for Michaelmas-Day 1771.

"And shall I yield? Shall that enraptur'd vow." (46)

L Eve Post, Sep 21, 1771.

Blank verse. London freemen resolve to continue the fight for the cause of freedom secured by King William against the Stuarts, and confirmed against the rebel Scots. Crosby is cited.

71-45. Free(th), John.
The Vicar of Brentford. Tune, The Vicar of Bray.

"In George the Third's illustrious reign." (80)

PA, Aug 10, 1771; The Warwickshire Medley (1776), pp. 95-7.

Song. Satire on Horne for deserting Wilkes and opposing his election to Sheriff of London. See 71-129.

71-46. Horace. Book I. Ode XXII. Quoted by an Honourable Colonel, to illustrate the Character of Sancho.

"The Man, that's neither brave nor just." (40)

Freeman's J, Mar 14, 1771; Baratariana (Dublin, 1777), pp. 138-40.

Regular ode. Imitation of Horace. A character of a cowardly and sleazy politician (George Townshend, Lord Lieutenant of Ireland, 1767-72) who is Ireland's bane and the enemy of civil rights but a supporter of the ministry. Canada and Wolfe are mentioned.

71-47. [Horne proves Wilkes and Wilkes proves Horne.]

"Horne proves Wilkes, and Wilkes proves Horne." (6)

"Pray, pray, Johnny Wilkes, why all this Pother." (4)

PA, Jun 12, 1771.

Two epigrams. Disgust with the dispute between Wilkes and Horne.

71-48. Hymn to Liberty. Intended for the Lord Mayor on his Enlargement from the Tower.

"O Liberty, divinest Name." (16)

St J's C, May 4, 1771.

Quatrains, in praise of liberty and those who refuse to truckle to arbitrary power -- like Brass Crosby, the Lord Mayor of London.

71-49. [If Wilkes in the Side of the King is a Thorn.]

"If Wilkes in the Side of the King is a Thorn." (4)

BWJ, Sep 21, 1771; MJ, Aug 31, 1771; PA, Sep 3, 1771.

Epigram. Wilkes makes Horne suffer far more than he made the King suffer.

71-50. Impromptu, on the number of Addresses presented, and Visits paid, to the Lord Mayor in the Tower.

"The ministry, thro' their oppression and malice." (6)

L Chron 29 (Apr 11, 1771), 360; WM 12 (Apr 25, 1771), 116-7.

Epigram. "Slaves" go to the court, but freemen visit Crosby in the Tower.

71-51. Impromptu, On the Report of a Certain Unpopular Nobleman intending soon to return to this Kingdom.

"Shall minions of a slavish court." (18)

G Eve Post, May 16, 1771.

Sixains. Satire on Bute who is responsible for the subversion of English liberty.

71-52. Ins and Outs.

"The patriots aver that this ministry's out." (4)

L Chron 29 (Feb 9, 1771), 151; WM 11 (Feb 21, 1771), 244.

Quatrain. Epigram. The patriots create a fuss simply because they are not in power.

71-53. Inscription written under the Statue of Charles II. lately erected in the Fish-Market at Newcastle.

"Sacred to the Memory /Of Charles Stuart." (c. 35)

BWJ, Jun 29, 1771; L Eve Post, Jun 22, 1771; Ox M 7 (Jul 1771), 33.

A pasquinade satirizing the Stuarts in the figure of Charles II, a dissolute and abandoned tyrant.

71-54. Instructions for Drawing a Picture.

"A Frightful old Hecate draw." (12)

BWJ, Feb 16, 1771.

OC. All public evils in England are the result of Scotch oppression.

71-55. [Is Junius dead, for all his Pains.]

"Is Junius dead, for all his Pains." (2)

PA, Nov 14, 1771.

Epigram. Junius deserves ignominious hanging.

71-56. [John Wilkes and Horne two quondam Friends behold.]

"John Wilkes and Horne, two quondam Friends behold." (6)

St J's C, Jun 17, 1771.

HC. The quarrel between two supposedly wise men, Wilkes and Horne, is inexcusable.

71-57. [John Wilkes is steady in his Plan.]

"John Wilkes is steady in his Plan." (4)
"The Diff'rence lies, as far as I can see." (4)

PA, Feb 22, 1771; May 25, 1771.

Two epigrams. For and against Wilkes in his dispute with Horne.

71-58. Lines Addressed to the Just and Brave Magistrates of the City of London.

"Freedom with Fortitude will e'er be join'd." (12)

L Eve Post, Mar 16, 1771.

HC. The patriots defend the laws and obey all legal power; but tyranny and despotism are not acceptable to Britons.

71-59. Lord North in the House of Commons speaking one day of the public character of Lord Sandwich.

"For form's sake I pray." (12)

Sixains. The persona of North defends Sandwich from the change of embezzling public money. The year is said to be 1771. In Jeffery Dunstan (pseud.), Fugitive Pieces (1789), pp. 30-1. See 89-2.

71-60. Monsieur Squinton.

"Le nom seul de Monsieur Squinton." (41)

MJ, Jun 29, 1771.

In French. Light satire on Wilkes.

71-61. A new Song, Addressed to John Wilkes, Esq; Member of Parliament for Middlesex, Alderman of Farringdon Ward Without, and who was July 1st, 1771, with Frederick Bull, Esq; elected Sheriff of London and Middlesex, by a respectable majority of the Livery. To the tune of "Blow, blow, thou Winter's Wind, &c."

O Liberty, e'er while." (36)

Ox M 6 (Supp 1771), 274.

Song. Celebrates Wilkes and Bull, chosen sheriffs, against the wishes of Bute and the court.

71-62. Oakman, J.
The Frogs and King. A Fable. To a Friend in the Country.

"Why does my friend, in country blest." (100)

Lloyd's 28 (Feb 22, 1771), 188.

Hudibrastics. Animal fable that illustrates a moral in defence of the King for his pacific nature.

71-63. Ode.

"As Britannia sat a-wailing." (40)

MJ, Nov 2, 1771; PA, Nov 4, 1771.

Regular ode in double quatrains. Britain complains of corrupt and oppressive government, and hopes for its end and the end of civil discord.

71-64. An Ode.

"Can the good dust of Alfred sleep." (64)

L Eve Post, Mar 28, 1771.

Irregular Pindaric ode, in defense of England's traditional laws traceable to Alfred and Magna Charta against those who would undermine them -- Mansfield, the Foxes (Charles James, Stephen, Henry), Weymouth, Luttrell, Onslow, Bute. Praise, however, of Wilkes, Crosby, Oliver, the patriots.

71-65. Ode on the Enlargement of the Right Honourable the Lord Mayor and Alderman Oliver.

"Hail! happy morn, with fairest freedom crown'd." (40)

L Eve Post, May 7, 1771.

Not quite regular ode, expressing pleasure in the release of Crosby and Oliver from the Tower, with a warning to Parliament that England may suffer the doom of Greece and Rome if oppression persists.

71-66. Ode to a Friend in the Country, on a late Commitment to the Tower.

"Peevish in these polluted Days." (18)

St J's C, Apr 18, 1771.

Sixains. Wilkes, thought to be incomparable, is less popular now than Oliver and Crosby, who are imprisoned in the Tower.

71-67. Ode, To Mr. Alderman Oliver. By a Lady.

"No more to join in festive dance." (66)

L Eve Post, Apr 9, 1771; MJ, Apr 9, 1771.

Regular ode in sixains. Praise of honest Oliver at a time when Britain, oppressive and corrupt, disgraces herself before Spain. (Richard Oliver, alderman, was called before the House of Commons with Wilkes and Crosby to answer for his conduct in arresting the messenger of the House in the Wilkes case. He was briefly committed to the Tower.)

71-68. Ode to the Lord Mayor in the Tower.

"Spirit of the Fathers, rise." (50)

St J's C, Apr 6, 1771.

Irregular Pindaric ode in defense of the City against the oppression of the court, especially of Lord Mayor Crosby, incorruptible Whig patriot in the tradition of Russel, Hampden, and Sidney.

71-69. Ode to the Right Hon. John Earl of Bute, on his Return to Britain.

"Hail, patron of the liberal arts!" (28)

L Chron 29 (May 30, 1771), 523; WM 12 (Jun 27, 1771), 403.

Pindaric ode, panegyric. Britannia greets Bute on his return (from Rome) and announces the end of faction, sedition, and party in his honor.

71-70. An Old Woman's Remonstrance. To one of the best of sublunary Beings; being as true, and, perhaps, _more_ important than any, or _all_, presented by the _loyal_ citizens of London.

"His faithful subject, Martha Bird." (52)

DJ, Aug 13, 1771; G Eve Post, Jul 30, 1771; GA, Aug 31, 1779.

OC. A petition to the King by one of the poor, complaining of high prices and taxes which force emigration to America, France, and Spain and encourage the people to turn to Wilkes. Asks for relief.

71-71. On a Late Grand Procession by Oliver Oddfish, Esq;

"It's just as I thought -- they went to the K[ing]." (6)

Lloyd's 29 (Jul 10, 1771), 47.

Hexameter couplets. The King rejects another protest at grievances suffered by petitioners. The title refers to Richard Oliver, alderman of London.

71-72. On a private Council.

"The Devil and N-rth in Conclave sat." (12)

St J's C, Jun 4, 1771.

Quatrains. The devil and Lord North have chosen Parson Horne to disgrace Wilkes and ruin the nation.

71-73. On Liberty. To Tories and Freethinkers. By a Revolution Whig.

"Almighty Liberty! we owe to thee." (14)

BWJ, Sep 28, 1771; L Eve Post, Sep 24, 1771.

HC. Liberty is the prime mover in divine nature, and so accounts for Wilkes's voice. (Wilkes's voice is sanctioned by the force of nature, liberty.)

71-74. On Seeing the Coffin, at a Late Masquerade.

"What means the stalking ghost of yonder slave." (6)

MJ, Feb 14, 1771.

HC. Ironic satire on Col. Henry Lawes Luttrell, who is presumed dead. (He died in 1821.) See Another Inscription for Col. Luttrell's Coffin: 71-10.

71-75. On Seeing the King at the Installation at Drury Lane Theatre.

"Garrick to view brings dull old rules." (4)

L Eve Post, Nov 21, 1771.

Epigram. Satire on King George, who keeps only knaves at court.

71-76. On Seeing Wedderburne's Speech in the House of Commons last week.

"B[ute], tho' a villain, yet deserves applause." (19)

MJ, Apr 9, 1771.

HC. Bute is a consistent villain. But Wedderburne is a hypocrite -- out of London he talks like a patriot, in London like a venal and corrupt courtier.

71-77. On Serjeant Glynn's Motion for new Regulating the Law Proceedings in Westminster Hall, etc. December, 1770.

"When the grave Serjeant in his Fury." (33)

St J's C, Jan 1, 1771.

OC. Satire on Glynn as seditious populist reformer; defense of Mansfield.

71-78. On the Different Conduct of the French and Irish Parliaments. On the Emptiness of the Treasury.

"Strange Alterations! Gallic Senates strive." (8)

Freeman's J, Jun 22, 1771.

Two epigrams. The British Senate is mean and corrupt, guided by self-interest; and the Irish Treasury is bankrupt and Irish trade ruined.

71-79. On the Lord Mayor's Recovery; or, a Remedy for the Gout.

"Pretending to cure, the Quacks make a rout." (4)

Lloyd's 28 (May 3, 1771), 430.

Quatrain. Ironically, Crosby has recovered from the gout -- in the Tower!

71-80. On the Present Dispute between Mr. Wilkes and Mr. Horne.

"Horne says that Wilkes, a vile blasphemer." (6)

G Eve Post, May 21, 1771.

Epigram. Satire on the dispute between Wilkes and Horne -- the one an atheist, the other a blasphemer. There's nothing to choose between them.

71-81. On the Present Times.

"O Britain, whither do thy Vices end!" (11)

Lloyd's 29 (Jul 12, 1771), 52; PA, Jul 13, 1771.

HC. A protest against social insubordination, threats to the nobility and monarchy. The times are vicious. Luxury corrupts everyone. Class lines are being broken by the lower middle and middle class who are rising into the nobility and even threatening the monarchy.

71-82. On the Quarrel between Johnny Wilkes, and Parson Horne.

"Wilkes says that Horne's a worthless knave." (24)

St J's C, Apr 18, 1771.

Quatrains. Satire on the quarrel between Wilkes and Horne, formerly great friends, but who now abuse each other.

71-83. On the Times.

"Much has been wrote, much has been said." (c. 225)

WM 14 (Oct 3, 1771), 18-20.

OC. Objects to the noise and fuss created by party differences, by ins and outs; by Wilkes and Horne, "the tools of thwarted opposition." Objects also to worthless petitions by those who demean the King, who is good and gentle.

71-84. On three Grub-street Authors Attacking Mr. Wilkes.

"Have you not in an Evening seen." (14)

St J's C, Dec 19, 1771.

OC. The Grub-street authors attacking Wilkes are like dogs helplessly yelping at the serene moon.

71-85. Paradoxes.

"See, Cause of Grief to some, to others, Sport." (10)

St J's C, Sep 24, 1771.

HC. The King is deceived by his ministers, and the nation misled by Bute and the King's mother. Liberty is endangered by "A sober Prince, 'midst an abandon'd Court!"

71-86. [A Parliament of Knaves and Sots.]

"A Parliament of Knaves and Sots." (12)

Freeman's J, Jul 9, 1771.

Sixains. Satire on the Irish Parliament for corruption, for accepting bribes and betraying the nation.

71-87. Passive Obedience.

"Why should we dream of arbitrary Things." (6)

St J's C, Apr 16, 1771.

HC. Anti-royalist poem vs. tyranny. Only a king who is a god can have unlimited powers.

71-88. Patriotism in Adversity.

"The Patriots, who, up Popularity's hill." (36)

L Eve Post, Jan 29, 1771.

Quatrains. Satire on the dispute between Wilkes and Horne. The patriots fall out because of selfishness and greed.

71-89. A Poem on the Present Times.

"For some great curse executive as dread." (96)

Ox M 6 (Supp 1771), 275-6.

Quatrains. A farmer objects to "brutal Game-Acts" which deprive him of "his sacred liberties" and ravage his fields in order to favor the "pamper'd" wealthy.

71-90. The Poet's Dream.

"Last night I dreamt some men in power." (14)

MJ, Mar 21, 1771; Say's, Mar 30, 1771.

OC. The poet dreams of taxes not paid in England and America, of soldiers who run away and jails emptied; of rebellion and slaughter; of the execution of an important figure, a Great Man. (Is this vision prophetic of the American Rebellion?)

71-91. A Political Parody on Cato. Act V. Scene 1.

"It must be so, -- Johnson thou reason'st well." (31)

MJ, Oct 24, 1771; PA, Oct 26, 1771.

Parody in blank verse. The King soliloquizes over the dangers and attractions of supremacy, supported by Samuel Johnson's False Alarm but opposed by Junius's essays in the Public Advertiser and by Wilkes.

71-92. The Political Spira; Or, The Legal Apostate.

"Who was it that bow'd to learned Grenville's shrine." (19)

L Eve Post, Apr 4, 1771.

Blank verse. Satire on Alexander Wedderburn for sordid self-interest. (Wedderburn had supported Wilkes in 1769; but bought off by North, he joined the North ministry as solicitor general.)

71-93. [The Priest of Brentford, when he would cajole.]

"The Priest of Brentford, when he would cajole." (10)
"Wilkes wonders how he lost his friends." (4)

MJ, Jun 15, 1771.

Two epigrams. On the dispute between Wilkes and Horne. They divide on the election of the Sheriffs of London. (Poll was taken June 25, 1771.)

71-94. The Progress of Apostasy: A Poem, Inscribed to the Rev. John Horne.

"'Twixt geese and ducks, and turkies dropt." (c. 184)

L Eve Post, Jul 4, 1771; PA, Jul 8, 1771.

Doggerel Hudibrastics. Satire on Horne for selling out to the great Shelburne and his faction, including North (!), and for adopting royalist Tory views.

71-95. A Prophecy.

"When Horne shall teach the Way to Heaven." (20)

BWJ, Aug 24, 1771; PA, Aug 23, 1771.

Quatrains. Liberty will disappear when certain improbable events come to pass -- like Horne speaking the truth, merit preferred at court, England no more the target of an alliance between France and Spain, etc.

71-96. A Prophecy found in the Library of Trinity-College, in Cambridge, being judged to have lain some hundred years.

"When here a Scot shall think his throne to set." (64)

MJ, Jan 22, 1771.

HC. A series of ambiguous predictions beginning with a hostile remark on the Scotch influence. Cited is the Parliament.

71-97. The Resolve.

"Say, shall I from Wilkes retire." (20)

L Eve Post, Aug 29, 1771.

Quatrains. Attack on Horne for lying about Wilkes and insulting one of Wilkes's supporters in Parliament, James Townsend.

71-98. The Revolution in the Kingdom of Frogs; a Fable, Address'd to the Malecontents of the present Times.

"Old Aesop tells, (nor think the story strange)." (16)

MJ, Nov 30, 1771.

HC. Animal fable. The British should be satisfied with their King, despite his faults -- dullness and lack of fire.

The Rising Glory of America. See 72-14, 78-73, 89-2.

71-99. Sharp, Jun., William.
To the Right Honourable the Lord Mayor.

"If words are far unequal to describe." (68)

L Eve Post, Nov 2, 1771.

HC. Panegyric on Mayor Crosby, who remains true to Wilkes and freedom, in spite of the apostasy of Horne to Shelburne.

71-100. The Sheriffs-Chain. Extempore.

"Wilkes wore the Ministerial chain." (8)

PA, Oct 16, 1771.

Epigram. Quatrains. Despite govermental opposition, Wilkes has his way and is chosen Sheriff of London.

71-101. A Song on Messrs. Wilkes and Bull being chosen Sheriffs. To the Tune of Hearts of Oak.

"Come cheer up my lads, for we've conquer'd at last." (38)

G, Jul 9, 1771; L Chron 30 (Jul 6, 1771), 32; MJ, Jul 6, 1771; Say's, Jul 20, 1771.

Despite oppression and court bribes, freedom has won, for Wilkes and Bull will be sheriffs. The King should turn from the ways of the Stuarts.

71-102. Stanzas, addressed to the released Magistrates.

"From the rude grasp of lawless pow'r." (114)

MJ, May 11, 1771.

Sixains. Praise of Mayor Crosby and Alderman Oliver, released from the Tower; and abuse of the government -- North, Gower, Grafton, Wedderburne, Charles James Fox.

71-103. Stanzas, addressed to the Right Hon. the Lord Mayor.

"With harsh ungen'rous insult spurn'd." (32)

L Chron 29 (Mar 21, 1771), 285; MJ, Mar 21, 1771; WM 12 (Apr 4, 1771), 21.

Quatrains. Support of Crosby whose fight for freedom has earned him a place in the Tower. Britain mourns.

71-104. A Supplication, Addressed to St. Stephen.

"Bestow a Protector to weed this foul place." (2)

G Eve Post, Apr 2, 1771.

Satire on the venality of Parliament. Begs the patron saint of Parliament, St. Stephen, to cleanse it of corruption.

71-105. Tait, John.
Ode on the Anniversary of his Majesty's Birthday, June 4, 1771.

"Loud raise your voices, British swains." (78)

WM 12 (Jun 6, 1771), 307.

Regular ode in sixains. An Establishment poem by a "loyal" Scot, in praise of the King who "repels the rude embrace/Of faction's sons, a grov'ling race."

71-106. The Three Parsons. A Parody.

"Three Parsons in one pious age were born." (6)

G Eve Post, Aug 3, 1771.

Parody on Dryden's epitaph on Milton. Satire on Horne for hypocrisy and impudence.

71-107. [Three Parsons, at three different Periods born.]

"Three Parsons, at three different Periods born." (6)

PA, Oct 4, 1771.

Parody on Dryden's epitaph on Milton. Satire on Horne, enemy of liberty.

71-108. The Times.

"Fornication, Seduction, Crim. Con. and the like." (12)

PA, Nov 23, 1771.

Epigram. Quatrains. Satire on the year 1771, characterized by immorality, licentiousness and criminality. (Possible allusion to Grafton's behavior.)

71-109. The Times.

"The sounding Horn." (96)

MJ, Feb 16, 1771.

Sixains. During these times, Wilkes is irrelevant; but North and Britain are behaving cowardly before France and Spain, against the wishes of Charles James Fox.

71-110. To Alderman Oliver in the Tower.

"Hark! heard ye not yon raging cries." (132)

LM 40 (Apr 1771), 228-9; MJ, Apr 11, 1771.

Regular ode in sixains. Invoking the sacred shades of the Whig past, Cromwell and Sidney, the poet fears for (Whig) liberty in the present that is overwhelmed with political evil and that forced Alderman Oliver into the Tower. The LM version omits four stanzas in which the poet asks for the assassination of North! See 71-4, Ode to Alderman Oliver in the Tower.

71-111. To John Wilkes, Esq;

"Proceed, thou Hero, in bright Freedom's Cause." (8)

PA, Nov 7, 1771.

HC. A panegyric on Wilkes who has recently been chosen sheriff. He will now "Secure" British rights, liberties, and laws.

71-112. To Lord [Mansfield.]

"My Lord, an impeachment." (36)

BWJ, Jan 5, 1771.

Regular ode in sixains. Judge Mansfield is threatened with impeachment and execution for encouraging oppression.

71-113. To Mr. Harley, and the Recorder of London.

"I told you Friend Harley, and you the Recorder." (12)

St J's C, Jan 17, 1771.

Quatrains. Thomas Harley, alderman of the City of London, and the Recorder, are praised, while the idols of faction, Wilkes and Horne, who are now throwing dirt at each other, are criticized.

71-114. To Mr. Wilkes, on his being elected Sheriff with Mr. Bull.

"All Contest is now at an end." (8)

L Chron 30 (Jul 23, 1771), 84; MJ, Jul 23, 1771; St J's C, Jul 20, 1771.

Quatrains. Epigram. Wilkes is congratulated upon being elected sheriff with Frederick Bull, and admonished to be still a friend to liberty. Wilkes split from Horne over this election.

71-115. To Nunnington.

"Thou whom th' enamour'd Muse invites." (18)

PA, Oct 29, 1771.

OC. Ironic lines praising the poet who had written a panegyrical address to Crosby in the Public Advertiser, Oct 11, 1771: "To the Right Hon. the Lord-Mayor." See 71-122.

71-116. To that Righte Worthie Man Master John Wilkes.

"John Wilkes, I pray." (48)

MJ, Apr 13, 1771.

Sixains. An imitation of medieval verses in Chatterton's style urging Wilkes to resist the Commons like Crosby and Oliver.

71-117. To the King.

"Would your Majesty please to attend to our woes." (10)

Lloyd's 28 (Apr 10, 1771), 348.

Hexameter couplets. A petition to the King to attend to the people's grievances, to banish North and Fox who would betray him and to accept honest men.

71-118. To the Lord Mayor.

"While you, by arbitrary power." (36)

L Chron 29 (Apr 11, 1771), 359; Lloyd's 28 (Apr 10, 1771), 348.

Regular ode in sixains. Panegyric on Mayor Brass Crosby, martyr to liberty who is imprisoned in the Tower.

71-119. To the Rev. Mr. Horne.

"In spite of Wilkes thou yet shalt rise." (12)

PA, Sep 5, 1771.

Sixains. In spite of Wilkes and Junius, Parson Horne deserves to be honored and respected for his integrity and independence.

71-120. To the Right Honourable Brass Crosby, Esq; Lord Mayor of London.

"Freedom, by Beckford's death, received a blow." (10)

L Eve Post, Mar 23, 1771.

HC. Brass Crosby is praised as a worthy successor of Beckford in opposing arbitrary, that is, "illegal pow'r."

71-121. To the Right Hon. Lord N[ort]h.

"With keeness trac'd, with nice attention try'd." (16)

WM 11 (Feb 28, 1771), 403.

HC. Questions all the criticism that North receives -- all undeserved and made by selfish men.

71-122. To the Right Hon. the Lord-Mayor.

"Dear Crosby, hail! accept the honest Lay." (40)

PA, Oct 11, 1771.

HC, signed Nunnington, praising Crosby for suffering imprisonment because he refused to submit to the tyranny of a corrupt government: he had supported the printers in their struggle for the freedom of the press. (Crosby consistently opposed the ministry in the Commons and in City politics -- regarding the use of press gangs in the City as well as the London printers who had printed Parlimentary debates. He defended the chartered privileges of the City.)

71-123. To those two most prodigious worthy Patriots John Wilkes, Esq; and the Rev. Mr. Horne.

"When Men with Principles like you." (4)

PA, Feb 9, 1771.

Epigram. On the dispute between Wilkes and Horne. Who is "honest," who is "right"?

71-124. Cancelled.

71-125. The Union.

"The meager Scots, in days of yore." (40)

L Eve Post, Jun 13, 1771.

Hudibrastics. Satire on the Scotch who have succeeded in feathering their nests at English expense. Bute and Mansfield are cited.

71-126. Upon Lord Halifax's Recovery.

"Had Halifax the Debt to Nature paid." (6)

St J's C, May 18, 1771.

HC. Epigram. If Halifax (George M. Dunk) had died, he would have been praised and his worth acknowledged; but now that he has recovered, he has lost this opportunity. (Halifax helped in the prosecution of Wilkes from the beginning in 1763. He died June 12, 1771.)

71-127. Vestis pretiosa: Or Parson Horne's old Clothes. A new song to an old Tune: "If any Wench Venus's Girdle wear."

"Parson Horne has lost the old Clothes." (16)

PA, Jun 1, 1771.

Song. Satire on Parson Horne for being a turncoat, allegedly selling himself to the devil, the government Tories.

71-128. The Vicar of Bray.

"The infectious hand the pious Parson hates." (4)

MJ, Jul 18, 1771.

Epigram. Parson Horne hypocritically pays homage to Lord Bute.

71-129. The Vicar of Brentford. A New Song, to the Tune of the Vicar of Bray.

"In young King George's Tory day." (58)

G, Aug 10, 1771.

Song. Another version of the old song, "The Vicar of Bray," a satire on Horne who deserted Wilkes for Shelburne. See 71-45.

71-130. The Vice-Roy. A Poetical Caricatura. Addressed to Lord Townshend.

"While you, against both wind and tide." (c. 275)

BWJ, Dec 21, 1771; Baratariana (Dublin, 1773), pp. 311-29 & (Dublin, 1777), pp. 284-305.

OC. Satire on George, 1st Marquis Townshend, Viceroy of Ireland (Oct 1767-Oct 1772), for his harsh administration of Ireland. A protest at the undeserved terrible treatment of the country by the exploiting English.

71-131. [Warton, Thomas.]
The Oxford Newsman's Address to his worthy Masters and Mistresses, 1771, supposed to have been written by a Gentleman of Oxford, well known in the Poetical World.

"Delicious News -- A War with Spain." (36)

PA, Jan 1, 1771.

OC. Ironic praise of the benefits accruing from the coming war with Spain. All the old themes and names will disappear from the news: Horne, Wilkes, Ins and Outs, etc.

71-132. [When France stands Umpire for proud Spain.]

"When France stands Umpire for proud Spain." (6)

MJ, Jan 24, 1771.

OC. Epigram. Satire on the ministry's weak and uncertain policy regarding Spain and the Falkland Islands. Britain is "little," not "great."

71-133. [Where is now that haughty flow'r.]

"Where is now that haughty flow'r." (40)

MJ, Apr 25, 1771.

Ballad, fable of the British rose (once guarded by liberty now banished by despotic power) which is destroyed by the Scotch thistle.

71-134. Whig and Tory.

"Whig and Tory scratch and bite." (4)

Lloyd's 29 (Oct 28, 1771), 419.

Epigram. Whigs and Tories are greedy for favors -- getting them, they no longer disagree.

71-135. Whitehead, William.
Ode for the New Year.

"Again returns the circl'ing year." (42)

BLJ, Jan 5, 1771; BWJ, Jan 5, 1771; G Eve Post, Dec 30, 1770-Jan 1, 1771; GM 41 (Jan 1771), 39; Lloyd's 28 (Dec 31, 1770-Jan 2, 1771), 1; L Chron 29 (Dec 29, 1770-Jan 1, 1771), 8; LM 40 (Jan 1771), 51; Say's, Jan 5, 1771.

Pindaric ode. The laureat celebrates the union of "Thrones, independence, laws, and liberty," bound by a "triple cord," King, Lords, and Commons. This "sacred union" will endure despite occasional "jars intestine," let no British enemies forget that!

71-136. A Wish without a Hope.

"While the Court-ninnies gain, for Wilkes, his ends." (48)

PA, Jul 10, 1771.

HC. The King must rid himself of his blundering ministry, which is merely guided by self-interest. He must assert his power, because his ministers do not know how to cope with Wilkes.

Prints

71-137. Britannia Congratulating the Right Hon. Brass Crosby, Esq. Lord Mayor, and Mr. Alderman Oliver, on their Releasement from the Tower, at the Rising of Parliament, May 8, 1771.

"Joy to my Sons and Patriots! -- high in fame." (36)

Broadside with HC. June 15, 1771.

George 4864 (V, 16-17).

Crosby and Oliver were imprisoned because of the dispute caused by the publication of parliamentary debates. They also received the support of the American colonies and joined other patriots -- Chatham, Camden, and Beckford.

1772   Books & Pamphlets

72-1. [Delamayne, Thomas Hallie]
   The Senators: Or, A Candid Examination into the Merits of the Principal Performers of St. Stephen's Chapel.
   London: Kearsly, 1772. 36p.

   "Long has the stage provok'd the critic's ire." (c. 630)

   Notices: CR 33 (May 1772), 410; MR 46 (May 1772), 539; Freeman's J, Jun 2 & 11, 1772; L Eve Post, May 21, 1772; L Chron 31 (May 5, 1772), 437; LM 41 (Jun 1772), 287; MJ, May 5, 1772; PA, May 9, 1772.

   Evans 12372 (Philadelphia, 1772); Sabin 79095.

   Copies: BL 11586.t.14, 11632.h.1 (4), 1346.i.5; Bod Godwyn Pamph 1498 (1); NUC CtY, DLC, IU, InU, MH, RPJCB.

   HC. Concerned basically with oratory as well as character, D. balances for the most part praise and blame as he takes up the major performers in the House of Commons: Fletcher Norton, Onslow (the son of the former speaker of the House), Jeremiah Dyson, Jenkinson, Townsend, Dowdeswell (only praised), Barre, Sawbridge, Cornwall, Fox, North, Thurloe, Dunning, Serjeant Glynn (colonies mentioned in this character), Wedderburne, Savile (only praised), Mawbey, Clare, Germaine, Rigby, Barrington (the man responsible for the St. George's Fields' massacre, May 10, 1768), Burke (praised), and Conway. Closes with a prayer that the minority will continue to guard the rights of Englishmen against the corrupt enemies of liberty (including "the King's friends"). (Five editions in 1772, one in Philadelphia 1772. The 2nd and later include additions—Conway, for example—for a total of 42p.) See 72-6, 72-7. (See also 73-4, 73-10.)

72-2. The Epocha, or the Review MDCCLXXII.
   London: Bladon, 1772.

   Notices: CR 33 (Apr 1772), 328; MR 46 (Apr 1772), 455.

   Copies: none located.

72-3. Evans, Nathaniel.
   Panegyric Ode to the Memory of General Wolfe, Slain at the Siege of Quebec.

   "What theme propitious to the lay." (86)

In 72-4: Poems on Several Occasions, pp. 12-16.

Irregular Pindaric ode. Patriotic celebration of Wolfe's great victory over the French.

72-4. -----.
Poems on Several Occasions. With Some other Compositions.
Philadelphia: Dunlap, 1772. xxviii + 160 + 24 + 2p.

Evans 12386.

Copies: BL 11686.d.23; NUC CtY, DLC, ICN, IU, MH, MiU-C.

For the relevant poems, see above 61-2, 62-3, 62-4, 63-5, 72-3.

72-5. Junius, pseud.
Political Poems: A Compilation.
London: Crowder, 1772. 46p.

Notices: CR 33 (Apr 1772), 329; MR 46 (Apr 1772), 455.

Copies: NUC OClW.

Junius' miscellany of "spirited poetic pieces," moral and political, calculated to inspire us with "true patriotism," by Churchill, Mason, Goldsmith, and Addison. Also included are "Thoughts on True Nobility and False" and an extract from The Poor Man's Prayer.

72-6. A Review of the Poem intitled "The Senators:" Or, A Re-Examination into the Merits of the Principal Performers of St. Stephen's Chapel. Part I.
London: Wilkie, 1772. 25p.

"When lesser Men against their Betters write." (c. 470)

See 72-7.

72-7. -----. Part II.
London: Wilkie, 1772. 30p.

"Hail! white robed Candour! of celestial birth." (c. 550)

Notices: CR 34 (Jul 1772), 70; MR 47 (Aug 1772), 151; L Chron 25 (Jul 25 & Aug 25, 1772), 89, 193-4; LM 41 (Aug & Sep 1772), 388, 440; M Chron, Aug 15, 1772.

Copies: NUC CtY, ICN (Pt. a only), NjP.

See 72-1. These possibly by Delamayne. HC. Part I. Rambling, discursive estimates of the personalities in the House of Commons. Berates poets who write of the politicians and their debates only through biased, second-hand reports in the newspapers, as in The Senators, which this work reviews. Characters of various kinds on Norton, Thurloe, North, Dunning, Burke, Germaine (Sackville); others, more briefly, are Saville, Wilkes, Mawbey, Barrington, Dyson, Jenkinson, Rigby.

Part II. Begins with remarks on party spirit, then proceeds to characters of Sir John Barnard, Beckford, Oliver and Brass Crosby, Wilkes, Clive (an extensive essay), and Conway. (See also 73-4, 73-10.)

Serials

72-8. Agricola. A Poem. Spoken at Merchant-Taylors School, on Election-Day, June 11.

"E'er Avarice, with rapacious hands." (89)

MJ, Jun 30, 1772.

Irregular stanzas. An objection to "Monopoly," the result of "Avarice" and "Luxury," because it deprives farmers of "the village green and common land," ruining their livelihood, spoiling the land, and forcing them to emigrate.

72-9. The Alderman in Retirement.

"Tir'd of debate, of party, and of pow'r." (38)

L Eve Post, Jan 28, 1772.

HC. An alderman who had supported Wilkes retires from politics, preferring rural quiet "To all the applause and pomp of civil war."

72-10. Another Sketch of the Times.

"Empty Churches." (19)

L Chron 32 (Jul 19, 1772), 40; KG, Jul 11, 1772.

Prose poem. A severe survey of the times -- immoral and absurd, including the politics: "A ministry without Abilities, An Opposition without Meaning."

72-11. [Assist, O Muse, the Praise of Wolfe to sing.]

"Assist, O Muse, the Praise of Wolfe to sing." (16)

St J's C, Aug 25, 1772.

Quatrains. Wolfe's fame and honor shall never die, untainted by the corruption of an ungrateful King and vile politicians.

72-12. Barnard's Ghost. A Poem. By a Gentleman of Oxford.

"In clumsy state, where the proud columns rise." (c. 400)

LM 41 (Aug & Sep 1772), 389-92 & 440-3; SM 34 (Sep 1772), 492-6.

HC. A Tory satire on Beckford, the so-called democratic patriot who wishes to destroy the monarchy, who encourages the crowd to rebel: "Freedom his plea, but anarchy his aim." Also attacks Wilkes, Junius, and Macaulay, among others, who like Cromwell all want a civil war. Sir John Barnard (c. 1685-1764) was an alderman and Lord Mayor of London. See DNB.

72-13. [Be this inscription / Sacred to the memory of General Wolfe.]

"Be this inscription / Sacred to the memory of General Wolfe." (c. 20)

MJ, Aug 18, 1772.

Wolfe and Pitt are joined in this memorial stressing their contribution to imperial growth.

72-14. [Brackenridge, Hugh Henry and Philip Freneau.]
The Rising Glory of America.

"No more of Memphis and her mighty kings." (c. 275)

New Foundling Hospital for Wit (1786), IV, 247-57; Jeffrey Dunstan (pseud.), Fugitive Pieces (1789), pp. 37-46.

Published first in America as A Poem, On The Rising Glory of America; Being An Exercise Delivered At The Public Commencement At Nassau-Hall, September 25, 1771 (Philadelphia: J. Crukshank for R. Aitken, 1772). 27 p. Sabin 25904, 7190. Evans 12398. The American edition is in the form of a blank verse dialogue with three speakers: Leander, Acasto, and Eugenio. The English editions in the miscellanies omit the speakers. -- Two young American poets trace the history of North America in this commencement poem, exalt the American spirit, and assert a new theme, "The rising glory of the western world." Freedom and commerce contribute to its great future as the new Jerusalem. Wolfe, Braddock, Washington, Franklin are cited; and Boston is celebrated for opposing tyranny.

72-15. Britannia's Epitaph for her beloved Wolfe.

"Marble! to thee, my darling I intrust." (14)

L Chron 32 (Nov 3, 1772), 436; WM 18 (Nov 5, 1772), 178.

HC. Wolfe will be remembered for his victory at Quebec.

72-16. The Church's Lamentation.

"A Learned Divine." (78)

BWJ, Feb 22, 1772; L Eve Post, Feb 18, 1772; LM 41 (Feb 1772), 89.

Sixains. A complaint, ironically presented, that the Established Church is about to be weakened by (secular) law. (A complaint at those who wish to remove the Test.)

72-17. The Death of Wolfe.

"Now to decide America thy fate." (c. 90)

T&C 4 (Dec 1772), 663-4.

HC. An account of the victory over the French in Canada, thereby giving to America its civil and religious liberty.

Delamayne, Thomas Hallie.

The Oliviad (1762). Excerpt 42 ll.

PA, Oct 24, 1772.

This excerpt gives an account of the action before Quebec, the basis for the praise of Wolfe's leadership. See 62-A, for Delamayne's long poem.

72-18. The Devil and Premier. A Ballad.

"At Bushy-park hall there dwelt a young Lord." (48)

BWJ, Jul 18, 1772; L Eve Post, Jul 9, 1772.

Ballad satire on North's corruption and Machiavellian politics.

72-19. Dialogue between a Frenchman and his Son.

"Why will you leave our France's climate mild." (22)

L Eve Post, Dec 15, 1772; W Misc 1 (Oct 18, 1773), 64.

HC. A young Frenchman leaves his country for England in order to share in its liberties and to join Wilkes.

72-20. Dialogue between a Patriot and Majority-Man.

"Pat. You sell your Country, Self, and all that's dear." (9)

St J's C, May 16, 1772.

HC. Satire on corruption, accepted by the Majority but rejected by the Patriots.

72-21. Epigram.

"A. How does great Britain, Mistress of the Deep." (2)

L Chron 32 (Sep 26, 1772), 308; St J's C, Sep 24, 1772.

HC. Britain is asleep.

72-22. Epigram.

"Israel's and Britain's Factious curs." (8)

KG, Jan 4, 1772.

Quatrains. Against Wilkes and Brass Crosby.

72-23. Epigram.

"Thus zealot James in holy Ardour pray'd." (5)

BLJ, May 16, 1772; St J's C, May 12, 1772.

James II wished his subjects to be slaves or Catholics; Bute wants both; but King George simply wishes his subjects to be slaves.

72-24. Epigram[s], Addressed to a certain Wise Assembly.

"You, in your Wisdome, have thought fit." (12)

St J's C, Mar 14, 1772.

Sixains. Satire on the 39 Articles, directed to Parliament (debating relief from subscription to them by the Dissenters).

72-25. An Epigram of Martial modernised, by a Youth of Fifteen, upon hearing of the Minister's sordid Avarice.

"Insatiate North! thou hast a rich man's store." (4)

LP, Feb 28, 1772.

HC. Satire on North for his greed.

72-26. Epigram on the Epitaphs for General Wolfe.

"The muse, a shameless mercenary jade." (4)

WM 18 (Nov 12, 1772), 212.

By R. Fergusson. Negative comment on the prize money offered for the best epitaph on Wolfe.

[Epitaph.]

Beginning in July 1772 and extending to the end of the year, and even in many instances into 1773, the serial publications printed numerous epitaphs and inscriptions commemorating the death of Wolfe and his many victories in Canada. They were written in competition for the award of £100 "offered by the Nobleman's Club at Almack's." These appeared often in multiples, as in the GM (16); often almost in every issue, as in Lloyd's (25); PA (12); St J's C (19). These figures are simply meant to be suggestive. Likewise, the entries of these poems in this bibliography are suggestive; not every epitaph printed has been included.

72-27. Epitaph.

"Be this monumental Inscription." (c. 40)

PA, Aug 4, 1772.

Epitaph on Wolfe. Pitt, who is severely castigated, should be blamed for Wolfe's death.

72-28. Epitaph for General Wolfe.

"This monument was erected." (c. 30)

UM 51 (Nov 1772), 264.

Inscription honoring a "noble Commander . . . Who curb'd his foes, and calm'd his country's breast."

72-29. Epitaph for General Wolfe.

"To read this monumental verse, approach." (17)

L Eve Post, Aug 20, 1772.

72-30. Epitaph for General Wolfe's Monument.

"If tender pity in your bosom dwell." (12)

WM 18 (Dec 24, 1772), 402.

HC. Eulogy on Wolfe who "with his blood a noble vict'ry bought."

72-31. Epitaph for the Monument of General Wolfe.

"O ripe in virtue! Britain's early boast." (10)

L Chron 32 (Oct 29, 1772), 424; WM 18 (Nov 5, 1772), 178.

HC. Wolfe is an inspiration to youth.

72-32. Epitaph for the Monument of Gen. Wolfe.

"Stay, Briton, stay! nor blush to shed a tear." (14)

GM 42 (Oct 1772), 487.

HC. Wolfe wanted to live just long enough to know that the British had conquered the French. "Then sunk the glorious patriot, Britain's pride."

72-33. Epitaph for the Monument of General Wolfe.

"When grateful Britons bid the marble rise." (18)

G Eve Post, Sep 26, 1772.

72-34. Epitaph. For the Monument of Wolfe.

"Rest, Warrior, rest. What Wonders hast thou done." (8)

HM 2 (Nov 1772), 619.

HC. Wolfe "restor'd [his] country and an Empire won."

72-35. Epitaph, In Memory of General Wolfe.

"An empire lost, a Montcalm slain." (14)

GM 42 (Sep 1772), 430-1; L Chron 32 (Sep 10, 1772), 253; L Eve Post, Sep 12, 1772.

OC. France lost an empire and Montcalm; Britain gained an empire but lost their general. King George did not believe Canada repaid that loss.

72-36. Epitaph in Memory of General Wolfe.

"Here, gen'rous Briton, drop the manly tear." (18)

GM 42 (Sep 1772), 430.

HC. Mourn for Wolfe who died for his country. Each soldier should emulate his deeds.

72-37. Epitaph in Memory of General Wolfe.

"If patriot worth, or emulation's fire." (12)

GM 42 (Sep 1772), 431-2.

Quatrains. Wolfe died at the moment of victory over France.

72-38. Epitaph in Memory of General Wolfe.

"O Passenger! if e'er thy breast has burn'd." (16)

GM 42 (Sep 1772), 431; St J's C, Aug 29, 1772.

Blank verse. Mourn for Wolfe, the chief and the man. -- Admonishes the gentleman gamblers at Almack's to model themselves on Wolfe.

72-39. Epitaph Intended for the Monument of General Wolfe.

"Stay, sons of heaven! -- quit vice's busy stage." (20)

LP, Sep 16 & 18, 1772. (Text corrected on Sep 18/72).

Epitaph signed with the name of Junius. Quatrains. Wolfe teaches us how to live and how to die, defending his country's freedom "from the tyrant's pow'r."

72-40. Epitaph on General James Wolfe, in the Military Style of Scripture. By the Reverend James De La Cour.

"Here lies a man of war, bred from his youth." (16)

BLJ, Nov 21, 1772.

HC. An unusual epitaph on Wolfe in the military style of the Old Testament.

72-41. Epitaph on General Wolfe.

"Briton, approach in sorrow's silent gloom." (4)

GM 42 (Dec 1772), 588.

HC. Brave Wolfe lies here. "He came, he saw, he conquer'd -- and he died!"

72-42. Epitaph on General Wolfe.

"Here rests thy corpse, O Wolfe! that once inclos'd." (24)

GM 42 (Oct 1772), 487-8.

HC. Brave Wolfe fought and led well at Louisbourg and Quebec, where he died. The King will erect a monument to his memory.

72-43. Epitaph on General Wolfe.

"His country Devotes this monument." (c. 25)

GM 42 (Sep 1772), 432; MJ, Sep 3, 1772; PA, Sep 3, 1772.

Wolfe succeeded in subduing "one fourth / Of the vast creation, America!"

72-44. Epitaph on General Wolfe.

"In worth exceeding, and in virtue great." (4)

WM 18 (Nov 12, 1772), 212.

Words cannot effectively praise Wolfe's greatness. By R. Fergusson.

72-45. Epitaph on General Wolfe.

"Oh! Stranger, stay, if e'er thy friendly eye." (14)

Say's, Aug 29, 1772; G Eve Post, Aug 13, 1772; GM 42 (Sep 1772), 430; KG, Aug 15, 1772; Lloyd's 31 (Aug 7, 1772), 140.

This is the first of numerous epitaphs on Wolfe appearing in Lloyd's -- 19 and one epigram. HC. Celebrates Wolfe's modesty at Quebec, where he died.

72-46. Epitaph on General Wolfe.

"O Wolfe / if e'er thy friends." (c. 25)

M Chron, Nov 26, 1772.

A panegyrical inscription on Wolfe by "An American."

72-47. Epitaph on General Wolfe.

"To thee, great Wolfe, who with thy warlike train." (11)

G, Sep 17, 1772.

HC. Wolfe's fame shall be immortal.

72-48. Epitaph on General Wolfe.

"Will any Briton pass unheeding by." (20)

GM 42 (Oct 1772), 487.

HC. The tale of Wolfe's victory and death at Quebec is narrated.

72-49. Epitaph on General Wolfe. By Sir William Draper.

"Immortal Wolfe! Sculpture, thy laurel'd bust." (12)

BWJ, Aug 8, 1772; G Eve Post, Aug 13, 1772; GM 42 (Sep 1772), 431; Say's, Aug 29, 1772; WM 17 (Sep 3, 1772), 305.

HC. Quebec is Wolfe's monument.

72-50. Epitaph. On the Death of Junius.

"Faction lament, Sedition drop a Tear." (32)

G Eve Post, Feb 6, 1772; PA, Feb 6, 1772.

HC. Satire on Junius. When this seditious writer attacked Mansfield, he wounded himself fatally.

72-51. Epitaph on the Late General Wolfe.

"Noble in arms to Wolfe this tomb is rais'd." (21)

LP, Sep 30, 1772.

HC. Praise of Wolfe for the manner and circumstances of his death.

72-52. Fergusson, R.
The King's Birth-Day in Edinburgh.

"I sing the day sae aften sung." (96)

WM 16 (Jun 4, 1772), 305.

Sixains. A Scotch poet loyally and humorously celebrates George III's birthday in modified dialect.

72-53. Former Times Compared with the Present.

"In Monkish Days we read of Borough-Men." (24)

BLJ, Jun 13, 1772.

HC. Satire on the times -- presented ironically. The past was full of corruption in public life; the present is not much better.

72-54. Great Beckford's Speech to the Livery, on the late Election.

"Behold my Statue, Beckford cries." (64)

St J's C, Oct 10, 1772.

Quatrains. The spirit of Beckford, former Mayor of London, warns the livery of North's attempts to bribe and corrupt MP's and thereby undermine liberty. Wilkes is cited.

72-55. Grub Street in Arms.

"The Subject started -- Wit flies out apace." (12)

St J's C, Oct 1, 1772.

HC. Satire on the poor versifyers competing for the prize for the best epitaph on Wolfe.

72-56. Impromptu, on reading an Epitaph offered to the Society at Almack's, for General Wolfe.

"The Muse replies, no cause there is to mourn." (22)

GM 42 (Oct 1772), 488.

HC. Wolfe's achievements render him immortal: "dying, [he] serv'd his Country and his King."

72-57. Index for 1772.

"Ch[atha]m neglected." (12)

DJ, Jan 7, 1773; L Eve Post, Dec 31, 1772; MJ, Dec 29, 1772.

Comment on the economic and political scene -- Chatham neglected, Camden respected, Wilkes rejected, North "erected," Mansfield "affected," bankers dissected, and credit dejected.

72-58. Inscription for the Monument of the Right Hon. G*****, E--- of ********.

"If e'er thy soul, oh passenger, could feel." (84)

L Eve Post, Oct 27, 1772.

HC. Satire on George Townshend, his terrible career as a soldier. He does not deserve honors like Wolfe. See On the Three New Marquises: 72-81. (He made the mistake of criticizing the generalship of a national hero.)

72-59. Inscription for Wolfe.

"What Epitaph or Monumental Pile." (8)

St J's C, Sep 29, 1772.

Quatrains. The only monument worthy of Wolfe is "the Nation's Glory" -- of which America is a part: "the Western Continent," or "America, which was fought for and won when Wolfe lost his life."

72-60. An Inscription proposed for General Wolfe's Monument.

"Be this Inscription / Sacred to the Memory of General Wolfe." (c. 35)

GM 42 (Sep 1772), 431.

Wolfe's heroic leadership is praised. Appointed by Pitt, Wolfe elevated the British empire "To the highest pitch of Glory."

72-61. Liberty of the Press.

"Hail, greatest Blessing Royalty can bring." (12)

DJ, Sep 29, 1772.

HC. Eulogizes the press for its freedom to expose dangers to truth in government.

72-62. A Literal Translation of a Late Speech into plain English.

"My good Lords and Sirs, I can scarce find expression." (74)

LP, Jun 19, 1772.

Hexameter couplets. Ironic satire through the King's persona on King George (portrayed as a subtle Machiavellian knave who has contempt for the people), the Marriage Act, George's wish to increase his prerogative, taxes and the budget, and the need for passive obedience and oppression. Wilkes is called a "blackguard" and "patriots . . . fools."

72-63. The Man of Kent. A Song. Wrote in the Year 1745.

"Augmented still in story." (57)

KG, Apr 25, 1772.

Song. Two stanzas are added to a song written in 1745 -- stanzas on Wolfe who was born in Westerham, Kent. Wolfe's name and fame are used to help Sawbridge (who owned large estates in Kent).

72-64. A New Modern Alphabet For the Use of Grown Children who study Politicks.

"A was an Allen, was cowardly shot." (21)

LP, Jan 31, 1772.

HC. A medley of satire and praise, a variety of people and events: Allen, Chatham, Grafton, Junius, the King, Mansfield, Wilkes, etc.

72-65. A New Song. On the Election for the Lord Mayor of London. To the tune of Nancy Dawson.

"Observe brave Wilkes and Townsend rise." (40)

M Chron, Oct 8, 1772.

Song honoring James Townsend, elected Lord Mayor of London. The history of the fight for freedom against corrupt placemen, "lawless Gen'ral Warrants," etc., is reviewed.

72-66. An Ode to a great Number of Great Men, in the time of Sir R. Walpole.

"See a new progeny descends." (102)

L Chron 31 (Mar 26, 1772), 300; WM 16 (Apr 16, 1772), 82-3.

Regular ode in sixains, originally dated August 1742. Satire on the new ministry upon Sir Robert Walpole's fall from power. The "great men," the new leaders, are fools. As these reprinted verses demonstrate, the Ins and the Outs can scarcely be distinguished. But only the impartial and disinterested, who "Unite all hearts, appease each storm," deserve applause.

72-67. Old England Turned Upside Down.

"Of this pure isle, the prosp'rous state." (104)

M Chron, Nov 11, 1772.

Quatrains. Objects to the hypocrisy of the anti-popery dissenters who mask their real intention to destroy the church. In politics, corruption controls places, and here, too, "godliness and gain" serve each other conveniently. Joining with atheists and deists, modern Whigs are like the old Puritans and plot Satanically to destroy the church.

72-68. On a late Promotion.

"When North appears with Star and Ribbon drest." (4)

St J's C, May 2, 1772.

Epigram. Satire on Lord North for corruption.

72-69. On a Premium of One Hundred Pounds being offered by the Noblemen's Club at Almack's, for the best Epitaph on General Wolfe.

"One hundred pounds -- too small a boon." (6)

BWJ, Aug 15, 1772; L Eve Post, Aug 11, 1772; PA, Aug 14, 1772.

The £100 award for the best epitaph on Wolfe does not correspond to the greatness of Wolfe.

72-70. On Mr. Wilkes's Last Address to the Livery.
A Simile.

"Hark! what faint voice is that? -- 'tis he." (26)

M Chron, Apr 10, 1772.

Octosyllabic couplets. Wilkes is neglected and forgotten, like an old mangy mongrel.

72-71. On Reading the Laureat's Ode.

"For two such meals of fulsome lies." (4)

MJ, Jan 2, 1772.

Epigram. Satire. The King pays Whitehead £100 for two odes a year; -- he overpays!

72-72. On Seeing many different Inscriptions to the Memory of General Wolfe. By a Lady.

"Silence, ye Bards, your various Contests cease." (4)

St J's C, Sep 17, 1772.

Advice to the versifiers to cease competing for the prize offered to the best epitaph on Wolfe -- for nothing they can do will add to his honours.

72-73. On the Approaching Mayoralty.

"Behold the Time is come to mock at Form." (25)

PA, Oct 24, 1772.

Blank verse attacking Wilkes the populist for causing anarchy by levelling all distinctions in rank.

72-74. On the Death of General Wolfe.

"Let Rome her Caesars and her Pompey boast." (34)

PA, Sep 4, 1772.

HC. In praise of the patriot hero Wolfe, "Call'd forth by Pitt."

72-75. On the Determination of the Negro Cause.

"Tyrants, no more the servile yoke prepare." (4)

M Chron, Jun 26, 1772.

Epigram. Slavery cannot be tolerated in Britain. Freedom prevails against Dunning (?), as slavery is declared illegal.

72-76. On the Election of the Duke of Grafton, Chancellor of Cambridge when Prime Minister, the Oxonians reflected upon the Time-servers as under:
. . . . Upon the Election of Lord North at Oxford, the Cantabrigians retorted.

"Good sister Cambridge, with regret we see." (4 + 4)

UM 51 (Nov 1772), 265.

Epigram. Satire. Cambridge and Oxford accuse each other of truckling to power.

72-77. On the late celebrated Mr. Charles Churchill.

"Sweet were the notes once Churchill sung." (16)

BWJ, Jul 4, 1772; MJ, Jul 2, 1772; M Chron, Jul 3, 1772.

Octosyllabic couplets. Churchill is praised and linked with Wilkes and the cause of freedom.

72-78. On the Present Age. 1772.

"No more, my friends, of vain applause." (72)

MJ, Oct 1, 1772; Ox M 8 (Feb 1772), 73-4.

Quatrains. Ironic lines on the state of the nation, everyone apparently honest, moral, and contented; but it is not really so.

72-79. On the present Coalition of Patriots.

"In some Apothecary's Shop." (20)

PA, Jul 18, 1772.

Octosyllabic couplets. Ironic satire on the foul union of a "motley Patriot-Rabble."

72-80. On the Report there would be no Lord Mayor's Day. A New City Election Song. To the Tune of Room for Cuckolds, here comes my Lord Mayor.

"Great the majority had Wilkes, that lad o'wax." (36)

M Chron, Oct 27, 1772.

Song. The writer assures us that there will be a day celebrating the election of a Lord Mayor, and everyone will have good food and "booze." Townsend and Wilkes are cited.

72-81. On the Three New Marquises. Ode. To the Tune of Pretty Sally.

"Illustrious Theme, what Oh! awake." (40)

L Eve Post, Dec 19, 1772.

Song. A protest at the promotion to the honor of marquis of three undeserving wretches and cowards -- Lord North, Earl of Hertford (Francis Seymour Conway), and George Townshend (who had in a letter severely criticized Wolfe's military ability). See Inscription for the Monument, . . . 72-58.

72-82. Parody on the King's Speech.

"It gives me ample satisfaction." (62)

BWJ, Feb 1, 1772.

Doggerel, tetrameter couplets. The King admits to the influence of his "Friends." He makes his opening speech, remarking that the threat of war with Spain has disappeared, but hopes that the navy will not be neglected and that Parliament will provide supplies proposed by his "sincerest Friends."

72-83. The Patriot's Soliloquy. A Parody.

"Oh Liberty! my boasted End and Aim." (18)

BLJ, Apr 11, 1772; St J's C, Apr 4, 1772.

HC. Satire on the patriot (apparently Wilkes) who cannot find liberty.

72-84. [The People's manners, an old Poet sings.]

"The People's manners, an old Poet sings." (8)

MJ, Feb 27, 1772.

HC. Why does the King, who is a good virtuous man, have such an evil court? George cannot be the King.

72-85. Pictures of the Present Times.

"A Deluge of Circulating Paper." (12)

BWJ, Jul 11, 1772; DJ, Jul 14, 1772; KG, Jul 7, 1772; L Chron 32 (Jul 7, 1772),

32; Say's, Jul 11, 1772.

Prose poem. A severe survey of the evils of the times -- in the economy, religion, and politics -- corruption, hypocrisy, and the like, including "Want driving Industry into Exile."

72-86. [Rest, happy shade! while round thy early tomb.]

"Rest, happy shade! while round thy early tomb." (8)

G Eve Post, Jul 30, 1772.

Epitaph on Wolfe: "Here shall Canada with Britain weep."

72-87. A Scheme for reducing the high price of Provision. A Cantata. Wrote in the year 1772. To the Tune of Cupid's Recruiting Serjeant.

"Come, Liberty's sons, and hear what I propose." (90)

T&C 4 (Dec 1772), 662-3; WM 19 (Jan 21, 1773), 113-4; The Caledoniad. A Collection of Poems Written Chiefly by Scottish Authors (London: W. Hay, 1775), III, 64-8.

Song. Satire on Wilkes and his followers and associates: Bull, Allen, Beckford, Glynn, Horne. The idea is to get rid of them and all will be well -- prices will tumble, the "mechanics" will work, beer will be plentiful, taxes can be paid cheerfully.

72-88. Song. [To the tune of "Rule Britannia."]

"Let haughty Monarchs of the world." (26)

L Eve Post, Oct 17, 1772.

Song, celebrates the victory of James Townsend (Lord Mayor of London, 1772-3) and Wilkes (Sheriff 1771-2) at the polls. Grafton and North, "and each court knave," are denigrated.

72-89. Stevens, George Alexander.
Politics. Tune, -- 'Tis a Twelvemonth ago, nay, perhaps it is twain.

"As an Englishman ought, I wish well to my King." (32)

Songs, Comic, and Satyrical (Oxford: For the Author, 1772), pp. 175-6.

A cynical song about politics -- the prevalence of bribery, and the wisdom of being In rather than Out (the distinction between the two being negligible).

72-90. [Sweet Willy Whitehead who with medium stile.]

"Sweet Willy Whitehead who with medium stile." (10)

G Eve Post, Jan 2, 1772; MJ, Jan 2, 1772.

HC. Satire on Whitehead's laureat poems: "simply chaste" and "delicately dull." Whitehead writes "smoothly" and sweetly. A pensioned poet, he wings "milkwarm praises of a milkwarm King."

72-91. To a certain Country.

"O Land corrupted, dastard, out of Heart." (20)

Lloyd's 31 (Oct 5, 1772), 340; St J's C, Sep 19, 1772.

HC. Something is terribly wrong with the nation that allows its people to starve. Cited are corruption, the ministry, the King.

72-92. To a Friend in an High Office.

"To make thee truly happy in thy trust." (11)

G Eve Post, Jun 6, 1772.

HC. Advice to a minister simply to be strictly just -- never to deprive others of their rights.

72-93. To John Wilkes, Esquire.

"Thou who 'mongst lesser Patriots shone." (42)

PA, Mar 20, 1772.

Sixains. Satire on Wilkes, infamous turncoat and fraud, deserted by friend and foe. Cited are Crosby, Glynn, Horne, Sawbridge, Townsend, Pitt.

72-94. To Junius.

"Junius, where art thou now? to thee we owe." (8)

St J's C, Sep 24, 1772.

HC. Junius should reappear to expose corrupt politicians, wicked and in high place.

72-95. To Lord Camden.

"Yes, to the Relish of the gen'rous Muse." (35)

PA, Mar 21, 1772.

Blank verse panegyric on Charles Pratt, Lord Camden, in the Whig tradition of Sydney, Locke, Somers, and protector of civil rights, as opposed to William Murray, Lord Mansfield, Scottish Tory.

72-96. To My Lord --------. [Mansfield.]

"Permit me, my good Lord, as the duty I owe." (86)

MJ, Mar 17, 1772.

Hexameter couplets. Satire on Judge Mansfield who is modelled on Judge Jeffries.

72-97. To the Admirer of Junius, on his calling Junius the invisible Deity of the Literary World.

"How, Junius deified! Tis odd." (6)

KG, Jan 4, 1772.

Junius is a devil.

72-98. To the Great.

"O Nobles, would you wonder, should you see." (17)

St J's C, May 28, 1772.

HC and quatrains. The nobility should prevent the poor from starving. Neither the King nor the laws are helping the starving poor. Bute (or his policy) is to blame.

72-99. To the Memory of General Wolfe.

"Soldiers and Sailors, pray make room." (4)

LP, Sep 9, 1772.

Epitaph on Wolfe. Cites Montreal as scene of his glorious victory!

72-100. To the Memory of General Wolfe . . . .

"Stop, soldier, stop; -- your hero's sacred dust." (6)

G Eve Post, Aug 18, 1772; GM 42 (Aug 1772), 383.

HC. Epitaph. Wolfe "heard the shout of victory, -- and fell."

72-101. To the Memory of General Wolfe.

"This tomb is rais'd to crown the hero's worth." (48)

UM 51 (Nov 1772), 263.

HC. Heroic Wolfe, "The price of Britain, and the scourge of France," died "in his country's cause."

72-102. To the Memory of Lieutenant General Wolfe.

"Here, peaceful, rests beneath this Marble Stone." (16)

PA, Jul 24, 1772.

HC. Praise of the heroic General Wolfe -- "noble, valourous and good."

72-103. To the Right Hon. The Earl of Sandwich, First Lord of the Admiralty, &c. &c. on his re-visiting the Docks and Ships of War at the several Ports in June, 1772.

"The Pow'r which lights all-cheering Rays bestows." (29)

M Chron, Jul 22, 1772; PA, Jul 15, 1772.

HC. Praise of the Earl of Sandwich for attending to the business of the navy, securing English commerce and bringing prosperity to "the Poor."

72-104. The Trimmers Double-faced Professions.

"I hold for Faith." (8)

PA, May 23, 1772; Lloyd's 30 (May 22, 1772), 499.

It is difficult to be sure of the trimmer's professions of faith -- for or against North, for or against the policies of the ministry, for or against the King.

72-105. [True friend to Liberty, accept the lays.]

"True friend to Liberty, accept the lays." (34)

L Eve Post, Nov 3, 1772.

HC. General satire on the powerful and rich great man who is evil in contrast with the good man who enjoys freedom for himself and others.

72-106. [When first, well-counsell'd, James the sceptre try'd.]

"When first, well-counsell'd, James the sceptre try'd." (24)

L Eve Post, Dec 12, 1772.

HC. Ironic satire on King and court who keep a standing army and reduce the power of the navy. (A standing army in America was a source of irritation.) Corruption and taxes are cited.

72-107. Whitehead, William.
Ode for the New Year, Jan 1, 1772. As performed before their Majesties and the Royal Family. Written by William Whitehead, Esq. and set to Music by Dr. Boyce.

"At length the fleeting year is o'er." (36)

BLJ, Jan 4, 1772; BWJ, Jan 4, 1772; G Eve Post, Dec 31/71-Jan 2, 1772; GM 42 (Jan 1772), 38; KG, Dec 31/71-Jan 4, 1772; Lloyd's 30 (Dec 30/70-Jan 1, 1772), 7; L Chron 31 (Dec 31, 1771-Jan 2, 1772), 2; L Eve Post, Dec 31, 1771-Jan 2, 1772; LM 41 (Jan 1772), 36; St J's C, Dec 31, 1771-Jan 2, 1772.

Irregular ode of sixains and quatrains. The laureat announces a time of quiet -- no more wars or tumults. Should Britain be true to herself, she will have no foreign foes to fear and will secure "domestic ease."

1773 Books & Pamphlets

73-1. City Patriotism Displayed: A Poem. Addressed To The Rt. Hon. Frederick Lord North.
London: Dixwell, [1773]. 5-24p.

"Whilst you, my Lord, in Bushy's cool Retreat." (c. 340)

Notices: CR 36 (Oct 1773), 316; MR 49 (Sep 1773), 231; KG, Sep 25, 1773; L Chron 34 (Sep 18, 1773), 281; LM 42 (Sep 1773), 456; LP, Sep 20, 1773.

Copies: NUC IEN.

HC. Satire on London City political leaders--John Wilkes, Brass Crosby, Frederick Bull, James Townsend, and others. Accuses Wilkes of hypocrisy--when rejected by Bute, to whom he had "meanly stoop'd for Favors," he became a patriot and demagogue, inflaming the mob and the press. His sole motive is self-interest; "the only Cause" of his politics "Disappointment and Contempt of Laws." Joining his "factious cause" are Crosby, Bull, Townsend, et al.--their creed made up of "Fictitious Wrongs," and to gain their point they excite sedition and subversion, transform Wilkes into a saint and the King into a Jacobite.

73-2. [Day, Thomas]
The Dying Negro. A Poetical Epistle, Supposed to be Written by a Black to his Intended Wife.
London: Flexney, 1773. 19p.

"Arm'd with thy sad last gift--the power to die." (c. 470)

Notices: CR 36 (Jul 1773), 70; MR 49 (Jul 1773), 63; GM 43 (Oct 1773), 503-5; L Chron 33 (Jun 22, 1773), 597; LP, Jul 5, 1773; M Chron, Jul 8, 1773; PA, Jul 8, 1773.

Sabin 18987 (1793 ed).

Copies: BL 11602.gg.1 (14); NUC CSmH, CtY, MB, MH, TxU.

3 eds to 1775; 2nd ed (1774) "with additions," viii + 22p.; 3rd ed (1775) "corrected and enlarged," iii-x + 24p., entitled The Dying Negro, A Poem (BL copy, 11630.e.6 [2], attributed in a MS note to T. Day and J. Bicknell).
HC. A monologue. A Negro slave, resolved to die and end his suffering, bequeaths his love to his absent bride. He vows that it is better to die than to endure again the brutal existence of a plantation slave "beyond the western main." He describes the sordid slave traffic before he kills himself.

73-3. [Delamayne, Thomas Hallie]
 The City-Patricians. A Poem.
 London: Allen, 1773. 39p.

"Say! shall the advent'rous Muse attempt to soar." (c. 600)

Notices: CR 36 (Sep 1773), 234-5; MR 49 (Sep 1773), 230; L Chron 34 (Sep 23, 1773), 297; L Mag 42 (Oct 1773), 509; LP, Sep 22 & 24, 1773.

Copies: BL 1500/2.

HC. Satire and panegyric on the politicians, the aldermen, of London, similar to The Senators (72-1) on the commoners in Parliament and The Patricians (73-4) on the peers at court. Emphasizes the baseness, venality, and servility of many aldermen since Beckford's time: James Townsend, who is accused of being the tool of Shelburne and Horne; George Bellas; Robert Ladbroke, a tool of North; Brass Crosby, and others. However, praises Barlow Trecothick, Serjeant John Glynn, John Kirkman, and John Sawbridge for honesty and other virtues, especially the last alderman. Wilkes is criticized for his apparent insincerity, living only in "anarchy and noise," but praised for his brave and strenuous resistance to oppression.

73-4. [-----]
 The Patricians: Or, A Candid Examination into the Merits of the Principal Speakers of the House of Lords. By the Author of The Senators.
 London: Kearsly, 1773. 34p.

"Let puling Poets rack their lovesick brains." (c. 600)

Notices: CR 35 (Feb 1773), 159; MR 48 (Feb 1773), 160; L Chron 33 (Feb 20, 1773), 181; L Mag 42 (Feb 1773), 92; PA, Mar 10, 1773.

Copies: BL 11602.h.21 (6); Bod Godwyn Pamph 1488 (2), Vet A5d.256 (4); NUC CtY, IU, InU, & MH (1st ed), ICN & NN (2nd ed, 1773).

HC. Inspired by freedom, Delamayne dares expose peers guilty of corruption and tyranny, "unaw'd by pow'r--uncheck'd by modern law"--Grafton (power-mad, undermined "Free-born Rights"), Gower, Suffolk (apostate, "dishonoured by a place"), Denbigh (barbaric), Pomfret, Weymouth (drinking brute, approved the St. George's Fields' massacre), the Bishops--excepting Exeter and Bangor (who vote for place and oppression, not conscience), Mansfield (tyrant), Hillsborough ("tyrant . . . made sacred freedom groan," yet generous and honest), Sandwich (shameless, pleasure-loving). Praised for their love of freedom are Camden, Temple, Lyttelton, Richmond, Shelburne (?), and Rockingham. Concludes with an exhortation to Chatham to take the lead of government and be the savior of Britain again. See 73-10. (See also 72-1, 72-6, & 72-7.)

73-5. English, Robert.
  The Naval Review. A Poem. Inscribed to the Right Honourable Sir Charles Saunders, Knight of the Bath, and Admiral of the Blue Squadron of His Majesty's Fleet.
  London: Becket, 1773. 22p.

  2nd & 3rd eds, 1774, 5-23p.

  "In higher sphere the Muse ambitious strays." (c. 120).

  Notices: CR 36 (Aug 1773), 155; MR 49 (Aug 1773), 148; G Eve Post, May 31, 1774; L Eve Post, Aug 9, 1774; St J's Chron, Aug 9 & 17, 1774; L Chron 34 (Aug 21, 1773), 189, & 35 (Jun 4, 1774), 544; LM 42 (Sep 1773), 456.

  Copies: Bod Godwyn Pamph 1711 (5) (3rd ed); NUC CtY (2nd ed), ICN (1st & 3rd eds).

  HC. At a time when "storms collecting frown on Albion's Plains," celebrates British naval victories over Spain and France at Quebec, Belleisle, Manila, Africa, Louisbourg. Praises Anson, Hawke, Keppel, Saunders, Wolfe. Concludes with patriotic pride in Britain's rule over the main, keeping "the jarring World in awe." Saunders and Wolfe cooperated at Quebec; Keppel contributed to English victories at Goree, Africa, and Bellisle, the fortress off the coast of France.

73-6. [Hurd, Richard]
  Discord: A Satire.
  London: Woodyer, Beecroft, et al., 1773. 5-16p.

  "Curst hour, when Discord by the Wrath of Jove." (c. 200)

  Notices: CR 36 (Dec 1773), 475; MR 49 (Dec 1773), 504-5; L Chron 34 (Dec 7, 1773), 557; L Mag 42 (Dec 1773), 611.

  Copies: BL 840.1.4 (7).

  HC. A generalized protest at the spirit of Discord, by the Bishop of Worcester, that destroys the happiness of individuals. But more horrifying is the furious discord that brings war and destroys nations. Concludes with Hollis's (the Duke of Newcastle's) denunciation of seditious and anarchic faction (when "Reproach shall reign, rude rhetoric, low intrigue"), in which it is clear that he has Wilkes in mind, the "lewd leader" undermining the prestige of George III, "a youthful Monarch."

73-7. [Mason, William]
  An Heroic Epistle to Sir William Chambers, Knight, Comptroller General of His Majesty's Works, and Author of a late Dissertation on Oriental Gardening.
  London: Almon, 1773. 19p.

  "Knight of the Polar Star! by Fortune plac'd." (146)

Notices: CR 35 (Jun 1773), 465-70; MR 48 (Apr 1773), 314-15; GM 43 (Jun 1773), 290-1; L Eve Post, Mar 11, 1773; L Chron 33 (Mar 30, 1773), 305; L Mag 42 (Apr 1773), 196-7.

Copies: BL 840.1.17 (1), 11660.c.8 (8th ed), 11657.g.54 (10th ed), et al.; Bod Godwyn Pamph 1492 (18), 1720 (10) (3rd ed), 1720 (9) (5th ed), 1736 (3) (7th ed), 1720 (14) (13th ed); NUC MH (2nd ed), KU (3rd ed), ICU & NNC (4th ed), CtY & TxU (5th ed), IU & MB (6th ed), CtY, InU, & TxU (7th ed), et al.

11 eds in 1773, 14 to 1777; the above is a 2nd ed; I have not seen a first.
HC. Satire on Tory taste, politicians, and writers; ostensibly a satire on the taste for Chinese gardening. Mason really directs his satire against the Scots, raised to various positions of power by the King, especially the Tory politics of Bute, the summary justice of Mansfield. Also satirized are Sandwich and a host of Tory writers--David Mallet, John Shebbeare, James Scott (Anti-Sejanus), Samuel Johnson, James Macpherson, and Tobias Smollett. Wilkes, too, appears. The satire is very allusive.

73-8. The Patriot. A Poem. Inscribed to the Supporters of the Bill of Rights. London: Evans, [1773]. 5-19p.

"Whilst crouds aspire to patriotic fame." (c. 300)

Notices: PA, Dec 19, 1772.

Copies: BL 11658.h.20.

HC. The tradition of true patriotism in England runs from Wilkes to Russell, Sidney, Hampden, Pym, and Raleigh. Describes the close friendship between Churchill and Wilkes, and the proceeds to satire on false patriots--Wedderburne, Fletcher Norton, North, and Charles Fox. Concludes with a denunciation of corruption; for freedom, he insists, depends on public virtue. North is considered Bute's "most pliant and obsequious tool," and Fox, now only at the beginning of his career, is considered only as a supporter of "ministerial measures."

73-9. Public Spirit, An Ode. By Verovicensis Senescens. Birmingham: Aris; London: Baldwin, 1773. [ii] + 12p.

"Strike the loud shell, Pierian maid." (171)

Notices: CR 35 (Aug 1773), 155; MR 48 (May 1773), 410.

Copies: NUC PU.

Regular Horatian ode. Invokes Clio, the muse of history, to inspire the present times, corrupted by luxury. Urges for Britons the models of Roman heroes who had been lovers of liberty. Calls for honest and independent English politics, the incorruptible rectitude of the republicans of classical Rome being the measure. Cited are King Alfred, Beaufort, Shippen, Henry (?) Digby.

73-10. A Review of the Poem, Intitled "The Patricians." Or, A Re-Examination into the Merits of the Principal Speakers of the House of Lords. By the Author of The Review of the Poem of the Senators.
London: Wilkie, 1773. 3-7 + 9-43p.

"Call'd forth from bus'ness, where the quiv'ring fate." (c. 600)

Notices: CR 35 (Jun 1773), 474; MR 49 (Jun 1773), 65.

Copies: NUC ICN, IU, TxU.

See 73-4. This probably not by Delamayne. HC. The poet objects to much of The Patricians as he remarks on several political characters from his own point of view. He is hostile to Wilkes, who debauches liberty and transforms it into license, and hostile to needless and weak city petitions and remonstrances which, in his opinion, the King rightfully rejects. Tries to set proper bounds for liberty in law and virtue, including the freedom of the press. The major characters he presents are those of Grafton, Camden, Weymouth, Mansfield and Sandwich (both defended and praised), and Chatham. He remarks on "our mad Colonists" when he praises Lord Hillsborough for dealing firmly with them. (See also 72-1, 72-6, 72-7.)

Verovicensis Senescens. See 73-9.

73-11. Wheatley, Phillis.
Poems on Various Subjects, Religious and Moral. By Phillis Wheatley, Negro Servant to Mr. John Wheatley of Boston, in New England.
London: Bell, 1773. [9]-124p.

To the Right Honourable William, Earl of Dartmouth, His Majesty's Principal Secretary of State for North America, &c. "Hail, happy day, when smiling like the morn." (43) pp. 73-5.

Notices: CR 36 (Sep 1773), 232-3; MR 49 (Dec 1773), 457-9; AM 7 (Jul 1784), 394-5. For other Wheatley poems in this collection, see also AR, 1772, 214-5; BLJ, Sep 25, 1773; GM 43 (Sep 1773), 456; HM 2 (Apr 1772), 219-20; L Chron 34 (Jul 1, Sep 16, Oct 5, 1773), 13, 277, 341; LM 42 (Sep 1773), 456.

Evans 19913 (1786 Amer. ed); Sabin 103136.

Copies: BL 992.a.34, 239.e.11; NUC CSmH, CtY, MH, NN, RPJCB, et al.

The poem to Dartmouth was written late in 1772. HC. Wheatley hopes that

Dartmouth's appointment as Secretary of State for North America (Aug 14, 1772) will help the cause of freedom, even for slaves. See 68-26: "To the King's Most Excellent Majesty."

Serials

73-12. Another Prophecy. In Answer to Merlin. See our last.

"When Stewart's blest Race shall return." (20)

St J's C, Sep 25, 1773.

OC. When the Stuarts return, there will be tyranny and corruption, and a loss of freedom and true religion. See "A Prophecy of Reformation in the year 1773": 73-87.

73-13. [Anstey, Christopher.]
A Parody on the Laureat's Ode for the New Year.

"Wrapt in stole of sable grain." (25)

West M 1 (Jan 1773), 105-6; WM 19 (Feb 11, 1773), 211.

Whitehead is called "the leaden Laureat of the day" because of his dull odes.

[The Boston Massacre.] "Canst thou, spectator, view this crimson'd scene." (24) Freeman's J, Jun 5, 1773; M Chron, Jun 1, 1773. An American report of a Boston service commemorating the Boston Massacre of March 5, 1770. See 73-16.

73-14. Bribery and Corruption. Extracted from a Satire published about 40 years ago.

"We all at bribery and corruption rail." (14)

L Eve Post, Oct 23, 1773.

HC. Protest at the sale of votes (bribery and corruption).

73-15. The Budget Solus.

"Before I pay off the national debt." (c. 150)

M Chron, Jul 7, 1773.

Dactylic meter, four or five stress couplets. Satire on Lord North. The persona of Lord North declares he is unfit to be a minister of state because he knows nothing about finance. But he wants to help "that Great Company," the East India Company.

73-16. [Canst thou, spectator, view this crimson'd scene.]

"Canst thou, spectator, view this crimson'd scene." (24)

Freeman's J, Jun 5, 1773; M Chron, Jun 1, 1773.

Quatrains in couplets from an American report of a Boston service commemorating the Boston Massacre of March 5, 1770. The key ideological issue stressed is the violent effect of maintaining a standing army in a peaceful community.

73-17. Clio to Lord North.

"On that fam'd Hill, where soft poetic Strains." (50)

PA, Mar 2, 1773.

HC. The Muse of History, Clio, praises Lord North, the premier, for his excellent statesmanship in guiding Britain. The colonies are not neglected, the prose preceding the verses declare.

73-18. [Come and listen awhile, and I'll tell you anon.]

"Come and listen awhile, and I'll tell you anon." (76)

PA, Dec 6, 1773.

Song. Ballad satirizing John Wilkes in a review of his career from the time when he was encouraged by Pitt and Lord Temple, sought help from the Duke of Newcastle, Francis Dashwood, and even Lord Bute! -- before he used his journalism to make a name for himself. The narrative includes his exile in Paris, his return and candidacy for a seat in the Commons, his expulsion, his running for alderman. His motive is always money.

73-19. [Come simple Whitehead, with thy simpler lays.]

"Come simple Whitehead, with thy simpler lays." (22)

L Eve Post, May 1, 1773.

HC. Ironic praise of Whitehead's "chaste and sober Muse."

73-20. Corsica Loquitur.

"Gens animosa virum, modo rupibus acriar ipsis." (96)

GM 43 (Mar 1773), 143.

One of the occasional Latin poems on the times: on the Corsican struggle against the French.

73-21. An Elegy to the Memory of the Late ----.

"Peace to thy royal shade, illustrious ---- ----" [King]. (56)

L Eve Post, Dec 23, 1773.

Heroic, elegiac, stanzas. When the present King George came to the throne, he was influenced by Bute. Perhaps he can be taught a lesson by the execution of Charles I -- and drive traitors from the court.

73-22. Epigram.

"History tells us of a vile intent." (4)

L Eve Post, Jun 29, 1773.

Parliament is subversive, and will blow up the nation -- unlike Guy Fawkes who tried to blow up Parliament.

73-23. Epigam.

"Three hundred placemen sitting in a row." (5)

L Eve Post, Nov 9, 1773.

Satire on the numerous placemen speaking for the nation in Parliament. They deserve hanging. (The theme is corruption.)

73-24. Epigram. Inscribed to John Wilkes, Esq;

"When patriots strike at palace or at steeple." (14)

L Chron 34 (Oct 16, 1773), 381; MJ, Oct 14, 1773.

Sonnet in couplets. When patriots come to power with the help of the people, they (like Cromwell) turn against them: a warning to Wilkes.

73-25. Epigram. On the late First Rate productions of Sir John Dalrymple, Bart. and James Macpherson, Esq.

"Sure Science's fall was reserved for those days." (6)

L Eve Post, Apr 8, 1773.

Hexameter couplets. A complaint against two Scots authors, Dalrymple for slandering Algernon Sidney and Lord William Russell; and Macpherson for disfiguring Homer.

73-26. An Epistle from the Author to his Mistress.

"You I love, my dearest life." (40)

GM 43 (Jan 1773), 40; WM 19 (Feb 11, 1773), 211; Under title of Protestation, also in L Eve Post, Jan 16, 1773; MJ, Jan 16, 1773; PA, Jan 19, 1773.

Trochaic tetrameter couplets. The poet professes a greater love of his wife than of all sorts of people with political associations -- the King, Pitt, North, Bute, Fox, Hillsborough, Camden, Grafton, Tories, Whigs.

73-27. [Epitaph on General Wolfe.]

"Gallia exulting echo'd loud his Death." (6)

St J's C, Mar 4, 1773.

73-28. Epitaph on General Wolfe.

"O pass not on -- 'tis Virtue bids thee stay." (14)

GM 43 (Jan 1773), 39.

73-29. An Epitaph on the late Lord Lyttelton.

"If worth exalted to thy soul be dear." (15)

W Misc 1 (Oct 4, 1773), 16.

Epitaph panegyric in HC on Lord George Lyttelton, a genuine patriot who withstood "oppressive pow'r." (But in 1766 he voted against repeal of the Stamp Act.)

73-30. Epitaph. On the Patriotic Lord Lyttleton.

"Sacred to the Memory of the Right Honourable/George Lord Lyttleton." (c. 20)

MJ, Sep 16, 1773.

Panegyric on Lord Lyttleton, a geniune patriot who was above party -- died Aug. 27, 1773: "Incorruptible by Interest, /Uninfluenced by Power."

73-31. Epitaph. On Wolfe.

"Conquerer of Quebec." (c. 20)

Lloyd's 32 (Jan 4, 1773), 20.

Inscription on Wolfe, who helped win an empire by subduing France. With prose remarks on the epitaph as an art form.

73-32. An Epitaph. To the Memory of General Wolfe.

"Britannia, weeping o'er his honour'd Bier." (18)

BLJ, Jan 9, 1773; St J's C, Jan 5, 1773.

HC. Wolfe died and conquered France at the same time -- "A British Hero" as great and noble as Roman Cato.

73-33. Extempore on the Patriot's Abuse at Mile End.

"Says Parson Horne to Johnny Wilkes." (8)

M Chron, May 7, 1773.

A humorous reflection on the dispute between Horne and Wilkes that indicates its triviality.

73-34. Farewell to 1772.

"Now the leaden year is gone." (34)

Lloyd's 32 (Jan 6, 1773), 28.

Doggerel (three stress) couplets. The year 1772 is characterized by venality.

73-35. [Farewell to Townshend, Welcome to Harcourt.]

"The Muse! that upon youthful thought takes flight." (129)

Freeman's J, Jan 7, 1773.

HC. Criticism of Lord Lieutenant George Townshend's corrupt regime in Ireland. But there is hope that the new viceroy or governor, Simon Harcourt, will be an improvement and will restore prosperity to Ireland.

73-36. Good Advice.

"Says B[ut]e to Lord North, see, all Faction is dead." (4)

St J's C, Apr 15, 1773; BLJ, Apr 17, 1773.

Quatrain. North resists Bute's attempt to be premier in these politically quiet times when faction has disappeared. In effect, he advises Bute to keep out of politics.

73-37. Green, Henry.
The Wooden Naval Walls of England. By Henry Green, Purser of his Majesty's Ship Ramillies.

"When Britain on her Sea-girt Shore." (40)

G Eve Post, Jun 24, 1773; KG, Jun 26, 1773; L Chron 33 (Jun 24, 1773), 607; L Eve Post, Jun 24, 1773; LM 42 (Aug 1773), 407; LP, Jun 23, 1773; MJ, Jun 24, 1773; PA, Jun 26, 1773.

Song. Britain's best defence was her navy, from the time of the ancient Druids; and now it must defend King George's empire. See "On Reading an ingenious copy of Verses, . . ." 73-69. Reprinted, 80-155.

73-38. A Guildhall Ballad. To the Tune of A Begging we will go, will go, &c.

"My honest Brother-Liverymen." (40)

MJ, Nov 30, 1773.

Song. The Liverymen will support Bull and Wilkes against the government's nominee, Thomas Harley, for Lord Mayor.

73-39. Hamlet's Soliloquy Imitated.

"To print -- or not to print -- that is the question." (32)

L Eve Post, Sep 25, 1773.

Blank verse. Parody. A contributor to newspapers has doubts about whether to print with J. Miller, printer of the London Evening Post.

73-40. Hastings, Thomas.
Ode on the Birthday of his Royal Highness the Prince of Wales.

"Hail to the bright, th'auspicious Day! (42)

PA, Aug 12, 1773.

Sixains in couplets. All good things happen on the birthday of George, Prince of Wales, including the end of faction at home and disaffection in America.

73-41. [How can the muse restrain the satir'd pen.]

"How can the muse restrain the satir'd pen." (14)

L Eve Post, Jun 22, 1773.

HC. Satire on the "dirty Scots" in all the places of government and even the church.

73-42. [Howard, Frederick, Fourth Earl of Carlisle.]
Verses, Composed by L--d C-----le, in praise of his select School-fellow friends, on leaving Eton.

"This plunder, O! indulgent Pope, forgive." (56)

GM 43 (Feb 1773), 93-4.

HC. The Earl of Carlisle, who later headed the Peace Commission to America (1778), here praises his Eton friends, among them Charles James Fox.

73-43. Impromptu. In answer to a Lady, who spoke disrespectfully of Mr. Wilkes, and complained of his Libertinism.

"Wilkes wanton roves from fair to fair." (8)

L Eve Post, May 4, 1773.

Quatrains. Wilkes' politics are defended, despite his licentiousness.

73-44. Inscription for General Wolfe's Monument. By a Lady.

"Sacred to Wolfe, this marble shrine we raise." (13)

GM 43 (Oct 1773), 511.

HC. Epitaph. "Quebec was conquer'd, but the hero dy'd," etc.

73-45. Inscription to the Memory of General Wolfe.

"To the Memory of / James Wolfe." (13)

Edin M&R 1 (Jan 1774), 166; Sent M 1 (Dec 1773), 473.

Epitaph. Inscription on the monument in Westminister Abbey to the memory of Gen. Wolfe.

73-46. J. Wolfe, Ob. A. D. Aet.

"It matters little where Wolfe's ashes lie." (4)

L Eve Post, Jan 21, 1773.

HC. It matters little where Wolfe is buried, for Canada is his monumental tomb.

73-47. Johnson, Samuel.
Present State of Great Britain.

"A thousand horrid prodigies foretold it." (4)

The Fugitive Miscellany (London: Almon, 1774), p. 57.

Prose poem. A gloomy description of a "sinking" nation -- "A feeble government," "A factious populace, luxurious nobles," etc. Probably written in 1773.

73-48. King Charles the First to a Poetaster that Rak'd his Ashes the 30th of January 1773.

"Avaunt! thou ugly grisly Shade." (12)

PA, Feb 3, 1773; Lloyd's 32 (Feb 5, 1773), 131.

OC. A Tory defense of Charles the Martyr against the Whig poet who attacked him and royalist principles in "An Ode for the 30th of January [1773]." Lloyd's does not carry the ode against Charles I. See 73-64.

73-49. Lewis, ------.
The Voice of Ireland: Or, The Viceroy: A Congratulatory Poem. Addressed to his Excellency Earl Harcourt.

"Rejoice, Ierne, happy isle." (256)

Freeman's J, Mar 18, 20, 23, 1773.

Quatrains, celebrating the appointment of the new viceroy of Ireland, Earl Harcourt, and the return of happiness to the nation; of justice, freedom, and health, as in the past under Chesterfield (Stanhope) and Northumberland (Percy). A blueprint for a liberal administration is given. -- Lewis, "corrector of the press," wrote many poems on Ireland for the Freeman's J. He may be called "the voice of Ireland."

73-50. Lines Written upon the Walls of the Theatre at Oxford, during the Exercises at the late Encoenia there.

"Lo! here the Place where many an Oxford Baynes." (9)

St J's C, Jul 13, 1773.

Two short poems -- couplets and quatrain. Satire on Lord North during his ceremonial installation as chancellor of Oxford -- for being corrupt: "a dirty Lord" bedaubed "with dirty praise."

73-51. A List of the Principal Supporters of the Bill of Rights.

"There's honest Jack Wilkes." (40)

PA, Jul 15, 1773.

Three-stress couplets describe several outstanding City members of the Bill of Rights Society -- Wilkes, Bull, Crosby, Glynn, and two Yankees (both Sheriffs of London), Stephen Sayre and William Lee. Cited are the words "Yanky" and "Yanky-doodle."

73-52. [Lord North (says his Worship).]

"Lord North (says his Worship)." (12)

L Eve Post, Sep 14, 1773.

Quatrains. Satire on bribery (the purchase of votes), which will not work where money is plenty and the people stupid.

73-53. The Loss of Freedom: A Monody.

"To you! ye friends of sacred Freedom's name." (24)

L Eve Post, Dec 21, 1773.

Quatrains. The freedom gained by Hampden against the Stuarts has been "lost in this degen'rate age," as a result of corruption.

73-54. The Monkey; or, Recreant Parson. A Tale.

"Who e'er with curious eye has rang'd." (32)

MJ, Jun 12, 1773.

Quatrains. Satire on Horne, a contemptible monkey.

73-55. Musical Intelligence Extraordinary.

"In commemoration of the alliance between England, France, and Spain." (c. 35)

KG, Apr 10, 1773; L Eve Post, Apr 8, 1773.

Three songs satirizing the Administration and Lord North. George is shown as under the influence of the Scotch, and corruption plays an important role.

73-56. National Ruin a National Act, or every Kingdom its own Deliverance.

"Tho' Tyrants -- Traitors -- Prince and Priests combine." (20)

L Eve Post, Jun 3, 1773.

HC. A threat to have the nation rise and destroy the despotic enemies (of freedom), the tyrants who "subvert its Right."

73-57. A New Ode For the New Year, 1773. By Cibberius Secundus.

"Dy'd in dulness' deepest grain." (34)

MJ, Jan 4, 1773.

Pindaric ode. Satire on Whitehead for his dullness, his frigid June and January odes.

73-58. A New Song, on the present Contest in the City. Tune -- Rule Britannia.

"Come Liberty, our souls inspire." (32)

Lloyd's 33 (Nov 29, 1773), 526.

An election song for the City of London in support of Frederick Bull (Ld. Mayor, 1773-4).

73-59. [O Father of thy Country, bid them stay.]

"O Father of thy Country, bid them stay." (6)

BLJ, Feb 26, 1773.

HC. The King must help the starving poor, or else they rightfully will emigrate.

73-60. The Occasional Address.

"All you liberty boys." (30)

L Chron 34 (Nov 27, 1773), 527; WM 22 (Dec 9, 1773), 338.

Sixains. Urges the "liberty boys," the voters, to spurn bribes and turn away from Wilkes and Bull.

73-61. Ode, As It Ought To Have Been Performed At The Encoenia Held at Oxford, July 1773.

"Sons of Corruption, who obedient hail." (100)

L Eve Post, Jul 20, 1773; The Fugitive Miscellany (London: Almon, 1774), pp. 96-100; New Foundling Hospital for Wit (1786), V, 69-74.

Irregular Pindaric ode, parody on "Ode at the Encoenia, Held at Oxford, July 1773". See 73-62. Satire on North. Objects to the war against the Caribs on St. Vincent's. Cited are St. George's Fields massacre, Charles James Fox, Mansfield, the King, Wilkes and Horne.

73-62. Ode At the Encoenia, Held At Oxford, July 1773, For The Reception Of The Right Hon. Frederic Lord North, Chancellor Of The University: Written By Dr. Wheeler, Professor Of Poetry; And Set To Music By Dr. Hayes.

"Daughters of Beauty, who enraptur'd hail." (100)

BLJ, Jul 10, 1773; G Eve Post, Jul 8, 1773; GM 43 (Jul 1773), 343; HM 3 (Aug 1773), 441-2; KG, Jul 10, 1773; Lloyd's 33 (Jul 7, 1773), 30-1; L Eve Post, Jul 6, 1773; M Chron, Jul 9, 1773; Ox M 10 (Jul 1773), 285-6; PA, Jul 9, 1773; St J's C, Jul 6, 1773; The Fugitive Miscellany (London: Almon, 1774), pp. 91-6; New Foundling Hospital for Wit (1786), V, 64-9. Also L Chron 34 (Jul 8, 1773), 36; LM 42 (Jul 1773, 355-6.

Irregular Pindaric ode. A patriotic Establishment poem honoring Lord North for his election as Chancellor of Oxford. See the parody above, 73-61.

73-63. An Ode For Liberty-Hall, Newcastle.

"Avaunt, ye selfish crew." (26)

L Eve Post, Aug 28, 1773.

Irregular Pindaric ode. Honor to (Serjeant) John Glynn, honest freedom fighter.

73-64. An Ode for the 30th of January.

"On this renown'd, illustrious Day." (68)

PA, Jan 30, 1773.

Sixains, except last stanza. In this genuine Whig poem, the poet defends the Commonwealth cause of liberty against tyranny and monarchy by reviewing the resistance to Charles I and his political principles. He uses the day meant to commemorate Charle's execution to warn kings who in the future might attempt to assume excessive power.

73-65. [Of Wolfe I think we've had enough.]

"Of Wolfe I think we've had enough." (24)

G Eve Post, Oct 14, 1773, (Reply Oct 16, 1773); Lloyd's 33 (Oct 4, 1773), 332; L Chron 34 (Oct 2, 1773), 335, (Reply Oct 5, 1773, p. 343).

Quatrains. Light satire. A woman believes there's enough poetry about Wolfe, and now, therefore, she writes about herself -- asking for marriage.

73-66. On General Wolfe.

"General Wolfe and his troops were very particular." (13)

LP, Apr 16, 1773.

Doggerel, fourteeners. Wolfe's death is explained in this light poem -- Wolfe went searching for the dead French in "the next world."

73-67. On Mr. Wilkes going to demand his Seat in the House.

"Alas! Johnny Wilkes, that apostate John Horn." (4)

LP, Apr 30, 1773.

Quatrain. Horne is obstructing Wilkes's return to the House of Commons.

73-68. On Phillis Wheatley.

"From Ind's waste wilds behold a mirror rise." (60)

LP, Nov 17, 1773.

HC. An admonition to Europeans, especially the English, to give recognition to Negroes for their cultural accomplishments,

73-69. On Reading an ingenious Copy of Verses in the London Evening Post of last Saturday, by Mr. Green, Purser of the Ramillies Man of War, and by him presented to the King, on his arrival at Portsmouth for the Naval Review.

"Are wooden Walls, not wooden heads." (28)

L Eve Post, Jul 1, 1773.

Quatrains. Satire on the Scots dominated Administration for weakening the navy. See song by Henry Green, 73-37.

73-70. On Reading the Naval Review by Mr. English.

"Pray, who do you say wrote the Naval Review." (4)

MJ, Sep 2, 1773.

Epigram. English's _Naval Review_ is not written well.

73-71. On seeing the skull of one of the rebel Chiefs, now lying on the very edge of the leads on the outside of Temple Bar, and which was lately blown from the pole whereon it was affixed.

"Hah, hah, old boy! and are you there." (32)

M Chron, Aug 18, 1773.

Quatrains. An address to the executed rebel Scots leader of the '45, critical of the Stuart cause for its tyranny. Bute deserves the same fate.

73-72. On the approaching General Election.

"Hail, glorious time." (24)

GM 43 (Nov 1773), 571. (18 ll.); Lloyd's 33 (Nov 10, 1773), 462; L Chron 34 (Nov 9, 1773), 464; L Eve Post, Nov 9, 1773; WM 22 (Nov 18, 1773), 462.

Regular ode in sixains. Satire on the electoral process, especially the hypocrisy and bribery.

73-73. On the Celebration of King Charles's Martyrdom.

"How can we be surpriz'd that G[eorg]e." (4)

Freeman's J, Feb 2, 1773.

Epigram. If we still mourn the death of a tyrant, the slain Charles I, then we should not be surprised that George III makes us his slaves.

73-74. On the Clerical Petition.

"Shall we admire that piety decays." (18)

Sent M 1 (May 1773), 141.

An expression of hostile sentiment against Dissenters, who were petitioning at this time for relief, for relaxation of the Thirty-nine Articles. Also attacks deism and reason in religion. (Regarding America, the relationship is to the Dissenters in New England.)

73-75. On the numerous Epitaphs on General Wolfe.

"Ah cease, ye Bards, your mournful Strain." (12)

St J's C, May 11, 1773.

Quatrains. Advice to cease writing epitaphs for Wolfe. They are terribly written in "feeble Rhyme," or, at best, "fetter'd prose."

73-76. On the Premier. An Epigram.

"Lord N--th appears the first in Geers." (8)

St J's C, May 8, 1773.

Quatrains. Lord North is a powerful premier, a strong leader.

73-77. On the Presentation of a new Remonstrance.

"To please the Cits, out of their Wits." (8)

St J's C, Mar 23, 1773.

Quatrains. The "Cits" petition the King for a triennial Parliament -- and should be granted their wish. They really don't know what they want and will soon beg for the septennial Parliament.

73-78. On the Tears of a Minister.

"Musick drew savage Tears from Pluto's Eyes." (6)

BLJ, Jun 26, 1773; St J's C, Jun 22, 1773.

HC. Satire. The minister weeps (hypocritically) over the problems of the country.

On True Nobility and False.

See 64-85: "Serious Thoughts on True Nobility and False."

73-79. Parody. From Julius Caesar. Act IV. Scene I. (Being a couterpart to the parody of Rich III. in our's of Thursday last.)

"North. Are all the several places in the public offices disposed of?" (c. 60)

L Eve Post, Nov 30, 1773.

Blank verse and prose. Satire on court bribery and corruption -- North, Jenkinson, the King, upon the coming election.

73-80. A Parody from Richard III. Act V.

"Magistrato. Here pitch our tents, e'en on Guildhall plain." (39)

KG, Nov 24, 1773; L Eve Post, Nov 23, 1773.

Blank verse. Crosby, present Lord Mayor of London, organizes his forces for the coming election -- against the corrupt court, its hirelings and placemen.

73-81. Parody of the first Song in Midas. Chorus.

"George on his throne." (18)

LP, Jul 14, 1773.

Song. King George (the navy) will have sovereignty over the seas against France, Spain, and Holland.

73-82. Parody on part of the third Epistle of Mr. Pope's Essay on Man, from ver. 236 to ver. 256.

"By this our God, not G[eorge] is understood." (20)

L Eve Post, Jun 5, 1773.

HC. Blames the Jacobite Scots for enslaving the English nation.

73-83. Parody on the first 28, and the 14 concluding lines of the first epistle of Mr. Pope's Essay on Man.

"Awake, my Wilkes! discuss all trifling things." (42)

L Eve Post, May 25, 1773.

HC. Asks Wilkes to support the Opposition to the Court (Administration), and the King, Bute and the Jacobites, and to the corruption of buying votes.

73-84. The Patriots.

"In Seventeen Hundred and Forty-five." (28)

BLJ, May 29, 1773; St J's C, May 27, 1773.

Tetrameter couplets. Ironic satire. A soldier and a prisoner in debtor's prison complain of the Scotch rebels who will destroy freedom and the state religion.

73-85. The Plaints of Runny-Mead. To the Memory of those renowned Barons who opposed the Tyranny of King John.

"All on old Thames's willow-fringed bank." (52)

L Eve Post, Jan 5, 1773.

Quatrains. A vision of how Magna Charta was won, but it is spoiled by the degenerate reality of present times, by the loss of freedom as a result of the bribery and corruption of "slaves."

73-86. A Political Genealogy.

"Arbitrary power begot Oppression." (7)

MJ, Nov 6, 1773; Say's, Nov 13, 1773; New Foundling Hospital for Wit (1786), IV, 101.

Prose poem. Tyranny can cause lawless murder. (These lines could apply to the St. George's Fields' massacre in 1768, and to the Boston massacre in 1770.) See 69-A and 70-164.

73-87. A Prophesy of Reformation in the Year 1773.

"When Britannia's dread Th[ro]ne a dread M[onar]ch adorns." (18)

St J's C, Sep 18, 1773.

Hexameter couplets. When the nation improves in several different ways regarding corruption, awarding merit, the Triennial Bill, oppression, then it will be free.

73-88. The Purchase of Votes the Perdition of Freedom; Or, The Receivers of Bribes, the Betrayers of Liberty. An Epigram.

"Ye venal tribes! ye shame of horned cattle'" (10)

Ox M 10 (Jun 1773), 245.

HC. Those who accept bribes are like cattle driven to market.

73-89. A Receipt to make a Patriot.

"Take a man that's a Whig, quite brimful of spirit." (24)

MJ, Nov 2, 1773.

Hexameter couplets. Tories are favored over Whigs by Lord North.

73-90. [Round honest North, beset with factious Stings.]

"Round honest North, beset with factious Stings." (4)

PA, Aug 7, 1773.

HC. Praise of "honest" Lord North, beset by the factious criticism of "Hydras."

73-91. A Sailor's Description of the House of Commons. Written upon the Presentation of the Captains Petition for an Increase of their Half-pay, the 11th of February, 1773.

"I heard a petition was going to be made." (72)

GM 43 (Mar 1773), 143-4; Lloyd's 32 (Mar 10, 1773), 246; West M 1 (Feb 1773), 164.

Quatrains. Sailor's diction is used to describe the vote on the petition for a pension increase.

73-92. [See, the legal Member comes.]

"See, the legal Member comes." (16)

G Eve Post, Dec 9, 1773; KG, Dec 11, 1773.

Another election song for Sir Watkin Lewes of Worcester: vs. bribery and corruption, but for "freedom of election."

73-93. A Song. To the Tune of, Hark Away, &c.

"Now again we brave Freemen rejoice." (24)

L Chron 34 (Nov 23, 1773), 512; LP, Nov 24, 1773.

An election song for Sir Watkin Lewes of Worcester, who stood for the independent interests and was defeated. He was a member of the Bill of Rights Society, and Alderman of London from 1772 to death in 1796.

73-94. Sonnet.

"Who, that has oft admir'd some reverend Oak." (14)

BLJ, May 1, 1773.

Sonnet. Italian style. A defense of Algernon Sidney, Whig martyr, from Sir John Dalrymple, Bart., who branded him traitor in his recently published history.

73-95. [Stop, read, smile, admire.]

"Stop, read, smile, admire." (c. 15)

LP, Feb 3, 1773.

A humorous "canned" epitaph -- which may be a satiric commentary on the spate of epitaphs appearing on Wolfe.

73-96. To Lord North.

"Great Pilot of the British State." (4)

PA, Mar 30, 1773.

Praise of Lord North, the Premier, "lov'd and rever'd by Whig and Tory."

73-97. To the Author of a much admired heroic Epistle.

"Sweet Swan of Albion, whose harmonious vein." (30)

L Eve Post, Mar 11, 1773.

HC. Praise of Mason's Heroic Epistle to Sir William Chambers. Satire on the Scots. See 73-7.

73-98. To the Author of a Poem just published, entitled The Dying Negro.

"Accept, pathetic Bard, these generous Lays." (c. 100)

PA, Jul 8, 1773.

HC. Praise of Thomas Day for his anti-slavery poem, The Dying Negro; encourages the rebellion of West Indian slaves against ruthless Christians. See 73-2.

73-99. To the British Nation.

"For Freedom the Sham Patriot raves." (4)

St J's C, Jan 23, 1773.

Quatrain. An admonition to genuine patriots to be honest and free.

73-100. To the ingenious Author of The Patricians.

"Go on, great Censor, let thy probing Page." (14)

PA, Mar 10, 1773.

HC. Delamayne is praised for his satire, his nice irony, that spares no high persons and knows no distinction in rank. See 73-4.

73-101. To Thomas Hutchinson, Esq. Governor of Boston, New England, (who has lately been unmasked.)

"What is the hope of an hypocrite though he hath gained." (16)

MP, Aug 10, 1773.

Prose poem, imitation of the Bible. Damns Governor Hutchinson as a wicked and deceitful hypocrite. (The reference is Benjamin Franklin's use of Hutchinson's correspondence to expose his duplicity.)

73-102. Verses addressed to John Wilkes, Esq; on his being a second Time chosen Lord-Mayor, by a Majority of Votes of the Liverymen of the City of London.

"Again, great Wilkes! the People's Voice." (24)

PA, Oct 8, 1773.

Sixains. Wilkes stands for freedom and the rights of the people against the corrupt court; therefore he deserves support. (Wilkes was London alderman in 1769, sheriff 1771-2, and lord mayor 1774-5.)

73-103. Verses extempore on reading a Paragraph in Yesterday's Paper, comparing Dr. Johnson to Dr. Young's Centaur not Fabulous.

"The Doctor compar'd to half Man and half Horse." (6)

PA, Nov 12, 1773.

Hexameter couplets. Satire on Johnson, inspired by the Scotch, "a mean servile Drudge," and "a hir'd State Slave," his own definition of "Pensioner."

73-104. Verses to the Right Hon. George Lord Lyttelton, written immediately after his being introduced to his Majesty.

"Ere on thy Father's Tomb the pensive Bust." (62)

PA, Dec 18, 1773.

HC. Panegyric on the young Lord Lyttelton, who advanced to the title after his father's death. He is asked to join with others in zealously asserting freedom's cause and to save the "drooping Country." (Thomas Lyttelton [1744-79] was the only son of George Lyttelton.)

The Voice of Ireland; or, The Viceroy: . . . "Rejoice, Ierne, happy isle." (256) Freeman's J, Mar 18, 20, 23, 1773. Celebrates the appointment of a new viceroy of Ireland and provides a blueprint for a liberal administration. See Lewis 73-49.

73-105. The Weavers Lamentation, or a Farewell to Ireland. [To the tune of Lochabar.]

"Farewell Donegal! And farewell O Belfast." (48)

Freeman's J, Sep 21, 1773.

Song. Ballad on the emigration to America and its causes -- poverty and distress, arbitrary government and tyranny (the "curst Riot-Act"). The weaver is sure "America's sons, both industrious and free," will welcome him.

73-106. [What's all the dazzling pomp of state.]

"What's all the dazzling pomp of state." (24)

L Eve Post, Aug 21, 1773.

Regular ode in sixains. The struggle for liberty continues, especially in Middlesex, and has little to do with "the pomp of state," "titled slaves," "the splendid trifles of the great." See 64-85.

Wheeler, --------. Ode at the Encoenia, . . . "Daughters of Beauty, who enraptured hail." (100) GM 43 (Jul 1773), 343; and many other sources. A patriotic Establishment poem honoring Lord North. See 73-62.

73-107. [When one, and two-fold seven, and mystic three.]

"When one, and two-fold seven, and mystic three." (62)

L Eve Post, May 11, 1773.

HC. Merlin prophecies that when France and England form an alliance, when the Scots dominate England, liberty should be fearful. Algernon Sydney is defended; and luxury and corruption criticized, as well as gambling.

73-108. [While heavy D---, dark and loud.]

"While heavy D---, dark and loud." (10)

St J's C, Feb 2, 1773.

Octosyllabic couplets. A warning that English trade is declining and the nation's debt mounting while politicians debate.

73-109. Whitehead, William.
Ode for the New Year 1773. Written by W. Whitehead, Esq. Performed before their Majesties.

"Wrapt in the stole of sable grain." (34)

BLJ, Jan 2, 1773; BWJ, Jan 2, 1773; GM 43 (Jan 1773), 39; KG, Dec 30, 1772-Jan 2, 1773; Lloyd's 32 (Dec 30, 1772-Jan 1, 1773), 7; L Eve Post, Dec 31, 1772-Jan 2, 1773; LP, Dec 30, 1772-Jan 1, 1773; PA, Jan 1, 1773; St J's C, Jan 2, 1773; Say's, Jan 2, 1773. Also L Chron 33 (Dec 31, 1772-Jan 2, 1773), 2.

Irregular Pindaric ode. An innocuous laureat poem about the seasons, winter changing to spring. Parodied twice: 73-13, 73-57.

73-110. Whitehead, William.
Ode on his Majesty's Birth-Day, June 4, 1773.

"Born for millions are the Kings." (38)

GM 43 (Jun 1773), 293; KG, Jun 5, 1773; Lloyd's 32 (Jun 2, 1773), 535; L Eve Post, Jun 3, 1773; LP, Jun 2, 1773; Ox M 10 (Jun 1773), 245; PA, Jun 4, 1773; Say's, Jun 5, 1773. Also L Chron 33 (Jun 3, 1773), 530; LM 42 (Jun 1773), 305.

Irregular Pindaric ode. King George is hailed as a monarch at one with the people over whom he rules. His is "delegated power" limited by law.

73-111. [Why, Citizens, this mighty Noise.]

"Why, Citizens, this mighty Noise." (28)

PA, Oct 5, 1773.

Quatrains. The City politicians, the aldermen contending for the mayoralty -- Wilkes, Bull, Sawbridge, Oliver -- are selfish. They are not genuine patriots, for they have no concern for the needy. None merit any votes.

The Wooden Naval Walls of England. "When Britain on her Sea-girt Shore." (40) G Eve Post, Jun 24, 1773; and many other sources. Song. Britain's best defence, her navy, must now defend King George's empire. See Henry Green, 73-37.

73-112. [Yon axe with gore distain'd, at one dire act.]

"Yon axe with gore distain'd, at one dire act." (32)

L Eve Post, Apr 1, 1773.

Blank verse. A tribute to Algernon Sidney and Lord William Russell, Whig martyrs, executed by James II (Sidney) and Charles II (Russell). See Sonnet, 73-94.

1774 Books & Pamphlets

74-1. Allen, William.
  The American Crisis: A Letter Addressed by Permission to the Earl Gower.
  London: Cadell, 1774. 72p.

  "While other Nations soft Refinements prize." (69)

  Notices: CR 37 (Jun 1774), 463-8; MR 50 (Apr 1774), 324.

  Sabin 884.

  Copies: BL 102.e.70; NUC DLC, ICN, MiU-C, RPJCB.

  HC. At the end of the prose essay and just before the prose postscript, Allen concludes his argument for the use of force (see pp. 54-56). A loyalist, he urges the strongest measures against the American colonies, which he wishes to see "reduc'd to Reason." He urges the King to take vigorous measures to quell faction and to establish order, liberty, and love.

74-2. Britannia. A Poem. In Two Parts. By an Eaton Scholar.
  London: Harris, Matthews, 1774. 16p.

  "While some, contented with more humble themes." (179)

  Notices: CR 38 (Nov 1774), 392; MR 53 (Aug 1775), 192, & (Oct 1775), 356.

  Copies: BL 11633.g.7; NUC DLC.

  HC. A criticism of the venal patriots and of the inhabitants of Boston for rebelling without just cause. Urges the "men of Boston" to "Reject rebellious war" and to keep Britain and the colonies united.

74-3. [Courtenay, John]
  An Epistle (Moral and Philosophical) from an Officer at Otaheite. To Lady Gr*s**n*r. With Notes, Critical and Historical. By the Author of the Rape of Pomona.
  London: Evans, 1774. 31p.

  "Can I forget the beauteous Emma's charms." (294)

  See 74-4.

428

74-4. [-----]
-----. A New Edition, corrected and enlarged.
London: Evans, 1775. 33p.

Notices: CR 39 (Jun 1775), 507; MR 52 (Feb 1775), 188.

Copies: BL 1490.e.46 (1st ed); NUC CLU, DFo, ICN, MB, & MH (1st ed), MB (2nd ed).

HC. Begins with an account of the sexual customs of Tahitian natives, then digresses with a prayer that the spoilers' oppression and exploitation of India not occur in Tahiti: it must be free. English liberty, in the tradition of Russell, Sidney, Hampden, and Milton should preside over the union of "Albion's realms," and its spirit should "Restore her children to a mother's breast." Thus, an allusion to the American troubles is in this section, ll. 206-40.

74-5. An Elegy on the Approaching Dissolution of Parliament.
London: Almon, 1774. 15p.

"Whilst other Bards compel the blushing muse." (c. 225)

Notices: CR 38 (Jun 1774), 472; L Chron 35 (Jun 7, 1774), 548; L Eve Post, Apr 26, 1774; LM 43 (May 1774), 244.

Copies: NUC NN.

HC. An allusive and elusive satire on Parliament. There are some allusions to the theme of corruption. But the major theme is simply the quiet of the House of Commons when certain MPs have gone--North, Barré, Pitt, Fox, Wedderburne, Norton. There is one glancing allusion to Boston and "her warriors with rebellious arms," the point being that Parliament provoked Boston with "their wild alarms." (CR attributes this poem to Delamayne.)

74-6. England's Tears: A Poem. Inscribed to Britannia. To which is added, Advice to the Voters of Great-Britain at the Approaching General Election.
London: Kearsly, 1774. iii + 15p.

"O Weeping Goddess, when wilt thou have rest." (c. 280)

Notices: CR 38 (Oct 1774), 319; MR 51 (Oct 1774), 317.

Copies: NUC TxU.

HC. Concerned over the disturbed state of affairs in England and America and over the spread of "Papacy" in Canada, the poet sees hope in the coming general parliamentary election, and urges electors to "restore our sully'd and dishonor'd name." Cited are Hutchinson, Gage, Luttrell, Wilkes, Boston, Hampden, Pryn, Lilburne, Allen and Clarke, and St. George's Fields.

74-7. [Hughes, Benjamin]
An Epistle to Junius.
London: Richardson & Urquhart, 1774. 27p.

"To lend a hand to prop up Dulness' Throne." (c. 520)

Notices: MR 50 (Feb 1774), 156.

Copies: BL 643.k.12 (12), T.661 (9).

HC. Begs Junius to return in order to perform his duty as a satirist, and discusses several targets that require his style and treatment--e.g., the wretched ministry (North, Sandwich, Jenkinson, Bute, Dyson, Welbore Ellis [?]), the city leaders Wilkes and Oliver, Scotsmen, lotteries, the hierarchy of the church, and the stage. (Signed by a contemporary hand on first page with the name of Benj. Hughes.)

74-8. Jingle, Bob, Esq., pseud.
The Association, &c. of the Delegates of the Colonies, at the Grand Congress, Held at Philadelphia, Sept. 1, 1774, Versified, and adapted to Music, Calculated For Grave and Gay Dispositions; With a Short Introduction. By Bob Jingle, Esq; Poet Laureat to the Congress.
N.p.: n.p., 1774. iii-iv + 5-22p.

"We, Loyal subjects of the King." (c. 345)

Notices: CR 39 (Feb 1775), 158; MR 52 (Mar 1775), 263; SM 37 (Feb 1775), 99, & (Mar 1775), 147; LR 1 (Appendix 1775), 510.

Copies: BL 1061.h.29 (7), 102.e.72; Bod Godwyn Pamph 280 (11); NUC CtY, ICN, MB, MH, NjP, RPJCB.

Ballad; Recitativo in dactylic tetrameter; Chorus in Hudibrastics. Satire on the First Continental Congress, particularly the Non-Importation Agreement. Adopting the persona of a delegate to the meeting in Philadelphia, September 1774, Jingle presents the non-importation agreement as finally adopted by Congress on October 20, 1774. In the course of the presentation, Jingle reviews the grievances which excited the Americans: the loss of habeas corpus and trial by jury, the Boston Port and Quebec Bills, acts involving taxation since the last war. (On the same subject, see The Poor Man's Advice to his Poor Neighbours [New York, 1774]. According to MR, this pamphlet is probably an American importation.)

74-9. Justice A Poem.
London: Kearsly, 1774. iii + 18p.

"What! shall I always hear, and ne'er reply." (c. 330)

Notices: CR 38 (Nov 1774), 392; MR 51 (Nov 1774), 394; L Chron 36 (Nov 10, 1774), 457; L Eve Post, Nov 12, 1774; PL, Nov 16, 1774.

Copies: Bod Godwyn Pamph 1730 (7); NUC IU.

HC. Inscribed to Frederick Bull, Lord Mayor of London. A satire in form of a dialogue on the enemies of freedom in the administration, it is a City poem. The author expresses fears that justice no longer exists, and implores the "sons of freedom" to assert their rights, prevent the use of force against America and the betrayal of freedom, "tho' it shake the THRONE," in the spirit of Cromwell, Hampden, Sidney. Attacked are North, Mansfield, Bute, Jenkinson, the "rule despotic" of the King, which extends to America, "the new world where freedom's sons had fled." Specifically objects to the preparations of "rule by force--the TYRANT's only law," and, at the beginning, singles out S. Johnson for denying there are threats to freedom in his False Alarm.

74-10. Cancelled.

[Langhorne, John]
The Country Justice. A Poem. By one of His Majesty's Justices of the Peace for the county of Somerset.
London: Becket, 1774.

This poem was published in three parts--1774, 1775, & 1777--of which the last is relevant. See 77-16.

74-11. [Mason, William]
An Heroic Postscript to the Public, Occasioned by their Favourable Reception of a Late Heroic Epistle to Sir William Chambers, Knt. &c. By the Author of that Epistle.
London: Almon, 1774. 14p.

"I that of late, Sir William's Bard, and Squire." (110)

Notices: CR 37 (Apr 1774), 313-14; MR 50 (Feb 1774), 154-5; GM 44 (Feb 1774), 85.

Copies: BL T.666 (6), 643.k.12, 1493.h.16; Bod Godwyn Pamph 1492 (21); NUC CtY, ICU, ICN, IU, MH.

8 eds in 1774, a 9th in 1777. HC. Slight satire. However, there are brief and general remarks on corrupt "hireling Peers" who prostitute themselves and their country--sell themselves and freedom, and betray the country. One of these peers is George William Hervey, Earl of Bristol ("Fannius").

74-12. The Muse in a Fright; Or, Britannia's Lamentation: A Rhapsody. Containing a Succinct Account of the Rise and Progress of British Liberty, and the Establishment of the Press; With the Methods Now Taking to Destroy it. In which will be displayed, A Number of Whole Length Characters, &c.
London: Bew, Axtell, et al., [1774]. 22p.

"Sol gave resplendently his chearful ray." (c. 550)

Notices: CR 37 (Apr 1774), 314; MR 50 (Apr 1774), 316.

Copies: NUC ICN.

HC. Traces British liberty to ancient times when the Celts fought the Romans, the Saxons allied with the Britons, and Alfred reigned. Hails the establishment of the printing press despite those who would suppress it. Statesmen, once true to Magna Carta but now corrupt, would banish liberty, esp. "Free Election," and censor the press by prosecuting, fining, and imprisoning the printers--Sandwich particularly is guilty. "A venal race the Commons now supply, / And wish to banish heav'n born Liberty." The poet also deplores the hapless state of Ireland, her local industry depressed and her inhabitants forced to emigrate to America; and the faction and discontent in America, which turn the land from its parent. Concludes with hope that Chatham, Germain (!), Junius, and Horace Walpole help crush oppression and restore liberty, and "reconcile the Americans to rest."

74-13. The Resurrection of Liberty; or, Advice to the Colonists: A Poem by the Ghost of Churchill.
London: Allen, 1774.

Notices: MR 51 (Oct 1774), 317; GM 44 (Nov 1774), 533; L Eve Post, Sep 24, 1774; L Mag 43 (Oct 1774), 504 & 44 (Jan 1775), 39.

Sabin 70128.

Copies: none located.

"Alas! poor Churchill! thy ghost's production is far unlike thy own, when in flesh. His advice to the colonists is, 'to return blow for blow.'" LM 44 (Jan 1775), 39.

74-14. Richardson, William.
  Poems, Chiefly Rural.
  Glasgow: Foulis; London: Murray, 1774. 140p.

  Notices: MR 51 (Aug 1774), 94-6.

  Copies: BL 11642.bbb.63, 11632.c.48 (4th ed, 1781); NUC CtY, IU, MH, MiU (2nd ed, 1775), TxU (2nd ed).

  4 eds by 1781. Includes his Corsica, 69-16.

Serials

74-15. The Able Doctor, or America Swallowing the Bitter Drought. An Explanation of a Political Print . . . .

"Behold America upon the ground." (28)

HM 4 (May 1774), 285. (Plate facing p. 250.)

HC. America is pinned down by Mansfield, Bute, and Sandwich as North forces tea down her throat. North rushes through Parliament "th'enslaving Bills" against Boston, and Britain weeps to see America's loss of her rights, while France and Spain grin happily. See M. D. George, Catalogue of Political and Personal Satires (London, 1935), # 5226 (V, 165-6), noting that the print also appears in the London Magazine 43 (Apr 1774), 184.

74-16. An Account of the Present State of the Political Thermometer.

"English spirit freezing." (11)

Say's, Dec 3, 1774.

A prose-poem based on a metaphor. A prophecy of storms to come because England does not respond to American anger.

74-17. An Address to Britannia's Sons.

"Fir'd with the glowing theme, my country's good." (c. 120)

Freeman's J, Jul 7, 1774.

Blank verse, praise of those in the tradition of liberty -- Chatham, Camden, Barre, Burke as well as Beckford, Granby, recently dead.

74-18. An Address to Sir E. D. [Edward Dering.]

"Tho' every pen conspires to shade." (16)

KG, Jul 27, 1774.

Quatrains. Dering is praised for merit, despite his loss of election and the vilification of his opponents.

74-19. Advertisement.

"If England's Fate, by Bribery o'ercast." (8)

St J's C, Feb 8, 1774.

HC. Protests bribery, which threatens the loss of liberty. Cited are North and Parliament.

74-20. Advice to Britons. A New Patriotic Song, adapted to the Tune of the old Song, called Hearts of Oak. By E. W.

"Come, Britons, unite; to each other be true." (37)

Say's, Nov 12, 1774.

Song. Protest at American Non-Importation agreement. Should Parliament have honest members, it will repeal all those acts against Boston that have hurt the Anglo-American trade. (Song revised and adapted to a later period of the American troubles. See Say's, May 4, 1776.)

74-21. Advices from Boston. Psalm 122.

"O 'twas a joyful sound to hear." (32)

PL, Jul 8, 1774.

Quatrains. The loyal congregation of the Church of England in Boston rejoice at the removal of the seat of government from Boston to Salem where they will be safe from the violence of "the Faction."

74-22. The Adviser. A Receipt for making a Nation Catholics or Slaves. For the Use of the English in the Year 1774. Written by an Irishman.

"First, let them be as wicked as they will." (36)

PL, Aug 24, 1774; St J's C, Jul 30, 1774.

HC. Another reaction to the Quebec Bill. Anti-Catholic sentiment linking tyranny with Popery and vice; but as soon as the English recover from their wickedness they will (again) give up Catholicism and slavery.

74-23. [Alarmed, with manly care, behold.]

"Alarmed, with manly care, behold." (18)

MJ, Aug 9, 1774.

Regular ode in sixains. Sympathy for Boston and the Americans who are consistent in their struggle for liberty in the tradition of Magna Charta. Cited are North and Mansfield.

74-24. [Alas! this Royal Oak's near doom'd to Fate.]

"Alas! this Royal Oak's near doom'd to Fate." (12)

PA, Aug 31, 1774.

Quatrains, epigram. A complaint against the Scottish influence (Mansfield), the cause of England's decline.

74-25. America: or, the Muse's Refuge: A Prophecy. Addressed to the Present Ministry.

"The Muse, offended at this age, these climes." (24)

WM 26 (Oct 13, 1774), 82; West M 2 (Sep 1774), 485.

Quatrains. Britain will decline, like former empires, and America will rise in glory: "Westward the course of Empire takes its way." An adaptation of Berkeley's famous verses. See 75-41.

74-26. An American Parody on the Old Song of "Rule Britannia."

"When Britons first, by Heaven's command." (54)

L Chron 37 (Jan 7, 1775), 32; Ox M 12 (Jan 1775), 23; SM 36 (Dec 1774), 666; W Misc 4 (Aug 7, 1775), 447-8.

Song. The Americans, keeping the example of the Mother Country in view, are inspired by freedom to resist tyranny and slavery.

74-27. [American Toasts.]

"A speedy and a lasting union between Great Britain and the Colonies."

KG, Dec 28, 1774.

Six American toasts on the American contest, remarking on the blind King, a corrupt minister, and an objection to "military government" and Scotch politics."

74-28. [And whither then is British Freedom fled.]

"And whither then is British Freedom fled." (46)

M Chron, Jun 16, 1774; L Eve Post, Jun 18, 1774; PA, Jun 3, 1774.

HC. A criticism of the King and North for corrupting an oppressive Parliament hostile to British liberty. (What is needed is the leadership of a republican like Algernon Sydney.)

74-29. [At Fancy's Call. Liberty's Address.]

"At Fancy's call I form a scene." (60)

MJ, Sep 13, 1774.

OC. Liberty addresses Albion asking that Boston be assisted, the tyrannical and corrupt ministry be cashiered and haunted by Allen's ghost. North, Mansfield, and the King are cited.

74-30. [Behold, to Shame th' Historic Page.]

"Behold, to Shame th' Historic Page." (8)

PA, Nov 9, 1774.

Epigram in quatrains. Satire on Wilkes and his slavish mob of supporters.

74-31. Boston.

"To be humane to Foes and fierce to Friends." (8)

St J's C, Sep 24, 1774.

HC. Boston treated us spitefully in dumping the tea. Now "sober tea" will be converted into a "Means of Vengeance."

74-32. The Boston Bill. A Ballad.

"If at a time to turn a rhyme." (32)

L Chron 36 (Jul 21, 1774), 76.

Song. Ballad, describes the haste in which North acted in pushing through the Boston Port Bill despite the opposition of Burke, Barre, Chatham, Leinster, Camden.

74-33. A Boston Epigram. To the Ministry.

"You've sent a rod to Massachusett." (4)

LM 43 (Jun 1774), 296; SM 36 (Jun 1774), 316; WM 25 (Jul 21, 1774), 114.

OC. The Boston Port Bill (enacted March 31) will backfire.

74-34. [Britain, America, at length be Friends.]

"Britain, America, at length be Friends." (10)

LM 43 (1774), Frontispiece, with verses.

HC. Britain and America have mutual interests and must be united. Together they will be omnipotent. See print, 74-219.

74-35. Britannia's Complaint. (Wrote in America, 1774.)

"Where Seraphs laud, and angels high adore." (62)

Cal Merc, Aug 13, 1781; G, Aug 27, 1781.

HC. Britain mourns the passage of laws that will oppress the American colonies, transform them into rebellious enemies and the situation into a civil war. Also mourns the fact that Pitt is not leading the government.

74-36. B[ute], M[ansfield], and N[orth].

"B[ute], M[ansfield], and N[orth], let me point out the men." (8)

MJ, Jun 21, 1774.

Anapest tetrameter couplets. Satire on the ministry -- expecially Bute, Mansfield, and North, who deserve assassination.

74-37. [By art and surprize, my Lord swears he'll succeed.]

"By art and surprize, my Lord swear's he'll succeed." (6)

M Chron, Oct 28, 1774.

Hexameter couplets. North dissolves the House in order to punish America with a new Parliament -- a dangerous tactic which may cause his downfall.

74-38. A Card, A Few of England's Evils: Or a Great Increase of the Under at this Time.

"Favourites, placemen and pensioners." (10)

M Chron, Aug 26, 1774.

Prose-poem. A list of evils and contradictions in English life at this time: a cynical survey including corruption, popery, taxes, and other grievances.

74-39. The Case is Altered.

"See how for Bribes yon' Christian Members run." (2)

St J's C, Jul 28, 1774.

Epigram. Even heathens would not vote like the bribed MP's. (This satiric epigram directed against bribes must reflect hostility towards those MP's who voted for the Quebec Bill.)

74-40. The Case Stated between England and America.

"The people of Boston our tea will not drink." (8)

LP, Sep 28, 1774.

The Americans are crazy to reject Britain and ask for war.

74-41. [Chatham, the Muse, ambitious of thy name.]

"Chatham, the Muse, ambitious of thy name." (59)

M Chron, Jun 24, 1774.

Blank verse. Praise of Chatham for his successful leadership in the war against France and Spain, and for his support of America against a corrupt court; and a defense of America's cause.

74-42. Chevy Chace. As now performing with general uproar at Covent Garden, and in the Liberties of Westminster. Being a New Song to an Old Tune.

"To the Hustings, ye Freemen, with spirit repair." (36)

LP, Oct 10, 1774.

Ballad, London election song for Humphrey Cotes, Mahon, and Mountmorres and against Lord Thomas Pelham Clinton and Hugh Percy. The point is that one group of candidates (Percy and Clinton) advocated "cutting America's throat," and these won the election.

74-43. The City March to the Guildhall, on a recent Day.

"Rise, rise, Britannia rise." (42)

Lloyd's 35 (Oct 26, 1774), 411.

Regular Horatian ode. Praise of Wilkes for his successful bid for the mayoralty. The patriots are pleased at this conclusion of the struggle against despotic power.

74-44. The City Poet of 1774.

"When Settle was the City Bard." (12)

L Chron 36 (Nov 8, 1774), 453; MJ, Nov 8, 1774; PA, Nov 9, 1774.

Quatrains. In the past the city poet fared well; but today the minor poets, inspired by Wilkes and Liberty, are ignored and starve.

74-45. [Come all loyal freemen who love King and land.]

"Come all loyal freemen who love King and land." (23)

L Eve Post, Aug 9, 1774; LP, Aug 10, 1774; M Chron, Aug 12, 1774.

An anti-Court election song for Newcastle freeholders, praising two candidates -- Phipps and Delaval -- and standing for Wilkes and freedom and integrity.

74-46. The Commons Outwitted. A New Ballad.

"A Comical circumstance happen'd of late." (35)

LP, Feb 18, 1774.

A ballad narrating the encounter of John Horne with Fletcher Norton and Lord North regarding the freedom of the press. The Boston tea-party is alluded to.

74-47. The Complaint: An Elegy on the present Northern Emigrations.

"Phoebe, the leader of the starry train." (84)

SM 36 (Oct 1774), 543-4; WM 26 (Oct 6, 1774), 49.

Quatrains. Scotland complains of the want and oppression that force the poor Scots to emigrate.

74-48. Congratulatory Song to the Members of the new Parliament, on their Acquisition of a Brother Representative, in Bob the Waiter.

"What signifies Latin or Greek, or such knowledge." (36)

Lloyd's 35 (Nov 4, 1774), 444; LP, Nov 2, 1774.

Song. Satire on Parliament. Bob (Robert Mackreth), a waiter at White's, the gambling club, was elected to the House of Commons. Who are his constituents? See "On Bob the Waiter's being elected" and "Poor ---'d's mad," 74-130, 74-158.

74-49. The Country Politicians.

"Had I my Wish, says honest Ned." (36)

Cumb Pacq, May 20, 1783; G Eve Post, Sep 20, 1774; PA, Sep 21, 1774.

Quatrains. Two farmers converse about the kind of country they wish they had -- a wise premier, an uncorrupt senate, an honest clergy, a humane judge, and a lower class that minds its place.

74-50. The Court Barometer for the Atmosphere of St. James's.

"The spirit of Liberty John Wilkes." (18)

LP, Feb 4, 1774.

Prose poem and couplets. A satiric metaphor (a barometer) reports the atmosphere of the court. Wilkes still represents liberty, America is much oppressed, etc. Concludes with satiric couplets on the King.

74-51. Cumberland, Richard.
Epilogue after the Entertainment called the Election, Written and Spoken by Mr. Cumberland.

"Such were the scenes, while base corruption stray'd." (22)

HM 4 (Dec 1774), 748.

HC. Satire on "base corruption" in a vile election, especially bribery.

74-52. Dialogue between A. and Thane.

"A. The Protestant Persuasion is my Joy." (6)

St J's C, Oct 25, 1774.

HC. Bute (the thane) challenges the Protestant religion. (This poem may be a reaction to the Quebec Act.)

74-53. Dialogue between an Englishman and a Minister.

"I've wonder'd oft at what's been done." (48)

M Chron, Dec 27, 1774.

Sixains. Satire on the ministry for declaring martial law and using specious reasons to justify its policies. Cited are America, taxes, sedition, Chatham.

74-54. A Dialogue between Frederick Lord North, and his Conscience, upon Passing the Quebec Bill.

"Thou canker wedded to my breast." (82)

L Eve Post, Jun 30, 1774; W Misc 2 (Sep 19, 1774), 598-600.

OC. The ghosts of Queen Elizabeth, William III, and Gen. Wolfe criticize North for the Quebec Act because it favors Roman Catholicism. North blames the Scots.

74-55. Dialogue between the Bostonians and Minister.

"B. Treat us like Foreigners! Deserves it slaughter." (6)

St J's C, May 10, 1774.

The Bostonians complain of the tea sent to them; but North replies by saying the Government needs money.

74-56. A Dialogue between two great trading Cities, Dantzick and Boston.

"Dantzick. Hola! Sister, I am besieg'd." (14)

Freeman's J, Sep 1, 1774; Lloyd's 35 (Aug 31, 1774), 220; LP, Aug 24, 1774.

Boston complains of the loss of its rights through oppression, ironically, by "The Best of Princes."

74-57. A Dialogue supposed to have been between James the Second and King William.

"James. If a mistaken Zeal has urg'd you on." (13)

Freeman's J, Jul 5, 1774; G, Jun 21, 1774; MJ, Jun 18, 1774; PA, Jun 22, 1774; St J's C, Jun 8, 1774.

HC. James II did wrong and, despite divine right, must forfeit his crown, which is operative only under law. (These lines assert the Whig doctrine of a limited monarchy, in effect a warning to George III and Tories who champion tyranny. The immediate occasion is the passing of the Quebec Act.)

74-58. Dissolution.

"What's this? Quebec the second to be pass'd." (14)

St J's C, Oct 22, 1774.

HC. Treachery may be expected from Lord Bute who still directs politics from behind the scenes.

74-59. The Election. A Fable. To Candidates.

"Elections, as they ought to be." (68)

HM 4 (Jan 1774), 53 & 7 (Appendix 1777), 886; WM 23 (Jan 13, 1774), 82.

OC. Animal fable illustrating the detrimental effects of bribery.

74-60. The Election. [A Song on Liberty.]

"Whilst happy in my native land." (20)

G Eve Post, Oct 18, 1774; Lady's M 5 (Oct 1774), 520; Lloyd's 35 (Oct 19, 1774), 385; MJ, Oct 18, 1774; Ox M 11 (Oct 1774), 310; Say's, Oct 22, 1774; W Misc 3 (Nov 28, 1774), 207-8; The Vocal Magazine (1778), Song 97, p. 29.

This popular song, from a musical Burletta Interlude, The Election, was "received with great applause." It is noteworthy for its opposition to election bribery and its refrain, "Or give me Death or Liberty." Did it inspire Patrick Henry?

74-61. [The Election at Worcester.] To the Tune of Rule Britannia.

"Crown'd with laurels see he comes." (18)

Lloyd's 35 (Feb 11, 1774), 149; LP, Feb 11, 1774.

Song. Sir Watkin Lewes is acclaimed as he joins in the election proceedings at Worcester. A patriot, he opposes a Nabob's corrupting influence.

74-62. Emigrants.

"Three Things we seek abroad, flying or fled." (4)

St J's C, Aug 2, 1774.

Epigram. The emigrants seek their religion, freedom, and prosperity abroad. They leave behind "Papists and Pensioners."

74-63. The Emigrants of Scotland's Farewell.

"Doom'd by Oppression's unrelenting band." (c. 120)

LM 43 (Dec 1774), 610-1.

HC. A sentimental reaction to the emigration of 800 persons to America "in the last spring from only the small shire of Galloway." The oppressed seek freedom and equality.

74-64. Epigram.

"Here lives a Man (write this upon his Door)." (8)

St J's C, Oct 27, 1774.

HC. Bute (Thane) is responsible for the policy of taxing "the Whiggish Colonists" and menacing them with the Quebec Act.

74-65. Epigram.

"It is not always Faction to oppose." (8)

St J's C, Aug 13, 1774.

Satire on Lord North, a knavish premier.

74-66. Epigram.

"Of Civil Ills in England hear the Rise." (8)

St J's C, Jan 11, 1774.

HC. Vicious tyrants will go the way of James II. (A warning to George.)

74-67. Epigram.

"Of future Times, whatever be the Lot." (4)

St J's C, Aug 2, 1774.

The present will be remembered as the time when America was "subdu'd," and when British honor was lost in India.

74-68. An Epigram.

"T'other day as old Quidnunc and Razon were walking." (10)

M Chron, Dec 20, 1774.

Fourteeners. Two men complain that the country is being ruined because of America, taxes, the debt.

74-69. Epigram. By an Hollander.

"Though, Countryman, we may perhaps awhile." (10)

St J's C, Sep 8, 1774.

HC. A Dutchman queries the wisdom of the Quebec Act and the action against Boston -- which appear to encourage the return of the Stuarts.

74-70. Epigram. On hearing the Duke of Richmond in the House of Lords . . . .

"Ye Patriots weep -- Lo! R-ch--nd Planet smit." (4)

PA, May 28, 1774.

The Duke of Richmond is linked with the Bostonians, whom he is unable to assist.

74-71. Epigram. On the Unanimous vote of the Right Reverend the Bench of Bishops to the Quebec Bill . . . .

"Old Nick, highly pleased at what yesterday past." (9)

KG, Jun 22, 1774; L Eve Post, Jun 21, 1774.

Satire on the bishops. The devil is pleased that the Bench of Bishops have encouraged Roman Catholicism by voting for the Quebec Bill.

74-72. Epigram(s).

"A Kingdom, such as thou never saw'st, O Sun." (16)

St J's C, Aug 9, 1774.

Four epigrams objecting to the Scottish influence, Bute, and Popery; corrupt peers; Quebec; George III. But William III is praised.

74-73. Epitaph, &c.

"To the Memory of A[lexande]r W[edderburn], Esq;" (c. 30)

Freeman's J, Jun 18, 1774; MJ, Jun 9, 1774; PA, Jun 11, 1774.

Inscription. Satiric attack on Wedderburn, solicitor general. He had twice defected from the cause of freedom and the colonies for venal reasons. His brutal treatment of Franklin (Jan 1774) for allegedly stealing Gov. Hutchinson's correspondence is alluded to. From "an American Paper."

74-74. Epitaph, &c.

"To the memory of / Thomas Hutchinson, Esq." (c. 30)

Freeman's J, Jun 18, 1774; LP, Jun 10, 1774; M Chron, Jun 13, 1774.

Inscription. Satire on Hutchinson, Governor of Massachusetts, as an enemy to his country for his attempt to abridge English liberties and destroy the charter of the province, an attempt which Franklin exposed.

74-75. Epitaph on the Late Parliament.

"Sacred / To the Second Parliament of George the Third / Who / In the infancy of their existence/." (c. 20)

Lloyd's 35 (Oct 21, 1774), 398; M Chron, Oct 24, 1774; PA, Oct 24, 1774.

Inscription. An ironic review of the second Parliament of George III's reign (1768-74), citing the expulsion of Wilkes, the failure to restore public credit and to eradicate corruption, the ill-fated attempt to assert the "superiority of the Mother Country over her rebellious offspring in America."

74-76. Epitaph on the Late Parliament.

"To the Memory of the / Second Parliament / Held in the Reign of / George the Third. / This Parliament, / Composed for the most part of / Unprincipled Villains/." (c. 80)

Freeman's J, Nov 1, 1774; L Eve Post, Oct 25, 1774; LP, Oct 25, 1774; MJ, Oct 22, 1774; PL, Oct 25, 1774.

Inscription. Also entitled "Another Epitaph on the Late Parliament." A satiric attack on the Parliament of 1768-74 for its corruption, its shameful violation of the rights of electors for expelling Wilkes ("for having opposed the Tyranny of the King's Highland Favourite"), its protection of Roman Catholicism in Canada, etc.

74-77. Epitaph on the Late Parliament.

"To the Memory of / The second Parliament, held in the Reign / of George the Third / . . ." (c. 20)

M Chron, Nov 1, 1774.

A hostile satiric inscription that simply records the demise of "this corrupted Body," October 7, 1774.

74-78. An Epitaph on the M[inistr]y.

"O Reader! / This tablet was erected." (c. 60)

LP, Sep 12, 1774.

Inscription, epitaph. Satire on the ministry, esp. Bute, Mansfield, North who, as Tories, strengthened the royal prerogative and oppressed the American colonies and the home country, encouraged corruption and self-interest.
-- Signed by "An American."

74-79. Extempore, On Reading some Scurrilous Paragraphs on Mr. Wilkes and the Bill of Rights Society, in some of the Papers.

"Observe, again the petty grubs." (18)

LP, Sep 14, 1774; M Chron, Sep 16, 1774.

Sixains. Satires on Wilkes are weak and ineffectual.

74-80. Extempore. On the Birth and Landing of King William.

"When Heaven, in Bounty to Mankind." (12)

PA, Nov 5, 1774.

Quatrains. A hope that King George will be like King William and maintain freedom in accord with the spirit of the Revolution.

74-81. Extempore on the Patriots' Abuse at Mile End.

"Says Parson Horne to Johnny Wilkes." (8)

M Chron, May 7, 1773.

OC. More on the quarrel between Wilkes and Horne.

74-82. Fable of a Wolf.

"A Wolf returning from Whitehall." (14)

W Misc 2 (Apr 4, 1774), 16.

OC. There are very few honest courtiers (politicians at court).

74-83. The Fall of Boston.

"Act I. Scene the last. (Lord North solus)." (21)

L Eve Post, Apr 2, 1774; KG, Apr 6, 1774.

Blank verse. North in a soliloquy vows to destroy Boston for crossing him.

74-84. Farewel[l] to the Highlands. A Song wrote on occasion of the present extraordinary emigration of the Highlanders.

"How bold were our fathers! how loud was their fame!" (22)

WM 25 (Jul 21, 1774), 113.

Song. A complaint that the brave highlanders are emigrating. (No cause is made specific.)

74-85. The First Psalm Parody'd.

"The man is blest that hath not lent." (28)

L Eve Post, Apr 26, 1774.

Quatrains. Parody. Praise of the man who is unbribed and independent and who supports liberty in Boston and at home.

74-86. Fragment of an Antient Prophecy. Discovered in the Year 1770.

"When husbandmen their rural toils forsake." (54)

L Eve Post, Jan 4, 1774; W Misc 1 (Jan 24, 1774), 401-2.

HC. A complaint at moral and political corruption in London -- especially bribery and venality -- which will bring ruin to the nation. Cited are losses to the treasury and a call by Patriots for an audit.

74-87. Freedom Revived. Tune -- Come haste to the Wedding.

"Ye Lads, for the Contest be quickly preparing." (22)

Song, broadside, [1774]. A lyric for the Parliamentary elections in Coventry, October 1774. From the Bodleian, Warwick b. 1 (190).

74-88. The Freeholders Memorial. Addressed to the Gentlemen, Clergy, and Freeholders of England, by T. S. To the Tune of, "Who's e'er been at Paris."

"Ye Muses who never your favours confine." (59)

L Chron 36 (Jul 30, 1774), 108; M Chron, Aug 1, 1774; W Misc 2 (Aug 15, 1774), 478-9.

Song with Derry down chorus. An election song against bribery and for honesty. The voters are urged to refuse to barter away their freedom by selling votes.

74-89. Free(th), John.
American Contest.

"Mother England's own child, a fine lusty grown lass." (50)

LP, Apr 18, 1774, (The song is entitled "The Times."); John Free(th), The Warwickshire Medley (Birmingham: Pearson & Rollason [c. 1776], pp. 1-3. Song 1. See 76-13.

Song with Derry down chorus. A review of the American controversy, in allegorical terms, between the mother country, England, and her daughter, the American colonies. Cited are luxury, tea, Boston tea-party, Intolerable Acts, Seven Years War, Parliament, taxes, Stamp Tax, Pitt, corruption, Ireland.
   Also in Free(th), The Political Songster (Birmingham: Pearson, 1790), pp. 18-19.
   The text varies. But this song is not the same as "The World Turned Upside Down," 66-134, 66-140. Nor is it the same as Freeth's "The Contest," 78-210.

74-90. Free(th), John.
The Pope's Address to his good Friends in England. Tune, As I was a driving my waggon one day.

"In Rome's rigid clime when it came to be known." (40)

The Warwickshire Medley (Birmingham: Pearson & Rollason, [1776], pp. 12-3. Reprinted in 1778: GA, Jul 20, 1778; L Eve Post, Jul 16, 1778.

Song. Satiric comment on the Quebec Act. The persona of the Pope expresses his satisfaction over the acts of the "heretic" George III which favor Popery. The "American broils" are being used to cover up the insidious Catholic and Tory attempt at power.

74-91. Free(th), John.
Prorogation.

"Hark, hark, the voice of royalty." (24)

The Warwickshire Medley (Birmingham: Pearson & Rollason, [1776], pp. 17-8.

Song. The Parliament adjourned in 1774. Half deserve to be tarred and feathered, as they implicitly follow the command of the premier, North. The cure for the ills of the land would be the execution of the knaves.

74-92. [Friend Luther, friend Conyers, if you love the honours.]

"Friend Luther, friend Conyers, if you love the honours." (28)

L Eve Post, Aug 2, 1774.

Quatrains. Instructions to MP's from Essex to vote on certain issues -- to repeal the Quebec Act -- and to be independent and honest.

74-93. A Friendly Hint.

"Unhappy G[eorg]e, by Tories led astray." (42)

Freeman's J, Nov 8, 1774.

HC. Criticizes the King for accepting the counsel of Tories (Bute, North, Sandwich), and asks that Chatham take the helm. Chatham will save the empire and prevent tyranny and papal power from overcoming the American colonies.

74-94. Friends, Neighbours, and Countrymen.

"Your well-weigh'd choice my heart with rapture fills." (2)

KG, Jul 23, 1774.

Epigram. Milles was elected representative in Parliament for the City of Canterbury; Dering was rejected.

74-95. [From 1746, to 1753.]

"From 1746, to 1753." (c. 25)

Freeman's J, Mar 24, 1774.

Inscription, in effect a mock pindaric ode, that compares the period 1746 to 1753, when Ireland was relatively stable and pleased with conditions, with the present, when conditions are worse. Cited are taxes, emigration, poor trade.

74-96. From the Greek.

"'Tis thought the Lust of Bribery without Measure." (7)

St J's C, Mar 8, 1774.

Epigram. Caustic comment on bribery, its effect on the Treasury and the next election.

74-97. The Genius of London Speaks.

"--Pluck down my offices, break my decrees." (20)

M Chron, Nov 8, 1774.

Blank verse imitation of Shakespeare. Criticism of Wilkes, now Lord Mayor, who will bring riot and anarchy to the City.

74-98. Goldsmith, Oliver.
Retaliation.

"Of old, when Scarron his companions invited." (146)

HM 4 (May 1774), 293-5.

Hexameter couplets. Fourteen lines on Edmund Burke, "For a patriot, too cool," but (according to Goldsmith) he was a party man. See 1774-A.

74-99. The Great Man in Decay.

"The great, good man, whom fortune will displace." (10)

W Misc 3 (Dec 19, 1774), 280.

HC. The great man -- the premier -- will still be respected even when fallen from office. Perhaps ironic.

74-100. [Have you not seen a tow'ring rock.]

"Have you not seen a tow'ring rock." (14)

L Eve Post, Jan 6, 1774.

Sonnet (non-standard). Praise of Wilkes, who stands firm against all hack criticism.

74-101. [Honor invites knaves to their rights.]

"Honor invites knaves to their rights." (6)

MJ, Apr 23, 1774.

Sixain. Satire on the practice of selling titles -- a mean business at court.

74-102. The Horns and the Tail; or, the M[inistr]y and the Americans. A Political Fable.

"Upon a time, a gad-fly stung." (60)

M Chron, Dec 23, 1774.

Sixains. A fable that illustrates the dilemma England suffers -- if it tries to suspend the rights of the colonies, it will ruin itself and lose its freedom.

74-103. An Impromptu.

"Could James the Second leave his grave." (6)

LP, Jul 8, 1774.

Sixain. The Stuart kings, Charles I and James II, would be amazed at a Parliament that passed the Quebec Bill. (Associate this poem with "On the Folly of the Times," LP, Jul 15, 1774, by the same writer: 74-141.)

74-104. Cancelled.

Johnson, Samuel. Present State of Great Britain. "A thousand prodigies foretold it." (4) The Fugitive Miscellany (London: Almon, 1774), p. 57. Prose poem. A pessimistic view of Britain, a "sinking" nation, declining because of corruption, "A feeble government," "A factious populace, luxurious nobles." Probably written in 1773. See 73-47.

74-105. A Late Speech Versified.

"My noble Lords and Gentlemen." (48)

LP, Jan 17, 1774.

OC. Ironic parody of the King's speech to open Parliament. He asks for money for the Crown and improvement of gold coin minting.

74-106. A Letter of Remonstrance and Condolence from a King George the Second's Light Guinea to its Cousin-german, a heavy King George the Third's.

"Not speak! when thus my brethren all are martyr'd!" (88)

HM 4 (Nov 1774), 685-6; T&C 6 (Oct 1774), 550-1.

Hexameter couplets. A protest at the passage of the Coinage Bill, briefly alluding to the destruction of Magna Charta and the rights of Englishmen, and breaking the hearts of the Bostonians. By J. D. Brewood.

74-107. Liberty.

"If, as some Heretics maintain, two Rules." (10)

St J's C, Oct 4, 1774.

HC. A protest at bribery, Scottish corruption, which threatens liberty in England.

74-108. Liberty Going.

"On Dover's Cliff, to mortal sight so steep," (46)

Freeman's J, Sep 6, 1774; L Eve Post, Aug 18, 1774.

HC, dialogue. Liberty threatens to quit Britain for America.

74-109. Marvell's Prophecy.

"America will be free." (4)

LP, Apr 29, 1774.

Quatrain. Marvell (a pseud.) predicts the loss of America to France and the restoration of the Stuarts there. (Marvell, a name assumed by a contemporary contributor to the newspapers, opposed the government's policy of coercion.)

74-110. Massie, J.
[Accounts of The Trade between London and Ireland.]

"Accounts of The Trade between London and Ireland." (c. 20)

G, Mar 10, 1774.

A memorial-type inscription in which Massie warns of the consequences of not understanding that the prosperity of the kingdom stands upon an American foundation.

74-111. The Modern Courtier.

"Pray say what's that, which smirking trips this way." (14)

L Chron 36 (Dec 6, 1774), 552; MJ, Dec 6, 1774.

HC. A Whig satire on a modern courtier, or politician, who, effeminate and servile to the king, cannot speak for the people or the people's right as explained in Magna Charta.

74-112. [Most, on Canada's Act, with anger frown.]

"Most, on Canada's Act, with anger frown." (7)

MJ, Jul 26, 1774.

Satiric objection to the Quebec Act.

74-113. A New Song. Supposed to have been sung by Goody N---h, by way of Lullaby to the Foundling Brat, the Popish Quebec Bill. To the Tune of "O my Kitten, my Kitten."

"O My baby, my baby." (39)

M Chron, Jul 2, 1774; St J's C, Jun 30, 1774; The Muses's Mirror (London: Baldwin, 1778), I, 164-5.

Song. A criticism of the bishops because they did not vote against the "Canada bill," that is, the Quebec bill. Cited are Bute, North, Chatham. The Quebec bill was enacted Jun 22, 1774.

74-114. A New Song. To the plaintive tune of Hosier's Ghost.

"As near beauteous Boston lying." (32)

LP, Apr 22, 1774; The Muse's Mirror (London: Baldwin, 1778), I, 202-3.

Song. A ballad narrating the Boston Tea Party, Dec 16, 1773, and asserting American rights. From the Pennsylvania Packet, Jan 3, 1774.

74-115. A New Song. To the Tune of, The Roast-Beef of Old England.

"When mighty roast-beef was the Englishman's food." (36)

LM 43 (Aug 1774), 400-1.

Song protesting the support by the bishops of "a popish bill," the power of "a venal majority" in Parliament, the failure of petitions -- while the Tories rule.

74-116. [The New Year.]

"The revolving Years proclaim to all." (68)

PA, Jan 1, 1774.

OC. Among other predictions is one that Parliament "shall her cause defend," meaning that it will insist on its rights.

74-117. The Oak & Arbutus. A Fable.

"In climes beneath remoter skies." (68)

L Chron 36 (Sep 27, 1774), 308; SM 36 (Sep 1774), 494-5; W Misc 4 (May 8, 1775), 140-1.

Quatrains. A botanical fable whose moral is that Britain's prosperity, the Oak, depends upon the health of the Arbutus, American trade.

74-118. An occasional Poem on the Conclusion of the Westminster Election; or an Advice from the Electors of that City to the Public. Concluding with an Address from the Author to the Duchess of Northumberland and Duke of Newcastle.

"When recr'ant rebels, fraught with vengeful ire." (40)

MP, Oct 29, 1774.

Quatrains. In support of the Court against the American rebels helped by factions in England -- especially of Lord Hugh Percy and Lord Thomas Pelham Clinton.

74-119. Ode.

"Hark! oh hark! the Muse's ear." (38)

Lloyd's 34 (Jun 8, 1774), 548.

Pindaric ode. A favorable reaction to America's objection to oppressive English colonial policies. Should the English give tax relief to the Americans, they will not rebel. This ode is a parody on Whitehead's birth-day ode, which it supports. But it is parodied satirically in the MJ, Jun 23, 1774: see 74-120.

74-120. [Ode.]

"Hark! (or does the Muse's ear)." (38)

MJ, Jun 23, 1774.

Pindaric ode. Parody on Whitehead's Birth-Day ode. The Americans are right to resist oppression and fight for freedom; and King George should learn from King John, and Bute from Mortimer. See 74-119, and 74-210.

74-121. Ode.

"Quoth Ralph to Hodge, what is this Rout." (84)

PA, Jun 20, 1774.

Quatrains, complaining that feeling is so high that even those who attempt to mediate between the two contending parties are menaced. This poem is meant as an answer to the "Paraphrase of Mr. Whitehead's Birth-Day Ode," 74-151. It expresses the need for union.

74-122. An Ode, Humbly inscribed to William Whitehead, Esq. Poet Laureat to George, King of Great Britain and America.

"Hark! or does the indignant ear." (40)

L Eve Post, Jun 7, 1774; LM 43 (Jul 1774), 351.

Pindaric ode, parody on Whitehead's birthday ode. Satire on Whitehead's dull venal verse that flatters tyranny. This poem asserts the virtue of freedom for America.

74-123. Ode on the Lord Mayor's Day for the Year 1774.

"Nature's green mantle on the ground is cast." (26)

PL, Nov 9, 1774.

Irregular Pindaric ode. "To Wilkes and to Fair LIBERTY" -- commonplace and conventional ode honoring Wilkes, the new Lord Mayor.

74-124. Ode On Wilkes's Election for the Lord Mayor.

"Ye patriot dames, rejoice and sing." (42)

The Muse's Mirror (London: Baldwin, 1778), I, 148-9.

Pindaric ode. Celebrates the election of Wilkes as Mayor of London.

74-125. Ode to Independence.

"Britons, if you pant for glory." (22)

T&C 6 (Oct 1774), 550-1.

Regular ode in sixains, plus chorus, in support of "Patriots," and against "Corruption's proud slaves." This is a Whig lyric invoking the spirit of the old Whig heroes, Hampden and Sidney.

74-126. Ode to the Mercury Packet-Boat, Occasioned by the Embarkation of his Excellency Governor Tryon, for England.

"Whilst all with duteous zeal contend." (78)

LP, Jun 8, 1774.

Regular Horatian ode. Panegyric on Gov. William Tryon of New York, who has left temporarily for England. Originally published in New York.

74-127. An Ode to the Right Honorable the Earl of Hillsborough.

"How long, great Hill! shall thy transcendent name." (40)

HM 4 (Oct 1774), 618.

Regular ode in octaves. Praise of Wills Hill, Earl of Hillsborough, the first secretary of state for the colonies (1768-72). His work contributed to peace and concord in America, according to this panegyric, and freedom and prosperity in Ireland.

74-128. Old New-Year's Day. An Irregular Burlesque Ode. By the Bellman.

"O never more abuse." (8)

M Chron, Jan 12, 1774.

Irregular Pindaric ode, satire on Whitehead for slavish flattery of the King, for "harping on Caesar." He should dedicate his lines to Bute or be quiet.

74-129. On a Late Speech.

"Awake, my Countrymen, awake." (30)

PA, Jan 27, 1774.

OC. Satire on the King's speech opening Parliament. It is ridiculed ironically for missing the point about important issues.

74-130. On Bob the Waiter's being elected to sit in P[arliamen]t.

"Bob cares not for his enemies a louse." (6)

G Eve Post, Nov 29, 1774.

Two epigrams. As an illustration of the corrupt nature of the Parliament of 1774, consider Robert Mackreth, a waiter at White's, a fashionable London club, being chosen to be the representative for Castle Rising. See "Congratulatory Song," "Poor -----d's mad," 74-48, 74-158.

Robert Mackreth, a waiter at White's, became proprietor of the Club in 1761. He became very rich through money-lending and land speculation. In Oct. 1774 he was nominated by Horace Walpole's nephew Lord Orford, who was heavily in debt to him, for Castle Rising, for which he sat until 1784. From 1784 to 1802 he sat for Ashburton. See Lewis Namier and John Brooke, The House of Commons 1754-1790 (1964), III, 89-90.

74-131. On certain late Preferments, additional Pensions and Employments, liberally conferred on the worthy Members of the Irish Parliament. See the London Gazette of Nov. 22, 1774.

"How prosp'rous now the pliant courtier's lot." (44)

Freeman's J, Dec 13, 1774.

HC. Disgusted with Irish passivity in face of the tyranny of a slavish Parliament, the poet holds up the example of Boston's resistance and struggle for her rights.

74-132. On Coffee House Politicians.

"The vulgar, who've always a spite at the great." (20)

L Chron 36 (Dec 29, 1774), 632; MJ, Dec 29, 1774.

Anapest tetrameter couplets. The fickle mob can never be entirely pleased. A defense, in effect, of Lord North's policies, especially his policy of taxing the colonies.

74-133. On Liberty.

"Be this my theme -- the darling of my song." (37)

MJ, Apr 21, 1774.

Blank verse. In accordance with tradition, Britons should resist any attempt to rob them of their rights. Their "fix'd resolve" should be liberty or death!

74-134. On Mr. Wilkes and Lord -- being sworn in together in the Commons House.

"When Wilkes and Lord -- first met in the House." (6)

St J's C, Dec 8, 1774.

Wilkes is sworn in to his seat in the House of Commons -- and behaves like a man.

74-135. On Patriotic Perseverance being Crowned with Success.

"No more of old Troy, and blind Homer's song." (5)

M Chron, Oct 12, 1774.

Epigram. Wilkes surpasses the heroes of Troy, for after ten years he finally triumphs.

74-136. On Reading an Account of the Late Politics of Two Great Cities.

"What, John Wilkes Lord Mayor! -- 'Tis shame and disgrace." (10)

WM 26 (Oct 20, 1774), 127.

Epigram. Wilkes is exalted in London, but the "rascal" really should be hanged. However, in Edinburgh only slaves are advanced.

74-137. On Reading the Monthly and Critical Reviews.

"What boundless erudition! how immense." (76)

GM 44 (Feb 1774), 87.

HC. Satire on the reviewers for their intellectual arrogance.

74-138. On seeing the Whigs Orange blended with the Tories Blue, at the late Elections for Essex and Hertfordshire.

"Strange sights we know sometimes arise." (20)

L Eve Post, Nov 12, 1774.

OC. "Lukewarm Whigs," dishonest Whigs, have allied with Tories in two counties -- Essex and Hertfordshire.

74-139. On the Author of the Boston Port Bill.

"Fierce Nimrod first the bloody chace began." (4)

KG, Apr 16, 1774.

Epigram. North is hunting down a whole people with his policies!

74-140. On the Emigration of our Manufacturers.

"O Fathers of your country, bid them stay." (6)

Lloyd's 34 (Feb 25, 1774), 196.

HC. The trade has been ruined, and so workers emigrate to avoid starvation. See objection to the "American war" in Lloyd's 35 (Nov 23, 1774), 505, for explanation of these verses.

74-141. On the Folly of the Times, and the Brimstone Supporters of those diabolical Amusements, called Fireworks, and Works of Fire.

"When mighty Rome was in a blaze." (18)

LP, Jul 15, 1774.

Sixains. The times are absurd. At a time of danger the court is providing amusements -- but the court is encouraging popery. See An Impromptu, LP, Jul 8, 1774: 74-103.

74-142. On the good People of B[osto]n.

"These B[oston]ites, who once could deign." (14)

M Chron, May 19, 1774.

OC. The people of Boston may regret their treatment of the King.

74-143. On the K[ing]'s Going to the House to Sign the Canada Bill.

"To please Old England with a bill of fare." (6)

MJ, Jul 23, 1774.

HC. Ironic comment on the people who enjoy seeing the King going to Parliament to sign the Canada (Quebec) Bill.

74-144. On the Meeting at the Guildhall of this City [Canterbury], on Monday Last.

"Freemen attend! -- 'tis honour's call." (36)

KG, Jul 16, 1774.

Quatrains. Election poem honoring Richard Milles -- who is honest, unlike his corrupt opponent Dering. (Whom are we to believe in this name-calling contest?)

74-145. On the New Speaker.

"Sir F[letche]r in the Chair! how I'm amaz'd." (6)

MJ, Nov 29, 1774.

Epigram. Satire on Sir Fletcher Norton, venal Speaker of the House of Commons, adept at corruption.

74-146. On the Perfidy of Scotchmen.

"That Scotchmen are false, we've a long time been told." (10)

MJ, May 31, 1774; St J's C, Jul 23, 1774 (with four additional lines).

Anapest tetrameter couplets. Scotchmen can not be trusted -- they rebelled against the First and Second Georges, and so now they will betray "in council," they will be "traitors in the cabinet." The St. George's Fields' massacre is cited. See 74-179.

74-147. On the Proceedings against America.

"Lost is our old simplicity of times." (36)

UM 55 (Nov 1774), 262.

HC. A complaint against anti-American policies that encourage Roman Catholicism and civil war and tyranny.

74-148. On the Quebec Bill.

"Well may proud Rome her late great honours boast." (8)

MJ, Sep 1, 1774.

HC. The Papists have won dominion over Canada through King George.

74-149. On the Stamp-Act.

"Stern Pluto grinning on his ebon throne." (34)

Freeman's J, May 12, 1774.

HC. In Hell a scheme is fomented for the oppression of Ireland -- for a stamp act, particularly, aimed at the liberty of the press.

74-150. The cxxxviith Psalm Paraphras'd. Super flumina.

"Beside the streams of Babylon her murmuring waters fall." (24)

M Chron, Aug 2, 1774.

Fourteeners. Signed G. S---D., Wandsworth, July 29. Protest at the harsh treatment of "Salem's sons."

74-151. Paraphrase of Mr. Whitehead's New Year's Ode.

"Behold! what martial Bands are those." (52)

LP, Jun 10, 1774; M Chron, Jun 14, 1774; PA, Jun 13, 1774.

Pindaric ode, parody. The title is clearly incorrect, the poem being a parody of Whitehead's ode printed for the King's birthday, June 4. This serious ode protests the coming civil war and begs for peace and friendship between America and Britain. See 74-121.

74-152. Parody on the Song of Chevy Chace.

"God prosper long our liberty." (60)

Freeman's J, Jul 14, 1774; L Eve Post, Jul 7, 1774.

Ballad narrates the story of the Popish Quebec Bill, inspired by Bute and Mansfield, and passed despite Chatham's protest. This is further evidence of oppression by a Parliament intent upon reducing English liberties.

74-153. A Patriotic Song. Addressed to the worthy and independent Electors of Great Britain.

"Ye guardians of freedom your duty attend." (28)

T&C 6 (Oct 1774), 549-50.

Song. A Whig lyric in support of honest and incorruptible patriots who refuse bribes. The spirit of Hampden and Sidney is invoked against the "haughty oppressor."

74-154. Patriotism. An Ode.

"When generous Greece, in virtue bold." (120)

LP, Sep 9, 1774.

Regular Horatian ode. Satire on the times from the Irish point of view. Cited are Flood, absentee landlords, emigration to America, discrimination or limitation of Irish trade by the English.

74-155. A Poetical Historical Account of England.

"James II. The second James, a furious Popish king." (52)

Freeman's J, Sep 24, 1774.

HC, presenting a panoramic history of England from James II to George III, concluding with a vision of catastrophe. Criticism of George III as an ineffectual ruler.

74-156. Political Directions for 1774.

"A. I cannot fiddle (said an ancient Wight)." (18)

St J's C, Feb 19, 1774.

HC. A pessimistic political view of what is to come for England in 1774 -- dearth, the domination by the court, weakness before its adversaries abroad, domestic troubles.

74-157. The Politicians.

"To the sage Smyrna, every day." (24)

LM 43 (Oct 1774), 504; West M 2 (Oct 1774), 538.

Octosyllabic triplets. A coffee-house complaint at the accomplishments of the politicians -- destruction of freedom, generation of war with the colonies, encouragement of Stuart despotism and Roman Catholicism.

74-158. [Poor ----'s mad! exclaim'd his friend.]

"Poor ----'s mad! exclaim'd his friend." (17)

L Eve Post, Nov 12, 1774.

OC. Satire on Lord Orford (Horace Walpole's nephew) who sent a waiter at White's (Bob Mackreth) to Parliament. See "Congratulatory Song" and "On Bob the Waiter's being elected," 74-48, 74-130.

74-159. Popular Toasts.

"May the British Military never be employed on an unconstitutional service. . . ."

Lloyd's 35 (Aug 17, 1774), 172.

Six toasts that favor the Americans and attack Parliament and the court. Gage is cited.

74-160. Portrait of a Gentleman fit to Represent his Country in Parliament.

"An understanding just, precise and clear." (12)

WM 26 (Oct 27, 1774), 146.

HC. An ideal portrait of a patriot who is independent and incorruptible.

74-161. The Printer's Farewell to his Country, on his Embarking for America.

"May conscious guilt distract his tortur'd breast." (62)

Freeman's J, Nov 5, 1774.

HC by a Limerick printer who, in protest at the Irish Stamp Act, gives up his business and departs for America -- but not before delivering this satiric invective at those local politicians responsible for his troubles.

74-162. Prophecy.

"If ever Slavery be England's Lot." (2)

St J's C, Nov 1, 1774.

Epigram. Satire on greedy Scotsmen, for they are responsible for the slavery coming to England.

74-163. A Prophecy.

"When Pow'r and Law in Scottish Hands are left." (6)

St J's C, Mar 22, 1774.

HC. Anti-Scots satire. When the Scots are in power, the political center will move from London to Edinburgh, the Highlanders will become Macaronies, and Newmarket races will be filled with Scottish ponies.

74-164. A Prophesy.

"When Rulers break their Oaths, and when the Cause." (8)

St J's C, Sep 22, 1774.

HC. A protest at the Quebec Act because it encourages "Popery." But conscience and the Scriptures prevent "Popery" from thriving in England.

74-165. [Pr----a, himself a r-bb-r vile, yet sage.]

"Pr----a, himself a r-bb-r vile, yet sage." (20)

G Eve Post, Feb 12, 1774.

HC. Franklin is compared to Prometheus -- for stealing Gov. Hutchinson's letters and firing up Massachusetts -- and deserves to be punished. (Pr----a = Prussia, the King of.)

74-166. Quebec.

"O Parliament! what Demon round thy Neck." (10)

St J's C, Jul 16, 1774.

HC. Protest at the Quebec Act for fixing Popery on English territory.

74-167. Quebec.

"O wretched State of Sovereignty's Height." (10)

St J's C, Jul 14, 1774.

HC. The King is warned that the passage of the Quebec Bill will bring in Popery and persecution. Parliament, it is protested, has done nothing to prevent this mistake.

74-168. Quebec.

"Quebec, O Protestants' eternal Shame." (10)

St J's C, Sep 6, 1774.

HC. Protest at the Quebec Act, the shame of Protestants, passed by bigots who favor Popery, who undermine "true Religion."

74-169. Quebec. To Certain Persons.

"What ye have gain'd hereby let others tell." (5)

St J's C, Aug 2, 1774.

Epigram. Passing the Quebec Bill has cost certain MP's the support of "some thousand honest English Hearts."

74-170. Queries to a Friend.

"Canst thou, O Friend, for sev'n Years more behold." (10)

St J's C, Jan 11, 1774.

HC. If conditions continue -- remonstrances ignored, oaths forsworn, the press gagged, and Parliament corrupted -- England will be worse than France and Spain.

74-171. A Short State of the Politics, Arts, &c. of this Country for the New Year.

"The K*** -- dozing" (15) [A Selection.]

L Eve Post, Dec 29, 1774.

Prose-poem. A review of the political state of affairs -- including corruption, the Scotch, the King, and the ministry.

74-172. [Since England's Prince, regardless of his state.]

"Since England's Prince, regardless of his state." (14)

MJ, Sep 24, 1774.

HC. A prophecy of doom, of the gathering storm. The country will be ruined because of the obstinacy of the King in refusing to heed petitions of grievances and for being under the influence of Bute.

74-173. Soliloquy. [Mr. R(igby), in an arbour on the summit of a hill, descending into a long woody valley.]

"Deep in the bosom of that nodding grove." (72)

L Eve Post, Jun 23, 1774.

Blank verse. Ironic satire on Rigby. Rigby meditates on corruption and Lord Bute's influence on the King.

A Song. Now Much in Vogue in North-America. To the Tune of -- Hearts of Oak, &c.

"Come, join hand in hand, brave Americans all." (43)

W Misc 3 (Dec 12, 1774), 255-6.

An American freedom song, from the Boston Gazette, refers to the tradition of freedom, placemen and pensioners (bribery and corruption), and the need for unity against oppression. (This is Dickinson's "Liberty Song," first pub. in 1768, and now reprinted without a change in the text.) See 68-95.

74-174. Song. To the Tune of Lillibullero.

"The great Men at Court so rampant are grown." (50)

PA, Dec 31, 1774.

Song. A protest at the excessive Scottish influence at court -- Bute, Mansfield, and others -- at English expense. These "makers of taxes" wish to enslave America before placing chains on England.

74-175. The Spirit of Popery Displayed. By Mr. Lewis, Corrector of the Press, (Whose poems are now printing by subscription.)

"The Romish Church commands her sons t'oppose." (34)

Freeman's J, Jan 11, 1774.

HC. A negative reaction to the debate on the bill for Roman Catholic relief. Lewis emphasizes cruel Catholic persecution. Cruel in the past, papists will continue to be cruel in the present and the future. They want only power.

74-176. State of Political Stocks this day at two o'clock.

"Royal Assurance -- high." (12)

L Eve Post, Nov 26, 1774.

Prose poem based on the metaphor of the stock market. "Royal assurance" is "high" and "Justice to America" is "shut." Corruption is "open" and Magna Charta "reduced one-half."

74-177. Tea: A New Song -- To an old Tune. Setting forth the obstinacy of the Americans, who refuse to take this emetic, because it is the pleasure of the British Parliament they shall drink tea whether it makes them sick or no.

"Ye Members of Parliament, trimmers of state." (42)

LP, Feb 16, 1774.

Song with Derry down chorus. The Americans sing their defiance to the British Parliament and refuse to drink East India tea. Cited are Stamp Act, Macaulay, Wilkes, Liberty, Pitt.

74-178. The Tears of ------. An Elegy Written in the Time of the Late Elections, on the Disappointment Arising to Venal Voters, by the making of Mr. Grenville's Bill for trying of Controverted Elections Perpetual.

"What heart-felt joys attend the peasant's lot." (108)

W Misc 3 (Dec 19, 1774), 281-3.

Parody of Gray's *Elegy*, elegiac stanzas. Grenville, responsible for the Stamp Act, is now curst for his attempt to reform the election laws.

74-179. [That Scotchmen are *false*, we've a long Time been told.]

"That Scotchmen are *false*, we've a long Time been told." (14)

St J's C, Jul 23, 1774.

Anapest tetrameter couplets. Anti-Scots satire. The Scots are rebels and traitors responsible for "the Massacre in St. George's Fields," and they are like the apostate bishops who voted for the Quebec Bill, Jul 19, 1774. See 74-146.

74-180. To a Certain Nobleman.

"Britannia's curse see here engraved thy name." (10)

MJ, Sep 6, 1774.

HC. Satire on an unidentified peer for criminal behavior.

74-181. To D[octo]r F[rankly]n.

"Thou base, ungrateful, cunning, upstart thing." (12)

G Eve Post, Jan 8, 1774.

HC. Satire on Franklin for double-dealing. Franklin, agent for Massachusetts and Postmaster of the American provinces, used his official position as postmaster to secure the private letters of Gov. Hutchinson and Lt. Gov. Oliver, returning them to Boston where they were read to the Boston Assembly and published, thereby exposing the anti-colonial duplicity of these officers. Massachusetts petitioned for their removal on the basis of this evidence secured by Franklin.

74-182. To John Wilkes, Esq; Member for Middlesex and Lord Mayor of London.

"The muse invites, and swells the welcome strain." (28)

L Eve Post, Dec 6, 1774.

HC. Panegyric on Wilkes, "faction's foe and freedom's friend," who as Lord Mayor of London is also MP for Middlesex.

74-183. To Lord North.

"Lest you should think me -- levis." (12)

G, Apr 9, 1774; G Eve Post, Apr 7, 1774.

In response to the destruction of tea in Boston harbor, North proposed the Boston Port Bill March 14, 1774; and it was enacted March 31. But this writer says it is impossible to enslave America because the country has great power and wealth and strong resolution.

74-184. To Mr. Wilkes.

"In vain contempt her poison'd Darts may throw." (10)

St J's C, Nov 12, 1774.

HC. Panegyric on Wilkes, London's new Lord Mayor -- despite his birth and conduct.

74-185. [To North, ye Britons, give uncommon praise.]

"To North, ye Britons, give uncommon praise." (20)

MJ, Jul 23, 1774.

HC. Ironic satire on the Quebec Bill, a victory for the French, over the protestations of Sir Joseph Yates (who resisted Mansfield).

74-186. To Paul Whitehead, Esq; Poet Laureat, on his Ode for the New Year 1774. Ode for the New Year 1774.

"'Pass but a few short fleeting years'." (32)

L Eve Post, Jan 11, 1774.

Pindaric ode. The writer objects to savage British barbarities in India, which Whitehead's ode does not justify. (William Whitehead, the poet laureat, was often confused with his contemporary, Paul Whitehead.)

74-187. To Sir Edward Dering.

"Pardon the Muse who only wreaths." (48)

KG, Jul 13, 1774.

Regular Horatian ode. An election poem in support of Dering, illustrating the nature of the electoral process in this critical period. Dering was running against Richard Milles for MP from the county of Kent. Dering was not of the court party.

74-188. To Sir E----- D[ering]. Occasioned by an Address to the Kentish Freeholders.

"My good friend, Sir Edward, a word in your ear." (4)

KG, Jul 20, 1774.

Advice to Dering, of Kent, not to bribe voters too heavily.

74-189. To the Earl of Ch[atha]m.

"'Tis known to all, O Pitt, that no Disgrace." (8)

St J's C, Oct 25, 1774.

HC. Pitt was driven from power by politics, but his noble virtues are recognized by a few, and he must endure disgraceful laws passed by ignorance (like the Quebec Act and the acts against Boston).

74-190. To the Electors of England.

"Friends, Brethren, Countrymen, attend." (62)

G Eve Post, Oct 13, 1774; Lloyd's 35 (Oct 7, 1774), 348.

Blank verse, parody of Shakespeare's Julius Caesar. The country is in a bad state -- freedom threatened, commerce poor. The poet asks for the end of corruption and for an honest election.

74-191. To the Honourable Thomas Maurice.

"When Panegyric forfeits, by Abuse." (48)

DJ, Aug 25, 1774.

HC. Praise of Thomas Fitzmaurice (brother of Earl of Shelburne) for his humane practices as an Irish landlord, thereby halting emigration of weavers.

74-192. To the Inhabitants of M[---------]t's-Bay.

"Ye vipers! from whose nest there springs." (14)

G Eve Post, Jan 29, 1774.

OC. Massachusetts was helped by England in her trials with French and Indians, but now she seeks independence. Perhaps England should let her seek her destiny alone.

74-193. To the King on the Affairs of America.

"Descending monarch, how I wait thy fame." (14)

LP, Oct 14, 1774.

HC. The King is ill-advised by his ministers and Bute to encourage civil war; he should repeal the acts that are responsible.

74-194. To the Right Hon. Frederick Bull, Esq; Lord Mayor.

"Happy the man, howe'er ordain'd his fate." (34)

L Eve Post, Jan 1, 1774.

HC. Praise of Lord Mayor Frederick Bull for standing firm for the freedom of the subject in the contest between an arbitrary Parliament and the City of London.

74-195. To the Town of Boston, in America.

"O Boston! seated on that Indian Sea." (8)

St J's C, May 10, 1774.

HC. A reaction to the tea party: the Bostonians were protesting English avarice; hence the destruction of tea was justified.

74-196. Cancelled.

74-197. The Triumvirate.

"F-x, H-e, P-p-k, strange triumvirate." (22)

MJ, Aug 16, 1774.

HC. Satiric characters of Charles James Fox, and two other persons. Fox's ambiguous nature is described: gambler and orator. But he is "devoid of principles."

74-198. Truth.

"That Nation never can continue long." (8)

St J's C, Aug 16, 1774.

HC. A protest against bribes and corruption, the Quebec Act, and hypocrisy.

74-199. Two Lines to the Worthy Electors of the City and Liberty of Westminster.

"Percy for Westminster again, upon my life." (2)

MJ, Oct 27, 1774.

Epigram. Lord Percy is running again for election to the House of Commons, but he is unfit for the seat.

74-200. Tyranny.

"Where Laws have fix'd the Bounds of Right and Wrong." (4)

St J's C, Feb 26, 1774.

HC. Where there is law, there is no tyranny; tyrants break the law and hurt their subjects.

74-201. Verses addressed to the City of London, on the Lord Mayor's Day, 1774.

"Great queen of nations! empress of the sea!" (28)

T&C 6 (Nov 1774), 607.

Quatrains. An objection to the present city administration who dishonor the dignity of their place, being factious and partisan.

74-202. Verses against the Satirical Scribblers of the Age.

"Ye wanton scribblers of the age." (12)

LP, Nov 14, 1774.

OC. Advice to satirists to cease vilifying men of merit.

74-203. Verses, occasioned by Mr. Wilkes's being elected to serve the Office of Lord Mayor of this City for the Year ensuing . . . .

"Once more, in sacred Freedom's Praise." (30)

PA, Oct 17, 1774.

Sixains. In support of Wilkes against those aldermen, "ministerial Tools," who had prevented Wilkes from being chosen twice before as mayor of London.

74-204. Verses occasioned by seeing the number of Songs in the public Papers, on the late Election for this County.

"Ye yeomen of Kent." (18)

KG, Nov 2, 1774.

Ode. Objection to the election songs in Kent for Thomas Knight and Edward Dering.

74-205. Verses on an Officer who Lost his Life at the Havannah. By a Lady.

"Virgins attend, and let kind pity move." (44)

Lady's M 5 (Jan 1774), 47.

HC. A young woman mourns the death of her lover at the Havannah, during the war against France and Spain. His corpse is returned to her!

74-206. Verses sacred to the Memory of the late General Wolfe.

"While Greece and Rome their dauntless heroes boast." (27)

St J's M 1 (Apr 1774), 143-4.

HC. Wolfe is not yet forgotten.

74-207. Versification of Gen. Gage's Proclamation for the Encouragement of Virtue, in Imitation of his Pious Sovereign. A Proclamation.

"To all the pretty girls and boys." (60)

L Eve Post, Nov 26, 1774.

Quatrains. Ironic satire on Gen. Gage (through his persona) who wishes to pacify the seditious colonists of Massachusetts. (Taken from the American Essex Gazette, printed at Salem.)

74-208. A Vision. The Colossus of the North; or The Striding Boreas.

"Rebelling rascals." (18)

HM 4 (Dec 1774), 695-6; LM 43 (Oct 1774), 520.

Quotes Marvell's lines on the Parliament of 1665 and applies them to the end of the present Parliament. Satire on North in original verses -- on North's power to bribe venal courtiers. See 74-220, the same verses in a print.

74-209. [When tyrants on the Continent were spread.]

"When tyrants on the Continent were spread." (11)

MJ, Aug 30, 1774.

HC. Liberty has gone west to America; and in the coming conflict America will win, despite Gage, Bernard, and Hutchinson.

74-210. Whitehead, William.
Ode for his Majesty's Birth-Day, June 4, 1774. By Wm. Whitehead, Esq; Poet-Laureat.

"Hark! -- or does the Muse's ear." (38)

Daily Advertiser, Jun 4, 1774; G, Jun 4, 1774; GM 44 (Jun 1774), 279; KG, Jun 4, 1774; Lady's M 5 (Jun 1774), 329; Lloyd's 34 (Jun 3, 1774), 530; L Eve Post, Jun 2, 1774; LP, Jun 3, 1774; M Chron, Jun 4, 1774; PA, Jun 4, 1774; PL, Jun 4, 1774: St J's C, Jun 2, 1774; St J's M 1 (Jun 1774), 239-40; Say's, Jun 11, 1774; & L Chron 35 (Jun 2-4, 1774), 534; LM 43 (Jun 1774), 296-7.

Pindaric ode. Whitehead prophesies the return of the prodigal to the parent, and of harmony and filial love.

74-211. Whitehead, William.
Ode for the New Year, Written by William Whitehead, Esq; Poet Laureat, and set to Music by Dr. Boyce, Master of the King's Band of Musicians.

"Pass but a few short fleeting years." (32)

G, Jan 1, 1774; GM 44 (Jan 1774), 37; KG, Jan 1, 1774; Lloyd's 34 (Dec 31, 1773-Jan 3, 1774), 5; L Chron 35 (Dec 30, 1773-Jan 1, 1774), 8; L Eve Post, Dec 30, 1773-Jan 1, 1774; LM 43 (Jan 1774), 42; LP, Dec 31, 1773-Jan 3, 1774; PA, Jan 1, 1774; St J's C, Dec 30, 1773-Jan 1, 1774.

Pindaric ode. Britain's mighty naval power is used to defend the country against "insulting foes" and to keep the peace in the world. See a critique of Whitehead's "New Year's Ode for 1774" in "To Paul Whitehead, Esq;" 74-186.

74-212. [Who has not seen a musket ramm'd.]

"Who has not seen a musket ramm'd." (12)

MJ, Sep 17, 1774.

Sixains, a simile. There will be an explosion because of oppressive tax bills -- and it will be at Boston.

74-213. Why are we daily pestered with Squibs flying about between the two Parties?

"Strange so much difference should be." (6)

KG, Nov 2, 1774.

OC. Cynicism about the division of parties in the Kent election (between Thomas Knight and Edward Dering). (These lines illustrate one type of attitude towards the election.)

74-214. Wilkes and Bull. Britannia to the Livery of London.

"Ye London Livery -- take care." (8)

M Chron, Oct 5, 1774.

OC. Advice to vote for Wilkes or Bull as Lord Mayor, not Esdaile or Kennet, because they will be "true to freedom."

74-215. Wilkes's Omnipotence. On the Illuminations on the Night of his Election for Middlesex.

"To shew our Power, my Friends, this glorious Night." (2)

St J's C, Oct 22, 1774.

Epigram. Wilkes celebrates his election to the House for Middlesex. All the lights go on, transforming night to day.

74-216. The Wise Men of Gotham, and the Goose. A Fable. By a Bostonian.

"Since speaking the truth is to danger allied." (c. 315)

T&C 6 (Jun 1774), 325-7; (July 1774), 381-2.

Anapest tetrameter couplets. Satire, in the form of a fable, on the British who will destroy the colonies because of greed. Cited are the Stamp Act, Boston.

74-217. A Wish.

"When shall we see again Religion's Pow'r." (2)

St J's C, Aug 13, 1774.

Epigram. Satire on the bishops who voted for the Quebec Bill.

74-218. The Wolf and the Porcupine: Or, The M[inistr]y and the Americans. Another Political Fable.

"A Wolfe of state, and on full scent." (90)

M Chron, Dec 31, 1774.

Sixains. An animal fable that illustrates the difficulty Britain will have in subduing the Americans.

Prints

74-219. [Britain, America, at length be Friends.]

"Britain, America, at length be Friends." (10)

LM 43 (1774), frontispiece.

HC. Britain and America have many things in common and must come to terms and unite, for together they will be omnipotent. See 74-34.

74-220. The Colossus of the North; or the Striding Boreas.

"See our Colossus stride with Trophies crown'd." (2 + 18)

Engr. with epigram in OC. LM 43 (Oct 1774), 520; HM 4 (Dec 1774), 695-6.

George 5242 (V, 175-6).

Lord North succeeds in bribing many MP's and securing a majority for his ministry in the late elections. See 74-208.

74-221. The Court Cotillion, or the Premiers New Parl*****T Jig.

"Rouze, Britons, Rouze! behold thy staggering State." (4)

Engr. for the Whimsical Repository, Dec 1, 1774.

George 5244 (V, 176-7).

Quatrains. America, England, and Scotland are being weakened and destroyed by disunity. Concord, however, will make Britain great.

74-222. A New Method of Macarony Making, as Practised at Boston.

"For the Custom House Officers landing the Tea." (4)

Engr. with anapest tetrameter couplets. October 12, 1774.

George 5232 (V, 168-9). Halsey, pp. 92, 94.

Satire on a Boston customs officer, here being tarred and feathered for trying to collect the duty on tea.

74-223. The St[ates]man on Stilts, or a Prime M[iniste]r in his Undress.

"A Lyon for Paws, for a Noddle an Ass." (4)

Engr. with epigram in couplets. December 1, 1774.

George 5243 (V, 176).

Satire on Lord North for ruining Britain, her financial state and her commerce.

1775 Books & Pamphlets

75-1. Barebones, Ebenezer, pseud.
Venality, A Poem.
London: Axtell, 1775. 5-30p.

"Thy Pow'r, O Gold! omnific all confess." (551)

Notices: L Chron 37 (Jun 29, 1775), 621.

Copies: NUC CtY.

HC. Allegorical satire on the corruption by the court and administration, particularly Grenville, Grafton, North, and (to a lesser degree) Sandwich. Those (political) savages would suppress "The Rights of Men, of God, of Nature," as they are venally motivated by gold. Allusion to the Boston Port Act (1. 186) and to Grenville's plan to tax America (11. 459-90). Cited also is Wilkes.

75-2. Battle of Bunker Hill. This Song was Composed by the British after the Engagement.
N.p.: n.p., [1775]. Broadside.

"It was on the seventeenth by break of day." (96)

Copies: CtY, MHi.

Ballad. Narrates, from the British point of view, the Battle of Bunker Hill, June 17, 1775. Cited are Yankees, Cop's Hill, Charlestown, Howe, Pigot, Boston, Beacon Hill. Refers to the Americans who put up a good fight as "stout whigs," and concludes that General Howe will make them run, and that if "King Hancock" and Adams are taken they will be hanged on "that hill call'd Bacon."

75-3. The Caledoniad. A Collection of Poems, Written Chiefly by Scottish Authors.
London: Hay, 1775. 3 vols.

Copies: BL 238.f.38; NUC CtY, DLC, IEN, MB, MH.

Falconer, "The Demagogue" (vol. 2, pp. 205-25). See 66-7.
[Song] "A Scheme for Reducing the High Price of Provisions. A Cantata" (vol. 3, pp. 64-8). See Serials 72-87.

75-4. Cave, Jane (afterwards Winscom).
On the First General Fast after the Commencement of the Late War.

"When direful judgments pour in like flood." (40)

In Poems on Various Subjects, Entertaining, Elegiac, and Religious (Winchester: Sadler, 1783), pp. 111-14. See 83-6.

Copies: BL 11632.aaa.10, 993.c.43 (1) (1786 ed); NUC CtY, ICN, IU, MB, MH, PU.

HC. When armies clash, only the shallow cannot see that God, who creates war and peace, is lord over all. On the Fast Day, when prayers go to God for aid, souls must be inspired by pure devotion, lest prayer be offensive. Then will "just petitions" be successful.

75-5. Civil War; A Poem. Written in the Year 1775.
N.p.: n.p., [1775]. 35p.

"O Ye of England, of each blessing heirs." (730)

Sabin 13165.

Copies: BL 11633.g.39; NUC RPJCB.

BL is the proof copy with copious MS corrections and revisions, written (spring 1775) before Germain's appointment (Nov 10, 1775) and before the fighting began. Blank verse. An introductory Italian sonnet explains the motivation compelling the author to write this poem--a complaint over a "nation's sorrows" and "a nation's wrongs." Believes the prosecution of "the American civil war" to be mad and ruinous, an "ideot battle" resulting in insurrection, loss of trade, calamities. Criticizes the deluded King who wishes to coerce the Americans. Britain's genius protests this unjust war and departs for America, a land fighting to be free. Generalized, no current individuals are cited.

75-6. Colvill, Robert.
Sacred to the Memory of Col. Abercrombie, of Major Pitcairne of Dysart, and their very gallant Fellow-Officers who fell in their Country's Cause in Pursuit of Victory against the Rebels at Bunker's Hill, July 17, 1775.

"What godlike form from yon imperial car." (34)

In 77-4: Atlanta, pp. 40-1; and in 79-7: The Caledonians, pp. 40-1.

HC. Dated Sept. 1775. First published in [Edinburgh] Weekly Magazine 32 (Apr 25, 1776), 146; London Chronicle 39 (Apr 25, 1776), 404. (Also in his Poetical Works [London: Dodsley, 1789], pp. 121-3.) Colvill mourns the death of his countrymen in the bloody action on Bunker's Hill, which occurred on Jun 17, 1775. Also see 76-83.

75-7. [Combe, William]
An Heroic Epistle to the Right Honourable the Lord Craven, on his Delivering the Following Sentence at the County Meeting at Abingdon, on Tuesday November 7, 1775. "I will have it known there is respect due to a Lord."
London: Wheble, 1775. 12p.

"Too long have Britain's sons with proud disdain." (c. 120)

Notices: CR 40 (Dec 1775), 481; MR 54 (Feb 1776), 163; L Mag 45 (Jan 1776), 46; LR 2 (Dec 1775), 495-6.

Copies: BL 840.1.17 (4) (2nd ed), T.667 (4) (3rd ed); NUC CtY, DLC, MH, & TxU (1st ed), ICN (2nd ed), NcD & WU (3rd ed).

2 eds in 1775, 3rd in 1776, another in 1785.
HC. Combe satirizes Craven's crass assumption of class superiority, and concludes ironically by asking how the Americans would receive the news of the "virtues of a British Peer." (Craven, in the Opposition, voted against the coercion of America.) Cited are Massachusetts Bay and "Yanky-doodle."

75-8. Drewe, Edward.
Lines, Addressed to a Friend, On the Author's Leaving Boston in 1775, for the Cure of his Wounds Sustained at Bunker's Hill.

"Oh, Dorilas, and must we part." (148)

In _Military Sketches_ (Exeter: Thorn; London: Debrett, 1784), pp. 117-24; and in _Poems, Chiefly by Gentlemen of Devonshire and Cornwall_ (Bath: Cruttwell, 1792), vol. I, pp. 123-9.

Notices: PA, Sep 5, 1776; St J's Chron, Aug 1, 1776; West Mag 4 (Oct 1776), 542-3; W Eve Post, Sep 10, 1776.

Copies: BL 992.d.32 (Poems); NUC CSmH, MU, & NN (_Military Sketches_), CtY, DLC, ICN, IU, MB, MH, NN, & TxU (_Poems_).

Elegiac quatrains. In early versions, Dorilas (who is his friend Colonel Simcoe, then a lieutenant) is called Lycidas. The structure of the poem resembles Milton's _Lycidas_. Drewe, writing to Simcoe, complains of having to leave his friend. He writes of Boston and daring "th'unequal war," and the slaughter and death at Bunker's Hill. He is hopeful that the rebellion will be crushed and peace restored. (The text varies in the serials.) See 81-12: Richard Polwhele.

75-9. The Genius of Britain. An Ode. In Allusion to the Present Times.
London: Almon, 1775. 3-14p.

"Where roams the Genius of the British Isle." (c. 150)

   Notices: CR 39 (Feb 1775), 159; MR 52 (Apr 1775), 353; G, Feb 8, 1775; GM 45 (Feb 1775), 93; L Chron 37 (Feb 14, 1775), 156; LM 44 (Feb 1775), 92; SM 37 (Mar 1775), 150.

   Sabin 26950.

   Copies: BL 164.n.33; Bod Godwyn Pamph 1725 (missing); NUC MH, NcD, PPRF.

   Irregular Pindaric ode. Where is Freedom, the Genius of Britain, to be found? Not in Sicily, Italy, Greece, France, Spain, Switzerland, or northern Europe, but "across th'Atlantic roar." But there rebellion raises its red flag, causing the "parent breast" to bleed. In the conclusion, asks Freedom to "Be firm, but calmly firm;--maintain the rights / That Nature gives and free-born manhood claims." And should it kindle too fierce a fire, Freedom should be tempered by mercy and pity. Also in New Foundling Hospital for Wit (1786), III, 271-9.

75-10. An Heroic Epistle From Omiah To The Queen of Otaheite; Being His Remarks on the English Nation. With Notes by the Editor.
   London: Evans, 1775. 44p.

   "To thee, Great Queen! whom happier realms obey." (746)

   Notices: CR 39 (Jun 1775), 508; MR 53 (Aug 1775), 187; C Chron, Jul 17, 1775; Freeman's J, Jun 29, 1775; HM 6 (Jan 1776), 50-1; L Chron 37 (Jun 22, 1775), 589; LP, Jun 14, 16, 19, 1775; W Misc 4 (Jul 10, 1775), 346-50; M Chron, Jun 21 & 23, 1775.

   Copies: BL 11630.e.11 (7); Bod Godwyn Pamph 1714 (9).

   HC. A satiric summary of English thought and behavior at the time--socially and culturally. However, Omiah visits Parliament and observes how often the fates of empire are decided by trivial causes and how Britain seems to be led by visionary schemes, especially regarding America. He hopes for an honest minister and a king who would "swear allegiance to the rights of man," and restrain corruption. The relevant section is to be found in ll. 569-618; cited are Richmond (praised), Chatham, Lyttleton, Sandwich (belittled), Boston, and the King.

75-11. [Jephson, Robert]
   An Heroic Epistle to A Great Orator.
   London: Hookham, 1775. 12p.

   "Quixote in grain! whose Patriotic rage." (194)

   Notices: CR 40 (Sep 1775), 245; MR 53 (Aug 1775), 187.

   Copies: MH.

HC. Satire on Chatham in the style of an ironic panegyric. Humorously ridicules Chatham, patriot and "imperious demagogue," his extravagant rhetoric, the ambiguity of his expression, and the inconsistency of his principles. America and tar and feathers are alluded to (ll. 150, 179). (Ascribed to Jephson in a contemporary hand.)

75-12. Nugent, Robert Craggs, Earl Clare.
Verses Addressed to the Queen with a New Year's Gift of Irish Manufacture.
London: Dodsley, 1775. 11p.

"Could poor Ierne gifts afford." (118)

Notices: CR 39 (Jan 1775), 77-8; MR 52 (Mar 1775), 269-71; DJ, Jan 12, 1775; G Eve Post, Jan 14, 1775; L Chron 37 (Jan 10, 1775), 33; LM 44 (Jan 1775), 39; LP, Jan 9, 1775; SM 37 (Jan 1775), 41.

Copies: BL T.655 (22), 161.1.43, 11641.g.18 (2nd ed); NUC CtY, ICU, MB, MiU, NcD, TxU.

Octosyllabic couplets. Complaint at the miserable state of the Irish because of English trade restraints. The American rebellion is mentioned and related to the Irish struggle for equality with the English in this plea for the abolition of British trade restrictions upon Irish manufactures. See the parody, 75-24.

75-13. Ode to the British Empire.
Dublin: Ewing, 1775. 15p.

"Lov'd Liberty! who oft in antient times." (210)

Notices: CR 39 (May 1775), 425; MR 53 (Jul 1775), 87; SM 37 (May 1775), 265.

Copies: NUC DLC, MH.

Regular Horatian ode. A vigorous criticism of the British government for its oppressive and tyrannical policy regarding America, in opposition to the spirit of Magna Carta and freedom. Places the blame for the direction Britain is taking towards ruin and the destruction of "charter'd Rights" upon a venal and corrupt Parliament. The temple where Pym, Hampden, Vane, Russell, and Sidney fanned freedom's fires is polluted; and these are the legislators who wish to enslave America! Ireland should help America in their struggle. Cited also are Scotland, Bute, Chatham, taxation, Wolfe, Braddock.

75-14. Penrose, Thomas.
Address to the Genius of Britain. By the Rev. Thomas Penrose, Curate of Newbury, Berks.
London: Crowder, [1775]. 5-15p.

"Come, genial spirit, to the earnest call." (162)

Notices: CR 40 (Jul 1775), 81; MR 53 (Aug 1775), 188; LM 44 (Nov 1775), 593; LR 2 (Jul 1775), 83-5; SM 37 (Jul 1775), 391; WM 56 (Jul 1782), 400-1.

Copies: BL 11633,ee,4; NUC CtY, MB.

Blank verse. Urges Britain to be reconciled with America, to remember the peaceful, prosperous times, in contrast to the present impoverished, depressed state of the colonies and England. Asks the spirit of Britain to whisper forgiveness and mercy in King George's ear. (Also in 81-8 : Poems, pp. 38-47.)

75-15. -----.
Donnington Castle.

"Blow the loud trump of war,--wide to the gale." (49)

In 81-8 : Poems, pp. 93-6.

Blank verse. Probably written at the time of the fighting early in 1775. Against the use of coercion in the American colonies. If anyone enjoys the destruction caused by civil war, let him view the ruins of Donnington Castle, which should teach an eloquent lesson. There Chaucer had entertained "the variegated groupe" within its ancient walls. But now all is changed!

75-16. -----.
Flights of Fancy.
London: Walter; Newbury: Willis, 1775. 22p.

The Helmets, A Fragment. "--'Twas midnight--every mortal eye was closed." (71) pp. 3-9.

The Carousal of Odin. "Fill the honeyed bev'rage high." (44) pp. 11-14.

Madness. "Swell the clarion, sweep the string." (91) pp. 15-22.

Notices: CR 39 (May 1775), 424; MR 53 (Aug 1775), 139-42; GM 46 (Jan 1776), 31; LR 1 (May 1775), 369-73; SM 37 (May 1775), 265.

Copies: BL 11630.d.5 (5); Bod Godwyn Pamph 1730 (8); NUC CtY, ICN, IU, MH, PU, TxU.

Blank verse, and two irregular odes. In three short poems, Penrose expresses his concern over strife and dissension in England and America. From the "Argument" of "The Helmets": "the Prognostication alludes to Civil Dissention, which some have foretold would arise in England, in consequence of the Disputes with America."

Penrose is "the agonizing Priest." "The Carousal"--Odin and his vassals celebrate war. "Madness"--the spirit of madness prevails throughout the land. (Also in 81-8: Poems, pp. 23-37.)

75-17. The Plaints of Runny-Mead: A Poem. In Honour of those gallant Spirits who opposed the Tyranny of King John.
  York: Etherington, [1775]. 9p.

"'Twas on old Thames's willow-fringed bank." (128)

Notices: CR 39 (Jun 1775), 507; MR 53 (Jul 1775), 87.

Copies: BL 11632.f.58.

Elegiac quatrains. "The nymph of Runny Mead" complains of the Scotch influence that, by means of "slavery and gold," has banished freedom and virtue. Through their tyrannical policies, the servile members of Parliament have deprived the peasantry of their land and forced them to emigrate or to starve. Now these "scourgers of Britannia's land" are oppressing Americans, attempting to force them beneath the rod of their tyrant power. Criminal oppression is felt everywhere. Britons must resist in the spirit of the nobles of the past who gave us Magna Charta, and help "wounded Freedom"; else she will expire.

75-18. The Political Looking-Glass. Humbly Dedicated to the King.

Notices: CR 39 (Jun 1775), 508; M Chron, Nov 29, 1774; LR 1 (Apr 1775), 297-8.

Copies: none located.

75-19. Rebellion. A Poem. Addressed to J--- W-----, Esq; Late L--d M---r of the City of L----n.
  London: Mathews, 1775. 5-24p.

"That glorious flame, bright idol of the age." (c. 300)

Notices: CR 40 (Nov 1775), 405; MR 54 (Feb 1776), 165; LM 45 (Mar 1776), 160; SM 37 (Nov 1775), 622.

Copies: BL 11630.b.1 (2), 164.n.31; NUC CtY.

HC. A Tory satire. Condemns the infamous votaries of rebellion, "whether of Boston, London, or Mile-end," especially Wilkes, villainous demagogue, "great author of domestic woes." Objects to the "city harangues . . . entreating success to American rebellion." Accuses the City magistrates and aldermen of being republicans and traitors, fostering Boston's discord and sedition and Britain's fall.

Cited are Hancock (compared with Wilkes), Warren, Sawbridge, P---r, Maskell, and C[amde]n (?).

75-20. Regatta. A Poem. Dedicated to the Right Honourable Thomas Lord Lyttelton.
London: Kearsly, 1775. 14p.

"When genial zephyrs sport on purple wings." (c. 200)

Notices: CR 39 (Jun 1775), 507; MR 52 (Jun 1775), 553; L Chron 37 (Jun 22, 1775), 581; LP Jun 26, 1775.

Copies: NUC CSmH.

HC. A description of the regatta on the Thames and the festivities associated with it at Ranelagh presents an optimistic view of the increasing glory of England. But the poet concludes with an ominous warning that faction and discord, the nation's "deadly foe," will cause division, decline, and ruin--all that ancient Rome suffered.

75-21. Sharp, William, Jr.
Verses to the Right Honourable John Wilkes, Lord Mayor.
London: E. & C. Dilly, [1775]. 5-14p.

"Superior to that study hard." (100)

Notices: CR 40 (Aug 1775), 162; MR 53 (Sep 1775), 263; LM 44 (Oct 1775), 536; LR 2 (Jul 1775), 86; SM 37 (Sep 1775), 509.

Copies: BL 1480.bb.1.

Prose dedication, dated May 20, 1775, to the London Livery. S. expresses his regard for them and contempt for "those Tyrants and their Abettors" who are undermining the constitution of "our once free country." He takes pleasure in "the firmness and fortitude of America," and in "the spirited exertions of the Livery of London . . . and the Freeholders of Middlesex."
Octosyllabic couplets. The verses defend Wilkes, still a patriot, although Lord Mayor of London. Samuel Johnson is cited.

75-22. [Tait, John]
The Land of Liberty, An Allegorical Poem, In the Manner of Spenser. In Two Cantos. Dedicated to the People of Great Britain.
London: Davies, 1775. ii + 61 + 1 (Glossary) p.

"All hail! ye beings, bountiful and fair." (1080)

Notices: CR 39 (Feb 1775), 159; MR 53 (Sep 1775), 262; G Mar 11, 1775; WM 28 (Apr 13, 1775), 82-3; SM 37 (Feb, Sep 1775), 99, 509.

Copies: BL 163.m.19; Bod Godwyn Pamph 1730 (9); NUC CtY, ICN, InU, MH, NN, RPB.

2nd ed in Dublin, 1775. Spenserian stanzas, political allegory. A ruler, banished by his rebellious subjects, visits three isles--Monarchy, Aristocracy, and Democracy (transformed into Anarchy), where dissension, faction, and vices prevail. Despairing, he visits the Land of Freedom, where justice reigns, and peace and concord prevail. (Is the last America? No; America is undoubtedly Tait's "Democracy.")

[Trumbull, John]
 M'Fingal: A Modern Epic Poem. Canto First, Or The Town-Meeting.
 Philadelphia: W. & T. Bradford, 1775. 40p.

Evans 14528; Sabin 97210.

Copies: NUC CSmH, CtY, DLC, MWA, PHi, RPJCB.

75-23. [-----]
 McFingal: A Modern Epic Poem. Or the Town Meeting.
 Philadelphia, Printed: London, Reprinted for J. Almon, 1776. 44p.

"When Yankies, skill'd in martial rule." (c. 1350)

Notices: CR 41 (Jun 1776), 481; MR 54 (Jun 1776), 504; GM 46 (Aug 1776), 374; L Mag 45 (Aug 1776), 438-9; LR 3 (Appendix 1776), 536-7; SM 38 (Jun 1776), 326.

Copies: BL 164.n.36; Bod Godwyn Pamph 1280; NUC CSmH, DLC, MiU-C, NN, RPJCB.

Hudibrastics. The first of the four cantos in the completed poem, 1782. Satire on the American Loyalists. McFingal, leader of the Tory faction, debates with Honorius, leader of the Whig faction. He attacks rebellious Whigs who preach foul sedition, and he defends Gage's past failures. McFingal prophecies the defeat of the rebels and the ascendancy of the Tories to power. The meeting ends in chaos. The hero's name is an obvious allusion to the Scotch influence, and particularly to James Macpherson. (1782 ed of 4 cantos first printed in Hartford; reprinted London, 1792.)

75-24. Verses Addressed to the ----- [Queen]. With a New Year's Gift of Irish Potatoes. By Lord Knows Who. In Imitation of a Late Poem.
 London: Almon, 1775. 14p.

"Could a poor Hibernian dare." (126)

Notices: CR 39 (Feb 1775), 159; MR 52 (Mar 1775), 271-2; L Chron 37 (Feb 9, 1775), 137; L Mag 44 (Feb 1775), 91; LP, Feb 8, 1775; SM 37 (Mar 1775), 150.

Copies: BL 11630.e.9; NUC CtY, IU, MH, OCU, PU.

Parody of Lord Clare's poem, 75-12. Octosyllabic couplets. Also relates the American troubles to the Irish objections to trade restrictions, but lightly satirizes the King and royal family. There are ironic allusions to the King's wish to punish Boston for dumping tea into the ocean, to "tar and feather sacrifice," to the British rejection of the American Congress, to Dartmouth's wish to have the colonies promise to end their squabbling. Asks that English trade restrictions be lifted so that the Irish can eat meat and "hope for grace." Concludes with the gift of potatoes, all he can afford, and of these verses. Lord North is cited. (The entire poem appears in London Packet on February 8, 1775.)

75-25. Yankee Doodle, or (as now Christened by the Saints of New England) The Lexington March.
London: Skillern, [1777-79?]. Broadside.

"Brother Ephraim sold his Cow and bought him a Commission." (48)

Sabin 105958-60 (this version not cited).

Copies: NUC MB, RPB.

America's earliest national song, the first American tune to become known internationally. Probably the first publication of the words was a music sheet issued in London by "Sk," Thomas Skillern, reflecting the attitude of the English establishment when the American War began near Boston in 1775. As the subtitle suggests, the song was probably published between May 15 and July 15, 1775, when the news of the battles of Lexington (April 19) and Bunker's Hill (June 17) reached London.
The first stanza refers to the capture of Louisburg in 1745 (not Amherst's recapture of this French settlement in 1758) and plainly demeans the Yankee New Englander as a coward. This low opinion of the colonial British-Americans as soldiers was to change as the war progressed. The allusion to Dr. Warren is vulgar and equally demeaning to the Yankee. See Oscar Sonneck, Report on the Star-Spangled Banner . . . Yankee Doodle (Washington: Government Printing Office, 1909); Samuel Foster Damon, Yankee Doodle [Providence, R.I.: Brown University, 1959].

75-26. The Yankies War-Hoop, or Lord North's Te-Deum for The Victorious Defeat at Boston, on the 17th of June, 1775 . . . Written by an American.
London: Bladon, 1775. 15p.

"When white headed Chads first arriv'd off the Whight." (208)

Notices: CR 40 (Sep 1775), 245; MR 53 (Oct 1775), 376; LP, Sep 27, 1775; LR 2 (Appendix 1775), 553; SM 37 (Oct 1775), 577.

Sabin 105974.

Copies: NUC CSmH, MiU-C, & RPJCB (1st ed), MH & MiU-C (2nd ed).

Dactylic tetrameter. A rollicking satiric narrative of the way in which the news of the Battle of Bunker's Hill reached the court in Gen. Gage's letter to Lord Dartmouth. Ridicules the claim of victory by the English at Bunker's Hill, although Gage had called it a defeat because so many British soldiers had died in the battle--about 2,000, including at least 92 officers, while the Americans had lost only 130. Concludes with an expression of defiance of Sandwich and all the soldiers his navy will transport, for American General Putnam "will murder 'em all." Praise of Putnam's leadership. Gower is also cited. (Captain Chads of the Cerberus brought General Gage's letter with the news about the purported victory at Bunker's Hill.)

Serials

75-27. An Acrostic Wish. [Putnam.]

"P-ut far away from this our land." (6)

KG, Jul 29, 1775.

The voice of Americans wishes the ministry to be exiled to some slavish country.

75-28. Address of the C[or]p[oration] of W[orceste]r to the K[ing].

"While suppliant realms approach'd thy Royal ear." (84)

L Eve Post, Nov 30, 1775.

HC. Satire on the loyal addressers of (Worcester) to the King.

75-29. An Address to the American Patriots.

"In lofty numbers godlike Milton sung." (30)

L Eve Post, Nov 4, 1775.

HC. Praise of the American leaders -- Washington, Putnam, Hancock -- who oppose the King's legions. Also Arthur Lee and Sam Adams are included. All are in the tradition of Cromwell who was praised by Milton, Dryden, and Waller, who inspire this poet. Satiric allusion to "pension'd Johnson, and the slave Shebbeare."

75-30. Addressed to Two Vain Disputants.

"I swell with laughter, when in warm debate." (8)

Cumb Pacq, Aug 31, 1775.

HC. Two disputants, blinded by party-rancour, cannot see the right solution to the American contest. Cited are Washington, Gage, taxes, freedom.

75-31. [Alas we mourn! Shall Liberty no more.]

"Alas we mourn! Shall Liberty no more." (23)

KG, Mar 4, 1775.

HC. A complaint that British shipwrights are given a cursed task -- to support tyranny.

75-32. Alexander's _Tears_ _and_ _Sighs_ _reversed_.

"Great [George] our [King], most pious man." (4)

LP, Oct 4, 1775.

Epigram. Satire. King George will ingloriously lose an empire.

75-33. An Alphabet for Little Masters and Misses.

"A Stands for Americans-who for Freedom fight." (21)

Freeman's Journal, Aug 29, 1775; L Eve Post, Aug 12, 1775.

An alphabet poem which pictures the present situation -- a civil war caused by the tyranny of Bute and the Scotch and a King ruled by corrupt placemen.

75-34. An Alphabet for little Masters and Misses.

"A Stands for Americans-who scorn to be slaves." (22)

L Eve Post, May 13, 1775; W Misc 4 (Jun 5, 1775), 232.

An abecedarian poem which emphasizes the justice of the American cause and blames those British responsible for the conflict. Cited are Congress, Boston, King George, Mansfield, North, Stuart (Bute), Tories, Wilkes, Archbishop of York.

75-35. Alphabetical Characters of Some of the Principal Persons in both Houses of Parliament.

"A -- was an Apsley -- a lawyer by grace." (22)
"A -- was an Abingdon -- who spoke his mind." (22)

L Eve Post, Apr 6, 1775.

Two lists. The second is more relevant -- Abingdon, Burke, Chatham, Effingham, Fox, Hartley, Richmond, Savile.

75-36. America. An Elegy.

"Tenders of Peace, and lenient means withstood." (92)

Lloyd's 37 (Aug 21, 1775), 177.

Elegiac quatrains. The poet begs for peace unlike the fanatics on both sides who push for destructive war. America must admit that it is partially wrong and that it needs Britain's parental care.

75-37. America, To General Lee.

"Let others strive, by servile arts, to gain." (24)

MJ, Apr 22, 1775; MP, Apr 24, 1775.

Elegiac quatrains. The persona America praises Gen. Lee for coming to her assistance and to fight for freedom against the tyranny of Parliament. Cited also is Gage.

75-38. American Epigram.

"Some mice deep intrench'd in a rich Cheshire cheese." (24)

New Found. Hospital for Wit (1786), IV, 239-40.

Quatrains. "From a Boston news-paper printed in October, 1775." An animal fable illustrating the moral that Americans must be free to choose their own government.

75-39. A Ballad recommended to the use of the Freeholders of Essex, on the day when their Ministerial Candidate shall be nominated by his Ministerial Uncle.

"Ye Essex Freeholders, ye good men and true." (30)

L Eve Post, Oct 7, 1775.

Song. Satire on a courtier from Essex, a supporter of North, who is politicking for his nephew. Evidence of corruption, nepotism.

75-40. [Be not surpriz'd, O Isle! thy present Woe.]

"Be not surpriz'd, O Isle! thy present Woe." (14)

St J's C, Jan 12, 1775.

HC. Anti-Scots satire. Bute, the Scottish thane, is responsible for the troubles. He should leave Britain for Rome.

75-41. Berkeley, George (Bishop of Cloyne).
Verses on the Prospect of Planting Arts and Learning in America.

"The Muse, disgusted at an age and clime." (24)

C Chron, Oct 30, 1775; Eng Chron, Sep 25, 1783; L Chron 39 (May 18, 1776), 485; SM 38 (May 1776), 266; GA, Mar 23 & Dec 8, 1778; New Foundling Hospital for Wit (1786), IV, 257-8.

Reprintings of Berkeley's famous quatrains prophetic of the great future of America: "Westward the course of empire takes its way." The Chester Chronicle reprints the verses for "this period particularly."

75-42. The Berkshire Petition Versified; to the Intent that the Children of English and American Patriots may the more easily learn it by Heart.

"We your Majesty's Subjects, most loyal in Duty." (60)

St J's C, Dec 7, 1775.

Fourteener couplets. Sir Willoughby Bertie (Earl of Abingdon) and Lord William Craven side with the Patriots against the American War; and because the Americans are unrepresented in Parliament, they believe the rebellion is justified.

75-43. The Blue-Box. Inscribed to Lord M[ansfiel]d.

"In days of yore, a fell old Witch." (16)

St J's C, Feb 16, 1775.

Quatrains. Pandora's box, source of ills, is as bad as Lord Mansfield's blue-box, which brings evil upon the country.

75-44. The Bostonians Defended.

"Why blame the wise Bostonians, pray?" (6)

G, Jan 27, 1775; KG, Mar 25, 1775.

Epigram. The Bostonians refuse to pay for Britain's security and to accept subjection.

75-45. The Bostonians to the Ministry.

"Cunning, regardless you of Civil Rules." (10)

St J's C, Jan 12, 1775.

HC. The Bostonians reject the ministerial plan, which is simply a trap to catch and punish them.

75-46. [Brave race of men! that lately shewed.]

"Brave race of men! that lately shewed." (6)

M Chron, Jul 14, 1775.

OC. A congratulation to the Americans on their victory at Ticonderoga and a wish that God grant their "just designs success."

75-47. Britain's Lamentation. See Jer. Chap. iv.

"Round all our coasts is heard the voice of woe." (36)

T&C 7 (Supp. 1775), 710-1.

Quatrains and sixains. Britain mourns the war, "stern Discord's stormy roar."

75-48. Britannia's Address to the Sons of Liberty in New England. In the Character of the Goddess of Liberty. A Parody on Shakespeare's Mulberry Tree.

"Behold here the fruit, which grace this fair tree." (48)

M Chron, Aug 27, 1779.

Song, "published at Boston in the year 1775." Britain threatens to hang the rebel leaders on the Liberty Tree -- Sam Adams, Hancock, Warren, and others.

75-49. Britannia's Charge. Addressed to the Minority Members, previous to their Meeting in Parliament on Thursday next.

"My happier sons! whom yet Corruption has." (53)

L Eve Post, Oct 21, 1775.

Blank verse. Parodied from passages of Shakespeare. Advice to Chatham to lead the opposition, supported by Rockingham and Richmond, Shelburne and Burke. This union will be effective against tyrants.

75-50. Britannia's Genius.

"In sable robes Britannia's Genius stands." (64)

L Chron 38 (Jul 18, 1775), 69; SM 37 (Jul 1775). 393.

Elegiac quatrains. Untitled in L Chron. The poet protests the American rebellion because it is not justified. He expresses fears that France, Spain, and Austria will help the rebels, and indignation that it is supported by traitors at home. He concludes with the hope that it will be crushed. Probably by William Woty.

75-51. A Cabinet Dialogue.

"Says D--nb--gh to D--dl--y, I'll talk to those Fellows." (8)

MJ, Nov 23, 1775; PA, Nov 25, 1775.

Hexameter couplets. Ironic satire. These members of the "cabinet," Basil Feilding (Earl of Denbigh) and John Ward (Viscount Dudley), both Tories, worry that Lord North may not persevere. Signed "Americanus."

75-52. Caesar's Lamentation and Consolation. A Loyal Song. Tune -- Oh that I ne'er had been married, &c.

"O that I ne'er had been crowned." (48)

M Chron, Aug 12, 1775.

Song. Quatrains with chorus. Satire on the King, whose persona insists the colonial rebellion must be suppressed with the aid of his "friends, the [Scotch] Jacobites" and Roman Catholics. He enjoys the prospect of "French Canadians" subduing the Protestants and his soldiers enslaving Boston. Cited are Mansfield, Bute, North, and Parliament.

75-53. The Cans. A Song. By G--S--C--. Tune -- Ye Warwickshire Lads, &c.

"Come listen each grave politician." (48)

HM 5 (April 1775), 249; MP, Mar 2, 1775.

A drinking song belittling the Americans, yet at the same time warning British soldiers to be careful lest they be "pickled in feathers and tar."

75-54. Casca's Epistle to Lord Mansfield.

"Can you, my Lord, who serve despotic Ends." (c. 320)

Crisis 17 (May 13, 1775), 109-16.

Revised for pamphlet publication in 1778: see 78-15.

75-55. Casca's Epistle to Lord North.

"To you, my Lord, these honest Lines I send." (c. 240)

Crisis 18 (May 20, 1775), 117-22.

HC. Satire on the court: the King, Bute, and his tool North. Accuses North of corrupting MP's to secure their votes against America; and the King, under Bute's influence, of oppressing America. Cited are Boston, Mansfield, "Tory" Samuel Johnson who called those traitors who wished success to America.

75-56. Christmas.

"Hail social season! cries the man of mirth." (8)

L Eve Post, Dec 21, 1775.

HC. The savage war against America does not mix well with the Christmas spirit.

75-57. Cole, R.
Thirtieth of January for Ever and Ever.

"That day, when, smote by patriotic power." (24)

M Chron, Feb 3, 1775.

Quatrains. A Tory defense of the day commemorating the execution of Charles I. Satire on the dissenting "saints" and patriots who are ready for another martyrdom in their attempts to destroy the Episcopal Church. Wilkes is cited. Answered in the M Chron, Feb 9, 1775, by one who obviously detests Charles the Martyr.

75-58. A Colloquial Extempore, by the Three Heads of Cerberus, On a Late Conference at St. James's.

"Britons of old one George could boast." (12)

L Eve Post, Dec 21, 1775.

Quatrains. Satire on Germain and the King. George Townsend (Viscount Temple), George Germain, and George III confer -- the first helped conquer Quebec; the second saved his neck at Minden ("Alas! for poor America!"); but of the third nothing can be said.

75-59. [The Colonists are fixed as any rock.]

"The Colonists are fixed as any rock." (4)

G, Jan 12, 1775.

Epigram. English merchants, suffering from the American boycott, object to the government's policies.

Colvill, Robert.

Sacred to the Memory of those most gallant Officers and Soldiers who fell in their Country's Cause . . . , [Bunker's Hill], June 17, 1775.

See Colvill, 76-83.

75-60. A Common Prayer for the Present Times.

"A Common prayer for the present times." (28)

HM 6 (Jan 1776), 64; LM 44 (Dec 1775), 655; WM 31 (Feb 1, 1776), 178.

Hymn in quatrains. A prayer that America and Britain re-unite because they are "Ally'd by blood, and interest too" and that God bring to light all rebels, including rebels to God and to man (meaning those who wage war).

75-61. Congratulatory Ode, addressed to Lord G[eorg]e G[er]m[ain]e.

"My Lord, I hail your spotless Fame." (54)

PA, Dec 5 & 7, 1775; An Asylum for Fugitives (1776), I, 91-3; New Foundling Hospital for Wit (1786), II, 92-5.

The first printing in PA was corrected and enlarged in the second; and the New Foundling Hospital prints a version of sixty lines. -- Regular (Horatian) ode in sixains. A severe personal satire on Lord George Germain, recently appointed Secretary of State for the Colonies, after Dartmouth's resignation. Germain's Minden past is exploited; however, his reputation was saved by his duel with Governor George Johnstone, Dec 17, 1770.

75-62. A Congratulatory Ode, addressed to Lord North.

"Sam Johnson in the true Sublime." (36)

PA, Oct 27, 1775; New Foundling Hospital for Wit (1786), II, 87-9.

Regular ode in sixains. A Whig patriot ironically satirizes the premier Lord North, his cause and his supporters -- Samuel Johnson, Jacobites, Birmingham, Whitehead, Shebbeare. Also cited are Stephen Sayre (an American, once Sheriff of London), sent to the Tower for instigating a plot to seize George III; Catherine Macaulay, Gage. This ode could be by William Mason.

75-63. The Contrast.
(Occasioned by the publication of an Answer to Mr. Burke's celebrated Speech on Taxation, wherein the author Modestly asserts, all that Gentleman's reasonings are Entirely Refuted.)

"Shebbeare and Burke, let none compare ye." (6)

L Eve Post, Apr 22, 1775.

Little Shebbeare cannot be compared to the celebrated and great patriot Burke.

75-64. The Counter Addressers. Extempore.

"The Citizens meet, and combining their Votes." (8)

Lloyds 37 (Oct 20, 1775), 382; L Chron 38 (Oct 19, 1775), 392; LM 44 (Nov 1775), 597; PA, Oct 20, 1775; SM 37 (Oct 1775), 579.

Epigram. Petitioners disagree on the Americans; but the King, agent of heaven, will know what to do.

75-65. A Curse.

"May all the evils of Pandora's box." (20)

M Chron, Mar 8, 1775.

HC. These couplets place a violent curse on all the corrupt priests and politicians of the government.

75-66. The Decree.

"As Jupiter in a council decreed." (30)

Freeman's J, May 23, 1775.

Hexameter couplets. Classical fable, on the dangers of force in the conflict between Britain and America. America may suffer the same fate as Ireland. Bute, North, and Mansfield are cited.

75-67. A Dialogue.

"Says dame Joan to her spouse, Of what use can it be." (16)

MP, Jul 26, 1775.

Quatrains. Husband and wife object to the Court's war policy, favoring Scot Jacobites, encouraging civil war, endangering the throne. Cited are the King, rebels, ministers.

75-68. The Dilemma.

"In ev'ry civil war this hazard's run." (6)

DJ, Jul 4, 1776; Freeman's J, Jul 20, 1775; KG, Jun 28, 1775; L Chron 37 (Jun 27, 1775), 615; St J's C, Jun 25, 1775.

Epigram. Those advocating a ruinous civil war, from which nothing can be gained, must be mad.

75-69. An Englishman's Prayer.

"O Watchful Heav'n! if Thane and Co. intend." (8)

St J's C, Aug 10, 1775.

HC. A prayer that if Bute intends to bring in Roman Catholicism through the Quebec Act, "another William" will come. (King William; and William, Duke of Cumberland.)

75-70. Epigram.

"Do justice to thyself, O English wight." (8)

Freeman's J, Jul 11, 1775; St J's C, Apr 29, 1775.

HC. On the conflict with the colonies. The King and his subjects must know what their rights and responsibilities are; otherwise there will be tyranny or rebellion.

75-71. Epigram.

"One being ask'd, what part Great Britain bore." (4)

L Chron 37 (Jan 14, 1775), 53; St J's C, Jan 12, 1775.

Britain no longer has integrity: consider the evidence of Boston and Quebec. (Britain encourages "fraud and superstition.")

75-72. An Epigram.

"Sir Courtly Plume, a borough town to buy." (8)

W Misc 3 (Feb 13, 1775), 472.

HC. Satire. Evidence of election corruption (buying votes) that backfires.

75-73. Epigram.

"Stuck on a Pole thy Head at Temple-Bar." (12)

Freeman's J, Jul 20, 1775; St J's C, Jun 27, 1775.

HC. England needs new leadership; North must go, and Massachusetts would then be happy.

75-74. Epigram.

"Your Money or your Life, on Shooter's Hill." (6)

St J's C, Aug 10, 1775.

Satire on Parliament. What is considered robbery here, our senate says is proper in America.

75-75. Epigram. By an Hollander.

"Though, countryman, we may perhaps awhile." (10)

Freeman's J, Jul 8, 1775.

HC. Thoughts or fears of a Dutch protestant that the present English government is acting irrationally and against the protestant cause. Boston, Quebec, the Stuarts are cited.

75-76. An Epigram designed as an Apology for the Rancour and Inveteracy which the Scotch express against the Americans.

"Sweet Scotia, weep, and thy hard Fate deplore." (6)

PA, Aug 28, 1775; MJ, Aug 26, 1775.

Ironic lines against the Scotch who are now hostile towards "stubborn Yankies" because the Americans have displaced them as rebel subjects of the King.

75-77. Epigram. John Bull, the Clothier, in the Colonies.

"John having hurt his patrimonial Store." (6)

Freeman's J, Aug 1, 1775; St J's C, Mar 18, 1775.

England has tried to "remedy" its economy by bribery and by taxing America, but has only succeeded in starting a civil war.

75-78. Epigram on a Late Publication, entitled, "An Answer to the printed Speech of Edmund Burke, Esq;"

"Let Burke, let Barre -- all the patriot band." (4)

L Eve Post, May 4, 1775.

Satire on John Shebbeare, the hired Tory pamphleteer who wrote against Burke and Barre. N.B. the pun on Shebbeare's name: Old Crop, Shabby Ears.

75-79. Epigram. On our Late Glorious Losses in America.

"'The World well lost!' -- While Anthony could gain." (4)

LP, Sep 27, 1775.

King George is losing his empire but gaining the hatred of his subjects.

75-80. Epigram. On Reading the Late Protest.

"The Americans are Cowards, and will yield." (4)

PA, Apr 3, 1775.

Irony directed at the ministry on the supposed cowardice of the Americans. (The "protest" refers to the minority assertions that the Americans are being driven to fight.) Mansfield, Sackville, and Sandwich are cited, and it was Sandwich who had declared (March 16, 1775) that the Americans were cowards, easily coerced.

75-81. Epigram on the Advice given by a great Lawyer to continue the War with America.

"Grant we are wrong, says M[ansfiel]d, we must fight." (4)

St J's C, Dec 28, 1775.

Lord Mansfield is wrong to advise war with America.

75-82. Epigram. On the Contest between Great Britain and America.

"Very few are so brave, as to willingly fight." (4)

St J's C, Nov 23, 1775.

Hexameter couplets. Britons are absurd to fight America, because they are sure to lose. (In a civil war the country inevitably is the loser.)

75-83. Epigram on the Difference of Times.

"In antient times, the Roman laws decreed." (8)

L Eve Post, Dec 14, 1775.

Quatrains in couplets. Satire on war mongers. In Roman times, he who saved a life was honored; in England today, he who takes away a life is honored.

75-84. Epigram. On the Lords agreeing in Conference with the Commons, to the Amendments of the New-England Fishery Bill.

"What news to-day, says Patriot Will." (4)

L Eve Post, Mar 28, 1775.

Epigram. Both houses of Parliament should be damned for passing the New-England Fishery Bill (enacted March 30, 1775). This bill prohibited the four New England provinces from the New Foundland fishery.

75-85. Epigram on the Presentation of the Huntingdon Address, by G. Woombeel, Esq.

"Why plead thus W[oombee]l human blood to spill." (2)

L Eve Post, Dec 2, 1775.

HC. Satire on a resident merchant of Huntingdon who supports the war policy because it will mean a contract from the government. (Spelling=Wombwell.)

75-86. Epigram. To the Boston Women.

"O Boston Wives and Maids, draw near and see." (4)

Freeman's J, Aug 24, 1775; St J's C, May 20, 1775.

Satire on the English for forcing the Boston women to drink tea, or die.

75-87. Epigram. Upon Lieutenant Nun, of the Navy, being Dispatched to England by General Gage with the Account of the Defeat of the King's Troops.

"The Gen'ral, to prove all his actions are just." (4)

LP, Jun 12, 1775.

Quatrain. The news from Gage about the engagement at Lexington and Concord reaches the court.

75-88. An Epistle from John Hancock, Esq; to the Right Hon. John Wilkes, Esq; concerning the dispute between the mother country and her children.

Sent M 3 (Jun 1775), 288.

A report of a poem which was not published.

75-89. Epitaph. On a Modern Minister.

"Here lies a Statesman to his Country true." (32)

PA, Jun 22, 1775.

HC. An ironic epitaph on the death of an honest and selfless politician concerned only for the welfare of the country. Such a person never really existed.

75-90. Epitaph on the cruel Death of Crisis.

"Here to the flames poor CRISIS was consign'd." (4)

MP, Mar 8, 1775.

The journal Crisis, ordered burned by the common hangman, cannot die -- truth never dies. (No. 3 Crisis was burned March 6, 1775. But the journal continued to be printed until October 12, 1776.)

75-91. The Ethereal Orator. On Reading Mr. B[urk]e's Speeches on American Affairs.

"This pompous bubble with rhetoric blast." (13)

M Chron, Jul 11, 1775.

HC. Satire on the vacuous rhetoric of Burke, with a hint that even he cannot consider what he says is serious and true.

75-92. The Evil Effects of Rebellion and Pretended Patriotism.

"The rabble forward to rebel." (56)

M Chron, Nov 21, 1775.

Hudibrastics, imitation of Samuel Butler's Hudibras. Satire on the mob of Americans who like their ancestors, Puritan "republican fanaticks," are misled by hypocritical demagogues to criticize the government. Cited are North, Wilkes, (Samuel) Adams, Wat Tyler and Jack Straw.

75-93. Extempore.

"A Late Gazette pretends to say." (4)

PA, Jul 12, 1775.

Epigram. False news of atrocities against our soldiers generate hatred against the Americans.

75-94. An Extempore.

"To frustrate all Lord Squintum's Toils." (18)

PA, Jul 12, 1775.

Quatrains and a sixain. A vulgar solution for the conflict between the King and the City. Wilkes, "Lord Squintum," is cited.

75-95. Extempore.

"To rectify all our transmarine Disputes." (4)

PA, Jul 4, 1775.

The solution to the American problem is the execution of the ministry -- "the Mansfields, Norths, and Butes." Thus will "stop all the Discord at Concord."

75-96. Extempore Epigram on a Late Promotion.

"Let me have blood, says [George], knee-deep in blood I'll ----." (2)

L Eve Post, Nov 14, 1775.

Couplet. Objection to Germain's appointment as Secretary of State for the American Colonies -- by a King who lusts for blood. Germain is portrayed as a cruel coward.

75-97. Extempore: On Mr. W[esley]'s Calm Address.

"Great North, Lord of the milk of Alma Mater." (4)

L Chron 38 (Dec 2, 1775), 544.

Epigram. This writer abhors Wesley's Tory views on the King's divine right, views supporting tyranny which renders subjects into slaves.

75-98. Extempore. On Reading the List of the Manchester Subscriptions.

"When Manchester People subscribe." (8)

PA, Dec 8, 1775.

Epigram. Quatrains. Manchester (like Birmingham) supported the government's policy of the coercion of America. There must have been a bribe by the court.

75-99. Extempore on Seeing the Home of a Row of Houses in the New Road, changed within this week from Happy-Man Row to King's Row.

"When Kings shall cease to cherish their own brood." (4)

LP, Jan 30, 1775.

Epigram. When Kings cease to take care of their children -- the Americans, they can no longer be happy.

75-100. Extempore. On Some Dispatches being sent by General Gage with Captain Coffin.

"Alas! Lord North, deplorable's thy case." (4)

KG, Jul 12, 1775; LP, Jul 10, 1775.

Epigram. Lord North is being defied by America, and Gage sends sad tidings with his messenger Capt. Coffin.

75-101. An Extempore Song, composed in a Jovial Company. To the tune of, A light heart and a thin pair of breeches goes through the world, brave boys.

"Ye sons of true freedom and spirit." (24)

Freeman's J, Aug 26, 1775.

An American song defies Bute, North, Gage, and the court, and asserts faith in the leadership of Congress.

75-102. An Extempore to the Lord Mayor.

"Advance to mighty honours! now thy fame's compleat." (7)

G, Feb 17, 1775.

HC (irregular). Wilkes, the modern Cato, is urged to speak for the City against the threats of "a servile Court."

75-103. A Fable. Addressed to the Right Hon. Lord N--th.

"Whoever makes an unjust Claim." (42)

St J's C, Feb 7, 1775.

OC. The fable of the goose that laid golden eggs has a moral that should be applied to Anglo-American relations.

75-104. A Familiar Epistle from a Lady in the Country to her Friend in Town.

"I grant 'tis a circumstance truly vexatious." (4)

L Eve Post, Mar 30, 1775.

HC. Extract. If we continue to oppress Britons, they will revolt. (Allusion to the coercive measures of Administration in a gossipy, ostensibly non-political poem.)

75-105. A Familiar Ode, Addressed to Lord North.

"The Colour of a Boston Shilling." (54)

Ox M 12 (Nov 1775), 348; PA, Nov 8, 1775; An Asylum for Fugitives (1776), I, 87-9.

Regular (Horatian) ode in sixains. The version in Ox M lacks three stanzas and the notes. -- Satire on Lord North and his supporters, including the bishops. The King must call upon Chatham to save the state and "To end this shameful Quarrel" with America.

75-106. [Fire, Water, Women, says Van Bruin.]

"Fire, Water, Women, says Van Bruin." (6)

L Eve Post, Jul 1, 1775.

Extempore. England and America shall fall by fire and water -- meaning war between the two.

75-107. Fish and Tea. A New Song -- To an Old Tune.

"What a Court hath Old England of folly and sin." (40)

LP, Apr 26, 1775.

Song. The British intend to force taxes on America -- taxes on fish and tea -- regardless of the Opposition (Chatham, Camden, Barre, Burke, Wilkes, Glynn). But the Americans will be free. Cited are Sandwich, Johnson, and the three Generals -- Clinton, Howe, and Burgoyne.

75-108. The following Abstract of the Resolves of the General Congress, assembled at Philadelphia in 1775, is put into Metre, for the Help of Weak Memories.

"The Congress Resolves to acknowledge the King." (111)

PA, Dec 13, 1775.

Hexameter couplets. On the Declaration of the Causes and Necessity of Taking Up Arms, July 6, 1775. The resolutions of the Continental Congress are ironically parodied in order to expose the hypocritical and ridiculous motives of the rebellious Yankees. Franklin is particularly cited. The Quebec Act is also significant.

75-109. The following impudent Ballad, on the taking of Ticonderago, by the free and loyal English Americans, is now sung about the streets of London.

"The Chiefs were met, the Planters came," (44)

M Chron, Aug 14, 1775.

A ballad narrates the American capture of Fort Ticonderoga (May 13, 1775). Cited is American Gen. Easton.

75-110. The following Lines were spoken Extempore by an American Lady, on hearing that the Conquering Hero was on his passage home to England.

"From Boston comes the frighted cow." (13)

MP, Oct 5, 1775.

OC. Satire on Howe, Clinton, Burgoyne, Percy -- but praise of the American officers, Putnam, Ward, and Lee, guardians of liberty.

75-111. The following Prophecy, which from the spelling appears to have been written several hundred years back, was lately discovered in the Burying Ground of St. George the Martyr.

"In seventyne hundreyd and seventie fore." (10)

L Eve Post, Jun 13, 1775.

Irregular meter, couplets. A prophecy of corruption and civil war in 1774.

75-112. The following was sung at the Meeting of his Majesty's Tradesmen, on his Birth-day . . . To the King.

"Pardon, Great George, what here is writ." (24)

Lloyd's 36 (Jun 23, 1775), 606.

Song in triplets with a tail. Advice to the King not to surrender to the Americans, and to use all means necessary to maintain English honor.

75-113. [For he who hangs or beats out's brains.]

"For he who hangs or beats out's brains." (2)

G, Aug 10, 1775.

A defense of an attempted suicide in order to avoid fighting Americans. The prose commentary indicates that the City supports such measures expressive of opposition to the civil war.

75-114. Forty-One Lines to ---- the ----.

"Alarm'd at Woes our bleeding Brethren feel." (41)

L Eve Post, Jan 5, 1775; PA, Jan 7, 1775.

HC. A plea to King George to rid himself of such supporters as Dalrymple, Shebbeare, and Johnson, and the King's Friends, and save his honor and the people's rights at home and in America. Signed "The Ape of the Ape of Junius" in L Eve Post.

75-115. Free(th), John.
Bunker's Hill, or the Soldier's Lamentation. Tune, The Muffled Bells of Bow and Bride.

"I am a jolly soldier." (60)

The Warwickshire Medley (1776), pp. 18-20; The Political Songster, or, A Touch on the Times (Birmingham: Pearson, 1784), pp. 12-14, and (Birmingham: Pearson, 1790), pp. 26-8.

Song. Freeth, through a common soldier's persona, complains of the great losses suffered by the British at Bunker's Hill. The battle occurred on June 17, 1775; news about it reached London July 25, 1775.

75-116. Free(th), John.
A Dialogue. Tune, Push about the brisk bowl.

"To judge at this crisis which England's the best." (32)

The Warwickshire Medley (1776), pp. 56-7.

Song. Probably written late 1774-early 1775. An American and Briton dispute over "which England's the best," the Briton declaring the country spent its treasure protecting America from France, and the American responding with objections to any tax whatsoever.

75-117. Free(th), John.
Lord G[eorg]e S[ackvill]e's Promotion. Or, Minden Bravery Rewarded. Tune, Roast Beef of Old England.

"When dastards are plac'd in the list of promotions." (22)

The Warwickshire Medley (1776), pp. 65-6.

Song. Freeth objects to the appointment of Sackville to the position of Secretary of State for the Colonies, taking Dartmouth's place (Nov 10, 1775). Sackville, he says, should have been ordered executed by George II for the Minden affair. Sandwich, too, should not preside over the navy. Both men should be sent to America.

75-118. Free(th), John.
The Soldier's Complaint. Tune, The Old Woman of Grimstone.

"In pitiful plight." (48)

The Warwickshire Medley (1776), pp. 129-30.

Song. Satire on a contractor, court appointed tool of North and Bute, whom the government chooses to represent Herefordshire and the poor. The soldier, after Bunker's Hill, protests this exploitation of the poor people. The Scotch are also included in the satire.

75-119. Free(th), John.
The Times.

"'Tis a shame to the land, and a cursed vexation." (30)

The Warwickshire Medley (1776), pp. 24-5; L Chron 19 (Feb 25, 1766), 200.

Song. A complaint at the starvation of the poor caused by corruption, enclosures, decline of commerce, oppressive taxation. Reprints 66-A, Freeth.

75-120. From St. Stephen's Chapel, Nov. 21. An Ode. Addressed to the Author of the Monody in this Day's Public Advertiser.

"O Bard! whene'er you rhime again." (66)

PA, Nov 24, 1775; New Foundling Hospital for Wit (1786), II, 135-7.

Regular ode in sixains. An answer to "A Monody in the House of Commons," 75-158. Satire on the leaders of the majority -- Sandwich (butcher and robber), Sackville, Cornwall, the "Scotch gang": Gilbert Elliot, Dundas, Wedderburne, Welbore Ellis, Thurloe; Rigby, and North. The point is that the ship of state will founder as such leaders plan to destroy America.

75-121. A General Index to the Occurrences in June 1775, in Mock Heroic Verse.

"The trial and condemnation of the two Perreaus." (22)

M Chron, Jul 3, 1775.

Hexameter couplets; "mock heroic" review of events and attitudes in June 1775, including comment on the coercive measures against the colonies, the maladministration of the North cabinet that subverts English freedom and ruins commerce, the City's petition against coercion rejected by the King, and the rearming of France and Spain.

75-122. The Ghost of America, A Vision.

"Methought, dreaming I entered the gallery of St. Stephen." (c. 60)

LM 44 (Jan 1775), 40-1.

Imitation of the banquet scene in Shakespeare's Macbeth, III, iv. The ghost of America startles Lord North at the Boston banquet. Cited are Fletcher Norton, Jenkinson.

75-123. The Gypsies. Sung at the Goosetree Club Masquerade.

"As we Gypsies pretend to that wonderful art." (32)

L Chron 37 (Mar 4, 1775), 220; MP, Mar 3, 1775; Ox M 12 (Mar 1775), 88.

Song. The gypsies declare they can divine anything, even the rise and fall of politicians, despite what may be happening in Boston and with Gage. (An example of the American problem entering the most innocent of works.)

75-124. [Hail Boston! Of the saints thou blest retreat.]

"Hail Boston! Of the saints thou blest retreat." (8)

LP, Jul 5, 1775.

Hexameter couplets. Praise of Boston, the home of pious and virtuous "saints."

75-125. [Half dunce, half rebel, thy envenom'd sting.]

"Half dunce, half rebel, thy envenom'd sting." (9)

MP, Nov 27, 1775.

HC. Satire. A loyal defense of the King from malevolent attacks in the press.

75-126. Hastings, Thomas.
On his Majesty's Coronation Day, September 22, 1775.

"High on the hostile hill." (65)

M Chron, Sep 22, 1775.

Irregular Pindaric ode. A prayer that America will be crushed, peace restored, and a reconciliation between America and Britain effected.

75-127. [He that can levy War with all Mankind.]

"He that can levy War with all Mankind." (30)

Crisis 20 (Jun 3, 1775), 133-4.

HC. Concluding verses to a prose essay portray a vicious tyrant. The point is unmistakable as the essay begins with a remark on Administration ordering the "Cerberus" with the three generals -- Burgoyne, Howe, and Clinton -- to America and an attack on Samuel Johnson for his anti-Whig dogmatic ideology.

75-128. The Hen and the Golden Egg; a Fable; Addressed to the Minister.

"Had Aesop been living, what mortal so able." (32)

New Found. Hospital for Wit (1786), IV, 238-9; Jeffery Dunstan, Fugitive Pieces (1789), pp. 78-9.

Irregular lines. Satire on British attempt at taxing America. The fable blames British greed for destroying a profitable relationship between Americans and Britons.

75-129. History of the Brutish Ministry.

"In former days, when all the brute creation." (46)

L Eve Post, May 4, 1775.

HC. Animal satire directed against the Scotch, the despotic ministry; but supportive of the rebellious Americans and their sympathizers in England. Predicts that it will not be possible to subdue the Americans.

75-130. Horace's Seventh Ode Imitated. To the People of England.

"Where? Madmen, where? Why not this fury curb'd." (20)

W Misc 3 (Mar 27, 1775), 622-3.

HC. Objection to a mad civil war from which only France and Spain can gain.

75-131. Howard, Robert.
Almeyda, or the Rival Queens.

"Pronounce it not." (30)

Freeman's J, Feb 21, 1775.

Blank verse. Howard's 17th century play is quoted in reaction to the impending civil war with America. In effect, this quotation expresses opposition to administration policies.

75-132. Impromptu on a Late Pamphlet.

"Taxation is no Tyranny, I swear." (10)

L Eve Post, Apr 6, 1775.

HC (uneven or irregular). Attack on Jacobite Johnson for his Taxation No Tyranny -- Samuel Johnson writing for Bute, his master.

75-133. Impromptu on Hearing Alderman H[ayle]y had chartered his ship, the John Wilkes, Capt. Hall to carry troops to Boston.

"Hancock and Otis, patriots bold." (8)

MJ, Feb 7, 1775; MP, Feb 8, 1775.

Quatrains. A London alderman, George Hayley, who had chartered his ship named "John Wilkes" to carry troops to Boston, is berated for his betrayal. Hancock & Otis are cited. (Hayley was the brother-in-law of Wilkes.)

75-134. Impromptu. On Seeing Lord Mansfield's Picture in the Print Shops.

"To please the eye the sculptor's skill is seen." (6)

MJ, Oct 3, 1775.

HC. Lord Mansfield is cruel and heartless.

75-135. Impromptu. On the Sailing of the Cerberus, with the three General Officers on the American Expedition.

"Behold the Cerberus th' Atlantic plow." (3)

GM 45 (May 1775), 246; KG, Apr 22, 1775; L Eve Post, Apr 20, 1775; WM 28 (Jun 15, 1775), 370.

Ironic satire(?). Generals Burgoyne, Clinton, and Howe sail to America for the first campaign against the Americans. "Bow, wow, wow" in the last line is the title of a popular song at the time and ironically refers to the name of the vessel, the Cerberus.

75-136. [In former times the poets feign'd.]

"In former times the poets feign'd." (28)

L Eve Post, Apr 25, 1775.

Quatrains. The ministry have ordered the three generals to proceed on the hellish Cerberus to do the bloody deed, to impose a tyranny on America.

75-137. [In George's days, there liv'd a wight.]

"In George's days, there liv'd a wight." (44)

MP, Jul 5, 1775.

Ballad. We Britons must uphold North and his policies against the (minority) patriots and Americans. We drove the French out with Wolfe, and never thought the Bostonians would take this "land of plenty" from us. We must now fight again to re-possess the land.

75-138. [Indians assert, that wheresoe'er they roam.]

"Indians assert, that wheresoe'er they roam." (4)

KG, Sep 27, 1775.

Epigram. Satire on the Scotch. The Scotch would not fight if, upon death, their spirits had to return home, as Indians believe.

75-139. Ingratum si dixeris, omnia dixeris. By a Lad of Twelve Years of Age.

"Be grateful to your friends -- is Nature's voice." (12)

GM 45 (Aug 1775), 396.

HC. Americans should heed the dictate of nature and be grateful for the friendship of Britain. They should be "grateful subjects, to a gracious King."

75-140. Innocent the Third.

"Chaste, pious, Innocent the Third." (48)

LP, Jan 23, 1775.

Quatrains. Satire on George III who, to convince his subjects that he is manly, will destroy the colonies and England.

75-141. [Inscription: To the Memory of . . . .]

"To the Memory of / Robert Monroe, Jonas Parker."

PA, Jun 1, 1775.

A suggested epitaph for those Americans killed at Lexington to be placed in Westminister Abbey by the leaders of the Opposition -- Rockingham, Shelburne, Chatham.

75-142. An Irishman's Answer to the American Address to his Countrymen, in which they are called Brethren and Fellow-Subjects.

"No Brethren you! -- Subject to none." (48)

MP, Sep 29, 1775.

Regular ode in sixains. Denies that the Irish have anything in common with Americans, and so will not join them in treason or adversity. Several animal fables illustrate the theme.

75-143. The Irishman's Epistle to the Officers and Troops at Boston.

"By my faith, but I think ye're all makers of bulls." (22)

Cumb Pacq, Sep 14, 1775; L Chron 38 (Oct 19, 1775), 391; LM 44 (Nov 1775), 597; Ox M 12 (Oct 1775), 317; W Misc 5 (Nov 6, 1775), 136.

Anapest tetrameter couplets. Satire on the British forces besieged and helpless in Boston. From the South Carolina Gazette, the Virginia Gazette, and Pennsylvania Magazine.

75-144. Irregular Ode, on the posture of affairs, 1775.

"Mourn, O Britannia! mourn." (54)

SM 37 (Sep 1775), 512.

Irregular Pindaric ode. Mourns the civil war for all the death and despair it causes. This is reason enough for peace and all its joys.

75-145. Jenkinson and Burke.

"Burke lifts the olive branch, peace is his plea." (6)

MJ, Dec 7, 1775.

Epigram. The policies of Burke and Jenkinson are contrasted -- Burke for peace, Jenkinson for war.

75-146. Jenny and her Mother. An English Story. In Answer to the American Fable.

"A brisk young girl, by nature wild." (56)

LP, Sep 13, 1775; M Chron, Sep 16, 1775.

OC. A moral fable about daughter Jenny (the American colonies) justifiably rebelling against her tyrannical mother (Britain), but prostituting herself with "Spaniard, Dutch, or French." The mother, in despair, deplores her loss. The moral is clear: "use the rod, to save the child." See "The Lioness and her Whelps," 75-151.

A Junto Song. "'Tis money makes the member vote." (45) L Chron 38 (Jul 15, 1775), 61; L Eve Post, Mar 2, 1775; and three other sources. Satire on Parliament for taxing the Colonies at will. See "A Song. By the Tory Junto": 75-251.

75-147. [King and No King was once a play.]

"King and No King was once a play." (12)

L Eve Post, Sep 23, 1775.

Quatrains. The King is the slave of his ministers; and they should resign.

75-148. The Lamentation of a Bostonian. Addressed to England.

"O Wretched Boston! well may'st thou deplore." (52)

T&C 7 (May 1775), 269-70.

HC. A resident of Boston mourns British oppression, despite American contributions to the empire. Invokes Chatham's aid.

75-149. Libel and Bludgeon, or the Royal Supporters.

"Scoundrels and venal wretches rise in place." (28)

L Eve Post, May 30, 1775.

HC. Extract presumably from a MS satirizing the corrupt ministry for using force: Only gentleness will be effective.

75-150. Liberty. A Poem. Addressed to the People of England.

"Descend sweet inspiration from thy seat." (110)

M Chron, Oct 6, 1775.

Blank verse. In praise of liberty and its American defenders against a corrupt administration, "the monsters of a court / who dare to rob them of their sacred laws." Favorably cited are Chatham, Camden, Effingham, Richmond, Washington, Putnam, Adams, Hancock.

75-151. The Lioness and Her Whelps: An American Fable.

"John Wilkes alone, without a blind." (28)

LP, Sep 9, 1775; M Chron, Sep 12, 1775.

OC. Animal fable, illustrating the need for children to defend themselves from a tyrannical and cruel parent. See answer in "Jenny and her Mother. An English Story," M Chron, Sep 16, 1775: 75-146.

75-152. [Lord North, the Phaeton of these our Days.]

"Lord North, the Phaeton of these our Days." (12)

MJ, Oct 3, 1775.

HC. Lord North is the political leader but the King's puppet. He will be famous because of America.

75-153. The Manchester Wags. A Song.

"Ye Lancashire lads and ye lasses." (35)

L Eve Post, Oct 7, 1775.

Ironic satire on the Tories who presented the loyal Manchester Address to the government in support of its coercive policies. Anti-Stuart sentiment.

75-154. The Massachusetts Congress's Address to General Washington versified by an Independent Whig.

"The Massachusetts Congress, full." (62)

PA, Sep 6, 1775.

OC. Ironic satire that emphasizes the negative character of the colonial struggle when Washington assumed command -- a nasty rabble for an army and an impious and illegal cause.

75-155. The Ministerial Gazette; or, Sukey North in the Dumps.

"Ten thousand men by Smith led out." (90)

L Eve Post, Jun 8, 1775.

Hudibrastics. Satire on the ministry upon the news of fighting at Lexington and Concord. "Sukey" is the name of the ship carrying the dispatches for Administration. Cited are Col. Smith of the regulars, North, Dartmouth, Sandwich, the King.

75-156. The Modern Courtier.

"Pray say what's that, which smirking trips this way." (14)

W Misc 4 (Aug 28, 1775), 518.

HC. Satire on the modern English courtier, who does not care for the people's rights and who fails to support Magna Charta liberties.

75-157. The Modern *Veni, Vidi, Vici*.

"We came, we saw, but could not beat." (8)

PA, Jul 29, 1775.

Epigram. OC. The British won only a Pyrrhic victory at Bunker's Hill -- if it was a victory at all.

75-158. A Monody in the House of Commons.

"Urg'd to come down, and press'd to stay." (60)

PA, Nov 21, 1775; New Foundling Hospital for Wit (1786), II, 132-4.

Sixains. A satire on the oratory of the patriot opposition in the House of Commons -- Sawbridge, Adair, Charles Fox, Burke, Thomas Townshend, Barre, Dunning, Hartley. See answer, "From St. Stephen's Chapel, Nov 21. An Ode, Addressed to the Author of the Monody": 75-120.

75-159. Necessity has no Law.

"The three Estates they for our Brethren carve." (9)

St J's C, Jul 4, 1775.

HC. Ironic satire. The Americans are severely treated because the corrupted Parliament cannot allow them to believe their property was their own: "necessity has no law."

75-160. A New Song.

"Two Heroes renown'd." (42)

MP, Dec 29, 1775.

A song that satirizes Germain, recently appointed by North to head the war effort, to the undoubted displeasure of Prince Ferdinand, George II, and Granby. Britain "has a very bad chance" with her foes when cowards are advanced to important places.

75-161. A New Song. On the City's Petitioning in Favour of the Americans. Tune, -- Sir John he got him an ambling nag.

"As Johnny of late went up in great state." (16)

M Chron, Apr 15, 1775.

Song. Wilkes goes to court with a petition for America, and, disturbed by his reception, reports to the City that Jacobites and Scots dominate it. See "On the Answer to a Late Remonstrance": 75-189.

75-162. A New Song, To the old Tune of "O my Kitten, my Kitten."

"O my Yankee, my Yankee." (48)

LP, Aug 4, 1775; The Muse's Mirror (London: Baldwin, 1778), I, 220-2.

A review of the events from Concord to Bunker's Hill and the unsuccessful attempts of the British -- the King, North, Gage, Howe -- to deal with the Colonies, esp. Boston. Putnam is the central figure.

75-163. A New Song upon a Late Promotion. To the tune of "A Cobler there was," &c.

"Ye poor silly people, who foolishly think." (36)

MP, Nov 13, 1775.

Quatrains with "Derry down" chorus. Satire on Sackville, just appointed by North as Secretary of State for the American Colonies with the responsibility of executing the war policy against the American rebels. This satire emphasizes Sackville's alleged cowardice at Minden. Sackville assumed the name Germain in 1770 upon inheriting the estate of his parents' friend, Lady Betty Germain.

75-164. The North-Highland Volunteers. A new warlike song. Tune: -- *In the Garb of Old Gaul*, &c.

"To humble Rebellion, establish the laws." (36)

SM 37 (Dec 1755), 677.

Song. The loyal Scotch fight for liberty and "defy Rebel Congress to alter our laws." They will cross the ocean "To conquer America over again."

75-165. Ode.

"'Twas near a lofty mansion's side." (42)

MP, Apr 27, 1775.

Parody on Gray's "Ode on the Death of a Favourite Cat." Belinda (England) is attracted to a vase with feathers floating in what appears to be water, reaches for it, and falls in only to drown in tar. (The allusion is to tar and feathers, the American Colonies.)

75-166. Ode, Addressed to the Earl of Dartmouth.

"My Lord, your filley's hardly broke." (36)

PA, Oct 31, 1775; An Asylum for Fugitives (1776), I, 89-90; New Foundling Hospital for Wit (1786), II, 90-2.

Regular (Horatian) ode in sixains. Ironic stanzas on the inability of Lord Dartmouth to pacify the rebellious American colonists, "the saints" and "stubborn Yankies." Alludes to Gage's forces trapped in Boston. -- Dartmouth, Secretary of State for the Colonies (until Germain took his place in 1775), objected to harsh measures. This ode may be the work of William Mason.

75-167. Ode for the 30th of January.

"The rolling year once more makes known." (46)

L Eve Post, Feb 7, 1775.

Regular (Horatian) ode. On the anniversary of the execution of Charles I. Those who stopped a tyrant's mad career should be praised, and emulated.

75-168. Ode For the 26th of October 1775. To John, Earl of Bute.

"Bellona late Minerva meeting." (18)

L Eve Post, Oct 24, 1775.

Regular ode in sixains (with introduction). Minerva, Goddess of Wisdom, warns the war god not to act hastily regarding Boston.

75-169. Ode inscribed to General Lee.

"Of dire events from sanguine schemes." (48)

MP, Mar 21, 1775.

Regular (Horatian) ode in sixains deplores the oncoming civil war brought on by the ministry; but patriot Lee deserves praise for fighting for freedom against tyrant power. Gage is cited.

75-170. An Ode of Condolence Addressed to Lord G[eorg]e G[er]m[ai]ne.

"My Lord, you're *hurt* by foolish Praise." (48)

PA, Dec 23, 1775.

Regular (Horatian) ode in sixains. Satire on the character and career of Germaine. Cited are Dartmouth, Richmond, Shelburne. An answer to "On some Late Publications," 75-187, and a defense of the Opposition.

75-171. Ode to Care. Written in the year 1775.

"Care, from Selmo, child of grief." (36)

L Cour, Jan 28, 1780.

Regular ode in quatrains. Advice to the monarch not to be proud and ambitious, cruel and bloody, not to spill the blood of brothers. Appears to be applicable to the situation just before or after the outbreak of the shooting.

75-172. Ode to Liberty.

"Fair Liberty, whom Heaven gave." (36)

PA, Nov 9, 1775.

Regular ode in quatrains. The rebels know nothing of genuine liberty, being fools, tools of seditious incendiaries, villains, and republicans.

75-173. Ode to the Memory of Dr. Warren. The Celebrated Orator, Who was Slain upon the Heights of Charles-Town, fighting for the Liberties of America, on the 17th of June, 1775.

"O Great Reverse of Tully's coward heart." (20)

LP, Jul 31, 1775; M Chron, Aug 3, 1775.

Regular (Horatian) ode in elegiac quatrains. Praise of Warren for his heroic oratory and his heroic death at Bunker's Hill. Criticism of North, Sandwich, and King George.

75-174. On a Gentleman's Asking of Another What Brought so Many Americans to Land.

"Ask you, What brought these Tories 'cross the sea." (2)

LP, Dec 8, 1775.

HC. Epigram. Satire on American loyalists. American Tories have flocked to London to drink their tea.

75-175. On a Lark.

"Hail, sweetest songster of the feather'd throng." (12)

KG, Dec 9, 1775.

Quatrains. A nature lyric that is non-political, "free from the political disputes of Whigs and Tories." (A "pure" poem is affected by the context of politics!)

75-176. On a Late Embarkation.

"The infernal Cerberus, tho' bred in Hell." (4)

L Eve Post, Apr 25, 1775.

Impromptu. The generals have embarked for America on the Cerberus -- hell's monsters!

75-177. On Colonel Barre's late Secession to Bath.

"O Thou, who late 'midst Patriots shone." (36)

PA, Dec 11, 1775.

Ode in sixains. Does not believe Barre is leaving the House of Commons because of illness and urges him, as a Patriot, to return in order to continue the opposition to the King and his ministers.

75-178. On Dr. Johnson's Credulity and Scepticism.

"Royal Charles the merry, the witty, and idle." (6)

M Chron, Apr 14, 1775.

Epigram. Satire. The credulous and sceptical Samuel Johnson, the orthodox believer, does not believe in the authenticity of Macpherson's Ossian, but "trusts second sight."

75-179. On Lord North's Conciliatory Motion for an Accommodation of all Differences with America.

"Vengeance and war, inflam'd, Bute's vassal row'd." (16)

Freeman's J, Mar 9, 1775.

HC. North should be distrusted for his rapidly shifting policies regarding America -- peaceful and warlike.

75-180. On Mr. Jacob Vredenbergh, a Barber, of New York, his refusing to compleat the operation of shaving on Capt. John Croser, on discovering him to be Commander of one of the transports.

"O Vredenbergh! a sacred name." (24)

MP, Jan 11, 1775.

Sixains. Satire rendering absurd the episode in which a New York barber refused to complete shaving a captain of a British transport ship. Cf. the print "The Patriotick Barber of New York," which reprints the last stanza: Feb 8, 1775. See 75-319.

75-181. On Mr. Wesley's Address to the Americans.

"O strange reverse! Shall Wesley stand display'd." (12)

Cumb Pacq, Nov 2, 1775.

HC. Ironic satire on Wesley who now receives applause from the government for his Calm Address to our American Colonies (1775).

75-182. On Modern Patriots.

"When Words convey'd their real Meaning, how." (4)

St J's C, Nov 7, 1775.

Epigram. Satire on the patriots -- who are parricides.

75-183. On Reading Mr. Wesley's Calm Address.

"Soon as the pious man explain'd the cause." (6)

Cumb Pacq, Oct 26, 1775.

Two epigrams. Wesley's Calm Address is persuasive, more effective than Tucker's essays or Johnson's pamphlet.

75-184. On Reading Mrs. Macaulay's late Address upon the Present Alarming State of Affairs.

"Whilst Britain's sons immers'd in pleasure lie." (58)

L Eve Post, Jan 26, 1775.

HC. Mrs. Macaulay is praised for her attempt to awaken the nation to its danger created by Tories -- Bute, Mansfield, North, Johnson, Shebbeare.

75-185. On Reading "That a considerable detachment of the Regulars were returned safe to the camp at Boston, with 1800 sheep -- prisoners."

"In days of yore the British troops." (8)

L Chron 38 (Oct 3, 1775), 328; L Eve Post, Sep 30, 1775; MJ, Sep 30, 1775; Ox M 12 (Oct 1775), 318.

Epigram. Satire on the British soldiers, surrounded in Boston and able only to conquer sheep.

75-186. On Reading that Inimitable Speech of Dr. Jonathan Shipley, the present Illustrious Bishop of St. Asaph, intended to have been Spoken in the House of Lords, on the Subject of altering the Charter of Massachusetts Bay.

"Hail, sacred Bard, who Virtue thus unites." (12)

L Eve Post, Aug 26, 1775.

HC. The Bishop of St. Asaph, a consistent opponent of the war, is praised for his attempt to resolve the differences between America and England without risking war and the loss of liberty. Cited are Stuarts and Bishops.

On Seeing the name ----- joined with Liberty, among the toasts at a late public entertainment. See "Qui capit ille facit": 75-232.

75-187. On Some Late Publications.

"Curs'd be the Pen by Faction sway'd." (36)

PA, Dec 19, 1775; New Foundling Hospital for Wit (1786), II, 130-1.

Ode in sixains. Praise for Lord Germain recently appointed, at a sacrifice to the serenity of his peaceful personal life, as Secretary of State for the American Colonies, taking the place of "timid Dartmouth," in order to suppress "foul Rebellion" and to save the empire.

75-188. On the American Expedition.

"Our political wrong-heads to shew themselves frantic." (16)

L Eve Post, Jul 29, 1775.

Fourteener couplets. An expression of sympathy for the Americans, after the Battle of Bunker Hill. Cited are Gens. Gage and Putnam, taxes.

75-189. On the Answer to a Late Remonstrance.

"The Court's astonish'd in this land, to find." (4)

MJ, Apr 20, 1775; MP, Apr 21, 1775.

Satire. Bitter ironic comment on a formal protest (presented by Wilkes) against court policy -- the City petition for the Americans rejected by the King. See "A New Song, On the City's Petitioning . . . .": 75-161.

75-190. On the Conduct of Administration respecting America.

"'Twould please me to see." (6)

M Chron, Feb 22, 1775.

Epigram. North and Bute should be tarred and feathered, perhaps even executed.

75-191. On the Death of Lord Clive.

"Life's a Surface, slipp'ry, glassy." (6)

DJ, Jan 7, 1775; L Chron 37 (Dec 31, 1774-Jan 3, 1775), 8.

Satire on nabob corruption. Clive could not bribe Death to let him live. (Robert Clive died a suicide, November 22, 1774.)

75-192. On the Grand Resolvers in England and Ireland.

"How blest are we in this bright age." (12)

Lloyd's 37 (Oct 6, 1775), 340; MJ, Oct 5, 1775; L Chron 38 (Oct 5, 1775), 343.

Sixains. Ironic satire on the lower classes, the mechanics, for talking] politics and presenting petitions.

75-193. On the Growing Oppressions of a Tory Administration.

"Townshend was wretched Ireland's curse." (48)

Freeman's J, Apr 20, 1775.

OC. Contrasts America's active resistance to oppression with Irish passivity. Boston should provide the example.

75-194. On the Infamous Triumvirate from Whence our National Apprehensions Arise.

"B[ute]! M[ansfield]! and N[orth]! need I point out the men." (20)

MJ, Jan 28, 1775; MP, Jan 31, 1775.

Hexameter couplets. Satire on Bute, Mansfield, and North who are responsible for all the trouble and who deserve to be tarred and feathered.

75-195. On the King's ordering Elliott's light horse, Preston's light dragoons, and three regiments of foot to reinforce his army before Boston.

"In arms and discipline compleat." (18)

Freeman's J, Feb 2, 1775.

OC express an optimistic view of the effect of reinforcements sent to Gage in Boston.

75-196. On the Late Additional Window Tax, 176-.

"God gave us Light, and bade that Light to roll." (4)

KG, Apr 22, 1775; St J's C, Apr 18, 1775.

Epigram. Protest at the politicians who have imposed an additional window tax.

75-197. On the Later Numerous Subscriptions of the London Merchants for the Relief of Boston.

"Erring, perverted, obstinate, and blind." (10)

Freeman's J, Mar 2, 1775.

Epigram. HC. Amazement that the London merchants would openly support the rebellious Bostonians. Suffolk, the Duke of Grafton, would hang them all, and so would Parliament.

75-198. On the Loss of North America in one Campaign.

"Of two Columbuses let Europe boast." (2+6)

LM 44 (Nov 1775), 597; PA, Oct 31, 1775.

Two epigrams. North has lost America, which Chatham had gained for Britain.

75-199. On the Marquis of Granby's Speech on One of the American Restraining Bills.

"To serve his Country in a time of need." (20)

L Eve Post, May 11, 1775.

HC. John Manners, the Marquis of Granby, the hero of Minden, is praised for speaking out against the ministry's coercive measures, especially the blockade of Boston. Cited are the Scotch.

75-200. On the Martyrdom of Charles the First.

"Heav'n in revenge for hapless Strafford's fate." (12)

LP, Feb 1, 1775.

HC. A warning by a Republican (signed Sidney) that (on the anniversary -- Jan 30 -- of the execution of Charles I) Kings must not be beyond the law. (Charles was executed Jan 30, 1649.) Cromwell is cited.

75-201. On the Patriots.

"Oh for a muse -- a muse of fire." (148)

M Chron, Dec 27, 28, 1775. (Two installments.)

Hudibrastic couplets. Satire on the Opposition (the Patriots) who support the American cause. Reviews the causes of the war, especially the American wish to avoid paying any taxes whatsoever, because they wish to be free of "Supreme Authority," meaning Parliament. The conclusion is that anarchy sets in should the supreme authority be defied.

75-202. On the Present Disturbances in America.

"Some ill-concerted plans, untimely laid." (24)

Cumb Pacq, Mar 2, 1775.

HC. Gentler means must be found to subdue the Americans.

75-203. On the Prospect of a War with France and Spain.

"Awake, Britannia's guardian pow'r." (20)

LP, Aug 14, 1775.

Quatrains. Now that Britain is at war with its colonies, it has to fear the prospect of war with France and Spain; but Britain's navy is still supreme on the main.

75-204. On the Storm of Thunder and Lightning on Tuesday the 18th instant, the day the Generals embarked for America.

"The Chiefs embark, and clouds involve the skies." (14)

MJ, Apr 20, 1775; GM 45 (May 1775), 246; KG, Apr 22, 1775; MP, Apr 22, 1775.

HC. Signed Hamden. Support of the American cause. Those guilty of fomenting civil war should be punished.

75-205. On the Tears of a Minister.

"Music drew savage tears from Pluto's eyes." (6)

LM 44 (Nov 1775), 597.

Epigram. A minister weeps over Britain's "woes."

75-206. The Pandaemonium, or Council of July 5, 1775.

"Faction and Folly, Arrogance and Pride." (40)

L Chron 38 (Jul 4-6, 1775), 24; SM 37 (Jul 1775), 393.

HC. Satire on Parliament, dominated by faction and folly, arrogance and pride. What is needed is common sense.

75-207. A Panegyric on Great-Britain.

"When science first on British regions smil'd." (30)

HM 5 (Jul 1775), 431.

HC. A bland panegyric on Great Britain for bringing civilization, prosperity and freedom, to the world.

75-208. The Paradox Solved.

"Loans, taxes, grants, th'encumber'd realm sustain'd." (14)

Limerick Chron, Nov 23, 1775.

HC. A satire on English oppression of Ireland through its corrupt leaders. A protest at English exploitation of Irish resources, which some corrupt Irish encourage.

75-209. Paraphrase of a late celebrated Oration. [By Lord North.]

"My Lords and Gemmen, -- America's present situation." (48)

MP, Nov 9, 1775.

Fourteener couplets. Ironic satire through the persona of Lord North who declares he will wage war upon the American colonies, that he will hire mercenaries, that France and Spain will not interfere so long as "we are each other's throats . . . a-cutting."

75-210. The Parody -- addressed to both Houses.

"To fight, or not to fight -- that's the Question." (13)

PA, Nov 3, 1775.

The question is (in this parody of Hamlet's celebrated soliloquy) whether to fight or not to fight the Americans -- for their rifled guns puzzle our officers and cause them to fear for their lives. They "rather stay in Boston Town / Than seek the Enemy on Bunker's Hill."

75-211. A Parody, On the Celebrated Ballad of Chevy Chace, inscribed to the Duke of Northumberland, and the Freemen of Westminster, who honourably and disinterestedly elected Lord Percy to be their Member in this noble, persevering, and honourable Parliament.

"To drive our friends with sword and gun." (96)

LP, Jun 2, 1775; KG, Jun 3, 1775.

Ballad, parody, narrates the fray at Lexington and Concord in which the provincials proved they were not cowards, but Lord Percy retreated; and so the absurd war began. Title is ironic.

75-212. Paulus. A Monody. See the miscellany Fugitive Pieces, Written by Sir Jeffrey Dunstan, 89-2.

75-213. A Picture of a Bostonian Saint.

"In Boston streets is often seen." (118)

M Chron, Feb 20, 1775.

Hudibrastic couplets. Satiric character of a Boston saint, a hypocritical, knavish, cheating mad dissenter and rebel who uses religion as a disguise for his villainies. May Parliament suppress such rebels and preserve the church and throne from this faction.

75-214. Pistol's Extempore Rondeau upon the Rifle-Men.

"Again, I say it, and again." (18)

KG, Sep 13, 1775; LP, Sep 11, 1775; M Chron, Sep 11, 1775.

OC. The American way of fighting -- guerrilla tactics, "bush-fighting" -- is objectionable to English soldiers: the riflemen hide behind a wall or hedge and select their targets. "A paltry, base, unwarlike plan!"

75-215. A Poetical Epistle to a Friend.

"From the banks of the Orwell, my friend Hal, I greet you." (76)

M Chron, Jul 13, 1775.

Hexameter couplets. An allusion (eight lines) to the Boston troubles, the threat of France and Spain, the quarrel between Administration and Opposition, which will not disturb the peace of the poet's stay in the country, the poet declares.

75-216. A Political Comparison. Semper Eadem et Idem.

"When Satan plann'd our parents' death." (40)

Freeman's J, Jan 9, 1776; L Eve Post, Sep 7, 1775.

Quatrains. A warning to the King not to go the way of the tyrannical Stuarts -- especially Charles I. Reference to the Quebec Bill, "the Canadian Catholics," in a note.

75-217. The Politicians.

"Old Brickbat and Frisseur, two great Politicians." (32)

KG, Dec 9, 1775.

HC. Satire. A barber and a bricklayer visit an ale-house to read the papers about Massachusetts, but scarcely can make out what they read -- being almost illiterate. (Illustrates the excitement of the American theme.)

75-218. A Prescription for Grievances.

"Where M[ansfie1]d and B[u]te, and the rest of the Tribe." (4)

St J's C, Apr 15, 1775.

Epigram. Satire. Were Bute, Mansfield and other Scots executed, trade would resume and make us prosperous. Such execution is a method far more effective than petitions.

75-219. The Present Age.

"No more, my friends of vain applause." (72)

KG, Oct 14, 1775; L Chron 38 (Oct 10, 1775), 357; LM 44 (Dec 1775), 656; New Foundling Hospital for Wit (1786), III, 301-3; W Misc 9 (Mar 16, 1778), 575-6.

Originally printed in August 1767, this satiric ode, reprinted in 1775, reviews the immorality of the times in all classes and professions and notes that, despite the recession in the economy, "luxury" is still apparent. See 67-38.

75-220. A Print of a celebrated Chancellor of the Exchequer . . . the following Parody on Pope's Inscription on Secretary Craggs.

"Statesman made up of littleness and fear." (6)

L Eve Post, Jun 3, 1775.

HC. Satire on North; Boston alluded to.

75-221. A Prophecy.

"Hail, happy Britain! freedom's blest retreat." (9)

KG, Aug 12, 1775.

HC. Britain is declining, and America is rising to take its place in greatness, wealth, and power.

75-222. A Prophecy.

"An Horseman shall an Island rule." (16)

L Eve Post, Mar 23 & 25, 1775.

OC. The Stuarts will return, bringing Catholicism with them. Ireland and the colonies will flourish and Britain be dismembered. (A dire warning.)

75-223. The Prophecy of Ruin, A Poem.

"Should e're a Prince the British Empire sway." (c. 460)

Crisis 12 (Apr 8, 1775), 67-78.

HC. Satire on the King in whose reign many political evils have been perpetrated: the persecution of Wilkes, the attack on the liberties of Boston, the Bishops' support of Popery. Objects to the subversion of "the natural rights of Man" by a king who knows no law but that of force, prefers rebel Scots to loyal Britons, and has turned out "that great Patriot Pitt" in favor of Bute in order to conclude "a shameful peace." Cited also are St. George's Fields and Allen, Spain and the Falkland Islands, bribery and corruption. Should men like Chatham, Burke, and Glynn fail to end corruption and tyranny, and Britons be slaves, the empire will fall in ruin. (The original text has "e're," clearly intending "e'er.")

75-224. A Prophecy Written by a learned Seer, two hundred years ago, and now very near its fulfilling.

"Long having deeply groan'd at visions sad." (14)

LP, Jan 4, 1775.

An English sonnet. America, it is predicted, will be the ruin of London.

75-225. A Prophesy.

"Englishmen are not wont to hear those notes." (11)

Freeman's J, Jul 11, 1775; St J's C, Apr 29, 1775.

HC. North and Bute, responsible for the violence against America, should beware.

75-226. The Prophet.

"Curs'd be his hand that arm'd with murd'rous rage." (22)

Freeman's J, Aug 26, 1775.

HC. The prophet urges Ireland, following the example of America, to rebel against corrupt and oppressive government. The King will grow wise and understand that North and Bute must be cashiered.

75-227. A Proposal. Addressed to the Americans, or a M---l Plan of Accommodation.

"Brave countrymen of England New." (99)

M Chron, Jan 31, 1775.

OC. Ironic satire on the ministry. The ministers propose that America surrender all its liberties, religious and civil, thereby effecting an accommodation. After all, the British have already done so. Cited are Bute, Boston, North, Liberty, Gage, tea, tax, dissent, Chatham, tar-and-feathering.

75-228. The Quarrel with America familiarly Stated.

"Rudely forc'd to drink tea, Massachusett in anger." (6)

L Eve Post, Aug 10, 1775.

A familiar view of tea as the cause of the American contest. Who is the aggressor? Who has begun the war?

75-229. A Quatrain occasioned by the annual Sermon on the 30th of January.

"A certain annual sermon preach'd this day." (8)

M Chron, Feb 1, 1775.

Quatrains satirizing the Stuarts for opposing religious and civil liberty. Charles I deserved execution.

75-230. Quebec.

"Quebec, O Protestants' eternal shame." (10)

Freeman's J, Aug 15, 1775.

HC. An Irish protest against the shameful papist Quebec Act.

75-231. A Question Answered.

"What is the Origin of England's Woes." (2)

St J's C, Dec 21, 1775.

Epigram. The cause of England's woes is that the King hates his friends but loves his enemies. (The meaning is that he favors his real enemies, the Tory Scotch; but hates his real friends, the Whigs who wish to keep the empire intact.)

75-232. *Qui capit ille facit*. On seeing the name ---- joined with Liberty, among the toasts at a late public entertainment.

"Mezentius the cruel, a tyrant of old." (8)

MP, Oct 9, 1775.

Hexameter couplets. An objection to joining liberty with a political figure who is an abettor of treason. (Could this be Wilkes?)

75-233. The Real Patriot's Prayer.

"Parent of all, Omnipotent." (24)

MJ, Sep 7, 1775.

Quatrains. A prayer for freedom, impartiality, and justice -- and a hope that the supplicant will stand for the right, even against the government.

75-234. [Remember him, the Villain, righteous Heav'n!]

"Remember him, the Villain, righteous Heav'n." (21)

MJ, Jun 13, 1775.

Rough blank verse. A soliloquy. Objection to those who would foment civil war in America.

75-235. Reply to the Author of the Lines inserted in the Public Advertiser last Tuesday, respecting Lord G[eorge] G[ermain]e.

"Curs'd is the Wretch whose vile Attempts." (36)

PA, Dec 23, 1775.

Ode in sixains. Germaine, the coward of Minden, cruelly assails the colonies fighting for the noble cause of freedom. He will destroy the empire. See "On Some Late Publications," on which this poem is a parody: 75-187.

75-236. The Returning Prodigal's Address on his being Introduced at Court.

"Great Sire, regard with melting eye." (18)

Freeman's J, Oct 14, 1775; Lloyd's 36 (Feb 22, 1775), 188; St J's C, Feb 16, 1775.

OC. Ironic satire. A patriot, once influenced by Wilkes, now becomes a turncoat and supporter of administration, and begs to share in the spoils.

75-237. Robinson Crusoe and his Man Friday: Or the Great Depth of Court Politics.

"The King, when viewing his perplext affairs." (72)

Freeman's J, Jul 20, 1775.

Mock oratorio. Satire. The King and North sing to each other about the difficulty of subduing the Americans.

75-238. Rondeau extempore, on reading a copy of extempore Verses in one of Wednesday's Papers.

"If Putnam, Ward, and Marshal Lee." (11)

PA, Oct 18, 1775.

The newly appointed American generals, Putnam, Ward, and Lee, must fight well or liberty will disappear and they will be hanged.

75-239. A Rough Sketch For the Royal Academy.

"Shut not the Door, good Hertford, I'm but One." (c. 220)

Crisis 32 (Aug 26, 1775), 209-14.

HC. Satire on the court, including the King, Mansfield, North, Bute as well as Whitehead and Samuel Johnson ("for his infamous pamphlet, Taxation No Tyranny"). The poet hopes that America will be victorious, free and independent at the end of the civil war. Grenville is also included.

75-240. The Royal Cow-Keeper. A Fragment. Being the Ninth and Last Canterbury Tale.

"Our Author, says a Potentate." (118)

M Chron, Mar 27, 1775.

OC. An allegorical fable about a King who wishes to have unlimited power over his domain, east and west (India and America); and he tries to get it by corrupting Parliament and intolerable acts against America. The event is uncertain. All the significant figures are cited -- Burke, Wilkes, Richmond, Pratt, Pitt, North as well as taxes, tyranny, representation, Jacobite, Tory.

75-241. Royal Virtue. An Excellent New Ballad, just imported from London.

"Come, let us sing." (72)

Freeman's J, Feb 25, 1775.

Ballad. Satire on the King: his virtues as a dull cit and buttonmaker and his willingness to spare no cost to crush rebellious Boston.

75-242. The Sailor's Address. To the Tune of "Hearts of Oak."

"Come listen, my cocks, to a brother and friend." (38)

KG, Apr 8, 1775; L Eve Post, Mar 11, 1775; LP, Jul 10, 1775; M Chron, Jul 12, 1775; An Asylum for Fugitives (1776), I, 144-6; New Foundling Hospital for Wit (1786), IV, 241-3.

Song. It is not right to fight against the Americans, who are our friends: "If New England we conquer, Old England's undone." We become the tools of such Jacobite Tories as Sandwich, should we perform their "dirty work."

75-243. [Says the Duchess of Kingston, No longer I'll wait.]

"Says the Duchess of Kingston, No longer I'll wait." (4)

G Eve Post, May 13, 1775.

Epigram. The infamous Duchess of Kingston (tried for bigamy) decides to return to England and drive the envious Englishmen to despair with her American fashion of feather and tar. (Pun.)

75-244. Scotch Admirals, Scotch Generals, Scotch Officers, in every department numberless.

"A Scotch Commander in Chief, North Britain." (18)

PL, Jul 19, 1775.

Prose poem. A list of Scotch in office. The Scotch are blamed for undermining the prosperity of the empire.

75-245. Scotch Casuistry.

"'Take and do what you please, says Thane, because." (14)

St J's C, Oct 28, 1775.

HC. An objection to Bute's Tory insistence on the King's Prerogative or Divine Right, against civil rights.

75-246. Scotch Loyalty always the Same. Addressed to Lord Mansfield.

"Scotchmen are virtual Rebels their own way." (4)

PA, Aug 30, 1775; MJ, Aug 29, 1775.

Epigram. The Scotch are to be distrusted -- they encourage force and they engage in fraud.

75-247. A Short State of the Politics, Arts, &c. of this Country for the New Year.

"The K[ing] -- dozing." (10. A selection.)

G, Jan 2, 1775; G Eve Post, Dec 31/74-Jan 3, 1775; LP, Dec 30/74-Jan 2, 1775; M Chron, Jan 2, 1775.

Prose-poem. The British spirit is adulterated; but the American is full proof; and corruption and Scots responsibility for American policy are still demoralizing factors.

75-248. Similar Occurrences in 1715, 1745, and 1775.

"Sev'nteen Hundred Fifteen, we knew, was a year." (12)

Lloyd's 37 (Sep 15, 1775), 269.

This "loyal" poet hopes that the third George like his two predecessors who suppressed the Scots rebels, will crush the American rebellion.

75-249. Simple Strains. Submitted to the Sense of the true Friends of Old England.

"The Boston Saints, most holy men," (48)

M Chron, Jan 14, 1775.

Sixains. Should the rebels try to fight the British, they will behave cowardly in the field. -- The causes of the conflict are reviewed -- taxes, smuggling, non-importation, coercion.

75-250. The Soldier's Fortune; or the Miseries of a Military Profession: Humbly Addressed to his Excellency Lord Harcourt.

"The youthful train to distant climes convey'd." (54)

Freeman's J, Feb 14, 1775.

HC. Now neglected, the brave soldier who fought bravely in the several American campaigns in the last war -- Canada and Cuba -- deserves the gratitude of his country. Harcourt was Lord Lieutenant of Ireland.

75-251. A Song. By the Tory Junto. To the Tune of A Begging we will go, will go, &c.

"'Tis money makes the member vote." (45)

L Chron 38 (Jul 15, 1775), 61; L Eve Post, Mar 2, 1775; LM 44 (Aug 1775), 431; SM 37 (Jul 1775), 392; WM 29 (Aug 3, 1775), 178.

Also entitled "A Junto Song," and originally published in the Pennsylvania Ledger. An ironic satire. This corrupt Parliament, its members bribed, has sovereignty over the Colonies and may tax them at will, using "force and fraud" to have its way.

75-252. A Song. Composed at a Town-meeting in Chester, Burlington County, July 1774. (From the Pennsylvania Ledger.)

"Come join in hand, all ye true loyal souls." (26)

L Chron 38 (Jul 8, 1775), 40; SM 37 (Jul 1775), 394.

Song. The Americans damn Wedderburne and North and will fight for freedom led by Franklin.

75-253. Stanzas written on Christmas-Day, 1775.

"While Britain's Sons, with Feast and Song." (28)

L Chron 38 (Dec 23-26, 1775), 616; LM 45 (Feb 1776), 106; MJ, Dec 23-26, 1775; PA, Dec 26, 1775; W Misc 5 (Jan 8, 1776), 384-5.

Quatrains. There is joy in Britain, but cheerless gloom and anger in America on Christmas Day. It is shameful that the British should be waging war against their protestant brethren and friends "on Freedom's latest shore."

75-254. The State Conjurers, an Impromptu, addressed to the Earl of D--NB--GH.

"My Lords, hems soft D--dl--y, "staunch Birmingham fails." (10)

PA, Nov 20, 1775.

Hexameter couplets. Birmingham, the city which supported the war against America, must now get a government contract for the production and sale of goods it can no longer market in the colonies.

75-255. Supporters of the Bill of Rights.

"Welcome, welcome Brother Lewes." (77)

PA, Jan 18, 1775.

Song. Ironic satire on the leaders of the Society for the Defense of the Bill of Rights defeated in the last Parliamentary election -- Sir Joseph Mawbey, Sir Watkin Lewes, Arthur Lee, Brass Crosby, Philip Stanhope (Viscount Mahon), John Sawbridge -- but not Wilkes.

75-256. [Tait, John.]
The Banks of the Dee.

"'Twas summer and softly the breezes were blowing." (24)
With "Additions By a Lady." (32)

Calliope: or, The Musical Miscellany (London: Elliot and Kay, 1788), pp. 98-100. (With music.)

Song, by a "fair maid," mourning the departure of a Scots soldier "To quell the proud rebels" in America, where he will die. Jamie left her "From unjust rebellion his country to free," according to the "Additions by a Lady."

75-257. Taxation No Tyranny.

"How sweet the Rambler under Virtue's lure." (22)

Freeman's J, Apr 18, 1775; L Eve Post, Apr 6, 1775; MJ, Apr 4, 1775.

HC. Causidicus criticizes Samuel Johnson's change for the worse because of his adoption of evil Borgian politics in the pamphlet Taxation No Tyranny.

75-258. A Taylor's Epigram of Manchester Velvet.

"Ye olde Yorkish Clothes, and ye gay Norwich stuffs." (8)
"This motley old Fashion all Whigs must condemn." (4)

LP, Sep 20, Oct 11, 1775.

Two epigrams with the same title. The court is Tory and influenced by Lord Bute, and the Whigs are unwelcome there. The allusion is to the loyal Manchester address.

75-259. The Tears of Britain.

"If for to die in Virtue's cause be just." (28)

L Eve Post, May 2, 1775.

HC. Now it is right and just to resist oppression. -- "Britons awake!"

75-260. [That some turn robbers, there's no doubt.]

"That some turn robbers, there's no doubt." (2)

G, Jan 4, 1775.

Epigram. On the effect of American Non-Intercourse. The American boycott of British goods is the cause of increase of robberies.

75-261. [These Mighty Crimes will sure ere long Provoke.]

"These Mighty Crimes will sure ere long Provoke." (38)

Crisis 2 (Jan 28, 1775), 11-12.

HC. Verses at the conclusion of an essay attacking "A Bloody Court, A Bloody Ministry, And A Bloody Parliament" for "crimes" which "should soon compel / America and England to Rebel." The crimes are oppressive taxes and lawless power. Cited are Bute, Stuart, King George.

Thirtieth of January, for Ever and Ever. See 75-57.

75-262. Thompson, Edward.
To the Memory of Mr. James Moore, who commanded a tender belonging to the Preston man of war, and who gallantly fell in action with the Provincials at sea . . .

"If sense in youth, mature as mellow'd age." (6)

LP, Nov 20, 1775.

HC. Epitaph. Eulogy of a young man killed at sea by the American rebels, possibly one of the first sea fatalities in the first naval battle of the American war.

75-263. To a Certain Nation.

"'Tis said, good folks, your constitution's gone." (18)

Freeman's J, Jul 11, 1775; St J's C, Apr 29, 1775.

HC. The English constitution has in effect made the King supreme; and Parliament, being corrupt, does not care. It is interested only in "pay" -- i.e., bribes.

75-264. To General Gage.

"These polish'd times, we must allow." (16)

St J's C, Sep 21, 1775; The Muse's Mirror (London: Baldwin, 1778), I, 132.

Quatrains. Satire. General Gage may have been eloquent, but he was a poor fighter.

75-265. To her Majesty on her Birth Day.

"Then since this day will not be seen." (14)

LP, Jan 18, 1775.

Tetrameter couplets. Asks the Queen to restore liberty, "Remove oppression from the land," and satisfy the Americans.

75-266. To Lord Chatham.

"Demosthenes, bold Orator of old." (27)

MP, Feb 9, 1775.

HC. Demosthenes, Cicero, Chatham are all great orators who spoke for freedom -- the last for the American colonies, "For th'injur'd Colonists' invaded rights."

75-267. To Lord [George Germaine.]

"Accept these Lines, thou British Mars." (36)

L Eve Post, Dec 14, 1775.

Regular (Horatian) ode in sixains. Satire on Germaine, the new Secretary of State for the American Colonies, for his alleged cowardice at Minden.

75-268. To Lord M--F--D.

"M[ansfiel]d beware, remember Jefferies' Fate." (2)

St J's C, Dec 23, 1775.

Epigram. Judge Mansfield is warned that he may share Judge Jeffrey's fate -- the Tower, execution. (George Jeffreys died in the Tower, April 18, 1689, imprisoned by the supporters of William of Orange when James II escaped to France.)

75-269. To Lord North.

"If yet thy mind can presage future woe." (70)

L Eve Post, Jul 13, 1775.

HC. North should be cautious about engaging the Americans in war. -- War is hell, especially civil war.

75-270. To Stephen Sayre, Esq.

"The wise, the good, in every age." (28)

M Chron, Oct 27, 1775.

Ode in quatrains, honors Stephen Sayre, an American who had once been London's sheriff, for asserting freedom's cause against North, Bute, and Mansfield, and the hired bravo assassins, Balfe and Macquirk. The poem also asserts Sayre's innocence in the alleged plot to seize the King. But although the evidence was perjured, Sayre was sent to the Tower.

75-271. [To Stop the Progress of fair Freedom's Foes.]

"To stop the Progress of fair Freedom's Foes," (14)

PA, Jul 5, 1775.

HC. Praise of Wilkes, who deserves fame as a freedom-fighter for the rights of Britons.

75-272. To the Duke of G[rafton] on his rejoining the Minority.

"Haste G[rafton]! make the Port again." (32)

St J's C, Nov 9, 1775.

Quatrains. Satire on the Duke of Grafton for joining the Minority Opposition and aiding the cause of rebellion. A response to a poem with the same title printed a week before. See 75-273.

75-273. To the Duke of Grafton, on his rejoining the Minority.

"Welcome to Honour's Course once more." (28)

St J's C, Nov 2, 1775.

Quatrains praising Fitzroy, Duke of Grafton, for returning to the Minority Opposition and taking up the cause against corruption and for America. He should speak for Chatham.

75-274. To the Earl of Chatham. Occasioned by the illiberal invectives thrown on his Lordship in the Newspapers.

"Gentle, tho' great; grave, not austere." (12)

Freeman's J, Mar 25, 1775; LP, Feb 17, 1775.

Quatrains in defense of Chatham against malicious criticism in the papers.

75-275. To the Friend of his Country and Mankind, Dr. Benjamin Franklin, on his Arrival from England, May 6, 1775.

"------ Welcome! once more." (16)

L Chron 38 (Jul 18, 1775), 72; WM 29 (Jul 27, 1775), 145.

HC. Originally printed in the Pennsylvania Packet, May 8, 1775. Franklin is welcomed home where he can "fan the flame which Liberty inspires." Americans owe a good deal to Wedderburn for Franklin's return home.

75-276. To the King.

"Reform thy Conduct, Monarch, or attend." (c. 200)
"Once more to stay the Fury of the Sword." (c. 200)

Crisis 27 & 29 (Jul 22 & Aug 5, 1775), 171-6, 183-8.

HC. A two-part state poem. 1. Reviews the politics of George's reign and begs George to "reform" his conduct or be doomed. Blames the King for "Civil Rage," the war that has begun in Concord. 2. Asks King George to return to a peace policy and accept the American petitions. The King and his Court are solely responsible for spilling blood.

75-277. To the Memory of Mr. William Bard [Baird], late Lieutenant in the Light Infantry Company of the 35th regiment, who was killed at the attack upon the American entrenchments near Boston. Addressed to Edward Drewe, Esq; his Captain, who received several wounds in the same engagement.

"Why unlamented should the valiant bleed." (48)

GM 45 (Aug 1775), 396-7; Lloyd's 37 (Aug 30, 1775), 214; LP, Jan 29, 1776; SM 37 (Aug 1775), 449; WM 29 (Sep 7, 1775), 338.

Elegiac quatrains. Mourns the death of a British officer who died bravely in the Battle of Bunker's Hill. See account of the fight that explains part of the poem in GM 45 (Aug 1775), 397. For Drewe, see 75-8.

75-278. To the M[inistry].

"The conduct which you now pursue." (9)

LP, Jun 9, 1775.

OC. Advice to the ministry to change its colonial policy -- to fight Spain, not the colonies.

75-279. To the People of Birmingham who Petition'd against America.

"You petition'd the King against Liberty, truth." (16)

LP, Apr 24, 1775.

Quatrains. Satire on the City of Birmingham for petitioning the King to coerce the colonies to obey the laws.

75-280. To the Queen, respecting the great Fog on her Birth-Day.

"No mortal Titles can command the Skies." (14)

St J's C, Jan 26, 1775.

HC. The great fog on the Queen's natal day suggests that the Court is perpetrating great wrongs upon America, for which Heaven is blaming England.

75-281. To the Rev. Dean Tucker, on his Late Publication against America.

"Hail, pious Tucker! true to ev'ry vow." (16)

L Eve Post, Aug 19, 1775.

HC. Satire on Josiah Tucker for writing against the Americans and having in mind his reward, elevation to a bishopric.

75-282. To the Reverend Mr. W[esley.]

"In early youth, when Oxford fondly saw." (32)

LM 44 (Dec 1775), 656.

HC. A satire on Wesley and Johnson for their Tory political principles -- the one motivated by a bishopric, the other by a pension. Both "human nature dare degrade," in their support of tyranny.

75-283. To the Right Hon. and Hon. the Members of both Houses of Parliament. The humble Petition of Timothy Talecatch, Paragraph-monger and Citizen, in Behalf of Himself and Others.

"Sheweth, That the Acts of the Mob he's been us'd to record." (20)

DJ, Feb 28, 1775; L Chron 37 (Feb 21, 1775), 183; PA, Feb 23, 1775; SM 37 (Feb 1775), 102.

Quatrains. Begs the political orators to abbreviate their speeches in this time of great excitement so that ordinary news could be printed and "our Fears" abated.

75-284. To the Right Hon. Lord North.

"Go on, my Lord, to guide the Helm of State." (18)

St J's C, Sep 7, 1775.

HC. A defence of North and the ministry's position on law and order, against anarchy and faction.

75-285. To the Right Hon. the Lord Mayor, Court of Aldermen, &c. of the City of London.

"You always are wrong, when you go to the King." (4)

L Eve Post, Jul 8, 1775.

Epigram. The Mayor and Aldermen of London must not go to the King with their petitions, but to Bute.

75-286. To the tune of the Highland March to St. James's.

"In the garb of old Gaul, with the fire of old Rome." (20)

LP, Dec 27, 1775.

Song. Satire on the Scotch for their greed.

75-287. [Toasts.]

"Unanimity and Firmness to our American colonies." (11)

L Eve Post, Jan 28, Feb 25, 1775.

Toasts. Pro-American and anti-Court (North, Mansfield, Bute) in sentiment. Tarring and feathering cited.

75-288. Tom Gage's Proclamation, or Blustering Denunciation.

"Whereas the Rebels hereabout." (70)

Freeman's J, Aug 10, 1775.

OC. Satiric parody of Gage's menacing proclamation establishing martial law for the inhabitants of Boston. "Taken from an American print of the 28th of June."

75-289. The Triumph of America: An Ode.

"Rejoice, ye Guardian Powers, with joyful note." (80)

G, Jun 29, 1775; UM 56 (Supp 1775), 371.

Regular (Horatian) ode in dixains. An ode of defiance against Britain's oppression, as the fighting begins in earnest. Probably written by an American.

75-290. The True Patriot in Retirement. Inscribed to Lord Chatham.

"Enough to glory and his country giv'n." (17)

MP, Nov 8, 1775.

HC. Chatham, the true patriot in retirement, seeks his God in nature, unlike North who seeks glory in a civil war.

75-291. A Truth.

"What a refinement do our Great contrive!" (2)

PA, Dec 26, 1775.

Epigram. Satire on the "Great" men at court. Printed over "Stanzas Written on Christmas Day, 1775," which justify the American rebellion: 75-253.

75-292. [Two James's, Charles's two, might well suffice.]

"Two James's, Charles's two, might well suffice." (6)

St J's C, May 27, 1775.

Epigram. The experience with the four Scottish Stuart kings, two James's and two Charles's, demonstrates the need for eternal vigilance; otherwise the English will lose their liberties to tyranny and Popery.

75-293. [Two Welchmen, partners in one cow.]

"Two Welchmen, partners in one cow." (52)

W Misc 4 (Sep 18, 1775), 590-1.

Quatrains. Vulgar folk tale that illustrates the waste and stupidity of the American war.

75-294. Upon a certain military gentleman, himself not very young, and his wife not twenty, being obliged a fortnight after marriage to leave his young bride, and embark upon the expedition against -------. (America?)

"Chloe in tears, Love's moon not half yspent." (6)

KG, Aug 26, 1775.

Epigram. A newly married couple are torn apart by the war.

75-295. Upon Lord E--be interesting himself in the county of Hampshire to procure an Address to the throne against the oppressed, and injured Americans.

"But two hundred and one to your list, my good Lord." (4)

LP, Nov 20, 1775.

Epigram. Quatrain. Satire on a landowner who had canvassed for votes to petition against the Americans.

75-296. Variations on a Monosyllable.

"Strike the lyre, prepare the song." (28)

L Eve Post, Nov 23, 1775.

Quatrains ending with Gage as rhyme. Satire on General Gage, court appointed Governor of Massachusetts.

75-297. Verses.

"Receive, O consecrated strand." (76)

M Chron, Jun 10, 1775.

Quatrains. A Whig republican poem. Freedom's persona urges the Americans to resist clerical and royal tyranny and oppression in the tradition of the ancient Spartans, Romans, and Hampden and Sidney of the English Revolution.

75-298. Verses by a Young Lady Twelve Years Old on her Father, now an Officer at Boston.

"Keep my father safe, O God." (24)

Lady's M 6 (Aug 1775), 439.

Tetrameter couplets. A young girl prays that her father, an officer at Boston, will not be killed by the American traitors and rebels, and that the war will end.

75-299. Verses made by a Young Lady on the Departure of her Lover to America.

"Ah soft awhile! in plaintive strain." (36)

Lady's M 6 (Dec 1775), 672.

Regular ode. Sentimental stanzas about a woman's grief upon separation from her lover gone to America.

75-300. Verses occasioned by the late Warlike Preparations.

"Hark the English Lion roars." (32)

LP, May 22, 1775; M Chron, May 24, 1775.

Quatrains. Patriotic lines encouraging war against France and Spain; probably an old song that could be adapted to the present times.

75-301. Verses occasioned by the Spanish Armament.

"Britons! rouse, for haughty Spain." (32)

M Chron, Jun 5, 1775.

Patriotic quatrains directed against the menaces of Spain and France. But the British navy, led by Keppel, Rodney, Saunders, and others, will repel them.

75-302. Verses to the Memory of Dr. Warren, the Celebrated Orator, who was slain upon the Heights of Charles-town, Gloriously Fighting against Mercenary Troops for the Liberties of America. On the 17th of June, 1775.

"O Great reverse of Tully's coward heart." (20)

LP, Jul 31, 1775.

Ode in heroic quatrains. Panegyric on Joseph Warren, the American leader who gave his life on Bunker's Hill in support of his expressed ideals.

75-303. Vox Populi, Vox Dei.

"Deluded M[onar]ch! say how long." (24)

Freeman's J, Oct 5, 1775.

Quatrains. A criticism of King George for the tyranny that is responsible for the destructive war (with America); but he should know that the people will resist, for the voice of the people is the voice of God.

75-304. [Warm is the contest of the Patriots now.]

"Warm is the contest of the Patriots now." (10)

L Eve Post, Aug 3, 1775.

Epigram. Satire. A comment on "the [London] Livery's late contest to see the King on the Throne," concluding with a wish to see the King deposed.

75-305. [Wesley, John (?).]
On the Troubles in America.

"The gath'ring clouds with aspect dark." (36)

Mat M & West M 1 (Sep 1775), 494-5.

A Methodist hymn deplores the beginning of civil war and asks that we pray for God's protection.

75-306. [What consolation can afford relief!]

"What consolation can afford relief." (14)

MP, Jun 12, 1775.

HC. A criticism of Sandwich and the Scot Junto at court for lying about the American will to resist oppression, to stand and fight bravely. Sandwich had lied about Dr. Warren and the alleged cowardice of Bostonians.

75-307. [What faithless Gaul and Power of haughty Spain.]

"What faithless Gaul and Power of haughty Spain." (16)

Freeman's J, Jul 20, 1775; St J's C, Jun 13, 1775.

HC. The present King and Parliament, venal and corrupt, have succeeded in imposing an arbitrary government on England.

75-308. [When Charles the Second held the Ball.]

"When Charles the Second held the Ball." (4)

Freeman's J, Oct 14, 1775; St J's C, Feb 4, 1775.

Epigram. The despotic court is now called "the Junto," not the "Cabal."

75-309. [When mutual passions fire the mind.]

"When mutual passions fire the mind." (20)

The Vocal Magazine (London: Harrison, Bew, 1778), pp. 151-4.

Song. Probably late 1775. Anger causes unnatural behavior and the end of society. America and Britain should compromise their views and end the bloody contest.

75-310. [While George surrounded by his minions.]

"While George surrounded by his minions." (21)

Freeman's J, Aug 24, 1775.

Tetrameter couplets. We in Ireland and Britain must rebel against a venal Scotch government and fight for liberty.

75-311. [While Pleasure reigns unrival'd on this Shore.]

"While Pleasure reigns unrival'd on this Shore." (28)

St J's C, Jul 29, 1775.

HC. We in England must stop this cruel and atrocious war. Scenes of carnage are imagined in Boston streets.

75-312. A Whim. Vice Triumphant; or Impudence, Faction, Profaneness, and Debauchery Rewarded . . .

"To spread sedition far and wide O," (12)

M Chron, Feb 4, 1775.

OC. Ironic satire on Wilkes. The persona of Wilkes speaks, explaining his subversive political and social views.

75-313. Whitehead, William.
Ode for his Majesty's Birth-Day, 1775.

"Ye Powers, who rule o'er States and Kings." (30)

C Chron, Jun 16, 1775; Cumb Pacq, Jun 29, 1775; G, Jun 22, 1775; G Eve Post, Jun 20, 1775; KG, Jun 21, 1775; Lady's M 6 (Jun 1775), 326; L Chron 37 (Jun 20, 1775), 592; L Eve Post, Jun 20, 1775; LP, Jun 21, 1775; MJ, Jun 20, 1775; M Chron, Jun 22, 1775; MP, Jun 22, 1775; PA, Jun 22, 1775; St J's C, Jun 20, 1775; also LM 44 (Jun 1775), 317.

Regular (Horatian) ode in sixains. Whitehead prays for peace, for union and concord.

75-314. [Who fram'd these cursed acts? The Patriots cry.]

"Who fram'd these cursed acts? the Patriots cry." (4)

MJ, Feb 28, 1775; MP, Mar 1, 1775.

Epigram. Only the devil could have framed the Intolerable Acts -- not that Jacobite Mansfield or the King's lawyers.

75-315. Written in America, on General Gage's fourth Paragraph against Immorality.

"Why, what in the name of Old Nick can he mean." (8)

The Muse's Mirror (London: Baldwin, 1778), II, 39.

Quatrains. Satire on Gen. Thomas Gage.

75-316. Written June 4, 1775.

"Propitious us'd to rise the morn." (16)

L Chron 37 (Jun 3, 1775), 535; PA, Jun 5, 1775; WM 28 (Jun 15, 1775), 370.

Regular ode, written for the King's birthday. Begs for an end to the civil war and the restoration of peace.

75-317. [Ye Sylvan Nymphs who haunt the woodland glades.]

"Ye Sylvan Nymphs who haunt the woodland glades." (32)

MP, Dec 6, 1775.

Quatrains. Pitt does not speak any more for America and freedom; nor does North care for peace and freedom. Boston objects to several British acts against America -- the Stamp Act, the Quebec Act, the Intolerable Acts, and peace and freedom disappear from America.

75-318. [You, my Lords, at this season, you gentlemen all.]

"You, my Lords, at this season, you gentlemen all." (33)

L Eve Post, Oct 31, 1775.

Hexameter couplets. Satire on the King's speech asserting the right to fight for empire, to fight against the American rebels.

Prints

75-319. The Patriotick Barber of New York, or the Captain in the Suds.

"Thou Patriot grand, maintain thy Stand." (6)

Engr. with sixain. February 8, 1775.

George 5284 (V, 194-6). Dolmetsch, pp. 76-7. Halsey, pp. 215, 217.

Capt. Crozer, commander of a British naval vessel, is refused a shave by a New York barber, a Son of Liberty. Camden and Chatham look on approvingly. See the complete poem, "On Mr. Jacob Vredenbergh," Morning Post, Jan 11, 1775, 75-180.

75-320. Six-Pence a Day.

"If you Gent^n Soldiers should die and be damn'd." (6)

Engr. with one couplet and one quatrain. October 26, 1775.

George 5295 (V, 202-3).

An anti-recruiting satire picturing the distress to which the English common soldier is subjected: he is starving, shot at by the Americans, and exploited by the Scotch.

75-321. [When Fell Debate and Civil Wars Shall Cease.]

"When fell Debate and civil Wars shall cease." (6)

Engr. with HC. LM 44 (1775), frontispiece.

George 5283 (V, 194).

A hope that Britain will be reconciled with America and that trade will be resumed, and France and Spain defied.

1776 Books & Pamphlets

76-1. [Arnot, Hugo]
The XLV. Chapter of the Prophecies of Thomas the Rhymer, in Verse; with Notes and Illustrations. Dedicated to Doctor Silverspoon, Preacher of Sedition in America.
  Edinburgh: Elliot, 1776. 19p.

"In distant climes in days of yore." (c. 130)

Notices: LR 4 (Jul 1776), 78.

Sabin 66006.

Copies: BL 11632.f.63; NUC CSmH, CtY, N, NjP, RPJCB.

Mixed verse forms. Ironic satire expressed in the figure of a persona who favors rebellion. Ridicules the zealous Presbyterian supporters of the rebellious Americans, those who foment discord and sedition--republicans (those who hate kings and murdered Charles I) and bigots (those who oppose the Quebec Act, that is, "the liberal and humane purposes of allowing the French in Canada their own laws and religion")--all who rejoice at the death of kings and at treason in America. Dr. Witherspoon has contributed to this civil discord, treason, and murder. The point is that the American Rebellion is rooted, according to the poet, in Puritan Presbyterian fanaticism, hostility towards monarchy and the established order, and willingness to start a civil war. (Dr. Silverspoon is Dr. John Witherspoon, a signer of the Declaration of Independence and President of the College of New Jersey. This verse pamphlet was evidently one of the results of a sermon by Witherspoon at Princeton, N.J., on May 17, 1776--The Dominion of Providence over the Passions of Men. . . . To Which is Added, An Address to the Natives of Scotland residing in America [Philadelphia: Aitken, 1776].)

76-2. Bedlam, A Ball, and Dr. Price's Observations on the Nature of Civil Liberty. A Poetical Medley.
  London: Dodsley, 1776. i + 5-23p.

"An Indian, who, from morn to night." (c. 300)

Notices: CR 41 (Apr 1776), 320; MR 54 (May 1776), 421; LM 45 (Jun 1776), 326; LR 3 (May 1776), 414; PA, Apr 10 & 23, 1776.

Sabin 4284.

Copies: BL 163.1.29; Bod Godwyn Pamph 1725; NUC DLC, NN, RPJCB.

Octosyllabic couplets. Satirizes frivolity and corruption, and at the same time Richard Price's egalitarian notions that reduce all to a natural state and justify colonial rebellion. One of the two responses in verse to Price's Observations on the Nature of Civil Liberty (1776). See 76-34: Tait's The Flight of Freedom, a poem which favors Price's humane views. There were over thirty replies to Price's polemic.

76-3. Champion, J[oseph].
   The Progress of Freedom; A Poem.
   London: Davis, 1776. 5-14p.

"For years unnumber'd Freedom view'd mankind." (180)

Notices: CR 42 (Sep 1776), 231; MR 55 (Aug 1776), 157; L Chron 40 (Aug 10, 1776), 148; LR 4(Sep 1776), 232; SM 38 (Aug 1776), 448.

Copies: BL 162.1.61, 161.1.22.

The inscription to the King is signed "J. Champion." HC. The spirit of freedom wandered from Greece to Carthage, Rome, the barbaric Middle Ages in Europe, and then finally to Britain, her proper seat, especially under the House of Hanover. Now it is "the noblest part" of George III "To punish rebels," because "Rebellion" is the "foe of Freedom." Chatham is faulted--his speeches raise sedition. But North is praised--his policies regarding taxation will bring concord and order, helped by Britain's fleets and armies. Concludes with the hope that King George will crush the rebellion.

76-4. [Combe, William ?]
   The Heroic Epistle Answered: By the R[ight] H[onourable] Lord C[raven].
   London: Wilkie, 1776. 3-11p.

"Hiss on, hiss on, ye needy Wags." (c. 180)

Notices: CR 41 (Feb 1776), 153; MR 54 (Mar 1776), 240; L Eve Post, Feb 13, 1776; LR 3 (Apr 1776), 333.

Copies: BL T.667 (5), 162.1.73; NUC CtY, DFo, MH, NN.

Hudibrastics. Doggerel satire on Craven for his arrogance and cowardice, great wealth and pride in his peerage, which noble status, he believes, excepts him from criticism of his poor behavior, including his defence of the Americans. On the last page his pro-American posture is described ironically. This poem continues the satire on Lord Craven in Combe's Heroic Epistle, 75-7.

76-5. The Complaint: Or Britannia lamenting the Loss of her Children. An Elegy. Inscribed to That learned Philosopher and able Statesman, Benjamin Franklin, LL.D. F.R.S.
   London: Brewman & Marriner, [1776]. 7p.

   "Sorrowing, upon Hibernia's sea-girt strand." (68)

   Copies: BL 11630.e.12 (15); NUC MH, MiU-C.

   Elegiac quatrains. Britannia, sitting upon the shore of Ireland, mourns "The King's War," i.e., the civil war with America; the death of Montgomery and Warren; and the death of many at Lexington and at Bunker's Hill. The ministry, according to the poet, is waging an unjust war. But the motives of the Americans are also suspect. Closes with an expression of hope for peace and reconciliation, and the return of the Americans to Britain's "bosom." (The poem was written in 1776, as the allusion to Gen. Montgomery's death indicates. Franklin does not appear in the poem, and there is no separate inscription. It may be America Lost, 78-1.)

76-6. [Day, Thomas ?]
   America, An Ode. To the People of England.
   London: Almon, 1776. 10p.

   "Far o'er the western azure main." (114)

   Notices: CR 42 (Jul 1776), 73; MR 55 (Jul 1776), 72; GM 46 (Jul 1776), 374; L Mag 45 (Sep 1776), 495.

   Sabin 1009.

   Copies: BL 164.n.39; NUC CtY, DLC, MiU-C, NN, RPJCB.

   Regular Pindaric ode; imitation of Gray's Bard. English ships with "hostile legions" approach American shores and are greeted by shrieks and sounds of woe and by the spirit of William Penn, founder of Pennsylvania, who speaks of strife to come in Freedom's cause and prophesies doom for a corrupt Britain, as happened to Spain in Peru. The war against America is unjust and unnatural. But America fights in the spirit of Alfred, Magna Charta, Hampden, and Sydney. Cited are Boston and Congress. (Reprinted in New Foundling Hospital for Wit [1786], IV, 263-70.)

76-7. [Day, Thomas]
   The Devoted Legions: A Poem. Addressed to Lord Germaine, and the Commanders of the Forces against America.
   London: Ridley & Kearsly, 1776. ii + 8p.

   "When sordid CRASSUS led his destin'd band." (135)

   See 76-8.

76-8. [-----]
-----. [2nd & 3rd eds]
London: Kearsly & Ridley, 1776. iii + 14p.

"When sordid CRASSUS led his destin'd band." (215)

Notices: CR 41 (Feb 1776), 153-4; MR 54 (Mar 1776), 242; LP, Jun 3 & 5, 1776; LR 3 (Apr 1776), 333.

Sabin 18982.

Copies: BL 163.1.59 (1st ed); NUC DLC, MH, MiU-C, PHi, & RPJCB (1st ed), CtY, NjP, RPJCB (2nd or 3rd eds).

The "Argument," as it stresses luxury and corruption, tyranny and slavery, is in effect addressed to the political and moral state of Britain.
HC. Crassus, an ancient Roman general, prepares an expedition against the Parthians, allies of Rome. A tribune, Atteius, opposing the war, confronts him and prophesies destruction of the legions and their leader for breaking the treaty. Implies thus the same fate for Lord Germaine and the forces sailing for America.

76-9. [Edwards, Bryan]
Ode for the New Year, 1776.
London: Almon, 1776. 9p.

"Genius of Albion! whither art thou fled." (123)

Notices: CR 41 (Feb 1776), 154; MR 54 (Apr 1776), 339-40; KG, Mar 2, 1776; L Chron 39 (Feb 29, 1776), 213; L Eve Post, Feb 29, 1776; L Mag 45 (Apr 1776), 212; LR 3 (Feb 1776), 154-5; SM 38 (Apr 1776), 211.

Sabin 56699.

Copies: BL 11633.g.5, 164.n.37; NUC CtY, MB, MiU-C, NN.

Irregular Pindaric Ode. The poet invokes the spirit of Britain to return to save the nation from corruption, discord, luxury, and ruin. This spirit inspires America to be free. France is now taking her revenge. In vain did Prince William defeat the Scots at Culloden, King William force the tyrant James II to flee, and Hampden and Sydney die. Admiral Saunders (who has just died), wept that "Stuart pride" lost the empire he had won. In America there is an unnatural war--Britain "Turns on herself, and drinks her children's gore!" Victory, under the circumstances, is defeat; Spain and France exult over this war. But the future will show America great and powerful, generously nourishing "Th'expiring parent." As Justice damns the guilty parricides responsible for this conflict, "perjur'd senators" and "venal lords," the spirits of Sydney and Russell approve the patriot cause and express pleasure at American victory.

(Also in his Poems, Written Chiefly in the West-Indies [Kingston, Jamaica: Aikman, 1792], pp. 48-52 as "Ode, Written in England, during the American War"; and in New Foundling Hospital for Wit [1786], VI, 7-12.)

76-10. An Elegiac Epistle from an Unfortunate Elector of Germany to his Friend Mr. Pinchbeck.
London: Douce, 1776. i-iii + 5-27p.

"I, who in glory's radiant lists enroll'd." (c. 400)

Copies: BL 840.1.17 (6); NUC CSmH, CtY, DLC.

HC. Ironic satire on King George III. Imagines that George, forcibly returned to his German dominions, writes to Pinchbeck about his "melancholy situation," deprived of the power and glory of kingship. He reviews some past history in this complaint, alluding to such painful events as Wilkes' release from the Tower, the St. George's Fields Riot, Beckford's insulting snub, and American victories in Canada (!). He is frightened by the vision of Charles I's execution and the violent death of oppressive rulers. Clearly, George is "A sovereign fitted to a Stuart's heart," having succeeded in tyrannizing by law where the Stuarts had failed. But still the threat of revolt is real in Luttrell, Horne, Wilkes. He begs for Pinchbeck to contrive a pair of wings that could set him free so that upon his restoration he could hang or burn "These curs'd republicans." There are general allusions to Scots he favored and Scots in search of a place. (The satire is too severe for an attribution to Mason.)

76-11. Four Excellent New Songs, I. The Britons Resolution to conquer their Rebels in North America. II. Britannia's Address to her children. III. The Lover's Parting. IV. The New Broom.
Newcastle: n.p., 1776. 8p.

I. "Come all you valiant soldiers and bold British tars." (78)

II. "Rouse rouse my dear sons, and no more languid lie." (36)

Copies: BL 11621.a.5 (6).

Only two songs are relevant, the first, hostile to the Americans, and the second, favoring them. I. Urges the defeat of the rebels and justifies the war and the need to reinforce Gen. Gage. American cowardice in the French and Indian war, American unwillingness to share the burden of the expense of protection against the French by paying taxes, and Puritan Republicanism are evidence of the hostile attitude which justifies the British cause. Cited are Hancock, "the traitor Lee," Adams, Washington, Putnam, and loss of trade.
II. Britannia urges Britons to go to America to live in freedom because the ministry is oppressive and despotic, and the bishops support slavery with their votes.

76-12. Freedom, Sacred to the Memory of General Richard Montgomery, Commander in Chief of the Continental Forces, in the Reduction of Popery and Canada. Whose Glorious Fall, in the Support of Constitutional Liberty, against the Encroachments of Arbitrary Power, (In the Storm of Quebec, on Sunday the 31st of December) closed the Important Year, 1775.
  Dublin: Bingley, 1776. [4-6] + 7-36, 39-42, 41-42p. (pagination imperfect at end)

"Urg'd in Defence of Freedom, and of Life." (540)

Notices: HM 6 (Jun 1776), 420-2.

Copies: NUC ICN, MiU-C.

HC. Eulogizes Chatham and Burke, reviews flight of the oppressed to the New World because of Stuart oppression, and notes their desire to remain loyal to Britain. But because of Scotch influence and North's ministry, Britain is determined to tax and crush the Americans. Congress thereupon requests Montgomery to lead an expedition against Popery and Canada where, at Quebec, he falls, joining an equally illustrious hero, Wolfe, in death. Both died for freedom, and Montgomery is mourned in England as well as in America. Believes that the extension of the Royal Prerogative (the King's power over Parliament) will destroy constitutional liberty. Cited are Goldsmith's <u>Deserted Village</u>, Richard Price, Stamp Tax, Tea, Mansfield, Gage, and the Quebec Act.

76-13. Free[th], John.
  The Warwickshire Medley: Or, Convivial Songster. Being a Collection of Original Songs, Political, Humourous, and Satyrical. Together with Many Other Select Pieces: Calculated for the Times. By J. Free.
  Birmingham: Pearson & Rollason, [1776]. viii + 142p.

Copies: BL 11601.b.44; NUC DFo, MH.

85 songs. This medley is largely a collection of Freeth's lyrics written 1765-75, with one exception: "Dudley Rout. A Song. On the Celebration of the Victory on Long Island" (1776). The following songs are particularly selected for their relevance, quality, and significance:

The American Contest	Pope's Address to his good Friends
Bunker's Hill	in England
A Dialogue	Prorogation
Hard Times	The Soldier's Complaint
The Ins and Outs	The State Jockeys
Lord G[eorg]e S[ackville]'s	The Statesmen
Promotion	The Times.

Most of these songs appear in the serials, which should be consulted.
  Freeth's songs appeared in many editions, the 6th in 1790; each collection

changed according to the times. See 82-10: Modern Songs and 83-15: A Touch on the Times.

76-14. The Genius of Britain, To General Howe, The Night Before the Battle At Long-Island. An Ode.
   London: Sewell, Wallis & Stonehouse, 1776. 13p.

   "The raven, on the darksome yew." (124)

   Notices: CR 42 (Nov 1776), 389; MR 55 (Dec 1776), 481-2; GM 47 (Jul 1777), 332; LM 45 (Dec 1776), 663; LR 5 (Feb 1777), 150; SM 38 (Nov 1776), 608.

   Copies: BL C.141.aa.1.

   Introduction of 2 sixains + 28 quatrains. A ballad more than ode. A loyal poem. Britain prays that Howe will prevail in the battle to come, destroy "Riot," and subdue the rebels. The Americans are execrated; they are not inspired by liberty. The spirit contrasts the past happy state of the colonies, its peace and prosperity, with the sad reverse of fortune in the present violence and danger. Nations defeated by Britain in the last war are now delighted. "By her children pierc'd, [Britain] bleeds" and they hope to "rise" by ruining her. Criticizes Chatham who, an "apostate" moved by "mean ambition," "infant wish for pow'r," encourages this war and "exalt[s] her foes." But praises North and Howe, their work approved by the gods, by Justice and Virtue.

76-15. Liberty: A Poem. To Which is Added The Modern Politician. By the Same Author.
   York: Flexney, 1776. 3-9 + 11-14p.

   "In yonder mead where silence reigns." (48)

   Copies: NUC NN.

   ("Liberty," a non-political poem about license and licentiousness of drunken brawlers, etc., is not included.) "The Modern Politician"--quatrains. The poet inquires of the "Modern Politician" the nature of contemporary politics, and is informed that self-interest, not the common good, motivates the dominant party. Having deceived the King, statesmen rule as they please. But those in the Opposition are "Traitors" who "Pretend allegiance to the King."

76-16. Lord Ch-----m's Prophecy. An Ode; Addressed to Lieutenant General G-ge. With Explanatory and Critical Notes, By the Editor.
   London: Almon, 1776. 5-16p.

   "When boasting G-ge was hurry'd o'er." (210)

   Notices: CR 41 (May 1776), 405; MR 54 (Jun 1776), 504; GA, Mar 21, 1778; GM 46 (May 1776), 228; LR 3 (May 1776), 411; SM 38 (May 1776), 265.

Copies: BL 163.1.60; Bod Godwyn Pamph 1692 (13); NUC CtY, DLC, MH, MiU-C.

Also "A New Edition" in 1776 (Sabin 63094--NUC NN). Six-line stanzas. Dedication to Richard Price, dated April 16, 1776. Chatham harangues Gage, sent to America where British troops have fallen. Franklin inspires the Americans. France and Spain will no longer dread or respect Britain. America will break "degenerate Britain's chain" and teach the world that "the people alone are supreme." Cited are Bute, Lord Percy, Putnam, Battle of Lexington, Bunker's Hill, "Yankies," Warren, Corsica, Saunders, Wolfe, Quebec Bill (Canada Bill), Dunmore, Montgomery, Shelburne, Richmond, Burke, Grafton, Tories, Mansfield, Rigby, Amherst. (Also in New Foundling Hospital for Wit [1786], II, 75-80.) Attributed to William Mason. See Advt, Dean and Squire, 82-13.

76-17. [Mason, William ?]
A Congratulatory Poem On the Late Successes Of The British Arms, Particularly The Triumphant Evacuation of Boston.
London: Baldwin, 1776. 16p.

"While temper'd wisdom at the helm presides." (242)

Notices: CR 42 (Jul 1776), 153; MR 55 (Sep 1776), 237; GM 46 (Nov 1776), 522; L Mag 45 (Sep 1776), 493-4; LR 4 (Sep 1776), 233; PA, Aug 3, 1776; SM 38 (Aug 1776), 448.

Sabin 15476.

Copies: BL 163.1.61, 11643.aaa.1 (2). Under pseud. of Malcolm McGreggor.

See 76-18.

76-18. [-----]
-----. To Which Is Added, An Ode to Mr. Pinchbeck, Upon His Newly-Invented Patent Candle-Snuffers.
Dublin: Wilson, 1776. 27p.

Copies: BL 11643.aaa.1 (2), 12330.aaa.11 (3); NUC DLC, ICN, MB, MH, MiU-C.

See 76-19 for Mason's Ode to Mr. Pinchbeck, of which the above is a reprint. The following is of A Congratulatory Poem. HC. Satire on the Court and its indefensible war policy. An independent bard ironically congratulates Britain on her victories (really defeats) in America. The war against the rebels is self-defeating, for--should Britain really win--she will have the right to tax "a barren plain." Concludes with expression of disgust over the obstinacy with which Britain pursues the irrational war: "And boast . . . a firmness in the wrong." The satire is also directed at the Scots, the King, North, Germain, and the pro-government writers--Shebbeare, Tucker, and Samuel Johnson (appearing as Churchill's Pomposo).

76-19. [-----]
Ode to Mr. Pinchbeck, Upon his Newly Invented Patent Candle-Snuffers, By Malcolm M'Greggor, Esq; Author of the Heroic Epistle to Sir William Chambers, and the Heroic Postscript.
London: Almon, 1776. 9p. [other eds 11p.]

"Illustrious Pinchbeck! condescend." (96)

Notices: CR 41 (May 1776), 405; MR 54 (Dec 1776), 504; GM 46 (Aug 1776), 371; L Mag 45 (Jun 1776), 325-6; LR 3 (May 1776), 385-8; WM 32 (Jun 13, 1776), 369-70; W Misc 6 (Jun 10, 1776), 259-62. Also SM 38 (Jun 1776), 326.

Copies: BL 11602.gg.25 (8) (5th ed); Bod Godwyn Pamph 1713 (7) (4th ed), 1493 (5th ed); NUC NcD (1st ed), CtY, IU, MiU-C, NjP, & RPJCB (2nd ed).

5 London eds in 1776; I use the 5th. Regular Horatian ode. Satire on England and its campaign to suppress the American rebellion. Imagines the possible aid of Pinchbeck's new snuffers to the state of affairs--implores him to "snuff the candle of the state," which once burned bright until "Bute dared to snuff it." Pinchbeck is also requested to "trim Old England's candle" of every "tory Chief." Then in North America, the poet asks "Our lady of Quebec" to snuff the flames of Boston with a huge extinguisher supplied by the inventor. Cited also are North, Mansfield, Sandwich, King George, Germain, et al.

76-20. Maurice, Thomas.
Hagley. A Descriptive Poem.
Oxford: Fletcher et al.; London: Dodsley & Kearsly, 1776. 41p.

"Once more, with trembling hand, I strike the lyre." (c. 570)

Notices: CR 41 (Dec 1776), 474; MR 56 (Feb 1777), 156-7; G Eve Post, Jun 30, 1778; L Chron 41 (Jan 16, 1777), 57; LM 46 (Apr 1777), 216.

Copies: BL 161.m.6, 11630.f.36; NUC CtY, InU, MH.

HC. Dedication dated Sept. 1, 1776. A topographical, descriptive, historical poem about the late Lord Lyttelton's estate near Birmingham. Maurice provides, in the last 18 lines, a typical patriotic, anti-Bourbon sentiment--he writes hopefully of peace with America to come soon and of Britain united triumphant over France and Spain. In the revision--in his Poems and Miscellaneous Pieces (London: Kearsly et al., 1779), pp. 109-34--this conclusion was reduced to 6 lines in which Maurice simply expresses the hope that the King will settle the American troubles and bring concord.

76-21. [Nugent, Nicholas]
An Answer to the Tears of the Foot Guards, In which that respectable Corps are vindicated from the Charges of Puppyism and Cowardice. Inscribed to Capt. Horneck and Ensign Richardson.
London: Kearsly, 1776. 5-21p.

"Of Men, renown'd in Arms, the Poet sings." (c. 180)

Notices: CR 41 (Apr 1776), 319; MR 54 (May 1776), 422; L Mag 45 (Jun 1776), 326; LR 3 (May 1776), 412.

Sabin 94569.

Copies: BL 164.n.40, 11620.gg.25 (10); Bod Godwyn Pamph 1691 (6), 1709 (4); NUC CSmH, IU, MiU-C, NN, RPJCB.

Nugent was Lieutenant in the First Regiment of Foot Guards. HC. Praises the "glorious few" who go to battle, forsaking pleasure and mock war maneuvers at home, and defends them from petty critics, like the author of Tears of the Foot Guards (see 76-37), who have charged them with effeminacy. Hancock and Bute are alluded to.

76-22. Ogden, James.
The Contest, A Poem, In Two Parts.
Newcastle upon Tyne: Robson, 1776. 70p.

"The Man's ambition, Muse, advent'rous sing." (c. 1530)

Copies: NUC ICN, MiU-C, RPJCB.

HC. A little epic in the style of the Miltonic sublime. Deplores an ambitious King who set Britain and its colonies at odds; attacks Bute, his rise to power after the fall of Pitt, his introducing Tories and Jacobites to Court; criticizes Grenville for blundering, introducing taxes into America, and forcing the colonists to unite and resist in defense of their rights; the Rockingham ministry is ineffective in its attempt to stop the troubles. The colonists unite--some in fear of tar and feathers--their forces march, led by Washington, appointed chief by Congress. Concludes with account of the campaign that led to British flight from Boston to Halifax. Other significant citations: the tea tax, Stamp Act, Burke and Conway, the Intolerable Acts (embargo on trade with Boston), Hancock and Samuel Adams, the Battle of Lexington, Putnam, corruption, Bunker's Hill, and John Dickenson.

76-23. The Patriot's Progress, or the Post of Honour Disputed: A Familiar Epistle, Inscribed to John Wilkes, Esq.
London: Wallis & Stonehouse, 1776.

Notices: CR 42 (Nov 1776), 389; MR 55 (Dec 1776), 480-1; SM 38 (Nov 1776), 608.

Copies: none located.

"A squib for the domestic incendiaries, and American demagogues." (From the Critical Review, and repeated in Scots Magazine.)

76-24. A Poetical Address to Almighty God. Supposed to be delivered by His Most Sacred Majesty, George III. Occasioned by the Present Troubles in America. And intended to convey a just Idea of the Character and Conduct of that Great Monarch, To Every Subject in the British Empire. By a Lover of His Country.
London: Harrison, Bladon, et al., 1777 [i.e. 1776]. i + i-iv + 12p.

"Great Sov'reign of the World! to Thee." (209)

Notices: CR 42 (Dec 1776), 474.

Copies: BL 643.k.6 (7), 162.m.66.

Inscription dated Dec. 24, 1776. Octosyllabic couplets. In the prose Preface, the poet expresses his disapproval of the revolt by the American colonies; therefore wishing to prevent others from joining them, he paints a favorable picture of the King and "his upright and judicious ministers," knowing full well that he espouses "the unpopular Opinion." In the poem, the persona of the King prays to God and defends his reign, his concern for his subjects' welfare, his judgment in choosing judges and ministers--especially North, "The real friend of liberty" who, it is hoped, will "stop rebellion's rapid force." The persona also defends his concern for the church and religious tolerance, and for the people's rights, so that he cannot understand why "They would from my protection fly."

76-25. [Pottinger, Israel]
The Duenna: A Comic Opera, in Three Acts. As it is performed, By his Majesty's Servants.
London: Johnson, 1776. 43p.

Song. Boreas. Tune. Give Isaac the Nymph. "Give Boreas the man who no honour can boast." (16) p. 16.

Glee and Chorus. Tune. This bottle's the sun of our table. "Canting John. This pamphlet shall answer 'em all, Sirs." (8) pp. 38-9.

Notices: CR 42 (Aug 1776), 152; MR 55 (Aug 1776), 156.

Copies: BL 11777.c.34; NUC DLC & MiU (1st ed), DLC, MB, MiU, NN, & TxU ("A New Edition" [1776]).

A satire on the ministry, including the King and Bute, with references to the American War, ironically indicating the absurdity of this weak and ineffectual administration's attempt to conquer America. Two songs illustrate the satire, one sung by the persona of Lord North and the other by John Wesley. The first emphasizes the corruption of North, the second Wesley's inhumanity: his Calm Address "proves that murder's right" and soon "swords of steel / Will bring the Yankies down." (Not to be confused with Sheridan's Duenna, which this parodies to some extent.) See 76-26.

76-26. [-----]
The Political Duenna: A Comic Opera, In Three Acts, As it is performed by the Servants of his Britannic Majesty, With Lord North's Recantation. To which are Added. I. A Letter to Mr. John Wesley on his Calm Address to the Americans, supposed to be written by the celebrated Junius. II. A Letter from an Irish Gentleman in London to his Friend and Countryman, in his Britannic Majesty's Service in America.
Philadelphia: Bell, 1778. 56p.

Evans 16017; Sabin 63764.

Copies: NUC CtY, MB, MH, PHi, RPJCB.

The American edition of Pottinger's Duenna. A Letter to Wesley, signed "Americus" (Arthur Lee), is taken from the Gentleman's Magazine 45 (Dec 1775), 561-4. The song Lord North's Recantation first appeared in the London Evening Post, March 5-7, 1778, and was reprinted in the General Advertiser, March 9, 1778.

76-27. [-----]
The General Fast; A Lyric Ode: With A Form of Prayer Proper for the Occasion; And a Dedication to the King. By the Author of the Duenna.
[London]: Fielding, Walker, et al., [1776]. iv + 12p.

"Genius of Britain guide my song." (138)

Notices: CR 42 (Dec 1776), 473-4; MR 55 (Dec 1776), 481; L Mag 45 (Dec 1776), 664; LR 5 (Jan 1777), 80; SM 38 (Dec 1776), 661.

Sabin 26877.

Copies: BL 11632.g.17; Bod Firth d.6 (11); NUC TxU.

The attribution to Pottinger is more likely in view of the nature of his Duenna (in the NUC this is under Richard Sheridan). The King proclaimed December 13, 1776, as a Fast Day--a day of "General Fast and Humiliation"--because of "the just and necessary Measure of Force which We are obliged to use against our rebellious

Subjects in our Colonies." But the Dedication to the King insists that "the American war" was "founded in injustice." It is also foolish because the Americans are "our equals" in arms and arts.

Regular Horatian ode. Once freedom was dear to Britain; but now--guided by Bute, Mansfield, Sandwich--Britain is debauched and impotent, the realm sinking. The colonies, an asylum for freedom, have their heroes: Putnam, Washington, Lee, Arnold, Montgomery. Closes with a toast to freedom, and a prayer for the success of "our American brethren." Incidentally, objects to the purchase of German mercenaries. Also cited are North and Germain.

76-28. Pro-Pinchbeck's Answer to the Ode From the Author of the Heroic Epistle to Sir William Chambers.
London: Ridley, 1776. i-ii + 5-12p.

"He who of late a Bard and 'Squire." (120)

Notices: MR 55 (Jul 1776), 72; LR 5 (Appendix 1777), 527.

Copies: BL 162.1.74, 1493.h.14; Bod Godwyn Pamph 1423; NUC CtY, MH, PU, TxU.

Six-line stanzas, regular Horatian ode. A Tory answer to Mason's anti-court poems. Ironically sings of the supposedly venal court and deluded Kings, whose tyranny is withstood by freedom's sons--Wilkes, Wat Tyler, and Jack Straw. Mason's satirical muse is inspired by Catharine Macaulay, her brother John Sawbridge, Richard Price, and liberty in the wilds of America.

76-29. Reflections on Government, With Respect to America. To Which is Added, Carmen Latinum.
London: Lewis, 1776. 32p.

Carmen. "Frustra infidelis concidit Allebrox." (44) pp. 29-32.

Notices: CR 41 (Apr 1776), 323; MR 54 (Apr 1776), 332.

Sabin 68694.

Copies: BL 102.g.33; NUC RPJCB.

In the prose essay, the author argues for lenity in treating the Americans, not for war. He believes that they, as British subjects, must be represented before they can be taxed. To him, the war is "unjust and ruinous." A "secret" influence is at work, through which the King's prerogative operates, and undermines Parliament. The poem continues the objection to the war, citing Burke, Chatham, and Camden. A zealous patriot, he wishes all British warships wrecked on the American coast. He also declares that America should willingly pay taxes if represented in Parliament.

76-30. Robinson, Mary M.
Elegiac Verses to a Young Lady, On the Death of her Brother; Who was Slain in the Late Engagement at Boston.
London: Johnson, 1776. 6-17p.

"While the fond tear bedews a Brother's shade." (120)

Notices: CR 40 (Dec 1775), 480; MR 54 (Feb 1776), 163; UM 57 (Supplement 1775), 373-4.

Copies: NUC ICN, InU, MB, NN, RPJCB.

The Advertisement is dated November 1775. The poem was written soon after the Battle of Bunker Hill. Elegiac quatrains. The poet consoles her grief-stricken friend, but she does not believe the soldier's cause is just. Britain is wrong to coerce the colonies, "To force allegiance to despotic sway," and its cause is "inglorious." Britain has wronged injured Liberty.

76-31. The South Wiltshire Petitioners, A Mock Heroic Poem, attempted after the Manner of Hudibras.
[London]: Snagg, [1776].

Notices: HM 6 (Jul 1776), 491; L Mag 45 (Jun 1776), 326.

Copies: none located.

"A satyr on a West country knight, stiled in the poem, Sir Bluster, for interesting himself in procuring a petition to Parliament, for conciliatory measures with America." (From the Hibernian Magazine.)

76-32. Stevenson, John Hall.
An Essay Upon the King's Friends, With An Account of Some Discoveries Made in Italy, And Found in a Virgil, Concerning the Tories. To Dr. S----l J-----n.
London: Almon, 1776. 36p.

"Treading the dreary waste, with feet unblest." (c. 100)

Notices: CR 41 (May 1776), 247; MR 54 (Apr 1776), 338; L Mag 45 (Sep 1776), 494; LR 3 (Appendix 1776), 537.

Sabin 22977.

Copies: BL T.1159 (5), 110.e.49; NUC CtY, DLC, MH, RPJCB.

A mixture of prose and verse (HC), burlesque of Samuel Johnson's Marmor Norfolciense and satire of his Tory principles expressed in Taxation No Tyranny, particularly that of virtual representation as applied to the colonies. Satirizes also the court dominated by Scotch Tories. (Also in his Works [London: Debrett, 1795], vol. I, pp. 249-88. Part of A Fragment of an Epic Poem. Book IV, published from the author's MS, appears herein and in his Works, II, 149-70.)

76-33. Stevenson, William, M.D.
   An Ode to Peace: occasioned by the present Crisis of the British Empire.
   Dublin: Stewart, 1776.

   Notices: Freeman's J, May 25, 1776.

   Copies: none located.

   See 78-39 (main entry) and 82-25 for later editions.

76-34. [Tait, John ?]
   The Flight of Freedom. A Fragment.
   London: Williams, 1776. iii + 18p.

   "As Caesar ridicul'd the words he heard." (c. 450)

   Notices: CR 42 (Sep 1776), 231; MR 55 (Aug 1776), 159-60; L Mag 45 (Oct 1776), 550; LR 3 (May 1776), 414; SM 38 (Aug 1776), 448.

   Copies: NUC ICN, NN, PHi.

Dedication to Richard Price. Blank verse allegory. An Old Man meets dejected Liberty, banished from various countries and now England. Disbelieving, he confirms the absence of Liberty from England--debtor's prisons, forfeitures for failing to pay taxes, venal magistrates, parliamentary bribery; so he plans to seek another land with heroes like Hampden, Wilkes, Pitt, Wolfe, Camden, but regretfully no Shelburne, who will remain to save the colonies, however. Thereupon he sees Liberty leave for America. Luxury also figures as a basic cause of the troubles.

76-35. [-----]
   Poetical Legends: Containing The American Captive, and The Fatal Feud. To which is added, The Fall of Faction, A Poetical Vision. By the Author of the Cave of Morar.
   London: Donaldson, 1776. 48p.

   The American Captive. "Turn, turn, said Jessy, Henry turn." (160) pp. 9-19.

   The Fall of Faction; A Poetical Vision. "Now Sleep had clos'd the peasant's eye." (140) pp. 37-44.

   Notices: CR 41 (May 1776), 405; MR 54 (Jun 1776), 504; L Mag 45 (Jul 1776), 384; LR 3 (Appendix 1776), 535; SM 38 (May 1776), 264.

   Sabin 63647.

   Copies: BL 643.k.12 (3); Bod W71 Jur (1); NUC CSmH, DLC, MH, MiU-C, NN, RPJCB.

Advertisement dated February 29, 1776. The narratives are meant to effect "An honourable Reconciliation between insurgent America and Britain" by stressing "the clemency and mercy of our benevolent Sovereign." The profits of the book's sale are promised to the "Fund for the Relief of sick and wounded Troops, and of the Widows and Orphans of the Soldiers Slain in America, fighting for the Laws of their Country." The American Captive: ballad narrative. Henry leaves Jessy to join the rebel Americans in "Freedom's glorious cause." Captured with many others, he and they are condemned to hang as traitors. But upon Jessy's intercession Henry is spared--and the rest--by the merciful British general. All are freed, and Henry regrets his defiance of King and country.

The Fall of Faction: sixain stanzas (ababcc), allegory. Faction, with its American lies about the English taking up arms against the King, is eventually displaced by Concord, Truth, and Liberty, aided by Justice and Mercy.

76-36. The Tears of Britannia. A Pindaric Ode. On the present American War. Written in the year 1776.

"High o'er a sea-bleach'd, rocky steep." (220)

In Poems on Various Subjects (Edinburgh: Gordon & Murray, 1780), pp. 110-21.

Copies: BL 1467.c.24.

Regular Pindaric ode. Britannia mourns the destructive civil war with America and utters a diatribe against luxury and corruption.

76-37. The Tears of the Foot Guards, upon their Departure for America: Written by an Ensign of the Army.
London: Kearsly, 1776. iv + 5-12p.

Notices: CR 41 (Apr 1776), 319; MR 54 (Apr 1776), 338; L Mag 45 (Jun 1776), 326; LR 3 (May 1776), 411; SM 38 (Apr 1776), 211.

Sabin 94569.

Copies: BL 164.n.38; NUC CSmH, CtY, DLC, MB, MH, MiU-C.

See 76-38.

76-38. -----: Written by an Ensign of the Provincial Army. The Second Edition, with Additions and Improvements.
London: Kearsly, 1776. iii-viii + 9-16p.

"Were I, like Niobe, all tears--I'd weep." (c. 125)

Copies: BL 11630.d.11 (5), 11632.g.70; Bod 1700 (12); NUC CSmH, CtY, DLC, NN, PHi, RPJCB.

HC. Satire on timid, effeminate military officers. An officer of the Foot Guards petitions "Lady H---" to intercede to prevent his being sent to fight the Americans. He cites the savage Indians, Bunker's Hill, Lexington, Boston. He has no ambition for a civil war or desire for honor, preferring the pleasures of female society at home. He wishes the Scots to fight; he does not care to be "A Mark for Riflemen in <u>Boston</u> Field." Cited also are Gower, Sandwich, Joseph Warren, Montgomery. The addition of one word in the title of the 2nd ed suggests a revision of point of view. (For a reply, see 76-21.)

76-39. Thistlethwaite, James.
The Prediction of Liberty.
London: Williams, [1776]. i + 39p.

"Soft breath'd th'ambrosial sigh that kiss'd the trees." (c. 760)

Notices: CR 41 (Mar 1776), 239; MR 54 (Apr 1776), 338; LR 3 (Mar 1776), 230-4.

Copies: BL 11630.e.16 (5); Bod Godwyn Pamph 1728 (20), 1734 (12); NUC DLC, MB, MH, NN, PU.

Dedication dated Feb. 26, 1776, to Henry Cruger, MP for Bristol. HC. Liberty speaks of ruin, depopulation, famine, destruction, and prophecies of England's devastation by war because corruption rules the realm; mourns England ruled by despots; defends rebellion when Freedom is the prize and the King, aided by Bute and Mansfield, rules insensibly, blind to impending destruction. America invites those few devoted to freedom. Her rebellion is justified. Characters of King George, Bute, and Mansfield are presented. Cited are Hampden, Sydney, Wilkes, the Scots, and the Stamp Act.

76-40. Three Excelent [sic] New Songs. I. A Mournful Song Upon the Battles of America 29th of April, 17th of June. II. The King Lay Musing Upon his Bed. III. The Turkish Lady.
N.p.: n.p., 1776. 8p.

A New Song on the Battle of America. "Good people all I pray draw near." (96)

Sabin 95736.

Copies: NUC NN.

Only the first song is relevant. Ballad in octosyllabic couplets, mourning the conflict in which many died for "Britain's rights in America." Gage exhorts his troops against Putnam's brave but outnumbered Americans. Mourns great British losses in the Battles of Lexington and Bunker's Hill. Concludes with a wish that Parliament be guided by "right heads" and with a prayer for peace.

76-41. Wells, Christopher.
  Address to the Genius of America. By the Rev. Christopher Wells, Lecturer of Penryn, Cornwall.
  London: Baldwin; Falmouth: Allison; Bristol: Cadell, [1776]. 8p.

  "Come, genial spirit, hear the earnest call." (110)

  Notices: CR 41 (Apr 1776), 319-20; MR 54 (May 1776), 421; L Mag 45 (Jun 1776), 326; LR 3 (May 1776), 414.

  Copies: NUC RPJCB.

  Blank verse. Why has youthful America turned against Britain, unmindful of the feelings of "the affected parent"? America prospered under Britain's protective wing--surely she must be blessed with content. Now, however, ills advance upon "this devoted country," while "Science" and "Plenty" leave it. The Genius of America must "return / To duty and to bliss," beg for pardon and mercy from "power parental," from Britain "Who weeps while she corrects." See 81-16, for annotation of the 2nd ed, considerably enlarged.

76-42. The Whig. A Poem.
  London: Dixwell, 1776. v-xiii + 15-30p.

  "On prostrate Rome when fierce Octavius stood." (244)

  Notices: CR 41 (Feb 1776), 154; MR 54 (Apr 1776), 338; L Chron 39 (Mar 5, 1776), 225; LR 3 (Feb 1776), 170; SM 38 (Apr 1776), 211.

  Copies: BL 163.m.31; NUC CSmH, CtY, TxU.

  (Half title="Detection of Discord: Or, The Whig.") In the prose preface, the author states his Whig view that the principles of the British constitution have of late been neglected or attacked, that the measures of the present ministry do not merit approval. He wishes that taxation of America be abandoned and that the old system of trade and control through the Navigation Act be restored. He approves the repeal of the Stamp Act by the Rockingham administration. He cannot accept the present ministry's policy of forcing America to submit. He would retire the ministry to private life.
  HC. In the poem, he objects to the American War, a civil war, which a just King would oppose. He berates the Scots, too eager to wage this war. Rockingham, Richmond, and Effingham can save the country. Others praised for defending the English constitution are Camden, Bentinck (Cavendish), Shelburne, Savile. Concludes with wish that those responsible for "an impious war," "false couns'lors," be removed from the throne; then discord across the Atlantic will end.

Serials

76-43. [A. stands for America, struggling hard for freedom.]

"A. stands for America, struggling hard for freedom." (34)

Freeman's J, May 23, 1776.

An abcedarian poem for politicians and the situation regarding the American War. King George and Mansfield are threatened with vengeance. Also cited are Boston, Canada, Carleton, Effingham, Ireland, Montgomery, North, Quebec, King Charles.

76-44. The Address of Britannia to General Carleton, on his Defeat of the Rebels before Quebeck.

"With tears of gratitude to thee I bend." (82)

M Chron, Sep 5, 1776.

HC. Praise of General Carleton for his repulse of the American attack on Quebec; satire on the opposition -- possibly Barre -- for treason.

76-45. Advice to a Painter. A Fragment.

"Painter now perform thy part." (66)

M Chron, Jul 17, 1776.

Three-stress couplets. Contrast of the glorious past with the dismal present -- the king deceived by flattering courtiers, by Bute and North, by others seeking their self-interest at the expense of American blood. Concludes with comment on the civil war and a pathetic hope for peace.

76-46. Advice to Britons. A New Song, adapted to the Tune of an Old Song, called Hearts of Oak.

"Come Britons unite in the national cause." (37)

Say's, May 4, 1776.

Song. While the war with America progresses, English traders and workers suffer, commerce being at a standstill. The war should end, the troops recalled, so that all may enjoy the blessings of peace. A revision of the same song, Nov. 12, 1774: 74-20.

76-47. Advice to the Patriots. With the Happy Effects of a Well-Disposed Flagellation. Exemplified in the Conduct of a Great Character.

"The more Lord N[or]th is flogg'd by Patriot zeal." (16)

MJ, May 25, 1776.

HC by Causidicus. The more Lord North is flogged by the patriots, the more vigorous he appears to become.

[Almighty Lord of Hosts, by whose commands.] G Eve Post, Sep 28, 1776. HC. An old prayer adapted by the late John Byrom is now applied "to the present unhappy contentions in America." See 76-78.

76-48. An Alphabet for Little Masters and Misses.

"A Stands for America -- now for ever gone." (22)

L Eve Post, Sep 7, 1776.

An abcedarian poem against the court and the American War which Bute began. Cited are the King, Mansfield, North, corruption, New York.

76-49. An Alphabet for Little Masters and Misses.

"A stands for Americans -- fighting to be free." (21)

L Eve Post, Jan 9, 1776.

Hexameter couplets. Abcedarian poem. A summary of the situation, the civil war, the fight against oppression, from the anti-court position. Cited are King George, the clergy, Mansfield, North, corrupt Parliament, rights.

76-50. American Civil War.

"Pride with Injustice (hear what's said) writes." (10)

St J's C, Jul 25, 1776; Freeman's J, Sep 5, 1776.

HC. England fights with the colonies only because of pride; but no one can win the civil war. Both may be wrong, but both cannot be right.

76-51. An American Parody on the Song of "Rule Britannia."

"When Britons first, by Heaven's Command." (54)

Freeman's J, Nov 5, 1776; St J's C, Oct 5, 1776; UM 59 (Sep 1776), 146.

Song. The Americans have learned from Britons that they will never tolerate tyranny and never be slaves.

76-52. The American Prayer.

"Father Supreme, whose loving care." (36)

L Eve Post, Apr 20, 1776.

Quatrains. A prayer (or hymn) that America have peace and liberty and that she adhere to Britain. Allusion to William Smith's celebrated <u>Sermon on the Present Situation of American Affairs</u> (1775).

76-53. American Rebellion, and Highland Loyalty.

"Why should our Col'nies madly run." (48)

SM 38 (Mar 1776), 148.

The same poem as "Verses on the American War," 76-380.

76-54. An Ancient Prophecy of Merlin.

"When a white horse shall o'er the lion rule." (10)

Freeman's J, May 30, 1776; L Eve Post, May 23, 1776.

HC. England will fall because of the King's obstinacy, the disunion of the people, and the use of mercenaries to fight its battles.

76-55. An Ancient Prophecy of Merlin.

"When the rank thistle shall in sweets surpass the rose." (10)

G, Aug 12, 1776; L Eve Post, Aug 8, 1776.

Hexameter couplets. Lines prophetic of the disintegration of the empire and of the loss of America when certain events transpire, such as the assertion of Scotch power over the English.

76-56. [And vast transactions contemplating.]

"And vast transactions contemplating." (6)

M Chron, Aug 17, 1776.

OC. A fragment of verse on the peace commission of the Howe brothers. They were planning to meet the rebel representatives on Staten Island; and it is indicated that the Americans were "Seduc'd by Patriots to rebel."

76-57. Another Ode for 1776.

"On the green banks which guard her strand." (26)

HM 6 (Jan 1776), 63; L Chron 39 (Dec 30/75-Jan 2, 1776), 7; L Eve Post, Dec 30/75-Jan 2, 1776; MJ, Dec 30/75-Jan 2, 1776; M Chron, Jan 3, 1776; PA, Jan 2, 1776; T&C 7 (Supp 1775), 710; WM 31 (Jan 11, 1776), 81; Asylum for Fugitives (London: Almon, 1776), I, 55-6; New Foundling Hospital for Wit (1786), IV, 216-7.

Parody of Whitehead's New Year's Ode, 1776. America protests the attack on her rights and her freedom. She denies that her sons rebel. The British are "deceiv'd, mistaken men" to think that Americans will yield to force. America insists that commerce is the basis of a fruitful relationship with Britain and that the war is entirely Britain's fault.

76-58. An Answer to a Late Tale. The Provoked Steed; or, An Able and Good-Natured Rider may (happen to) get a Fall.

"The Man who plann'd the chariot-pin." (64)

West M 4 (Feb 1776), 101.

Quatrains. An answer to Jenyns' poem on America: 76-190. The horse America, mistreated and provoked by several acts of the British (Stamp Act and Proclamation of Rebellion), throws its rider. Let us hope the rider can regain the horse. But there is a better and gentler way to control America by not abusing "nat'ral rights."

76-59. An Antient Prophecy Found among the old Papers Lately Discovered in Somerset-House.

"The time will come, old wizards say." (29)

M Chron, Jun 6, 1776.

OC. A prophecy that the Scotch Jacobites will dominate the government and the Americans will rebel.

76-60. An Apology for the Alteration of a Great Man's Conduct.

"At Minden, the enemy just at my nose." (4)

L Eve Post, Feb 13, 1776.

HC. Satire on Germain for cowardice: he does not fear American riflemen three thousand miles away.

76-61. An Apostrophe.

"Say, shall this age when Germaine lives, not claim." (12)

MP, Jun 19, 1776.

HC. Satire on Germain.

76-62. At a Consultation of the Junto.

"Jenk. Curse on these cowards -- how they fight." (9)

L Eve Post, Sep 7, 1776.

Tetrameter couplets. Ironic satire on the ministry. The court advisors -- or junto (Jenkinson, Gilbert Elliott, Mansfield) curse the Americans for fighting too well. They promise another campaign against the "Yankies" with the assistance of mercenaries -- Russian, German, and even Turkish.

76-63. At a Masquerade Ball Given at Ranelagh June 14, 1776 . . . .

"My laurels I cropt to bring hither to you." (8)

HM 6 (Jul 1776), 472-3.

Hexameter couplets, on America. Honor to Carleton for saving Quebec, and "success to Old England, and death to its foes!"

76-64. A Ballad.

"At *** late." (42)

MJ, May 30, 1776.

Song. Satire on those in the East Riding of Yorkshire who wish to present a loyal address to the King, favoring the government's policy of coercion against America.

76-65. A Ballad, Written, or Rather Spoken, By a Gentleman, at Coming into a Coffee-House, from the Above Musical Entertainment. [Whitehead's Ode for his Majesty's Birth-Day, June 4, 1776.]

"Say no more of the breezes -- some wine and tobacco." (24)

An Asylum for Fugitives (1776), I, 148-9; New Foundling Hospital for Wit (1786), II, 143-4.

Quatrains. Not a parody or satire on Whitehead's birthday ode for 1776, but a positive reaction to the government's coercive measures. The poet urges vigorous and consistent measures.

76-66. The Bellman's Cantata. As it Was Sung or Said at the Royal Exchange.

"O Yes! O Yes! O Yes!" (25)

M Chron, Aug 19, 1776.

The news of Admiral Howe's safe landing on Staten Island sends the stock market up. ("Bulls, Bears, and Jews" react favorably to the prospect of peace.)

76-67. The Birth Day. [June 4, 1776?]

"Round [George]'s chair, in triple rows." (8)

New Foundling Hospital for Wit (1786), II, 131.

Quatrains. Satire on the flattery lavished on the King.

76-68. Blooming Dale: An American Soliloquy.

"Hark! hark, the hostile Band I hear." (28)

PA, Nov 16, 1776; Jeffery Dunstan, Fugitive Pieces (1789), pp. 46-7.

Ballad on the beginning of the American war which destroys the life of pastoral simplicity of young American lovers. They are separated and the woman complains. See 89-2.

76-69. A Bot Mot of Dr. Price's, Versified. See Dr. Price's Pamphlet.

"Scotch Machiavel in Tory spleen grown old." (22)

Freeman's J, May 25, 1776; L Eve Post, May 18, 1776; MJ, May 21, 1776.

HC. Causidicus opposes to Mansfield's words that the colonies must be conquered Price's celebrated saying that the British fight for dominion over the colonies but that the colonies fight for the noble cause of self-dominion. (Richard Price, Observations on The Nature of Civil Liberty . . . [1776].)

76-70. Boston in Distress.

"While pleasure reigns unrival'd on this shore." (28)

GM 46 (Mar 1776), 135; HM 6 (Apr 1776), 283; SM 38 (Mar 1776), 147; WM 32 (Apr 25, 1776), 147.

HC. Imagines all sorts of atrocities committed by the British in Boston and begs for the end of "this cruel carnage," this fratricidal struggle.

76-71. [Britain! my country! whence these dire alarms.]

"Britain! my country! whence these dire alarms." (86)

W Misc 5 (Jan 22, 1776), 433-5.

HC. A sermon in verse. The American rebellion is one of a combination of factors contributing to lower moral standards. Britain must have moral reform before conditions will improve.

76-72. Britain's Fate.

"To warn poor Britain of her fate." (4)

New Morning Post, Dec 13, 1776.

Epigram. An objection to the attempts being made to enslave Britain -- such as the proclamation of a Fast Day for December 13, 1776.

76-73. Britannia. An Ode to Dr. Myersbach. To be Sung or Said in the Several Streets and Lanes throughout the Cities of London and Westminster. Tune -- All in the Land of Essex.

"To Myersbach, great Piss--kyker." (40)

St J's C, Oct 17, 1776.

Song in quatrains. Satire on the Tory Scots and Jacobites who, like quacks, are ruining the country and causing her to mistreat the American colonies. "The Whigs desclaim the War"; but because Toryism and Popery have poisoned and blinded Britain, she requires a purge of her eyes. Cited are Sam Johnson, Shebbeare, Stuart, Bute.

76-74. Britannia. A Vision.

"In solemn silence, at the midnight hour." (68)

W Misc 6 (Jul 22, 1776), 404-5.

Blank verse. A vision of Liberty deserting Britannia for America; Tyranny thereupon tears Britannia to pieces.

76-75. [Britannia cries, O sons, you scarce can know.]

"Britannia cries, O sons, you scarce can know." (23)

St J's C, Jul 20, 1776.

HC. Britain is in a shambles now, although it was prosperous and free fifteen years ago. Who is to blame? -- "Scotch politicians" who engage in bribery.

76-76. Britannia's Caution to Lord G. Germaine.

"So -- so." (6)

L Eve Post, Jan 20, 1776.

Another snap at Germain after "The Times are Altered," L Eve Post, Jan 18, 1776. He deserves execution. See 76-338.

76-77. Burgoyne, John.
A Prologue, written by General Burgoyne, spoken at Boston in New England, before the Tragedy of Zara, performed by Officers of the Army for a public charity.

"In Britain once -- it stains th' historic page." (36)

HM 6 (Apr 1776), 279-80.

HC. The Prologue to Zara, a tragedy by Aaron Hill, was spoken by Lord Rawdon at the opening of the theatre at Boston when it was garrisoned by British troops under the command of Sir William Howe. Boston was under siege at the time. Burgoyne's anti-Puritan remarks on the closing of the theatre in Cromwell's day, "quell'd by the bigots' roar," have a peculiar relevance for this bibliography. However, the epilogue, also written by Burgoyne, is not particularly relevant. -- There are textual variants in the version of the prologue appearing in The Dramatic and Poetical Works of the Late Lieut. Gen. J. Burgoyne (London: Whittington, 1808), II, 238-9. Reprinted often in 1782: see 82-55.

76-78. Byrom, John.
[Almighty Lord of Hosts, by whose commands.]

"Almighty Lord of Hosts, by whose commands." (24)

G Eve Post, Sep 28, 1776.

HC. A prayer of Francis the First when at war with the Emperor Charles the Fifth was adapted by the late John Byrom and now is applied "to the present unhappy contentions in America."

76-79. The Campaign; An Ode on the Triumphal Return of Gen. Gage from the Wars, with three Addresses, humbly inscribed to that HERO.

"Strike loud the harp to General Gage." (66)

Freeman's J, Jan 2, 1776; L Eve Post, Apr 11, 1776.

Regular (Horatian) ode in sixains. Satire on General Gage and the administration that underestimated the martial courage of the colonists besieging the British in Boston.

76-80. The Canada or Quebec Bill.

"Stand fast, O Head, upon that Subject's Neck." (8)

MP, Mar 14, 1776; St J's C, Feb 1, 1776.

HC. An objection to the Quebec Act, a Popish Act that will bring Catholic persecution. Burke, Wilkes, Dunning, Glynn should try to do something about this act that Bute favored.

76-81. A Character. Taken from a Poem Speedily to be Published, called, The Portrait of the Times.

"Yet why should Satire thus engross the Muse." (36)

MJ, May 28, 1776.

HC. The age is dominated by satire, but there are some men who can sustain praise -- Richmond and Chatham.

76-82. Col. B[arre] and Lord N[orth]. A Parliamentary Tiff.

"Restore! roar'd Bar-e t'other day." (26)

MP, Mar 14, 1776.

Dialogue in quatrains. Col. Barre complains of poor leadership that has lost America, urging the appointment of Shelburne; but North defends himself.

76-83. Colvill, Robert.
Sacred to the Memory of Col. Abercrombie, of Major Pitcairne of Dysart, and their very gallant Fellow-Officers and Soldiers who fell in their Country's Cause in pursuit of Victory against the Rebels at Bunker's Hill, July 17, 1775. [June 17, 1775.]

"What godlike form from yon imperial car." (34)

L Chron 39 (Apr 25, 1776), 404; WM 32 (Apr 25, 1776), 146. Also in Robert Colvill, Atalanta A Poem (London: Bew, 1777), pp. 40-1; The Caledonians: A Poem (Edinburgh, 1779), pp. 40-1; The Poetical Works (London: Dodsley et al; 1789), pp. 121-3. Revised in the last.

Colvill mourns the death of his Scots countrymen in the Battle of Bunker's Hill.

76-84. [Constitutional Toasts.]

"May the Incendiaries of Old England -- be Hanged." (10)

L Eve Post, Sep 17, 1776; MJ, Sep 19, 1776.

Three anti-government toasts, including a wish that the American cause prosper.

76-85. The Contented Man.

"If fortune smile, if fortune frown." (24)

KG, Jan 31, 1776; L Chron 39 (Jan 25, 1776), 96.

Sixains. The simple and sincere contented man does not fear the fleets of France or Spain, or cares not for the defeat of Hancock or North, or fights not for fame like Percy. He enjoys love and the simple life.

76-86. [Cooper, Myles.]
Stanzas written on the Evening of the 10th of May, 1776. By an Exile from America.

"To thee, O God, by whom I live." (96)

GM 46 (Jul 1776), 326-7; SM 38 (Jul 1776), 384; WM 33 (Aug 8, 1776), 207-8.

Sixains. The Rev. Myles Cooper, President of King's College [Columbia], New York, and a loyalist, narrates the story of his harrowing escape from a Whig mob in New York, 1775.

76-87. A Country Man's Exclamation on Hearing that Long Island was Taken.

"Long Island -- have they only taken now." (2)

LP, Oct 23, 1776.

Extempore. Howe has taken too long to win Long Island.

76-88. [The _cowardly_ Colonists pray to the Lord.]

"The _cowardly_ Colonists pray to the Lord." (17)

M Chron, Jan 18, 1776.

Ironic hexameter couplets on the alleged cowardice of the colonists who fight fearlessly, motivated by freedom; but the British have only the phantom of honor to fight for. Gage and Mansfield are cited.

76-89. The Decision: Or the American Controversy Settled. A Tale.

"A Monkey once of sober life." (c. 330)

An Asylum for Fugitives (London: Almon, 1776), I, 30-40.

OC. An animal fable about a family argument begun by the father taking advantage of his prosperous son. The father asserts his rights or prerogative; the son makes concessions, but refuses to be a slave and to allow the rest of the family to prey upon him. A compromise is suggested whereby the father's superior position is respected, but his dominion is used "for wholesome ends."

76-90. De Quo Narrandum Audiat.

"At the play! when the News of the slaughter arriv'd." (24)

L Eve Post, Nov 19, 1776.

Hexameter couplets. A satire on the King for enjoying the theater while there's slaughter on Long Island and elsewhere in America.

76-91. The Dialogue. A New Song; between A. Wedderburne and Sir G[ilber]t E[lliot]t.

"As Sawney was passing by Westminster Abbey." (50)

M Chron, Jan 19, 1776.

Song on the selfish Scotch who hope to make the most out of the war with the colonies -- Wedderburne and Gilbert Elliott as exemplars.

76-92. Dialogue between L[or]d N[ort]h and C[harle]s F[o]x, Esq.

"Says Charles Fox to Lord North, as together they sat." (52)

M Chron, Jan 10, 1776.

Hexameter couplets. Fox counsels North to give up Germain and accept the help of Burke and Barre.

76-93. Dialogue. Thane. Americans.

"Th. Send, send, says Thane, more troops and ships away." (7)

St J's C, Jul 27, 1776.

HC. Thane (Bute) encourages the war against the Americans, who insist they will "fight" Popery and tyranny.

Drewe, Edward. Lycidas. An Elegy. "Oh, Dorilas, and must we part." (148) PA, Sep 5, 1776; St J's C, Aug 1, 1776; West Mag 4 (Oct 1776), 542-3; W Eve Post, Sep 10, 1776. Elegiac quatrains. Drewe writes of Boston and the slaughter at Bunker's Hill. See 75-8.

76-94. The Eagle and Rebellious Birds. A Fable.

"Old Aesop made the feather'd train." (66)

L Chron 39 (Jan 23, 1776), 85; Ox M 13 (Jan 1776), 419-20.

OC. Animal fable. The moral is that the colonies have gone too far, despite all the help from the parent country, and now their rebellion will be crushed, and "the upstart race" will be reduced "To tameness, poverty, and peace."

76-95. Election Song. By an Independent Freeholder. Tune, -- "Jolly Mortals fill your Glasses."

"Jolly sons of Mirth and Freedom." (36)

L Eve Post, Jan 11, 1776.

Objects to having a contractor, who is supported by a corrupt ministry (North, Harley) as MP. Themes are corruption, North, Parliament.

76-96. Electioneering Songs.

"Curst be the wretch that's bought and sold." (12)
"Britons who boast your country's love." (12)
"The expences of war, and corruptions of peace." (16)

Freeman's J, Jun 20, 1776.

Three Irish election songs: 1. Vs. bribery and corruption. 2. Vs. tyranny and the ministry, for free elections. 3. Vs. the old Parliament, its taxes and corruption, and for a new. The old Parliament is also damned for making "Popish laws."

76-97. An Elegy on the Death of Doctor Warren.

"He's gone! Great Warren's soul from earth is fled." (68)

HM 6 (Mar 1776), 211-2.

HC. Dated from Philadelphia, June 28, 1775. Panegyric on Dr. Joseph Warren, who died in the Battle of Bunker's Hill. He is compared with Hampden, Raleigh, Russel, Sidney. With Adams and Hancock he was "united in great freedom's cause."

76-98. Elegy to the Memory of the Late King.

"Peace to thy royal Shade, illustrious King." (56)

L Eve Post, May 9, 1776.

Elegiac quatrains. The Scotch, especially Bute, are to blame for the sinking state and for the King's abuse of his power. George must learn the lesson of Charles I. (The late King is George III, before he came under the wrong influence.)

76-99. The Emigrant. An Eclogue. Occasioned by the late numerous emigrations from the Highlands of Scotland.

"Fast by the margin of a mossy rill." (128)

SM 38 (Apr 1776), 213-4; WM 31 (Mar 21, 1776), 399-400.

HC. A protest at the Scottish emigrations to America -- caused by "hard oppression," ruthless monopoly, "barb'rous avarice," a change to crop production from raising sheep and goats.

76-100. English to the Colonists.

"We're very much in Wrath, regard our Votes." (2)

St J's C, Mar 26, 1776.

Epigram. The colonists should heed Parliament; otherwise they can be executed as rebels.

76-101. Epigram.

"Alas, alas, this poor deserted nation." (4)

Cumb Pacq, May 9, 1776; G Eve Post, Apr 30, 1776.

Quatrain. The patriots, supported by Richard Price, are endangering the nation.

76-102. An Epigram.

"Alas! we find it is too true." (6)

MJ, Nov 12, 1776; PA, Nov 14, 1776.

Sixain. "The Scotch Faction" ruthlessly and relentlessly pursue the war against America so far as to push it to Hell Gate. Allusion to Howe's tactics in the Battle of Long Island: he pursued the retreating provincials to Hell Gate (on Long Island).

76-103. Epigram.

"The Americans try'd first of all." (4)

Freeman's J, Oct 19, 1776.

Quatrain. Now that the Americans have melted down the King's statue for lead, Howe and Percy should beware.

76-104. An Epigram.

"As a little old Man, in a narrow cap'd Hat." (10)

Cumb Pacq, May 2, 1776.

Hexameter couplets. An objection to the panegyrics on Montgomery. On the other hand, Burgoyne will earn praise.

76-105. Epigram.

"Behold! The elements against us interpose." (4)

L Eve Post, Aug 24, 1776.

Quatrain. Even the elements are against Britain in this unnatural war, as the rising waters at Charlestown, S. C., bar prevented the British troops from engaging the rebels.

76-106. Epigram.

"Carlton, we've told, hath pass'd the Lakes." (4)

Freeman's J, Oct 1, 1776.

Quatrain. It is incredible that Carleton's campaign, his invasion of the colonies from Canada, is progressing so rapidly.

76-107. An Epigram.

"The CONGRESS so proud." (6)

MP, Oct 21, 1776.

On the Long Island campaign. The bold British army will drive Congress, who merely write well, from New York.

76-108. Epigram.

"The Congress thought to melt the King." (4)

Freemans' J, Oct 19, 1776.

Quatrain. Congress did not succeed in making the King show compassion; so now they melt his statue in order to shoot up the Howes.

76-109. Epigram.

"Flourish, O Brib'ry; Justice be thou dumb." (4)

St J's C, Jun 20, 1776.

This Parliament is not doing, nor will do anything, about bribery in the seven years of its duration.

76-110. Epigram.

"The Ministry have rais'd, the People say." (4)

Freeman's J, Jul 16, 1776; St J's C, Jun 20, 1776.

The ministry (North et al.) must pay with their lives for their country's freedom and safety.

76-111. Epigram.

"No victory was ever more compleat." (4)

Freeman's J, Dec 5, 1776; L Eve Post, Nov 28, 1776.

Quatrain. On the British victory over the Americans on Lake Champlain -- which was fruitless.

76-112. Epigram.

"Quoth Jack to Tom on the Fast-Day." (4)

L Eve Post, Nov 21, 1776; MJ, Nov 23, 1776.

Satire on the Fast Day, Dec 13, 1776. We fast for Scotch crimes and pray for better times.

76-113. Epigram.

"Tho' rebels of their courage boast." (4)

L Eve Post, Nov 7, 1776.

Quatrain. Satire on debates in Parliament. Perhaps by means of a speech we can cause the rebels to fly.

76-114. An Epigram.

"Tyrants account, and call it power to kill." (4)

Freeman's J, Oct 1, 1776.

HC. An objection to the tyrannical politics of murder and fraud.

76-115. Epigram.

"Were we to tax America." (4)

PA, Nov 23, 1776.

On unlimited sovereignty. If the British were to tax America without limitation, only the ministers would profit (with places and pensions, and the power to bribe).

76-116. Epigram.

"What, to his People, says the Tyrant-Man." (4)

St J's C, Aug 6, 1776.

HC. Should the tyrant do as he pleases, even against the laws, the people will try him. (On tyranny and the prerogative.)

76-117. Epigram, Addressed to the Partial Paragraphist of the Gazette, who after being obliged to recount the rapid march, bravery, and conduct of Col. Arnold, thought to obscure his merit by calling him "one Arnold."

"One Arnold! and is this the hero's praise." (4)

L Eve Post, Jan 9, 1776.

Quatrain. Praise of Arnold for his heroic march into Canada in order to take Quebec: the source of the expression "one Arnold."

76-118. Epigram. America and England. [And] America.

"America is destin'd to the Chain." (4)
"Thus speaks America to all her Sons." (11)

St J's C, Jan 27, 1776; Freeman's C, Aug 31, 1776.

Epigrams. Britons must rejoice that their attempts to enslave America are unsuccessful for this would simply mean enslaving themselves. America is inspired by traditional liberty, and shall conquer injustice and oppression.

76-119. Epigram applied to the American Rebellion.

"Treason doth never prosper -- What's the Reason." (2)

KG, Jun 12, 1776; St J's C, Jun 8, 1776.

Should treason prosper, it would not be treason.

76-120. Epigram. By an Hollander.

"We standers-by with less Emotion hear." (6)

St J's C, Apr 30, 1776.

HC. The corrupt Parliament is bribed to vote for war against America; but Parliament would treat the colonists worse if they were Dutch.

76-121. Epigram on a Late Treaty, or the Difference between the Years 1714 and 1776.

"One Brunswick was call'd in to save the British Crown." (2)

L Eve Post, Mar 7, 1776.

The Crown is being threatened in 1776.

76-122. Epigram on a Wanton and Ill-founded Abuse of Mr. Burke's Public Character.

"As Constans rails without a cause." (8)

L Eve Post, Apr 13, 1776.

Quatrains. Satire on a newspaper writer who, without cause, vilified Burke.

76-123. Epigram On Sir Peter Parker's Wound Off Sullivan's Island.

"If honour in the breech is lodg'd." (4)

New Foundling Hospital for Wit (1786), IV, 243.

Satire on Admiral Parker whose breeches were torn off, his thigh and knee wounded, in the action against Sullivan's Island, June 28, 1776. See "A New War-Song": 76-214.

76-124. Epigram. On the Dilatory Proceedings of the Army in America.

"The British troops can surely never move too slow." (3)

L Eve Post, Aug 27, 1776.

Triplet. Satire on Germain for his poor leadership of the American campaigns: the army does nothing.

76-125. Epigram on the Jure Divino of Kings.

"Kings rule by right divine, nor can do evil." (3)

L Eve Post, Aug 8, 1776.

Epigram. Triplet. Satire on the monarchy. Objects to the divine right of Kings to do evil.

76-126. Epigram. On the Prospect of a French Invasion, while Great Britain is engaged with America.

"Now whilst the Quarrel with our Sons." (8)

PA, Nov 23, 1776.

Quatrains. The British do not fear the French or their threatened invasion.

76-127. Epigram on the 13th of December 1776.

"If praying would pay the Debt of the Nation." (4)

PA, Nov 23, 1776.

Objects to prayers on the Fast Day for the slaughter of American brethren.

76-128. Epigram. Spoken Extempore. On Reading the Proclamation for a General Fast.

"What needs a Proclamation for a Fast." (6)

Sent M 4 (Nov 1776), 526.

HC. Satire on the fast. Because of the expense of the war, we shall have nothing left to eat. A fast will soon be unnecessary.

76-129. An Epigram. The Quintessance of the Arch-Patriot's Speech to the Livery, at the Close of the Poll.

"Fair Liberty, cries W[ilkes], retires." (4)

G Eve Post, Jul 4, 1776.

Quatrain. Satire on Wilkes, defeated for election as Chamberlain. He no longer has the liberty to cheat.

76-130. Epigram. Upon W[IL]KES's last speech in Parliament.

"Hancock and Adams traitors are." (8)

G Eve Post, Jan 25, 1776; KG, Jan 27, 1776; St J's C, Jan 25, 1776.

Quatrains. Wilkes is a traitor for praising Hancock and Adams. He deserves to be executed.

76-131. An Epigramatic Dialogue Between two great Characters. On the Approaching Fast.

"No news arriv'd? -- Such nerveless drones." (8)

MP, Dec 2, 1776.

Quatrains. The King assures Germain that Howe and the soldiers will win.

76-132. Epigrammatical Postscript of a Letter from an Officer at Long Island to his Friend and Patron in the Ministry.

"Tho' you and your colleagues, by night and by day." (6)

L Eve Post, Oct 19, 1776.

Sixain. The ministry should act more quickly; otherwise the soldiers will go to hell. Pun on Hell-gate (a channel of the East River leading to Long Island Sound), and the reference is to the American defeat on Long Island.

76-133. An Epistle From A Martyr In The Shades, To Whom It May Concern Upon Earth.

"Yet then! before the fatal sword be drawn." (c. 600)

An Asylum for Fugitives (1776), I. 62-83.

Written probably in late 1775 or early 1776, as an allusion to Gen. Montgomery suggests. Dedication to Edmund Burke, "Defender of Liberty, Virtue, and the Rights of Humanity." HC. Charles I's ghost calls for an end to the war against America. He confesses to tyranny -- the use of divine right, prerogative, and influence to rule. But now contrite and repentant, he prays that England be saved from hypocrites, gold and fraud, and accepts his own execution which "left his country free." However, civil war has begun with the Battle of Lexington, despite the justice of the "righteous rebel" American cause, the just complaint against "legal wrong" and oppression. The war against him was justified, he admits, because Parliament was then free. Now freedom "rears her vagrant head" in the west, where right resists power, as in the Battle of Lexington.

76-134. Epistle from a Young Lady in Town to a correspondent at Canterbury.

"So I went to the House -- as you know I intended." (120)

LP, Mar 8, 1776; PA, Mar 9, 1776.

Anapest tetrameter couplets. Light satire on the debates in the House of Commons -- e.g., North's bill for hiring German mercenaries. The question is also raised about the right to tax and enslave the colonial Americans. Signed Louisa Chaucer.

76-135. An Epistle to Lord G. Minden.

"While you, my Lord, your faded honours wear." (44)

L Eve Post, Feb 10, 1776.

Elegiac quatrains. A woman complains of Germain's barbaric and unneighborly behavior. He had her hunting dogs killed.

76-136. Epitaph for Captain Morris.

"The World's Example, and his Country's Pride." (16)

PA, Sep 4, 1776.

HC. This officer died for an unworthy cause.

76-137. Epitaph on a Modern Patriot.

"Here lies John Wilkes! -- good passenger attend." (8)

MP, Nov 26, 1776.

HC. Satire on Wilkes. Ironic lines in praise of Wilkes -- prematurely dead.

76-138. Epitaph on General Montgomery.

"Dear Warrior-shade! Whom Fate's untimely hand." (10)

L Eve Post, Mar 12, 1776.

HC. The death of Gen. Montgomery, American patriot, will inspire "gen'rous youth" to avenge their country's wrong. He was killed before Quebec, Dec 31, 1776.

76-139. [Epitaph on General Montgomery.]

"To sects no bigot, of a liberal mind." (8)

L Eve Post, Mar 23, 1776.

HC. From the conclusion of an essay on Montgomery's life. Montgomery, Wolfe, Hampden all fought for freedom. Montgomery is not a "rebel."

76-140. An Epitaph on the Political Death of the Arch Patriot.

"Here lyeth / To the great Joy of Public and Private Society." (c. 40)

MP, Jul 10, 1776.

Epitaph. Inscription. An attack on Wilkes, who is here consigned to oblivion in a review of his career.

76-141. [Epitaph on the Political Death of Wilkes.]

"On Monday, July 1, 1776 / Departed this Political Life." (c. 25)

MP, Jul 18, 1776.

Epitaph. Inscription. Satire on Alderman Wilkes, having lost the election for the office of City Chamberlain.

76-142. Exhortation to Britain.

"Britain! thou envy of the polish'd world." (23)

MP, Sep 2, 1776.

HC. The poet views the rebellious colonists with disdain and calls on the British to defend their honor and law by "scourging the upstarts" through war.

76-143. An Extempore.

"Whilst villainous pensioners sit at the helm."

M Chron, Jan 25, 1776.

Epigram. Placemen simply want new taxes "to pay their d[amn']d pensions."

76-144. An Extempore Epigrammatic Question: To Which An Answer Is Desired.

"When George shall o'er America succeed." (2)

An Asylum for Fugitives (1776), I, 146.

Epigram. Satire on King George, who will be "a merry king indeed" when he succeeds over America.

76-145. Extempore. In Answer to the Lines Signed P. Addressed to the Congress, inserted in the Morning Chronicle of Yesterday.

"Thou worst of all the rhiming train." (12)

M Chron, Jan 12, 1776.

Quatrains. Satire on P., the author of "To the Congress," for his dullness. See answer in "To Q," Jan 18, 1776. See 76-355 & 76-352.

76-146. Extempore, on Lord Dunmore's issuing his Proclamation from on Board a Ship.

"Hail mighty Dunmore! great Viceroy!" (8)

MJ, Jan 11, 1776; PA, Jan 12, 1776.

Quatrains. Satire on John Murray, 4th Earl of Dunmore, the loyal Governor of Virginia, for attempting to enforce obedience on the colonists from a naval warship.

76-147. Extempore. On Observing that England is to Fast one Day after the Scotch.

"In former days, the Scots, they say." (6)

MJ, Dec 3, 1776.

Sixain. Epigram. The Scotch eat while the British fast.

76-148. Extempore, on Reading that Lord North was flung from his horse and broke his arm.

"Does not this omen threaten something worse." (14)

LP, Sep 23, 1776.

Four extempore poems on Lord North's accident. That Lord North broke his arm was of some interest to the wits for various reasons -- for its effect on the Junto (cabinet) and court and nation.

76-149. Extempore on reading that the Duchess of Gloucester was Delivered of a Prince at Rome.

"Ye powers that o'er our realm preside." (8)

G Eve Post, Feb 6, 1776; KG, Feb 7, 1776.

Quatrains. Fears of a Stuart pretender, fears for Protestantism in Britain, now that the wife of Charles Stuart, the present pretender, has given birth to a son.

76-150. Extempore. On the Late Retreat from Boston.

"Howe, witnessing in Boston his troops palpitation." (4)

M Chron, May 29, 1776; PL, May 16, 1776.

Epigram. Satire on Howe's evacuation of Boston.

76-151. Extempore, on the Review of the 1st and 2nd Battalions of Troops, in Frosty-Weather.

"Zeal may exclude the Dread of Cold." (8)

Lloyd's, Jan 17, 1776; PA, Jan 16, 1776.

Epigram. A complaint at the low pay of the common soldiers.

76-152. Extempore Verses.

"How distinguish'd that man is, both valiant and wise." (4)

W Eve Post, Dec 31, 1776.

Hexameter couplets. How can we reward a man of valor who promotes his country's glory?

76-153. Extempore Verses on the Poet Laureate's Ode for 1776.

"Alas! poor Master Laureate." (12)

L Eve Post, Jan 9, 1776.

Quatrains, chiding the laureate for not bragging of victories (over the rebels).

76-154. Extempore. Written the Anniversary of the Royal Accession.

"Ere while the House to Britain dear." (20)

L Chron 40 (Oct 24, 1776), 407; PA Oct 26, 1776.

Quatrains, celebrating the accession of George III. King George II and Prince Frederick died, and now another George is king. May he reign for many years! "Old Freedom's Parent, and her Prop."

76-155. A Fable. Addressed to the Right Hon. Lord N[or]th.

"Whoever makes an unjust claim." (42)

Freeman's J, Dec 6, 1776.

OC. The moral fable of greed that killed the goose that laid golden eggs has a lesson that can be applied to current events.

76-156. A Familiar Epistle from America.

"Excuse me, dear friend, I can't think it true." (51)

GM 46 (Jun 1776), 279; Lloyd's 38 (Jun 10, 1776); SM 38 (Jun 1776), 327.

Hexameter couplets. A loyalist satire on South Carolina rebels.

76-157. The Fast.

"The King proclaims a Fast to-day." (14)

MP, Dec 13, 1776.

Two epigrams. Satiric commentary on the Fast Day, December 13, 1776.

76-158. The Fast Day.

"When Abraham, full of sacred awe." (28)

G, Dec 13, 1776; Lloyd's 39 (Dec 11, 1776); L Chron 40 (Dec 12, 1776), 572; WM 34 (Dec 19, 1776), 402.

A hymn in quatrains. A serious Fast Day prayer to God to accept the petition of "guilty" Britain (for success in the American War).

76-159. The Fate of the British Lion; Or, the Difference between Last War and the Present.

"Last war he roar'd so loud, and look'd so grim." (4)

L Eve Post, Apr 4, 1776.

Epigram. In the last war Britain was brave and fearless; in this war, she is pessimistic and fearful.

76-160. The Female Remonstrance: An Ode. By a Lady. Set to the Music of The free and accepted Mason.

"In a hot civil war." (90)

L Eve Post, Mar 19, 1776.

Ode in sixains, song. A demand that the war should end and the soldiers and sailors return home. The woman's point of view regarding the American war.

76-161. The Following Lines were Lately Stuck on the Door of St. Stephen's Chapel.

"Britons of old, as antient records tell." (4)

W Misc 7 (Nov 25, 1776), 192.

Epigram. Satire on Britons, on MP's, who no longer care for freedom. They "barter liberty for sordid gains."

76-162. The following Lines were wrote with charcoal, on the walls of the new gaol in Philadelphia by an Officer [Captain (J.F.D.) Smyth, of the Queen's Rangers], and one of the first in it: . . .

"Confinement hail! in honour's justest cause." (24)

M Chron, Nov 6, 1782.

HC. Dated from Philadelphia Prison, Jan. 20, 1776. A British officer deplores "the days of Cromwell, puritannic (sic) rage" that has resulted in the colonial rebellion against "freedom, government, and laws."

76-163. [For what great end must Britons fast and pray.]

"For what great end must Britons fast and pray." (20)

L Eve Post, Dec 3, 1776.

Elegiac quatrains. Objection to the King's proclamation for a fast and for success in the American war on the grounds of its hypocrisy.

76-164. [Freeth, John.]
Dudley Rout. A Song. On the Celebration of the Victory on Long Island.

"Dudley's a loyal spot. (52)

A Warwickshire Medley (1776), pp. 137-9.

Dudley, a loyal borough in Worcestershire, celebrates Howe's victory on Long Island. The loyal inhabitants wish New York were taken and all the rebels and Presbyterians slain.

76-165. Gardner's Ghost, A Prophetic Ballad found in Merlin's Cave, Richmond.

"Let little villains conscience gor'd." (56)

Crisis 64 (Apr 6, 1776), 407-9.

Ballad. Col. Thomas Gardner, of Massachusetts, wounded at Bunker's Hill, June 17, 1775, died July 3. His ghost appears before the sleeping King George and predicts the rise of France and the downfall of Britain, frightening George "to attone his guilt" and bid "Gage go butcher [no?] more." George is also warned of the fate of Charles I and informed that he fights for Scotchmen.

76-166. General Washington. A New Favourite Song at the American Camp. To the Tune of "The British Grenadiers."

"Vain Britons boast no longer, with proud indignity." (48)

M Chron, Jul 20, 1776.

Song. An American song reprinted to illustrate the boastfulness of the rebels who must be chastised into obedience. Cited are North, George Washington, Wolfe, Hancock, France, Spain, Howe, Carleton.

76-167. Gibraltar; or, News from Madrid.

"Let's take Occasion from the present Hap." (10)

St J's C, Jul 23, 1776; Freeman's J, Sep 12, 1776.

HC. The pretender Charles will learn from King George who has increased his prerogatives upon the advice of Bute. Pitt no longer provides leadership and the nation is corrupted. (Note to "wicked": "See General Lee's excellent letter to General Burgoyne, in the St. James's Chronicle. Sat. Aug. 12, 1775.")

76-168. A Great Personage to Mr. Hartley, on his Experiment.

"I see, Sir, that the Flame you raise." (4)

MJ, Aug 17, 1776; PA, Aug 20, 1776.

Epigram. Hartley should teach Germain the art of putting out fires.

76-169. [Hail, Pennsylvania! from raging seas once more.]

"Hail, Pennsylvania! from raging seas once more." (18)

KG, Apr 6, 1776.

HC. Praise of Pennsylvania by a native returning from England, and a prayer that British ills and oppression will never enter there. Cited is the "tyrant mother."

76-170. Hastings, Thomas.
The Coronation. An Irregular Ode.

"To welcome in the auspicious morn." (34)

M Chron, Sep 21, 1776.

A loyal Pindaric ode.

76-171. Hastings, Thomas.
Ode for the Birth-Day of His Majesty.

"When first the tow'ring mountains rose." (64)

M Chron, Jun 5, 1776.

Pindaric ode. Stanza 4 briefly alludes to the American struggle.

76-172. Hastings, Thomas.
Ode for the Birth-Day of his Royal Highness George Prince of Wales, August 12, 1776.

"Hail Liberty! thou basis of delight!" (56)

M Chron, Aug 12, 1776.

Pindaric ode. Brief allusion to internal faction and trouble.

76-173. Hastings, Thomas.
Ode for the Birth-Day of his Royal Highness the Duke of Gloucester, November 25, 1776.

"Now bent to chear the southern clime." (32)

M Chron, Nov 25, 1776.

Another irregular Pindaric ode by Hastings, the volunteer loyalist laureat.

76-174. Hastings, Thomas.
On the Birth-Day of her Majesty, May 19, 1776. An Irregular Ode.

"Hark! 'tis the voice of Heav'n! Cease false alarms." (28)

M Chron, May 18, 1776.

Irregular Pindaric ode. The misled Americans should return to reason, Britain and peace.

76-175. The Heads: Or the Year 1776.

"Ye wrong heads, and strong heads, attend to my strains." (40)

G Eve Post, Nov 21, 1776; HM 6 (Dec 1776), 859; KG, Nov 27, 1776; Ox M 13 (Nov 1776), 664-5; SM 38 (Nov 1776), 610; UM 59 (Nov 1776), 262; WM 34 (Dec 5, 1776), 337-8; W Misc 7 (Dec 16, 1776), 250-1; West M 4 (Nov 1776), 618-9. Also L Chron 40 (Nov 19, 1776), 495; LM 46 (Feb 1777), 104-5; Jeffery Dunstan, Fugitive Pieces (1789), pp. 31-3. Title varies: "Heads of the Year 1777."

Song with Derry down chorus. A popular lyric on George Alexander Stevens' lecture on heads which includes comments on corruption, rebellion, loss of liberty in Britain, and a drastic solution to a medical problem, amputation, that reflects the American troubles. See Jeffery Dunstan, 89-2.

76-176. An Heroic Epistle to the Supposed Author of the Heroic Epistle to Lord Craven.

"Well may we smile, when men whom Nature made." (132)

L Eve Post, Feb 13, 1776.

HC. Satire on those who supported the administration's war policy. Illustrates the indignant reactions to the local support received by the court for its American War. The poet favors Abingdon and Craven. See Combe, 75-7, 76-4.

76-177. [Homer and Horace, ancient Authors say.]

"Homer and Horace, ancient Authors say." (18)

St J's C, Jun 18, 1776.

HC. England is ruled by evil men who wish to gain their point at any cost -- even the destruction of the country and the colonies.

76-178. Hope Revived. <u>Tandem</u> <u>resurget</u>. Britannia, recovering from a Fit of Sickness, rises from the Couch, and says,

"When Sons ungrateful to kind Parents prove." (18)

Lloyd's 39 (Oct 16, 1776), 372; L Chron 40 (Oct 15, 1776), 372; MJ, Oct 12, 1776; MP, Oct 15, 1776; PA, Oct 15, 1776.

HC. There is hope that the victories of General William Howe and his brother Admiral Sir Richard will bring peace with America (after the New York campaign). Also entitled "Soliloquy. By Britannia, on Recovering from a Fit of Despondency," MP, Oct 15, 1776.

76-179. An Impromptu.

"Jack Wilkes and the Premier sincerely I hate." (4)

M Chron, Mar 28, 1776; WM 32 (Apr 11, 1776), 82.

Epigram. Wilkes and North both deserve hanging; both are "rogues."

76-180. An Impromptu congratulatory Ode on the Late Arrival of a celebrated American Governor.

"He's come! -- He's come! -- He's come." (6)

L Eve Post, Dec 21, 1776.

Sixain. Satire on Lord Dunmore, former Governor of Virginia, who has returned to England.

76-181. An Impromptu on Raising the Land-Tax for 1776.

"Four shillings in the pound we see." (8)

LP, May 10, 1776; An Asylum for Fugitives (1776), I, 56.

Quatrains. Epigram. Thanks North, ironically, for taxing us not to fight Spain and France and for leaving us some money.

76-182. Impromptu. On Seeing a Soldier's Strum walking down the Strand with his Firelock on her Shoulder.

"Gin and the Trull I sing, the first who bore." (2)

LP, Mar 27, 1776.

Satire. Imitation of first lines of Virgil's Aeneid, referring to the fighting in Boston.

76-183. [In Abram's plains there lie interr'd.]

"In Abram's plains there lie interr'd." (20)

L Chron 39 (May 21, 1776), 496; SM 38 (May 1776), 267; W Misc (Jun 17, 1776), 285.

Quatrains. A celebration of the American officers killed in the campaign against Canada -- Montgomery, Macpherson, Cheeseman, Hendricks. "From the Pennsylvania Packet."

76-184. [In vain with weeping eyes, Britannia stood.]

"In vain with weeping eyes, Britannia stood." (53)

Freeman's J, Jun 11, 1776.

HC. Britannia complains of English war against the undeserving Americans who wish only to be free, and blames the troubles upon the Scotch Jacobites who believe it is to their Tory cause to divide America from Britain. Cited are Mansfield, North, Bute, foreign mercenaries, Churchill.

76-185. Independence: A Song. Tune: "When Britain first at Heaven's command."

"Where old Edina's turrets rise." (24)

Cal Merc, Sep 23, 1776.

A patriotic Scottish song of independence and freedom.

76-186. Index virtutis Bellona: An Epigram.

"Whom Heav'n protects as worthy of its care." (6)

L Eve Post, Oct 8, 1776.

HC. Heaven protects the Americans and their just cause.

76-187. [Ingratitude! -- the cause of all the woe.]

"Ingratitude! -- the cause of all the woe." (4)

G Eve Post, Sep 17, 1776.

Lines at the end of a moral sermon. The Americans are responsible for the war because of their ingratitude.

76-188. [Inscription at Boston.]

"After having been cooped up two winters." (c. 10)

Freeman's J, May 28, 1776; G, May 24, 1776; L Eve Post, May 21, 1776; MJ, May 23, 1776.

A provincial monument commemorates the British evacuation of Boston under pressure from Washington's forces.

76-189. [Inscription for Bradshaw.]

"Stranger, / Ere thou pass, contemplate this Cannon." (25)

MJ, Jun 29, 1776.

Epitaph honoring John Bradshaw, one of the judges who condemned the tyrant Charles I to death. His experience teaches us "That Rebellion to Tyrants, / Is Obedience to God."

76-190. Jenyns, Soame, Esq.
America. Addressed to the Rev. Dean Tucker.

"Crown'd be the man with lasting praise." (40)

AR 1776, pp. 204-5; GM 46 (Mar 1776), 133; L Chron 39 (Jan 4, 1776), 16; L Eve Post, Feb 1, 1776; St J's C, Jan 30, 1776; SM 38 (Feb 1776), 98; WM 31 (Jan 11, 1776), 81; Asylum for Fugitives (London: Almon, 1776), I, 23-4; New Foundling Hospital for Wit (1786), I, 70-1.

Quatrains. Animal fable. Entitled variously: "The Last Resource," "The Pin," "On the Chaise-Pin Contrivance," "A New Ballad, adapted to the Times," "America," "The American Coachman," or "Verses." Jenyns agrees with Josiah Tucker that it is better to let the colonies go rather than fight for them, on the analogy of freeing mad horses from a chaise in order to save the lives of the passengers within. The two writers predict that as soon as they are free the colonies will drift apart, but eventually will return to Britain. See 76-58 & 76-195.

76-191. Jerry Jingle's Rhiming Journal.

"Thro' thick and thin my Muse must dash." (62)

LP, May 3, 1776; M Chron, May 7, 1776.

Tetrameter couplets, doggerel. Among other news (e.g., the Duchess of Kingston), the British army has evacuated Boston, and the court is worried (Germain); but Jingle has faith in the Howe brothers.

76-192. King Hackabout's Speech to Both Gangs of Gypsies.

"The bus'ness of rapine, and plunder compleated." (24)

Freeman's J, May 30, 1776; L Eve Post, May 23, 1776.

Hexameter couplets. Ironic lines about the gypsies which, as a total metaphor, are applicable to the present situation: gypsy lack of public spirit, gypsy thievery and plundering relate to the British involved in the American War.

76-193. [Know all, it is our Royal will.]

"Know all, it is our Royal will." (28)

Freeman's J, Dec 10, 1776.

Quatrains. An ironic objection to the fast planned for December 13, 1776. The war is deemed criminal, for which no penance can atone.)

76-194. The Last Dying Speech of J--n W---es, Esq.

"O Liberty, Heav'n's best and greatest good." (32)

MJ, May 18, 1776.

HC. A Whig state poem, praising English constitutional liberty and defending it from the attacks of Tory Samuel Johnson, John Shebbeare, and Lord North in the Stuart tradition of tyranny. Cited are Hampden, King William.

Liberty. An Elegy. "From a black cliff, where bold Cornubia's shore." (168) Dunstan, Fugitive Pieces (1789), pp. 118-26. Elegiac quatrains. Liberty bewails oppression in the reign of George III and praises all her defenders: Wilkes, Camden, Beckford, Chatham, Burke, Effingham, and many others of the minority opposition. Liberty notes how the war against America began -- her petitions were denied and then America was accused of treason. See Dunstan, 89-2, the main entry.

76-195. Lines Addressed to S[oame] J[enyns], Esq; occasioned by his verses to Dean Tucker.

"A cap and bells for him produce." (40)

Jeffery Dunstan, Fugitive Pieces (1789), pp. 84-6.

Quatrains. Against Jenyns' belief that freedom for America means anarchy; asks that America be treated justly, controlled gently with a "silken rein." See Jenyns, 76-190; Dunstan, 89-2.

76-196. Lines on Sedition and American Bravery.

"Now from the rod of Justice, Treason flies." (49)

MP, Dec 27, 1776.

HC. Satire on American treason and sedition and the British "fraudful Patriots" responsible for this miserable war. These lines were undoubtedly inspired by the American defeat in the New York and Long Island campaign. Probably by Thomas Stewart, the dramatist.

76-197. The Lion and His Rebellious Subjects, a Fable. Addressed to Both Parties.

"Deep in a wood's romantic maze." (60)

MP, Nov 9, 1776.

OC. Animal fable. The civil war will encourage England's enemies to take action. The King must be strong and firm to unite and save the country from destruction.

76-198. Little Britain; a Poem.

"In ancient times, no matter where." (24)

G Eve Post, Aug 27, 1776; KG, Sep 11, 1776; L Chron 40 (Aug 20, 1776), 183; LM 45 (Sep 1776), 498; PA, Aug 21, 1776; WM 33 (Sep 19, 1776), 402; W Eve Post, Aug 20, 1776.

Quatrains. A protest against social abuses in "little" or petty or small-minded Britain -- inhumane game laws and imprisonment for debt, and the absurd war against America over taxes.

76-199. [Long as old Troy its siege, had Britain stood.]

"Long as old Troy its siege, had Britain stood." (78)

Freeman's J, Dec 12, 1776.

HC. Satire on the government, the King and his ministers, for their unjust war on America, resulting in "The empire disunited now for ever." Cited are taxation, Papists, Scotch.

76-200. The Long Island Prisoners, An Irregular Ode.

"Washington, admir'd by all." (40)

L Chron 40 (Nov 19, 1776), 496; SM 38 (Nov 1776), 610; WM 34 (Dec 1776), 337.

Irregular Pindaric ode. Meditative verses on the Battle of Long Island. General Howe should not boast of his victory on Long Island, which netted three American generals -- William Alexander (Lord Stirling), John Sullivan, and Nathaniel Woodhull. But the Americans will never yield "To unconditional despotic sway." "Conciliation" is the basis to build the British empire on.

76-201. Lord N----'s Soliloquy.

"The Exchequer empty -- eighteen millions wanted." (6)

L Eve Post, Sep 7, 1776.

HC. Ironic satire on North whose persona betrays himself -- he cannot beat the Americans. Cited are Charles-Town bar, Germain, American War.

76-202. The Loyal Briton. A New Song. Tune of -- Lumps of Pudding.

"Come chear up your hearts, boys, our country commands." (32)

M Chron, Nov 20, 1776.

Song. The loyal Britons will conquer America again -- as demonstrated by victories at Bunker's Hill, Staten Island, and New York, despite Barre's speeches and the "Sham Patriots." Cited are the Howes, Washington, Sandwich, North, the King.

76-203. The Meeting after the Recess; a Poem.

"With Christmas Mirth, and Christmas Cheer." (32)

G Eve Post, Jan 23, 1776; L Chron 39 (Jan 23, 1776), 88; MJ, Jan 23, 1776; PA, Jan 24, 1776; W Misc 5 (Feb 12, 1776), 505.

Quatrains. May be a song. It is not possible to defeat the Americans -- they conquer while running away.

76-204. Midsummer Day Verses, To the Worthy Livery.

"'Chang'd are the times, no more with dread alarms."

L Eve Post, Jun 22, 1776.

HC. Praise of unchanging and unyielding Wilkes, still the honorable freedom-loving public servant.

76-205. [Milton, John. Paradise Lost.]

"O Shame to men! devil with devil damn'd." (13)

L Eve Post, Feb 20, 1776.

Lines from Milton's Paradise Lost are selected to cast a slur on the ministry for its responsibility in starting a civil war. Another quotation from Milton -- Paradise Regained III, 72 ff. -- appears in L Eve Post, Jun 4, 1776, as a comment on the present situation and the nature of monarchy.

76-206. The Minister's Campaign. A Ditty.

"Of great Germaine." (60)

PL, Jun 11, 1776.

Song. An ironic review of the fighting -- Lexington, Bunker's Hill, Boston, and now Germain plans a new campaign to take Charleston, S.C., in June 1776.

76-207. The Ministry.

"The Minden Hero bears the belle." (4)

MP, Feb 21, 1776.

Epigram. Satire on Germain, North, Sandwich.

76-208. The Miracle near Sullivan's Island.

"By the Red Sea the Hebrew Host detain'd." (8)

St J's C, Oct 8, 1776.

Quatrains. General Clinton's attack on Sullivan's Island, Charleston, S.C. (on June 28, 1776), is miraculously repelled by the Americans.

76-209. A Modern Character.

"Let proud Pomposo 'gainst his Conscience write." (38)

MJ, Nov 9, 1776.

HC. Satire on Samuel Johnson, renegade to the ideals of his youth for writing Taxation No Tyranny.

76-210. [Montgomery dies; -- from his ill-boding fall.]

"Montgomery dies; -- from his ill-boding fall." (10)

G Eve Post, Mar 30, 1776.

HC, counter to the encomiums on the rebel General Montgomery, killed in Canada, December 31, 1775. In his death is a lesson for General Lee, a traitor.

76-211. [Montgomery falls! Let no fond breast repine.]

"Montgomery falls! Let no fond breast repine." (6)

SM 38 (Feb 1776), 98; WM 31 (Mar 28, 1776), 414; New Foundling Hospital for Wit (1786), VI, 7.

Epitaph by Bryan Edwards. Montgomery, who died in the expedition against Canada in December 1775, is in the tradition of Hampden. See 92-1.

76-212. [My bra lads! see your foes! lo, yonder they be.]

"My bra lads! see your foes! lo, yonder they be." (2)

G Eve Post, May 21, 1776.

Hexameter couplet. A Scottish general's harangue to his soldiers upon engaging with the American enemy -- kill or be killed: a good summary of the present situation with the Americans as seen by some British.

76-213. A New Scheme to raise a New Corps and supply the Loss of a Scotch Militia. Addressed to Lord Barrington.

"Of Arms and wond'rous Tribes I sing." (102)

LP, May 15, 1776; PA, May 15, 1776; An Asylum for Fugitives (1776), I, 57-61; New Foundling Hospital for Wit (1786), II, 81-5.

Sixains. Satire on the Scots and the court. A humorous way of checking the depopulation of Scotland is proposed -- the use of "Ouran Outangs." Germain can even use them "for his Yankey war," thereby avoiding the need of Russian mercenaries.

76-214. A New War-Song. By Sir P-t-r P-rk-r. Tune -- Well met, brother Tar.

"My Lords, with your leave." (36)

L Chron 40 (Aug 29, 1776), 212; L Eve Post, Aug 27, 1776; MJ, Aug 29, 1776; SM 38 (Sep 1776), 495; WM 33 (Sep 19, 1776), 402.

The persona of Admiral Parker complains of "cowardly Yankies" who inflicted a defeat upon his squadron of ships supporting General Clinton's assault on Charleston, S.C., and its fort on Sullivan's Island. (Admiral Parker, June 28, 1776, led a fleet in support of Clinton's attack on the fort on Sullivan's Island guarding the harbor. This attack failed because of vigorous American resistance.) Parker declares that the British will take the whole continent, "If the cowardly Yankies will let us."

76-215. N[or]th and Ger[mai]ne; or, the Whimsical Union.

"In different Trades N[or]th and Germ[ai]ne were bred." (12)

G, Jan 23, 1776.

HC. North and Germain unite. But neither is effective -- North not at diplomacy or Germain at war.

76-216. O Navis, Referent in Mare te, etc. Horace Ode 14. Lib. 1.

"Britannia, every way compleat." (12)

G Eve Post, Jan 30, 1776; KG, Jan 31, 1776.

Imitation of Horace; Horatian ode. North will steer the ship of state safely into port.

76-217. Ode.

"Tremble, ye Patriots! at my nod." (46)

L Eve Post, Jun 8, 1776.

Song in sixains. Satire on Whitehead's birthday ode and the poor leadership of the ministry -- Sandwich, Germain, Mansfield, Jenkinson -- who failed at Bunker's Hill and Boston. Cited are the King, Pinchbeck, Washington.

76-218. Ode. Addressed to General Lee.

"To Lee I tune the Heart-felt Lays." (48)

PA, Oct 2, 1776; An Asylum for Fugitives (1776), I, 151-4.

Regular ode in sixains. Panegyric on American General Lee who, with Washington and Hampden, will achieve immortal fame, while Sandwich and Germain will be damned. Allusion to the failure of Admiral Parker and the failure to cross the Charlestown ford, Dunmore and Negroes ("our good allies"), British atrocities and Indian scalping, Bunker's Hill.

76-219. An Ode, Addressed to Lord G[eorg]e G[ermain]e, on his Approaching Dissolution.

"My Lord to celebrate your Praise." (30)

PA, Jan 13, 1776; New Foundling Hospital for Wit (1786), II, 128-9.

Ode in sixains. Personal ironic satire on Lord Germain; his cowardice at Minden will not be forgotten.

76-220. Ode for his Majesty's Birth-Day, 1776. Which was performed at Hampstead.

"What moments roll so happy to a throne." (62)

LM 45 (Jun 1776), 330-1.

Pindaric ode. A celebration of George's birthday with remarks, from the point of view of the court, on the rebellion of ungrateful subjects. The King awaits their return to duty and their repentance so that he can show clemency to them.

76-221. Ode for the 4th of June, 1776.

"To earn an annual butt of sack." (48)

L Eve Post, Jun 4, 1776; MP, Jun 5, 1776.

Regular (Horatian) ode in sixains. Satire on King George. Ironic stanzas on the King who stubbornly keeps to his American policy despite destruction of the empire. Germain and Whitehead are cited, as well as the Scotch.

76-222. Ode for the Queen's Birth-Day.

"This day we hail, as that which gave." (36)

Lloyd's 38 (Jan 17, 1776); L Chron 39 (Jan 16, 1776), 64; MJ, Jan 16, 1776; PA, Jan 18, 1776; WM 31 (Jan 25, 1775), 146-7; W Misc 5 (Feb 12, 1776), 499-500.

Irregular ode in praise of Queen Charlotte including some lines prophetic of a reconciliation between Britain and America to which the Queen contributes.

76-223. Ode Occasioned By Sir William Browne's Legacy of Two Gold Medals, To Be Disposed Of Annually, For The Encouragement of Poetry In The University of Cambridge.

"Fair Granta! bid thy sons rehearse." (108)

New Foundling Hospital for Wit (1786), III, 293-300.

The Advertisement is dated June 10, 1776. Regular (Horatian) ode in sixains. The poet waxes ironic over the Tories who have chosen as the subject for the prize poems -- in Latin and Greek -- "Bellum Americanum," The American War: "Who could a nobler subject chuse / To animate a classic Muse?" Then he proceeds to mention Gage's army, the war in Boston; Percy, and the possibility of a "Yankee maid" falling in love; the socalled "Vict'ries" at Concord and Bunker's Hill; Howe's retreat from Boston; Carleton's anticipated retreat from Quebec; and the beginning of the New York campaign.

76-224. Ode on Fame.

"The human mind is bent on Fame." (32)

L Eve Post, Jun 27, 1776.

Regular (Horatian) ode. Fame cannot be pursued by such monstrous acts as the instigation of an inhumane civil war.

76-225. An Ode on his Majesty's late Birth-Day, (as it should have been written) by William Whitehead, Esq.

"Ye northern winds, whose baneful power." (34)

MP, Jul 8, 1776; T&C 8 (Jul 1776), 384; W Misc 6 (Jul 29, 1776), 427-8.

Irregular Pindaric ode. Parody. A complaint of the Scotch influence through Bute which is causing Britain to fail: she "conquers not, tho' stain'd in blood."

76-226. Ode to Lord G[eorge] G[e]rm[ai]ne.

"All hail G[e]rm[ai]ne; G[e]rm[ai]ne all hail." (108)

L Eve Post, May 23, 1776; W Misc 6 (Jul 29, 1776), 428-9.

Regular (Horatian) ode in sixains. Satire on Germain and the other ministers -- Sandwich and Dartmouth, and ministerial writers -- Samuel Johnson, Macpherson, Shebbeare, Hugh Kelly, and Generals Cornwallis, Howe, Clinton, Burgoyne, who are unable to defeat and suppress the rebels.

76-227. Ode to my Lords the Bishops, on the approaching Fast.

"'Tis well, my Lords, we're glad to find." (45)

L Eve Post, Nov 26, 1776.

Regular (Horatian) ode in sixains. Satire on the Bishops who support the American War, "blood and murder," including a threat to the "traitors," Tories and Jacobites, who are responsible for it, a threat to execute them like those executed in the '45 Rebellion.

76-228. Ode to Peace. By a Lady.

"Come, gentle peace, with calmest brow." (24)

Lady's M 7 (Jul 1776), 382.

Ode in quatrains. A prayer that America will yield and pay just tribute (taxes), thereby bringing peace.

76-229. An Old Fable New Turned.

"In days of yore, when mice could speak." (36)

MP, Dec 18, 1776.

OC. Animal fable, warning the Americans to be content with British rule because the alternative -- French arbitrary government -- is worse.

76-230. The Old Woman and her Two Daughters. An unfinished Canterbury Tale.

"Upon a time (our author says)." (c. 250)

LM 45 (Jun 1776), 328-30; M Chron, Jan 2, 1776.

OC. Moral fable about England (the old woman) and Freedom and Prerogative (her two daughters). The latter chases Freedom to America, where she thrives, until trouble begins -- caused by "Th'ill-favour'd daughter and the dame." The patriots are favored.

76-231. Omiah: An Ode. Addressed to Charlotte Hayes.

"Of Statesman's Wiles I scorn to sing." (84)

LP, May 22, 1776; PA, May 24, 1776.

Ode in sixains. Ironic social satire on the visit of the south-sea islander Omiah to England. He is made viceroy of Quebec and Boston. (Only the last stanza is pertinent.)

76-232. On a Certain American in Harley Street.

"Alas! my friend, what changes riches make." (10)

M Chron, Sep 14, 1776.

Epigram. The American loyalist in Britain has lost his wealth -- and his friends.

76-233. On a Late Fall.

"[North], by a fall hath broke his arm." (4)

L Eve Post, Oct 1, 1776.

Quatrain. Epigram. Satire on North. North has broken his arm; his neck is saved for the future.

76-234. On a Secession.

"When bribery in both Houses shall give law." (4)

Freeman's J, Sep 10, 1776; L Eve Post, Aug 31, 1776.

Quatrain. Epigram. Because the majority in Parliament has been bribed, "the virtuous" can do nothing but secede. (The allusion is to the secession of the Rockinghamites.)

76-235. On an approaching Festival. See Isaiah 58, quite through.

"Is this the Fast that Heav'n has chose." (28)

L Eve Post, Dec 7, 1776.

Quatrains. Hymn. Another objection to the hypocritical fast -- a fast proclaimed for December 13, 1776. This is a prayer for mercy and peace, not for success in a fratricidal war.

76-236. On an Intended Fast.

"I will not fast, nor Dare I pray." (5)

MJ, Nov 12, 1776; PA, Nov 14, 1776.

Extempore. The writer will not pray for victory as he objects to the fast; he will rejoice only when peace is restored. The King proclaimed a general fast on December 13, 1776, for victory against the rebels.

76-237. On Dr. Franklin's Sailing to Europe, on Pretence of Negociating with the French.

"Had Franklin's true reasons for sailing away." (8)

G Eve Post, Dec 29, 1776; MP, Dec 30, 1776.

Epigram. Satire on Franklin. Franklin's true reason for leaving America is to enjoy himself in France.

76-238. On Dr. Price's Observations.

"No more I trust what Laymen love to say." (4)

St J's C, Feb 29, 1776.

Epigram. Dr. Richard Price is unlike most clergy -- he revolts from convention and seeks to improve the reputation of priests. A favorable comment on Price's Observations on The Nature of Civil Liberty . . . and The Justice and Policy of the War with America (1776).

76-239. On hearing of the Loss of the Windsor, Experiment, and Actaeon, on Carolina-Bar.

"What an Experiment, alas! we've made." (4)

L Eve Post, Aug 22, 1776; LP, Aug 22, 1776; PA, Aug 24, 1776.

Three naval vessels have been lost in the attack on Charleston, S. C. Now only ruin can end "this bloody civil war."

76-240. On Hearing that Lord Sandwich had painted the characters of our Honest and Religious Sailors in a Moral Light.

"Praise him, ye Tars -- for he to you has given." (6)

LP, Mar 22, 1776.

Ironic lines on immoral Sandwich defending the morality of sailors. (See "On Lord Sandwich Pleading the Morals of our Sailors," L Eve Post, Mar 18/76.)

76-241. On His Majesty's Statue being Melted down in America to make Bullets.

"To melt into balls his Majesty down." (4)

L Eve Post, Oct 1, 1776.

Quatrain. Epigram. It is ironic that the King's statue is being melted for rebel bullets in order to kill the King's subjects.

76-242. On Lord S[andwich] pleading the Morals of our Sailors.

"Can we succeed in these dire civil wars." (2)

LP, Mar 18, 1776.

Epigram. It is ironic that immoral Sandwich should defend the morals of English sailors.

76-243. On One Arnold's being taken Prisoner: An Irregular Ode.

"Come ye who erst, in Charles's Days." (58)

PA, Mar 1, 1776.

Irregular Pindaric ode. Satire on the alleged capture of General Arnold before Quebec and on the struggle for colonial independence. The poet could not care less for the end of Montgomery and "Independency."

76-244. On reading in the publick prints, that those Heroes of Scotland, Lords Dunmore and William Campbell, were arrived from America.

"If Britain sings, America must weep." (14)

LP, Dec 25, 1776.

HC. Satire on Dunmore and Campbell, Scotch government officers in America, who have been forced to go home. Dunmore was Governor of Virginia. Campbell was Governor of South Carolina (but he had died from wounds received in the attack on Charleston by Admiral Parker and General Clinton!).

76-245. On Reading the Gazette Extraordinary. Extempore.

"What shall I, ye sacred Nine." (16)

G Eve Post, Oct 10, 1776; MP, Oct 12, 1776.

Three-stress couplets. Praise of the Howe brothers who have defeated the Americans on Long Island. See "Stanzas On Seeing the Lines in the Morning Post of Saturday last," MP, Oct 15, 1776: 76-332.

76-246. On Seeing the Foot Guards on their March for the Embarkation to America.

"Our King's brave guards -- the heroes of his pay." (6)

LP, Mar 18, 1776.

HC. Satire on the drunken foot-guards embarking for America -- a nasty picture.

76-247. On Sir William Howe's amazing Activity, Martial Ardour, and Rapidity in Reducing the American Rebels, and forcing their Entrenchments at King's bridge.

"Intrepid Howe like rapid light'ning flew." (63)

Freeman's J, Dec 21, 1776.

HC. Satire on Gen. William Howe. Ironic commentary on Howe's successes in his cruel campaign to seize New York and crush the rebel army. But he fails to move quickly enough (and so a complete victory is not gained).

76-248. On the American Rebellion.

"Why beams the helmet o'er Britannia's brow." (48)

SM 38 (Mar 1776), 147.

Quatrains. An attack on "false America's perfidious bands" who commit parricide. Their vile propaganda disguises "their dark designs." Signed by W. W[atki]ns. See "Why beams the helmet o'er Britannia's brow," the same poem, 76-389.

76-249. On the American War.

"We gamble in this war against all chance." (4)

Freeman's J, Sep 10, 1776; L Eve Post, Aug 31, 1776; W Misc 6 (Sep 23, 1776), 624.

Quatrain. Epigram. In the American War the dice are loaded against us, win or lose -- loaded with lead.

76-250. On the Approaching Fast.

"When parents and the children fight." (20)

W Eve Post, Nov 26, 1776.

Quatrains. Lord North should think of Bute when he tries to make peace with the American rebels. He should be careful not to be outwitted by the Congress.

76-251. On the Approaching Fast. An Epigram.

"Who would not jump to fast and pray." (4)

L Eve Post, Nov 19, 1776.

Satire on the war. The King has proclaimed a fast (Dec. 13, 1776), which will be good, for our food is washed down with blood.

76-252. On the Approaching Ministerial Fast.

"Attend, (cries North) while we proclaim our will." (22)

Freeman's J, Dec 3, 1776.

Satire on the North ministry. An ironic objection to the proclaimed fast in support of government's policy of force to suppress the colonial rebellion. The King, Carleton, Gage, and Washington are cited.

76-253. On the Birth-Day.

"Flatt'ry begone! to a good King." (8)

L Eve Post, Jun 1, 1776; West J, Jun 8, 1776.

Quatrains. Objects to the flattery of the King in the laureat's birthday odes and asks for the end of the civil war so that George can "reign in his people's hearts," not by bloody tyrannical force.

76-254. On the Death of General Montgomery.

"Oh may a prince reluctant honours pay." (10)

WM 32 (May 9, 1776), 209.

Epitaph on Montgomery who fought heroically against tyranny.

76-255. On the Death of the American General, Montgomery.

"Deck'd be his tomb with ever-vivent bays." (14)

MP, Mar 26, 1776.

Epitaph. HC. Panegyric on General Montgomery, compared with Wolfe; both fell before Quebec.

76-256. On the Death of the Late Admiral Saunders.

"Here rests the man, who living dar'd be brave." (10)

Freeman's J, Jan 18, 1776; KG, Jan 10, 1776; L Eve Post, Jan 6, 1776.

Epitaph. HC. Admiral Saunders, who had helped conquer Canada, has died (Dec 7, 1775), unhappy at the civil discord that will lose what he had won.

76-257. On the Defeat of the Americans at Long Island.

"Hark! vengeance rears her awful head." (24)

Lloyd's 39 (Oct 11, 1776), 364; LP, Oct 11, 1776; M Chron, Oct 12, 1776.

Regular ode in sixains. Praise of the British who fight "In liberty's and justice' cause" for their victory over the rebel forces, "Faction's coward Sons," in the Battle of Long Island. Indians and Negroes are pleased "To see their tyrants bleed." This battle was fought Aug 27, 1776.

76-258. On the Expedition to America.

"Blow, Eurus, blow, and with propitious gales." (26)

G Eve Post, Apr 9, 1776; GM 46 (Apr 1776), 178; MJ, Apr 4, 1776; SM 38 (Apr 1776), 214.

HC. Wolfe's ghost haunts Hancock and angrily berates him for the bloody and unjustified rebellion. Asks the Americans to cease fighting and beg for mercy from Howe.

76-259. On the Frequent Review of the Troops.

"Reviews are gaudy shews -- allow'd." (12)

L Chron 39 (Apr 2, 1776), 319; LM 45 (Apr 1776), 218; PA, Mar 30, 1776; SM 38 (Mar 1776), 148; WM 32 (May 9, 1776), 209.

Quatrains. War is wasteful -- of lives and money.

76-260. On the Happiness of a Kingdom ruled by a Virtuous and a tender Sovereign.

"That land is blest, and happy is the nation." (18)

Say's, Apr 13, 1776.

HC. Advice to the King to change his ways -- seek prudent advice and learn that the war against America, rash and misguided, will ruin the land.

76-261. On the Late Majorities in favour of the Address.

"Do three to one your first Majorities run." (2)

L Eve Post, Nov 9, 1776.

Epigram. Satire on Parliament where the majority for the destructive war policy is running three to one.

76-262. On the late Victory in America [and] Answer to the Above.

"Much applause and much honour to brave gen'ral Howe." (16)

WM 34 (Oct 24, 1776), 146.

Hexameter couplets. The British lost a Lieutenant Ragg to the Yankees on Long Island, but they captured Lord Stirling.

76-263. On the Military Disgrace of the Provincial Generals, Washington, -- Putnam, -- Wooster, -- and Lee.

"By many great actions of many _great_ men." (6)

MP, Oct 22, 1776.

Epigram. Ironic verses on the defeat of the American forces on Long Island.

76-264. On the Origin and Loss of Liberty.

"Behold how the sun spreads its rays unconfin'd." (48)

L Eve Post, Dec 31, 1776-Jan 2, 1777.

Song. Ballad satire on the government, narrates the story of Liberty that has migrated from Britain to America, for the Americans are now in the "old English" spirit; also of the National Fast of December 13, 1776, a fast initiated by crooked hypocrites, the present state-leaders, and of corruption in Parliament, concluding with a toast to the Whig martyrs, the models of integrity, Russell and Sidney.

76-265. On the Regatta at Richmond.

"Alas! Alas! what can prevent our Fall?" (4)

L Eve Post, Aug 22, 1776; LP, Aug 22, 1776; PA, Aug 24, 1776.

Quatrain. Satire on the King who enjoys himself at the regatta ball while the nation suffers in a bloody civil war.

76-266. On the Report of Lord N[orth]'s Resignation.

"What profits, Britain! N--th should rule no more." (8)

Say's, Mar 2, 1776.

HC. The Tories are responsible for a tyranny that is causing the country's wretchedness. Should North resign, he will only be replaced by Germain, another Tory -- so Bute has "decreed."

76-267. On the Report of Mr. James Twitcher's Leaving the Admiralty. A Sea Epigram.

"Turn out, my boys, and give three cheers." (4)

LP, Feb 19, 1776.

Epigram. Cheers for the report of Lord Sandwich's resignation.

76-268. On the Sanguine Expectation formed of General Howe's Army.

"Whilst all the Junto sit with smoothen'd brow." (6)

L Eve Post, Aug 10, 1776.

HC. Epigram. Unlike the ministers, a Yankee sympathizer predicts the defeat of Gen. Howe. See 76-385, the same poem.

76-269. On the Taking Long-Island, and New York. Addressed to General Howe. By a Lady.

"A _Female_ Bard! great chieftain! deign to hear." (48)

MP, Nov 6, 1776.

Regular (Horatian) ode in octaves. The triumph of the Howes over the Americans on Long Island may bring peace and the restoration of good relations between the colonies and Britain. A warning to the Americans not to seek foreign aid is included.

76-270. On the Three Estates of the Kingdom of Utopia.

"Of Three Estates, we know it to our cost." (9)

MP, Jan 16, 1776.

HC. Parliament is corrupt, the King has too much power -- as seen by a republican.

76-271. On the Total Eclipse of the Moon, July 30, 1776.

"The Moon was at her full; the Stars were bright." (56)

C Chron, Aug 9, 1776.

HC. Hopes that the eclipse does not portend something dreadful to the King, and prays for peace and an end to the American rebellion.

76-272. On the universal Forwardness of the present military Disposition.

"I'll list for a soldier, says Robin to Sue." (4)

L Chron 39 (Mar 9, 1776), 248; Ox M 13 (Mar 1776), 90; SM 38 (Mar 1776), 148.

An old epigram is applied to the present times. Robin threatens to leave his wife and sign up for army service; his wife threatens to "raise . . . fresh recruits." In GM 37 (May 1767), 273, it is entitled merely "An Epigram."

76-273. On the war with the Colonies.

"Our Colonies embroil'd affairs." (36)

G Eve Post, Nov 30, 1776; L Chron 40 (Nov 28, 1776), 525; New Morning Post, Dec 2, 1776; SM 38 (Nov 1776), 609.

Regular (Horatian) ode in sixains. Urges unity in the struggle to bring America "back to loyalty and truth," Percy and Cornwallis providing heroic models. But it is better to negotiate an end to the war by treaty and cease wasting strength when "a foreign foe [France is] so near." This poem is untitled in some versions.

76-274. [On the white rocks which guard her coast.]

"On the white rocks which guard her coast." (29)

Freeman's J, Jan 11, 1776.

Parody of Whitehead's New Year's Ode, 1776. Irregular ode, begging for peace between America and Britain, for a favorable attitude towards American petitions.

[Our Colonies embroil'd affairs.] G Eve Post, Nov 30, 1776; etc. Ode in six-ains. Urges unity in the struggle to bring America "back to loyalty and truth." In some versions entitled "On the War with the colonies": 76-273.

76-275. [Our song thus chearfully we sing.]

"Our song thus chearfully we sing." (22)

L Eve Post, Sep 10, 1776.

Song. An American song of freedom. Taxes are cited as a prime issue.

76-276. [Paine, Thomas.]
Song on Liberty Tree, from the Pennsylvanian Magazine. Tune -- The Gods of the Greeks, etc.

"In a chariot of light, from the regions of day." (32)

WM 33 (Aug 15, 1776), 241.

The goddess Liberty planted the Liberty Tree in America, which Britain, "King, commons, and lords," wishes to cut down.

76-277. A Panegyric on a Late Expedition.

"Sir Peter made a brave retreat." (20)

L Eve Post, Sep 5, 1776; MP, Sep 25, 1776.

OC. A satire on Sir Peter Parker, admiral of the British fleet that failed in the attack on Charlestown, S.C.

76-278. A Parody on the much admired Song, called the Jolly Young Waterman.

"And did you not hear of a dext'rous Minister." (32)

L Eve Post, Dec 12, 1776.

Satire on North who with his majority in Parliament can do what he pleases and who works with contractors and jobbers enriched by the American war. And the war is being enlarged and taxes are increasing.

76-279. A Pastoral, suited to the Times. In the Caledonian Dialect, with a Glossary.

"Roger. Well nibour Branky, are you here your lane." (166)

WM 31 (Jan 25, 1776), 145-6.

HC. A Scottish dialect poem, generally anti-American in sentiment, on "Britannia fightin' wi' America." Cited are the King and Hancock.

76-280. The Pausing American Loyalist. A Parody on the Soliloquy of Hamlet.

"To sign, or not to sign? That is the Question." (33)

MJ, Jan 30, 1776; PA, Jan 30, 1776.

Blank verse. The American loyalist fears he must support Congress's Non-Exportation Act forbidding trade with Britain.

76-281. Peace. An Ode.

"O Peace! the offspring of the skies." (48)

Cumb Pacq, May 16, 1776; L Eve Post, Jul 18, 1776.

Regular ode in twelve-line stanzas. An anti-court poem. A prayer for peace, the end of discord and faction. The ministry is risking the future with its war policies. Liberty must protect "the natural rights of Men."

76-282. The Pennsylvania March. To the Tune of the Scotch Song, -- "I winna marry any lad, but Sandy o'er the Lea."

"We are the troops that ne'er will stoop." (28)

Freeman's J, Jun 20, 1776; L Eve Post, Jun 13, 1776.

An American song stresses the theme of the fight for freedom against British tyranny.

76-283. A Poem on John Wilkes.

"Let hireling pens corruption's sway defend." (24)

Say's, May 18, 1776.

Quatrains. Asks Wilkes to "assume a pow'r" and end discord in Britain.

76-284. [The Poetical Medley: Additional Verses on Richard Price.]

"And, from the Hands of the Creator." (27)

Lloyd's 38 (May 3, 1776); PA, May 4, 1776.

Tetrameter couplets. Comment on Price's <u>Observations on the Nature of Civil Liberty</u> and the basic premise: all political power resides naturally in the people. The poem stresses the anarchy and confusion resulting from this Whig political principle.

76-285. A Political Genealogy.

"A Revolution begot a Free Choice." (9)

Freeman's J, Sep 10, 1776; L Eve Post, Sep 3, 1776; MJ, Sep 8, 1776; PA, Sep 6, 1776.

Prose poem. The present civil war is traced back, step by step to the Glorious Revolution, Scotchmen, arbitrary power, and oppression. See 69-A, 73-86.

76-286. Political Maturation; Or, Colonies Grown into Kingdoms. An Epigram.

"States are like children, who ere yet they stand." (8)

L Eve Post, Nov 19, 1776.

Epigram. The colonies are maturing into kingdoms that could have taken care of their parent, if treated carefully and kindly.

76-287. A Prescription for Grievances.

"Where M[ansfiel]d and B[u]te, and the rest of the tribe." (4)

Freeman's J, Dec 6, 1776.

Quatrain. Epigram. Petitions will be heard and commerce will bring prosperity upon the execution of Mansfield and Bute.

76-288. The present State of England.

"As sure as Bribery is Corruption's Brother." (2)

St J's C, Mar 19, 1776.

Epigram. Satire. Bribery is the brother of corruption; thus one half of England's paid to rob the other half.

76-289. The Prince's Nativity. -- A Pindaric.

"As on this day all-beauteous Heaven." (34)

G Eve Post, Aug 10, 1776; LM 45 (Aug 1776), 442.

Irregular Pindaric ode. A loyal poem on Prince George's birth. The loyal bard does not wish a painful event, like the American rebellion, to interrupt the festivities celebrating the birthday of the Prince of Wales.

76-290. A Prophecy by America.

"When the fair Maid shall slight her flatt'ring Glass." (40)

PA, May 2, 1776.

HC. When all sorts of improbable events occur, then America will be a friend to Britain. Mentioned are Sandwich, Fox, Burke, Barre, Rockingham, Wilkes, Saville, the King's Friends, and arbitrary schemes, etc. (Next to this poem in the PA is a prose reaction to Tom Paine's Common Sense.)

76-291. A Prophecy for the year 1776.

"North, Jeffreys, the Thane, Jenkinson, and Jemmy Twitcher." (2)

LP, Feb 26, 1776.

Epigram. The ministry will destroy the country: North, Mansfield, Bute, Jenkinson, Sandwich.

76-292. A Prophecy of Merlin.

"When a black dog shall on a white horse ride." (27)

Freeman's J, Jan 30, 1776; L Eve Post, Jan 18, 1776.

HC. A prophecy of civil war caused by the Scots, resulting in the destruction of the empire.

76-293. A Prophecy said to be found behind an old Arras in lately fitting up the Royal Apartments at Windsor.

"In the same year when seven and six." (20)

Freeman's J, Sep 19, 1776; L Eve Post, Sep 10, 1776; MJ, Sep 12, 1776; PA, Sep 14, 1776.

OC. A prediction of the country's ruin because of the civil war, Parliament and the church contributing to the ruin.

76-294. Prophesy concerning the Event of the present Civil War.

"Eng. Conquer, I'm ruin'd; conquer'd, I'm undone." (10)

St J's C, Mar 30, 1776.

HC. Dialogue between England and Foreigner. England faces a dilemma in the civil war. It is now declining, but America is rising. Yet only justice and honor can prolong a nation's life.

76-295. The Quack.

"John Bull, a 'Squire of Eminence and Worth." (8)

St J's C, Nov 12, 1776; LM 52 (Jun 1783), 297.

HC. John Bull (Britain) hired a quack (Scotch physician) for a cure, but it proved too severe. Alludes to Tory "Severity and Despotism" advocated by the Scottish politicians. See "The Quack," 83-A, enlarged to eighteen lines and improved.

76-296. Quebec Taken by Wolfe in 1759, and Defended by Carleton in 1776.

"Dying, heroic Wolfe this conquest gain'd." (4)

St J's C, Jul 16, 1776.

HC. General Carleton saved Quebec, which Wolfe had conquered before.

76-297. A Question.

"When, for remonstrances and humble prayers." (8)

L Eve Post, May 25, 1776; W Misc 6 (Jul 15, 1776), 381-2.

HC. In this critical time, when the King refuses to accept petitions and remonstrances, and the nobility is concerned only with self-interest, who will protect the constitution and how can Englishmen be free?

76-298. [Quite deafen'd and frighted, with Fifing and Drumming.]

"Quite deafen'd and frighted, with Fifing and Drumming." (48)

St J's C, Jan 13, 1776.

Hexameter couplets. A good review of the situation from the Whig position. The Tories are friends of the King; the Whigs are being attacked, even in America. Cited are S. Johnson, Shebbeare, Alg. Sidney, King William, Canada and Quebec Act, corruption, American Whigs, Bute, Gage, North, Hancock, Adams, Bunker's Hill.

76-299. A Real Scene between a Great Personage and a Great Artist.

"Pinchey. Good morning to your Highness." (c. 35)

L Eve Post, Mar 23, 1776.

Blank verse. Parody on Shakespeare's Macbeth. Satire on the King and Pinchbeck, with the American rebellion at the heart of it. The King is in a quandary about the Americans, but decides to snuff out the rebellion. See William Mason, 76-18.

76-300. A Recipe for Making a Birth-day Ode.

"Take of the western gales a pound." (36)

LP, Jun 21, 1776; M Chron, Jun 24, 1776.

Regular (Horatian) ode in sixains. Satire on laureat Whitehead, particularly his style. But a question is also raised about the justice and effectiveness of the war.

76-301. A Recipe. To Governors. To the English. &c.

"When Men become superior to the Laws." (8)

Freeman's J, Jun 13 & 18, 1776; St J's C, Mar 14, 1776.

Four epigrams critical of the government -- for tyranny (the Stuarts are tyrants), maladministration, bribery (bribery brings ruin -- this Parliament should know).

76-302. [Regal philanthropy here's shewn indeed.]

"Regal philanthropy here's shewn indeed." (2)

L Eve Post, Oct 10, 1776.

Epigram. Satire on the King, who is being entertained while his subjects suffer.

76-303. The Resolution, March 2, 1776.

"Three moons the earth was bound in frost." (66)

L Eve Post, May 21, 1776; W Misc 6 (Jun 24, 1776), 309-11.

Sixains with repeated rhyme on "Resolution." A satiric account of the British besieged in Boston, and their evacuation of the city by boat after American pressure became too much for them to withstand.

76-304. The Restoration; or May 29.

"When James the Pedant rul'd this Isle." (36)

G Eve Post, May 28, 1776; M.T, May 28, 1776; PA, May 29, 1776.

Ballad, quatrains. Ironic satire on the ministry placed in the historical context of the failed Stuarts. Thus Germain, Sandwich, and North are demeaned.

76-305. Retaliation: On Hearing the Account of the Reception of General Fraser's Regiment in Boston.

"Pray what makes you growl so? said Sandy to Dick." (12)

Cal Merc, Aug 21, 1776.

Quatrains. The Americans, who had been "drummed" out of the home country, now retaliate and drum the British forces out of Boston.

76-306. The Retreat. An Epigram.

"While Franklin, with Electric Toys." (6)

PA, Nov 27, 1776.

Sixain. On the Battle of Long Island. Franklin diverted Howe so that Washington could escape.

76-307. The Retreat of the Ten Thousand: A Consolatary Ode, Addressed to Lord G. G. By the Author of Lord Ch--m's Prophecy.

"Courage, my Lord -- tho' Howe is fled." (96)

LP, May 13, 1776; M Chron, May 13, 1776; PA, May 11, 1776; An Asylum for Fugitives (1776), I, 104-8; New Foundling Hospital for Wit (1786), II, 96-102.

Regular ode in sixains. Satire on the government, all those supporting the war against America, and General Howe who has just been compelled to evacuate Boston. See 76-16.

76-308. The Revolution Anthem. [Or, The Vicar of Bray.]

"When James assuming [asserting] right from God." (52)

Freeman's J, Jul 9 & Aug 13, 1776; L Eve Post, Aug 6, 1776.

A song in defense of William and the Glorious Revolution, but against Papists, Stuarts, and Tories. (Also entitled "An Old Song Revived. The Vicar of Bray," L Eve Post, Aug 6, 1776 and Freeman's J, Aug 13, 1776.) The point is that the American Whig tradition is traceable to the Glorious Revolution, as well as the Puritan Revolution.

76-309. [The Sages of Old, in Prophecy, told.]

"The Sages of Old, in Prophecy, told." (16)

G Eve Post, Jun 22, 1776; L Chron 39 (Jun 20, 1776), 600; MJ, Jun 20, 1776.

Quatrains. A plea for peace between America and England. This old poem, applied to the present times, preaches against division, faction, civil war, and prays for success to the British in this crisis.

76-310. St. Stephen's Orders to the Keeper of his Chapel.

"Some hold that Saints may stray from Heaven." (36)

MP, Jun 19, 1776.

Quatrains. St. Stephen orders that his chapel, in which Parliament sits, be kept "clean" of pensioners and placemen; but the keeper complains that it is impossible to rid the place of bribery.

76-311. See Saw; Or, The Present State of the Ministry.

"North, conscious of each blunder." (10)

L Eve Post, Mar 30, 1776.

Three-stress couplets. North and Germain (supported by Bute) cannot agree on the way to pursue the war against America. Evidence of poor leadership when the ministry was disabled by internal quarrels.

76-312. A Serious Hint to the Reverend Clergy of Ireland, on the Approaching Ministerial Fast.

"Pause, Preacher, pause, reflect e'er you begin." (48)

Freeman's J, Nov 21, 1776.

HC. Devotion in a wrongful cause is sin -- the clergy must consider what their support of the coming Fast signifies. The poet is sympathetic with the American cause.

76-313. [Shakespeare, William. Cymbeline.]

"The following scene from Shakespeare's play of Cymbeline, King of Britain, is so applicable to the present times, and the behaviour of the Britons so like the Americans, that you'll oblige a reader if you will lay it before the public." [Cymbeline and his Court face the Roman Ambassador.] (c. 40)

LP, Jan 17, 1776.

Extract: Act III, Scene i, from Cymbeline. The British commissioners, the Howe brothers, are like the Romans; and the Americans are like the ancient Britons who refuse to pay tribute.

76-314. The Ship with Two Rudders. A Political Fable; addressed to Dr. Price.

"A Gallant ship as ever stood." (56)

M Chron, Feb 23, 1776.

OC. The crew of the ship of state added a second rudder, making steering impossible; thereupon the captain took command, controlled the rebels, broke the added rudder, allowing the ships to sail properly. The British empire cannot tolerate Congress. Richard Price should understand the moral.

76-315. The Siege of Quebec.

"Goddess! or Muse! -- whate'er thy name." (c. 160)

MP, Sep 4, 1776.

OC. Satiric narrative on the American soldiers who failed in their attack on Quebec (in the winter of 1775-6): Montgomery, Campbell, Thompson, Arnold vs. Carleton, Maclane, Hamilton. Others cited are Price, Paine (Common Sense).

76-316. The Snow-Ball; a Poem.

"The Blue-faced Boys, with eager Haste." (24)

G Eve Post, Jan 13, 1776; KG, Jan 20, 1776; Lloyd's 38 (Jan 15, 1776), 59; L Chron 39 (Jan 16, 1776), 55; MJ, Jan 13, 1776); PA, Jan 16, 1776; Say's, Jan 20, 1776.

Quatrains. On the similarity between the difficulty of rolling a large snow ball and moving the ball of state, when the patriots refuse to help.

Soliloquy. By Britannia, on Recovering from a Fit of Despondency. "When Sons ungrateful to kind Parents prove." (18) MP, Oct 15, 1776; and other sources. A hope that the victories of the Howes will bring peace. See 76-178.

76-317. Some Additional Lines, which were recited at the Caractacan Meeting, at Longnor, in Shropshire, in July, 1776.

"So sung the bard who, in Silurian groves." (30)

GM 46 (Sep 1776), 427.

Blank verse. The rebellion of the Americans is unjustified. If Britain should triumph in the war, it should be merciful and should forgive "e'en blind deluded zeal." Then peace and prosperity "can Return again to bless Columbia's shores," and the empire be reunited and powerful once more.

76-318. Some Lines addressed to the very worthy Patriots in Opposition.

"To you who for Rebels in senate oft' plead." (30)

M Chron, Sep 14, 1776.

Hexameter couplets. Satire on the Opposition who, simply using the American issue in order to get into place, are not to be trusted.

76-319. [Some news, my dear friend, is come over at last.]

"Some news, my dear friend, is come over at last." (14)

L Eve Post, Oct 17, 1776.

Hexameter couplets. News about the American defeat on Long Island.

76-320. A Song.

"When ministerial fools or knaves." (28)

KG, Oct 16, 1776.

Quatrains. An expression of hope for the end of corrupt cheats in the administration, and an end to the war. Cited are Chatham, Gov. Dunmore of Virginia, hulks on the Thames.

76-321. A Song made by the Soldiers in Garrison at Quebec, after Gen. Montgomery's Defeat. Tune: Highland March.

"Come chear up my lads! 'tis for freedom we fight." (54)

WM 33 (Aug 1, 1776), 177-8.

A song celebrating the victory over Arnold and Montgomery by Carleton and his forces.

Song on Liberty Tree . . .

See Thomas Paine, 76-276.

76-322. A Song sung at Portsmouth, on hearing that Mr. James Twitcher was shortly to resign.

"Ye sons of the main, who yet true to the cause." (15)

LP, Feb 21, 1776.

An expression of pleasure that Sandwich may resign as Secretary of Navy. Adm. Richard Howe may help turn Sandwich out of office.

76-323. A Song. Sung at the Hampshire Club (instituted for the support of public liberty) Nov. 4, 1776, being the anniversary of the birth-day of King William the Third, of glorious memory.

"All hail to the day when great Nassau was born." (40)

L Eve Post, Dec 17, 1776.

An attack on Scotchmen, Tories and Jacobites, who would destroy Whig rights and freedom.

76-324. A Song. To an Old Tune.

"Rouse, Britons! Rouse!" (30)

New Morning Post, Dec 10, 1776.

The Howe brothers will be victorious over the rebels, and then over the French.

76-325. Song. To the tune of Bessy Bell and Mary Gray.

"O Gage, Burgoyne, so great ye are." (32)

PA, Jan 13, 1776.

Ironic lyric on the poor leadership of Gage and Burgoyne, whose starving troops in Boston are besieged by the Americans under Putnam, Ward, and Washington.

76-326. Sonnet. Written at the Grave of Algernon Sydney, at Penshurst.

"In this retir'd and solitary nook." (14)

MP, Nov 18, 1776.

Modified Italian sonnet, honoring the Whig martyr Algernon Sydney, executed in reign of Charles II, after the exposure of the Rye-House plot. This poem appears to counteract the effect of the anti-Whig lines "To their High Mightinesses, the American Congress," 76-366.

76-327. Sonnet. Written at the Village of Auburn, in 1775.

"When, lovely spot! thy beauties I recount." (14)

MP, Nov 13, 1776.

Sonnet, modified Italian. A sentimental lyric on the emigration to America from Goldsmith's Auburn, only to have oppression follow the emigrants there -- and war.

76-328. A Specific for Modern Patriotism. To Lord N[ort]h.

"The flaming patriot blackens with disgrace." (22)

MJ, May 7, 1776.

HC. Bribes and places will stop patriots from criticizing the government.

76-329. Stanzas for New Year's Day, 1776.

"Bifronted Janus leads the smiling Year." (24)

PA, Jan 1, 1776.

Heroic quatrains. The poet asks why, when England is blest with peace and plenty, there should be rebellion across the Atlantic; it is freedom for which the colonists are fighting, and the English should have "the Virtue" to leave off fighting and "to be right."

76-330. Stanzas for the Thirtieth of January.

"Mem'ry recal (sic) the solemn Day." (24)

L Chron 39 (Jan 30, 1776), 112; PA, Jan 31, 1776.

Quatrains. The present King, unlike stupid Charles I, a stubborn tyrant who opposed "His faithful Commons," has the support of the country. (January 30th was the day set aside for the commemoration of Charles I's execution.)

76-331. Stanzas humbly inscribed to the Right Hon. Earl Mansfield, Lord Chief Justice of the King's Bench.

"O Thou! in whom each brighter virtue joins." (36)

L Chron 40 (Dec 26, 1776), 621; Cal Merc, Jan 6, 1777.

Heroic quatrains. Panegyric on Mansfield for all the virtues -- humanity, patriotism, dignity, oratory, justice, manly sense.

76-332. Stanzas On Seeing the Lines in the Morning Post of Saturday Last.

"Say! shall Gratitude divine." (18)

MP, Oct 15, 1776.

Irregular ode. Generals Clinton and Percy deserve as much applause as the Howes -- all are heroic. See "On Reading the Gazette Extraordinary," MP, Oct 12, 1776: 76-245.

76-333. The State of Europe. A Poem.

"The Spaniard of his Shipping brags." (40)

G Eve Post, Feb 17, 1776; KG, Feb 14, 1776; Lloyd's 38 (Feb 13, 1776); MJ, Feb 10, 1776; PA, Feb 13, 1776.

Quatrains. Should England end the war, it will do good and achieve fame.

76-334. The Statesman; An Irregular Ode.

"Bute loves arbitrary rule." (64)

Freeman's J, Sep 26, 1776; L Eve Post, Sep 19, 1776; An Asylum for Fugitives (1776), I, 154-5; New Foundling Hospital for Wit (1786), II, 147-8.

Sixains, and some quatrains and cinquains. Satire on the court. A complaint directed at the court leaders, tracing their Tory ideology of arbitrary rule back to Bute: North, Germain, Rigby, Weymouth, Suffolk, Mansfield, Jenkinson, Thurloe, Wedderburne, Sandwich. (The miscellanies print only 50 lines.)

76-335. The Suicide.

"Where, where, alas! are Britain's Laurels fled." (8)

Freeman's J, Sep 28, 1776; St J's C, Sep 21, 1776.

HC. An objection to the civil war against America because it means suicide for Britain. Cited are mercenaries.

76-336. A Tale. Sermons are less read than Tales.

"We spent the Night at Hancock's Head." (50)

L Eve Post, Oct 12, 1776; PA, Oct 17, 1776.

OC. The fable illuminates the fact that the British intend to force their sovereignty over America, a tyrannical solution which John Hampden and Lord Camden deplore.

76-337. The Temple of Liberty. Written at an Inn.

"Let Stavely and Saxby, on Freedom declaim." (18)

G Eve Post, Jul 2, 1776; M Chron, Jul 3, 1776.

Hexameter couplets. Real liberty is found at an English inn, not anywhere else in England or America, despite what others may say: Stavely, Saxby, Johnson, Price, Burke, Shebbeare, Wilkes.

76-338. The Times are Altered; Or, An Epigram on a Great Minister of State coming to Town in the Snow.

"Through hills of snow (such now's his patriot flame)." (3)

L Eve Post, Jan 18, 1776.

Satire on Germain, the coward of Minden. See "Britannia's Caution," L Eve Post, Jan 20/76, another satire on Germain: 76-76.

76-339. To Britons. Hor. Epode 7. *Quo, quo scelesti, ruitis?* &c. imitated. On the Present Unnatural War.

"What daemon, jealous of Britannia's weal." (32)

Freeman's J, Sep 26, 1776; KG, Sep 7, 1776; St J's C, Sep 5, 1776.

Ode in heroic quatrains. Imitation of Horace. The war is counter to the tradition of freedom fostered by Hampden, Russell, Sidney. It is not against the Bourbons, France, or Spain, but against English subjects. It is an oppressive civil war caused by the Jacobite Scotch.

76-340. To Captain Nugent.

"Thrice dauntless youth, who durst the state withstand." (16)

LP, Mar 25, 1776.

HC. Panegyrical epitaph honoring a brave American officer killed at Bunker's Hill: -- Captain Nugent. (Patrick Nugent, in the Connecticut Regiment that fought at Bunker's Hill, was probably wounded, not killed.)

76-341. To Doctor Shebbeare, On his Laborious Pamphlet, in Answer to the Late Minority Writers.

"Your sheets I've perus'd." (18)

MP, Jul 24, 1776.

Regular (Horatian) ode in sixains. A satire on John Shebbeare, writer for the Tories. Shebbeare wrote against Burke in 1775, and against Price in 1776.

76-342. To his Excellency Major General Carleton, on his Defeat of the Rebels before Quebec.

"For future laurels, sav'd by heav'n from harms." (20)

L Chron 40 (Jul 6, 1776), 31; SM 38 (Jun 1776), 328.

HC. Praise of General Carleton for stopping Montgomery and Arnold at Quebec where he had been wounded before and Wolfe killed.

76-343. To James Wilson, Esq; a Member in the Irish Parliament, late a Captain of Marines . . . .

"When young Achilles shunn'd the war of Troy." (20)

LP, Apr 19, 1776.

HC. Praise of James Wilson, MP in the Irish Parliament, for surrendering his commission in the marines rather than participate in the American War, "an unnatural civil war." Cited is Bute.

76-344. To John Wilkes, Esq;

"Should you, Doctor Wilkes, these Lines peruse." (52)

PA, Jul 5, 1776.

Ballad. Satire on Wilkes, who is advised to go Boston for friendship, because his reputation is lost in Britain and he is forgotten.

76-345. To Lord G. G. on his Bragging Gazette.

"You boast, from Gen'ral Carlton (sic) and Sir Guy." (13)

Freeman's J, Aug 8, 1776; L Eve Post, Aug 1, 1776.

HC. Satire on Germain. A defence of the rebels who prudently retreated from Carleton's offensive, like Germain at Minden.

76-346. To Lord Mansfield.

"M--F--D beware, remember Jefferies fate." (4)

Freeman's J, Jul 16, 1776.

Two epigrams. A cruel Mansfield and a "loathed Ministry" are blamed for the American War.

76-347. To L[ord North].

"In this black moment of extreme distress." (34)

MJ, Jun 6, 1776.

HC. On the tragic waste of a civil war from which only Chatham can save the country.

76-348. To Lord N[orth].

"Oft have the Patriots for the war." (4)

W Eve Post, Nov 26, 1776.

Epigram. A warning to Lord North to beware when negotiating a peace (with America).

76-349. To Miss H. H---. Written by a young Gentleman who embarked lately for America.

"When o'er the wide tempestuous main I'm borne." (26)

HM 6 (Oct 1776), 714.

HC. A young man complains of leaving his beloved "for a distant shore."

76-350. To Miss H---- M----.

"E'er this sad scrawl thy weeping eyes explore." (32)

MP, Dec 23, 1776.

HC. On his way to war in America, a soldier bids farewell to his fiancée and protests his love. He died in the Battle of Bunker's Hill with her name on his lips.

76-351. To My Friend, Capt. B--m, On his Departure from England.

"Ere the sweet breath of genial winds arise." (12)

MP, Nov 12, 1776.

Quatrains. A wife bids farewell to her husband and begs he return to her arms safely from the war with the American rebels.

76-352. To Q. In this Paper of Friday Last.

"Hah! Why so angry, Master Q." (8)

M Chron, Jan 18, 1776.

OC. The same author of "To the Congress," Jan. 11, 1776, responds to the invective of "Extempore. In Answer," January 12, 1776: 76-145.

76-353. To S. J. Esq. on his late Definition of Patriotism.

"I next thee sat a tedious year." (24)

W Eve Post, Aug 22, 1776.

Regular ode in sixains. Satire on Soame Jenyns for his cynical definition of patriotism ("No virtue in a patriot-deed"), which explains why he votes for North and the court and against Saville.

76-354. To that Fanatical, political, physical, enthusiast Patriot and Physician, the Reverend Mr. W[esle]y.

"As in some country town we often find." (74)

LP, Aug 2, 1776.

HC. Satire on Wesley for his hypocrisy, largely for his Primitive Physic. Ten lines allude to his Calm Address to our American Colonies (1775).

76-355. To the Congress.

"Ere Northern cities are destroy'd." (12)

M Chron, Jan 11, 1776.

Quatrains. The Americans are foolishly obstinate and should submit before their country is destroyed. See "Extempore. In Answer . . ." 76-145.

76-356. To the Gentlemen in Opposition, the following Hudibrastick Lines are Humbly Dedicated.

"Ye worthy Candidates for place and pence." (81) + (77)

M Chron, Mar 14, 21, 1776.

Hudibrastic verses. Two installments. Satire on the Minority Opposition, guided by self-interest and betraying the country. The conclusion stresses the need to uphold the country's cause, Britain's legal rights, before France and Spain will support Congress. Besides, the poet cynically adds, the patriots will soon take their turn at places. They must be patient.

76-357. To the Island of Great Britain. [And] To General Lee.

"Thy Fate, on ev're Side, seems pretty clear." (2)
"Thou seems't to have at Heart thy Country's Fate." (2)

St J's C, Mar 9, 1776.

Two epigrams. Unless Britain is lucky, its fate is gloomy. If only Gen. Lee were premier, he would avert this fate.

76-358. To the K[ing].

"Nor France, or Spain, Vienna, Sweden, Russia." (16)

MJ, Jul 16, 1776.

HC. Only peace between Britain and her colonies can guarantee the impregnable strength of the mother country.

76-359. To the Memory of General Montgomery.

"With noble Brutus Roman virtue fled." (16)

LP, Mar 25, 1776.

HC. Panegyric on Montgomery who is in the tradition of great rebels -- Brutus, Cromwell, Sydney, Marvell -- all against tyranny.

76-360. To the Memory of Sir Charles Saunders. Written by Captain Thompson, 1776.

"Within this sculptur'd marble rests from war." (12)

LP, Apr 5, 1776.

Epitaph. Panegyric on brave Admiral Saunders, recently dead. (By Capt. Edward Thompson.)

76-361. To the People of England.

"Hear Hampden's spirit calling from the dead." (10)

L Eve Post, Jul 18, 1776.

HC. Objection to the King's war policy. Hampden's spirit urges Britons to fight Stuart policy that encourages tyranny and slavery.

76-362. To the People of England.

"Your continent is gone, your islands going." (4)

Freemans' J, Aug 27, 1776.

Epigram. Satire on Bute, who is the root cause of the grief suffered by the people of England -- the loss of America and the West Indies and increasing grievances at home.

76-363. To the People of Great Britain and America: In Imitation of Horace, Book V. Ode vii. _Detestatio belli civilis._

"Say, Britons! what wild frenzy draws." (28)

T&C 8 (Nov 1776), 606-7; WM 34 (Dec 12, 1776), 369-70.

Regular (Horatian) ode in quatrains. Enough British blood has been spilt in Canada! Why must British brothers now fight each other only to benefit France and Spain? "Mad Faction" is responsible for this detestable civil war. Let there be peace and unity in freedom again.

76-364. To the Poet Laureat. An Ode Parodied.

"In the black caverns of our coast." (24)

L Chron 38 (Jan 11, 1776), 44; LM 45 (Mar 1776), 164; MJ, Jan 11, 1776.

Parody of Whitehead's New Year's Ode, 1776. Britain's "Evil Genius" demands bloody war "of trait'rous and oppressive men."

76-365. To the Valetudinarians of Bath, upon their Rejoicings for the defeat of the Provincials on Long Island.

"Upon politick, sober themes." (12)

LP, Oct 28, 1776.

OC. A severe criticism of residents of Bath for their celebration of the bloody British victory on Long Island.

76-366. To their High Mightinesses, the American Congress.

"Would you know what a Whig is, and always was." (24)

M Chron, Nov 15, 1776.

Octaves in couplets. Satire on seditious Whigs who derive from the devil. Thus the Americans in Congress are seditious devils. See 76-326.

76-367. To those whom it may concern.

"I've oft observ'd, especially of late." (15)

St J's C, Jun 13, 1776.

HC. England is falling, because of a corrupt Parliament, a civil war, and Scottish leadership.

76-368. A Toast.

"May the King and his People live together in concord." (3)

LP, Aug 12, 1776.

Triplet. May all rivals for places be hanged. (Interested politicians stand between "the King and his People.")

76-369. The Tool of the Bloody Junto.

"N[orth] hopes his treason will be soon forgot." (6)

L Eve Post, Mar 2, 1776.

HC. Invective against Lord North, the Scotchmen's tool who wished "to be employ'd / In murd'rous plans, where millions are destroy'd!"

76-370. ['Twixt English Kin, whence does such Mischief come.]

"'Twixt English Kin, whence does such Mischief come." (2)

St J's C, Mar 23, 1776.

Epigram. The source of the trouble between America and Britain is Bute and Popery.

76-371. Uniticus on the Times. An Acrostic.

"O ppression and despotic mighty sway." (10)

Say's, May 18, 1776.

HC. Acrostic on the times -- oppressive because of a despotic government that causes rebellion and now proceeds with war. (The best commentary on this poem is the King's Speech, May 23, 1776, on the "great National Cause," the struggle for "Constitutional Subordination.")

76-372. Upon Lord Mulgrave being appointed to the command of the Ardent man of war, and violently defending, in the House of Commons, the naval administration of Lord Sandwich.

"What a change is perform'd by a voy'ge to the pole." (10)

LP, Nov 9, 1776.

Hexameter couplets. Lord Mulgrave (Constantine John Phipps) has been bribed to support Sandwich and the naval administration.

76-373. Upon Reading in the Papers that Government had lost the Hope Transport, with seventy Stand of Arms.

"O say what foul Aeolian mouth." (12)

LP, Jul 15, 1776.

Sixains. Extempore. Satire on the ministry. An important transport vessel was lost in a storm, and now Sandwich's plans are gone awry.

76-374. Upon Reading that Gen. Washington's Horse was Shot under him when reconnoitring the King's Forces.

"'Tis true that Washington hath lost his Horse." (4)

LP, Sep 16, 1776.

Epigram. Washington's horse was shot; but Admiral Parker and General Clinton lost both ships and men.

76-375. Upon reading that the Tobacconists in Dublin had raised the price of snuff two-pence an ounce, on account of the American war.

"This proves the Yankees are our fellest foes." (2)

LP, Sep 13, 1776.

Epigram. The price of tobacco has risen even in Dublin as a result of the American war. The Yankees have the British by the nose.

76-376. Upon Seeing a Proclamation for a Fast, &c.

"[King George], in order the Yankies to quell." (18)

L Eve Post, Dec 5, 1776.

Hexameter couplets. The British through their Scotch agents have solicited the aid of hell -- German mercenaries and Indians -- to quell the rebellion, but the Americans have God on their side and cannot be defeated. Cited also are Negroes and Papists.

76-377. Upon the late attempt at Charles-Town.

"Our late expedition in fact does appear." (26)

G, Sep 3, 1776.

Hexameter couplets. An account of the British failure under Clinton, who landed on Sullivan's Island, to storm Charles-Town, S. C., because of a miscalculation of the depth of the ford the troops were to wade over.

76-378. Use of Bribery to the Americans. *Pecunia Vincit Omnia*.

"Less spilling of blood." (22)

M Chron, Sep 6, 1776.

Dimeter couplets. Cynical satire. The Americans might have been conquered by bribery; thus our trade could have been protected.

76-379. Verses addressed to Mr. Tait, on reading his *Poetical Legends*, lately published.

"How sweet are the strains of the muse." (28)

SM 38 (Jun 1776), 328; WM 32 (May 30, 1776), 305.

Quatrains. John Tait is praised for his humanitarian offer of the profits from the sale of *Poetical Legends* for the relief of sick and wounded troops and of widows and orphans of soldiers slain in America. For Tait's *Poetical Legends*, see 76-35. Tait responded to these verses in SM 38 (Jun 1776), 329.

76-380. Verses on the American War.

"Why should our Col'nies madly run." (48)

L Chron 39 (Mar 14, 1776), 261; Ox M 13 (Mar 1776), 89.

Regular ode in sixains. Britain will assert its right to enforce "just subjection to the parent state." On the other hand, the Americans do "assert Britannia's cause." Now is the time for clemency. See "American Rebellion, and Highland Loyalty," 76-53, the same poem. Signed S. S---.

76-381. Verses on the Approaching Fast.

"Behold a solemn Fast proclaim'd." (28)

L Eve Post, Nov 23, 1776.

Quatrains. Satire in the style of the hymns of Sternhold and Hopkins, on the bloody-minded King and ministry for a fast proclaimed for the wrong reasons, for taxes. Supports the Americans and their freedom.

76-382. Watkins, T.
On the American Rebellion.

"The rocks majestic, from their craggy beds." (110)

T&C 8 (May 1776), 269-70.

HC. Not the same poem as that by W. Watkins, 76-248. The American rebels are criticized as impious, "basely ingrate," "False to those bonds that sacred duty draws," "Licentious," and their behavior is unjust and unnecessary because Britain is not tyrannical. The ruler is "a patriot monarch" who extends the olive wreath and offers mercy. If the Americans refuse peace, he will use a terrifying force against them.

76-383. Wesley, John.
To A Friend On Some Late Infamous Publications In The Newspapers. [1776.]

"You ask the cause of all this pother." (22)

The Poetical Works of John and Charles Wesley, ed. G. Osborn (London: Wesleyan-Methodist Conference Office, 1870), VIII, 446-7.

OC. Wesley complains of the smear tactics of "patriots elect" who are trying to ruin his reputation for opening "people's eyes" in his Calm Address to Our American Colonies (1775). He thinks of himself as "the nation's undeceiver." -- In a letter to me, Frank Baker says this poem is in the MS 4to volume, "Hymns & Verses on Modern Patriotism, & the American Rebellion and Independancy &c," p. 24. See Baker's Representative Verse of Charles Wesley (London: Epworth Press, 1962), p. 393 (#112).

76-384. [When Hurd was a Whig in a thirsty old Caxon.]

"When Hurd was a Whig in a thirsty old Caxon." (6)

L Chron 39 (Apr 9, 1776), 352; St. J's C, Apr 13, 1776.

Hexameter couplets. Richard Hurd, formerly a Whig but now a Tory bishop, votes for the Government's attempts to suppress the Americans. But it is questionable whether he votes according to God's wish. Entitled in L Chron, "Ductor Dubitantium: Black and All Black."

76-385. [Whilst all the Junto sit with smoothen'd brow.]

"Whilst all the Junto sit with smoothen'd brow." (6)

Freeman's J, Aug 27, 1776; L Eve Post, Aug 20, 1776.

HC. Epigram. The Ministerial Junto expect Howe to win and end the war, but "A New-York Yankee" declares that Howe will be beaten. See 76-268, the same poem.

76-386. Whitehead, William.
Ode for his Majesty's Birth-Day; Written by William Whitehead, Esq. Poet Laureat, and Performed at St. James's on the 4th of June, 1776, By his Majesty's Band of Musicians.

"Ye western gales, whose genial breath." (34)

AR, 1776, p. 2(3; Cumb Pacq, Jun 13, 1776; G, Jun 4, 1776; G Eve Post, Jun 1, 1776; GM 46 (Jun 1776), 279; KG, Jun 5, 1776; Lady's M 7 (Jun 1776), 325; Lloyd's 38 (Jun 3, 1776); L Eve Post, Jun 1-4, 1776; LP, Jun 3, 1776; MJ, Jun 1-4, 1776; M Chron, Jun 4, 1776; MP, Jun 4, 1776; Ox M 13 (Jun 1776), 201; PA, Jun 4, 1776; St J's C, Jun 1-4, 1776; SM 38 (May 1776), 267; Sent M 4 (Jun 1776), 277; WM 32 (Jun 13, 1776), 369; West J, Jun 8, 1776; L Chron 39 (Jun 1-4, 1776), 536; LM 45 (Jun 1776), 332; Asylum for Fugitives (1776), I, 147-8.

Irregular Pindaric Ode. The laureat waits impatiently for news from America. He is worried: "Can Britain fail?" he asks, during a pause in the struggle. But he insists upon Britain's "rightful sway." See W. Mason's comment on this ode and the others by Whitehead in Works of the English Poets, ed. S. Johnson (London: Wright), 1790), LXXIII, 123-4.

76-387. Whitehead, William.
Ode for the New-Year. Written by William Whitehead, Esq; and set to Music by Dr. Boyce.

"On the white rocks which guard her coast." (26)

AR, 1776, p. 202; Cumb Pacq, Jan 11, 1776; Freeman's J, Jan 6, 1776; G, Jan 1, 1776; G Eve Post, Dec 30/75-Jan 2, 1776; GM 46 (Jan 1776), 36; HM 6 (Jan 1776), 63; KG, Dec 30/75-Jan 3, 1776; Lady's M 6 (Supp 1775), 724; Lloyd's 38 (Dec 29/75 -Jan 1, 1776); L Eve Post, Dec 30/75-Jan 2, 1776; LP, Dec 29/75-Jan 1, 1776; MJ, Dec 30/75-Jan 1, 1776; M Chron, Jan 1, 1776; MP, Jan 1, 1776; Ox M 13 (Jan 1776), 419; PA, Jan 1, 1776; St J's C, Dec 30/75-Jan 2, 1776; Sent M 4 (Jan 1776), 40; T&C 7 (Supp 1775), 710; UM 57 (Supp 1775), 372; WM 31 (Jan 11, 1776), 80-1; West J, Jan 6, 1776; L Chron 39 (Dec 30, 1775-Jan 2, 1776), 2; LM 45 (Jan 1776), 50; Asylum for Fugitives (1776), I, 54-5.

Irregular Pindaric ode. Britain begs the Americans, "deceiv'd, mistaken men," to stop the fighting because the British are not fostering tyranny. The war is blamed on "the madness of a few." (Alternate title: "On Monday January 1, at noon, was performed before their Majesties and Royal Family, the following Ode, written by Wm. Whitehead, Esq; Poet Laureat, and set to Music by Dr. Boyce, Master of the King's Band of Musicians.")

76-388. [Whoe'er could say that, with Disgrace.]

"Whoe'er could say that, with Disgrace." (4)

PA, May 13, 1776.

Epigram. General Howe was not fired from his place; he had resigned. (The reference is the evacuation of Boston.)

76-389. [Why beams the helmet o'er Britannia's brow?]

"Why beams the helmet o'er Britannia's brow?" (48)

L Chron 39 (Apr 2, 1776), 328; SM 38 (Mar 1776), 147; Sent M 4 (Jun 4, 1776), 277.

Quatrains. A protest at the Americans for fomenting a civil war, and for their lying and their vile propaganda, their campaign of hate against Britain. See "On the American Rebellion," 76-248.

[Why should our Col'nies madly run.]

See "Verses on the American War," 76-380.

76-390. Wilk. and Libertina. A Burlesque Dialogue.

"Whether Phoebus that morn o'er the City shone bright." (c. 100)

MP, Jul 17, 1776.

On Wilkes's diminishing popularity, resulting in his loss of the election to the post of City Chamberlain to Benjamin Hopkins. Libertina is critical of America, refusing to join with Hancock and Adams, and with Dissenters.

76-391. Wilkes Chamberlain; Or, Freedom Triumphant.

"Wilkes chosen Chamberlain -- O rare!" (18)

L Eve Post, Feb 17, 1776.

Ode in sixains. Let us honor Wilkes, elected Chamberlain of London. (But he was elected in 1779 on his fourth attempt at this office!)

76-392. [Would'st thou improve in regal Skill, O King.]

"Would'st thou improve in regal Skill, O King!" (4)

St J's C, Mar 30, 1776.

Epigram. HC. The King should learn from a violinist tuning his instrument how to improve his skill in government.

76-393. [Write on, Great Dodd, who writ'st so fast.]

"Write on, Great Dodd, who writ'st so fast." (16)

KG, Jan 13, 1776.

Quatrains. The Rev. Dr. Dodd is used as a vehicle to satirize Bute -- regarding his chief responsibility for the Peace of 1763.

76-394. Written under the Picture of a Lady, represented in the Character of Liberty, dressed in a Cloak and Bonnet.

"Dear parent, wont to nurse me in thy arms." (20)

L Eve Post, Nov 26, 1776.

HC. Liberty bids farewell to Britain (presumably leaving for America).

76-395. Wrote on Viewing, from Dumbarton-Castle, the Transports in the Clyde, having the Troops on Board destined for America.

"What charming prospect feeds my wond'ring eyes." (28)

WM 32 (May 9, 1776), 209.

HC. Prays that the troops reach America safely and be protected by guardian angels as they fight for their country's laws and rights.

76-396. Yankee Doodle's Extempore Address to his American Brethren, on the Defeat upon Lake Champlain.

"While I your fleet's disastrous lot." (16)

New Morning Post, Nov 25, 1776.

Quatrains. Satire on the Americans. Named after Washington, Lee, and the Congress, American ships seized on Lake Champlain are portrayed as possibly evil characters. (The New Morning Post began publication late in 1776 in an attempt to undermine the reputation and circulation of the Morning Post. The poem was included in the eighteenth issue.)

76-397. [Ye grave medical tribe, stand well to my call.]

"Ye grave medical tribe, stand well to my call." (32)

G, Aug 7, 1776.

Hexameter couplets. Wesley is a hypocrite, politician, and quack; inconsistent on the American question, he now defends the government and is unable to persuade "Yankee Heroes" to surrender their rights.

Prints

76-398. The Catch Singers: Sir William Howe, Lord Richard Howe, Lord George Sackville, Lord North.

"Sir W. Howe: Ha, Ha, He." (6)

Engr. with catch verses. 1776.

George 5342 (V, 226).

America is roughed out on a map on the background wall, and the men sing of their greed for gold. (Relate to George 5399, on the Howes' wish to prolong the war.)

76-399. The Wise Men of Gotham and their Goose.

"In Gotham once the Story goes." (30)

Mezzotint with OC. February 16, 1776.

George 5326 (V, 216-217). Halsey, pp. 43, 45-6; Wynn Jones, p. 75; Spirit of 'Seventy-Six, ed. Commager and Morris (1958), I, 572.

The old fable of the goose that laid the golden eggs is applied to America and Britain. The greed of the British (Bute, Archbishop Markham, Germain, Sandwich, and others) killed the American goose.

76-400. The Yankie Doodles Intrenchments near Boston 1776.

"Behold, the Yankies in there Ditch's." (12)

Engr. with triplets. 1776.

George 5329 (V, 218-19). Repr. Wynn Jones, p. 79; Bailey, British Public Opinion on the American War in Prints [London:] British Museum, n.d., facsimile; The British Look at America During the Age of Samuel Johnson (1971), #88.

A satire on cowardly Americans and their leaders, a hypocritical parson and thieving Putnam.

1777 Books & Pamphlets

77-1. The Asses Ears, A Fable. Addressed to the Author of The Goat's Beard.
London: Riley, 1777. 11p.

"Immortal Bard, ordain'd to sit." (c. 180)

Notices: CR 43 (Mar 1777), 234; MR 56 (Mar 1777), 193-4.

Copies: BL 163.1.10; NUC CtY, IU, NN, PU.

Hudibrastics. Satire on the poet laureate William Whitehead and on Samuel Johnson, Establishment authors. Relates how Jove assembles birds and beasts to complain that no poet expresses proper respect for him. Orders a contest of poets and awards the prize to the Ass whose poetry, devoid of sense, includes "New-Year songs and Birth-day Odes"--for which the laureate was famous. Johnson is ridiculed in the figure of the Bear, especially his "tracts of politics."

77-2. Britannia's Garland, Containing four excellent New Songs. I. Britannia's Call to Her Sons on Expectation of a French War. II. The Dusky Night. III. The Soldiers Farewell. IV. Collin Stole my Heart Away.
N.p.: n.p., n.d. 8p.

I. Tune--Come then all ye social powers. "Come ye lads who wish to shine." (31)

III. "My dearest girls we are now amarching." (45)

Copies: BL 11621.c.2 (3), 11621.c.7 (21).

These two songs are relevant. The first, a recruiting song by John Freeth, says that Britain united can defy France and Spain, as well as the world. It appeared in some London newspapers during April 1778, was often reprinted, and also appeared in Freeth's collections. See Freeth, 78-211.
The third song, however, has not been located in any serial, journal or newspaper; here, believing their cause is just, the soldiers leave for America "to fight for Britain's glory." BL dates this pamphlet 1775 (?) and locates the place of publication at Newcastle; perhaps a more reasonable date would be late 1777 to early 1778.

77-3. The Ciceroniad. A Poem. Inscribed to William Earl of Mansfield: With a Dedication to his Lordship.
London: Carnegy & Bew, 1777. v-viii + 9-35p.

"O! Thou who once, in Rome's degenerate days." (c. 460)

Notices: CR 44 (Nov 1777), 393-5; MR 58 (Jan 1778), 74; GM 48 (Jan 1778), 48; L Mag 46 (Nov 1777), 573; SM 39 (Appendix 1777), 714.

Copies: BL 163.m.48; NUC IU, NcU.

HC. Cicero is sent from the shades to determine the different pretensions of British bar orators to the prize allotted to superiority of merit in their profession. The pleaders assemble and assert their respective claims; their characters are sketched and some are ridiculed, others praised. The palm is bestowed on Lord Mansfield. Although the American troubles are not mentioned, this poem is of interest because it berates Britons for denying merit to Scotland, which helped conquer Canada (pp. 28-30) and because it praises Wedderburne and Mansfield, the talents of the latter having inspired the envy and hatred of "a desperate faction."

77-4. Colvill, Robert.
Atalanta. A Poem. Canto 1.
London: Bew, 1777. 41p.

"Of Albion's reign, with delegated sway." (c. 1050)

Notices: L Chron 42 (Jun 28, 1777), 4.

Copies: BL 11657.g.56 (2); NUC MiU-C.

Dedicated to Earl Percy, who had fought at Lexington and Concord. Blank verse. Epic, Miltonic imitation, with echoes of James Thomson. Colvill writes not about the war so much as the period preceding, during which the war was brewed. In occasional interludes, as he looks ahead, the war does figure in the narrative. The poem is incomplete--only one canto was written and published, although Colvill did contemplate additional cantos.
  He writes of the British "sway" in America, which the Americans usurped in their rebellion. Asserts that the Mother Country was responsible for the prosperity of the colonies; insists upon subordination; describes the development of the colonies and the greatness of the provincial states and cities (Boston, New York, Philadelphia); concludes with the Genius of Britain admonishing his children that the King rules them only for their good, that they are being seduced by "Siren traitors" to rebel. Thereupon, Britain spreads over the provinces "the shield of Safety"--that is, the war begins.
  Atalanta concludes on p. 37. The following pages include "To the Memory of the Hon. W[illiam] L[eslie]," "Sacred to the Memory of Col. Abercrombie . . . Bunker's Hill, July 17, 1775," and "Verses for General Wolfe's Monument" (Sept. 7, 1760), pp. 38-41. See 59-1, 75-6, & 79-7.

77-5. [Combe, William]
The Justification: A Poem. By the Author of The Diaboliad.
London: Bew & Gardner, 1777. vii + 39.

"What ails my Friend?--what means th'exploring eye." (c. 700)

Notices: CR 44 (Dec 1777), 474; MR 57 (Dec 1777), 486-8; L Mag 46 (Appendix 1777), 664: LR 6 (Dec 1777), 451-5.

Copies: BL 163.m.11 & 11630.c.9 (17) (1st ed), 992.g.1 (8) & 12330.aaa.14 (3) (another ed); NUC CSmH, CtY, DLC, ICN, IU, MH, TxU.

HC. A defense of satire; an Opposition poem. Dialogue between the satiric poet "P" and his friend "L." Satire is written in vain: it is ineffective, cruel, and inhumane, "L" declares. But "P" will not surrender the satirical mode: it is really benevolent, he insists, defending virtue and exposing vice. "L" asks if any deserve praise, and "P" replies there are some incorruptible senators who do—Savile, Camden, Rockingham, and Chatham. Also Bishop Lowth is praised. There is one brief allusion to the American war and its effect on friendship (p. 3); the poet contrasts himself with Whitehead, the soothing flatterer (p. 37).

77-6. Darwall, John.
Political Lamentations Written in the Years 1775 and 1776, Respectfully inscribed to The Right Honourable Lord North, and The Right Reverend and Honourable Brownlow (North) Lord Bishop of Worcester: To which is annexed A Political Sermon Preached in the Parish-Church of Walsall December the 13th, 1776, being the Day appointed by His Majesty for a General Fast. . .
London: Nicoll, [1777]. 5 + 13 + 13 + 20p.

Political Lamentation. Written in 1775. "Heav'n prosper long our noble King." (176)

Political Lamentation. Written in 1776. "Whence come these Wars and fightings dire." (176)

Notices: CR 43 (Apr 1777), 315; MR 56 (May 1777), 390; L Mag 46 (Jun 1777), 328; SM 39 (Jun 1777), 324.

Sabin 18644.

Copies: BL 161.1.30, 11659.cc.1 (9); NUC MiU, NN, RPJCB.

In the preface, Darwall condemns the Americans for their bloody rebellion and their "domestic insidious Abettors." He does not believe there is just cause for the civil strife, the cry of liberty but mere pretence. Each "Political Lamentation" is in ballad meter. In the first, he defends British policy on America, taxation and subordination, and execrates the Americans for asserting "Lawless Independency," for religious hypocrisy, and for brutal violence to loyalist opponents (tarring and feathering, riding a pole, blinding). In the second, he declares the fundamental source of the American War is sin: all the evil passions of man. In the sermon, he defends the King from the charge of tyranny, damns the Americans for their willingness to shed blood, and argues the justice of British policy. But, as in the second poem, the ultimate source of the present calamities is the burden not of a tax, but of our sins.

77-7. [Dawes, Matthew]
   The Prospect from Malvern Hill: Or, Liberty Bewailing Her Injuries In America.
A Poem. By A Gentleman of the Inner Temple.
   London: Bew, 1777. i-iv + 28p.

   "Hence, idle Sleep! hence from my slumb'ring soul." (c. 480)

   Notices: CR 44 (Dec 1777), 475-7; MR 58 (Mar 1778), 237; GM 48 (Apr 1778), 192;
LR 6 (Appendix 1777), 521-2; M Chron, Dec 27, 1777.

   Sabin 66068.

   Copies: NUC CtY, IEN, MH, NN.

In the dedication to the Earl of Abingdon, Dawes approves his <u>Thoughts on Burke's
Letter to the Sheriffs of Bristol, respecting the Affairs of America</u>, agreeing that
attempts to reduce Americans to unconditional surrender are improper and ruinous.
HC. A descriptive poem, a significant part commenting on current politics, especially
on the American War. Attacks the bribed court for its "sordid deeds," its bloody
measures against Americans only because they reject oppression. The court, both fraudulent Whig and only "less impudent" Tory, assails liberty. Success in the war will
endanger the throne. The Americans are not rebels--they simply resist tyranny. Liberty
can be found now only in America; in England the constitution is undermined. The war
is waged by the Scotch, who fought a Stuart cause, were rebels to British laws, and
are reputed to have fomented the war. Concludes by asking the King to banish "the
Whig and Tory train" from his court, to maintain the people's rights by law, and to
let freedom reign. Pays tribute to Chatham and Camden.

77-8. [Day, Thomas]
   The Desolation of America: A Poem.
   London: Kearsly, Richardson & Urquahart, & Flexney, 1777. 26p.

   "Through the dim shades by frantic terror led." (c. 520)

   Notices: CR 44 (Nov 1777), 391-2; MR 57 (Dec 1777), 424-8; Freeman's J, Jan 13,
1778; G, Dec 2, 1777; GM 47 (Feb 1778), 83-5; HM 8 (Jan 1778), 55-6; L Chron 42
(Nov 29, 1777), 532; L Mag 46 (Appendix 1777), 664; LR 6 (Dec 1777), 457-9; SM 39
(Appendix 1777), 715-6.

   Sabin 18980-1.

   Copies: BL 163.m.24; NUC CtY, DLC, ICN, MH, MiU-C, NN, RPJCB.

   The first printing, also 26p., was published by E. & C. Dilly, J. Wilkie, and G.
Kearsly in 1777. The second was as above. (See Adams 77-35 a & b about the difference.)

HC. An American family is described fleeing the ravages of war. Mother implores the British to end the war against "kindred blood," exhorts American women to go like Sabine wives to the battlefield and implore the enemy to cease fighting. But she recognizes the futility of such an act. Father, fleeing the English, reviews their tyranny over America, the last refuge of freedom. He curses Britain and vows to struggle on to victory.

77-9. Duché, Jacob.
Episode, From The Indian Treaty, A Poem.

"Rosetta, fairest maid that grac'd the plains." (68)

In Caspipina's Letters; Containing Observations on a Variety of Subjects, Literary, Moral, and Religious. Written by a Gentleman Who Resided some Time in Philadelphia (Bath; rpt. London: Cruttwell & Dilly, 1777), vol. II, pp. 28, 30-33.

Notices: CR 43 (May 1777), 381-3; MR 57 (Oct 1777), 301-2; Lloyd's Eve Post 41 (July 4, 1777), 20; LR 5 (May 1777), 410-15.

Evans 13258-9; Sabin 21048.

Copies: BL 246.g.8; NUC CtY, DLC, ICN, MH, MiU-C.

Caspipina's Letters first published in Philadelphia, 1774; 3rd ed London: Leighton, 1791; 2nd ed dedicated to Richard Penn, Late Governor of Pennsylvania. For comment on the poem, see "Letter XIII. Three Specimens of American Poetry" (1777), II, 28.
Elegiac quatrains. Narrates an incident in America of two young, colonial lovers, Rosetta and Doris, captured and separated by Indians. Later, at a meeting of Indian nations, they are brought together and six English captives are to yield their lives. At the Indian feast, Doris, tied to a tree, dies, as does Rosetta, succumbing to grief.

77-10. English, Robert.
An Elegy, On the Death of the Right Honourable Sir Charles Saunders, Knight of the Bath, Admiral of the White Squadron of His Majesty's Fleet. By the Rev. Robert English, M.A. Chaplain to the Twelfth Regiment of Foot; and to the Right Honourable Edward Lord Hawke.
London: Becket, 1777. 17p.

"How vain the transient scene of pomp and praise." (119)

Notices: CR 43 (Jun 1777), 472; MR 56 (Jun 1777), 478; GM 47 (Aug 1777), 388; Lloyd's Eve Post 42 (Apr 20, 1778), 382; L Eve Post, Aug 1, 1778; L Mag 46 (Jul 1777), 372-3; LR 5 (Appendix 1777), 535; St J's Chron, Apr 18, 1778.

Copies: BL T.669 (8), 162.1 (11); NUC CtY, MH.

HC. A review of Admiral Saunders' successful naval career. He is eulogized for his service to his country in the navy and in Parliament. Saunders served at Quebec against France, and was a friend of Admiral Keppel, who fought heroically under his command.

77-11. Fifth Ode of the K[in]g of P[russia]'s Works Paraphrased. On the Present War.
London: Printed for the Author, 1777. 11p.

"How long oh Europe, in this vicious age." (88)

Notices: CR 45 (Jan 1778), 76; MR 58 (Mar 1778), 236; LR 7 (May 1778), 382; SM 40 (Jan 1778), 36.

Copies: BL C.136.f.7.

8-line stanzas in HC. Published in December 1777, this poem predicts the extension of the American War into another European war fought around the world. It protests the European proclivity for savage warfare, condemns English aggression against America. Only mild government produces beneficial and peaceful results. The tragic civil war in America is condemned.

77-12. [Freeman, S.], pseud.
England's Glory, A Poem to the King.
London: Fielding & Walker, [1777]. iii-iv + 38p.

"Long had Britannia mourn'd her native Isle." (c. 810)

Notices: CR 46 (Sep 1778), 236; MR 58 (Jan 1778), 75; GM 48 (Feb 1778), 96; LR 7 (Mar 1778), 211.

Copies: BL 11602.gg.25 (14); NUC ICN.

Dedication to George III dated September 1777, signed "S. Freeman." HC. A loyal Tory poem, reviewing past divisions and internal strife in England, a land ruled as a monarchy by "the wisest and best Government," where the Prince's and people's interest is identical, in contrast to a democracy, a source of popular tyranny. Admonishes Britain to banish discord, self-interest, faction, religious dissension; exhorts the people to stand up for the King and oppose "inbred Factions and domestic Foes." Praise of Lord Percy, Archbishop of York (Markham), Bathurst, North, Mansfield, General Howe, and Whitehead.

A Gentleman of the Inner Temple. See 77-7.

77-13. [Inglis, John ?]
The Patriots: Or, An Evening Prospect on the Atlantic. In which Some Noted Political Characters are delineated; with Strictures on those Ladies who have distinguished themselves in the Fashionable Modes of Gallantry.
London: Cadell; Edinburgh: Drummond, 1777. xi + 5-54p.

"Broad o'er the wide Atlantic stream." (924)

Notices: RWM, Jul 31, 1777.

Copies: BL 11642.eee.25; Bod Godwyn Pamph 1722 (10); NUC PPRF.

In the prose essay dedicated to Lord North, the author opposes the Americans and criticizes Chatham for fomenting sedition and rebellion, Fox ("the mighty patriot and assertor of American liberty") for his improvident and dissolute behavior, Barrè, and Wilkes, who are set against "a glorious band of men" possessing all the virtues: North, Germaine, Wedderburne, and Dundas. America cannot withstand superior British might or the British spirit as expressed in Britain's constitution.
Octosyllabic couplets. Revealing himself a Scot, the poet imagines false patriots who, speaking for liberty, abuse the King and hide rebellion in their hearts--among them Barrè, Fox, and Chatham. Then he praises Prime Minister North, who urges "British thunder" against the rebels. He also presents the King as forbearing, merciful, humane, and regretful of the need to use force against America.

77-14. Jamaica, A Poem, In Three Parts. Written in that Island, in the Year MDCCLXXVI. To Which Is Annexed, A Poetical Epistle From the Author in that Island to a Friend in England.
London: Nicoll, 1777. 43p.

"Let some, enraptur'd with poetic strains." (408)

Notices: CR 45 (Mar 1778), 230-1; MR 58 (Feb 1777), 142-4.

Copies: BL T.25 (6).

HC. Celebrates the beauty and productivity of Jamaica, but damns the barbarous cruelty of the planters and the miseries of their Negro slaves. Fears the revenge of the tortured slaves in the epistle. Praises Lord Mansfield's famous decision to grant Negroes freedom in Britain. America is mentioned once as being engaged in the slave trade (Pt. 3, l. 75--p. 31), but the American War is not mentioned.

77-15. John the Painter's Ghost: How He Appeared on the Night of His Execution to Lord Temple; and How His Lordship Did Communicate the Same at Full Court, to the Astonishment of All Present: Now Partially and Circumstantially Related.
London: Williams, 1777. 19p.

"'Twas at the silent solemn hour." (204)

Notices: CR 43 (May 1777), 389; MR 56 (Jun 1777), 478; LR 5 (Appendix 1777), 525, & 6 (Aug 1777), 157.

Copies: BL 164.n.43, 11602.gg.25 (11); Bod Godwyn Pamph 1737 (10); NUC CtY, MiU-C.

Ballad, imitation of Mallet's *William and Margaret*. James Aitken was executed for an attempt to burn naval property at Portsmouth, motivated by republicanism and sympathy for the American cause. His confession was obtained through Lord Temple. In the ballad, his ghost, as "John the Painter," takes revenge. He appears before Temple and says other "culprits of state" should have been considered--Bute and Germain. He declares he died a republican, hating all monarchs. Temple, frightened, tells the King of the ghost's appearance and repeats John's remark that America will be victorious. Noting that the strife began over a tea tax, Temple advises George to "break" Parliament. The Preface attacks the Scots, Aitken being of Scottish origin. Cited also are Grenville, Sandwich. See "The Confession of James Aitken" in *Public Advertiser*, March 18, 1777.

77-16. [Langhorne, John]
The Country Justice. A Poem. By One of His Majesty's Justices of the Peace for the County of Somerset. Part the Third.
London: Becket, 1777. 17p.

"O, No! Sir John--the Muse's gentle Art." (144)

Notices: CR 43 (Jul 1777), 79; MR 56 (Jun 1777), 477; LR 5 (Appendix 1777), 520.

Copies: NUC CtY, ICN, InU, MH, RPB.

HC. The poem was published in three parts--1774, 1775, & 1777--but only the last part has comments on British policies and politics regarding America, some 30 lines. Langhorne regrets Parliament's mistaken policies that drove America from Britain, but he has no confidence in the patriots who misled America. He is dismayed that Parliament "hurt" and "Dishonoured" liberty and "tore a Daughter from her Parent's Heart," but he also blames the patriots for their "wild Illusions" that sank commerce and misled America, "Lost in the Rage of Anarchy and Arms." Particularly, he blames Chatham for encouraging rebellion, for vanity's sake--a statue! This section of the poem, entitled "Depraedation," also provides evidence of abuse in India.

77-17. Lucas, Henry.
The Tears of Alnwick; A Pastoral Elegy in Memory of the Late Elizabeth, Dutchess of Northumberland. Dedicated, by permission, to Earl Percy.
London: Dodsley, 1777. 23p.

Notices: CR 42 (Dec 1776), 475; MR 56 (Jan 1777), 68; L Mag 46 (Apr 1777), 216.

Copies: BL 11630.b.1 (7); NUC MH, PU. (All are 2nd eds.)

I have not located a 1st ed. Dedication to Percy dated June 14, 1777. Only pp. 18-19 are relevant. HC. After lavishing praise on the deceased duchess, Lucas turns to her son Percy and expresses hope for a victorious peace so he can really indulge his tendency to sublime panegyric. The present time being inappropriate, he is led to remark that Britons are not afraid to fight, but they fear to fight the Americans: they are troubled by "that generous sympathy of mind / That fear to wound their own offending kind." Percy is congratulated on his return from the fighting in New England and New York; his support of Germain's leadership which "rebel schemes defy" is confirmed. A loyal view of the struggle. A more complex view of Percy's thoughts on the war may be seen in Lewis Namier & John Brooke, The House of Commons 1754-1790 (New York: Oxford University Press, 1964), III, 269-70.

Macgreggor, Malcolm. See 77-18.

77-18. [Mason, William]
   An Epistle to Dr. Shebbeare: To Which Is Added An Ode to Sir Fletcher Norton, In Imitation of Horace, Ode VIII. Book IV. By Malcolm Macgreggor, of Knightsbridge, Esq. Author of the Heroic Epistle to Sir Wm. Chambers, &c.
   London: Almon, 1777. [3] + 5-27p.

"O for a thousand tongues! and every tongue." (221)

"Muse! were we rich in land, or stocks." (72)

Notices: CR 44 (Jul 1777), 75-7; MR 57 (Dec 1777), 488; GM 47 (Jul 1777), 338-9; LR 6 (Jul 1777), 26-31; SM 39 (Aug 1777), 442.

Copies: BL T.666 (4), 840.1.14 (4), 840.1.17 (8), 11630.d.17 (22); Bod Godwyn Pamph 1713 (8) (1st ed), Godwyn Pamph 1490 (12) (2nd ed), Godwyn Pamph 1490 (13) (3rd ed); NUC CtY, DLC, MH, NN, & TxU (1st ed), CSmH, CtY, DLC, MH, & MiU-C (2nd ed).

4 eds, same imprint, 1777. Anti-Tory satires. The Epistle: HC. Ironically addressing Shebbeare, an Administration writer (e.g., his newspaper articles attacking Price), Mason ridicules North and the war against America, where England will be vanquished; also Samuel Johnson and his Tory ideas; Mansfield (a "true Tory" who perverted Liberty); the "weazel Scots"; North and his bribed House of Commons; the Irish policy (citing Nugent's 1775 poem on Ireland); taxation at home; and greedy ministers. Freedom, he concludes, has departed England for America.
   The Ode: octosyllabic couplets. Asks what good the American war will do, even though the Howe brothers should rout Washington, for it will not reduce taxes. Johnson is ridiculed regarding Macpherson's Ossian. (Norton was speaker of the House of Commons.)

77-19. [Maurice, Thomas]
 A Monody Sacred to the Memory of Elizabeth, Dutchess of Northumberland. Addressed to His Grace the Duke of Northumberland.
  Oxford: Fletcher, Prince,& Parker; London: Dodsley,& Kearsly, 1777. 14p.

 "Hark!--Whence that loud, funereal Yell." (270)

 Notices: CR 43 (Feb 1777), 158; MR 56 (Mar 1777), 235.

 Copies: BL 162.1.35; NUC CU, CtY, ICN, MH.

 HC. In ten lines the poet alludes to the Duchess' mourning husband who thinks of his brave son Hugh Percy fighting the American rebels "in insulted Britain's glorious Cause."

77-20. Poetical Excursions In The Isle Of Wight.
  London: Conant, 1777. v-ix + 42p.

 "Once more, Elysian Isle." (c. 660)

 Notices: CR 43 (Mar 1777), 233; L Mag 46 (Jun 1777), 328.

 Copies: BL 163.m.3; Bod Godwyn Pamph 1730 (10); NUC DLC, OrU.

 Mixed verse, decasyllabic and octosyllabic couplets. Brief comment near the end (pp. 37-40), in prose note and in verse, on the American War. The poet imagines flying "in Fancy, to a distant Strand," America, pursuing his "favourite Object . . . Fair Freedom." He does not "yet" anticipate "the Subjugation of our Colonies." America is inspired by freedom and the Whig martyrs--Hampden, Sidney, Russell--who "march undaunted forth to Liberty, or Death." He consigns to lasting infamy Sir John Dalrymple for maligning these leaders in a recently published history, and attacks the Scotch. Also included is a eulogy of Wilkes.

77-21. [Preston, William]
  The Age of Loyalty: An Historical Panegyric. With Explanatory Notes.
  London: Wallis, 1777. 26p.

 "Hence to the desart, and the trackless grove." (342)

 Notices: CR 43 (May 1777), 389; MR 57 (Oct 1777), 325; LR 5 (Appendix 1777), 526.

 Copies: BL 163.1.62; NUC ICN.

 See 77-22.

77-22. [-----]
  The Court Mirrors: Or, The Age of Loyalty. An Historical Panegyric. With Explanatory Notes.
    Dublin: Marchbank, 1777. 23p.

  Copies: Bod Vet A5e.2743 (5).

  Another edition of 77-21. HC. Ironically praises a "Loyal Age" having no thirst for freedom or patriotism. In a corrupt, pleasure-loving England, virtues are pretence, honor is cunning. So Preston urges the King to bribe a "sinful race" of Britons into goodness. Ironically praises the Scots and the doctrine of arbitrary right, a "gospel of despotic sway." England is now so corrupted that only the structure of state remains; but it has lost its soul. Occasional cynical comments on the American War, fought over "a paltry tax"--e.g., the shamefully garbled news about it in official dispatches, the bloodthirsty and unchristian attitude towards it, officers and higher clergy rejoicing at the carnage. Cited are German mercenaries and West-Indian islands.

77-23. Public Spirit: An Essay.
    London: Almon & Kearsly, 1777. 37p.

  "Luckless the Wretch, in an abandon'd Age." (c. 580)

  Notices: MR 58 (Mar 1778), 236; GM 48 (Apr 1778), 192; LR 7 (May 1778), 382.

  Copies: BL 164.n.42; NUC ViW.

  HC. Satire on the corrupt times. The source of all this evil is Bute and his ambition. Wishes an honest Christian spirit to expose hypocritical justifications of the American War as monstrous viciousness. The court is corrupt; even "servile Priests," desiring power, "teach again/ The exploded Doctrines of the Stuart's reign." Yet a faithful few (traced to the barons who secured Magna Charta, Sidney, Locke, "the Camdens of their day") provide models of public spirit and will reclaim the land from foul oppression--Rockingham, Portland, Richmond, Shelburne, Chatham, Manchester, Camden, and Dunning. These he defends from damning lies. But public spirit has deserted Britain for America, flying "O'er western waves to happier, kinder Skies." Junius and the patriot opposition must unite to remove the wicked from the throne and save the land.

77-24. Six Odes, Presented to that justly-celebrated Historian, Mrs. Catharine Macaulay, on her Birth-Day, And publicly read to a polite and brilliant Audience, Assembled April the Second, at Alfred House, Bath, To congratulate that Lady on the happy Occasion.
    Bath: Cruttwell; London: Dilly, Walter, et al., [1777]. 48p.

  An Irregular Ode, Respectfully inscribed to Mrs. Macaulay, And presented on her Birth-Day, April 2d, 1777. "As high above the starry sphere." (111) pp. 20-7.

A Vision. "My mind, with low'ring heavy clouds deprest." (53) pp. 35-8.

Britannia's Reward. A Vision. "As late I wander'd o'er the upland lawn." (119) pp. 39-45.

Notices: CR 43 (May 1777), 389; MR 57 (Jul 1777), 145-9; LR 5 (Jun 1777), 476.

Copies: BL 11631.f.22; NUC CtY, DLC, MH, OCU, TxU.

Irregular Pindaric, HC, HC. These three poems may be relevant because they emphasize the major themes of Macaulay's writings: her hatred of despotism, love of freedom, and her impartial treatment of royalty who, although great, may be vicious and vile. The Stuarts are cited. She is praised for her bold assessment of the great and her exposure of hypocrisy, servility, and corruption. Hampden should be pleased by the achievement of this "Child of Liberty," and is asked to proclaim her triumph in the skies.

77-25. The Sixteenth Ode of the Third Book of Horace Imitated. With a Dedication to the Right Honourable the Lord N[ort]h.
London: Almon, Bew, & Sewell, 1777. 23p.

"Acrisius, grown exceeding jealous." (c. 120)

Copies: BL 161.m.71; NUC DLC.

Ode, imitation of Horace. Fictitiously dedicated to Lord North, dated June 2, 1777, and signed S----l J-----n. Light satire on Samuel Johnson, his corruption (pension), with glancing allusions to politics, America, tea, and taxation. Johnson's persona in the ironic dedication announces "gold" as the ode's subject, declares his veneration of North's principles, and congratulates North on becoming "under the tuition of the Scotch and Bedford Junto, as orthodox a Tory as the K[ing], the A[rch] B[isho]p of Y[or]k, and myself." In the poem, the persona begins with the story of Jove and Danae, and proceeds to describe how gold corrupted many famous people similarly. But, indifferent to wealth because of his pension, he writes an occasional pamphlet filled with lies "To damn the Whigs and praise the Tories" and to pay for his "stock of tea." He pays his taxes with his pension, but admits that he will not again insist "That Tyranny is Not Taxation."

77-26. The Voice of the People. Inscribed to Henry Cruger, and Edmund Burke, Esqrs.
Bristol: Printed for the Author, and sold by the Booksellers, [1777?]. 11p.

"Perish the slave, whatever his degree." (161)

Sabin 100675.

Copies: NUC NN.

Cruger and Burke were MP's for Bristol. HC. The voters of Bristol are urged to return Burke and Cruger, sincere "sons of liberty," as their representatives in the new Parliament.

77-27. Warwick, Thomas.
  The Rights of Sovereignty Asserted. An Ode. By Thomas Warwick, Esq; of University College, Oxford.
  London: Dodsley; Oxford: Fletcher, 1777. [5]-16p.

"Monster! whose unfilial hand." (90)

Notices: CR 43 (Jun 1777), 472; MR 57 (Jul 1777), 78; L Mag 46 (Jul 1777), 373; LR 5 (Appendix 1777), 523.

Copies: BL 162.1.19, 11630.e.2 (2); NUC CtY, MB.

Dedication to the Duke of Northumberland and his son Earl Percy dated May 15, 1777. Regular Pindaric ode. Britannia demands that America cease fighting. But America--misled by hellish design, fraudulent freedom and piety, ambition, avarice, distrust, and discontent--insists upon continuing, the result being anarchy. Britannia begs America to return, citing her help in the French and Indian War and her contribution to American prosperity. Then withdrawing her protection, she lets America seek the French--i.e., become prey to France. The Howe brothers will succeed, despite a bloody struggle, "civil gore," aided by the heroic deeds of Earl Percy.

77-28. [Whitaker, John]
  Manchester, An Ode.

"When first Rebellion rear'd his crest." (48)

In Richard Polwhele, ed., Poems, Chiefly by Gentlemen of Devonshire and Cornwall (Bath: Cruttwell; London: Cadell, 1792), vol. II, pp. 74-6.

Copies: BL 11660.ee.24; NUC CtY, DLC, IU, MH, MiU, NN.

Regular Horatian ode. Written c. December 1777, after Burgoyne's defeat, to help recruit officers and men for a new regiment to support continuing the war. A note alludes to Manchester "presenting the first address to the King for reducing the American rebels" (in 1775). This poem was first entitled "The Praises of Manchester. An Ode. Calculated to be set to Music," in Lloyd's 42 (Mar 20, 1778), 275: see 78-423.

Serials

77-29. The Abingdon Garland. [Tune. "As I went to Abingdon."]

"Have you read Abingdon, heigh, Sir, ho, Sir." (75)

PA, Nov 14, 1777.

Song. A satire on Bertie, the Earl of Abingdon's attacks on Burke and Government, especially the Archbishop of York, and his expressions of support for sedition, Franklin and Price. These lines are supposedly a revision of the "Parody on the Old Song" appearing in the PA, Oct 11, 1777: 77-245. They simply parody the first so-called "Parody."

77-30. Advice on the Present Situation of Affairs.

"Humanity, that bleeds for home-felt woe." (8)

W Misc 7 (Jan 20, 1777), 387-8.

HC. Weary of war, the writer asks for humane peace.

77-31. Advice to Modern Patriots. Written by the Editor.

"Ye sage politicians, who're never content." (16)

Vocal Magazine (1778), Song #432, p. 115.

Song. Advice to the Opposition to give up, for it cannot withstand the power and deceit of the premier, North. (The editor may be John Bew, the publisher.)

77-32. [All joy to great Caesar, the Howe's are found.]

"All joy to great Caesar, the Howe's are found." (11)

L Eve Post, Nov 1, 1777.

Satire on the Howe brothers who are not having much success in their campaign against America. "The Scotch and the Tories / Have lost him an empire, and crown'd him with glories."

77-33. An Alphabet for little Masters and Misses.

"A Stands for America--which seems to be going." (21)

Freeman's J, Oct 11, 1777; L Eve Post, Sep 30, 1777.

An abecedarian poem listing people and circumstances involved in the loss of America: Bute, Carleton, the French, Germain, the King, Jacobites, Mansfield, North, places and pensions. The war "which pursued, will be the ruin of us all."

77-34. The American War. An Epigram.

"When brothers fall out about trifles of state." (8)

Freeman's J, Sep 27, 1777; L Chron 42 (Sep 11, 1777), 264; PA, Sep 12, 1777; St J's C, Sep 11, 1777.

Quatrains. The Americans and British should peacefully compromise their conflicting wishes.

77-35. Another New War Song. By S[ir Peter Parker].

"Now, my Lords, once again." (36)

L Eve Post, Feb 1, 1777.

Song. A satiric and comical continuation of Admiral Parker's experiences after Sullivan's Island off Charleston, S. C., last year: now his attack on Rhode Island is described.

77-36. The Beau of 1777.

"The dress of Beaus it were hard to reduce." (20)

W Eve Post, Sep 18, 1777.

Quatrains. Satire on the Beau of 1777 (in contrast with more serious problems of the day).

77-37. [Blust'ring, bloody (Burgoyne), who such mighty things boasted.]

"Blust'ring, bloody [Burgoyne], who such mighty things boasted." (4)

L Eve Post, Nov 11, 1777.

Irregular couplets. Some of Burgoyne's officers objected to his strategy and especially to his proclamation. These verses, which they wrote, declare that Burgoyne, because of his bloody acts--arming Indians and Devils--is now justly made to suffer.

77-38. Bon Mot of an American. On General Howe.

"Men easily imitate others, they say." (4)

G Eve Post, Mar 15, 1777; L Chron 41 (Mar 15, 1777), 264; MP, Mar 18, 1777.

Epigram. General Howe intimidates the Americans, who do not care to fight him (as a result of his victories in New York).

77-39. [Brave Gates, where in Saratoga's fair Field.]

"Brave Gates, where in Saratoga's fair Field." (4)

PA, Dec 29, 1777.

Extempore. HC. Gates treated Burgoyne and his army generously at the surrender in Saratoga.

77-40. Britannia, a New Cantata.

"Britannia, sov'reign Queen of Isles." (20)

G, May 22, 1777; Lloyd's 40 (May 26, 1777), 510; M Chron, May 23, 1777; PA, May 26, 1777.

Song. A loyal lyric urging Britons to fight in the honorable and just cause of maintaining their rights in the American colonies.

77-41. Britannia to Dr. Price.

"Say, gloomy Sage! what future Meed." (24)

G Eve Post, Apr 8, 1777; PA, Apr 5, 1777.

Ode in sixains. Attack on Richard Price for being a traitor to the church and the state and for encouraging (America to commit) parricide.

77-42. The British Sailor's Appeal.

"While British valour still by all confest." (40)

G, Jul 7, 1777.

Heroic quatrains. An objection to press warrants, evidence of inhumane oppression.

The Budget. A Song. See [Freeth]: 77-131.

77-43. Burgoyne (?), John.
A Vaudeville. Sung by the Characters at the Conclusion of a new Farce, call'd the Boston Blockade. Performed by the British Officers at Boston during the Siege of that Garrison. Said to be written by General B-------.

"Ye Critics, who wait for an end of the scene." (45)

MP, Jul 30, 1777.

Song. The British in Boston entertain themselves while being besieged by the Americans.

77-44. [Burgoyne's] Proclamation.

"The forces under my command." (92)

Lloyd's 41 (Aug 15, 1777), 163; MP, Aug 13, 1777; West G, Aug 12, 1777.

Hudibrastics (OC). Burgoyne's bombastic proclamation, June 29, 1777, versified. This version appears to be ironic because the style of burlesque Hudibrastic couplets is at variance with the content. He threatens "dreadful vengeance" upon the colonists who misbehave. Burgoyne was at the beginning of his campaign to march from Canada to New York in order to isolate New England from the other colonies. Another version appeared in September: see 77-45.

77-45. Burgoyne's Proclamation Versified.

"Be it known unto you all that here I come." (26)

Freeman's J, Sep 27, 1777; L Eve Post, Sep 11, 1777; MJ, Sep 13, 1777; PA, Sep 13, 1777.

Hexameter couplets. Satiric parody, through the persona of Burgoyne, on Burgoyne's ferocious proclamation to the inhabitants of New York at the beginning of his campaign to cut off New England. See another version, 77-44.

77-46. The Cabinet Debate: An Epigram.

"What the Devil, says North, to his Colleague Germaine." (14)

LP, Oct 15, 1777; PA, Oct 17, 1777.

Hexameter couplets. North, Germaine, and Sandwich debate on how to raise additional money for an American campaign. Germaine recommends using the wealth of India, but North says Germaine's leadership is unproductive. The point is that Britain does not have the power to defeat America, as King George appears to believe.

77-47. A Cabinet Repartee.

"To North the Lean, says George the Wise." (4)

PA, Dec 5, 1777.

Epigram. North, in speaking to the King, is grateful that there is only one General Arnold to contend with.

77-48. The Campaign -- Extempore.

"From trifling causes vast events." (12)

LP, Nov 26, 1777; PA, Nov 27, 1777; Sent M 5 (Nov 1777), 328; W Eve Post, Nov 27, 1777.

Quatrains. Ironic comment on the trifling cause of the American War--a pound of tea. The war has cost many lives and should be stopped.

77-49. Celia's Complaint for the Loss of her Shepherd.

"What sadness reigns over the plain." (48)

Musical Companion, or Songster's Magazine for the Year 1777 (1777), pp. 31-2.

Song. A girl weeps over the loss of her sweetheart, gone to fight in America.

77-50. A Certain Speech Transversed.

"My Lords, and my Gentlemen! 'tis with great joy." (68)

Freeman's J, Dec 30, 1777.

Anapest tetrameter couplets. Satire on the King and ministry. After Burgoyne's defeat, the King's persona speaks to Parliament begging for continued funding for another campaign against America, despite failure to subdue the obstinate rebels.

77-51. A Certain Speech Versified.

"Tax'd as we are beyond our strength." (8)

G, May 19, 1777; L Chron 41 (May 17, 1777), 471; PA, May 21, 1777.

Quatrains. Satire on Parliament, especially the House of Commons, which cheerfully votes additional taxes.

77-52. Charade.

"My First, was half-Hypocrite! -- Tyrant! -- and Martyr." (12)

MP, Jan 10, 1777.

Satire on Charles James Fox, "that rough monster."

77-53. Christmas Day. (Parodied from Milton.)

"This is the month, and this the happy morn." (15)

L Eve Post, Dec 23, 1777.

Imitation of John Milton's "On the Morning of Christ's Nativity." Advice to the rulers of the country to grant peace to Britain and her "children," or colonies. Only this resolution is meaningful.

77-54. A Christmas Presentation from the Bellman of St. James's.

"Queen of the World! Opinion! hear my Pray'r." (60)

PA, Dec 26, 1777.

HC. A criticism of those who obstinately insist upon carrying on the American War even to the point of ruin for the country.

77-55. The Christmas Recess: A Poem.

"The doors are clos'd; heard ye the sound." (44)

G, Dec 16, 1777; Lloyd's 41 (Dec 24, 1777), 611; WM 39 (Jan 28, 1778), 112.

Quatrains. On the Parliamentary recess which will provide relief to North and Government from the criticism of Opposition, Burke and Abingdon.

77-56. The City Politician.

"No torture, sure, is so intense." (44)

AWCour, Nov 25, 1777; Lloyd's 41 (Nov 14, 1777), 476.

OC. Satire on the newspapers. Instead of good serious news about the Howes, the Morning Post prints trivia and pessimistic reports on Burgoyne's campaign. The poet wishes to punish North and Bute.

77-57. The Cobler's Prophecy in 1634, Anno Dom.

"In some future pious reign." (8)

Freeman's J, Jan 16, 1777; L Eve Post, Jan 7, 1777.

Mixed OC and HC. Satire on the times. Foretells that in the reign of pious George III there will be a victory of papists, Jacobites, and Tories over true Whigs, bringing suffering for the poor and profits for the rich, and bloody persecution.

77-58. Colvill, Robert.
To the Memory of the Hon. William Leslie, Captain in the gallant 17th Regiment, who was unfortunately slain when his Battalion forced their way through the Rebel Army, Jan. 3, 1777.

"Sweet William was an earl's son." (240)

WM 36 (Apr 3 & 10), 48-9, 81-2. Also in 89-1: his Poetical Works, pp. 131-42 (revised).

Two cantos, in ballad style. A loyal poem in praise of the brave Scots officers who fought against the American rebels--Sir Alexander Murray, General Grant, Captain Scott, General Percy, Colonel Mawhood, as well as Captain William Leslie. It is the Battle of Princeton that is described, January 3, 1777, when Colonel Mawhood's British troops were overpowered and obliged to retreat.

77-59. [Come, my boys, let us sing.]

"Come, my boys, let us sing." (24)

L Eve Post, Mar 18, 1777.

Song. A satirical, topical reaction to Howe's campaign in New Jersey--Trenton and the Delaware and the Raritan. Mentioned are Lee's capture, the bill to suspend habeas corpus, and Cornwallis.

77-60. A Comment on the New Year's Ode.

"The year begins--well, Mr. Printer." (56)

M Chron, Jan 14, 1777.

Ballad, ironically remarking on the diction and thought of Whitehead's laureat ode for the new year, 1777.

77-61. The Comparison: A State-Epigram.

"While North is snoring, in his Nest." (8)

PA, Nov 19, 1777.

Quatrains. In this time of crisis, who deserves more applause: sleeping North or amorous Sandwich?

77-62. The Compromise.

"When mutual passions fire the mind." (20)

PA, Aug 11, 1777; Sent M 5 (Aug 1777), 182.

Quatrains. If both America and Britain agree that they are mistaken, their unnatural war will be quickly ended.

77-63. A Consolatory Address to General Lee.

"If many dangers do environ." (23)

MP, Apr 23, 1777.

OC, consoling General Charles Lee, pessimistic about the outcome of the struggle. Lee, a deserter, falls a just victim to his country's laws. (Lee had been captured December 13, 1776.)

77-64. Corydon's Farewell on his Embarkation for America.

"Farewell the bell upon a ram's neck hung." (66)

T&C 9 (Jul 1777), 384.

HC. A young recruit bids a sentimental farewell to his home and its natural surroundings, his country chores and pleasures.

77-65. The Council of Taylors: A Fragment of an Opera. Act Last, Scene Third.

"Mr. Absque. We are met to hear and to debate." (c. 100)

L Eve Post, Oct 7, 1777.

Recitatives and songs. Satire on the Cabinet or Ministry (Apsley, Rigby, North, Germaine) who all are delighted with the war against America for several selfish reasons, basically corrupt.

77-66. A Countryman's Description of a Raree-Show in London.

"As I pass'd thro' the City, a crowd was gather'd." (40)

Freeman's J, Dec 30, 1777; L Eve Post, Dec 23, 1777.

Ballad, with "Derry down" chorus. An ironic narrative of Burgoyne's campaign, concluding in the Yankee capture of his army and the execution of those responsible: Mansfield, Bute, North, Germain. Also cited are Washington, Arnold, and Frazer.

77-67. The Courtly Congress.

"B[u]te is a firebrand--M[ans]f[iel]d is a knave." (8)

L Eve Post, Dec 6, 1777.

Satire on the court. All the members of the court deserve hanging: Bute, Mansfield, Germaine, North, Rigby, Jenkinson, Sandwich, Suffolk, Thurloe, Ellis, Stanley, and Wedderbourn.

The Death of Alico, an African Slave. See Bryan Edwards: 77-74.

77-68. Description of a Modern Circle at St. James's.

"Mark the train around attending." (8)

Freeman's J, Apr 24, 1777; L Eve Post, Apr 8, 1777.

Trochaic tetrameter couplets. General satire on the fawning court at the King's St. James's Palace: all these rich and powerful support tyranny.

77-69. Description of America, in Reference to its Past and Present State.

"Sorrow was a stranger here." (24)

L Chron 41 (Jan 16, 1777), 64; W Misc 7 (Jan 13, 1777), 357; New Foundling Hospital for Wit (1786), V, 166-7.

Quatrains. Before America was blessed with pastoral bliss; now, at war, it is desolate. Death and danger are everywhere.

77-70. The Devil and John the Painter.

"Says Old Nick to Jack as he stood in the cart." (4)

LP, Jun 16, 1777.

Epigram. Anapest tetrameter couplets. The devil encourages John the Painter, the arsonist, on the way to his execution March 10, 1777.

77-71. A Dialogue between General Prescot and the Officer of the Party that took him Prisoner.

"Prescot. Says the General when taken, to him who commanded." (28)

L Chron 42 (Sep 30, 1777), 324; L Eve Post, Sep 27, 1777.

Quatrains. Gen. Richard Prescott is critical of the American way of fighting; but the American officer defends himself effectively: it brings results, as seen at Lexington, Bunker's Hill, Trenton, and Boston.

77-72. The Disappointed Scotchman. A Satire.

"Sae, Sawney, guid faith! as I tauld you, ye coof." (41)

MP, Jun 4, 1777.

Hexameter couplets. Satire on those canny Scotsmen who encourage the rebellion, wish to split the country, and gain at the expense of the English. The Scotch are as sly as Wilkes but not so fat as Johnson.

77-73. A Dream, in the American Style (Stile).

"Rare news from the Island, the tables are turn'd." (30)

L Chron 41 (Feb 18, 1777), 172; WM 36 (Mar 27, 1777), 18.

Hexameter couplets. A dream that the minority has come into place and that the tables are turned as the colonies dominate Great Britain.

77-74. Edwards, Bryan.
Stanzas occasioned by the Death of Alico, an African Slave, condemned for Rebellion in Jamaica, 1762.

"'Tis past: -- Ah! calm thy cares to rest!" (40)

Freeman's J, Oct 2, 1777; LP, Sep 22, 1777; SM 39 (Nov 1777), 614; UM 61 (Nov 1777), 270-1; WM 38 (Oct 30, 1777), 111-12. Also in New Foundling Hospital for Wit (1786), VI, 13-15; The Muse's Mirror (London: Baldwin, 1778), II, 249-51; The Muse's Pocket Companion (Carlisle: Milliken, 1785), pp. 249-50.

Quatrains. Anti-slavery poem. The persona of a Negro slave condemns his captors, Christian tyrants, for their cruel denial of freedom to oppressed Africans. He is burned alive. See 92-1: Edwards' Poems Written Chiefly in the West-Indies, pp. 37-8.

77-75. Elegy. Addressed to the Revolted Colonies.

"Hark! o'er the billowy western main." (107)

SM 39 (Feb 1777), 103; T&C 9 (Jan 1777), 45; WM 35 (Feb 27, 1777), 305.

Irregular Pindaric ode. The poet has Britain beg the American colonies to cease their obstinacy, admit their guilt, and submit--"Let not th'event of war decide." Britain will forgive the prodigal who returns in peace. (This is not an elegy!)

77-76. Elegy On the Death of Brigadier General Mercer, of Virginia, Slain in the Action Near Princeton, January 3, 1777.

"Another patriot claims the votive strain." (68)

New Foundling Hospital for Wit (1786), IV, 244-7.

Elegiac quatrains, on the death of American general Hugh Mercer, killed in action near Princeton, January 3, 1777. (Actually, he was badly wounded and died January 12, 1777.)

77-77. The Engagement.

"When erst Britannia's hardy sons arose." (58)

Cumb Pacq, Sep 16, 1777; LP, Sep 19, 1777.

HC. A spirited narrative of a battle between an armed British merchantman and an American privateer.

77-78. England's Hue and Cry after the Howes.

"Where do ye lie." (14)

L Eve Post, Oct 21, 1777.

Dimeter couplets. Satire on the Howes who do not fight and who do not keep the government informed. Where are they?

77-79. An Epigram.

"Burke often Scripture quotes, as Christians shou'd." (4)

MP, Jan 8, 1777.

HC. Stresses Burke's self-interest, desire of material gain.

77-80. An Epigram.

"The idle Rabble oft inquire." (6)

PA, May 1, 1777.

Sixain. Washington, admired by Whigs, chose the title of dictator because he dictates to his enemies, not to his friends.

77-81. Epigram.

"The number forty-five seven years ago." (4)

L Eve Post, Jul 1, 1777.

Wilkes has little support now; the Court has bought off his followers.

77-82. An Epigram.

"'Tis said, that Rigby t'other night." (8)

L Eve Post, Jul 8, 1777; PA, Jul 10, 1777.

Quatrains. Satire on the ministry, especially Rigby and North -- the former without brains, the latter without courage and conviction. (Richard Rigby, in charge of the Pay Office, was an active instigator of the American War.)

77-83. An Epigram.

"A Wag, who thinks his Wit is nice." (8)

PA, Oct 22, 1777.

OC. Satire on the Howes who run before the Yankees.

77-84. An Epigram.

"When first the fatal War began." (8)

PA, Oct 11, 1777; W Eve Post, Oct 9, 1777.

Quatrains. It seemed a joke that the American War began over a quarrel about a pound of tea; but now all of India's tea would not end this war!

77-85. An Epigram.

"Whilst Abingdon and frothy Burke." (6)

PA, Nov 8, 1777.

Sixain. The quarrel between Abingdon and Burke shows that both are wrong.

77-86. An Epigram.

"Whilst you, great G[eorg]e, for Knowledge hunt." (6)

PA, Nov 10, 1777; St J's C, Nov 6, 1777.

Sixain. While King George looks for wisdom, the empire disintegrates. Franklin, however, knows what to do and keeps to the point.

77-87. An Epigram: The Brothers.

"The Brother-Stars of former Days." (10)

PA, Oct 11, 1777; W Eve Post, Oct 9, 1777.

OC. On the quandary of Britain (expressed in a metaphor), unable to find the proper direction for the ship of state.

77-88. An Epigram. Extempore. On Hearing that Lord Abingdon's Horse Washington, was beat by Mr. O'Kelly's Filly Venus, at Lewes Races.

"At Lewes, Washington was beat." (4)

L Eve Post, Aug 12, 1777; MP, Aug 14, 1777.

Quatrain. Washington is "famous for retreat," but he "ne'er will run." (Abingdon, in the Opposition, favored Washington.)

77-89. An Epigram. The False Conception.

"North t'other Day I chanc'd to spy." (8)

St J's C, Jun 14, 1777.

Quatrains. Satire on Lord North for his appearance and for his political deception.

77-90. An Epigram on General Sir William Howe's Retreats.

"When William of Nassau was beaten by France." (8)

L Eve Post, Oct 14, 1777.

Quatrains. Satire on Gen. Howe, who retreats before the Americans, very poor soldiers; unlike King William, who had to retreat before French troops, the best in Europe.

77-91. Epigram. On One Part of Our Army Being Made Captives under General Burgoyne; and the Other Part, under General Howe, attacking Mud Island, in order to keep up a communication with Philadelphia.

"That we're all in the dirt, or as good." (4)

L Eve Post, Dec 11, 1777.

Quatrain. Satire on Burgoyne's defeat and on Howe's Mud Island attack, November 1777.

77-92. An Epigram. On Reading in the News-papers that Lord Howe had Employed General Lee in soliciting an Accommodation with the Americans.

"In Holy Writ, I've heard, 'tis told." (8)

PA, May 8, 1777.

Quatrains. General Howe will never succeed in gaining America by taking to the sea or by asking General Lee to intercede for peace. (Howe planned a sea maneuver for the capture of Philadelphia. After his capture, Lee was persuaded by Howe to go over to the British side.)

77-93. Epigram. On the Capture of a Certain General.

"A Gen'ral of late has been vilely abus'd." (4)

M Chron, Sep 26, 1777.

Satire on British General Prescott, captured when in bed with a woman.

77-94. Epigram on the Head-Ach of a certain Gentleman.

"What three times blooded in a day." (4)

L Eve Post, Mar 13, 1777.

OC. North deserves to bleed, because he was responsible for the American War.

77-95. An Epigram. On the ingenious Poems written at Oxford against Lord Abingdon's Pamphlet.

"In merry Songs, that only draw a Tear." (6)

PA, Dec 20, 1777.

Sixain. The poems written at Oxford against Lord Abingdon are like intestinal gas.

77-96. Epigram on the Ministry.

"They may sleep safely in their beds." (4)

Freeman's J, Aug 19, 1777; L Eve Post, Aug 5, 1777.

Quatrain. The ministers are safe from execution, for they have no heads to lose.

77-97. Epigram. On the Parliament's Paying the King's Debts.

"What the Crown asks, shall we not give." (4)

L Eve Post, Feb 11, 1777.

OC. Satire on King and Parliament. Parliament's financial grants to the King benefit half of its members. Reference is corruption, bribery and pensions.

77-98. An Epigram. On the Publication of Some Seditious Speeches of the Arch-Patriot in the City.

"Thy speeches, Wilkes, -- how fine they read." (4)

MP, Dec 19, 1777.

Quatrain. Satire on Wilkes' speeches for wanting sincerity.

77-99. Epigram. On the Sudden and Secret Arrival of Dr. Franklin in London.

"'Twas said, last Night, that Franklin came." (8)

PA, Feb 5, 1777.

Quatrains. On the rumor that Franklin is in London negotiating conciliation with North. (But in fact he had gone to France to negotiate a loan.)

77-100. Epigram. To Doctor Shebbeare.

"Once, Shebbeare, once in Verse and Prose." (4)

PA, May 20, 1777.

Shebbeare (now a government writer) censures those who censure the enemies of the people. (Now "venal," he has become a Tory.)

77-101. Epigram upon General Prescott's (when he was taken Prisoner) calling out for his Breeches.

"'The Handkerchief!' -- Othello cries." (6)

Cal Merc, Sep 29, 1777; L Chron 42 (Sep 23, 1777), 304; L Eve Post, Sep 20, 1777; PA, Sep 24, 1777.

Sixain. A satire on Prescott because of his embarrassing and humiliating predicament.

77-102. Epigramma. In Bostoniam et Trentoniam, a Georgio Washington, Dictatore, sine clade, captas, et Germanis libertatem datam. [On the Capture of Boston and Trenton without Bloodshed. . . .]

"Vicit Dictator Caesar quiq; vicit & Afrus." (4)

L Eve Post, Apr 24, 1777.

One of the occasional Latin poems published on the American War: about Washington's capture of Boston and Trenton without bloodshed and setting the German troops (captured at Trenton) free.

77-103. [An Epigraph for an Essay on the American Colonies.]

"To glorious Liberty America these days." (2)

L Eve Post, Jun 24, 1777.

Couplet. America is preparing "a deep foundation" for liberty by means of the war, "By bold attempts."

77-104. An Epistle from a Gentleman in London to his Friend, a Surgeon's Mate at Portsmouth, on his Departure for New York.

"When once you set sail." (30)

L Eve Post, Jul 26, 1777.

Sixains. Humorous advice to a surgeon's mate on how to be a successful physician--including remarks on his training at New York.

77-105. An Epistle from a Young Lady to an Officer With his Majesty's Army in Canada.

"Ye prosp'rous winds! propitious gales arise." (86)

MP, Jun 26, 1777.

HC. A young woman complains of her separation from her lover with the army in Canada. (Burgoyne began his march southward to isolate New England by linking up with Howe on June 13, 1777.)

77-106. An Epistle to the American Insurgents.

"Tell me now, ye Boston blades." (48)

G, Dec 25, 1777; W Eve Post, Dec 25, 1777.

Quatrains. An English translation of the French "Epitre aux Insurgens." Light ironic comment on the barbaric Americans who, despite Europe and its acceptance of tyranny, fight for freedom in the old Roman republican tradition. See "Epistle to the Americans," 77-107, and "Translation, or rather Paraphrase of the Epitre aux Insurgents," 77-312.

77-107. An Epistle to the Americans, from an Inhabitant of Paris. Inscribed to Dr. Franklin.

"Ye factious sons of Boston, tell us." (56)

Freeman's J, Oct 11, 1777; L Eve Post, Oct 2, 1777.

OC and quatrains. An ironic comment on the barbaric and primitive Americans who, despite Europe and its tyranny, are fighting for freedom in the old Roman republican tradition. England, on the contrary, now willingly accepts tyranny.
The French original, "Epitre aux Insurgens," appeared in the London Evening Post, December 20, 1777. Two other translations are printed at the end of the year. See "An Epistle to the American Insurgents," 77-106, and "Translation, or rather Paraphrase of the Epitre aux Insurgents," 77-312.

77-108. Epitaph.

"Here lies, Without Hope of Resurrection." (c. 40)

PA, Apr 7, 1777.

Inscription. The King's friends who govern by means of favoritism are destroying the political order, Parliament and the court, and are responsible for the rebellion and the dismemberment of Britain.

77-109. Extempore.

"America--our Royalists say." (8)

PA, Oct 11, 1777.

Quatrains. Howe cannot defeat the Americans, despite the boasting claims of the royalists.

77-110. Extempore.

"At length th'important News arrives." (8)

PA, Oct 31, 1777.

Quatrains. Epigram. The Howes are unsuccessful; some support them, and some do not.

77-111. Extempore.

"The Holy Scriptures wisely say." (12)

PA, Jun 13, 1777; W Eve Post, Jun 12, 1777.

Quatrains. Scriptures and common sense require that the war against America be ended, despite the war-mongering courtiers. Common sense says, "Mind the Words of Chatham."

77-112. Extempore.

"In ancient times, when England's fame." (12)

Sent M 5 (Aug 1777), 182; The Vocal Magazine (1778), Song #582, p. 153.

Song. Quatrains. On Britain's decline from power. Before England was feared by France; but now, being weak, she is mocked, and the reverse is true.

77-113. Extempore.

"When *Anne* the British Sceptre wielded." (16)

PA, Aug 4, 1777.

Quatrains. The war with America should end so that the French will not gain from it.

77-114. Extempore.

"When Fame of old, with fulgent Wings." (24)

PA, Oct 20, 1777; W Eve Post, Oct 18, 1777.

Quatrains. Formerly Britain was prosperous, free, and strong; but because of Scotch corruption, she now faces ruin.

77-115. Extempore.

"When first went Abroad our brave Soldiers and Tars." (16)

LP, Oct 13, 1777; PA, Oct 15, 1777; Sent M 5 (Oct 1777), 278-9.

Quatrains. Britain is unable to defeat the American rebels, and so the war should be ended.

77-116. Extempore.

"When great Eliza rul'd this Land." (12)

PA, Jul 28, 1777; W Eve Post, Jul 26, 1777.

Quatrains. On French provocation. The French need to be faced with the resolution like that with which England faced Spain in Elizabeth's day.

77-117. Extempore.

"When Tea to Boston first was sent." (24)

PA, Jul 26, 1777; W Eve Post, Jul 24, 1777.

Quatrains. Tea as a cause of the American War is trivial. Surely it is not too late to bring the war to an end.

77-118. Extempore. On a Late Debate.

"Shall impudent People without Doors aspire." (12)

L Chron 41 (May 1, 1777), 423; PA, May 3, 1777.

Quatrains. A challenge of privilege, the custom of not allowing the people, who are the real masters and who provide the money, to question what is happening in Parliament.

77-119. Extempore, on hearing that a Noble Lord, high in Office, invited a certain Col[one]l in Opposition to dine with him, after receiving much Abuse from him at a certain Sporting Club.

"Tho' humble N[or]th, a Slave to Fear." (8)

PA, Dec 16, 1777.

Quatrains. Satire on North for (apparently) fearing "one Irish Bully," Barre.

77-120. Extempore, on reading that, as soon as one General appeared on the Back Settlements, another disappeared on the Coast of the Jerseys.

"Our Gen'rals, noted for disasters." (8)

Freeman's J, Sep 27, 1777; L Chron 42 (Sep 13, 1777), 264.

Satire on Generals Howe and Burgoyne who have failed to link their forces. Unless they do, they are warned, the British will lose America.

77-121. Extempore, on the frequent Assurances of the Pacific Intentions of the French.

"The French are pacific, they tell us." (24)

G, Jul 3, 1777; G Eve Post, Jul 1, 1777; PA, Jul 2, 1777; W Eve Post, Jul 1, 1777.

Quatrains. Advises the end of "the war Trans-Atlantic," so that England can attend to its true enemy, France.

77-122. Extempore, on the Report of a speedy Reconciliation between Great Britain and her Colonies.

"And shall the bloody contest end?" (20)

G Eve Post, Jun 28, 1777; PA, Jul 1, 1777; W Eve Post, Jun 28, 1777.

Quatrains. Hopes that the news of a reconciliation between America and Britain is true and that the civil war will end.

77-123. Extempore. On the Report that Earl Percy is to have a Blue Ribbon.

"Some two years ago, on America's strand." (8)

L Eve Post, Jun 10, 1777; PA, Jun 11, 1777; W Eve Post, Jun 10, 1777.

Quatrains. Epigram. Two years ago, Percy, who commanded the troops at Lexington and Concord, tried to hang the American rebels; but now, as a reward for his services in America, he is to receive a title.

77-124. A Favourite Song of the Rebels. To the Air of "The Watry God."

"The watry God, great Neptune lay." (54)

M Chron, Jan 6, 1777; St J's C, Jan 4, 1777.

Song. Esek Hopkins, the American naval captain, defeats Admiral Howe in battle. But young America has other heroes, too--Washington, Putnam, Lee.

77-125. The First Ode of the Second Book of Horace imitated. Addressed to a celebrated Orator and Letter Writer.

"Our civil Discord, which began." (47)

M Chron, Oct 9, 1777; PA, Oct 10, 1777.

OC. Imitation of Horace. Satire on Burke for encouraging the Americans. The civil war was caused by "Grenville's wild Revenue Plan," the Stamp Act, and then tea. Asks Burke to be quiet and inactive for a while.

77-126. The following is a short State of the Flourishing Condition of the British Empire.

"Burgoyne in a wood." (10)

Freeman's J, Nov 27, 1777.

Dimeter couplets that are placed in accounts of the difficulties and defeats suffered by Burgoyne's forces, August-October 1777, the bewilderment of the British who, confused, know not what to do.

77-127. The following Poem was composed by a Gentleman, on hearing that Lord and General Howe were sailed on a secret Expedition.

"The two Brothers are sail'd, but no one knows where." (15)

Freeman's J, Sep 13, 1777; L Eve Post, Sep 6, 1777.

Triplets. On the difficulty of learning what the Howes have adopted as their strategy. Cited are Boston, Hell Gate, New Jersey.

77-128. The following Song, it is supposed, was written by the Author of a certain Pamphlet. To the Tune of "To all ye Ladies," etc.

"To all you Yankeys in the Land." (63)

PA, Oct 6, 1777; St J's C, Oct 2, 1777.

Ironic song about Yankee sympathizer Willoughby Bertie, Earl of Abingdon, who wrote a pamphlet Thoughts On The Letter of Edmund Burke, Esq; To the Sheriffs of Bristol, On The Affairs of America (1777). Abingdon raced a horse called "Washington." Markham and Franklin are cited.

77-129. The following Song was composed by a loyal Subject, for the 4th day of June, 1777, and sung that day in America. Tune, "Rule Britannia!"

"Blest cause of genial life, arise." (28)

L Chron 42 (Jul 22, 1777), 88; MP, Jul 24, 1777.

Song for the King's birthday by an obedient American loyalist who hopes that "traitors may receive their final doom." Could be by Jonathan Odell.

77-130. Fragment on the Fast.

"But suppose that the King had instead of a fast." (12)

Freeman's J, Feb 1, 1777.

Anapest tetrameter couplets. Satire on the King and his ministers, Mansfield and North. Instead of a fast, a purge is recommended. Signed "Anti-Bute."

77-131. [Freeth, J.]
The Budget. A Song.

"On matters of state, 'mongst those who debate." (48)

Freeman's J, Sep 2, 1777; L Eve Post, Aug 19, 1777.

Ballad. Critical remarks on the war budget. The war cost dearly. Cited are the King, North, French, rebellion, and taxes.

77-132. Freeth, John.
Prescot's Breeches: Or, The Old Soldier's Voyage to America. Tune.--The Chace of Killruddy.

"We set sail from Portsmouth on Candlemas-day." (40)

Freeth, Modern Songs on Various Subjects (1782), pp. 14-16; and The Political Songster (1790), pp. 31-2.

Song. Ballad narrating the experience of a soldier who has gone to fight in America and who questions the capture of Prescott (on July 10, 1777): "where was his guard?" He notes that Howe and Clinton are not making progress against Washington. See Freeth, 82-10.

77-133. [From New-York for Westchester.]

"From New-York for Westchester." (32)

G, Jan 4, 1777.

Ballad. On the fighting between Generals Howe and Washington in 1776, the New York campaign, concluding with a wry comment that Congress has ordered Washington not to risk a battle until France joins America in an alliance.

77-134. A full and true Account of the Matchless Retreats of General Howe, and the Cowardice of the Yankees.

"I sing of how the times are alter'd of late." (48)

L Eve Post, Oct 4, 1777.

Regular (Horatian) ode in double quatrains. A narrative of the beginning of the war--Gage in Boston, Lexington (Percy, Burgoyne, Hancock, Adams), the cowardice of the Yankees, New York (the Howe brothers)--emphasizing British failure.

77-135. General [Burgoyne]'s Letter.

"A Thirst for blood, and sword in hand." (12)

Freeman's J, Sep 4, 1777; L Eve Post, Aug 25, 1777.

Triplets. Satire on Burgoyne (through his persona) for encouraging the Indians to engage in their savage practice of scalping.

77-136. General Burgoyne's Soliloquy.

"My sword once drawn, it shall not be in vain." (24)

Freeman's J, Sep 13, 1777; L Eve Post, Sep 6, 1777.

HC. An ironic parody, through his persona, of Burgoyne's proclamation. Burgoyne boasts that he will kill every American rebel, including the aged, women, and children. See "[Burgoyne's] Proclamation": 77-44, 77-45.

77-137. General St. Clair's Letter to Congress, Fort Edward, July 14. Versified.

"Congress, perhaps, good Sir, may think." (114)

M Chron, Oct 3, 1777.

OC, doggerel. Versified letter of American Gen. St. Clair to Congress about his retreat from Ticonderoga, July 5, 1777, as a result of Burgoyne's invasion from Canada. The verses emphasize American cowardice. Cited are many American officers, especially Gen. Schuyler, and British officers, especially Gen. Frazer.

77-138. Glee sung by a Society of Citizens, on Tuesday, July 29.

"Come let us drink." (12)

PA, Aug 1, 1777.

Song: glee. Includes an ironic allusion to more Yankee campaigns, taxes and expenditures; so carpe diem!

77-139. Graham, Catharine Macaulay.
An Ode.

"When Nature first, with vivifying heat." (48)

UM 60 (May 1777), 263-4.

Regular ode in sixains. Mrs. Macaulay begs Britannia its "rage forego" and end the civil war with Americans: they "will their rights maintain," whatever force is used against them.

77-140. [Great are the Howes at playing leave and take.]

"Great are the Howes at playing leave and take." (19)

Freeman's J, Sep 2, 1777.

HC. A criticism of the erratic and questionable operations of the Howe brothers in America.

77-141. A Great Man's Soliloquy.

"Ti-con-de-ra-go." (6)

Freeman's J, Sep 4, 1777; L Eve Post, Aug 25, 1777.

Epigram. Burgoyne's capture of Fort Ticonderoga pleases Lord North, because it will enable him to increase the budget for next year.

77-142. The Habeas Corpus: An Epigram.

"The Habeas Corpus, it is said." (6)

PA, Mar 1, 1777.

Negative reaction to proposed suspension of the Habeas Corpus Act by the proposed American High Treason Bill. This epigram is followed by another on the amendment of the new bill by a "patriot," Dunning. See "A Late Petition Versified," 77-160.

77-143. [Haggard Report, with raven wing.]

"Haggard Report, with raven wing." (40)

Freeman's J, Sep 13, 1777; L Eve Post, Sep 6, 1777.

OC. Reports of big and bloody battles (probably Burgoyne's) reach Britain. The Scotch and German mercenaries and the Indians led by Burgoyne and the "tyrants," like Germain, will be defeated by Washington.

77-144. The Halcyon Days of Old England; Or, The Wisdom of Administration demonstrated: A Ballad. To the tune of -- Ye Medley of Mortals.

"Give ear to my song, I'll not tell you a story." (47)

Freeman's J, Jan 3, 1778; L Cour, Dec 31, 1779; L Eve Post, Dec 25, 1777, & Dec 30, 1779; LP, Dec 31, 1779.

Song, with additions in the three 1779 sources above. Satire on the absurd and unsuccessful war of the ministry fought over "a tax of three pence." Cited are Burgoyne and Howe and their failures. See 79-205.

77-145. [Hard is his lot! If peace or war, his views.]

"Hard is his lot! If peace or war, his views." (6)

G, Jan 3, 1777.

Epigram. HC. The politician has a difficult time with criticism -- in peace and war.

77-146. Hastings, Thomas.
Irregular Ode on the Birth-Day of his Majesty. June 4, 1777.

"In vain, whilst ratt'ling thunders fly." (14)

M Chron, Jun 4, 1777.

In two stanzas, the loyal Tory poet complains of internal faction encouraging the American enemy.

77-147. Hastings, Thomas.
Ode for the Birth-Day of his Royal Highness the Prince of Wales, Aug. 12.

"Suspend your rage, Ye sons of war!" (42)

G, Aug 12, 1777; L Chron 42 (Aug 9, 1777), 151; M Chron, Aug 12, 1777; PA, Aug 12, 1777.

Irregular Pindaric ode. Hastings, in another loyal ode, asks the young Prince of Wales to behave like the Black Prince and "face thy foes." He celebrates the "Brunswick line" and wants Britons to unite.

77-148. The Heroes; Or, the Glory of the Present War.

"The war is well supported by the Howes." (30)

LP, Nov 24, 1777.

HC. Satire on the cowardice and poor leadership of Lord Germaine, against whom the Americans stand no chance of winning (ironically, of course). The point is that the Americans cannot be defeated by the Howes or Germaine because their cause is just.

77-149. An Hint to the Patriots.

"No Triumphs of our gracious King." (96)

PA, Dec 27, 1777.

Regular ode in sixains. An answer from government's side to its detractors -- to "Ode on the Success of his Majesty's Arms" (77-183) and "A Supplemental Ode, or a Hint to Lord North" (77-292). The state of affairs is reviewed and the American War defended: Howe victorious in the Jerseys, Burgoyne defeated in New York, "Clinton and Vaughan not in Sight," Franklin in France "instructing" Beaumarchais. North and Germaine must go on with the war, and we can absorb the debts (costs). Shelburne, Barre, and Burke should be gagged with Rockingham's

Declaratory Act. We must not waver or be inconstant.

77-150. Howe's Magnificent Boast; or, Great Cry and Little Wool.

"Quoth Howe, 'As sure as death we'll slay.'" (30)

Freeman's J, Jan 7, 1777.

Tetrameter couplets. Ironic satire on Gen. William Howe. The persona of Howe boasts that he will crush the rebels ("Cromwellians, Puritans, and Round-heads," republicans) and end the war. But has all this happened? Reference to Kings-Bridge (north of Manhattan), the New York campaign.

77-151. [I think I see the pointed steel.]

"I think I see the pointed steel." (12)

Freeman's J, Sep 27, 1777.

Quatrains. An anti-war poem. Let us "drive jarring principles away" and have peace.

77-152. Impromptu on the Ode for the New Year.

"Imperial winter's sway." (12)

L Eve Post, Jan 2, 1777.

Sixains. Satire on laureat Whitehead for wanting poetic inspiration.

77-153. Inscription for a Column at Runingmede, between Stains and Windsor where Magna Charta, or the Great Charter of Liberties, was obtained by the Barons in Arms from King John.

"Thou, who the verdant plain dost traverse here." (16)

W Misc 9 (Oct 27, 1777), 95.

Blank verse. The sacred rights won by the Barons from tyrannical King John, preserved in Magna Charta, must be transmitted to our posterity.

77-154. [Inscriptions on a Statue of Mrs. Catherine Macaulay.]

"Government is a Power delegated for the Happiness of Mankind." (c. 20)

Freeman's J, Sep 13, 1777; L Eve Post, Sep 6, 1777; LP, Sep 8, 1777; West J, Sep 13, 1777; W Eve Post, Sep 9, 1777.

A statue of Mrs. Macaulay in the character of History has been erected in her honor.

77-155. [Inspir'd by Virtue, and the sacred call.]

"Inspir'd by Virtue, and the sacred call." (62)

Freeman's J, Jul 24, 1777.

HC. Britain succeeded through her industry and commerce, invention, arts, and sciences. But corruption followed upon prosperity, bringing bribery of the senate and oppression at home and abroad in America. But the attack on America, the civil war, fails. The rebels will be viewed by History as patriots who fought for liberty and equality.

77-156. The Irresistible Enemy.

"Let Poets sing, in lofty rhymes." (18)

G Eve Post, Nov 22, 1777.

OC. In the battle between the sexes, Celia's eyes are irresistible, the cause of the poet's defeat: a better subject than the campaigns of Howe or Burgoyne.

77-157. Jack Tar's Address to Fortune, When Going to Sea on a Cruize.

"Fortune! next cruize propitious prove." (20)

M Chron, Jul 8, 1777; W Misc 9 (Mar 23, 1778), 600.

OC. A British sailor begs for a rich Yankee prize so that he can impress his sweetheart with expensive gifts.

77-158. John the Painter's Ghost, to all (if there can be any so wretched) who may be inclined to render themselves as Miserable, and their memory as Detestable as He hath done.

"Ye poor deluded, guilty souls." (28)

G Eve Post, Mar 18, 1777; L Eve Post, Mar 15, 1777.

Quatrains. The persona ghost of James Aitken (John the Painter, hanged for treason) warns the British to beware his fate. Cited are America, France, Spain, who cannot help a traitor.

77-159. A King's Answer to a Subject who asked him if he had any feeling.

"If thousands die for me, must I be sore." (6)

GA, Dec 13, 1777.

HC. Satire on tyrannical and inhumane monarchs who do not care for their subjects.

77-160. A Late Petition Versified.

"We, the Lord-Mayor and Aldermen, in Common Council." (38)

G Eve Post, Feb 27, 1777.

Satire. Irony. Hostile versification of a petition against the bill to suspend habeas corpus. Satire on Richard Price, John Sawbridge, Wilkes, Watkyn Lewes, Thomas Hallifax. (This bill was introduced February 6, 1777.)

77-161. A Late Remarkable Speech Versified.

"Most graceless Sovereign, / This Bill I present, because 'tis my duty." (40)

L Eve Post, May 10, 1777.

Hexameter couplets. Satire on Parliament and the King. Sir Fletcher Norton begs the King for his assent to a bill to provide the Royal Family with funds, particularly the King with funds for bribing Parliament, thereby making friends for himself. (Norton, Speaker of the House of Commons, made the speech at the delivery of the Civil List Money Bill to the King, May 7, 1777.)
In the same issue, fourteen more lines on the same subject appear, entitled "A Spurious Speech which appeared in a morning paper a few days ago, versified": see 77-A.

77-162. A Letter from Capt. Bligh, Of the Wasp sloop, to Rodolphus Green, Esq; Versified.

"Be pleas'd Rodolphus, to make known." (18)

M Chron, Sep 26, 1777.

Doggerel. OC. Ironic versified letter from Capt. Bligh, telling the Irish not to fear, for he and his small ship and crew will protect the Irish channel from Yankee marauders.

77-163. [Listen North, attend Germaine.]

"Listen North, attend Germaine." (6)

PA, Nov 17, 1777.

Sixain. Lines at the conclusion of an essay urging firm action against America and its allies in the war.

77-164. [Lo! Civil War with more than common Rage.]

"Lo! Civil War, with more than common Rage." (87)

St J's C, Oct 11, 1777.

Blank verse. A review of the situation in 1777. A criticism of the "simulated Patriots" who provoke the contest with America and inflame the quarrel. These are the politicians in the Minority Opposition. The Howe brothers are blamed for not being active enough. Asks America to return to Britain, and turn from France.

77-165. The Longest Day.

"The sun, superior, rides on high." (32)

W Eve Post, Jun 19, 1777.

Quatrains. A criticism of the warlike court in a pastoral. The courtiers go to the country to enjoy the scene, but were they to behave harmlessly like the shepherds, Britain's woes would end.

77-166. Lord North's Levee.--To the Tune of Christ Church Bells, as it is sung at many patriotic Clubs in the City.

"See the cringing Coxcombs come." (14)

PA, Jul 5, 1777.

Song. Satire on the basely fawning courtiers at Lord North's reception.

77-167. The Lunatic.

"Come here to me, ye fighting Fools." (26)

PA, Sep 5, 1777; New Foundling Hospital for Wit (1786), IV, 219; Jeffery Dunstan, Fugitive Pieces (1789), pp. 55-6.

Irregular lyric ode. Satire on the madness of war, dedicated to "fighting Fools," all those who love war: Yankees, Congress, and several generals -- Washington, Lee, and Howe. See 89-2.

Macaulay, Catherine. An Ode. See Catherine Macaulay Graham, 77-139.

77-168. Martha Mark'em to Kitty Curious.

"Dear Kitty, On Thursday just after I gave you a Call." (52)

Lloyd's 41 (Dec 22, 1777), 604; PA, Dec 23, 1777.

Four stress, or anapestic tetrameter couplets. Light satire on the debates in Parliament on pressing, describing the behavior of the Minority Opposition.

77-169. Midsummer Day.

"Is there a man, who wishing to do well." (24)

L Eve Post, Jun 24, 1777.

HC. Praise of Wilkes, freedom-fighter. (Wilkes wished to be chosen Chamberlain of the City of London. The poll of the London Independent Livery was being taken at this time.) Britons pray Wilkes will continue to combat despotic power.

77-170. A Military Repartee.

"Surrounded thus, who can escape?" (6)

PA, Dec 23, 1777.

Epigram. Sixain. On Burgoyne's surrender at Saratoga to General Gates.

77-171. [The Ministerial toast of the day.]

"The Ministerial toast of the day, is,--'May the Americans be conquered, and never forget Howe.'" (4)

L Eve Post, Jun 26, 1777.

The Ministry toasts Howe; the Americans say they will have freedom despite Howe.

77-172. Monody to the Memory of the Officers who Fell in the Storm of Forts Clinton and Montgomery. October 6th, 1777.

"I pant, I burn to pour the fervid strain." (70)

M Chron, Dec 24, 1777.

Irregular Pindaric ode. Panegyric on the brave officers who were killed in the storming of American Forts Clinton and Montgomery, two strong points on the Hudson River. British General Clinton is cited. Originally printed in James Rivington's Royal Gazette, New York, Nov. 15, 1777.

77-173. Montgomery's Ghost. A New Song from America.

"In Chesapeak Bay, as at Anchor we lay." (32)

PA, Nov 18, 1777.

Song. The ghost of Gen. Montgomery speaks to the British who, venal and corrupt unlike Pitt, would enslave their brothers in America, and he urges them to retreat before they are crushed. Gen. Howe is cited.

77-174. A New Song.

"Ye jobbers exalt both your hearts and your voice." (40)

L Eve Post, Oct 14, 1777.

Song. Satire on the contractors who profit from a prolonged war with America. An objection to the continuation of a ruinous war. Cited are contractors, Howe, Delaware, Scotchmen, taxes.

77-175. Ode.

"Hail! C--------d, whose cumb'rous Loads." (36)

PA, Feb 13, 1777.

Regular ode in sixains. An ironic answer to "The Patriotic Secession" in the form of a personal satire on the author, Richard Cumberland, the playwright and poet. (Cumberland was clerk and secretary to the Board of Trade and Plantations, 1761-76, and he acted as private agent for Germain when the latter was secretary of state for the colonies.) See 77-249.

77-176. Ode.

"In what remote, sequester'd Glade." (36)

PA, Mar 1, 1777.

Regular ode in sixains. Satire on the Earl of Chatham, in eclipse.

77-177. An Ode.

"Yes, Winter now terrific reigns." (32)

L Eve Post, Jan 21, 1777.

Regular ode in octaves. Asks Britain to end hostilities, because the Americans are inspired by Liberty.

77-178. Ode for the New Year, by N. E. Poet Laureate to the Congress of Liberty; Set to Music by Benedicto Arnoldo.

"The year revolves; the Fav'rite's sway." (32)

Freeman's J, Jan 16, 1777.

Regular (Horatian) ode in octaves. Satire on Bute who again exerts his baneful influence on the King, undermines the constitution, imposes a tyranny on the English, and commits a parricide on inoffensive America.

77-179. Ode for the New Year, January 1, 1778. (Not the Laureat's).

"On the white rocks which guard her coast." (40)

L Eve Post, Dec 27-30, 1777.

Irregular ode. Britannia mourns her loss, her captured army at Saratoga, but insists her real enemies are (the ministers) at court; and if they are spurned, Britain will be free again.

77-180. Ode for the New Year, 1777.

"Why number months? why mark the years?" (56)

LM 45 (Dec 1776), 664-5; WM 35 (Jan 16, 1777), 113.

Pindaric ode. Asks that the Americans, "Sister subjects," stop the war.

77-181. Ode on Shooting.

"When summer's past, and Sol more faintly shines." (40)

LP, Sep 26, 1777.

Regular (Horatian) ode, unrhymed. The hunting season means no animal is safe from "ruthless man." And the British "wage a civil war" across the seas. Let peace come soon.

77-182. Ode on the Birth-Day of his Most Sacred Majesty, George III. King of Great Britain, &c.

"Again the rolling Year returns the Day." (34)

PA, Jun 5, 1777.

Irregular Pindaric ode. A loyal poem in praise of the King's virtues that encourage the arts and learning despite internal discord and "dire contention" caused by "hostile Kindred Bands." By J. H. Wynne.

77-183. Ode, On the Success of his Majesty's Arms.

"Sing Io Paeans, thro' the Land." (96)

GA, Dec 12, 1777; L Eve Post, Dec 9, 1777; PA, Dec 11, 1777; W Eve Post, Dec 16, 1777; New Foundling Hospital for Wit (1786), II, 108-15; Sir Jeffery Dunstan, Fugitive Pieces (1789), pp. 6-11.

Regular (Horatian) ode in sixains, claimed by Jeffery Dunstan. After Burgoyne's defeat, the poet writes an ironic satire celebrating the defeat of the rebel forces and the severe punishment meted out to their leaders. For example, the members of Congress would be hanged and Samuel Johnson would preside on the scaffold. Others cited are Franklin, Washington, Arnold, Charles Lee. Thereupon the opposing British politicians would be reconciled (Fox and Germaine) and faction cease in Parliament, and Wilkes become friends with Bute, etc.
"A Supplemental Ode, or A Hint to Lord North" follows this ode: see 77-292.

77-184. Ode to Peace.

"Come, lovely nymph, whom gladsome gales." (54)

HM 7 (Jan 1777), 63.

Regular ode in sixains. Begs for peace and the end of the civil war. "Since Providence supports our side," let us be "more wise and good" so that "The present war be understood."

77-185. Ode to Peace.

"Sweet, smiling angel!--deck'd with ev'ry grace." (36)

CA, May 24, 1777.

Quatrains. A complaint at the civil war, its slaughter and devastation, and a call for peace under the aegis of Britain.

77-186. [Odell, Jonathan]
A Birth Day Song, By the Rev. J. O. M.A. New-York, June 4th, 1777.

"Time was when America hallow'd the morn." (32)

LM 46 (Nov 1777), 578-9; WM 38 (Dec 25, 1777), 303-4.

Song. Odell celebrates the King's birthday with a loyal song and complains of the "deluded multitude" taking up rebellion and loyalists imprisoned. To him, rebellion's "cause . . . is built on a lyc!"

77-187. Odell, Jonathan.
Inscription on a Curious Chamber Stove, in the Form of an Urn, contrived in such a Manner as to make the Flame descend instead of rise from the Fire, invented by the celebrated Dr. Benjamin Franklin. Written by the Rev. Mr. Odell, an Episcopal Clergyman, at Brunswick, in New-Jersey.

"Like a Newton sublimely he soar'd." (20)

Cumb Pacq, Apr 8, 1777; GM 47 (Apr 1777), 188; Lloyd's 40 (Mar 28, 1777), 307; LP, Mar 31, 1777; PA, Mar 29, 1777; W Eve Post, Mar 27, 1777. Also repr. MP, Nov 16, 1780; GA, Jul 1, 1783; LM (NS) 1 (Sep 1783), 233; St J's C, Jun 26, 1783; West M 11 (Dec 1783), 663-4.

Quatrains. Franklin's genius was perverted by political ambition, which "kindled the blaze of sedition." Like the poem above (77-186), repr. in Winthrop Sargent, The Loyal Verses of Joseph Stansbury and Doctor Jonathan Odell (Albany: Munsell, pp. 5-6 + n. 4.

77-188. Odell, Jonathan.
   Liberty.

   "Offspring of Heaven, O Liberty! whose name." (90)

   LP, Apr 4, 1777; PA, Apr 5, 1777.

   HC. Britain must not treat America as the French treated Corsica, driving the country by tyrannical acts to desperate measures. America will fight for liberty against venal ministerial oppressors.
   Liberty (Philadelphia: Goddard, 1769) is here reprinted in part to remind the English that the Rev. Odell was not always a supporter of the government.

77-189. [Odell, Jonathan]
   Song for St. George's Day, Composed by the Reverend I. O. A. M. And sung by a loyal Party at New York, April 23, 1777. Tune, Hail England, old England.

   "For ages the nations beheld with surprize." (65)

   LM 46 (Oct 1777), 530; WM 38 (Nov 20, 1777), 183.

   A patriotic cantata. An expression of hope that Howe will defeat the rebellious Americans.

77-190. On a Certain Celebrated Historian [Macaulay].

   "As Phoebus return'd from his tour t'other day." (12)

   Cumb Pacq, May 6, 1777; LP, Apr 18, 1777.

   Quatrains. Panegyric on Mrs. Catherine Macaulay, the historian. (Her birthday was April 2.)

77-191. On a Late Bequest.

   "Though not one shilling while I live." (8)

   G Eve Post, Jun 10, 1777.

   Quatrains. Epigram. A bequest of a fortune was made to the nation to pursue the war with America.

77-192. On a Late Capture.

   "Prescott with Arnold was so much enrag'd." (8)

Freeman's J, Sep 4, 1777; L Eve Post, Aug 25, 1777; PA, Aug 22, 1777.

Epigram. Prescott offered a reward for the capture of Arnold, who thereupon offered a smaller reward for Prescott. Prescott was captured July 10, 1777, in Rhode Island.

77-193. On a Late Capture.

"'Twixt Prescott and Lee." (6)

Freeman's J, Sep 4, 1777; PA, Aug 22, 1777.

Sixain. Epigram. British Gen. Prescott was captured while philandering, but American Gen. Lee was captured while performing his duty.

77-194. On a Late Extraordinary Gazette.

"Hill's regiment, it says, did for three hours engage." (4)

L Chron, 42 (Sep 13, 1777), 272.

Quatrain. Satire on an exaggerated victory report. It is incredible that a British regiment should engage a force six times its number, and prevail with but the loss of a few men.

77-195. On a Late Transaction in America.

"The intrepid Burgoyne many dangers went through." (6)

UM 61 (Supp 1777), 371; WM 39 (Mar 4, 1778), 232.

Epigram. Burgoyne was stopped by Gates.

77-196. On Capt. Pye, of the Guards (distinguished by the Name of Chicken-Pye) going to America.

"How good's the Minister to England's foes." (4)

LP, Mar 7, 1777.

Epigram. The starving Americans should be glad to learn that Capt. (Chicken) Pye is going overseas to fight them.

77-197. On Christmas.

"Welcome, thrice welcome, Christmas gay." (42)

L Chron 42 (Dec 25, 1777), 621.

OC. Probably ironic lines on the times: the country ruled by disinterested men of integrity, "Without a thought of place or pension," liberty suffering no diminution, Popery decreasing, the poor prosperous, etc.

77-198. On City Honours.

"There was a time, when traitors to their King." (16)

G Eve Post, Aug 19, 1777; L Chron 42 (Aug 19, 1777), 180; MP, Aug 19, 1777.

Quatrains. Anti-Wilkes. A hope that Wilkes (and his supporters) will be removed from City positions of trust.

77-199. On General Burgoyne's Army Being Surrounded by the Americans.

"Burgoyne embark'd with eager haste." (16)

LP, Dec 29, 1777.

Quatrains. Brief narrative of Burgoyne's campaign until his army was stopped by Gates and Arnold.

77-200. On General Howe's Army.

"Some men may think Howe's army is asleep." (2)

Freeman's J, Aug 19, 1777; L Eve Post, Aug 5, 1777.

Epigram. Howe's army appears to be asleep or playing games.

77-201. On General Prescott being carried off naked, "Unanointed, Unanealed."

"What various lures there are to ruin a man." (4)

L Chron 42 (Sep 27, 1777), 320.

Epigram. Quatrain. General Prescott was captured "without his breeches" because of a woman.

77-202. On G[uy] Carleton's Laborious March, Naval Victory, and Magnanimous Retreat from Lake Champlain to Quebec.

"O'er brakes, o'er bogs, o'er mountains, and o'er crags." (48)

Freeman's J, Jan 16, 1777.

HC. General Sir Guy Carleton has attempted to reach Howe in order to defeat Washington in New York; but he has failed and must prepare another campaign. Arnold is cited.

77-203. On hearing that General Burgoyne was defeated by General Arnold.

"It's well known Burgoyne is wise, loyal and brave." (4)

PA, Nov 21, 1777.

Epigram. Quatrain. A reaction to the rumor that Burgoyne was having difficulty in his New York campaign. Arnold may have proved too much for him.

77-204. On John the Painter.

"How sad this solemn gloom! -- no twinkling globes." (48)

G Eve Post, Oct 23, 1777.

Heroic quatrains. James Aitken (John the Painter) is imagined viewing with pleasure the results of his treason, his arson, just as the Americans see the ruin of Britain "with a guilty joy." But he is punished, like Catiline, for his crimes. Written by the youth who wrote "A Pastoral." See 77-247.

77-205. On Liberty.

"Liberty! Passion of the human Race." (8)

PA, Jan 25, 1777.

Epigram in quatrains. "Liberty's a Briton's element."

77-206. On L[or]d C[hatham]'s Late Motion in the H[ouse] of L[or]ds. [And] On the Same.

"With pride, ambition, envy, malice curs'd." (6)

"Foe to his King, his country, and her laws." (6)

G Eve Post, Jun 7, 1777.

HC. Two caustic and vulgar satires on the Earl of Chatham's motion for peace with America, May 30, 1777, before France joins the fray. (His motion was rejected, accepted only by the "Patriot Peers.")

77-207. On Lord North's Illness. Occasioned by Reading a Late Prophecy in one of the Newspapers.

"Who shall command." (34)

MP, Mar 12, 1777.

Ode. Mixed verse. Defense of North as an effective and honest leader, better than Rockingham, Shelburne, or Richmond, and his integrity more enduring than that of Burke and Wilkes.

77-208. On Lord North's Indisposition.

"When First Britannia heard the Rebel band." (33)

G, Mar 4, 1777; Lloyd's 40 (Mar 3, 1777), 220; PA, Mar 4, 1777.

HC. Lord North is ill, thereby endangering Britain's attempt to suppress the American rebellion. (A news report appearing in G, March 6, 1777, speculated that North's illness was caused by bad news from Howe and Cornwallis in America.)

77-209. On Mr. Horne's Trial [&] Answer.

"It is said, whilst on Horne Judge and Jury were sitting." (12)

G, Aug 7, 1777.

Hexameter couplets. The poet believes Horne is being unlawfully tried before Judge Mansfield for attempting to aid American prisoners.

77-210. On Mrs. Macaulay's Birth-Day. Celebrated at Alfred-House, Bath, April 2, 1777.

"Great patriot King! sage founder of our laws." (42)

L Eve Post, Apr 5, 1777.

HC. Praise of Mrs. Macaulay for her books on English history.

77-211. On Poor John the Painter, who was hanged for being a Fool, at the Gates of Portsmouth Dock, on Monday, March 10, 1777.

"When sanguine priests, with sanguine views." (24)

L Eve Post, Apr 1, 1777.

Quatrains. John the Painter bungled his work at arson and trapped himself; but he is like those who have "set America on fire."

77-212. On Reading a Pamphlet, called "A Calm Address to the Inhabitants of England."

"Did ever Pasquil so belie its name." (70)

L Eve Post, Jul 1, 1777.

HC. Critical of John Wesley for urging support of the war against America. Wesley was persuaded by Samuel Johnson to change his mind about America. Cited also is Markham, Archbishop of York.

77-213. On reading Admiral Montague's Account . . . of the taking of the Retaliation Privateer: An Epigram.

"While Montague was fast asleep." (12)

PA, Oct 17, 1777.

Sixains. On the capture of an American privateer that was preying on English fishing vessels.

77-214. On Reading B[urgoyne]'s Proclamation, Versified, in the Ledger.

"In times when wit flourish'd, where Athens now stands." (16)

L Eve Post, Sep 20, 1777.

Quatrains. A negative reaction to Burgoyne's proclamation as (recently) rendered in verse in the Public Ledger. (I have been unable to see the Ledger version of the proclamation.) See 77-44, 77-45.

77-215. On Reading Lord Abingdon's Thoughts on the Letter of Edmund Burke, Esq.

"Tho' venal Senators, for dirty pay." (65)

GA, Dec 11, 1777.

HC. Praise of Abingdon for defending Whig republican tenets against corrupt MP's, Tories and Scots guided by Bute and Mansfield; and for opposing the costly war against America.

77-216. On Reading Several Papers Published by Order of the Rebel Congress.

"Who in the field beholds your wond'rous deeds." (6)

Cal Merc, Sep 15, 1777; LP, Sep 19, 1777.

HC. The American cause is demeaned by the cowardly behavior of the Yankees in the field and by the scolding in Congress's papers.

77-217. On Seeing a Paragraph in the Papers, of Twelve Tories being **Condemned** to the Gallows by the Convention at New York.

"A Tory! quoth I, what animal's that." (4)

LP, Sep 24, 1777.

Extempore in couplets. Satire on the Tory character, savage and murderous (as it supports the American War).

77-218. On Taking General Lee. An Epigram.

"Ye American Rebels, don't obstinate be." (4)

MP, Mar 13, 1777.

Hexameter couplets. Satire on the capture of General Lee, and advice for him to get rid of Washington, to wash off the "filth of Rebellion."

77-219. On the American War.

"Will no Experience Britons teach." (8)

PA, Nov 21, 1777.

Epigram. Quatrains. The breach between America and Britain grows wider each year of the civil war, while France gains.

77-220. On the Breaking Up of Parliament.

"At length the golden synod ends." (42)

L Chron 42 (Dec 13, 1777), 584; WM 38 (Dec 25, 1777), 303.

Sixains. On the Parliamentary recess which will end debate and bring Christmas cheer and peace. The "patriots" will recruit their "force" and prepare for the new year (Richmond and Burke).

77-221. On the Captures of General Lee and General Prescot; the first as he was reconnoitering the Field of Mars, the second the Field of Venus.

"Brave Lee was surprized as he went out to see." (4)

PA, Aug 30, 1777.

Epigram. Gen. Lee was doing his duty when captured, but Gen. Prescott was in bed with a woman.

77-222. On the Death of Brigadier-General Fraser, who was killed near Saratoga, the 7th of October, 1777.

"When sound Advice and mild Remonstrance fail'd." (10)

Cal Merc, Jan 10, 1778; L Chron 43 (Jan 1, 1778), 15; PA, Dec 31, 1777; W Eve Post, Jan 1, 1778.

HC. Gen. Fraser died bravely, but perhaps he died "too soon." Corrected in PA, Jan 2, 1778.

77-223. On the Death of Cornet Geary, killed in a Skirmish with the Provincials.

"Martial ardour fir'd his breast." (12)

St J's C, Apr 12, 1777; UM 60 (Apr 1777), 206.

Epitaph in quatrains. Young Geary died bravely, facing the enemy. See the inscription "To the Memory / of / Cornet Francis Geary," 77-306.

77-224. On the Death of the late Adm. Saunders.

"Lo! Saunders mingles with the mighty dead." (41)

GM 47 (Mar 1777), 139.

Irregular Pindaric ode. Saunders, who had helped conquer Canada, weeps over the "foul impious war" with America that threatens to lose the empire that "his valour won." France and Spain are happy over this war.

77-225. On the Embarkation of the Officers, belonging to the Last Brigade of the Guards, for America. An Apostrophe.

"Mark but that train! so gallant, trim and bold." (20)

MP, Dec 12, 1777.

HC. Satire on a brigade of guards, effeminate and ill with venereal disease, off to fight in America.

77-226. On the Fate of the Two Captive Generals, Lee and Prescott.

"With arms and men above his par." (4)

Freeman's J, Sep 6, 1777; L Eve Post, Aug 30, 1777.

Epigram. Lee is captured while on duty, Prescott while sleeping with a woman.

77-227. On the following Line of Mr. Addison. "Sweet are the slumbers of a virtuous Man," Applied to the same Occasion [the Capture of Prescott].

"Had Cato's Sleep like Prescott's been." (4)

Freeman's J, Sep 4, 1777; L Eve Post, Aug 28, 1777; PA, Aug 22, 1777.

Even Cato would have been caught, had his sleep been like Prescott's.

77-228. On the Gazette, containing Sir Peter Parker's Last Letter.

"In a former Gazette, where Sir Peter's great deeds." (12)

L Eve Post, Feb 18, 1777.

Quatrains. Ironic account of Admiral Parker's escape from the American forces under Hopkins (in Rhode Island).

77-229. On the Head-Ach of a Certain Person in an High Office, Who is said to have been Blooded three Times in one Day.

"The head-ach! impossible! 'tis a mistake." (12)

L Eve Post, Mar 4, 1777.

Hexameter couplets. Satire on Lord North, who deserves execution--a beheading as a cure for his head-ache. See also 77-94.

77-230. On the Important News contained in Last Saturday's Gazette.

"Where's the Gazette? the Addresser joyous cries." (4)

L Eve Post, Oct 11, 1777.

Extempore. Satire on the war-party (the ministry) which is unable to defeat the Americans.

77-231. On the Intended Rejoicings for the Taking of Philadelphia, &c.

"Is there such cause for joy, ye sons of mirth." (19)

L Eve Post, Dec 20, 1777.

HC. On Howe's occupation of Philadelphia, September 26, 1777. There is no cause for rejoicing over Howe's victory because "this bloody war" is "accurs'd," "unnat'ral, ill-judg'd," fratricidal, and it should end.

77-232. On the Late Literary Correspondence between the Commanders of the British and Foreign Armies in America.

"The age is now grown so polite." (8)

L Chron 42 (Oct 18, 1777), 392; LP, Oct 20, 1777; WM 38 (Nov 6, 1777), 136.

OC. Epigram. Ironic satire on the way the war is fought -- a civil war managed by civil men.

77-233. On the Premier's late Retreat to Bushy-Park. An Epigram.

"When Boreas, to his Country-Seat." (12)

L Eve Post, Apr 3, 1777; PA, Apr 4, 1777.

Sixains. Satire on the leadership of Lord North, unable to guide the state which is threatened by Spain, France, and America.

77-234. On the Premier's present Head Ache. An Epigram.

"The World will think it quite absurd." (4)

PA, Feb 28, 1777.

OC. Satire on Lord North who was ill.

77-235. On the Present State of Affairs.

"Rise Britons! rise with all your father's might." (24)

M Chron, Aug 1, 1777.

HC. A complaint at French support of the Americans on the seas.

77-236. On the Present Unnatural War.

"Once more let fancy take her ample flight." (24)

LP, Oct 15, 1777.

Quatrains. In support of America. An objection to a great mistake, the civil war with America.

77-237. On the Provincials stealing General Prescot out of his Bed, and Carrying him, Spite of Tears and Intreaties, Naked, to General Arnold.

"The Handcock trap'd the Fox upon the deep." (18)

LP, Aug 20, 1777.

HC. Gen. Prescot was captured by Arnold's troops July 10, 1777, in Rhode Island. The British campaign against America is collapsing, and the King will rue the day he took Scotch advice (Mansfield and Bute).

77-238. On the 30th of January.

"Our Tory-Clergy on this Martyr's day." (6)

L Eve Post, Jan 28, 1777.

HC. On this anniversary of Charles I's death, the Tory clergy (in their sermons on Charles the Martyr) will damn Whig Revolution tenets and praise tyranny, absolute monarchy.

77-239. On Three Lords of the Admiralty going to Winchester to hang John the Painter, for setting fire to Portsmouth Dock-yard.

"Three noble Lords to Winchester are fled." (4)

LP, Mar 7, 1777.

Epigram. Quatrain. The three Lords of the Admiralty sentencing the arsonist James Aitken (John the Painter) should watch their heads. He was executed on March 10, 1777.

77-240. Our Commanders.

"Gage nothing did, and went to pot." (8)

GA, Dec 4, 1777; L Eve Post, Nov 29, 1777.

Epigram. OC. Satire on the failures and lack of progress of the military campaigns by Gage, Howe, Carleton, Dunmore, Clinton, Burgoyne. All have gotten us very little for our money.

77-241. The Panic.

"As when the Rapine of old Priam's Boy." (10)

PA, Oct 23, 1777; St J's C, Oct 21, 1777.

HC. Epigram. As the gods were divided among themselves during the Trojan War, so they are in the American War. Thus Gen. Howe retreats, unable to defeat the Americans who have Pallas Athena on their side.

77-242. Paraphrase of General Schuyler's Letter to General Washington.

"I lately sent, dear Sir, a Letter." (38)

Lloyd's 41 (Aug 29, 1777), 212; M Chron, Aug 29, 1777; PA, Aug 30, 1777.

OC, mixed verse. The persona of American Gen. Schuyler ironically parodies a letter about the retreat of Gen. St. Clair's forces from Fort Ticonderoga and their pursuit by Burgoyne's army. The letter is in Lloyd's 41 (Aug 25, 1777), 198.

77-243. A Paraphrase on the First Ten Verses of the LXXIId Psalm. Taken from a New-York Paper, of Feb. 13.

"God of all worlds! preserve the king." (32)

GM 47 (Apr 1777), 188; Lloyd's 40 (Mar 28, 1777), 307; WM 36 (Jun 5, 1777), 337.

Hymn. A loyal hymn which asserts that the rebel Americans, "unhappy sons of shame," will "Again aggrandize [King George's] name," will pay homage and bring tribute to him.

77-244. A Parody of the New Year's Ode for 1777, addressed to William Whitehead, Esq; Poet Laureat.

"Again imperial Winter's Sway." (32)

MP, Jan 4, 1777; PA, Jan 4, 1777.

Regular ode in octaves. Protests Whitehead's uninspired and gloomy odes on the rebellious colonies.

77-245. A Parody on the Old Song, "Have you been to Abingdon? Heigh Sir! hoa Sir!" &c.

"Who has read Abingdon, heigh Sir! hoa Sir!" (42)

G Eve Post, Oct 11, 1777; PA, Oct 11, 1777.

Song. Abingdon is praised for writing effectively against Burke (he pulled off Burke's mask and put him to bed), Markham (Archbishop of York), and the ministry (Mansfield, Germain, and North). See "corrected version," PA, Nov 14, 1777: 77-29.

77-246. Past, Present, and Future.

"There was a time, when Britain's daring sons." (24)

L Chron 42 (Jul 26, 1777), 104; MP, Jul 29, 1777; UM 61 (Aug 1777), 95-6.

Quatrains. The time will soon come when Britain by means of its powerful navy will chastise France for assisting America and Spain for its insults on the high seas.

77-247. A Pastoral. On the King's Birth-Day. By Boys of the First and Second Classes in the Free School, Lancaster, June 9, 1777.

"Damon. [George is] the Patron of fair Virtue's Cause." (32)

Cumb Pacq, Jun 24, 1777.

HC. Dialogue. Blames the ungrateful Americans for the war. Cited are the King and the Howes.

77-248. The Patriot Quelled, or the Flood Freezed by a North Wind: An Epigram.

"Says Fox to Burke, the blust'ring North." (6)

G Eve Post, Jan 28, 1777.

Sixain. The speeches of the patriots Fox and Burke are feeble before North's effective answers.

77-249. The Patriotic Secession: An Ode.

"The thirteen States submit, -- and B[urk]e." (24)

PA, Feb 6, 1777.

Regular ode in sixains. Ironic stanzas satirizing, censuring, the Minority (especially Burke) for seceding from both Houses of Parliament. (Those who seceded were the Rockinghamites.) Presumably written by Richard Cumberland; see 77-175.

77-250. The Peace of the County Restored.

"Two knights of spirit and true game." (30)

Freeman's J, Aug 21, 1777.

Sixains. Were the Irish to participate in the war between Britain and America, or between Whigs and Tories, they will suffer more. No matter who wins, the Irish lose.

77-251. The People's Address to Lord Boreas.

"Come blust'ring Boreas, let us know." (12)

L Eve Post, Aug 23, 1777.

Quatrains. Satire on North for failing to defeat the Americans; he should be replaced by Chatham.

77-252. A Poetical Address to the Mercantile City of Bristol.

"All hail to Bristol! -- Commerce's fam'd Retreat." (80)

PA, Aug 26, 1777.

HC. Traces the progress of the spirit of Commerce from Carthage, Greece, and Italy, to Britain where the monarchy rests on trade. But now "civil Discord" has caused the Atlantic trade to disappear. When will the war end "And Britons cease to shed their Brother's gore?" the poet asks. But the arts flourish--e.g., Chatterton (Rowley) and Hannah More.

77-253. A Political Conversation.

"Said Dick to Tom, pray tell me by what Laws." (4)

PA, Dec 30, 1777.

Epigram. HC. The cause of the American War is the insistence upon "Prerogative."

77-254. The Political Palinurus; An Epigram.

"Britannia's Knuckles get a Rap." (10)

PA, Oct 18, 1777.

OC. On Lord North's sleeping at the helm as the ship of state founders.

77-255. The Politicians and Time. A Fable.

"The sun was set and day-light gone." (58)

T&C 9 (Jul 1777), 382.

OC. A Scotsman, West Indian, and Englishman offer their opinions on the American War: the first declares that the Americans are violent, destructive rebels; the second that they are just in fighting for their birthright; and the third that the English will make American pride "knock under." But only time will tell what will happen.

Proclamation. See [Burgoyne's] Proclamation: 77-44.

77-256. Proclamation Extraordinary.

"Oyez, Oyez -- Good People all." (16)

L Mag 46 (Oct 1777), 531; LP, Oct 3, 1777; M Chron, Oct 6, 1777; PA, Oct 7, 1777.

OC. The King issues a proclamation offering a reward for information about General Howe, mysteriously disappeared. (Howe was on his way to Philadelphia, via the ocean.)

77-257. The Prudent Generals Compar'd: An Epigram.

"When Rome was urg'd, by adverse Fate." (8)

MJ, Jan 2, 1777; PA, Jan 2, 1777.

Quatrains. Satire on Gen. Howe. Fabius saved Rome by caution and delay; but Gen. Howe, using the same strategy, "can save" the thirteen colonies.

77-258. Punch's Speech.

"My Lords, and ye Gentlemen Commoners, know." (38)

PA, Nov 24, 1777.

Hexameter couplets. Ironic satire through the persona of the King on the situation at this time--Howe's disappointing news, Burgoyne's difficulties. The British are unable to achieve victory over America. See "The Audience's Answer to Punch's Speech," 78-64.

77-259. Quarter Day.

"When yonder Sun's protracted rays." (40)

Lloyd's 41 (Sep 26, 1777), 308; W Eve Post, Sep 27, 1777.

Quatrains. On the agricultural economy. Tenant farmers must pay rent to their landlords on Quarter Day at the end of the summer. It is a cause for complaint by industrious farmers and by those forced off the land by the unjust "Great" and powerful landlords concerned only for profit.

77-260. [Quarter Day] Another.

"This Day denies the wish'd repose." (32)

Lloyd's 41 (Sep 26, 1777), 308; W Eve Post, Sep 27, 1777.

Quatrains. Landlords should be sympathetic with the working poor who, starving, cannot afford to pay their rent. (A picture of oppression on the farm -- a cause of emigration.)

77-261. The Question proposed.

"America must be subdu'd." (4)

L Chron 42 (Oct 28, 1777), 421; St J's C, Oct 25, 1777.

Quatrain. A satire on Howe's dilatory tactics. Everyone believes America must be subdued; Administration believes Howe will succeed, but others ask when.

77-262. A Rebel Epitaph.

"Beneath / This humble Sod." (8)

MP, May 27, 1777.

Epitaph inscription. A protest at the base murder and inhumane scalping of four American patriots by Burgoyne's men: an incident in the war.

77-263. The Rebuke. Imitated from the Latin.

"What still, my friend, that brow of care." (40)

L Eve Post, Mar 20, 1777.

Regular (Horatian) ode. "William" complains of the hard times, of bankruptcies, etc., of the failure of government; but he should correct his own failings first. Cited are the patriots and the ministers who worry "Friend William."

77-264. A Receipt to make a Modern Minister of State.

"To form a min'ster the ingredients." (18)

WM 35 (Jan 2, 1777), 50.

OC. Satire on a modern minister for his ambiguous nature, a combination of

"Broker, Sycophant, and Trickster."

77-265. A Recruiting Song. Irregular.

"Come, come my brave boys, to your colours repair." (49)

M Chron, Sep 19, 1777.

A recruiting song urges support for England's cause against the American rebels and their allies, the French, England's "natural foes."

77-266. The Repartee. An Epigram.

"When North, in Senate, lately said." (6)

PA, Dec 9, 1777.

Sixain. Satire on North. North cannot sleep at home because he sleeps in the House of Commons.

77-267. The Restoration; or May 29th.

"In ancient times they made a boast." (16)

G Eve Post, May 27, 1777; PA, May 29, 1777; W Eve Post, May 27, 1777.

Quatrains. Charles II was restored on May 29 and the "King's Friends, a scurvy pack," ruled the nation. Now there are those who nostalgically yearn for the restoration of the Stuarts, although they "Deplore the cause."

77-268. The Retreat: A Simile.

"When Howe from Bounds-Brook's Lines retreats." (6)

St J's C, Sep 9, 1777.

OC. Howe retreats and defeats the Yankees, just as a woman conquers her pursuers.

77-269. Reynard's Disappointment. An Epigram.

"Charles reads the Papers -- deems 'tis true." (12)

G Eve Post, Feb 1, 1777; PA, Feb 1, 1777; The Muse's Mirror (London: Baldwin,

1778), I, 245.

   Sixains. Satire on Fox, who has gone to France (Dec. 1776) to meet Franklin and get the French King to pay his debts -- but without success.

77-270. A Scotch Repartee.

   "Though B[ur]ke and B[ar]re sweat and toil." (6)

   PA, Dec 22, 1777.

   Epigram. Satire on Burke and Barre, who talk about the good of Britain but are full of "Air."

77-271. [The Scotch Repartee Enlarged.]

   "True! B[ur]ke and B[a]rre have no Land." (12)

   PA, Dec 26, 1777.

   Epigram. Sixains. "A Scotch Repartee" is enlarged to include a criticism of Fox, who also has no property. Thus he hates Old England "And doats upon the New."

77-272. A Seasonable Epigram. Extempore -- on hearing the Affected Contempt with which a certain Minister chose to speak of Political Writers in general, in one of his late public Harangues.

   "When sputt'ring N[ort]h, who says he gives no Bribe." (4)

   PA, Dec 5, 1777.

   HC. Satire on North. The reason North dislikes political writers is that he never did anything good that was worth writing about.

77-273. The Selfish Growlers: A Simile.

   "When Dunghill-Cur or rav'nous Fox." (12)

   G Eve Post, Dec 30, 1777; PA, Dec 31, 1777.

   Sixains. The Patriot Opposition are simply guided by self-interest.

77-274. [Sent by our Sov'reign's mild, but firm command.]

   "Sent by our Sov'reign's mild, but firm command." (27)

MP, Mar 20, 1777.

HC. A soldier defends the war aims of government, and explains the role of the army in crushing the rebellion but at the same time being humane. "The sentiments therein contained," he believes, "to be pretty general throughout the British army."

77-275. [Shame on the Wretch who's bought and sold.]

"Shame on the Wretch who's bought and sold." (8)

Cumb Pacq, Apr 25, 1777.

OC. A complaint at the venality in the election market.

77-276. Shebbeare, John.
[That Cuckoo Tone.]

"That Cuckoo Tone." (14)

PA, Apr 17, 1777.

OC. Shebbeare, a government writer, attacks Richard Price as a Presbyterian hypocrite for fomenting treason against the King, Church, and State. These lines appear at the end of his "Letter VI. To Doctor Price." From <u>Hudibras</u>.

77-277. The Shortest Day: A Thought.

"Dark, dull, and gloomy are the Days." (20)

G Eve Post, Dec 20, 1777; PA, Dec 22, 1777; W Eve Post, Dec 20, 1777.

Quatrains. A prayer that peace with America will come next spring.

77-278. Simile.

"Two dogs were quarreling for meat." (12)

PA, Aug 6, 1777; W Eve Post, Aug 5, 1777.

Quatrains. While England and America are at war, France will gain her end, and "seize the prize" which undoubtedly is America.

77-279. Simkin Blunderhead's Epistle to his Friend at London. Charles Town, January 1776.

"Excuse me, dear -----, I can't think it true." (51)

M Chron, Aug 19, 1777.

Doggerel, four or five stress couplets. Satire on the hypocrisy of the Americans concerning slavery, on threats against freedom, on paper money, and on the low-class leadership. (Written January 1776.)

77-280. The Sleeping Conqueror: An Epigram.

"A _modern_ Statesman, once, alleg'd." (12)

PA, Oct 20, 1777.

Sixains. Pitt defeated America in Germany; North can defeat America only in the realms of sleep.

77-281. [So, Sirs, are ye come? I am glad at the heart!]

"So, Sirs, are ye come? I am glad at the heart." (40)

L Eve Post, Nov 27, 1777.

Anapestic tetrameter couplets. Satire on the King through his persona. The King's persona betrays him as a silly goose. However, these reactions to Burgoyne's defeat must have been conventional: that is, should the Americans yield now, he will end the war.

77-282. The Soldier's Farewel. A New Song. Written at the Desire of a young Lady, on Capt. **** embarking for America. Tune: -- Despairing beside a clear stream.

"From Glotta's blest harbour unmoor'd." (32)

WM 36 (Apr 3, 1777), 49.

Song. The soldier bids farewell to his lady because his country calls for his aid. She prays for his safe return from America.

77-283. The Soliloquy. An Epigram.

"Old Twitcher, sitting t'other Day." (12)

PA, Apr 4, 1777.

Sixains. Personal satire on the Earl of Sandwich who, unable to carry on with his mistress (Ray), turns to drink and amassing wealth.

77-284. [Some men with wry faces and confident air.]

"Some men with wry faces and confident air." (43)

Freeman's J, Aug 26, 1777.

Hexameter couplets. The future of the war is dim, all pessimistic. Therefore it is wise to end it. Cited are the King, the French, the Americans at Trenton, and privateers.

77-285. A Song.

"Let Patriots write." (48)

L Eve Post, Oct 23, 1777.

Song in sixains. There is little doubt that the Yankees will defeat the Howes and Burgoyne. The patriots (Opposition MP's) say the long delay in news presages disaster. Cited are Washington, Arnold, and (Thomas) Conway.

77-286. Song in The Quaker.

"Boreas. While the Lads of St. Stephen's shall angrily, ah." (20)

PA, Dec 5, 1777.

Parody of a song in The Quaker. Lord North and Lord Germain sing a duet about their possible impeachment by the House of Commons.

77-287. A Song. To the Tune of the Children in the Wood.

"Now ponder well, ye Yankees dear." (24)

Lloyd's 41 (Oct 22, 1777), 396.

Song in quatrains. Satire on Congress that allowed Franklin to seek French help and save himself from the gallows.

77-288. The Songs in the Beggar's Opera Parodied.

"Through all the employments at Court." (c. 75)

L Eve Post, Nov 18, 1775.

Parody on John Gay's Beggar's Opera. Satire on the ministry for being selfish and corrupt: including Toryism, the American War, the King, Germain, North, the Majority. Chatham is cited.

77-289. Stanzas. To the Memory of John the Painter.

"Long as thy name shall last in infamy." (12)

G Eve Post, Mar 18, 1777; MP, Mar 17, 1777.

Elegiac quatrains. A curse on James Aitken, known as the arsonist John the Painter. May the parricidal American rebels die on the gibbet like you, John the Painter.

77-290. The State Quacks.

"Britannia was sick, for a Doctor they sent." (20)

Freeman's J, Aug 23, 1777; L Eve Post, Jul 29, 1777; L Mag 46 (Aug 1777), 432; W Eve Post, Jul 29, 1777.

Quatrains. Britain is losing life and money and all the state quacks, the Scotch and the courtiers, cannot help her. Reprinted 79-443.

77-291. The Substance of Sir W[illia]m H[ow]e's last Letter, from New York, versified.

"As to kidnap the Congress, has long been my Aim." (32)

PA, Sep 5, 1777.

Song with Derry down chorus. Satire on General Howe for his inability to trap Washington in New Jersey.

77-292. A Supplemental Ode, or a Hint to Lord North, on the State of the Nation.

"The various Triumphs of our King." (90)

PA, Dec 19, 1777; New Foundling Hospital for Wit (1786), II, 116-23; Jeffery Dunstan, Fugitive Pieces, (1789), pp. 12-19.

Claimed by Jeffery Dunstan as a supplement to "Ode on the Success of his Majesty's Arms," 77-183.

Regular ode in sixains. Satire on the failure of British arms in America. Ironically transforms Burgoyne's defeat into victory and cites others, like Howe's at Red Bank and Mud Island. North will not give up, but will seek allies (Russia, Ireland, Scotland) and defeat America and its French ally. Then he will execute the Yankees (Sam Adams) and imprison Shelburne, Burke, and Barre. Cited also are Gates, Arnold, Hessians, Franklin, Sandwich, and Markham. Possibly answered by "An Hint to the Patriots," 77-149.

77-293. The Times.

"Come on! -- come on! -- ye Britons brave." (24)

MP, Jul 11, 1777.

Quatrains. The British legions will be victorious over the foe from France, America, or Spain.

77-294. To a Certain Great Person.

"Come, leave the odd whims of a nicknackatorious." (16)

L Eve Post, Dec 27, 1777.

Hexameter couplets. Advises the King to mature -- to turn from buttons and Bute, the Stuarts, Jacobites, and Scots; read Locke and Sidney, Russell, and Hampden; and become a Whig.

77-295. To a Great Person.

"Let me tell you, your Scotch education." (2)

L Eve Post, Sep 27, 1777.

HC. Epigram. The King has been poisoned by a "Scotch education," thereby ruining the nation.

77-296. To a Young Gentleman who lately went to America as a Voluntier in the Army.

"Where flies the stripling fond of arms." (48)

WM 35 (Jan 16, 1777), 113.

Quatrains. A youth not yet fifteen years old is asked to return to his mourning family and enjoy his life at home.

77-297. To Britain.

"Blush Britain! blush at thy inglorious war." (22)

Say's, 1777? Frank Moore, Songs and Ballads of the American Revolution (New York, 1855; repr. Port Washington, N. Y.: Kennikat Press, 1964), pp. 163-4.

Song. Moore locates this song in Say's for 1777, but does not give a precise date. I have not been able to locate it in the journals or newspapers of the period.
An objection to "this civil contest, this ignoble jar," this unjust war provoked by Britain's "cruel measures," for which Scotchmen are responsible.

77-298. [To fight! -- or not to fight! -- that is the question.]

"To fight! -- or not to fight! -- that is the question." (41)

MP, Jan 22, 1777.

Rough blank verse. Parody of Hamlet's speech applied to those refusing to fight against America. A satire on the Minority Opposition. Percy and Cornwallis are cited as brave exemplars, unlike cowards.

77-299. To Lord G[eorg]e G[ermain]e.

"While factious Crowds maliciously unite." (50)

PA, Dec 13, 1777.

HC. An ironic satire pretending to defend Germaine after Burgoyne's defeat and urging him to continue the struggle. Burke, Barre, and Fox are cited.

77-300. To Lord North.

"I write for ministerial use." (15)

L Chron 42 (Aug 19, 1777), 180; MP, Aug 19, 1777.

OC. Aesop's moral fable of the goose that laid golden eggs is addressed to Lord North and applied to the war against America.

77-301. To Peace.

"Guardian of Britain's Glory." (12)

PA, Nov 7, 1777.

Quatrains. Peace will bring trade and wealth, hopefully, by the end of the year. "Faction" is quiet and the "omens" are lucky.

77-302. To Sawndy Wedderbourn, and the Scots, who call out for the destruction of news-papers.

"Sawndy, a General Advertiser be thy bane." (4)

GA, Dec 4, 1777; L Eve Post, Nov 29, 1777.

Epigram. Satire on the Scots who wish to suppress freedom of speech (Wedderbourn, Bute, and Mansfield).

77-303. To the Citizens of London.

"Lull'd in security, you see." (8)

MP, Jun 24, 30, 1777.

Quatrains. Two epigrams on the election for London City Chamberlain, Wilkes vs. Hopkins. These lines satirize Wilkes' greed for money.

77-304. To the Earl of Abingdon.

"Thy principles, O noble Lord! are true." (4)

L Eve Post, Sep 4, 1777.

Quatrains. Praise of Abingdon for his principles. (In the Minority, he opposed Government's policies.)

77-305. To the [King].

"Would you America regain." (5)

Freeman's J, Mar 20, 1777.

Epigram. The King must avoid a war with France and Spain, or he will lose his empire forever.

77-306. [To the Memory / of / Cornet Francis Geary.]

"To the Memory / of / Cornet Francis Geary." (c. 17)

MP, Oct 13, 1777; W Eve Post, Oct 11, 1777.

Epitaphial inscription on the circumstances of the death of a brave young English officer, son of Admiral Geary, killed by the Americans in the Burgoyne campaign. See "On the Death of Cornet Geary," 77-223.

77-307. To the Patriots.

"Ye grumbling Patriots! hear the Muse." (68)

L Eve Post, Oct 28, 1777.

OC. Satire on the ministry, particularly the Army and Navy (Sandwich and Barrington), for its failure in the war.

77-308. To the P[remie]r. On hearing that he will certainly be called up to the House of Peers, at the close of the evening session.

"When Opposition o'er Power prevails." (6)

L Eve Post, Jul 17, 1777.

Extempore. Couplets. Satire on North. He will be executed, hanged or sent to the block, when the Opposition comes to power.

77-309. To the R. R. the B. of B.

"Are ye the pious Guardians of the Laws." (24)

St J's C, Dec 11, 1777.

Quatrains. A satire on the Bench of Bishops for their hypocrisy, for appearing to be meek but really being bloody-minded, except for John Hinchcliffe, Bishop of Peterborough, who opposed the government's American War.

77-310. To the Underwriters of the good ship the Britannia.

"Who says that Dangers can the Ship o'erwhelm." (12)

PA, Jul 19, 1777.

HC. North is sleeping at the helm of the foundering ship of state.

77-311. Tradesmen's Song. For His Majesty's Birthday, 1777. Tune -- When Britons first at Heaven's command.

"Again, my social friends, we meet." (30)

G, Jun 6, 1777.

A loyal song in praise of King George, who reigns with "firmness . . . o'er this jarring land," and even the colonies are happy to accept him as king.

77-312. Translation, or rather Paraphrase of the Epitre aux Insurgents.

"Messieurs of Boston tell me why." (48)

PA, Dec 29, 1777.

A third translation of the French Epitre aux Insurgents, in octaves (couplets and quatrains). See "An Epistle to the American Insurgents" and "An Epistle to the Americans": 77-106 and 77-107.

77-313. Tria juncta in uno. To the Tune of Shiling O'Geary. A New Song. Composed by Colonel Kane, set to musick by Lord Barrington, and sung by Lieut. Gen. Craig. . . .

"Come cheer up, my lads, you have nothing to fear." (48)

GA, Nov 20, 1777.

Song. Satire on Howe, Clinton, and Burgoyne because they are unable to beat the rebels decisively. Written before the news of Burgoyne's capture at Saratoga makes this song even more ironic. Cited are the Battles of Bunker's Hill, Long Island and New York, Trenton, Sullivan's Island (Charleston, S. C.), Burgoyne's campaign; officers Baum and Breymen (Hessians); and Mansfield and Bute, who "keep the direction" and will bring all the affairs "to the utmost perfection."

77-314. Try Every Thing; Or Nothing Like Perseverance.

"G[eorg]e merits universal praise." (58)

Freeman's J, Mar 18, 1777.

OC. An Irish Protestant review of the unavailing attempts to subdue the American rebels by King and Parliament (Gage, Howe, the mercenary Hessians, the denial of habeas corpus). And now the King will use Papists to purge heresy from the land: "From Puritans [Papists] will never run."

77-315. Twitcher and his Chairman.

"Old Twitcher, now in his Decline." (24)

PA, Oct 25, 1777.

Regular (Horatian) ode in sixains. Satire on the close friendship between Sandwich, Secretary of the Navy, and George Wombwell, a government contractor and East India director. Both are accused of corruption and avarice. For Wombwell, see Lewis Namier and John Brooke's The House of Commons 1754-1790 (1964), III, 654-5.

77-316. Verses addressed to the Author [William Combe] of the Justification, a Poem lately published.

"Have done, my Bard, no more rehearse." (18)

G Eve Post, Dec 18, 1777; PA, Dec 22, 1777.

Sixains. Signed "H. M." Combe should give up bitter satire for praise, for "higher Themes."

77-317. Verses, &c.

"Hail, Liberty! while others pay." (38)

L Eve Post, Nov 27, 1777.

OC. An invocation of the spirit of King William of Nassau (William III) to bring peace and freedom, especially peace and friendship with America. The protestant interest and freedom are here allied.

77-318. Verses occasioned by the Long Recess, in Times of the Utmost Danger.

"Great Pitt with Glory crown'd Britannia's Fame." (14)

PA, Dec 16, 1777.

HC. The government adjourns Parliament in time of danger, as a result of Burgoyne's defeat, in order to gag the opposition. Suffolk and Pitt are cited.

77-319. Verses on Mrs. Macaulay's Birth-Day, April 2.

"O let not Catharine's modest ear refuse." (20)

W Eve Post, Apr 10, 1777.

HC. Praise of Mrs. Macaulay as historian, in honor of her birthday.

77-320. Verses Written on the Twenty-ninth of May, being the Day of King Charles's Restoration.

"When madd'ning faction, and tyrannic sway." (40)

G, May 29, 1777.

Heroic quatrains. An assertion of the principle underlying the eighteenth-century constitution, the result of revolutionary events in the seventeenth century. Sidney and Russel died for liberty; and William III, a Stuart, "secur'd a Brunswick's reign."

77-321. Washington. A Poem.

"'Twas in the silent hour of Night." (84)

MP, Jan 6, 1777.

Ballad narrative about how Mrs. Maria Gibbons deceived Washington and spied for the British.

77-322. [What a puff the Tories make.]

"What a puff the Tories make." (18)

L Eve Post, Aug 12, 1777.

Regular ode in sixains. An ironic reaction to the loss of two battleships to the American navy.

77-323. [When England's patriot flame was dead.]

"When England's patriot flame was dead." (12)

L Eve Post, Sep 30, 1777.

Sixains. America is now the land of the free, not England. The British navy is weak and ineffectual, the result of the Ministry's incompetence.

77-324. [When John the Painter over Beer.]

"When John the Painter over Beer." (16)

PA, Aug 21, 1777.

Quatrains. An attempt at humor by a fanciful comparison: John the Painter with the Earl of Sandwich.

77-325. [When sly Jemmy Twitcher had smugg'd up his face.]

"When sly Jemmy Twitcher had smugg'd up his face." (30)

L Eve Post, Feb 22, 1777.

Doggerel. Six-stress iambics. Satire on Sandwich for his immorality, presumably by T. Gray, on the occasion of the Lord standing candidate for the Chancellorship of Cambridge in 1763.

77-326. [When York's Tory Prelate the Whigs would debase.]

"When York's Tory Prelate the Whigs would debase." (16)

G, Jun 16, 1777.

Quatrains. Satire on Bishop Markham of York for his Tory views of the church.

77-327. [Whether from fate, or some more potent cause.]

"Whether from fate, or some more potent cause." (14)

The Muse's Mirror. Being a Collection of Poems (London: Baldwin, 1778), I, 256.

Sonnet in couplets. A protest at the self-interested and disgraceful leadership of "Statesmen, and senators," locusts responsible for a "starving" land, "In one year eating up a seven year's toil."

77-328. Whitehead, William.
Ode for his Majesty's Birth-Day, Written by William Whitehead, Esq; And set to Music by Dr. Boyce.

"Driven out from Heav'n's etherial domes." (34)

AR, 1777, p. 197; G Eve Post, Jun 3, 1777; GM 46 (Jun 1777), 286; Lady's M 8 (Jun 1777), 326; Lloyd's 40 (Jun 2, 1777), 535; L Chron 41 (Jun 3, 1777), 530; L Eve Post, Jun 3, 1777; L Mag 46 (Jun 1777), 330; LP, Jun 2, 1777; M Chron, Jun 4, 1777; MP Jun 4, 1777; St J's C, Jun 3, 1777; Sent M 5 (Jun 5, 1777), 288-9.

Irregular Pindaric ode. The laureat invokes the spirit of Unanimity to drive away Discord. He has sung enough of war and slaughter, and he hopes for "happier hours."

77-329. -----.
Ode for the New Year, written by William Whitehead, Esq. and set to music by Dr. Boyce.

"Again imperial Winter's sway." (32)

AR 1777, p. 196; Cumb Pacq, Jan 9, 1777; Daily Advertiser, Jan 1, 1777; Freeman's J, Jan 16, 1777; G, Jan 1, 1777; GM 47 (Jan 1777), 38; Lady's M 7 (Supp 1776), 713-4; Lloyd's 40 (Dec 30, 1776-Jan 1, 1777), 7; L Chron 41 (Dec 31-1776-Jan 2, 1777), 3; L Eve Post, Dec 31, 1776-Jan 2, 1777; LP, Dec 31, 1776-Jan 2, 1777; M Chron, Jan 1, 1777; PA, Jan 1, 1777; St J's C, Dec 31, 1776-Jan 2, 1777; SM 5 (Jan 1777), 36; West J, Jan 4, 1777; W Eve Post, Dec 31, 1776-Jan 2, 1777. Also L Mag 46 (Feb 1777), 104.

Regular ode in octaves. Whitehead begs the American rebels, "wayward children" and "parricides," to stop the war and unite with Britain to seek the blessings of peace, "the Public Good." He does not believe freedom "can e'er be found where many a tyrant reigns." But "true liberty" is assured by "Britain's well-mix'd state."

77-330. A Word of Advice.

"O Britons! Britons! deign to think." (32)

PA, Jan 25, 1777.

Quatrains protest self-interest that will be the ruin of the country.

Wynne, J. H. See "Ode on the Birth-Day," 77-182.

Prints

77-331. The Captive Generals Soliloquy and Yankey's Advice.

"When pass'd the Rubicon, my Talents did with Ardour burn." (8)

Engr. with rough verse in couplets. C. October-December 1777.

Pierpont Morgan Collection (IV.51.261). Copy in Lewis-Walpole Library.

The British general (Burgoyne), defeated at Saratoga, wishes, in shame, that the bloody war were over and he back in England.

77-332. The Flight of the Congress.

"Impatient of Imperial sway." (18)

Engr. with OC in sixains. November 20, 1777.

George 5401 (V, 251-2). Repr. Wynn Jones, p. 97; Sidney George Fisher, The True History of the American Revolution (1902), p. 346.

Animal fable. General Howe occupied Philadelphia in September 1777 after the victory at Brandywine. This poem stresses the success of British arms over the rebels, despite their French alliance.

77-333. General Sanguinaire Mark-ham.

"Mark-ham whom Patriarch Noah cursed." (6)

Engr. with sixain. By M. Darly. October 28, 1777.

George 5400 (V, 250-1).

William Markham, consecrated Archbishop of York in June 1777, is here satirized for his bloodthirsty attitude towards the Americans and "Cannon Law."